Professional PHP4 XML

Luis Argerich
Ken Egervari
Matt Anton
Chris Lea
Charlie Killian
Chris Hubbard
James Fuller

Wrox Press Ltd ®

Professional PHP4 XML

© 2002 Wrox Press Ltd

wrox

Published by Wrox Press Ltd,
Arden House, 1102 Warwick Road, Acocks Green,
Birmingham, B27 6BH, UK
Printed in the United States
ISBN 1-86100-721-3

Trademark Acknowledgements

Credits

Authors
Luis Argerich
Ken Egervari
Matt Anton
Chris Lea
Charlie Killian
Chris Hubbard
James Fuller

Additional Material
Dilip Thomas

Technical Editors
Indu Britto
Rahul Shah
Matthew Moodie
Girish Sharangpani
Shivanand Nadkarni

Author Agent
Safiulla S.M.

Project Manager
Safiulla S.M.
Dilip Thomas

Editorial Thanks
Paul Cooper

Special Thanks
Christian Stocker

Content Architect
Dilip Thomas

Technical Reviewers
Sanjay Abraham
Matt Anton
Luis Argerich
Chuck Hagenbuch
Andrew Hill
Graeme Merrall
Jon Parise
Derick Rethans
Jonathan Stephens
Keith Vance

Proof Reader
Agnes Wiggers

Index
Adrian Axinte

Production Manager
Liz Toy

Production Coordinators
Pip Wonson
Rachel Taylor

Cover
Dawn Chellingworth
Santosh Haware

Illustrations
Santosh Haware
Manjiri Karande

About the Authors

Luis Argerich

Luis Argerich is a development and technology manager for Salutia, a leading health solutions provider for South America and a teacher at the University of Buenos Aires (UBA). He has also featured as a co-author on *Professional PHP4* (1861006918, Wrox Press) from Wrox Press. Luis has shown interest in PHP since version 2.0 and has used it in conjunction with XML for projects such as search engines, transactional systems, web applications, and web services.

Ken Egervari

Ken is a 22-year-old entrepreneur and author from Windsor, Ontario Canada who is a technology enthusiast and software architect. He has written several types of applications ranging from networking to entertainment and the enterprise. He has used various languages such as Assembly, C, C++, Java, SQL, PHP, DHTML, and others. Ken is co-author of a PHP framework library called eXtremePHP and is also co-author of *Professional PHP4* (1861006918,Wrox Press).

Matt Anton

Matt Anton (LAMP is literally his middle name) is a computer consultant and freelance writer. He leads a quiet life (so he thinks), loves his parents (so they think), and believes in God (so God thinks). He has worked as a co-author on Professional Apache 2.0 (1861007221, Wrox Press). His technology interests include XML, Mac OS X, J2EE technologies, and other web site deployment issues.

Chris Lea

Chris Lea is a developer currently living in Los Angeles, CA. He received a BS in Physics with Highest Honors and Distinction from UNC-CH in 1997, and has been sitting in front of a computer for a great deal of his time since then. Typically he uses Linux, which has been his platform of choice since sometime in college when he first bumped into it. He started in with PHP a few years after that and has worked on projects ranging from the entertainment industry to the financial sector. You can find out all you ever wanted to know and more at his personal web site http://www.chrislea.com/.

Charlie Killian

Charlie Killian is a freelance PHP programmer currently working in the San Francisco Bay Area. For the last 4 years, he has been specializing in the development of commercial and open source web applications for a variety of companies, both large and small. He divides his time between computer programming, travelling throughout India (and the rest of the world), and spending time with his friends and family.

Chris Hubbard

Chris is the founder and principal consultant for Wild Characters. Wild Characters provides web development to various clients in the telecom, health, gaming, and business consulting industries. Chris has been working with Internet-related technologies since 1994 and has worked on projects ranging from an HTML sweatshop to working with a couple of the largest web sites. Chris is happily married with two wonderful children.

James Fuller

James Fuller has 15 yrs commercial programming experience in a variety of languages. He has been technical director of some large Internet companies and currently holds this position at on-IDLE Ltd. He is a regular contributor to the XSL-List. He would like to play chess more and learn the Czech language.

Table of Contents

Chapter 1: Introduction   **1**

   Introducing XML   **1**

   Introducing PHP   **3**

   XML and PHP   **3**

   Useful Resources   **4**

   Book Roadmap   **5**

Chapter 2: PHP Fundamentals   **11**

   Basic PHP Syntax   **11**

   Variables   **12**
      Variable Types   12
      Assignment   20

   Constants   **21**

   Operators   **21**
      Arithmetic Operators   22
      Assignment, Increment, and Decrement Operators 22
      Comparison Operators   23
      Logical Operators   23
      Bitwise Operators   24
      String Operators   25
      Error Handler Operator   25

   Control Structures   **25**
      Conditional Structures   26
      Loops   27

   Functions   **29**
      User-Defined Functions   30
      Returning Values   31
      Variable Functions   32

   Classes and Objects   **32**
      Procedural vs. Object-Oriented Programs   33
      Classes   34

   File and Directory Access   **40**

   Summary   **44**

Table of Contents

Chapter 3: XML Fundamentals — 47

Data Representation — 47

Meta Data — 48

Markup Languages — 49

XML Syntax — 50
  The XML Body — 50

Reviewing the XML Structure of a Document — 59
  The XML Prolog — 59
  The XML Epilog — 60

Summary of the XML 1.0 Specification — 61

Designing XML Documents — 62
  Vocabularies — 62
  Validating XML Documents — 62

DTDs and Schemas — 63
  DTDs — 63
  Using DTDs — 75
  The Shortcomings of DTDs — 77
  Schemas — 78

Namespaces — 85

Summary — 87

Chapter 4: XML Derivatives — 89

Functional Classification of XML Derivatives — 90

Common Patterns for XML Processing — 90

Generic Derivatives — 92
  DOM — 92
  SAX — 93
  XPath — 95
  XSLT — 96

Presentation Vocabularies — 99
  XHTML — 99
  WML — 101
  SVG — 103
  VoiceXML — 106
  XUL/XBL — 106

The Semantic Web — 108
  RDF — 108
  RSS — 110

XLink and XPointer — 114
  XLink — 114
  XPointer — 116

Validating XML Documents — **118**
RELAX NG — 118
Schematron — 120

Web Services — **123**
XML-RPC — 123
SOAP — 124

Summary — **126**

Chapter 5: SAX — 129

Parsing XML — **129**
Types of Parsers — 130

What Is SAX? — **131**

How Does SAX Work? — **131**
Advantages — 133
Disadvantages — 134

Expat — **135**
Installing Expat on Windows and UNIX — 135
Parsing an XML Document with Expat — 136
Expat Functions — 137
Putting it Together — 145
Additional Expat Functions — 150

An Object-Oriented Approach — **156**
The eXtremePHP Framework — 157
The SaxParser Framework — 159
Writing the Parser — 160
Additional SaxParser Methods — 172

Problem Data — **173**
Handling Whitespace — 173
Non Well-Formed XML Content — 177
The Ampersand — 180

Summary — **181**

Chapter 6: DOM — 183

What is the Document Object Model (DOM)? — **183**
Advantages and Disadvantages — 186
SAX vs. DOM — 188

Getting Started — **189**
Installing DOM On Windows — 189
Installing DOM On UNIX — 190

Table of Contents

DOM Objects and Methods   **192**
The DOM Architecture   193
Tree Construction Methods   195
The DomDocument Class   198
The DomNode Class   205
The DomElement Class   221

Parsing XML Documents   **224**

Adding XML Content   **229**

Deleting XML Content   **236**

Limitations   **239**
Incomplete DOM Level 1 and Level 2 Standard   239
Unsound Architecture   240
Object-Oriented Capability   244

Summary   **245**

Chapter 7: XPath   **247**

XPath Defined   **248**

How XPath Works   **249**
XPath Syntax   250
Nodes   251
The XPath Representation of a Document   253

XPath Expressions   **255**
Writing XPath Expressions   255
    Location Paths   255
    Selecting Elements   256
    Selecting Text   257
    Selecting Processing Instructions   257
    Selecting Comments   257
    Selecting Attributes   257
    Wildcards   258
Extended Syntax   259

Axes   **259**

Predicates   **264**
Attributes in Predicates   265
XPath Functions   266
Applying a Function to an XPath Expression   269
Useful Predicates   270

Using XPath from PHP   **274**
Using XPath from the DOM Extension   275
Using XPath from XSLT   278

Summary   **280**

Chapter 8: XSL — 283

Transforming vs. Parsing — 284

XSL — 285
The XSLT Processor — 286
The XSL Language — 292
  Creating XSL Documents — 293
  A Simple Example — 294
  Using the XSLT PHP Extension — 300
Precedence Rules and Predefined Templates — 302
  Named Templates — 304
  Using XPath for Calculations — 309
XSL Instructions — 314
Creating Resultant XML Documents — 331

Sablotron Functions — 341
Output the Target Document to a File — 341
Using Variables Instead of Files — 342
An Object-Oriented Approach — 344
Ensuring Forward Compatibility — 349

Useful XSL Applications — 350
Multi-Tiered Applications — 350
Introduction of New Languages — 351
Document Conversion — 352
Publishing — 354

XSLT As a Functional Language — 355

Supporting Legacy Applications — 358

Summary — 360

Chapter 9: XML Classes — 363

Generic XML Parser Class — 363
Parsing the File — 364
Displaying the Results — 366
A Trimmed Down Bug List — 367

XMLFile — 370
A Trimmed-Down List Revisited — 372
A Simplified XML File — 374

XML Transformer — 376
Using the XML Transformer Class — 377

XPath with phpXML — 381
  One Last Trimmed-Down List — 381
  A Searchable Bug List — 383

Summary — 388

Chapter 10: Putting It Together   391

Programming XML Applications   392

Transforming XML   393
Using DOM for XML Transforming   395
Using XSLT for XML Transforming   395
Using SAX for XML Transforming   402
Choosing a Transformation Strategy   410
Abstracting XML Transformations   411

Modifying XML   411
Using DOM To Modify XML Files   412
Using SAX To Modify a Document   415
Using XSLT To Modify a Document   418
Abstracting the Modifications To an XML Document   420

Creating Objects from XML Files   420
Using SAX To Create PHP Objects from XML   422

Querying XML   424
Using DOM To Query an XML Document   425
Using XPath To Query a Document   426
Using XSLT To Query a Document   428
Using SAX To Query a Document   429
Other Querying Alternatives   430
Abstraction Again   431
Caching Strikes Back   431
Choosing a Querying Strategy   431

Writing XML   431
Manual Writing   432
Using DOM To Write XML Data   435
Using SAX To Write XML Data   436

Summary   437

Chapter 11: Syndicated Content   439

RSS   440
RSS Structure   440

The PEAR RSS Parser Class   442

A Simple RSS Application   443

Multiple Sources and Cached Content   446

A Simple RSS Generation Class   454

Summary   461

Chapter 12: XML to DB, DB to XML   463

Basic XML Storage   464
Flat Files   464
Simple Database Storage   465

XML to Database   466

Database to XML   480
Non-Nested Query   481
A Nested Query   483

Summary   486

Chapter 13: XML Storage   489

Analysis of an XML Storage Solution   489

Building our Own Storage Solution   490
Storing XML Documents   491
Organizing XML Documents   503
APIs   506

Using a Product for XML Storage   516
Relational Databases   516
Native XML Databases   517

Summary   534

Chapter 14: PHP As a Client   537

WDDX   537

PHP and TCP/IP   546

Jabber   550

PHP and Web Services   554

SOAP   563

Future of Web Services and PHP   586

Summary   587

Table of Contents

Chapter 15: SVG   589

SVG   589

SVG User Agents   590

SVG Basics   591
  MIME Type, File Extensions, Prolog, DTD, Namespace, and Document Structure   591
  Embedding SVG in HTML   593
  Errors   594
  Container Elements   596
  Coordinate System   597
  Style   603
  Creating Shapes   605
  Creating Basic Text   612
  Basic Animation   614

PHP SVG Class   616

A Bar Chart Using SVG   618

Summary   628

Chapter 16: XML-RPC   631

What Are RPCs?   631

What Is XML-RPC?   632

What Are Web Services?   632

The XML-RPC Protocol   633
  The Basic XML-RPC Protocol   633
  Extending the XML-RPC Protocol   634
  The Protocol Details   636

XML-RPC in PHP   649
  Using the XML-RPC Library from Usefulinc   650
  The Library Details   655
  Service Descriptions   657

Resources   664

Summary   664

Chapter 17: Case Study: A Calendar Server Using XML-RPC   667

The Calendar Application   667
  Methodology   668
  Technologies To Be Used   668
    Communication Protocol   669
    Web Server Application   670
    Server-Side Programming Language   670
    Storage   670

The Server Application (Iteration 1) **671**
The Database 672
User Management 675
Initializing the Server 676
Server Functions 677
Server Exceptions 690
Installing the Server 691

The Client Application **691**
Interface Design 692
Application Design 692
Developing the Client Application 693
Installing the Client 713

The Command-Line Client **713**

New Requirements (Iteration 2) **715**
Modifying the Server 717
Modifying the Web Client 719

Future Requirements **724**

Summary **728**

Appendix A: PHP4 XML Language Reference **731**

Common Steps When Employing XML Parser **732**

The PHP XML API **733**

XML Parsing Error Codes **743**

Appendix B: Installing PHP4 and Apache **747**

Windows Installation **749**

Installing on UNIX-Like Systems **760**

Further Resources **770**

Summary **771**

Appendix C: SAX 2.0: The Simple API for XML **773**

Class and Interface Hierarchies **774**

Appendix D: The XML DOM (Document Object Model) **827**

Fundamental Interfaces **827**

Extended Interfaces **838**

Table of Contents

Appendix E: XSLT Reference   841

Elements   841

Functions   873

Appendix F: XPath Reference   879

Axes   880

Node Tests   884

Functions   886

Appendix G: Object-Oriented Programming   899

Objects and Classes   900

    Members   900

    Methods   900

    Constructor   901

    Instances   902

    Calling Instance Methods   903

    Inheritance   904

Summary   917

Index   919

1

Introduction

Writing a book is always a challenge, and this book is no exception. One of the first challenges is to determine what information needs to be presented, and how it should be conveyed. In figuring this out we worked around a couple of facts:

❑ PHP is a good programming language

❑ XML is a good way of interacting with data

❑ The support within PHP for XML, while young, is sufficiently mature that the combination of the two is now viable

To determine what information to present, we looked at a lot of the PHP books on the market. Many of them included a chapter about XML. Also, there were a lot of books about XML and a few of them included a chapter on PHP; but most of them concentrate on Java or a Microsoft technology. At the time of going to print, there are no books on the market that discuss the working of PHP and XML together – this book is designed to fill that hole.

Introducing XML

XML, put in simple terms, is a data modeling language and as such it can be used for:

❑ Organizing information

❑ Representing information

❑ Exchanging information

❑ Processing information

Organizing Information

Normally, programmers use a database in their applications. When we thinks about using a database we automatically organize the data using the relational model, use an RDBMS to store the data, and use SQL to access and modify the data. If we think about using XML we will need to organize the information using a hierarchical model, use a native XML database to store the data, and use SAX, DOM, XPath, and XSLT to query and modify the data.

As you can see it is the same movie with different actors, and like actors can greatly improve a movie, so XML can greatly empower the application.

Representing Information

As an open standard, software vendors and developers quickly and widely adopted XML as a very practical way to represent information, to exchange information between parties, and to process information.

XML is a good way to represent information since it is based on a solid syntax where markup is used to convey meta data information that is represented hierarchically using XML elements and subelements.

Let's look at our first XML document:

```
<person ssn="83871">
  <name>John Smith</name>
  <age>27</age>
  <address>
    <street>State</street>
    <number>909</number>
    <apt>105</apt>
    <city>Houston</city>
    <state>Texas</state>
    <zip>90909</zip>
  </address>
</person>
```

This example describes a person. XML is a very easy representation since humans can read it easily. Also, programs easily understand XML documents since the rules for XML writing are very strict.

Since programs can easily process XML there are a lot of tools for XML processing and a lot of languages and derivatives based on XML that allow a programmer to do quite a number of things using XML documents. That's why we may not only need to use XML for a project but may also want to use it.

Exchanging Information

XML is also a good way to exchange information since:

❑ It is an open standard that any organization or individual can use to transport data

❑ It is vendor-neutral as it can be used to exchange information among systems written in different languages by different companies

Processing Information

XML makes it very easy to process information. There are languages to query XML documents, standards to process and parse XML documents, standards to transform and modify documents, native XML databases to store and retrieve documents, standards for implementing web services based on XML, messaging standards based on XML, and finally there are file formats for graphics, texts, and math formulas based on XML.

Some programmers say that XML is difficult. In fact it is not, but there are a variety of tools and selecting the right ones may be hard. We hope that this book will teach you how to choose a good solution for your problem. XML won't present you a problem, it will present a lot of solutions.

Introducing PHP

PHP is an interpreted scripting language used mostly for web-based applications. As a general scripting language, PHP provides many of the features that you can find in other languages such as Perl, Python, or Java.

PHP excels when used to write web-based applications. It can be easily used with almost all the important, free, or commercial web servers allowing web applications to be portable and operating system independent. Besides that, PHP code can be combined very easily with HTML to produce web pages without any programming effort. When used as a web server module PHP is faster and more efficient than CGI. It also has a very robust engine.

Another very interesting feature of PHP is that one can usually write applications, even complex ones, very fast using PHP. If the Perl motto is "There's More Than One Way To Do It" the PHP motto will be "There's a Fast Way to Do It". PHP provides a lot of extensions and built-in functions for very specific tasks that will require a hard-to-find library or a lot of code in other languages.

XML and PHP

For XML processing, PHP provides a SAX parser, a DOM extension that includes XPath and XPointer support, and an XSLT extension prepared to use different XSLT processors. Besides that, there are a lot of classes or libraries for using other XML derivatives from PHP. When this book was released there were classes for RSS, RDF, Schematron, XQuery, SAX filters, SOAP, XML-RPC, XUpdate, SVG, and WML. It is a certainty that many other libraries, tools, and classes will be added in the future.

So PHP is a dream language for web-based applications and it has a lot of built-in and external tools for XML processing. That's why, when you think about a web-based application using XML or a web front-end for a system using XML, we should consider PHP as a very convenient choice.

To sum up succinctly, by using PHP and XML together we will:

❑   Write less code
❑   Write the application faster
❑   Have a very efficient product at the end

Useful Resources

- ❏ To know the 'real rules' of XML it is best to get the official specifications at the W3C:

  - ❏ For a general search of specs refer to http://www.w3.org/
  - ❏ The XML 1.0 specification at http://www.w3.org/TR/2000/REC-xml-20001006/
  - ❏ The XPath specification can be located at http://www.w3.org/TR/xpath/
  - ❏ The DOM 1.0 spec is at http://www.w3.org/TR/1998/REC-DOM-Level-1-19981001/
  - ❏ The XSLT specification is at http://www.w3.org/TR/xslt/
  - ❏ The XHTML specification is at http://www.w3.org/MarkUp/
  - ❏ The SVG specification is at http://www.w3.org/Graphics/SVG/Overview.htm8
  - ❏ The RDF specification is at http://www.w3.org/TR/1999/REC-rdf-syntax-19990222/
  - ❏ SAX, a very useful API for XML processing, has its homepage at http://www.saxproject.org/
  - ❏ The documentation for PHP extensions using XML is at the PHP web site: http://www.php.net/

- ❏ Classes for XML processing using PHP can be found at:

  - ❏ http://www.phpclasses.org/
  - ❏ http://phpxmlclasses.sourceforge.net/
  - ❏ http://pear.php.net/manual/en/packages.xml.php

Who Is This Book for?

This book targets programmers whose PHP experience enables them to code and maintain small PHP web applications. Although the audience is expected to have this level of maturity, we will review the PHP syntax and general installation. We will also review the installation of the most recent versions of Apache, PHP, and MySQL. We are assuming that programmers reading this book will not need an introduction into the conceptual basis of programming. We have also assumed an interest in programming web and distributed applications. PHP developers who need to work with XML, or intend to do so in the future, will find this book useful.

What You Will Learn

This book will provide web developers and PHP programmers with the information necessary to create XML-based web applications, or to augment existing applications with XML. There are many XML derivatives and this book will explain XML and the various derivatives of XML that are relevant to PHP. Where a derivative is supported in PHP, we will explain what the derivative is and how to use it.

We will provide sufficient information about PHP and XML to show how to use these two technologies together. We hope that by doing so, more XML projects will use PHP instead of Java, or ASP, and that more PHP projects will use XML instead of flat files (`.ini` or `.conf`) or databases. The aim is to have more PHP projects that will provide an XML interface.

One reason why XML is confusing is its different flavors and aspects. We've been asked many times, "What is XML and what are all these other abbreviations like XSL, DTD, and XPath?". Our answer is that XML is a way of describing data. XML is a template language similar to HTML that is used to describe data. Almost all the related XML recommendations are written using XML. The one primary exception is the DTD, which doesn't follow the rules of XML. Admittedly this answer isn't enough. And we will discuss all this and more, in detail, in the chapters ahead.

This book answers the questions "What is XML?" and "How do I use XML within PHP?".

Book Roadmap

This book is packed with 16 chapters, 1 case study, and 7 appendices.

Let's have a quick run-down:

- ❏ *Chapter 2* is about the core of PHP. It walks us through the basic constructs of the PHP language, including data types, operators and variables, functions, arrays, and file operations.

- ❏ *Chapter 3* is a run-through of XML fundamentals and a look at Schemas, DTDs, and vocabularies.

- ❏ *Chapter 4* focuses on the different flavors of XML. It concerns itself with the generic XML derivatives, presentation vocabularies, the semantic web, XLink and XPointer, validating XML documents, and web services.

- ❏ *Chapter 5* concentrates on Expat, PHP's built-in SAX parser. It looks into the whys and wherefores of SAX being extremely viable for web development. It also deals with getting started with Expat and writing both procedural and object-oriented parsers.

- ❏ *Chapter 6* is a discussion on DOM as an alternative to SAX. It looks into parsing, adding, and deleting XML content using DOM.

- ❏ *Chapter 7* is an introduction to XPath and focuses on using XPath from PHP and XSLT too.

- ❏ *Chapter 8* veers away from traditional parsing methods to detail the benefits of using XSL. It details Sablotron, the XSLT processor that is bundled with PHP.

- ❏ *Chapter 9* examines some third-party classes for PHP like the generic XML parser class, XML File, XML Transformer, and phpXML.

- ❏ *Chapter 10* brings together all the knowledge gained from the previous 9 chapters to detail reading and writing XML. This chapter puts all that is detailed in the earlier chapters into practice, to show different solutions to the same problem using different technologies.

- ❏ *Chapter 11* examines RSS as a way to syndicate the content of the web site. It covers some basic techniques for getting and generating syndicated RSS content.

- ❏ *Chapter 12* deals with getting XML to interact with a database. Moving to the flip side of the coin, it also works with the powerful `xml_sql2xml` class that is part of the PHP PEAR libraries.

- ❏ *Chapter 13* complements the previous chapter and discusses some options for storing XML. It analyses different alternatives to store XML documents, the commercial and free products that offer XML storage, and Xindice too.

❑ *Chapter 14* examines how PHP can be used as a client to all sorts of XML server standards. It reviews a mixture of techniques for connecting, messaging, and integrating with XML-based client-server technologies and protocols. The chapter also spends some time in reviewing the fundamentals of SOAP and general issues that are related to Service Orientated Architectures.

❑ *Chapter 15* focuses on SVG, an XML presentation vocabulary, which can be used to create dynamic graphics in PHP. It also contains detailed examples on embedding the PHP directly in the SVG file, and using the PHP SVG class to generate an SVG document.

❑ *Chapter 16* concerns itself with how PHP can use XML-RPC as a server and a client to provide or access web services. In particular, it details using the Usefulinc library to write XML-RPC clients and servers and some small examples of XML-RPC clients and servers that can be used as skeletons to design our own services.

❑ *Chapter 17* builds upon Chapter 16 to show the power of XML-RPC and PHP when we build an extensible calendar server and two different kinds of client: one web-based, the other command-line based.

These are the 7 appendices:

❑ *Appendix A* is a PHP4 XML language reference

❑ *Appendix B* is all about getting PHP working with the Apache web server, both on UNIX and Windows environments

❑ *Appendix C* is a SAX 2.0 reference

❑ *Appendix D* is a DOM reference

❑ *Appendix E* is an XSLT language reference

❑ *Appendix F* is an XPath language reference

❑ *Appendix G* is an OO primer

Conventions

To help you get the most from the text and keep track of what's happening, we've used a number of conventions throughout the book.

For instance:

> **These boxes hold important, not-to-be-forgotten information, which is directly relevant to the surrounding text.**

While the background style is used for asides to the current discussion.

As for styles in the text:

❑ When we introduce them, we **highlight** important words

- ❑ We show keyboard strokes like this: *Ctrl-K*

- ❑ We show filenames and code within the text like so: `<element>`

- ❑ Text on user interfaces and URLs are shown as: Menu

We present code in two different ways:

```
In our code examples, the code foreground style shows new, important,
   pertinent code
while code background shows code that is less important in the present
   context or has been seen before.
```

Customer Support

We always value hearing from our readers, and we want to know what you think about this book: what you liked, what you didn't like, and what you think we can do better next time. You can send us your comments, either by returning the reply card in the back of the book, or by e-mail to feedback@wrox.com. Please be sure to mention the book title in your message.

How To Download the Sample Code

When you visit the Wrox site, http://www.wrox.com/, simply locate the title through our Search facility or by using one of the title lists. Click on Download in the Code column or on Download Code on the book's detail page.

The files that are available for download from our site have been archived using WinZip. When you have saved the attachments to a folder on your hard-drive, you need to extract the files using a decompression program such as WinZip or PKUnzip. When you extract the files, the code is usually extracted into chapter folders. When you start the extraction process, ensure your software (WinZip, and PKUnzip, for example) is set to use folder names.

Errata

We've made every effort to make sure that there are no errors in the text or in the code. However, no one is perfect and mistakes do occur. If you find an error in one of our books, like a spelling mistake or faulty piece of code, we would be very grateful for your feedback. By sending in errata you may save other readers hours of frustration, and of course, you will be helping us provide even higher quality information. Simply e-mail the information to support@wrox.com; your information will be checked and if correct, posted to the errata page for that title, or used in subsequent editions of the book.

To find errata on the web site, go to http://www.wrox.com/, and simply locate the title through our Advanced Search or title list. Click on the Book Errata link, which is below the cover graphic on the book's detail page.

E-Mail Support

If you wish to directly query a problem in the book with an expert who knows the book in detail then e-mail support@wrox.com, with the title of the book and the last four numbers of the ISBN in the subject field of the e-mail. A typical e-mail should include the following things:

❑ The **title of the book, last four digits of the ISBN**, and **page number** of the problem in the Subject field.

❑ Your **name, contact information**, and the **problem** in the body of the message.

We *won't* send you junk mail. We need the details to save your time and ours. When you send an e-mail message, it will go through the following chain of support:

❑ Customer Support – Your message is delivered to our customer support, and they are the first people to read it. They have files on most frequently asked questions and will answer anything general about the book or the web site immediately.

❑ Editorial – Deeper queries are forwarded to the technical editor responsible for that book. They have experience with the programming language or a particular product, and are able to answer detailed technical questions on the subject.

❑ The Authors – Finally, in the unlikely event that the technical editor cannot answer your problem, they will forward the request to the author. We do try to protect the authors from any distractions to their writing; however, we are quite happy to forward specific requests to them. All Wrox authors help with the support on their books. They will e-mail the customer and the editor with their response, and again all readers should benefit.

The Wrox support process can only offer support to issues directly pertinent to the content of our published title. Support for questions that fall outside the scope of normal book support is provided via the community lists of our http://p2p.wrox.com/ forum.

p2p.wrox.com

For author and peer discussion join the P2P mailing lists. Our unique system provides **Programmer to Programmer**™ contact on mailing lists, forums, and newsgroups, all in addition to our one-to-one e-mail support system. If you post a query to P2P, you can be confident that many Wrox authors and other industry experts who are present on our mailing lists are examining it. At p2p.wrox.com you will find a number of different lists to help you, not only while you read this book, but also as you develop your applications.

To subscribe to a mailing list just follow these steps:

1. Go to http://p2p.wrox.com/

2. Choose the appropriate category from the left menu bar

3. Click on the mailing list you wish to join

4. Follow the instructions to subscribe and fill in your e-mail address and password

5. Reply to the confirmation e-mail you receive

6. Use the subscription manager to join more lists and set your e-mail preferences

2

PHP Fundamentals

In this chapter, we are going to cover the basic syntax and control structures of the PHP programming language. Though we assume some familiarity with PHP, we will take some time to review issues such as file access that are used a great deal elsewhere in this book. Also, we will review basic techniques of object-oriented (OO) programming and discuss the principal differences between OO and procedural techniques. Thus this chapter, while not intended to be a complete tutorial in PHP syntax, will serve to refresh our basic PHP knowledge.

Basic PHP Syntax

In the context of a web page, PHP code sits embedded within the surrounding markup, which is probably, but not necessarily, HTML or XHTML. PHP code is within special tags that help distinguish it from the rest of the markup.

There are four sets of special tags that may be used to denote PHP code:

❑   `<script language="php">...</script>`

❑   `<?php...?>`

❑   `<?...?>`

❑   `<%...%>`

Of these four, only the HTML (`<script language="php"></script>`) and XML (`<?php...?>`) forms are always available. The short-form (`<?...?>`) and ASP style (`<%...%>`) are not as portable as the longer versions; they can be enabled or disabled in the `php.ini` file.

Throughout this book, since we are set to embed PHP code in XML or XHTML, we will use the `<?php...?>` form to conform to the XML. A sample would look like this:

```
<body>
  <?php
    // insert code here
  ?>
</body>
```

Variables

Variables can be used to store some data in PHP. In PHP all variables are represented by the use of a dollar sign ($) preceding the variable name. A valid PHP variable name starts with a letter or an underscore, followed by any number of letters, numbers, or underscores. A typical variable declaration in PHP looks like this:

```
$foo = "Christian";
```

Variable Types

There are eight distinct primitive variable types that can be used with PHP for storing data. The eight types are divided into three categories:

- ❏ Scalar types
- ❏ Compound types
- ❏ Special types

The $ sign is used for all types of variables, including compound types like arrays and objects.

We can use PHP's `gettype()` function to find the type of a particular variable:

```
<?php
$Variable = "This is some text";
print (gettype($Variable));
?>
```

This will print:

    string

We can also use the related `settype()` function to explicitly set the type. It requires the variable name followed by the type we wish to set it to:

```
<?php
$Variable = "2";
settype($Variable, integer);
```

```
print (gettype($Variable));
print ($Variable);
?>
```

PHP doesn't require us to declare variables before we use them, or to tell it what kind of data we plan to store in the variable. The same variable can, over the course of a program, store many different data types. A variable is created as soon as we assign it, and then exists for as long as the program is executing. In the case of a web page, that means it exists until the request has been completed.

The exceptions to this are functions, which have their own variable scope.

Scalar Types

A scalar type is used to hold a single item of data. This could be a number, a sentence, a single word or character, or another item appropriate to the scalar variable type that contains it.

The four scalar types are:

❑ Boolean

❑ Integer

❑ Floating Point

❑ String

Boolean

Boolean variables can have one of two values – TRUE or FALSE. Like all keywords in the PHP languages, these are case-insensitive. It is generally a convention to use all uppercase letters, hence we will be using uppercase throughout the book. A typical declaration would look like this:

```
$boolean_variable = TRUE;
```

Integer

Integer values can be specified in decimal, octal, or hexadecimal format using the standard conventions. Integers beginning with a leading zero (0) are interpreted as octal. Integers beginning with a leading zero followed by an x (0x) are interpreted as hexadecimal. In PHP, integers can be optionally preceded by a + or – sign. Also, all integers in PHP are 32 bits long and are signed – the range is from –2,147,483,646 to 2,147,483,647.

If we specify a number beyond the bounds of an integer, or perform an operation that results in a number that is beyond the bounds of an integer, it will be represented as **float**. In case of division, if both the numerator and denominator are integers, and the result comes out as an integer, then the return value will be an integer; otherwise the return value will be a float.

Hence the following code will assign an integer value of 2 to the variable $quotient:

```
$first_int = 4;
$second_int = 2;

$quotient = $first_int / $second_int;
```

Floating Point

Floating point number is also known as float, double, or real number. The exact size of a float is machine dependent though a precision of roughly 14 decimal places is common; this conforms to the 64-bit IEEE format.

A typical float declaration looks like this:

```
$float_variable = 3.1415;
```

However, it is important to note that in some cases the floating-point arithmetic in PHP is not as precise as one might like. To perform high precision calculations, we should use the appropriate mathematical functions available in the language. PHP provides a library of arbitrary precision math functions (the bc* family) that are useful for these situations. For more information refer to the online PHP language manual available at http://www.php.net/manual/en/ref.bc.php.

String

String variables are very easy to use in PHP, and there is a wide range of built-in functions to help us manipulate them. A typical declaration looks like this:

```
$string_variable = "Christian is a Balboa dancer.";
```

This example uses double quotes to specify a string literal – this is the most common method. However, PHP tries to expand any variables it sees within double-quoted strings. This code:

```
$dance_style = "Balboa";
$string_variable = "Christian is a $dance_style dancer";
print ($string_variable);
```

will print:

Christian is a Balboa dancer

There are a number of escape characters that PHP will recognize in double-quoted strings. Here is a list of the most commonly used ones:

Sequence	Meaning
\n	Linefeed
\r	Carriage return
\t	Horizontal tab
\\	Backslash
\$	Dollar sign
\'	Single quote
\"	Double quote

We can specify string literals with **single quotes**. However, PHP does not recognize the above escape characters and it will not try to expand variables. This example:

```
$dance_style = "Balboa";
$string_variable = 'Christian is a $dance_style dancer\n';
print ($string_variable);
```

will output:

Christian is a $dance_style dancer\n

There is a third method of creating string literals called **heredoc syntax**. It is useful when we have multiple-line strings, and employs the <<< notation. When creating the quotation, one provides an identifier after the <<<, then the string, and finally the same identifier to close. For example:

```
$str = <<<ENDQUOTE
    This is a multi-line string.
    Note that I don't have to escape any "quotes" here.
ENDQUOTE;
```

As with double-quoted strings, variables found in heredoc statements are expanded. In this code sample, the variable $str would have the value Hello, World!:

```
$foo = "World!";
$str = <<<ENDQUOTE
Hello, $foo
ENDQUOTE;
```

There are two very important and potentially problematic issues that must always be remembered when using heredoc syntax:

❑   The closing identifier must begin in the first column of the line it is on. It may not be indented with spaces or tabs.

❑   After the closing semicolon, there can be no other characters on the same line except for the linefeed (\n) character. This can cause problems when using Windows-based editors, as Windows uses the sequence \r\n as a line terminator that might make the code fail. Many of these editors have an option that lets us set the line terminator character. If this option is available, telling it to use UNIX-style terminators should fix the problem.

> **The semicolon at the end of the closing identifier of heredoc is optional, but it is good practice to use it for consistency with the rest of the PHP code.**

Compound Types

Compound types allow us to store more complicated things than a single item of data. PHP allows two compound types:

❏ **Array**
Arrays let us store groups of items

❏ **Object**
Objects are used to group data and the functions that operate on that data

Array

Arrays are an important part of the PHP language. They are in reality optimized ordered maps in PHP. This means that they can be used interchangeably as real arrays, hashes, dictionaries, lists, and so on, without any real work on the part of the programmer. It is one of the things that makes development in PHP so much faster than in languages such as C.

A new array can be created with the array() construct. Note that it is, in fact, a true language construct, though it looks just like a function. An array will contain a certain number of comma-separated 'key => value' pairs, where key is either a non-negative integer or a string, and value can be anything. Note that negative integers are allowed but are to be discouraged, simply because they can be confusing to handle. As with most languages, the preferred way of doing things is to have the first index of an array be 0 (zero) and start going up by one for each index after that.

Here is an example array declaration:

```
$arr_variable = array(0 => 'Person', 'name' => 'Doe', 'height' => 'tall');
```

We can also specify arrays using square bracket syntax. The above sample, with a square bracket declaration, looks like this:

```
$arr_variable[0] = 'Person';
$arr_variable['name'] = 'Doe';
$arr_variable['height'] = 'tall';
```

If $arr_variable doesn't exist yet, then it is created with the first declaration. Note that both arrays and scalar variables are designated with the dollar sign ($).

We can use the empty bracket ([]) syntax to push new values into an array. When this syntax is employed, PHP will put the assigned value into the array corresponding to an integer key. Taking the current maximum integer index and adding one to it determines this integer. If there are no existing integer indices then zero is used. This means that the above example is equivalent to:

```
$arr_variable[] = 'Person';
$arr_variable['name'] = 'Doe';
$arr_variable['height'] = 'tall';
```

Likewise, consider the following code snippet:

```
$design_sites[] = "newstoday.com";
$design_sites[] = "threeoh.com";
$design_sites[] = "k10k.net";
```

This is functionally identical to the following:

```php
$design_sites[0] = "newstoday.com";
$design_sites[1] = "threeoh.com";
$design_sites[2] = "k10k.net";
```

Arrays are very versatile and flexible in PHP. We often make use of multidimensional arrays that use compound square brackets notation as in C and other languages. A sample declaration for a multidimensional array looks like this:

```php
$compound_array['person']['name'] = "Scooter";
$compound_array['person']['occupation'] = "Actor";
$compound_array['cat']['name'] = "Doe";
$compound_array['cat']['occupation'] = "none";
```

This could also be declared using the array() construct as follows:

```php
$compund_array =
    array('person' => array('name' => 'Scooter', 'occupation' => 'Actor'),
    'cat' => array('name' => 'Doe', 'occupation' => 'none'));
```

Objects

Objects are instances of classes that group data and relevant methods together. A simple class declaration looks like this:

```php
class SimpleClass
{
    var $mReturn;
    function ShowReturn($str)
    {
        return $this->$mReturn;
    }
} // end class Simple Class
```

In this example, variable $mReturn is of type object. We will cover their usage in greater depth in the *Classes and Objects* section later in the chapter.

Special Types

PHP4 provides two special types:

❑ Resources

❑ NULL

Resources

Resources are created and handled by particular PHP functions, and hold a reference to some external resource (such as a database connection). In earlier versions of PHP, resources were primarily relevant because they sometimes had to be freed manually when no longer in use.

However, since PHP4, this is no longer an issue as there is a built-in garbage collector that takes care of these issues. The garbage collector may clear out the resource before the page is done executing if the resource is no longer needed. This issue is never a problem in a web-based development environment, but can be relevant when we are using something like PHP-GTK to write programs.

The exception to this is the case of persistent database connections that are left available for future use if employed.

A complete list of resource types is available at http://www.zend.com/manual/resource.php.

NULL

The case-insensitive NULL type represents a variable that has no value. Introduced with PHP4, this type has only one possible value, that is, NULL.

> *This is different than the value 0, FALSE, or the empty string " ". In each of these cases, there is a value in question. The value 0 is an integer, the value FALSE is a Boolean, and " " is a string with length zero.*

A NULL means that the variable has no value whatsoever. Therefore, the following two snippets are checking for different things:

```
if ($value == FALSE) {
  // execute code
}

if ($value == NULL) {
  //execute code
}
```

The first if statement is checking to see if $value has the Boolean value FALSE. The second is checking to see if $value has any value assigned at all.

Variables from the Outside

This is an important section as it reflects a recent change in how PHP handles variables in the global scope. A PHP program allows the use of predefined variables. They can be defined as properties of the web server, cookies for the current site, GET or POST variables transmitted from a form, or environment variables from the operating system.

In versions of PHP prior to 4.2, many of these were simply defined for the developer in the global scope at the beginning of the page execution. For example, if there was a cookie called namecookie with a value of "Rich Fremont" defined, then the code:

```
print ($namecookie);
```

would output:

Rich Fremont

The same idea was true for other kinds of variables. Among these, particularly important were the GET and POST variables that could be sent to a page via an HTML form.

Let's take a look at the following form:

```
<form name="theform" action="nextpage.php" method="post">
<input type="hidden" name="hisname" value="Jackie Stewart">
<input type="submit" value="Submit">
```

If the user submitted this form, then on the nextpage.php page, the variable $hisname would already be defined and have the value Jackie Stewart.

This was true as long as the register_globals attribute in php.ini was set to On, which was the default prior to PHP 4.2. The problem with the approach is that it could allow web site users to define arbitrary global values in developers' code, which can be a potential security risk.

Therefore, this behavior is not enabled by default in PHP 4.2 and higher. Variables from cookies, forms, and so on are not automatically defined for us any longer. This adds increased security, though it might add some inconvenience to development.

The PHP team did not leave developers in the lurch though. They have created several new constructs that will keep development simple.

Superglobal Arrays

The new constructs are called superglobal arrays. What makes them interesting is that they are always defined in the global scope of the program. It is never necessary to reference them as being global – PHP simply understands this for us and lets us write our code.

Each array is associative, with the key being the name of the variable and the value being the value of the variable. The table lists the set of arrays and their definitions:

Superglobal Array	Contents
$_GLOBALS	Holds references to every variable in the global scope of the program.
$_SERVER	All the variables that are set by the web server. Therefore, the contents are web server-dependent.
$_GET	Variables defined via HTTP GET, often from a form or URL.
$_POST	Variables defined via HTTP POST, often from a form.
$_COOKIE	Variables defined via HTTP cookies.
$_FILES	Variables defined via HTTP POST file uploads.
$_ENV	Variables defined by the machine environment. They are dependent on the machine and operating system.
$_REQUEST	Holds the contents of $_GET, $_POST, $_COOKIE, and $_FILES.
$_SESSION	Variables currently registered to the script's PHP session.

This may seem a little strange at the moment. Let's look at that previous form example again and see how we would handle it in PHP 4.2 and up. This is the form:

```
<form name="theform" action="nextpage.php" method="post">
<input type="hidden" name="hisname" value="Jackie Stewart">
<input type="submit" value="Submit">
```

Now, on the nextpage.php page, we could get to the variable using the superglobal arrays, like this:

```
print ($_POST["hisname"]);
```

This is slightly more typing than before, when we could have just said print ($hisname), but the security trade-off makes it more than worth it.

> *For more information on these new arrays, refer to the PHP web site at:*
> *http://www.php.net/manual/en/language.variables.predefined.php.*

Assignment

Variables can be assigned by value or by reference.

Assigning Variables By Value

Typically, in PHP, new variables are assigned by value. Consider the following snippet:

```
$name = 'Doe';
$second_name = $name;
```

The variables $name and $second_name would both hold the value Doe. However, subsequently changing the value of $second_name would have no effect on $name. This means that it is possible to make many copies of a particular value.

Assigning Variables By Reference

Although the standard assignment mechanism in PHP assigns variables by value, it is possible to assign variables by reference using the & syntax as follows:

```
$name = 'Doe';
$second_name = &$name;
```

Assigning a value by reference creates a pointer to the data in question. Here, $second_name and $name are synonyms for the same data. Changing the value of $name would change the value of $second_name and vice-versa.

Variable Variables

A powerful, but arguably underused, aspect of PHP is the ability to assign variable variables. This is another way of saying a variable whose name can be set by the language dynamically. A variable variable takes the value of one variable, and uses that as the name for a new variable.

Let us examine the following snippet:

```php
$name = 'john_doe';
$$name = 'programmer';
```

Here, we create two separate variables. The first is $name which has the value john_doe. The second is a variable named $john_doe with the value programmer.

This can give us some powerful options as a developer. However, it also gives us the ability to write code that is quite hard to follow. When we use these, it is best to include plenty of comments explaining exactly what is going on.

Constants

PHP provides the define() function for defining constants. Constants are often used when we have a value appearing in many places that never changes. A typical example might be when creating error codes.

Here is an example that defines a constant called AUTHOR_NAME:

```php
define("AUTHOR_NAME", "John Doe");
```

Once defined, PHP will replace any occurrence of AUTHOR_NAME with the string John Doe when it finds it:

```php
// prints out John Doe
print (AUTHOR_NAME);
```

We can declare PHP constants in one location, and execute different code later on depending on whether the constant was defined, or what value it was defined as. This is tested using the defined() function:

```php
if (defined("AUTHOR_NAME")) {
    print ("AUTHORNAME is defined");
} else {
    print ("AUTHORNAME is not defined");
}
```

Note that constants are not variables; we do not prefix them with a leading $ sign. By convention, constants are given all uppercase names, although this is only a convention, and we are free to choose any name that conforms to the variable naming rules.

Operators

Operators are parts of the language that take one or more values and return some kind of information. There are many different operators in PHP; we will briefly review the most useful of them here.

Arithmetic Operators

This class of operator takes two values and performs a mathematical function on them. This is a complete list of the available arithmetic operators:

Operator	Example	Name	Result
+	$a + $b	Addition	Sum of $a and $b
-	$a – $b	Subtraction	Difference of $a and $b
*	$a * $b	Multiplication	Product of $a and $b
/	$a / $b	Division	Quotient of $a and $b
%	$a % $b	Modulus	Remainder of $a divided by $b

Assignment, Increment, and Decrement Operators

The basic assignment operator is = and should not to be confused with the equality (==) operator. The = operator tries to assign the value on its right-hand side to whatever is on its left-hand side. The following will put the integer value 3 in the $a variable:

```
$a = 3;
```

However, the assignment 3 = $a will fail because we cannot assign a value to the constant 3.

In addition to the = operator, PHP supports the usual shorthand, that is, combined operators such as +=:

```
// the next two lines are equivalent
$a = $a + 3;
$a += 3;
```

There is a combined operator for each of the arithmetic operators listed above.

Finally, we have the standard increment and decrement operators, ++ and -- respectively. If the increment or decrement operator is placed after the variable it affects (a suffix), then the current expression is evaluated before the operation takes place:

```
$a = 2;
$b = $a++ - 1;
// $a now equals 3, $b now equals 1
```

If it is placed before the affected variable (a prefix), then the operation happens before the current expression is evaluated:

```
$a = 2;
$b = ++$a - 1;
// $a now equals 3, $b now equals 2
```

Comparison Operators

These are operators that take two values and return a Boolean result, based on some comparison between them. Here is a chart that lists all the comparison operators:

Operator	Example	Name	Result
==	$a == $b	Equal	TRUE if $a is equal to $b
!=	$a != $b	Not equal	TRUE if $a is not equal to $b
<>	$a <> $b	Not equal	TRUE if $a is not equal to $b
===	$a === $b	Identical	TRUE if $a is equal to $b, and they are of the same type
!==	$a !== $b	Not identical	TRUE if $a is not equal to $b, or they are not of the same type
<	$a < $b	Less than	TRUE if $a is less than $b
>	$a > $b	Greater than	TRUE if $a is greater than $b
<=	$a <= $b	Less than or equal to	TRUE if $a is less than or equal to $b
>=	$a >= $b	Greater than or equal to	TRUE if $a is greater than or equal to $b

As we can see, there is more than one way to write some of the operators. Alternativee syntaxes for things such as the <> operator were introduced to be the same as corresponding operators in other languages.

There is another conditional operator known as the **ternary operator** (? :), which operates in many other languages, such as C:

```
(expression1) ? (expression2) : (expression3);
```

This will return expression2 if expression1 evaluates as TRUE, or expression3 otherwise.

Comparison operators are usually used in context of a conditional control structure. We will cover these structures in the *Control Structures* section later in the chapter.

Logical Operators

These are similar to the comparison operators in that they also return Boolean values. Also, in the same vein, they are typically found within conditional control structures. This is a complete list of logical operators and evaluation rules:

Operator	Example	Name	Result
and	$a and $b	AND	TRUE if both $a and $b are TRUE
&&	$a && $b	AND	TRUE if both $a and $b are TRUE
or	$a or $b	OR	TRUE if either $a or $b is TRUE
||	$a || $b	OR	TRUE if either $a or $b is TRUE
!	! $a	NOT	TRUE if $a is TRUE
xor	$a xor $b	Exclusive OR	TRUE if either $a or $b is TRUE, but not both

An important note is that the && operator and the and operator are at different precedence levels, with && being higher. An analogous situation exists for || and or. If we write clean code and use parentheses properly, it shouldn't matter which one we use.

Bitwise Operators

These are operators that allow us to manipulate specific bits within integers. They look somewhat analogous to the logical operators we have already seen. In practice, these are rarely used in PHP programming, since they are typically more complicated to think about than other operators. The reward for this complication is that they are very, very fast.

If truly blinding speed is a requirement, then we should probably question whether or not PHP is the correct language for our application in the first place. A compiled language like C might suit our needs better.

The bitwise operators are summarized in the table below:

Operator	Example	Name	Result
&	$a & $b	AND	Bits set in both $a and $b are set.
|	$a | $b	OR	Bits set in either $a or $b are set.
^	$a ^ $b	Exclusive OR	Bits set in $a or $b but not both are set.
~	~ $a	NOT	Bits set in $a are unset, and vice versa.
<<	$a << $b	Left Shift	Shift the bits of $a $b steps to the left. Equivalent to multiplying by two $b times.
>>	$a >> $b	Right Shift	Shift the bits of $a $b steps to the right. Equivalent to dividing by two $b times.

These are used very often while defining error codes in a program. Here is an example:

```
define("NO_DB_CONNECTION", 1 << 0);      //NO_DB_CONNECTION is 1
define("NO_DB_DATA", 1 << 1);            //NO_DB_DATA is 2
define("NO_DATA_FILE", 1 << 2);          //NO_DATA_FILE is 4
define("HAS_READ_PERMS", 1 << 3);        //HAS_READ_PERMS is 8

if (NO_DB_CONNECTION | NO_DB_DATA) die("Check Database!");
if (NO_DATA_FILE & HAS_READ_PERMS) die("Data file missing!");
```

String Operators

There are two string operators that are very convenient in practical use. The first is the dot (.) operator that concatenates the strings on its left and right sides. The second is the concatenating assignment operator (.=) that appends the string on its right to the value on its left:

```
$a = "Go west ";
$b = $a . "young man";
// $b now equals "Go west young man"

$a = "Go west ";
$a .= "young man";
// $a now equals "Go west young man"
```

Error Handler Operator

There is a special operator that we can use to help handle issues with errors. By appending the @ symbol to an expression, we can suppress any error reporting that the expression might return. This is commonly used for functions that might generate an error. For example:

```
// mysql_connect() establishes a connection to a MySQL server.
$handle = @mysql_connect($server, $username, $password) or
    die("Couldn't make a database connection");
```

In this expression, the mysql_connect() function will not generate an error, if it fails for some reason.

We can use this operator in any expression that has the effect of assigning a value to something, though we should be careful. Remember that all error messages will be disregarded; this includes fatal errors that cause the script to stop executing. If we've suppressed such a message, then our script will simply die with no explanation of what happened.

Control Structures

A PHP program is a collection of statements. We can tell the program which statements to execute with the use of conditional control structures. We can also tell the program to perform a series of repetitive steps over and over based on some condition. We will look at both of these scenarios in this section. Before we start, we need just a moment to review code blocks.

A **code block** is a group of statements enclosed by opening and closing curly braces ({ }). PHP will execute the statements within the braces as one group. They are most often used in conjunction with control structures, because this allows executing a group of statements, possibly many times, based on some kind of test. We will see this in use right away.

Conditional Structures

Conditional structures such as `if` and `switch` allow different blocks of code to be executed depending on the circumstances at the time of the execution.

if

```
if (expression) statement;
```

The `if` statement is the simplest conditional structure. This allows us to execute a certain piece of code based on a test. Here, `expression` must provide a Boolean value to the `if` statement.

In this example:

```
if ("Debbie" == $name) {
    print ("\$name equals $name\n");
    print ("All done!\n");
}
```

Here two lines would be printed out if the variable $a held the value `Debbie`. However, we might want to be able to tell the program to do something different if the name was not `Debbie`. This is where the **else** structure comes into play:

```
if ("Debbie" == $name) {
    print ("\$name equals $name\n");
    print ("All done!\n");
}
else {
  print ("\$name is not Debbie\n");
  print ("All done!\n");
}
```

This gives us a fair amount of control. However, what happens if we want to check to see if the name is either `Debbie` or `Vinnie`, and act accordingly? In this case we can use the **elseif** control structure:

```
if ("Debbie" == $name) {
    print ("\$name equals $name\n");
    print ("All done!\n");
}
elseif ("Vinnie" == $name) {
    print ("\$name equals $name\n");
    print ("All done!\n");
}
else {
    print ("\$name is not Debbie or Vinnie\n");
    print ("All done!\n");
}
```

We can include as many `elseif` statements as necessary in the `if...elseif...else` sequences. This lets us test for a variety of different things.

switch

There may be situations where we need to test some variable for a variety of different values; in this case we might be better served by using the **switch** control structure. Then the above example would look like this:

```
switch ($name) {
case "Debbie":
    print ("\$name equals Debbie\n");
    print ("All done!\n");
    break;
case "Vinnie":
    print ("\$name = Vinnie\n");
    print ("All done!\n");
    break;
default:
    print ("\$name is not Debbie or Vinnie\n");
    print ("All done!\n)";
}
```

We may use as many `case` blocks as we like; just be sure to add `break` at the end of each one. Otherwise PHP will continue to cascade down each test until it finds either a `break` or a `default` block to execute. The **default block** is a special one that will always execute if PHP makes it that far into the `switch` statement.

Note that we do not need to put multiple statements inside curly braces when using `switch`. PHP regards everything between a `case` and its corresponding `break`, or between `default` and the end of the `switch` block (`}`), as a block, and will execute all the statements it finds.

Logically speaking, `if...elseif...else` structures and `switch...case...default` structures are identical. Anything we can accomplish with one, we should be able to do with the other. We should choose our structure based on what we are comfortable with, and what will produce the most legible code.

Loops

Loops allow a block of code to execute a given number of times, or until a certain condition is met. They are often used for tasks like accessing records from a database query, reading lines from a file, or traversing the elements of an array. There are four types of loop in PHP: `while`, `do ... while`, `for`, and `foreach`.

while

```
while (expression) statement;
```

`while` can help us perform specific actions many times over, very easily. Again, `expression` must provide a Boolean to the `while` structure. Here is an example:

```
$i = 1;
while ($i <= 10) {
    print ("\$i equals $i\n");
    $i++;
}
```

This will print out:

$i equals 1
$i equals 2
...
$i equals 10

Note that we had to increment the variable within the code block. Otherwise, we would have had an infinite loop situation. The variable $i would have kept the value 1, so the expression $i <= 10 would never have become False.

do. ..while

```
do {
    statement;
} while (expression);
```

Closely related to while is the **do ... while** structure. It basically works the same way, except that the Boolean expression is checked at the end of the loop iteration.

This means that with a do ... while loop, we are always guaranteed that the statement will be executed at least once. The above example could be written using this structure, like so:

```
$i = 1;
do {
    print ("\$i equals $i\n");
    $i++;
} while ($i < 10);
```

Note that the same potential problem with an infinite loop exists as described above.

for

```
for (expression1; expression2; expression3) {
    statements;
}
```

Although while and do ... while are very useful, the most common kind of loop used is the **for** loop. It is also the most complex control structure in PHP, though it behaves just like its counterparts in other languages.

When the loop iterates for the first time, expression1 is evaluated unconditionally. At every iteration of the loop, expression2 is evaluated as Boolean. If it returns TRUE then the loop continues and the statement is executed. Of course, statement could be a group of statements nested in a code block. Finally, after the loop iterates each time, expression3 is executed. The above example would look like this using a for loop:

```
for ($i = 1; $i <= 10; $i++) {
    print ("\$i equals $i\n");
}
```

foreach

```
foreach (array_expression as $value) statement;

foreach (array_expression as $key => $value) statement;
```

The special **foreach** operator is designed specifically to help us handle arrays in the simplest way possible. There are two syntaxes for the operator, the second being a minor (but useful) extension of the first:

❑ foreach (array_expression as $value) statement;
   This syntax simply loops through all the values of the array, and puts the current one in the $value variable for use in the statement.

❑ foreach (array_expression as $key => $value) statement;
   In this syntax, the array key is also put in the $key value. If the array has a string key in a particular slot, then that is used. If not, then the integer index is used.

A subtle but important note is that the foreach operator works on a copy of the array_expression, not the array itself. The internal array pointer is always set to the first element, so we do not need to use PHP's reset() function before putting the array into the operator.

Here is a simple example demonstrating the use of foreach:

```
$person['name'] = "John Doe";
$person['height'] = "Six foot five"
$person['guitar'] = "Les Paul Custom Sunburst";

// this will output
//
// name is John Doe
// height is Six foot five
// guitar is Les Paul Custom Sunburst

foreach ($person as $key => $value) {
    print ("$key is $value\n");
}
```

Functions

PHP has a huge wealth of built-in functions that are a part of the language. A great deal of our time as a PHP programmer will be spent writing functions to handle various tasks.

User-Defined Functions

```
function FunctionName($arg_1, $arg_2, ..., $arg_n)
{
    statement1;
    statement2;
    ...
}
```

Any valid PHP code can be put into the code block, including other functions or classes (we will look at them in a moment). Also, any number of arguments can be used for $arg_1, $arg_2, and so on and these arguments can be any type the programmer wishes. However, PHP does not support **function overloading**.

> **Function overloading means that several functions have the same name, but will behave differently depending on the number or type of the arguments supplied to them. As mentioned, the workaround in PHP is to have the same function behave differently, depending on its argument list.**

Typically, the arguments are passed to the function by value once the function has been defined. This means that in the usual case, PHP is working on a copy of the variable that we give to the function:

```
$foo = 2;
function AddTwo($num)
{
    $num += 2;
}
AddTwo($foo);
```

In this snippet, running the AddTwo() function on $foo does nothing. The value of $foo is not changed. However, we may explicitly pass variables by reference using the reference syntax on the argument. Consider this:

```
$foo = 2;
function AddTwo($num)
{
    $num += 2;
}
AddTwo(&$foo);
```

Here, $foo will now have the value of 4, once AddTwo() has been run on it.

At this point, we have not arrived at a very good solution for implementing our AddTwo() function for two reasons:

❑ If the PHP configuration allow_call_time_pass_reference is set to Off in the php.ini file, this will generate an error message. Since this particular configuration grants a speed increase, it is common to find this setup.

❑ The programmer must remember to always pass the argument by reference, or else it won't work as expected. Fortunately, PHP has a way around this as well. If we employ the reference syntax when we define the function, PHP will always force the argument to be passed by reference regardless of whether or not the programmer remembers to do it.

With this in mind, we modify our snippet to:

```
$foo = 2;
function AddTwo(&$num)
{
    $num += 2;
}
AddTwo($foo);
```

Again, $foo has the value 4 as expected. But we don't have to pass the argument by reference anymore since we defined the function to always use a reference.

In all of the above examples, the variable $num is scoped locally to the function. This means that it will not interfere with a $num variable that has been defined globally and is used elsewhere. Also, $num can be used as an argument when defining other functions with no troubles.

A last but important issue regarding functions is the ability to define functions with **default variables** for their arguments. Assigning variables to constant values when defining the function does this. For example:

```
function PersonFunction($age , $name = "John Doe")
{
    // statements
}
```

Having done this, we can call the function with one or two arguments. If we leave the second one out, the function will simply assume that $name is John Doe. However, if we do supply the second argument,then whatever we put in will override the default value.

The only thing to keep in mind is that PHP requires all arguments with default values to be stacked to the right of the argument list. The script will not execute otherwise.

Returning Values

Often, we will want to manipulate data that we give to a function and return our results. This is accomplished by the optional return keyword in PHP:

```
function DoubleNumber($num)
{
    return 2 * $num;
}
// will output 6
print (DoubleNumber(3));
```

We can return any of the primitive variable types, including arrays. Also, a function may be able to return more than one type of value, as in the following example:

```
function Divide($a, $b)
{
    if { (0 == $b)
        return FALSE;
    }
    return $a / b;
}
```

Here, the function will return the value of $a divided by $b (which will be an integer or a float), unless $b is zero. In that case, it will return the Boolean value, FALSE. This makes PHP more flexible than strictly typed languages where functions can only return one type of value, and we have to declare that type when we define the function.

It is also possible to return a reference from a PHP function, but we must use the reference operator & when we define the function and assign its return value to a variable:

```
function &ReturnReference()
{
    return $ReferenceVar;
}
$SomeReference = &ReturnReference();
```

Variable Functions

In a way analogous to PHP's variable variables, we can create and use variable functions. This is accomplished by putting parenthesis after a variable. When PHP sees this, it looks for a function with the appropriate name to execute:

```
function PrintHello()
{
    return "Hello!\n";
}

$FunctionVar = 'PrintHello';

// prints Hello!
print ($FunctionVar());
```

There is a very wide range of functionality that we can get out of user-defined functions in PHP. This is particularly powerful when used in conjunction with PHP's system of classes and objects, which we will cover next.

Classes and Objects

Before we start in with a technical definition of classes and objects, we should talk for a moment about a more basic issue, the difference between procedural and object-oriented programming (OOP).

The simple examples we have seen so far in this chapter are all procedural. That is to say, there was data, and we manipulated that data with various routines or functions. Sometimes these were functions provided by the language, and sometimes we had written them ourselves. In any case, the important thing to recognize is that the data held in the different variables we saw was not in any way connected or associated to the functions that acted on them. We start with some data, manipulate it in some way, do something with the results, and then the script ends. This is what the term **procedural programming** means.

This is a perfectly reasonable top-level approach to writing programs. However, as programs get larger, we may find that it has some drawbacks. Firstly, we may end up doing the same types of things over and over. Second, it is possible that we will have a great many functions and variables all over, and we will want to find a good way to help organize them. Finally, we may want to associate functions and the data they manipulate more closely. When this happens, we should code in an **object-oriented** style.

Procedural vs. Object-Oriented Programs

So what makes OOP different from procedural programming? When we code an application with functions, we create programs that are code-centric, applications that call function by function consecutively. The data is first sent as the input, the function does the actual transformation, and then it returns the corresponding output. OOP takes the opposite approach since it is data-centric.

Here is an illustration showing the two paradigms:

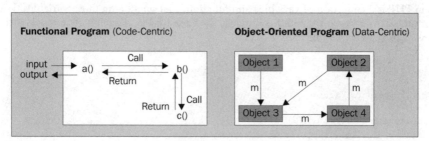

As we can see from the above diagram, input enters the function a(), which then calls the function b() using the output of a(). Function b() then calls c() using the output of b(). Then c() returns its output to b() which then returns its output to a(). Function a() finally produces the program output. Function a() would be the main function of a typical C program. In the object-oriented model, objects request the services of others, easily seen when Object 1 requests the service of Object 3. Object 3 in turn requests the service of Object 4 and so on, until Object 1 receives a reply from Object 3 of the end result, tracing backwards.

What's happening is that each object uses the services provided by the others within the program to receive information so it can do its own work, that is, make its own decisions based on asking other objects for information. The passing of these messages is the flow of the program in itself, the data and the methods or the functionality of the object are contained in one central location.

The difference between the two paradigms is that objects contain all the data and behavior that should exist together, while the data and functions are clearly separated in the functional paradigm. This makes object-oriented code very easy to trace during maintenance and increases the modularity of the project.

Now, this doesn't mean that procedural programs aren't maintainable, because they can be. It just requires a lot more thinking and organization on the architect's part to ensure that everything is located in the proper location. Also ensuring there are no global variables being manipulated in many of the project files if any should exist. The best thing about OOP is that we just make the objects as they make sense, follow some guidelines, and things should be pretty organized. With more complex applications, the use of special patterns can strengthen the design of the systems so we can reap added benefits.

Classes

In any program there are variables that hold data, and functions that perform some operation using these variables. In procedural programming, these variables and functions are thought of as separate entities, whereas in OOP, variables and functions are grouped together in distinct modules, called **classes**.

The class is made up of any number of properties (data) and methods (functions). Once we have defined the class, we can make any number of **objects** that belong to the class.

The object would be an **instance** of the class. The functions in that object are referred to as **methods** of the class, and the variables are called **member** variables. A method is a service (very similar to an implementation of a function) that an object guarantees to provide to its clients (other objects). When an object requests a service from another, it passes a message and receives a response.

A class in PHP is a collection of variables and functions that operate on those variables. We define a class with the class keyword, and then enclose the code for the class in a code block, just as for functions. This is a very simple class:

```
class FirstClass
{
    var $mReturnValue;

    function ShowReturnValue()
    {
        return $this->mReturnValue;
    }
} // end class FirstClass
```

Our class has one member variable $mReturnValue. The leading m at the beginning of the variable name is not required, but is customarily done when using classes to indicate that it is a member variable. The ShowReturnValue() method simply returns $mReturnValue.

In many languages such as PHP, the $this variable refers to the current object. Therefore, using $this->mReturnValue tells the function to return the object's $mReturnValue variable. If we hadn't used $this, then PHP would have looked for an $mReturnValue defined in the ShowReturnValue() method. Since that doesn't exist the function would always return nothing.

The **arrow** (->) **operator** lets us indicate what part of the $this object we are interested in. Note that there is no $ sign in front of mReturnValue when using $this->mReturnValue;.

A very important issue is that member variables in PHP can only have static initializers:

```
    var $mReturnValue = date();
```

If we use the above statement, our example would not have worked. However, we could have said:

```
    var $mReturnValue = 5;
```

and gotten a result, since 5 is a static variable.

When we want to make use of this class, we **instantiate** an object with the new keyword, like this:

```
$class_test = new FirstClass();
```

When an object has been created using the new operator, it is said that the object has been **instantiated**. Thus, the object is called an **instance** of the FirstClass class.

We can then make use of the member variables and methods through the -> operator:

```
$class_test->mReturnValue = 10;
// Outputs "10"
print ($class_test->ShowReturnValue());
```

Constructors

In the example above, we had to set the value of $mReturnValue ourselves after the object was created. This is typically undesirable. The correct way to avoid this is to use a **constructor** function.

Constructors are special functions in classes. In PHP, a constructor is a function that has the same name as the class it is defined in. It is executed automatically whenever an instance of that class is instantiated. This is very useful for setting up the initial state of the class. They can define default values and do all the things that normal functions can do:

```
class FirstClass
{
    var $mReturnValue;

    function FirstClass($num = 10)
    {
        $this->mReturnValue = $num;
    }

    function ShowReturnValue()
    {
        return $this->mReturnValue;
    }
} // end class FirstClass
```

This time we will instantiate two objects so that we can see how our new functionality can be used:

```
$class_test = new FirstClass();
$second_class_test = new FirstClass(4);

print ($class_test->ShowReturnValue());          // outputs "10"
print ($second_class_test->ShowReturnValue());   //outputs "4"
```

Here we didn't have to access the $mReturnValue directly from our program. The constructor set it up for us. In $class_test, we did not pass any arguments to the constructor, so it used the assigned default of 10. In $second_class_test, we gave the constructor an argument of 4, so it set $mReturnValue to that value.

The second very important issue to be aware of is that the two objects we set up do not share any data or methods. That is to say, the $mReturnValue and ShowReturnValue() of $class_test have nothing to do with their counterparts in $second_class_test. Although they share the same functionality, the two objects represent distinct data, and have methods that operate on their own data and nobody else's.

Technically speaking, we could have gotten the above output by simply going directly to the $mReturnValue variable, like this:

```
print ($class_test->mReturnValue);
```

But unlike some other object-oriented languages, PHP does not support the idea of public and private variables. In a language such as C++, we can be explicit about which variables are available to the outside and which are not by using public and private keywords.

At the time of writing, PHP does not support these declarations, so all member variables are essentially public. However, it is considered bad practice to access and/or modify member variables directly. Instead, we use methods such as ShowReturnValue() to get at the data. Likewise, if we wanted to modify the $mReturnValue variable after it was first defined, we would create a method like ModifyReturnValue() that would do the job for us.

Extending Classes

One of the most useful things about classes is the ability to extend them and add new functionality. This means that we can take an existing class and give it new member variables and methods while retaining all of the original things that made us use the class in the first place. It encourages code reuse that helps us save time by making use of code already written. Also, it is much more useful, in practice, to write pluggable modules such that we can easily swap in a different subclass and have a different implementation of something, but not change the rest of our code.

We accomplish this with the following syntax:

```
class B extends A
{
    // new code goes here
}
```

To see this in action, we will extend our `FirstClass()`, and give it a new method:

```
class SecondClass extends FirstClass
{
    function IncrementValue()
    {
        $this->mReturnValue++;
    }
}
```

Here we created a new kind of class called `SecondClass()`. It does everything that `FirstClass()` did, but has a new method that increments the `$mReturnValue`. Note that we didn't have to define that member variable since it was already given to us as a part of `FirstClass()`. We can instantiate an object from `SecondClass()`, just as we did before:

```
$class_test = new SecondClass();
$class_test->IncrementValue();        // $mReturnValue is now 11
print ($class_test->ShowReturnValue()); // outputs "11"
```

Also, we did not define a constructor for `SecondClass()`. What happens in this case is that PHP goes up the parental tree of classes looking for a constructor to execute. In this case, it found that `FirstClass()` had a constructor, so that was used. However, if we had defined a constructor in `SecondClass()` that would have been used instead.

The :: Operator

Sometimes, we want to make use of a method in a class, but we don't need it for anything else. In this case, we can use the `::` operator to access the method directly without even instantiating an object. This method is commonly referred to as **static method invocation**.

This happens very frequently in some cases, such as the PEAR database access classes that will be used later in this book. Here is a bare bones example:

```
class SuperSimple
{
    function ReturnName()
    {
        return "My name is John Doe.";
    }
}   // end class SuperSimple

// outputs "My name is John Doe."
print (SuperSimple::ReturnName());
```

Here we did not actually create an object of type `SuperSimple()`. Instead, we used the operator to directly access the `ReturnName()` method defined in the class. Note that this means that the `ReturnName()` function cannot make effective use of instance methods or variables.

The Parent Operator

Remember that in our `SecondClass()`, there was no constructor defined. Let us return to that example and put one in:

```
class SecondClass extends FirstClass
{
    function SecondClass()
    {
      // do nothing
    }

    function IncrementValue()
    {
      $this->mReturnValue++;
    }
}
```

Now we have eliminated any kind of constructor being called. The constructor for `SecondClass()` does nothing, but PHP will not look for any more constructors from parent classes. However, we can make PHP access a method from the parent of a particular class with the **parent** operator.

To regain the execution of the constructor from `FirstClass()`, we could do this:

```
class SecondClass extends FirstClass
{
    function SecondClass()
    {
        parent::FirstClass();
    }

    function IncrementValue()
    {
        $this->mReturnValue++;
    }
}
```

Now it behaves exactly as it did before.

> *This is similar to using the `super()` construct in Java; thus, PHP's implementation maps to other OO languages.*

There is a tremendous wealth of power that can be gained by using classes effectively in our program. We will employ them a great deal throughout the rest of this book.

Object/Class Functions

PHP provides us with several built-in functions that can be used to probe various parts of a given object. For example, we can use the `class_exists()` function to see if a particular class has already been defined:

```
// instantiate new object IF the class exists
if (class_exists("FirstClass")) {
    $fc = new FirstClass();
}
```

The full list of object class functions (except for a few deprecated ones) is as follows:

Function	Usage
boolean class_exists(string class_name)	Returns TRUE if the class referenced by class_name has been defined, FALSE otherwise.
string get_class(string object_name)	Returns the name of the class of which object_name is an instance, or FALSE if object_name is not an object.
array get_class_methods(mixed class_name)	Returns an array of all the method names in class_name. We can use either a string representing a class for class_name or an actual object that we've instantiated.
array get_class_vars(mixed class_name)	Analagous to get_class_methods(). Returns an array with the default properties of the class. Uninitialized properties are not reported.
array get_declared_classes(void)	Returns an array with the names of all the defined classes.
array get_object_vars(object object_name)	Returns an associative array with the names and values of all defined variables in an object. If a variable hasn't yet been assigned a value it is not reported.
string get_parent_class(mixed class_name)	Returns the name of the parent class. class_name can either be a string referring to a defined class or an instantiated object.
boolean is_a(object object_name, string class_name)	Returns TRUE if object_name is an object of type class_name or has class_name as one of its parent classes.
boolean is_subclass_of(object object_name, string class_name)	Returns TRUE if object_name belongs to a class that is a subclass of class_name.
boolean method_exists(object object_name, string method_name)	Returns TRUE if method_name is a method for the object object_name.

For a more detailed explanation, refer to the online PHP manual at:
http://www.php.net/manual/en/ref.classobj.php.

File and Directory Access

In this book, we will be working a great deal with external files both on the file system and at remote sources. Therefore, this section will detail reading to and writing from files. PHP has an enormous number of functions that help to manipulate files and directories, and we will look at a few of them in depth here. However, by the end of this section we should have little trouble learning about the other available methods if we are so inclined.

Whenever we deal with a file, there are always three basic steps to go through:

❑ Create a file handle for the file in question

❑ Read from or write to the file via the file handle

❑ Close the file

Creating a File Handle

The versatile `fopen()` function makes creating file handles a simple thing in PHP. If successful, it returns a file handle (sometimes called a **file pointer**) aimed at the beginning of the file in question. It returns FALSE on failure.

> **The file handle is a special resource data type.**

Let us look at how we can add the `fopen()` functionality:

```
fopen(string filename, string mode [, int use_include_path]);
```

The argument `filename` can be the name of the file, or its absolute path. If `filename` is the name of the file, then it is assumed that the file is in the current working directory.

The second argument `mode` indicates whether the file is to be opened for reading, writing, or appending. It can have one of the possible values. There are several available modes:

Mode	Meaning
r	Open for reading with the file pointer at the start of the file.
r+	Open for reading and writing with the file pointer at the start of the file.
w	Open the file for writing with the file pointer at the start of the file. Truncate the file length to zero. Attempt to create the file if it doesn't exist.
w+	Open the file for reading and writing with the file pointer at the start of the file. Truncate the file length to zero. Attempt to create the file if it doesn't exist.
a	Open the file for writing with the file pointer at the end of the file. Attempt to create the file if it doesn't exist.
a+	Open the file for reading and writing with the file pointer at the end of the file. Attempt to create the file if it doesn't exist.

In all of these cases, a b may be appended to the mode in fopen(). On systems that distinguish between binary and text files, the inclusion of a b tells PHP that it is handling a binary file. Use of b will have no effect whatsoever on UNIX systems, so it is wise to always add the b when writing portable scripts.

The third argument use_include_path specifies whether PHP should search for files in the include_path too. The include_path can be set in the php.ini configuration file.

A typical (but poorly implemented) usage is:

```
$fp = fopen("./myfile.txt", "r");
```

This tries to open a file called myfile.txt in the same directory as the script is running in for reading. We know that it is open for reading because the second argument for the mode is r.

Above, we noted that the fopen() example was poorly implemented. This is because the function is not guaranteed to succeed. It is always wise to check when using fopen() to make sure that a file handle was actually created. A much better implementation would be:

```
if (!($fp = fopen("./myfile.txt", "r"))) {
    die("Couldn't open file!");
}
```

That way, if something goes awry, we will know about it with a useful error message.

Another very appealing feature of this function is that it handles HTTP and FTP 'files' transparently, assuming that the fopen_wrappers configuration option is set to On (which is the default). Of course, in the case of http, the 'file' must be opened **Read Only**.

The following three statements are perfectly valid:

```
$fp = fopen("http://www.wrox.com/", "r");
```

```
$fp = fopen("ftp://somedomain.com/pub/datafile.xml", "r");
```

```
$fp = fopen("ftp://user:pass@somedomain.com/file.txt", "w");
```

This can make tasks like fetching syndicated content almost trivially simple. PHP treats a file pointer from an HTTP or FTP 'file' exactly the same as a file pointer for a file on the file system, so once we have opened it we can proceed as normal to work with the file.

When we are finished with a file handle, it is always a good idea to close it using the fclose() function. Technically speaking, this is not required since PHP will automatically free up resources once they are not being used. However, it is still a good idea because it will keep us from accidentally writing over something because we are using a file handle from a previous fopen() command. The syntax for fclose() is:

```
fclose(int filehandle);
```

Reading and Writing To a File

Now that we have a file handle safely in hand, we can go about reading from and/or writing to it. The most basic way of getting data from a file is with the `fread()` function:

```
fread(int filehandle , int length);
```

It will read up to `length` bytes from the file, and return those bytes as a string. Reading stops when `length` bytes have been read, or when the end of the file is reached, whichever comes first.

We can use the `filesize()` function to put the entire contents of a file into a variable:

```
$datafile = "./datafile.txt";
if (!($fp = fopen($datafile, "r"))) {
    die("Couldn't open $datafile");
}

$filecontents = fread($fp , filesize($filename));
fclose($fp);
```

Now, the entire file's contents are held in the `$filecontents` variable. However, there might be times when we don't want to read the entire file in, at once. For example, if it is a very long file, it might be too much of a memory hog to hold it all in one variable. In this case, we would want to read it in using smaller chunks and process the data in some streaming manner. This could be accomplished along these lines:

```
$datafile = "./bigdatafile.txt";
if (!($fp = fopen($datafile , "r"))) {
    die("Couldn't open $datafile");
}
while ($datachunk = fread($fp, 4096)) {
    // do something with the 4k of data in $datachunk

}
fclose($fp);
```

Here, we are reading in the contents of `bigdatafile.txt` located in the same directory four kilobytes at a time. The `while` loop will eventually terminate when there is no more data to be read because then `fread()` will return FALSE.

Now that we have seen how to get data out of a file, we should look at how to put some data into a file. The basic method is to use the counterpart of the `fread()` function – `fwrite()`:

```
fwrite(int filehandle , string data [, int length]);
```

The function will attempt to put the string represented by data into the file corresponding to the file-handle, and insert the data at the place in the file where file-handle is pointing. If the optional parameter length is included, `fwrite()` will only try to put `length` bytes in.

Here is a simple example:

```php
$datafile = "./character_traits.txt";
if (!($fp = fopen($datafile, "a"))) {
    die("Couldn't open $datafile");
}
$data_string = "Debbie wears crazy socks.\n"

fwrite($fp , $data_string);
fclose($fp);
```

Since the mode that we chose to open the file is a, the file pointer is set to the end of the file. Therefore, when we write our data to the file it appends it to the end. Keep in mind that PHP will try to create a character_traits.txt file, if it is not already there. This can potentially cause a problem depending on the platform we are using.

On UNIX systems, the 'write file' operation will fail if the web server process does not have write permissions for the directory we are writing to. Also, the file created will be owned by the web server process. We can use the chown and chmod commands to allow the server process to write to a directory. This can be accomplished by typing man chown and man chmod respectively at the command line.

Using the file() Function

There is one more function which provides a quick and dirty way to get at the contents of a file. The file() function is something of a combination of fopen() and fread(). It takes the contents of a file and returns an array with each line of the file corresponding to an array element. Mirroring the fopen() function, file() can read HTTP and FTP 'filenames' transparently:

```php
file(string filename [, int use_include_path]);
```

As before, if the optional second parameter is set to 1, then PHP will look for filename in the include path. Please note that we do not have to supply file() with a file handle. All we need is the file name, and PHP takes care of the rest.

This bit of code allows us to output the contents of a file using this function and include line numbers:

```php
$datafile = "./datafile.txt";

$datafile_contents = file($datafile);

foreach ($datafile_contents as $line_number => $line) {
    print ($line_number + 1) . ': ' . $line . '<br />';
}
```

We are adjusting the $line_number variable so that the output starts with line 1.

Keep in mind that the line terminators from the original file will still be in the strings contained in the $datafile_contents array. We can use the trim() function to remove these if we wish:

```php
for ($i=0 ; $i < count($datafile_contents) ; ++$i) {
    $datafile_contents[$i] = trim($datafile_contents[$i]);
}
```

Summary

This chapter has been a brief refresher on the PHP language.

First we looked at the basic PHP syntax. Then we saw how we can create variables and skirted through the different types. Later we considered constants. We also looked at the most commonly used operators.

Then we turned our attention to the structures that form the building block of any successful application:

❑ The conditional statements `if` and `switch` are used to test a condition and execute different blocks of code depending on the results.

❑ The loops `while`, `do ... while`, `for`, and `foreach` allow repetitive behavior. The `foreach` loop is specifically designed for traversing the elements of an array.

❑ Functions are reusable units of code that can be invoked as necessary to perform specific tasks. They make code more modular and maintainable.

Then we looked at OOP that is essential for PHP to survive as the web platform of tomorrow. We talked about how it differs from procedural programming and discussed its benefits – increased reusability and maintainability. We learned that objects contain methods, members, and a constructor and that they become instantiated in our program with PHP's operators.

The aspects of OOP that PHP supports make it possible to create large and complex applications in a full OOP framework. It is interesting to note that some of the most popular PHP-based libraries out there, such as PHPLib and PEAR, are implemented as OOP classes.

File systems are useful for storing simple data like configuration files and unstructured data like images or word processing documents. Finally, we looked at PHP's built-in functions for manipulating files in the server's file system.

There is an enormous amount of functionality built into the APIs that are available. In particular, it is always a good idea to read through the references for string manipulation functions, array manipulation functions, regular expressions, and file or directory access functions.

For a detailed treatment of the basics of PHP programming, refer to *Beginning PHP4* (*ISBN 1-861003-73-0*) and *Professional PHP4* (*ISBN 1-861006-91-8*) from *Wrox Press*. The most up-to-date information is always available on the official PHP web site at http://www.php.net/.

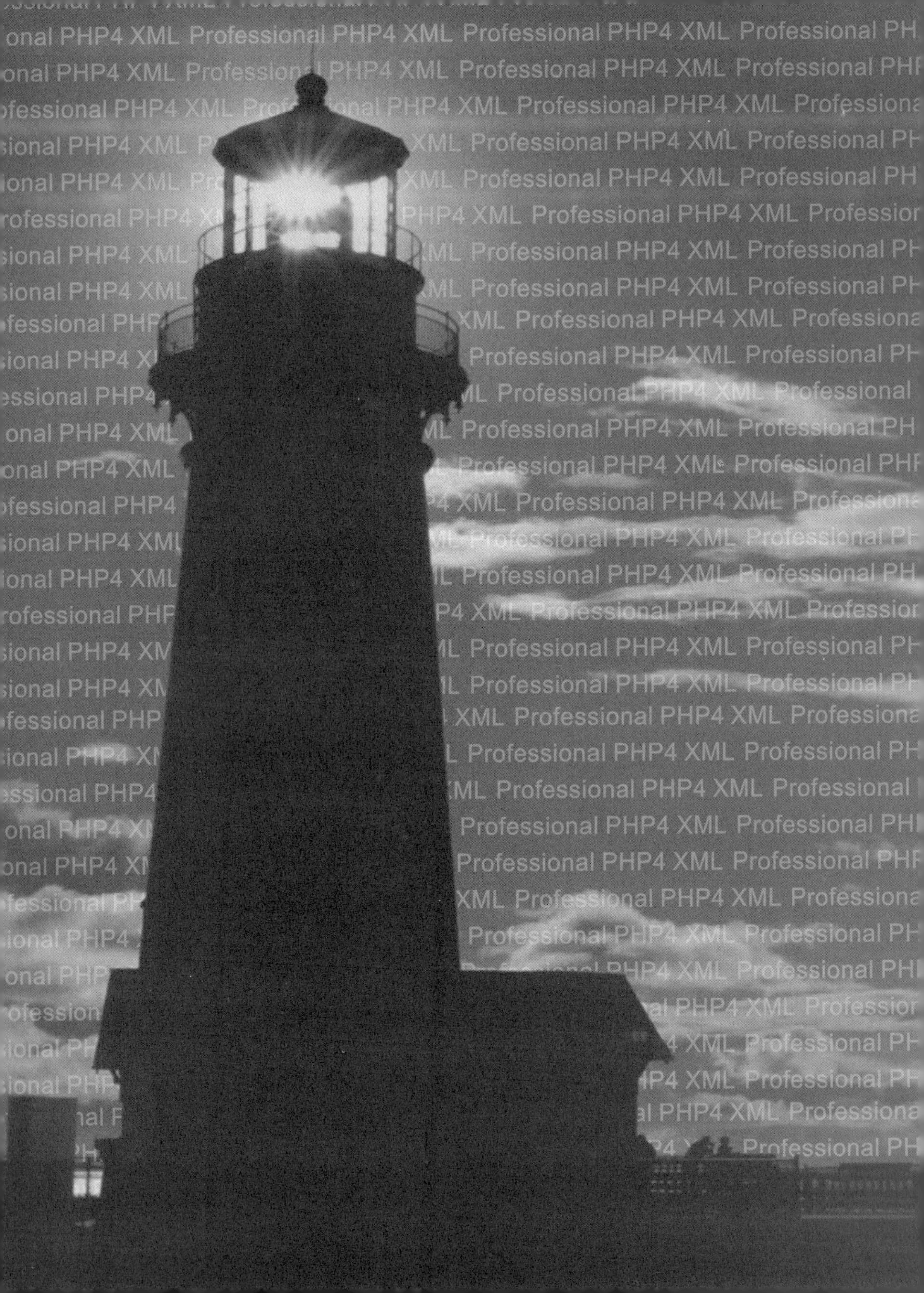
Professional PHP4 XML

3

XML Fundamentals

Welcome to XML! You may already have seen some XML documents before reading this chapter, and noticed that XML documents are easy to understand for humans since they tend to be self-describing. However, XML is not just tags and some text, there are a lot of very strict rules, definitions, and standards, defined to create the standard for data representation – XML.

In this chapter we'll be covering the fundamentals of the XML 1.0 specification by the W3C. We'll examine which are the rules to write well-formed documents according to the specification, and we'll learn what a valid document is and how to use DTDs or Schemas to define vocabularies, and validate documents against those vocabularies. We'll also cover namespaces that allow us to mix several vocabularies in the same document without collisions, and that are a key standard in modern XML documents. XML is a flexible way to create common information formats, and share both the format and the data on the World Wide Web, intranets, and elsewhere.

Data Representation

The storage, retrieval, and manipulation of data have been very important areas of computer science since its very beginning and are still important today.

Since the invention of the first computer, programmers have been dealing with data. Earlier, programmers used punch cards to store information and process it in computers. Later they had tapes and disks, and the information was stored in files. As more and more data needed to be processed by computers, databases emerged. Now we have many terabytes of data around us – we have digital books, digital pictures, digital movies, and digital audio, for example.

Relational databases have been the de facto standard to store and manipulate data since the late '80s. Since the Internet emerged in the early '90s, computers are being interconnected, systems becoming distributed, and data is not only being stored but also transmitted from one system to another.

While relational databases are very good solutions for static on-site data storage and retrieval, they aren't designed for sending or receiving information, or exchanging data between applications.

Extensible Markup Language (XML) is a new data modeling standard that has been specifically designed to allow data to flow between systems. XML can also be used to store and retrieve information. As a data modeling language XML is an alternative to relational databases and in many situations the use of XML is better for some applications than using a relational database. For other applications we can combine relational databases and XML documents for best results.

Meta Data

We've been talking about data, but it's very difficult to understand data without **meta data**. We call meta data the information that is not data itself, but that which is used to describe data. In simple terms we can call meta data **data about data**. For instance, the famous ASCII end-of-line and carriage return characters (0x0A and 0x0D) are meta data.

> **Meta data is data that describes the real data.**

Meta data exists in a variety of formats. Though computers can understand data without meta data, it is a very hard task, as they need more information while processing the data, like rules about the data, what it represents, or what it is for. Thus, when representing information on a computer, one important task is to add enough meta data to allow computer programs to process the information properly.

Look at this example:

Information without explicit meta data (unstructured)	Information with explicit meta data (structured)
Payment: please pay $25.67 to John Williams or Jimmy Smith from Foo. inc, the payment should be ready by the 25th of January. Thanks Frank.	Payment Amount: $25.67 Payto: John Williams Payto: Jimmy Smith Company: Foo.inc Due: 20020125 Authorized-by: Frank

In the left column we have a payment note that a manager wrote to his secretary. The secretary has all the required data to easily process the payment without asking any questions. If we use a computer system to process these payments, then the left column can be very difficult to process – we can write a program to parse the note and extract the information, but if the manager changes the way he writes his notes the parser will be useless, and the program will fail. In the right side we represented the same note but we added meta data; we used a plain text format where each line has the format 'meta data: data'. A computer program can easily understand this information, and process the payment without problems.

It's relatively easy for humans to extract meta data that's mixed in with the data itself, or to extrapolate it from context, but not so for a computer.

Markup Languages

Markup languages are very old, in fact, they are older than computers. When information was stored using paper, people used to mark some text from their papers, and maybe take notes on the margins. That's the origin of markup, and it's exactly the way in which markup languages work.

In 1969 while men were landing on the moon, Ed Mosher, Ray Lorie, and Charles F Goldfarb of IBM Research invented the first modern markup language – **Generalized Markup Language** (GML). This language was adopted in 1986 by ISO as a standard, and became ISO 8879 – **Standard Generalized Markup Language** (SGML), which used **tags** to describe meta data. SGML is not a document language in itself, but a description of how to specify one. In fact SGML is meta data.

This is an example of an SGML document:

```
<!DOCTYPE email [
<!ELEMENT email 0 0 ((to & from & date & subject?), text) >
<! ELEMENT text - 0 (para+) >
<!ELEMENT para 0 0 (#PCDATA) >
<!ELEMENT (to, from, date, subject) - 0 (#PCDATA) >
]>
<date>10/12/99
<to>john@foo.com
<from>Mike
<text>Hi, how are you?
```

SGML is a powerful and complex language that has been widely used by the US Government, and some very large organizations such as publishers of technical information and standards. The complexity of SGML was the reason why small organizations and individuals couldn't afford the cost of technology based on SGML.

In 1996 the World Wide Web Consortium (W3C) began the process of designing a simple markup language based on SGML. The result – XML. XML is based on SGML, and is actually a subset of SGML. XML is designed to be understood by humans and computers as well, and it is simple, so technologies based on XML would facilitate the adoption of the standard easily.

XML 1.0 became a W3C recommendation in February 1998. The formal specification is available on the Web from the W3C site at: http://www.w3.org/TR/REC-xml/.

In XML we use tags to indicate meta data or attributes of the tags (that is, text between tags for data).

We can write a payment note using XML, like this:

```xml
<?xml version="1.0"?>
<payment>
  <payees>
    <payto>John Williams</payto>
    <payto>Jimmy Smith</payto>
  </payees>
  <amount>25.67</amount>
  <company>Foo Inc.</company>
  <due>20020125</due>
  <authorizedby>Frank</authorizedby>
</payment>
```

XML is a plain-text format and hence human readable, also we can use the tools of our choice to read or edit it. As we can see, the information in the above payment note example can be understood both by humans and by computers.

> Markup is a method of conveying meta data. Markup languages use string literals or tags to delimit and describe this data.

XML Syntax

The XML 1.0 specification defines that a document must be **well-formed** to be an XML document. Also, the parsers must validate documents to be well-formed, and refuse to process documents that are not well-formed – this is to prevent XML implementations from allowing non-compliant XML documents to be processed, which is what happened with HTML.

A well-formed document is comprised of three parts:

❑   An optional Prolog

❑   A mandatory body in the form of a tree of XML elements

❑   An optional Epilog

XML documents are ordered as Prolog, Root Element, and Epilog. A document with nothing but a Root Element is perfectly acceptable. The Epilog on the other hand can contain any information that is covered in Prolog except for DOCTYPE and XML declarations. Since the Prolog and Epilog are optional, we'll describe the XML body first. Later in the chapter we will see more of the Prolog and Epilog.

The XML Body

The XML body is a tree of XML elements. The root element of the tree is known as the **document root element**. There must be only one root element in a well-formed XML document. This is the top-level element in an XML document, and all the other elements are called its **children**. The body is a mandatory part of the XML document.

Elements

An element is the basic building block of an XML document. Elements can contain several kinds of XML objects including other elements.

Tags delimit elements, and define the element by enclosing the string literal name in angle brackets (< >). Every element has a starting tag, an optional content, and an ending tag. If the element is empty, then it can start and end in the same tag. We'll see examples of this later.

This is an element named `name` that contains text (`John Smith`):

```
<name>John Smith</name>
```

and without content we could have written:

```
<name></name>
or
<name/>
```

See more details in the Elements section under DTDs and Schemas.

Empty Elements

Some elements cannot have content, for example, the `<br>` HTML element is used to signal a line break, and can't have any content. Since XML defines that all elements must have closing tags, we have to write empty elements in XML as:

```
<br></br>
```

or:

```
<br />
```

or:

```
<br/>
```

The first form can be used for an element that is empty. The second form is recommended since it explicitly indicates that the element can't have content. This convention is not mandatory, but recommended. The last form won't be accepted for older HTML-based browsers, so if we are rendering data to a browser we should use `<br />` instead of `<br/>` for compatibility reasons.

Nesting Elements

Elements can contain subelements; the XML specification defines that element nesting is valid up to any level as long as it is done properly. To have elements properly nested we have to follow one simple rule – when a closing tag is found, the name of the closing tag must match the name of the last opening tag found.

Here is an example of invalid nesting also known as crossed tags:

```
<paragraph>
  <italics>This is a test<bold>(</italics>
  <title>The way of the tiger</title>)</bold>
</paragraph>
```

Here is an example of valid nesting:

```
<paragraph>
  <italics>This is a test</italics><bold>(
  <title>The way of the tiger</title>)</bold>
</paragraph>
```

Characters

Since XML was designed to be used worldwide, valid characters are not restricted to the common Latin-ASCII set that most applications use. XML files can contain 16-bit Unicode characters. The following table lists the valid XML characters:

Character Values (hexadecimal)	Description
09	Horizontal tab
0A	Line-feed
0D	Carriage-return
20-7E	ASCII display characters
80-D7FF	Unicode characters
E000-F8FF	Private Use Area
F900-FFFD	CJK (Chinese-Japanese-Korean) characters

Names

Elements have names that are indicated in the start and end tag of the element. All names must begin with a letter, an underscore (_), or a colon (:), and can use valid name characters as well. Valid name characters also include digits, hyphens (-), and periods (.). Letters are not limited to English characters.

In practice, however, the colon character should not be used except as a namespace delimiter. Also, element names can't begin with the string XML, in any case format, for instance, 'xMl', and 'XMl', are not valid as element names.

> XML is case-sensitive; that is, <foo>, <fOo>, and <FOO> are all different element names in an XML document.

For example:

```
<directory.person>John Williams</directory.person>
<Foo>This is a test</Foo>
<greetings>Hello World</greetings>
```

Notice that the period is valid as a character for <tagnames>.

Character Data

Elements can also contain character data. Character data is anything that is not markup. It can contain any valid characters with the exception that some XML-specific characters must be escaped as XML entities.

For example the <, >, and & characters must be written as <, >, and & respectively. All XML-compliant parsers must respect this. We will discuss entities in more detail in the *Entities* section.

Here is an example of character data in an element:

```
<text>
   This is an element that contains some text.
   This text was written by John &amp; Will.
</text>
```

Mixing Elements and Character Data

Elements, subelements, and character data can be mixed in several ways. For example:

```
<text>
   <title>Hello world</title>

   This is some text in the middle...

   <paragraph>
     Here's a little story <footnote>very little</footnote>
     about a town where Jack &amp; Jill lived.
   </paragraph>

  More text in the middle...

</text>
```

While mixing text and subelements is allowed by the XML standard, some XML designers consider that it is preferred not to allow the mix so as to keep the XML file neat, both for parsers and for humans.

Attributes

Attributes are used to describe the properties of XML elements. An attribute can be written as follows:

```
<person age="25">Jimmy Smith</person>
```

An attribute is formed by an attribute name, an = sign, and an attribute value. A well-formed XML document must observe that:

❑ **Attributes have a value**
In older HTML versions we can find attributes without a value, for example:

```
<input type="checkbox" checked />
```

If we have to emulate an attribute without a value in XML we must use a dummy value such as:

```
<input type="checkbox" checked="checked" />
```

❑ **Values are enclosed between single or double quotes**
Attribute values can contain any valid XML characters. We can enclose attribute values between double or single quotes. The quotes should be escaped using the XML entities ' and " for ' and " respectively.

❑ **Attribute names as well as element names do not begin with any variety of the 'XML' word**

❑ **Attribute names are not repeated in an XML element**

Let's now look at some valid and invalid attributes:

Attribute	Validity
`<person age=25></person>`	Invalid (no quotes around value)
`<person age='25'></person>`	Valid
`<person name="John Williams"></person>`	Valid
`<person name="Peter" age='25' />`	Valid
`<company name='Johnson & Johnson' />`	Invalid (& must be escaped)
`<room number='145' tv-included />`	Invalid, attribute without value
`<company name="Foo Inc" name="Foo.com" />`	Invalid, two attributes called name

> If the name is the "noun" of an XML element, then attributes are its "adjectives".

Special Attributes

There're two special attributes defined by the XML recommendation – xml:space and xml:lang.

xml:space

This attribute can be used to tell the processing application how to treat whitespace in an XML document. An application can preserve or remove whitespace as needed since it is not data in an XML element; we will see more about whitespace in the next section.

The xml:space attribute may override the way applications deal with whitespace. This attribute can have two values:

- ❑ `xml:space=preserve`

- ❑ `xml:space=default`

The first one tells the application to preserve whitespace for this element and all of its children. The second one indicates that default whitespace processing can be applied. Therefore, if this attribute is used at the document root element it will affect the element that contains the attribute and all of its children, that is, it will affect the whole XML document.

Here is an example:

```
<letter>
  <from>J.Smith</from>
  <to>Jack Smith</to>
  <text xml:space="preserve">
      Dear Jack,
      ....
  </text>
</letter>
```

xml:lang

This attribute also applies to the element that contains the attribute and all of its children. It is used to indicate the language used in affected elements. The value of this attribute can follow several formats – the most common is the ISO-639 2-letter language code, for example, 'en' for English, 'ja' for Japanese, and so on.

For more information on code for the names of languages see:
http://sunsite.berkeley.edu/amher/iso_639.html.

Here is an example:

```
<comments>
  <comment>This is a comment</comment>
  <comment xm:lang="en">
    This is the English language value of attribute
  </comment>
</comments>
```

Whitespace

When using XML parsers, it is good to know how whitespace is treated. In XML the following characters are considered **whitespace**:

- ❑ The tab character 0x09

- ❑ The line feed character 0x0A

- ❑ The carriage return character 0x0D

- ❑ The space character 0x20

The rule for handling whitespace is very simple – all whitespace characters within the content are preserved while whitespace within element tags and attribute values may or may not be removed.

So, if we have the following XML document:

```
<foo>
  <data>
    <name>Data 1</name>
  </data>
  <data>
    <text>This is some text</text>
  </data>
</foo>
```

the application can receive either:

```
<foo>
  <data>
    <name>Data 1</name>
  </data>
  <data>
    <text>This is some text</text>
  </data>
</foo>
```

or:

```
<foo><data><name>Data 1</name></data><data><text>This is some
text</text></data></foo>
```

We have to be aware of how to deal with whitespace used for indentation at the application level since the parser is not obliged to remove it.

Character and Entity References

Sometimes, a character insertion may violate the well-formedness condition of the XML document. In such instances, it is best to use **character references** to insert characters in the XML document. There are two ways to use character references:

❑   &#NNNN;
     To indicate a character using its decimal Unicode value.

❑   &#xHHHH;
     To indicate a character using its hexadecimal Unicode value.

> *If you are familiar with ASCII, you can convert ASCII to Unicode by adding a 0x00 byte before the ASCII code of the character.*

  or   is equivalent to   and both represent the whitespace character.

Entity references allow the insertion of a string literal into elements or attribute values. Entity references are formed by the & sign followed by a legal XML name, and terminated by a semicolon (;).

Five entities are predefined in the XML specification:

❑   &

❑   <

❑   >

❑   '

❑   "

User-defined entity references are allowed as a way to use 'macros' to insert literals in an XML document – these entities must be defined in the XML document DTD (Document Type Definition). We shall detail DTDs later in this chapter.

Processing Instructions

Processing instructions (PIs) are a mechanism defined by the XML specification to pass specific information to the application about how to process a part, or the whole, of an XML document. Processing instructions are defined by the following syntax:

```
<?name value?>
```

name must be a valid XML name, while value can be any string; that's the complete definition of a processing instruction in the specification.

Here is an example:

```
<?validate schematron="sch1.xml"?>
<?php php code goes here ?>
<?render position="centered"?>
```

PHP (the wonderful language we are studying in this book) is inserted in HTML pages as an XML (or XHTML) processing instruction. While processing instructions are not commonly used in XML documents, some specific PIs are useful, for instance, to associate an XSLT stylesheet to an XML document.

Comments

Comments can be used to document or provide notes about an XML document. Comments can appear anywhere outside markup and can include any characters, including <, >, and & since they are not parsed. Comments follow this syntax:

```
<!-- comment-text -->
```

The XML specification allows, but doesn't require, an XML processor to provide a way for the application to retrieve comments. Therefore we should never use comments to transmit data, some kinds of PIs, or scripting elements, since the XML-compliant parser may remove the comments after parsing.

For example:

```
<foo>
<!-- now one data element for each piece of information -->
  <data>
    <!-- data may have a name and a text -->
    <name>The first data</name>
    <text>Hello world<!-- Simple text --></text>
  </data>
</foo>
```

> **XML parsers are not required by the XML specification to pass comments to the application. Comments are intended for humans, not for computers.**

CDATA Sections

CDATA sections are sections of text that must not be parsed, so we can include special characters such as <, >, and & in them. For example, if we want to write an HTML document inside an XML element, it can be very painful to escape all the < and > characters, so we can use a CDATA section and include the document as-is.

> **CDATA sections can appear anywhere but in markup.**

CDATA sections are defined in the following way:

```
<![CDATA[ DATA ]]>
```

For example:

```
<doc>
  <program>
    <name>Hello world</name>
    <language>HTML</language>
    <code><![CDATA[
      <html>
        Hello world
      </html>
    ]]></code>
  </program>
</doc>
```

CDATA sections are also useful to include XML fragments, code from programming languages, and non-parseable text. One problem, however, with CDATA sections is a browser that doesn't recognize XHTML will not know how to process the CDATA section, and will give a syntax error. To avoid this we can use forward slash (//) to comment out the CDATA section. The lines within a CDATA section although look suspiciously like markup, so an XML processor looking for markup will not scan them.

> CDATA sections should not be used to encode binary data since the binary data may contain the characters]] > indicating the end of a CDATA section. It is recommended that we use a normal XML element, and encode the binary data using base64 encoding.

Reviewing the XML Structure of a Document

Earlier in this chapter we have that a well-formed XML document is comprised of:

- ❑ An optional Prolog
- ❑ A mandatory body
- ❑ An optional Epilog

We have already discussed XML body earlier. In this section we will discuss Prolog and Epilog in detail.

The XML Prolog

The XML Prolog is that part of the XML document that is found before the document root element. The XML Prolog is important since many PIs or special directives on how to process the document are included at this level. The valid sections of the XML Prolog are:

- ❑ The XML declaration
- ❑ Processing instructions (PIs)
- ❑ Comments
- ❑ The Document Type Definition
- ❑ Internal subset declarations

We already know about processing instructions and comments, so we are going to focus on the new objects that are valid in the XML Prolog.

The XML Declaration

The XML declaration is, in fact, a processing instruction. All XML documents should begin with an XML declaration. Some XML parsers actually require the XML file to begin with the XML declaration, some don't. If present, the XML declaration must be right at the top of the document; not even whitespace is allowed before it. The XML declaration can indicate several characteristics about the XML document:

- ❑ The XML version in use:

```
<?xml version="1.0"?>
```

- ❑ The character set being used:

```
<?xml version="1.0" encoding="UTF-8"?>
```

Valid character sets are:

- ❏ UTF-8 (rq)
- ❏ UTF-16 (rq)
- ❏ ISO-8859-1

The standalone Declaration

A standalone document is a document without an **external markup declaration** (from the XML 1.0 spec). We can say that an external markup declaration is something that appears external to the document entity (the document root and its content), or in a parameter entity (explained later). Therefore, a document that doesn't have a DTD is usually a standalone document.

Here is an example:

```
<?xml version="1.0" encoding="UTF-8" standalone="yes" ?>
```

The Document Type Definition

We'll be studying what document type definitions do in detail when we study DTDs later in this chapter, but for now, think of them as a means to validate the structure of an XML document. They are declared in the Prolog as follows: the first snippet is an internal declaration, while the second shows two external declarations:

```
<!DOCTYPE Catalog [
  <!ENTITY copy "&#169;">
  <!ENTITY wrox "Wrox Press, Ltd.">
]>
```

```
<!DOCTYPE root_element_name SYSTEM "URI">
<!DOCTYPE root_element_name PUBLIC "URI">
```

The XML Epilog

The XML Epilog may contain comments, PIs, or whitespace. The Epilog is all that is found after the document root element closing tag.

For example:

```
<?xml version="1.0" ?>                          The XML Prolog
<!DOCTYPE team PUBLIC
"http://www.mysite.com/dtd/team.dtd" >

<team>                                          The XML body
  <name>
    <!-- team members follow -->
    <member>
      <name>John Smith</name>
    </member>

    <member>
      <name>Peter Smith</name>
    </member>
</team>

<!-- end of the document -->                    The XML Epilog
```

Summary of the XML 1.0 Specification

This is a very short summary of the XML specification that we've been describing in this chapter:

Concept	Example

There must be only one document root element. It must be an element that has no parent and no siblings enclosing all the XML elements in the document.	`<root>`
	`  <e1></e1>`
	`  <e2></e2>`
	`</root>`

All the element tags must be closed.	`<name>John Smith</name>`
Empty tags must be closed.	`<info status="ok" />`
Attributes must have values.	`<foo number="1">Hello</foo>`
Attribute values must be enclosed by single or double quotes.	`<foo number='10'` `name="John">Test</foo>`
We can't repeat attribute names in an element.	`<friends name="John" name="Peter />`
XML special characters must be escaped as entities.	`<company>Johnson &amp;` `Johnson</company>`

CDATA sections are not parsed.	`<source><![CDATA[`
	`  print("hello world");`
	`]]></source>`

Comments.	`<foo>`
	`  <!-- information about a person -->`
	`  <name>John Smith</name>`
	`</foo>`

Designing XML Documents

When we design an XML document, we must first define a root element and then the structure that the document must have – what elements can be found at the root level, what subelements are possible, what are the element names, attributes, and so on.

A common question when designing an XML document is when to use a subelement or an attribute. For example, if we have a `<person>` element describing a person, we can define the element as:

```
<person>
  <name>John</name>
  <age>27</age>
</person>
```

or:

```
<person name="John" age="27" />
```

For XML processing parsers, both formats are easy to handle. But the first one seems to be more descriptive, which is why good advice to XML document designers is to use attributes for information that is not relevant for humans but for computers (IDs, serial numbers, and so on). When the information is relevant to humans a subelement is recommended. We may also have to consider that a subelement may have sub-subelements while an attribute cannot be expanded; so if the data may later be expanded or described, a subelement is more flexible.

Vocabularies

When we create a set of XML document formats for a specific task we define an XML **vocabulary**.

An XML vocabulary defines the rules to describe information about a particular topic using XML. We may have a vocabulary to describe books, to list people that work in some company, or to write mathematical formulas, for example.

Some vocabularies dedicated to very specific topics can become a standard to describe that topic, or to write documents regarding the subject. There are many standardized and non-standardized XML vocabularies. When we use a standard vocabulary, we gain a lot of interoperability since we are able to interchange information with any application that supports that standard. This is why XML standards are a key technology for exchanging information between computer systems. In this book we'll cover some standardized vocabularies such as the **SVG** vocabulary for graphics, **WML** for WAP devices, and **RSS** for content syndication. We'll also use some non-standardized vocabularies, many of them invented for us to show examples of XML processing, and others are examples of XML documents based on non-standardized vocabularies.

Validating XML Documents

We've already learned what constitutes a well-formed XML document and that it can be valid or invalid. A valid document is a well-formed XML document that successfully instantiates an XML vocabulary. An invalid document is a document that is linked to an XML vocabulary but doesn't follow the rules defined in the vocabulary.

To validate an XML document we need a way to define an XML vocabulary, and a way to link the vocabulary to the document to allow validating parsers to check if the document follows the rules defined in the vocabulary.

When the XML 1.0 specification was launched, the W3C suggested DTDs as the way to describe XML vocabularies. DTDs are the easiest way to describe a vocabulary, but they may not be very specific. The need for tighter vocabularies led the W3C to define **XML Schemas** as the new method to define vocabularies and validate XML documents.

DTDs and Schemas

DTDs and Schemas are two ways to define an XML vocabulary. First, the W3C created DTDs and then introduced Schemas to provide a better definition of vocabularies. While it is accepted that Schemas are the best way to define an XML vocabulary and validate an XML document, there aren't many Schema implementations available yet. DTDs are handled by almost all validating parsers, and a lot of XML applications. They will be around for a long time and will probably co-exist with Schemas. We will describe the construction of DTDs first and then move on to Schemas.

DTDs

Let's take a look at a sample XML document, `bug_list.xml`:

```
<?xml version="1.0" encoding="iso-8859-1"?>
<bug_list>
  <application name="sportran compiler" version="1.1">
    <bugs>
      <bug_item>
        <title>It crashes when a string with more than 256 bytes is
              declared</title>
        <report_date>2002-01-28T10:15:00</report_date>
        <reported-by>John Smith</reported-by>
        <status>Open</status>
        <last_update>2002-01-28T10:16:00</last_update>
        <description>...</description>
        <severity>3</severity>
      </bug_item>
      <bug_item>
        <title>String concatenation fails if a string contains a dot</title>
        <report_date>2002-01-14T14:30:00</report_date>
        <reported-by>Mike Brown</reported-by>
        <status>Closed</status>
        <last_update>2002-01-16T18:30:00</last_update>
        <description>...</description>
        <severity>5</severity>
      </bug_item>
      <bug_item>
        <title>Error when summing two integers</title>
        <report_date>2002-01-14T16:30:00</report_date>
        <reported-by>Mike Brown</reported-by>
        <status>Open</status>
```

```
            <last_update>2002-01-14T16:30:00</last_update>
            <description>...</description>
            <severity>4</severity>
          </bug_item>
        </bugs>
      </application>
      <application name="SportyEditor" version="1.0">
        <bugs>
          <bug_item>
            <title>Cut and paste doesn't work</title>
            <report_date>2002-01-05T17:25:00</report_date>
            <reported-by>John Smith</reported-by>
            <status>closed</status>
            <last_update>2002-01-09T10:15:00</last_update>
            <description>...</description>
            <severity>5</severity>
          </bug_item>
          ...
        </bugs>
      </application>
    </bug_list>
```

In most of the examples later in this book, we'll be using this XML document so this is a good place to explain what it is. The document is generated by a theoretical bug database application. We may, or we may not, like the way the document is designed, but since it is generated by an application we can't ask the application to change it. We'll often be facing a problem where not-so-well-designed XML needs to be parsed.

The XML document lists all the applications in the database, and for each application it lists bugs indicating a title, when it was reported, and who reported the bug. Let's explain the XML vocabulary used by the bug-database XML:

The root element is <bug_list> and encloses all the <application> elements. In each <application> element we have name and version attributes describing the application and a <bugs> element enclosing all the bugs for that application.

Each <bugs> element may have one or many <bug_item> elements, and each <bug_item> element describes a bug for that application.

Each bug element contains the following:

❑   The bug <title>, or a short description of the problem.

❑   The <report_date> is the date when the bug was reported.

❑   <reported_by> is the name of the person who reported the bug.

❑   The <status> of the bug can be open or closed indicating if the problem was solved or not.

❑   <last_update> is the time when the bug was updated (changed status).

❑   The <description> is a detailed description of the bug.

❑   <severity> indicates how severe the bug is. A higher number indicates a more severe bug.

Let's now take a look at the syntax of DTDs, and then try to create a DTD for our sample XML document. This DTD can be used for applications that may want to use this XML format to list bugs or provide bug-management functionality – those applications can use the DTD to validate that, the XML document they receive is formatted as the application expects, and that it will be processed successfully.

Elements

The first thing we have to learn about DTDs is how an element is defined. An element is defined using the `<!ELEMENT >` construction:

```
<!ELEMENT element_name CONTENT >
```

CONTENT defines what is valid inside an element, and can be ANY or EMPTY, or a definition of subelements, including text, that the element may have. An `<EMPTY>` element is defined as:

```
<!ELEMENT foo EMPTY>
```

In this declaration we define the `<foo>` element to be empty; no text or subelements can be placed inside as children of `<foo>`. The element, however, can have attributes; the following are examples of empty foo elements:

```
<foo />
<foo></foo>
<foo type="text" />
<foo type="text" name="title" />
```

The ANY keyword declares an element to be always valid, regardless of what is inside that element. For example:

```
<!ELEMENT foo ANY>
```

The ANY keyword tells the parser not to validate the element since anything will be valid as content: subelements, sub-subelements, and text, for example.

Text Elements

If an element can contain only text, it should be declared as #PCDATA:

```
<!ELEMENT foo (#PCDATA) >
```

For example, this `<foo>` element can't contain subelements but may contain text:

```
<foo>
  Hey this is a test
</foo>
```

Sequences

We can indicate that an element is composed of a sequence of subelements by indicating the subelements between parentheses and separating them by commas:

```
<!ELEMENT foo (name,data,text) >
```

For example, in this declaration we declare that `<foo>` must have a `<name>` child, a `<data>` child, and a `<text>` child and that the subelements must occur in the given order:

```
<foo>
  <name>foo</name>-
  <data>Some data</data>
  <text>Some text</text>
</foo>
```

This `<foo>` element is valid. If we change the order of the subelements, or omit one of them, the element will be invalid and a validating parser will reject it.

Choices

We can use a `choice` to define the types of subelements that an element may have. Choices are written as a list of names between parentheses and are separated by pipes (|):

```
<!ELEMENT foo (name|data|text) >
```

In this declaration we define that the element `<foo>` may have a `<name>` child, a `<data>` child, or a `<text>` child. One of them must be present, and once one of them is present no other subelements can be valid inside `<foo>`.

Pipes are used in DTD declarations to express exclusive ORs, which means that we have to make an exclusive choice from the elements separated by pipes.

For example:

```
<foo>
  <text>some text</text>
</foo>
```

This is a valid `<foo>` element.

```
<foo>
  <name>Foo</name>
  <text>Some text</text>
</foo>
```

This is an invalid `<foo>` element.

Cardinality

To indicate how many occurrences of elements, sequences, or choices are valid, we need cardinality operators. Cardinality operators can qualify an element name, a `choice`, or a `sequence`. They are:

Operator	Description
?	0 or 1 occurrences are valid
+	1 or more occurrences are valid
*	0 or more occurrences are valid

This is similar to the syntax of regular expressions. You may be familiar with them if you have programmed PHP regexes. Only ?,+, or * are valid as cardinality operators in a DTD (we have more options using regular expressions).

Here is an example:

```
<!ELEMENT foo (name,data*) >
```

In this declaration, we define the <foo> element to have exactly one <name> element (that must appear), and 0 to n data elements.

The following examples are valid <foo> elements:

```
<foo>
   <name>Foo</name>
</foo>
```

```
<foo>
   <name>foo</name>
   <data>some data</data>
   <data>more data</data>
   <data>even more</data>
</foo>
```

Mixed Content

If an element allows text as well as subelements, then its content is said to be **mixed**. Mixed content elements must be defined as a choice (|) with * cardinality, and the #PCDATA keyword must be the first name in the choice group:

```
<!ELEMENT foo (#PCDATA|name)* >
```

In this declaration, <foo> can have text or a <name> element, and there can be many occurrences of <name>.

The following fragments are valid <foo> elements:

```
<foo>
  <name>foo</name>
  This is some text
</foo>
```

```
<foo>
  Text here
  <name>foo</name>
  More text
  <name>other name</name>
</foo>
```

Examples

Mixing sequences, choices, and the cardinality operators allow many combinations to be created. Let's now look at some element declarations and analyze what is valid, and what is not:

```
<!ELEMENT foo (A,(B|C)) >
```

First, `<foo>` must have an `<A>` subelement, and then a choice between `<B>` and `<C>`, but one of them must appear.

If we don't qualify a group or an element with a cardinality operator then 1 is assumed, and the element or group will be mandatory and can't repeat:

```
<!ELEMENT foo (A,(B|C,D)+) >
```

Again, `<A>` is mandatory at the beginning, and then there must be at least 1 or more occurrences of a group where B or C start the group and that element must be followed by D.

The following are valid `<foo>` elements:

```
<foo>
  <A />
  <B /><D />
</foo>
```

or:

```
<foo>
  <A/>
  <B/><D/><C/><D/><B/><D/>
</foo>
```

The following `<foo>` element must have an `<A>` child first, and a `<D>` child at the end. In the middle, 0 to n `<B>` elements, and an optional `<C>` element can be present. We can't have more than one `<C>` element; therefore if 1 to n `<B>` elements and `<C>` are present then `<C>` must be after the last `<B>`:

```
<!ELEMENT foo (A,B*,C?,D) >
```

The following are valid elements:

```
<foo>
  <A/>
  <B/><B/><B/>
  <D/>
</foo>
```

or:

```
<foo>
  <A/>
  <B/><B/><B/>
  <C/>
  <D/>
</foo>
```

or:

```
<foo>
  <A/>
  <C/>
  <D/>
</foo>
```

In this declaration, <foo> can start with an optional <A> subelement or with a group. If <A> is present then it must be followed by the group, and the group can occur only once. The group is formed by a choice of <B> or <C> followed by an optional <D> and a mandatory <E>:

```
<!ELEMENT foo (A?,(B|(C,D?,E))) >
```

For example:

```
<foo>
  <A/>
  <B/>
  <E />
</foo>
```

or:

```
<foo>
  <A/>
  <C/><D/><E/>
</foo>
```

or:

```
<foo>
  <C/><E/>
</foo>
```

Defining the Elements of Our Sample Vocabulary

Now that we know how to define elements in a DTD, we can try defining the elements we have in our bug-list example.

Let's start with the root.

The root of our vocabulary is `<bug_list>`; a `<bug_list>` element is composed of one or more `<application>` elements:

```
<!ELEMENT bug_list (application+) >
```

An `<application>` element has exactly one `<bugs>` element, and it's optional. An application may have zero bugs:

```
<!ELEMENT application (bugs?) >
```

A `<bugs>` element may have one or more `<bug_item>` elements. We force at least one `<bug_item>` because the `<bugs>` element is optional. An application without bugs should not have a `<bugs>` element, and if there is a `<bugs>` element then at least one `<bug_item>` must be found:

```
<!ELEMENT bugs (bug_item+) >
```

The `<bug_item>` element must contain a `<title>`, `<status>`, and `<severity>`. The `<report_date>`, `<last_update>`, `<reported-by>`, and `<description>` are optional:

```
<!ELEMENT bug_item (title,report_date?,reported-by?,status,
                    last_update?,description?,severity) >
```

In this declaration we allow only one `<title>`, `<status>`, and `<severity>` and make them mandatory; the rest are optional, but if they must appear they should do so in the order indicated in the DTD.

If we want to allow elements to appear in any order, we can use:

```
<!ELEMENT bug_item (title,report_date?,reported-by?,status,
                    last_update?,description?,severity) *>
```

but then we allow elements to repeat.

To restrict the occurrences of subelements to a maximum of one, and allow them to appear in any order, we'd need to write all the valid permutations of elements in a choice, allowing only one of the permutations to be valid. For example:

```
(title,report_date?,reported-by?,status,last_update?,description?,severity)
```

and:

```
(report_date?,tite,reported-by?,status,last_update?,description?,severity)
```

are two of the permutations; there are more than 5000, and to write about them all is really out of the scope of this chapter.

This is a limitation of DTDs – if we want subelements to be limited to only one occurrence, but in any order, we can do it easily for two or three subelements, but the work tends to be impossible when there are many subelements.

We must make a design choice, and allow elements to appear in any order, but repeating or limiting the number of occurrences to one and forcing the order in which elements must occur.

Our DTD so far looks like this:

```
<!ELEMENT bug_list (application+) >
<!ELEMENT application (bugs?) >
<!ELEMENT bugs (bug_item+) >
<!ELEMENT bug_item (title,report_date?,reported-by?,status,
                    last_update?,description?,severity) >
```

Attributes

DTDs can also be used to define what attributes can be used for a particular element. Attributes are defined using the following syntax:

```
<!ATTLIST elementName
  attributeName TYPE MODIFIER
  attributeName2 TYPE MODIFIER
  ...
>
```

The MODIFIER indicates if the attribute is optional or required, and whether there's a default value for the attribute.

The modifier can be:

Modifier	Meaning
#REQUIRED	The attribute must appear in every instance of the element.
#IMPLIED	The attribute may optionally appear.
#FIXED 'value'	The attribute must always have the default value indicated following the modifier. If the attribute doesn't appear then the default value is assumed, if it appears with another value then the element is invalid.
'value'	The attribute is optional, if it appears it may have any value, if it doesn't appear then the default value is used. So after parsing the attribute always has a value.

This example declares <foo> to have an optional attribute named color:

```
<!ATTLIST foo color CDATA #IMPLIED>
```

The four possible rules that we may use to describe our `color` attribute for the `<foo>` element are:

Syntax	Description
`<!ATTLIST foo color CDATA #IMPLIED>`	The attribute is optional; the value is the value the attribute is given if it appears.
`<!ATTLIST foo color CDATA "blue" >`	The attribute is optional, if it doesn't appear it's by default `blue`, if it appears it may have any value.
`<!ATTLIST foo color CDATA #REQUIRED>`	The attribute is required and may have any value.
`<!ATTLIST foo color CDATA #FIXED "blue">`	The attribute is optional but if it is used then there's only one value allowed. If it doesn't appear then the default value is assumed.

There are several attribute types we can use in an XML document. We have already seen the `CDATA` type for attributes in the examples. The allowed types for an attribute are:

Type	Description
`CDATA`	Character data (string).
`ID`	Name unique within a given document. If two attributes of type `ID` have the same value, then the XML parser should return an error.
`IDREF`	Reference to some element with an `ID` value the same as the `IDREF` attribute.
`IDREFS`	Many `IDREF`s separated by whitespace.
`ENTITY`	Name of a predefined external entity.
`ENTITIES`	Many entities separated by whitespace.
`NMTOKEN`	A name.
`NMTOKENS`	Many `NMTOKEN`s separated by whitespace.
`NOTATION`	Accepts one of a set of names indicating notation types declared in the DTD.
[Enumerated value]	Accepts one of a series of explicit user-defined values that the attribute can take.

Next we will move on to discussing each attribute type and some examples.

CDATA

A `CDATA` attribute:

- ❑ Can contain any string
- ❑ Cannot contain markup
- ❑ Has unlimited length

For example:

```
<!ATTLIST foo description CDATA #IMPLIED >
<foo description="This is some text" />
```

ID, IDREF, and IDREFS

The ID attribute is used to uniquely identify elements in a particular XML document. When an attribute is declared to be ID then the value for this attribute is unique among the document elements.

For example:

```
<!ATTLIST foo eid ID #REQUIRED>

<doc>
  <foo eid="15" />
  <foo eid="24" />
  <foo eid="33" />
</doc>
```

In the above example, if we had two `<foo>` elements with the same `eid` attribute value then the parser should tell us that the document is invalid.

IDs are fine for identifying elements; IDREFs are used to refer to those IDs.

An IDREF attribute indicates that the attribute value must be the value of an ID attribute somewhere in the document.

For example:

```
<!ATTLIST foo eid ID #REQUIRED>
<!ATTLIST note fooid IDREF #REQUIRED>

<doc>
  <foo eid="15" />
  <foo eid="24" />
  <foo eid="33" />
  <note fooid="24">This is a note</note>
</doc>
```

In the above example, we can see how we can use ID and IDREF attributes to make a `<note>` element refer to a `<foo>` element, without a parent-child relationship between the elements. This is somewhat analogous to a foreign key in a relational database.

An IDREFS type attribute is a list of IDREF attributes delimited by whitespace. For example:

```
<!ATTLIST foo eid ID #REQUIRED>
<!ATTLIST note fooid IDREFS #REQUIRED>

<doc>
  <foo eid="15" />
```

```
    <foo eid="24" />
    <foo eid="33" />
    <note fooid="24 15">This is a note</note>
</doc>
```

NMTOKEN and NMTOKENS

An NMTOKEN attribute is limited to be a valid XML name using the same rules we've seen for element names. The attribute value can use letters, digits, colons (:), underscores (_), periods (.), and hyphens (-). While element names can't begin with a punctuation mark, NMTOKENs can, so they are less restricted than element names. NMTOKENS don't have to be unique within a document, which gives us another means of grouping together elements apart from the element hierarchy.

For example:

```
<!ATTLIST foo name NMTOKEN #REQUIRED>

<foo name="john_smith" />
```

NOTATION

NOTATION type attributes are designed to provide a way in which XML documents can include external data and signal to the application – the name, URI (Uniform Resource Indicator), or path of an external application that can be used to process that data. Since they are seldom used, we are not going to discuss them in detail in this book.

Enumerations

We have seen that CDATA attributes can have any text as values, and NMTOKEN attribute limits the content to be a valid XML name. **Enumerations** can be used to restrict the valid values for an attribute to a list of valid values. For example:

```
<!ATTLIST foo isGood (yes|no) #REQUIRED >
```

In this declaration we are restricting the value of the isGood attribute of the <foo> element to two valid values – yes or no.

Entities

Other useful elements that can be used when writing DTDs are entities. DTDs use entities to reduce the amount of text that needs to be written for the DTD or the XML document. We can classify entities in two groups – **general entities** and **parameter entities**.

General Entities

A general entity is like a macro in many text editors. We define the entity to have some text and whenever the parser sees the entity appearing, it will be replaced by its content. Since the entity is defined in the DTD, only validating parsers are required to make the proper entity replacements; non-validating parsers can ignore entities.

A general entity can be defined as:

```
<!ENTITY wrox "Wrox PressLTD." >
```

Once the entity is declared we can use &wrox; in our XML document, and a validating parser will replace the entity by its value.

An entity can also refer its value to an external file defined by a URI:

```
<!ENTITY legal-note SYSTEM "http://mysite.com/texts/legal-note.txt" >
```

One restriction to observe is that entities cannot refer to themselves directly or indirectly (using another entity, for example in a circular reference).

Parameter Entities

Parameter entities can be used to define lists of attributes that are common to many elements in the document. For example, we can use the color and name attributes for many elements in a DTD. We can define them as follows:

```
<!ENTITY %color-name "color CDATA #IMPLIED name CDATA #REQUIRED" >
```

Note that parameter entities are named with a percent sign (%) and a valid name. Referring to parameter entities is a straightforward task:

```
<!ATTLIST foo %color-name; >
```

We could have defined more attributes for the <foo> element, referencing the %color-name; entity would automatically define the color and name attributes for the <foo> element.

Now we can add attributes to the DTD for our <bug_list> vocabulary:

```
<!ELEMENT bug_list (application+) >

<!ELEMENT application (bugs?) >

<!ELEMENT bugs (bug_item+) >

<!ELEMENT bug_item (title,report_date?,reported-
by?,status,last_update?,description?,severity) >

<!ATTLIST application name CDATA #REQUIRED version CDATA #IMPLIED>
```

Using DTDs

Now that we know how to write a DTD, we just need to know how to associate a DTD with an XML document. The DOCTYPE declaration in the XML Prolog can be used for this.

Internal DTDs

Internal DTDs define the DTD of the document in the document itself, that is, they are self-contained.

Internal DTDs are declared using the following syntax:

```
<!DOCTYPE root_element [ DTD-CONTENT ]>
```

For example:

```
<?xml version="1.0"?>
<!DOCTYPE doc [
  <!ELEMENT doc (foo*) >
  <!ELEMENT foo (#PCDATA)>
]>
<doc>
  <foo>Hello world</foo>
</doc>
```

In the above example, we declared an internal DTD for the <doc> element root. The DOCTYPE declaration always indicates the root element name and then <!ELEMENT> sections are used to define each element of the document including the root.

Internal DTDs are very useful, but present some problems:

❑ Internal DTDs can add a lot of information to medium- to large-sized XML vocabularies in the XML document. If each document must include the whole DTD then the documents can be very large and hard to handle.

❑ Internal DTDs compromise DTD maintenance. If the DTD needs to be changed, we may need to change each document that uses the DTD internally. This is not a very practical approach.

External DTDs

While internal DTDs can be used for some small applications, external DTDs are the most common solution to associating a DTD with a document. They are declared using this following syntax:

```
<!DOCTYPE root_element SYSTEM "URI">
```

For example:

```
<!DOCTYPE doc SYSTEM "http://www.mysite.com/doc.dtd">
```

External DTDs are used for creating a common DTD that can be shared by multiple documents. The advantage with this approach is that any change that takes place in the external DTD is automatically reflected on all the documents that reference it. There are two main types of external DTDs: **private** and **public**. However, there is one basic rule that we have to follow – if any elements, attributes, or entities used in the XML document are referenced or defined in an external DTD, (standalone="no"), the DTD must be included in the XML declaration.

Combining Internal and External DTDs

An XML document can use both internal and external DTD subsets. The internal DTD subset is specified between the square brackets of the DOCTYPE declaration. The declaration for the external DTD subset is placed before the square brackets immediately after the SYSTEM keyword.

Here is an example:

```
<?xml version="1.0" standalone="no" ?>

<!--define location - the open square bracket indicate internal DTD-->
<!DOCTYPE document SYSTEM "test.dtd" [

<!--the markup in the internal DTD referencing the external DTD-->
<!ATTLIST assessment assessment_type (exam | assignment | prac)>
<!ELEMENT results (#PCDATA)>

<!--close the DOCTYPE declaration-->
]>
```

The main advantage of combining an internal and external DTD is, if a publicly available DTD meets most, but not all, of our needs, we can reference it as an external DTD in our DOCTYPE declaration and then add our own declarations in an internal DTD to augment the public DTD.

> **Declaring an element with the same name in both the internal and external DTD subsets is invalid.**

The Shortcomings of DTDs

DTDs are a good way to define vocabularies, but there are some disadvantages that we have to mention:

❏ **The DTD content model is hard to manage**
In the DTD application we've seen how to define a list of subelements with cardinality 1, but allowing them to appear in any particular order is difficult.

❏ **DTDs are not XML**
This is a very big disadvantage. We can't use XML derivatives or applications to parse, build, or transform DTDs. If we want to write DTDs from a database or a document, it would be easier if they could be written in XML. Also, modifying DTDs would be easier if XML-related applications could be used.

❏ **DTDs cannot validate data types**
If we want to restrict an element or an attribute to be a number, a date, or some specific data type, we cannot do that because DTDs can use only the #PCDATA and CDATA data types.

❏ **DTDs cannot validate element contents**
We can use an enumeration to validate an attribute value against a list of admitted values, but we can't do the same with attributes. In many situations we want to define an element that can only have some specific values; this is very useful when we have to exchange information between different applications using XML.

❑   **DTDs cannot be used with namespaces**
    Namespaces are heavily used to combine two different vocabularies in the same XML
    document. Since our document can only refer to one external DTD, we can't use a DTD to
    validate a document that uses multiple namespaces. We'll study namespaces later in this chapter.

Let's look at the DTD for our `<bug_list>` vocabulary:

```
<!ELEMENT bug_list (application+) >

<!ELEMENT application (bugs?) >

<!ELEMENT bugs (bug_item+) >

<!ELEMENT bug_item (title,report_date?, reported-by?, status, last_update?,
description?, severity) >

<!ATTLIST application name CDATA #REQUIRED version CDATA #IMPLIED>
```

We can see that the following things are not considered by the DTD:

❑   The subelements of the `<bug_item>` element may appear in any order, the DTD constrains
    them to the given order

❑   Some elements may have a restriction in length; for example, `<title>` may be limited to 200
    characters

❑   The `<report_date>` and `<last_update>` elements should be a date in the ISO 8061 format

❑   The severity element must take a numeric value between 1 and 10

❑   The `<status>` element can be Open, Closed, open, or closed

Schemas

XML Schemas are the suggested standard by the W3C to substitute DTDs. Schemas can validate the
same things as DTDs while offering several advantages:

❑   XML Schemas are XML documents

❑   XML Schemas support data types

❑   XML Schemas support constraints for element and attribute values

❑   XML Schemas allow the use of namespaces

❑   Schemas can be inherited and reused

❑   New content models can be defined

Since a full coverage of XML Schemas can take the whole book, we are going to see an overview of
Schemas with the help of examples. In this section we will see how we can construct a Schema for our
bug_list vocabulary and thus circumvent all the disadvantages we had when using a DTD.

> An XML Schema is an XML document, and the file is usually saved as
> `something.xsd`.

Let's now write a skeleton Schema indicating that the root is the `<bug_list>` element, and that a
`<bug_list>` element may have an unlimited (non-zero) number of `<application>` subelements:

```
<?xml version="1.0" encoding="UTF-8"?>

<xs:schema xmlns:xs="http://www.w3.org/2001/XMLSchema" elementFormDefault=
                       "qualified" attributeFormDefault="unqualified">

  <xs:element name="bug_list">
    <xs:annotation>
      <xs:documentation>A vocabulary to list bugs</xs:documentation>
    </xs:annotation>

    <xs:complexType>
      <xs:sequence>
        <xs:element name="application" maxOccurs="unbounded"/>
      </xs:sequence>
    </xs:complexType>
  </xs:element>

</xs:schema>
```

`xmlns:xs="http://www.w3.org/2001/XMLSchema"` declares a namespace for tags, beginning
with `xs`. We'll explain namespaces later in this chapter. All the elements of the Schema are written in
the form `<xs:element_name>`, where `xs` is the namespace prefix we used.

The `<xs:complexType>` element is used to define elements that contain subelements. The
`<xs:sequence>` element defines that a `<bug_list>` contains at least one (it is the default), and as
many as unbounded `<application>` subelements. With the use of the `maxOccurs` and `minOccurs`
attributes, we can define any cardinality for an element in the Schema. For instance, we can restrict an
element to appear from 1 to 3 times.

Next, we'll indicate that each application element may have zero or more `<bugs>` elements. This is the
Schema:

```
<?xml version="1.0" encoding="UTF-8"?>

<xs:schema xmlns:xs="http://www.w3.org/2001/XMLSchema"
elementFormDefault="qualified" attributeFormDefault="unqualified">
  <xs:element name="bug_list">
    <xs:annotation>
      <xs:documentation>A vocabulary to list bugs</xs:documentation>
    </xs:annotation>
    <xs:complexType>
      <xs:sequence>
        <xs:element name="application" maxOccurs="unbounded">
          <xs:complexType>
```

```
                <xs:sequence>
                    <xs:element name="bugs" minOccurs="0" maxOccurs="unbounded"/>
                </xs:sequence>
            </xs:complexType>
        </xs:element>
    </xs:sequence>
</xs:complexType>
</xs:element>
</xs:schema>
```

Note how `<xs:element>`, `<xs:complexType>`, and `<xs:sequence>` were used, this time inside the `<application>` element definition to indicate that from zero to unbounded `<bugs>` elements can be found.

Now using the same procedure we indicate that each `<bugs>` element may have one or more `<bug_item>` elements:

```
<?xml version="1.0" encoding="UTF-8"?>

<xs:schema xmlns:xs="http://www.w3.org/2001/XMLSchema"
elementFormDefault="qualified" attributeFormDefault="unqualified">

    <xs:element name="bug_list">
        <xs:annotation>
            <xs:documentation>A vocabulary to list bugs</xs:documentation>
        </xs:annotation>
        <xs:complexType>
            <xs:sequence>
                <xs:element name="application" maxOccurs="unbounded">
                    <xs:complexType>
                        <xs:sequence>
                            <xs:element name="bugs" minOccurs="0" maxOccurs="unbounded">
                                <xs:complexType>
                                    <xs:sequence>
                                        <xs:element name="bug_item" maxOccurs="unbounded"/>
                                    </xs:sequence>
                                </xs:complexType>
                            </xs:element>
                        </xs:sequence>
                    </xs:complexType>
                </xs:element>
            </xs:sequence>
        </xs:complexType>
    </xs:element>
</xs:schema>
```

Then we indicate that each `<bug_item>` must have a `<title>`, `<status>`, and `<severity>`, and optionally `<reported-by>`, `<report_date>`, `<last_update>`, and `<description>`. These elements can appear in any order:

```
<?xml version="1.0" encoding="UTF-8"?>
<xs:schema xmlns:xs="http://www.w3.org/2001/XMLSchema"
elementFormDefault="qualified" attributeFormDefault="unqualified">
    <xs:element name="bug_list">
        <xs:annotation>
            <xs:documentation>A vocabulary to list bugs</xs:documentation>
```

```
        </xs:annotation>
        <xs:complexType>
          <xs:sequence>
            <xs:element name="application" maxOccurs="unbounded">
              <xs:complexType>
                <xs:sequence>
                  <xs:element name="bugs" minOccurs="0" maxOccurs="unbounded">
                    <xs:complexType>
                      <xs:sequence>
                        <xs:element name="bug_item" maxOccurs="unbounded">
                          <xs:complexType>
                            <xs:all>
                              <xs:element name="title"/>
                              <xs:element name="description" minOccurs="0"/>
                              <xs:element name="reported-by" minOccurs="0"/>
                              <xs:element name="last_update" minOccurs="0"/>
                              <xs:element name="report_date" minOccurs="0"/>
                              <xs:element name="status"/>
                              <xs:element name="severity"/>
                            </xs:all>
                          </xs:complexType>
                        </xs:element>
                      </xs:sequence>
                    </xs:complexType>
                  </xs:element>
                </xs:sequence>
              </xs:complexType>
            </xs:element>
          </xs:sequence>
        </xs:complexType>
      </xs:element>
    </xs:schema>
```

The <xs:all> container indicates that the list of elements is not a sequence where order is to be respected, rather it is a bag of elements that may appear in any order. We indicated the optional elements with a minOccurs="0" attribute, and since the maxOccurs attribute is not present it is defaulted to 1.

Now we add data types indicating:

❑   title is a string

❑   description is a string

❑   reported-by is a string

❑   last_update and report_date are dateTime which means they must be ISO 8601-formatted dates

❑   severity is an integer

❑   status is a string

This is the Schema with data types added:

```xml
<?xml version="1.0" encoding="UTF-8"?>
<xs:schema xmlns:xs="http://www.w3.org/2001/XMLSchema"
elementFormDefault="qualified" attributeFormDefault="unqualified">
  <xs:element name="bug_list">
    <xs:annotation>
      <xs:documentation>A vocabulary to list bugs</xs:documentation>
    </xs:annotation>
    <xs:complexType>
      <xs:sequence>
        <xs:element name="application" maxOccurs="unbounded">
          <xs:complexType>
            <xs:sequence>
              <xs:element name="bugs" minOccurs="0" maxOccurs="unbounded">
                <xs:complexType>
                  <xs:sequence>
                    <xs:element name="bug_item" maxOccurs="unbounded">
                      <xs:complexType>
                        <xs:all>
                          <xs:element name="title" type="xs:string"/>
                          <xs:element name="description" type="xs:string"
                                      minOccurs="0"/>
                          <xs:element name="reported-by" type="xs:string"
                                      minOccurs="0"/>
                          <xs:element name="last_update" type="xs:dateTime"
                                      minOccurs="0"/>
                          <xs:element name="report_date" type="xs:dateTime"
                                      minOccurs="0"/>
                          <xs:element name="status" type="xs:string"/>
                          <xs:element name="severity" type="xs:integer"/>
                        </xs:all>
                      </xs:complexType>
                    </xs:element>
                  </xs:sequence>
                </xs:complexType>
              </xs:element>
            </xs:sequence>
          </xs:complexType>
        </xs:element>
      </xs:sequence>
    </xs:complexType>
  </xs:element>
</xs:schema>
```

We then added attributes for the <application> element, adding the <version> and <name> elements as strings:

```xml
<?xml version="1.0" encoding="UTF-8"?>
<xs:schema xmlns:xs="http://www.w3.org/2001/XMLSchema"
elementFormDefault="qualified" attributeFormDefault="unqualified">
  <xs:element name="bug_list">
    <xs:annotation>
```

```
                  <xs:documentation>A vocabulary to list bugs</xs:documentation>
               </xs:annotation>
               <xs:complexType>
                 <xs:sequence>
                   <xs:element name="application" maxOccurs="unbounded">
                     <xs:complexType>
                       <xs:sequence>
                         <xs:element name="bugs" minOccurs="0" maxOccurs="unbounded">
                           <xs:complexType>
                             <xs:sequence>
                               <xs:element name="bug_item" maxOccurs="unbounded">
                                 <xs:complexType>
                                   <xs:all>
                                     <xs:element name="title" type="xs:string"/>
                                     <xs:element name="description" type="xs:string"
                                                 minOccurs="0"/>
                                     <xs:element name="reported-by" type="xs:string"
                                                 minOccurs="0"/>
                                     <xs:element name="last_update" type="xs:dateTime"
                                                 minOccurs="0"/>
                                     <xs:element name="report_date" type="xs:dateTime"
                                                 minOccurs="0"/>
                                     <xs:element name="status" type="xs:string"/>
                                     <xs:element name="severity" type="xs:integer"/>
                                   </xs:all>
                                 </xs:complexType>
                               </xs:element>
                             </xs:sequence>
                           </xs:complexType>
                         </xs:element>
                       </xs:sequence>
                       <xs:attribute name="version" type="xs:string" use="optional"/>
                       <xs:attribute name="name" type="xs:string" use="required"/>
                     </xs:complexType>
                   </xs:element>
                 </xs:sequence>
               </xs:complexType>
             </xs:element>
           </xs:schema>
```

Finally, we add some constraints:

❑   `title` has a maximum length of 200

❑   `severity` must be a value between 1 and 10

❑   `status` may be `open` or `Open`, `closed` or `Closed`

This is the final Schema:

```
<?xml version="1.0" encoding="UTF-8"?>
<xs:schema xmlns:xs="http://www.w3.org/2001/XMLSchema"
elementFormDefault="qualified" attributeFormDefault="unqualified">
  <xs:element name="bug_list">
    <xs:annotation>
      <xs:documentation>A vocabulary to list bugs</xs:documentation>
    </xs:annotation>
    <xs:complexType>
```

```
      <xs:sequence>
        <xs:element name="application" maxOccurs="unbounded">
          <xs:complexType>
            <xs:sequence>
              <xs:element name="bugs" minOccurs="0" maxOccurs="unbounded">
                <xs:complexType>
                  <xs:sequence>
                    <xs:element name="bug_item" maxOccurs="unbounded">
                      <xs:complexType>
                        <xs:all>
                          <xs:element name="title">
                            <xs:simpleType>
                              <xs:restriction base="xs:string">
                                <xs:maxLength value="200"/>
                              </xs:restriction>
                            </xs:simpleType>
                          </xs:element>
                          <xs:element name="description" type="xs:string"
                                        minOccurs="0"/>
                          <xs:element name="reported-by" type="xs:string"
                                        minOccurs="0"/>
                          <xs:element name="last_update" type="xs:dateTime"
                                        minOccurs="0"/>
                          <xs:element name="report_date" type="xs:dateTime"
                                        minOccurs="0"/>
                          <xs:element name="status">
                            <xs:simpleType>
                              <xs:restriction base="xs:string">
                                <xs:enumeration value="open"/>
                                <xs:enumeration value="Open"/>
                                <xs:enumeration value="closed"/>
                                <xs:enumeration value="Closed"/>
                              </xs:restriction>
                            </xs:simpleType>
                          </xs:element>
                          <xs:element name="severity">
                            <xs:simpleType>
                              <xs:restriction base="xs:integer">
                                <xs:minInclusive value="1"/>
                                <xs:maxInclusive value="10"/>
                              </xs:restriction>
                            </xs:simpleType>
                          </xs:element>
                        </xs:all>
                      </xs:complexType>
                    </xs:element>
                  </xs:sequence>
                </xs:complexType>
              </xs:element>
            </xs:sequence>
            <xs:attribute name="version" type="xs:string" use="optional"/>
            <xs:attribute name="name" type="xs:string" use="required"/>
          </xs:complexType>
        </xs:element>
      </xs:sequence>
    </xs:complexType>
  </xs:element>
</xs:schema>
```

Note how we can validate many things about an XML document using Schemas.

Namespaces

We've seen how we can define XML vocabularies using DTDs or Schemas. Since XML is a standard designed to provide great flexibility for interchanging data we may want to mix several vocabularies in the same XML document.

For example, we may want to use a publishing vocabulary to write a text about a car, and mix the publishing vocabulary tags with a car industry vocabulary used to describe cars. The problem arises when there might be ambiguities, or name collisions between vocabularies. If we use the attribute `color`, is it the color of a car or the color of the font? Restrictions can be completely different for the same element or attribute in two different vocabularies. Therefore, if the computer can't determine from which vocabulary an element or an attribute name originates, then it would be very difficult to validate the document since restrictions can be completely different for the same element or attribute in two different vocabularies.

Namespaces are the way to handle multiple vocabularies in one document. The use of namespaces is a standard by the W3C. A namespace is defined as: *a collection of names identified by a URI reference, which are used in XML documents as element types and attribute names.*

Declaring and Using Namespaces

An XML namespace is declared as an attribute of an element. The `xmlns` attribute name is used to declare an XML namespace. Note that we can't have a collision because attribute names beginning with `xml` are reserved by the XML standard.

A namespace is declared using:

```
<elementName xmlns:PREFIX="URI" >
```

For example:

```
<bug_list xmlns:buglist="http://www.bugseverywhere.com">
</bug_list>
```

Once a namespace is declared we can use qualified names in the form `prefix:name`. For example:

```
<bug_list xmlns:buglist="http://www.bugseverywhere.com">
  <buglist:application>

  </buglist:application>
</bug_list>
```

When we use a qualified name, we are indicating that the element name belongs to the namespace that was declared for the prefix used to qualify the element name.

Scope and Defaults

If we declare one namespace, we don't need to qualify element or attribute names inside the scope of that namespace. That is, the scope of a namespace includes the element, its attributes, and all elements and attributes, which are descendants of that element.

For example:

```
<bug_list xmlns:buglist="http://www.bugseverywhere.com">
  <buglist:application buglist:name="foo">

  </buglist:application>
</bug_list>
```

is the same as:

```
<bug_list xmlns:buglist="http://www.bugseverywhere.com">
  <application name="foo">

  </application>
</bug_list>
```

We can declare more than one namespace for an element. In this case the first namespace is the default; we may use the second namespace in the scope of the first, if we qualify names or attributes, when we use them.

The following example shows how to mix two different vocabularies in the same XML document, and how namespaces can be used to qualify attributes as well as elements:

```
<cars xmlns:car="URI"
  xmlns:units="URI">
  <car>
    <name>Turbo Car</name>
    <length units:units="inches">6543</length>
  </car>
</cars>
```

Here, the <name> and <length> element belong to the default namespace: car. The units attribute was qualified to belong to the units namespace.

Namespaces are important as XML vocabulary can be used from XML documents that may be using another vocabulary.

Summary

In this chapter, we've covered all the concepts regarding the XML 1.0 specification. We analyzed the structure of an XML document and enumerated all the rules that a document must follow to be a well-formed document.

We talked about XML vocabularies and valid XML documents, covering DTDs and Schemas as two ways to define an XML vocabulary and validate a document.

We created a DTD for our sample XML vocabulary. Then we went on to create a Schema for it by adding data types and other validations that weren't possible using DTDs.

Finally, we mentioned namespaces, and described why namespaces are useful and how can we use namespaces in our XML documents or vocabularies.

This chapter covered the core of the XML specification. There are a large number of XML derivatives that are very useful for programmers, and the next chapter will introduce XML derivatives and describe the most important XML derivatives.

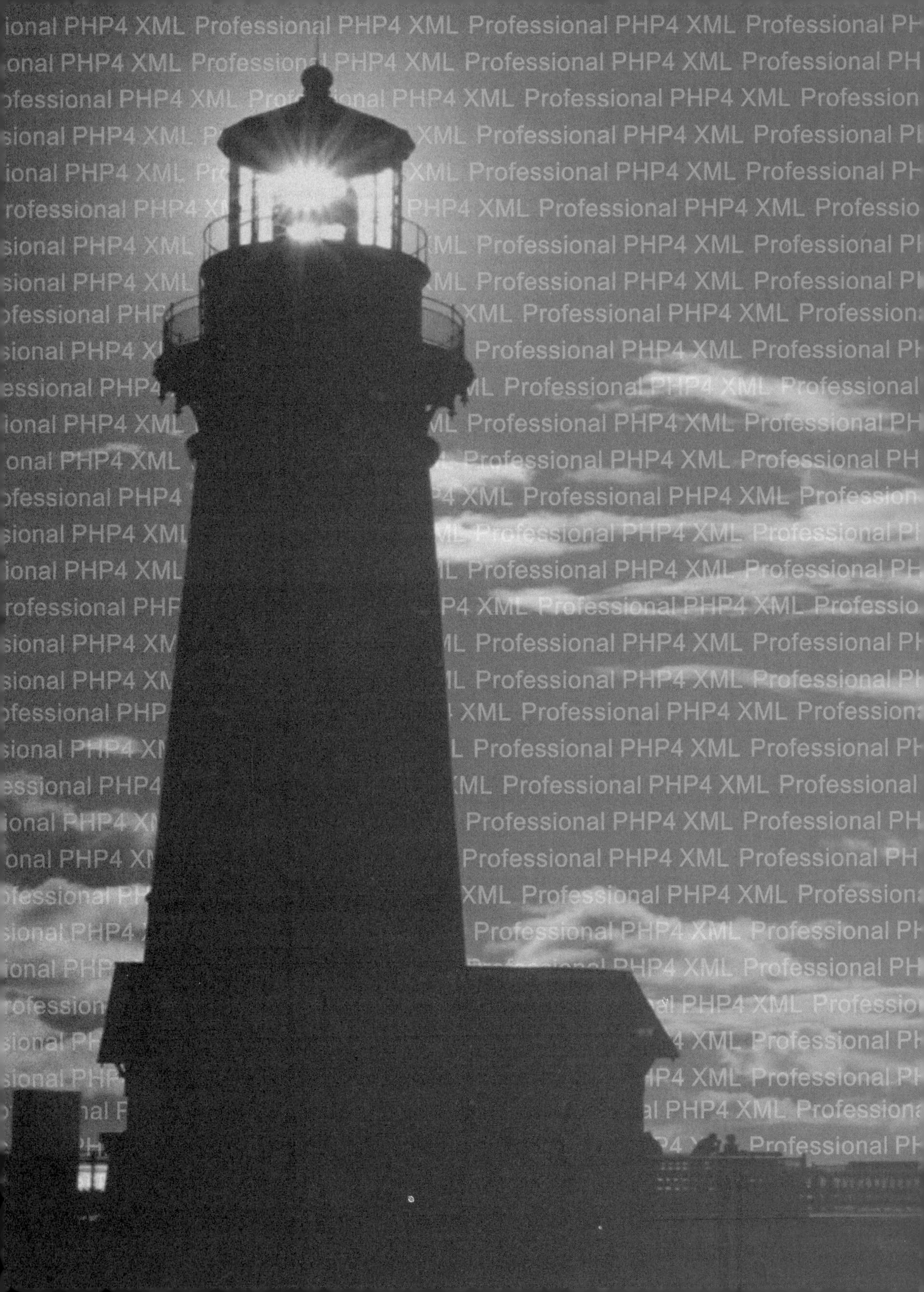
Professional PHP4 XML

4

XML Derivatives

XML is more than a tool for structuring information in documents. We can create languages that can standardize the treatment of any kind of information, for example, presentation of data, data transfer, and communication between applications. These languages are called XML derivatives. Since XML made its appearance into the world of markup languages, a lot of derivative standards, technologies, and tools have emerged. Developers often get lost when they have to decide which XML derivative should be used to solve a problem, as there is such a vast variety of them today. In this chapter we'll present the most relevant XML derivatives for programmers in general and PHP programmers in particular.

The first part of the chapter looks into the classification of derivatives and presents a mini-cookbook that can be used to understand the requirements to solve a particular problem.

The second part of the chapter looks into each derivative, and talks briefly about what it does, how we can put it to use, and how it fits together with PHP. This chapter is just an overview; the most commonly used derivatives are discussed later in the book. Take this chapter as the yellow pages of XML programming.

Functional Classification of XML Derivatives

Here is a table detailing the functional classification of XML derivatives:

Parsing	Using or Deploying Web Services	Presentation Vocabularies	Meta Data	Validating	Querying	Transforming XML Documents
DOM	SOAP	SVG	RDF	DTD	DOM	XSLT
SAX	XML-RPC	XHTML	RSS	Schema	XPath	DOM
XSLT		WML		Schematron	XPointer	
		VoiceXML		RELAX	XSLT	
		XUL		XSLT	SAX	
		XBL				

Common Patterns for XML Processing

Here is a list of some of the common patterns used for XML processing:

Problem	Derivatives	PHP Approach
Converting XML documents to HTML	XSLT	Use the PHP XSLT extension.
Converting XML documents to other XML vocabularies	XSLT	Use the PHP XSLT extension.
Converting XML documents to binary files or proprietary formats	XSLT	Use the PHP XSLT extension.
Deleting an element or many elements from an XML document	DOM	Option 1: Use the DOM extension to parse the document and delete the unwanted elements.
	XSLT	Option 2: Write an XSL stylesheet that converts the XML document to XML removing the unwanted elements.
	SAX	Option 3: Use Expat and build a SAX parser that ignores the unwanted elements.
Modifying values from an XML document	DOM	Option 1: Use the DOM extension, parse the document and modify the values that need to be changed.
	XSLT	Option 2: Write an XSL stylesheet and use the XSLT extension to change the XML document.

Problem	Derivatives	PHP Approach
Extracting content from an XML document, for example the value of `<foo>` elements	XPath	Option 1 (recommended): Write an XPath expression and use it to get all the necessary data from the document. Use the `xpath_eval()` function from the DOM extension to execute the XPath expression.
	DOM	Option 2: Use the DOM extension, parse the document and navigate the tree to pull the data from the XML.
	SAX	Option 3: Write a SAX parser using the Expat extension and use handlers to detect what content you want from the document.
	XSLT	Option 4 (for complex extraction): Write an XSLT file to convert the XML document to a representation of the data you need from the XML.
Performing basic computations on XML documents	XPath	Use the `xpath_eval()` function from the DOM extension and get the result using an XPath expression.
Performing heavy computations on XML documents	XSLT	Use the XSLT extension and write an XSLT stylesheet to perform the computation.
Making presentations or displaying graphic charts using XML	SVG	We can generate our graphic using a drawing application and save it as an SVG file. If the application doesn't support SVG we can try converting the file to SVG.
Creating graphical user interfaces (GUIs) and specifying the display and behavior of the elements comprising the interface	XUL, XBL	Use XUL namespace to place elements in the GUI layout file, XBL to define/describe event handlers, and CSS and DOM bindings to these elements.
Including graphic elements in XML documents, for example, a pie chart in an XML document summarizing sales	SVG	Option 1: Use namespaces and include the graphic as SVG in any element of the document.
	Binary Data	Option 2: Convert the file (JPG or GIF) to base64 and include it as a normal element in an XML document.
Converting non-XML data to XML	SAX	Write a SAX handler to produce SAX events for the non-XML format. We can use the basic SAX handlers to convert the data to XML.
Converting non-XML data to proprietary formats, binary files, or HTML	SAX and XSLT	Write a SAX handler to convert the data to XML and then use XSLT to convert the XML to anything we need.
Presenting XML documents in the browser	XSLT and XHTML	Use XSLT to convert the XML file to XHTML and display it in a browser as HTML.
Deploying web services	XML-RPC or SOAP	Use an XML-RPC or SOAP library; XML-RPC is easier to use than PHP.

Generic Derivatives

In this part of the chapter we'll cover some generic derivatives that can be used in many situations for parsing, processing, and transforming XML documents. We will be looking at:

- ❑ DOM (Document Object Model)
- ❑ SAX (Simple API for XML)
- ❑ XPath (XML Path Language)
- ❑ XSLT (Extensible Stylesheet Language Transformations)

DOM

DOM is a platform- and language-neutral interface that will allow programs and scripts to dynamically access and update the content, structure, and style of documents. The document can be further processed and the results of that processing can be incorporated back into the document (from the W3C specification).

Usage

DOM is used for:

- ❑ Parsing XML documents
- ❑ Modifying XML documents
- ❑ Querying/processing XML documents
- ❑ Writing XML documents
- ❑ Transforming XML documents

Description

The basic use of DOM is to obtain a parsed representation of an XML document known as the **DOM tree** and access or modify this tree as we want. We can use DOM to query/access elements of an XML document and also use it to alter/modify XML documents. Adding elements and attributes or modifying them is a good example of what we can do using DOM.

PHP and DOM

We can use the DOM extension of PHP to process XML documents with the DOM standard. The DOM extension of PHP can be used to process and parse XML documents, navigate the DOM tree, and access or modify XML objects as needed. While the DOM extension of PHP retains its experimental status, it should be used with care since it can change whenever a new PHP version is released.

Example

In this example we parse an XML document to get the name of the root element and the children of the root element:

```
<?php
$doc = domxml_open_mem($xml);
$root = $doc->document_element();
print ("The name of the root element is: " . $root->tagname . "<br />");
$nodes = $root->child_nodes();
print ("The children of the root element are:<br />");
foreach ($nodes as $node) {
    if ($node->node_type() == XML_ELEMENT_NODE) {
        print ($node->tagname() . "<br />");
    }
}?>
```

Resources

❑ Chapter 6 details DOM

❑ The DOM specification at http://www.w3.org/DOM/

❑ The PHP extension DOM documentation at http://www.php.net/domxml/

SAX

SAX is a standard interface for event-based XML parsing, developed collaboratively by the members of the XML-DEV mailing list (from the SAX authors' home page).

Usage

SAX is used for:

❑ Parsing and processing XML documents

❑ Transforming XML documents

❑ Querying XML documents

❑ Converting non-XML data to XML

Description

SAX is an event-driven parser for XML. This means that the parser will process the XML document and produce **events**; the programmer can intercept the events in which he is interested by setting **handlers**. Handler prototypes capture the data relevant to the event.

The basic SAX events are:

❑ **An XML element starts**
   This event is triggered when a tag such as <foo> is found; it gives the programmer the name of the element and its attributes

❑ **An XML element ends**
   This event is triggered when a tag such as </foo> appears in the document; the handler receives the name of the element

❑ **Text is found**
   This event is triggered whenever text is found inside an element; the SAX specification allows a parser to produce several text events for the same text inside an element

❑ **An XML comment is found**
This event is triggered when an XML comment is found in the document

❑ **An XML processing instruction is found**
This is triggered when the parser finds a processing instruction in the document

If we have the following XML document:

```
<?xml version="1.0"?>
<doc>
  <foo name="hey">
    This is some text
  </foo>
</doc>
```

A SAX parser will produce the following events in the given order when parsing the document:

❑ Document starts

❑ Element starts name: <doc>

❑ Element starts name: foo attributes: (name=>hey)

❑ Text data appears: This is some text

❑ Element ends name: </foo>

❑ Element ends name: </doc>

❑ Document ends

An interesting use of SAX is that we can write a SAX-compliant parser for non-XML data, thus allowing the data to be transformed to XML and processed for many tools that can use a SAX parser for input. You can see an example of a SAX parser for non-XML data in Chapter 10.

An important consideration is that SAX is stateless, if we receive a character data (text) event, SAX won't tell where the parser is when the text is found. This means that we won't know which element contains that text unless we keep track of the context. Tracking context is one of the very basic tasks to be done when using a SAX parser.

PHP and SAX

In PHP the XML parser function uses Expat, which is a SAX parser. We need to have Expat installed, configured, and compiled with PHP to use the XML extension. Check the PHP installation for your operating system to see if you need to install the Expat library to use the XML extension of PHP; it's not needed on Linux where Expat is bundled with Apache, and it's not needed under Windows where the .dll for the XML extension provides the Expat functionality.

Example

In this example we use the SAX parser to find <foo> elements in an XML document. This simple example shows how we can create a parser, set element handlers, and define the handlers. It also details the standard parsing procedure with error reporting:

```php
<?php
$file = "data.xml";

function startElement($parser, $name, $attrs)
{
    if($name == "FOO") {
        print ("A foo element is found!<br />");
    }
}

function endElement($parser, $name) {}

$xml_parser = xml_parser_create();
xml_set_element_handler($xml_parser, "startElement", "endElement");

if (!($fp = fopen($file, "r"))) {
    die("could not open XML input");
}

while ($data = fread($fp, 4096)) {
    if (!xml_parse($xml_parser, $data, feof($fp))) {
        die(sprintf("XML error: %s at line %d",
            xml_error_string(xml_get_error_code($xml_parser)),
            xml_get_current_line_number($xml_parser)));
    }
}
xml_parser_free($xml_parser);
?>
```

Please refer to Chapter 5 for an explanation of this example if needed. Note how we matched the element name against FOO because we didn't set the Expat case folding option.

Resources

❏ Chapter 5 details SAX

❏ SAX homepage at http://www.megginson.com/SAX/SAX1/index.html.

❏ PHP XML parser documentation, available at http://www.php.net/manual/en/ref.xml.php.

❏ Expat homepage at http://www.jclark.com/xml/expat.html.

XPath

"The XML Path Language is a language for addressing parts of an XML document, designed to be used both by XSL and XPointer." (from the W3C specification).

Usage

❏ Querying XML documents

❏ Accessing and selecting parts of the XML document from XSLT

Description

XPath is a syntax used to access objects from an XML document using location paths to obtain portions of the document and predicates to filter what parts of the document we want. XPath is based on XPath expressions – an expression returns a set of nodes known as the **node-set**, and then we process the nodes accordingly.

PHP and XPath

In PHP we can use XPath with the `xpath_eval()` function from the DOM extension. The `xpath_eval()` function will return an array of element nodes; we can iterate the array and process each node as we want.

For more information and instructions on how to use DOM nodes refer to Chapter 6 and the DOM extension documentation. Also, Chapter 7 has a full description and tutorial on the XPath syntax.

Example

In this example we parse the XML file and process an XPath expression to get all the `<title>` elements that have a node attribute with value `bold`:

```
$xml = 'SOME XML ....';
$doc = xmldoc($xml);
$ctx = XPath_new_context($doc);
$foo = xpath_eval($ctx, "//title[@mode='bold']");
print_r($foo);
```

The `print_r()` function prints the structure returned by `xpath_eval()` and this is an array of element nodes.

Resources

- ❑ Chapter 6 details DOM nodes
- ❑ Chapter 7 details XPath
- ❑ The XPath specification at http://www.w3.org/TR/XPath/
- ❑ The PHP manual page at http://www.php.net/manual/en/function.xpath-eval.php
- ❑ The DOM extension documentation at http://www.tallent.com/frontier/DOM/dox/default.html

XSLT

"Extended Stylesheet Language Transformation (XSLT) is a language for transforming XML documents into any representation." (from the W3C XSLT specification).

Usage

XSLT is used for:

- ❑ Querying XML documents
- ❑ Transforming XML documents
- ❑ Parsing/processing XML documents
- ❑ Validating XML documents

Description

XSLT is a language to process and transform XML documents. It is perhaps the most powerful derivative for XML programmers. XSLT demonstrates the power of XML as an information exchange standard and a very convenient representation of data that can have several presentations. We can build XSLT transformations to convert XML to other XML vocabularies, to HTML, to WML for WAP devices, to PDF files, to binary files, to SQL queries, to code in some language, and to text files. It can also be used to query documents, make computations, and validate XML documents.

XSLT is a functional language, so at times it is considered to be unfriendly for those programmers who are used to procedural programming. We can learn XSLT easily if we know Haskell, Lisp, Scheme, or some other functional language. We need to understand what XSLT does to be able to fully profit from it.

There are a lot of XSLT processors for different languages and many of them are free; we can be sure to find a free, ready-to-use XSLT processor for the more common programming languages. Sablotron, Xalan, Saxon, and XT are some of the widely used XSLT processors.

> **XSLT is also a declarative language, which allows us to transform a source document, or a data structure of an XML document, into a result tree for a new XML document. XSLT, however, is looked on as a functional language because it supports programming constructs like `if` conditions, `for` loops, and XPath functions.**

PHP and XSLT

PHP has an XSLT extension based on the Sablotron XSLT processor. Chapter 8 has rich detailing on XSLT and how it can be used from PHP. In the next section we will look at a small sample of XSLT from PHP.

Example

Let's take a sample XML file that lists some quotes from movies and books:

```
<?xml version="1.0" encoding="UTF-8"?>
<quotes>
  <quote>
    <text>You shall not pass!</text>
    <author>Gandalf, the Lord of the Rings</author>
  </quote>
  <quote>
    <text>If you want him come and claim him</text>
    <author>Arwen, the Lord of the Rings</author>
  </quote>
</quotes>
```

We can build an XSLT file to transform this XML file to HTML and see the quotes in a browser. The XSLT stylesheets work using templates.

We are going to use two templates in this example:

❑   The first template matches the root of the XML document and generates the root of the HTML output with the `<html>`, `<header>`, and `<body>` tags as well as the title for the output. Since XML documents have only one root element this template will be matched only once by the XSLT processor.

❑   The second template matches each quote and we format the `<text>` and `<author>` elements to display the quote with some basic HTML decorations.

This is the XSLT file:

```
<?xml version="1.0" encoding="UTF-8"?>
<xsl:stylesheet version="1.0" xmlns:xsl="http://www.w3.org/1999/XSL/Transform">
<xsl:output method="html" />

<xsl:template match="/">
  <html>
    <header><title>Quotes</title></header>
    <body>
      <h2>Some quotes from books and movies</h2>
      <xsl:apply-templates></xsl:apply-templates>
    </body>
  </html>
</xsl:template>

<xsl:template match="/quotes/quote">
<p><i><xsl:value-of select="text" /></i>
(<b><xsl:value-of select="author" />)</b></p>
</xsl:template>
</xsl:stylesheet>
```

and here is how we can make the transformation from PHP:

```
<?php
// Allocate a new XSLT processor
$xh = xslt_create();

// Process the document
if (xslt_process($xh, 'quotes.xml', 'quotes2html.xsl',
                 'result.html')) {
    readfile('result.html');
} else {
    print ("Sorry, quotes.xml could not be transformed
            by quotes2html.xsl into");
    print ("  result.xml the reason is that " .
            xslt_error($xh) . " and the ");
    print ("error code is " . xslt_errno($xh));
}
xslt_free($xh);
?>
```

The result, HTML looks like this:

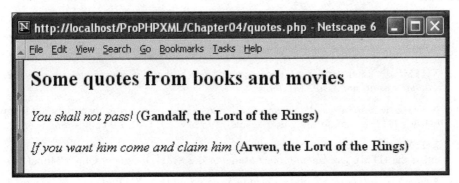

Resources

- ❑ The Sablotron page at http://www.gingerall.com/charlie/ga/xml/p_sab.xml
- ❑ The PHP XSLT extension at http://www.php.net/xslt/
- ❑ XSL homepage at the W3C at http://www.w3.org/Style/XSL/
- ❑ The XSLT specification at http://www.w3.org/TR/xslt/

Presentation Vocabularies

Between different XML derivatives there is a category with a huge number of members – XML vocabularies. We may find vocabularies for the health industry, e-commerce, EDI, engineering, and presentation vocabularies, for example. Presentation vocabularies are XML vocabularies designed to present data on some specific devices or rendering programs. For example, if we want to present data on a WAP cell phone we can use WML.

In this section we will look at some of the most important presentation vocabularies we may need.

A very common design methodology for content presentation is to transform data from any source to XML, then use XSLT to transform XML to the presentation languages that may be needed. This significantly eases a lot the process of adding a new presentation for our application since only an XSLT stylesheet will be needed.

XHTML

XHTML 1.0 is the first document type in the XHTML family. It is a reformulation of the three HTML 4 document types as applications of XML 1.0. It is intended to be used as a language for content that is both XML-conforming and, if some simple guidelines are followed, operates in HTML 4-conforming user agents (from the W3C specification).

Usage

XHTML is used for:

- ❑ Presentation of content in web browsers

Description

XHTML is a formalization of HTML as XML. It defines a set of rules we have to follow to write an HTML document that is XML-compliant. This leads to several advantages; the W3C mentions the following:

❑ XHTML documents are XML conforming. As such, they are readily viewed, edited, and validated using standard XML tools.

❑ XHTML documents can be written to operate as well as, or better than, they did before in existing HTML 4 conforming user agents, as in new XHTML 1.0-conforming user agents.

❑ XHTML documents can utilize applications (for instance, scripts and applets) that rely upon either the HTML Document Object Model or the XML Document Object Model.

❑ As the XHTML family evolves, documents conforming to XHTML 1.0 will be more likely to interoperate within and among various XHTML environments.

The most important advantage is that we will be able to validate our XHTML documents and parse and process them as XML. For example, we can use XSLT to transform an XHTML document to a PDF file or any other presentation.

HTML is good as a presentation language but it's not easy to process by computers. XHTML merges the presentation capabilities of HTML and the processing advantages of XML.

Differences with HTML

To write XHTML-compliant documents, we have to observe the following rules regarding the differences between XHTML and HTML:

❑ **Documents must be well-formed**
XHTML documents must be well-formed XML documents. For example, we can't overlap tags in XHTML.

❑ **Elements and attribute names must be in lowercase**
HTML is case-insensitive, whereas XHTML is case-sensitive because XML is case-sensitive.

❑ **End tags are required**
We can't have tags that are opened and never closed, and tags without content must be written following the XML rules. For example:

```
<img src="foo.gif>      INVALID
<img src="foo.gif" />   VALID
<br>    INVALID
<br/>   VALID
<br />  VALID
```

❑ **Attribute values must always be quoted**
We have to quote attribute values with single or double quotes, like this:

```
<input type='text' name='foo" />      INVALID
<input type="text" name="foo" />      VALID
```

❑ **We cannot omit attribute values**
In HTML we can place tags with attributes that don't have values, but this is invalid in XML. The solution is to use a dummy value for attributes that don't need one, like this:

```
<input type="checkbox" checked />          INVALID
<input type="checkbox" checked="checked" />  VALID (or checked="true")
```

❑ **Script elements must be contained in CDATA sections**
Since characters such as ", ', <, &, > must be escaped in XML, we may find a problem if we include script elements in our HTML page as, for example, JavaScript or VBScript code. We have to enclose scripting elements in CDATA sections to avoid this problem, like this:

```
<script><![CDATA[
...
]]></script>
```

Example

The following is an example of a valid XHTML document:

```
<?xml version="1.0" encoding="UTF-8" ?>

<!DOCTYPE html PUBLIC "-//W3C//DTD XHTML 1.0 Strict//EN"
"DTD/xhtml1-strict.dtd">

<html xmlns="http://www.w3.org/1999/xhtml">
  <head>
    <title>Sample</title>
  </head>
  <body>
    <p>Hello World</p>
  </body>
</html>
```

> Since XHTML is compatible with HTML 4 we can display XHTML in all the browsers that display regular HTML. Since XHTML has several advantages over HTML, it's a good idea to generate XHTML code from our applications and scripts instead of HTML.

Resources

❑ The XHTML 1.0 specification at http://www.w3.org/TR/xhtml1/

WML

"Wireless Markup Language (WML) is a presentation language for devices with little screens, small memory and reduced bandwidth capabilities. It was designed for cell phones but can be used for other devices supporting WML." (from the WAP forum).

101

Usage

WML is used for:

❑ Presentation of content and applications for WAP cell phones

❑ Interfaces for other wireless devices capable of rendering WML

Description

WML is a presentation language very common for WAP-enabled cell phones. In WML, each screen that will be rendered to the device is defined as a **card**. One WAP file can include several cards to minimize the number of connections the device has to make (think about a file with multiple HTML documents for a browser). We can have forms and results of forms in WML, we can process these forms as we process HTML forms, and thus create applications for cell phones.

We will need a WAP emulator to test our WML scripts. A lot of WAP emulators are freely available on the Web.

Example

In this example we use WML to create 3 cards.

The first one is a home-card that links to the other cards. We will look at how to define a card, how to display text in the cards, and how to define a link from one card to another one:

```
<?xml version="1.0"?>
<!DOCTYPE wml PUBLIC "-//WAPFORUM//DTD WML 1.1//EN"
"http://www.wapforum.org/DTD/wml_1.1.xml">
<wml>
  <card id="greeting">
    <p><img src="logo_welcome.wbmp" alt="Welcome" /></p>
    <p>WELCOME WAP!</p>
    <p><?print($HTTP_USER_AGENT);?></p>
    <p><a href="welcome.wml#news" title="News">News</a></p>
    <p><a href="welcome.wml#health24" title="Health24">Health24</a></p>
  </card>

  <card id="news">
    <p>The news</p>
  </card>
  <card id="health24">
    <p>The application</p>
  </card>
</wml>
```

The presented script creates two cards (screens), the first card greeting is displayed showing an image with the logo of some company, a title, and two links: one to the news section and the other to the Health24 section (an application). The WAP engine displays the first card and when one link is selected and activated it jumps to the card that has an ID equal to the # section of the link.

We can use PHP to generate WML in the same way we use PHP to generate HTML – we have to send the proper headers to the WAP device. For example:

```
<?php
header("Content-Type: text/vnd.wap.wml");
print ("<?xml version='1.0'?>");
print ("\n");
?>

<!DOCTYPE wml PUBLIC "-//WAPFORUM//DTD WML 1.1//EN"
"http://www.wapforum.org/DTD/wml_1.1.xml">
<wml>
  <card id="greeting">
    <p><img src="logo_welcome.wbmp" alt="Welcome" /></p>
    <p>WELCOME WAP!</p>
    <p><?print ($HTTP_USER_AGENT);?></p>
    <p><a href="welcome.wml#news" title="News">News</a></p>
    <p><a href="welcome.wml#health24" title="Health23">Health24</a></p>
  </card>

  <card id="news">
    <p>The news</p>
  </card>
  <card id="health24">
    <p>The application</p>
  </card>
</wml>
```

Resources

❑   WML Primer available at http://www.p2p.wrox.com/content/phpref/wml.asp

❑   The wireless development network at http://www.wirelessdevnet.com/channels/wap/

❑   Zvon's WML tutorial at http://www.zvon.org/xxl/WMLTutorial/Output/introduction.html

❑   The Openwave Developer Program page at http://developer.openwave.com/

❑   Case study in *Professional PHP4* from *Wrox Press (ISBN 1-861006-91-8)*

SVG

Scalable Vector Graphics (SVG) is a language for describing two-dimensional graphics in XML. SVG allows for three types of graphic objects – vector graphic shapes (for instance, paths consisting of straight lines and curves), images, and text. Graphical objects can be grouped, styled, transformed, and composited into previously rendered objects. The feature set includes nested transformations, clipping paths, alpha masks, filter effects, and template objects (from the W3C specification).

Usage

SVG is used for:

❑   Presentation of graphics and images in XML

❑   Animations

❑   Slideshows

Description

SVG is an XML vocabulary for graphics based on XML. In SVG we draw graphics using tags such as `<circle>`, `<poly>`, `<line>`, and so on. SVG is based on vector graphics instead of bitmaps that are commonly used in formats such as GIF and JPG.

In Raster or bitmap-based graphic formats the graphic is defined by specifying the color of each pixel in the graphic. In a vector graphic format we indicate lines, circles, polygons, and the formats they are drawn in on the screen.

The main characteristics of SVG are:

- ❑ **SVG sources are text files**
  We can edit and process SVG files with text editors, find/replace SVG sources to make changes, and so on.

- ❑ **SVG is XML**
  This carries all the advantages of XML to SVG. We can transform SVG files using XSLT (for example we can morph an SVG graphic or change colors with XSLT), parse an SVG file, extract graphic elements, and so on.

- ❑ **SVG is scalable and zoom-able**
  Since it's based on vectors, if we zoom-in or enlarge the image the resolution is maintained. This isn't true for bitmaps where the resolution is fixed – SVG has dynamic resolution.

- ❑ **Searchable and selectable text**
  We can search and select text elements and cut/paste them from an SVG graphic.

- ❑ **Scripting and animation**
  SVG provides scripting and animation features.

Example

Here we will draw a rectangle with a drawing application and export the graphic as SVG.

Let's look at the source:

```
<?xml version="1.0" standalone="no"?>
<!DOCTYPE svg PUBLIC "-//W3C//DTD SVG 1.0//EN"
  "http://www.w3.org/TR/2001/REC-SVG-20010904/DTD/svg10.dtd">
<svg width="100" height="100">
  <rect x="17" y="18" width="67" height="60"
        style="fill:rgb(0,0,255);stroke:rgb(0,0,0);stroke-width:1"/>
</svg>
```

If you want to test the source, create a file named `square.svg` with the above data, then point your browser to the file and if you have an SVG plug-in it should display a graphic.

This is the graphic viewed in a browser with an SVG plug-in (there's a good SVG plug-in for IE and Netscape at http://www.adobe.com/svg/viewer/install/main.html):

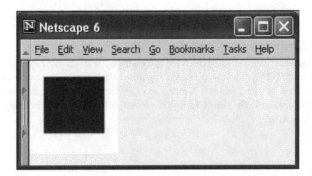

Now let's change the color and add some text:

```
<?xml version="1.0" standalone="no"?>
<!DOCTYPE svg PUBLIC "-//W3C//DTD SVG 1.0//EN"
  "http://www.w3.org/TR/2001/REC-SVG-20010904/DTD/svg10.dtd">
<svg width="100" height="100">
  <rect x="17" y="18" width="67" height="60"
  style="fill:rgb(192,0,0);stroke:rgb(0,0,0);stroke-width:1;fill-opacity:1"/>
  <text x="24px" y="38px"
    transform="translate(0 1) translate(0 1) translate(0 1) translate(0 1)
    translate(0 1) translate(0 1) translate(0 1) translate(0 1) translate(0 1)
    translate(0 1) translate(0 1)"

    style="fill:rgb(0,0,0);font-size:24;font-family:Arial">Wrox
  </text>
</svg>
```

and this is the result:

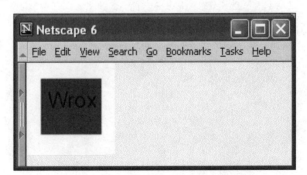

Resources

- ❑ The Batik project, a Java API for SVG, available at http://xml.apache.org/batik/index.html
- ❑ The SVG homepage at the W3C http://www.xml.com/pub/a/2002/01/23/svg/index.html
- ❑ Trajectory Pro, an SVG-native editor, available at http://www.jasc.com/
- ❑ Lot of resources, tutorials, and demos at the Sun web site at http://www.sun.com/ (search for SVG)
- ❑ A column about SVG graphics at http://www.xml.com/pub/a/2002/01/23/svg/index.html

VoiceXML

VoiceXML is a web-based markup language for representing human-computer dialogs, just like HTML. While HTML assumes a graphical web browser, with display, keyboard, and mouse, VoiceXML assumes a voice browser with audio output (computer-synthesized and/or recorded) and audio input (voice and/or keypad tones). VoiceXML leverages the Internet for voice application development and delivery, greatly simplifying these difficult tasks and creating new opportunities (from the VoiceXML forum).

Usage

VoiceXML is used for:

❑   Voice-enabled applications

Description

VoiceXML is a vocabulary for voice-enabled applications. VoiceXML can be used to generate scripts to play sound files, read tones from the phone, and perform actions based on user input. The device is the phone, the screens are sound files, and the keyboard is the phone pad.

VoiceXML allows the programmer to represent application flow, forms, and common tasks for voice applications in XML. It is expected that vendors will adopt XML to create applications that can be common for many different solutions.

Example

This simple example shows a form that plays the `hello.wav` sound file. It is a kind of "hello world" that can be played from a phone:

```
<?xml version="1.0"?>
<vxml application="foo" version="1.0">
  <form id="some">
    <block>
      <prompt>
        Hello world
        <audio src="hello.wav" />
      </prompt>
    </block>
  </form>
</vxml>
```

Resources

❑   The VoiceXML page at http://www.voicexml.org/

XUL/XBL

XUL (XML-based User-interface Language) is a cross-platform language for describing user interfaces of applications (from the Mozilla web site).

XBL (Extensible Bindings Language) is, as its name suggests, a markup language that defines special new elements, or **bindings**, for XUL widgets (and for HTML elements).

Usage

XUL and XBL can be used to create vendor-neutral user interface definitions; we have to then render these definitions using the proper tools depending on the platform you are using. In the Mozilla project, XUL and XBL are used to define the user interface that the browser (Mozilla) uses.

Description

XUL provides the ability to create most elements found in modern graphical interfaces. It is generic enough that it could be applied to the special needs of certain devices, and powerful enough that developers can create sophisticated interfaces with it.

Some elements that can be created are:

❏   Input controls such as textboxes

❏   Toolbars with buttons or any content

❏   Menus on a menu bar or pop-up menus

❏   Tabbed dialogs

❏   Trees for hierarchical or tabular information

❏   Keyboard shortcuts

The displayed content may be generated based either on the contents of a XUL file or from data from a data source. In Mozilla, such data sources include a user's mailbox, their bookmarks, and search results. The contents of menus, trees, and other elements can be populated with this data, or with your own data supplied in an RDF file.

Example

The following XUL file describes a window:

```
<?xml version="1.0"?>
<?xml-stylesheet href="chrome://global/skin/" type="text/css"?>

<window
    id="findfile-window"
    title="Find Files"
    orient="horizontal"
    xmlns="http://www.mozilla.org/keymaster/gatekeeper/there.is.only.xul">
...
</window>
```

And this one describes a button:

```
<button
    id="identifier"
    class="dialog"
    label="OK"
    image="image.gif"
    default="true"
    disabled="true"
    accesskey="t"/>
```

Resources

❑   http://www.mozilla.org/docs/xul/xulnotes/xulnote_xbl.html

❑   A tutorial on XUL http://www.xulplanet.com/tutorials/xultu/

❑   The Mozilla project home page http://www.mozilla.org/

The Semantic Web

The semantic web is a concept defined by Tim Berners-Lee, chair of the W3C. It is a concept that can't be described quickly, but we can put it into the following words.

The semantic web is the collection of meta data needed for machines to understand the Web. Today, the World Wide Web is a complex network of documents; the information contained in those documents can't easily be categorized, indexed, and processed by programs since there is not enough meta data to describe the documents. In this section we describe RDF (Resource Description Framework), the vocabulary designed by the W3C to create the semantic web.

RDF

One of the most important requirements for highly automated web services is a rich description mechanism. RDF is the best possible way for rapid implementation of web services based on the emerging standards such as WSDL, UDDI, and ebXML.

Definition

RDF is a foundation for processing meta data. It provides interoperability between applications that exchange information on the Web that machines can understand. RDF emphasizes facilities to enable automated processing of web resources. RDF can be used in a variety of application areas. For example, in resource discovery to provide better search engine capabilities, in cataloging for describing the content and content relationships available at a particular web site, page, or digital library, by intelligent software agents to facilitate knowledge sharing and exchange, in content rating, in describing collections of pages that represent a single logical document, for describing intellectual property rights of web pages, and for expressing the privacy preferences of a user as well as the privacy policies of a web site.

Usage

RDF is used for:

❑   Description of meta data on the Web

❑   Catalogs of information

❑   Description of web sites and documents

❑   Indexes of complete web sites

❑   Categorization of information

❑   Web directories

Description

The semantic web is an initiative from the W3C to formalize the definition of content on the web to contain documents and the description of what those documents contain. These descriptions are the semantic web, and meta data is the key to build them. The W3C has proposed the RDF syntax for meta data.

Why Do We Need Meta Data?

While humans easily understand documents on the Web, they are really complicated for computers. A program traversing the Web may find it very difficult to find, for example, pages where publications by a particular author are shown or pages where a certain topic is described. Categorization, classification, and specialized searching are difficult tasks because the Web provides data but not meta data (at least not enough) and machines do need meta data to understand what the data is about.

A Brief Introduction To RDF

The basic model of RDF consists of 3 objects – resources, properties, and sentences.

Resources are anything that can be described by RDF. A resource can be a web page, a collection of pages, a piece of information in a document, a book, an XML document, even a person. Resources are described by URIs, optionally followed by an anchor ID. Since URIs are extensible, every object in the world may have its own URI that can be described using RDF as a resource.

Properties are attributes of resources. Some resources may have some properties and some properties can be defined by more than one kind of resource. RDF defines these relationships in its data model using XML Schemas. Each property has a specific meaning.

Sentences are the combination of a resource, a property, and a value for that property.

Values can be any object, for example, they can be RDF resources, strings, numbers, and XML documents. Here is an example:

Resource	Property	Value	Sentence
Wrox Press, a company that publishes programming books	published	Professional PHP XML	Wrox Press published a book titled "Professional PHP XML"

Here we see how the value of the published property can be a resource, for example a book. A book may have several properties such as title, authors, and abstract. If we mix everything in an RDF document we can obtain a full description of every single book published by Wrox Press, and build several applications to use that information.

Using the RDF syntax we could write an XML document to describe that sentence:

```
<?xml version="1.0"?>
<rdf:RDF
  xmlns:rdf="http://www.w3.org/1999/02/22-rdf-syntax-ns#"
  xmlns:s="http://description.org/schema/">
  <rdf:Description about="http://www.wrox.com">
    <s:Published>http://www.wrox.com/books/Professional_PHP_XML</s:Published>
  </rdf:Description>
</rdf:RDF>
```

The book can be described as:

```
<rdf:RDF>
  <rdf:Description about="http://www/wrox.com/books/Professional_PHP_XML ">
    <s:Publisher>Wrox Press</s:Publisher>
    <s:Title>Professional PHP XML</s:Title>
    <s:Date>2002-XX-XXT02:27</s:Date>
  </rdf:Description>
</rdf:RDF>
```

> **Namespace and XML declaration are intentionally left out from the above example simply because we wanted to show RDF elements and how we can use them to describe information.**

Frequently we have to refer to a group of resources, for example a list of books or a collection of stamps. RDF provides **containers** to group resources. The containers may be:

❑ **Bags** – Bags are unordered lists of resources allowing duplicates, and without order between items

❑ **Sequences** – Sequences are ordered lists of resources

❑ **Alternatives** – Alternatives are lists of resources or literals for only one value or property

For example:

```
<rdf:RDF>
  <rdf:Description about="http://www.wrox.com">
    <s:books>
      <rdf:Bag>
        <rdf:li
          resource="http://www.wrox.com/books/Professional_PHP4"/>
        <rdf:li resource=" http://www.wrox.com/books/Professional_PHP_XML"/>
      </rdf:Bag>
    </s:books>
  </rdf:Description>
</rdf:RDF>
```

There is a lot of information, documents, derivatives, tools, and initiatives for the semantic web and the description of meta data. RDF is a very useful standard for meta data description.

Resources

❑ The RDF specification at http://www.w3.org/TR/1999/REC-rdf-syntax-19990222/

RSS

Rich Site Summary (RSS) – also referred to as RDF site summary – is a web content syndication format. It is a lightweight XML format designed for sharing headlines and other web content. It was originally developed by Netscape to fill channels for Netcenter.

Today, RSS has evolved into a popular means of sharing content between sites (for example, CNN, BBC, Slashdot, and ZDNet). Thus it solves a number of problems like increasing traffic and gathering and distributing news.

Usage

RSS is used for:

❏   Content syndication

❏   Meta information about web pages

Description

Many times we have seen sites with sidebar boxes announcing news from other sites, stock information, or meteorological information. It's easy to understand that not all of these sites can run their own news engines, meteorological services, and stock information services. So they are using information from other sites. Content syndication is the activity that permits applications or sites to use and reuse information provided by external sites.

RSS is one of the most used vocabularies for content syndication. With RSS we can describe pieces of content, their titles, associated images, and a link to the full content at the original site.

Let's see an example of an RSS file to understand the vocabulary:

```
<?xml version="1.0" ?>
<rdf:RDF xmlns:rdf="http://www.w3.org/1999/02/22-rdf-syntax-ns#"
         xmlns="http://purl.org/rss/1.0/">

  <channel rdf:about="http://www.foonews.org/foo.rdf">
    <title>World news</title>
    <link>http://www.foonews.org</link>
    <description>These are some news from around the world</description>
    <image rdf:resource="http://images.foonews.org/images/image.gif"/>
    <items>
      <rdf:Seq>
        <rdf:li
           resource="http://foonews.org/article.php?sid=02/05/06/0139258" />
      </rdf:Seq>
    </items>
    <textinput rdf:resource="http://foonews.org/search.php" />
  </channel>

  <image rdf:about="http://images.foonews.org/images/image.gif">
    <title>World news</title>
    <link>http://www.foonews.org</link>
    <url>http://images.foonews.org/images/image.gif</url>
  </image>

  <item rdf:about="http://foonews.org/article.php?sid=02/05/06/0139258">
    <title>Argentina changes president again</title>
    <link>http://foonews.org/article.php?sid=02/05/06/0139258</link>
    <description>
      Argentina has changed its president as the national
```

```
      crisis deepens.
    </description>
  </item>

  ... More items ...

  <textinput rdf:about="http://foonews.org/search.php">
    <title>Search FooNews</title>
    <description>Search FooNews's Archive</description>
    <name>search</name>
    <link>http://foonews.org/search.php</link>
  </textinput>
</rdf:RDF>
```

An RSS file has exactly one <channel> subelement describing the source of information. The <channel> describes the information provider and the <item> elements describe each piece of information.

The <channel> element has some mandatory subelements – <title>, <link>, <description>, <language>, and <image>:

❑ **title**
    Indicates the name of the channel, it's how people refer to our service. Normally we can use the name of our web site as the title for the channel. Maximum length is 100 characters.

❑ **link**
    A URI pointing to the source of information, for example our web site. The maximum allowed length is 500 characters.

❑ **description**
    A description of the site, service, or information source. Maximum length is 500 characters.

❑ **image**
    An XML element used to describe an image; we'll describe the image element later. An image contains or may contain the following subelements:

    ❑ **URL**
        The URI of the image, a GIF, JPG, or PNG image. Maximum length for the text in a URL is 500 characters.

    ❑ **title**
        Title describing the image, it's used in the ALT attribute of an HTML page where the image is displayed.

    ❑ **width**
        Optional width of the file, default is 88 and maximum is 144.

    ❑ **height**
        Optional height of the file, default is 31 and maximum is 400.

❑ **items**
    A list of the items that are contained in this channel

<channel> has an optional subelement too:

❑ **textinput**
    This is an XML element that provides some sort of interaction to the channel, we can indicate a mini-HTML form in this element.

Image

The main <image> element represents an image to be associated with an HTML rendering of the channel. This can then be displayed at the top of any listings as a link to the homepage of the channel's provider. An image may have the following subelements:

- ❏ **title**
  The alt text to be associated with the HTML rendering of the image

- ❏ **URL**
  The URL to be associated with the image

- ❏ **link**
  The link to the actual image itself

Items

A channel may contain any number of items; each item describes a particular piece of information of the described channel. An item may have the following subelements:

- ❏ **title**
  The title of the piece of news or information described in the item

- ❏ **link**
  Link to the full article

- ❏ **description**
  Description, abstract or summary for the item. Maximum length is 500 characters

Text Input

The optional <textinput> subelement describes the data to construct a search box for rendering along with the items in this channel. An text input may have the following subelements:

- ❏ **title**
  A title for the input box

- ❏ **description**
  A description of the input box

- ❏ **name**
  The variable name for the input box

- ❏ **link**
  The link to the search engine

PHP and RSS

PEAR has a class to parse RSS files and there is also a class to parse RSS 0.91 files at http://www.upperdesign.com/. Another good approach for RSS data is to transform the RSS file to the presentation we may need using XSLT. We can even transform the RSS file to SQL and insert the titles in a database and display them from our PHP pages.

Resources

❏ Chapter 12 describes RSS

❏ The specification for RSS at http://purl.org/rss/1.0/

❏ The RSS class for PHP at http://www.phpclasses.upperdesign.com/browse.html/package/61

❏ Another RSS class at http://www.horde.org/jonah/

❏ The PEAR class for RSS http://pear.php.net/package-info.php?pacid=22

XLink and XPointer

XLink and XPointer are two derivatives created by the W3C to provide a link from an XML document to another. This task was easily achieved in HTML with the <a> tag. The linking model for XML extends the functionality of <a> allowing several kinds of linkage between XML documents.

XPointer is a standard that allows defining a specific point in an XML document or a portion of an XML document defined by two points (a range); XPointer can be used from XLink to define links to sentences, elements, or any part of an XML document.

XLink

XLink is language created by the W3C that provides links between different XML documents.

Usage

XLink is used for:

❏ Linking between XML documents

❏ Establishing relationships between XML documents

Description

XLink is the W3C initiative to provide a standard for linking between XML documents. The basic use of XLink is to replace the HTML tag <a href=" "> with an XML vocabulary. However, its use extends to many other powerful applications of links.

A very basic XLink introduction must begin with the link:

```
<foo xmlns:XLink="http://www.w3.org/1999/XLink
  XLink:type="simple"
  XLink:href="desc.xml"
  XLink:role="description"
  XLink:title="product descriptoin"
  XLink:show="replace"
  XLink:actuate="onRequest">Some content
</foo>
```

The global attributes of the linking element define the type of the link and its properties. The global attributes are described as follows.

type

The type attribute defines the type of link for the element. Possible values are:

❑ simple – a simple link

❑ extended – an extended link that can link to many resources

❑ locator – a pointer to an external resource

❑ arc – a traversal rule between resources

❑ title – a descriptive title for another linking element

The type of link determines which global attributes are required and which are optional:

Global Attribute	simple	extended	locator	arc	resource	title
type	Required	Required	Required	Required	Required	Required
href	Optional		Required			
role	Optional	Optional	Optional		Optional	
arcrole	Optional			Optional		
title	Optional	Optional	Optional	Optional	Optional	
show	Optional			Optional		
actuate	Optional			Optional		
label			Optional		Optional	
from				Optional		
to				Optional		

href

The href attribute is used to contain the URI of the resource pointed to by the link.

role

The role attribute defines the function of the link defined by the application.

arcrole

This attribute is similar to role, but for arcs. The arcrole attribute defines the URI reference for some description of the arc role.

title

It contains a human readable string describing the link.

show

The show attribute indicates how the link is suposed to get rendered. Possible values are:

❑ new – the linked document should be rendered in a new context (for a browser in a new window)

❑ replace – the linked document replaced the actual context (a traditional HTML link replaces the document)

❑ embedded – the document pointed to should be inserted in the actual content in the position of the link

actuate

The actuate attribute defines when the link should be rendered. Possible values are:

❑ onRequest – the link will be interactively activated by the user

❑ onLoad – the link is automatically activated when the document is displayed

Extended Links

Extended links expand the link concept to the paths in a graph. An extended link may contain many locator type links, each one describing a resource that participates in the graph. For example, if we have a menu with five options we need five locators, one for each option. Each locator may contain an href, role, and title attributes.

Once locators are defined we define the paths between resources using **arcs**. An arc describes a path between two resources. Locator roles are used to define the from and to arcs to use, so a single arc may define several paths if there's more than one locator with the same role.

Example

This is an extended link describing a family:

```
<family xmlns:XLink="http://www.w3.org/1999/XLink" XLink:type="extended">
  <child XLink:role="child" XLink:href="john.xml" title="john" />
  <father XLink:role="father" XLink:href="peter.xml" title="peter" />
  <child XLink:role="child" XLink:href="mary.xml" title="mary" />
  <relationship XLink:type="arc" XLink:from="father" XLink:to="child"
                show="replace" actuate="onRequest" />
</family>
```

In this example the arc describes two arcs originating on the father, one for each child.

Resources

❑ The XLink specification at http://www.w3.org/TR/2001/REC-XLink-20010627/

XPointer

XPointer is a language defined to express fragment identifiers for any URI reference that locates a resource whose Internet media type is one of text/xml, application/xml, text/xml-external-parsed-entity, or application/external-parsed-entity. XPointer supports addressing both into the internal structures of XML documents and external parsed entities.

Usage

XPointer is used for:

❑ Referencing portions of the XML document

❑ Linking to portions of the XML document

Description

XPointer is a language used to identify fragments of XML documents. While XPath can address elements or attributes, XPointer can address portions of elements and attributes, for example, the first three characters of text inside the `<foo>` element.

XPointer can point to a particular position of an XML document or address a range of data in an XML document. XPointer is used from the XLink specification to address what is linked from an XLink link.

XPointer is built on top of XPath by adding features to address points and ranges. It can address nodes using XPath syntax and can address ranges and points that XPath cannot.

Full XPointer Syntax

The full syntax describes an XPointer expression as one or more XPointer parts, where each part can be like this:

```
XPointer: XPointer(//foo/data[1])
```

The above expression selects the first occurrence of a `<data>` element; it selects the child of the `<foo>` element.

XPointer By IDs

If the elements have an `id` attribute defined in the DTD we can select elements using this XPointer format:

```
XPointer:XPointer(id("x01"))
```

Child Sequences

We can select elements in XPointer by navigating the XML tree and indicating the position of the element to be selected. For example:

```
XPointer: /1/2/3 OR XPointer:/*[1]/*[2]/*[3]
```

This would select the third child of the second child of the root element.

Combination

We can combine the use of IDs and child sequences:

```
XPointer(id('x01')/*[2])
```

This would select the second child of the element with ID (`'x01'`). This is equivalent to:

```
XPointer: x01/2
```

Points

A point is defined by a node (addressed as described before) and an index. The node is called the **container** node. An index of zero indicates the point before any child elements of the container node:

```
XPointer: XPointer(start-point(//foo))
```

A non-zero index n indicates the point behind the nth child element:

```
XPointer: XPointer(end-point(range(//foo/data[2])))
```

Character Points

When indicating a node of an element that cannot have child elements, such as processing instructions, comments, or text nodes, the index of the point expression is an index into the string value of the node:

```
XPointer: XPointer(start-point(string-range(//*,'hello', 2, 0)))
```

This points to the second character of the string `hello` in the container node.

Ranges

A range in XPointer can be defined by two XPointer locators in the form:

```
XPointer:XPointer(expression) to (expression)
```

Resources

❑   The XPointer specification at the W3C: http://www.w3.org/TR/xptr/

Validating XML Documents

We will often want to make sure that our XML documents, or documents provided by a third-party, conform to a common vocabulary or standard. For example, we might want to check if a file is a valid RSS document before we parse it. If the document does not conform, then it could be unusable by our application.

RELAX NG

RELAX NG is a simple Schema language for XML, A RELAX NG Schema specifies a pattern for the structure and content of an XML document. A RELAX NG Schema thus identifies a class of XML documents consisting of those documents that match the pattern. This Schema in itself is an XML document (from the RELAX tutorial at Oasis).

Usage

RELAX NG is used for:

❑   Validating XML documents

Description

RELAX is a Schema-based language to validate XML documents, that is, in RELAX validating is done using an XML document. The RELAX language is fairly simple and very powerful. We won't cover the full RELAX language in this chapter but we will take a look at how it works.

The root of the RELAX document is a **module**. In the module we indicate the RELAX version in use, the namespace of RELAX, and the target namespace (if we are writing a validating script for a vocabulary in some namespace):

```
<module
  moduleVersion="1.2"
  RELAXCoreVersion="1.0"
  targetNamespace=""
  xmlns="http://www.xml.gr.jp/xmlns/RELAXCore">

  ....

</module>
```

The `<interface>` element is used to indicate the root element of the XML vocabulary that we are going to validate:

```
<interface>
  <export label="foo" />
</interface>
```

To indicate that the `<foo>` element must have a `data` string subelement:

```
<elementRule role="foo">
  <ref label="data" />
</elementRule>

<tag name="foo"/>

<elementRule role="data" type="string" />

<tag name="data" />
```

The `<ref>` element is used to indicate composition of elements.

If an element is composed of several subelements we have to define a **sequence**. For example, if we want to validate that each `<data>` element has a `name` and `text` we can use:

```
<elementRule role="data" label="data">
  <sequence>
    <ref label="name" />
    <ref label="text" />
  </sequence>
</elementRule>
```

We can use a `<choice>` to express that an element can contain a choice of subelements:

```
<elementRule role="foo">
  <choice>
    <ref label="data" />
    <ref label="text" />
  </choice>
</elementRule>
```

We can also indicate valid data types for elements, required or optional attributes, data types for attribute values, number of occurrences for elements, choices and sequences, valid ranges or valid values for element contents.

RELAX is a powerful yet simple language to validate XML documents. It requires a RELAX implementation to be able to use the RELAX language to validate documents. There aren't any RELAX implementations for PHP yet, but we'll surely see some in a very near future.

Resources

- ❑ Learning to RELAX at http://www.xml.com/pub/a/2000/10/16/RELAX/index.html
- ❑ RELAX quick reference available at http://www.xml.com/pub/a/2000/10/16/RELAX/quickref.html
- ❑ RELAX NG tutorial at Oasis http://www.oasis-open.org/committees/RELAX-ng/tutorial.html
- ❑ A tutorial available at http://catcode.com/RELAX_tut/1.html

Schematron

The Schematron is a simple and powerful Structural Schema Language. Rick Jeliffe says the Schematron is "A feather duster for the furthest corners of a room where the vacuum cleaner (DTD) cannot reach".

Usage

Schematron can be used for:

- ❑ Validating XML documents

Description

Schematron is a validating language for XML documents based on XSLT and XPath. We write validating scripts using the Schematron XML vocabulary, which allows the use of XSLT expressions and XPath. Then we use a predefined XSLT stylesheet to compile the validation and produce an XSLT file that can be used to validate XML documents.

Let's say it again: we use an XSLT stylesheet that produces another XSLT stylesheet. For example:

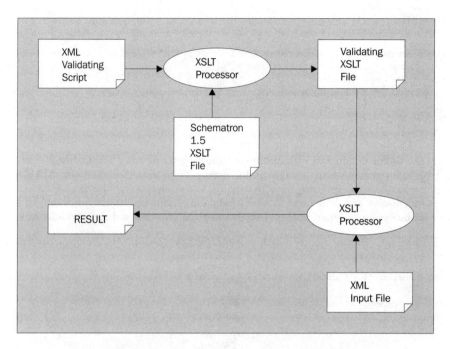

The Schematron language itself is very simple – it is based on **patterns**. Each pattern may contain several <rule context=""> subelements where context is an XSLT expression. It may also contain a mixed combination of <assert test=""> and <report test=""> where the test attribute is an XPath location path.

The Schematron language illustrates a very interesting pattern – using XSLT to validate XML, that's why we included XSLT as an option to validate XML files. Using Schematron we don't need to write XSLT files – we just write an XML script and there is an XSLT stylesheet to create the validating XSLT file. This is an interesting design pattern for XML processing too.

Example

In this example we build a validating script to check XML documents where each <AAA> element must have a <BBB> child:

```
<Schema xmlns="http://www.ascc.net/xml/schematron">
<pattern name="test1">
  <rule context="AAA">
    <assert test="BBB">The BBB element is not present</assert>
  </rule>
</pattern>
</schema>
```

In this example we test XML documents validating that `<edition>` elements must have a `version` attribute:

```
<schema xmlns="http://www.ascc.net/xml/schematron">
<pattern name="Structural vaidation">
  <rule context="edition">
    <assert test="@version">Version attribute missing</assert>
  </rule>
</pattern>
</schema>
```

If we want to validate documents with the above validating script using Schematron, we must generate an XSLT file that runs the validation against documents. To produce the validating XSLT stylesheet we transform the validating script using the `skeleton1.5.xsl` stylesheet. The `skeleton1.5.xsl` is the XSLT implementation of Schematron; it takes a validating script and transforms it into an XSLT file that can later be used to validate XML documents with the rules defined in the validating script.

When we run the `skeleton1.5.xsl` stylesheet on the above Schematron file we obtain the following XSLT:

```
<?xml version="1.0" encoding="UTF-8" standalone="yes"?>

<axsl:stylesheet xmlns:sch="http://www.ascc.net/xml/schematron"
xmlns:axsl="http://www.w3.org/1999/XSL/Transform" version="1.0
">

  <axsl:template match="*|@*" mode="schematron-get-full-path">
    <axsl:apply-templates select="parent::*" mode="schematron-get-full-path"/>
    <axsl:text>/</axsl:text>

    <axsl:if test="count(. | ../@*) = count(../@*)">@</axsl:if>
    <axsl:value-of select="name()"/>
    <axsl:text>[</axsl:text>

    <axsl:value-of select="1+count(preceding-
sibling::*[name()=name(current())])"/>
    <axsl:text>]</axsl:text>
  </axsl:template>

  <axsl:template match="/">
    <axsl:apply-templates select="/" mode="0"/>
  </axsl:template>

  <axsl:template match="edition" priority="4000" mode="0">
    <axsl:choose>
      <axsl:when test="@version"/>
      <axsl:otherwise>Version attribute missing</axsl:otherwise>
    </axsl:choose>
    <axsl:apply-templates mode="0"/>
  </axsl:template>

  <axsl:template match="text()" priority="-1" mode="0"/>
  <axsl:template match="text()" priority="-1"/>

</axsl:stylesheet>
```

Schematron is a very simple validating language that can be used for a lot of validation. Many semantic validations that are impossible to do with DTDs or difficult with Schemas, can be done with Schematron in a very simple way.

Schematron can validate:

❑ Number of elements, subelements, or attributes for a particular context
❑ Names of elements, subelements, or attributes
❑ Allowed or forbidden content for elements or attributes
❑ Data types of elements and attributes
❑ Relationships between elements

PHP and Schematron

Since Schematron is based on XSLT we can use it with the PHP XSLT extension. To validate an XML document against a Schematron file we have to first build an initial XSLT file using the Schematron XML and the `skeleton1.5.xsl` stylesheet. Then we need to run the generated XSLT file with the input XML file to produce the result of the validation. We can either precompile the Schematron files or use a kind of cache to reduce the number of XSLT transformations we have to make. Once a Schematron file is compiled into the validating XSLT we don't need to do that transformation any more. We can just use the generated XSLT stylesheet to validate the XML documents.

Resources

❑ The Schematron homepage at http://www.ascc.net/xml/schematron/
❑ A tutorial available at http://xml.ascc.net/xml/resource/schematron/schematron.html

Web Services

A web service is a function that can be accessed from a machine connected to the Web. A protocol is used to encapsulate the way the connection is established, how parameters are passed, and how values are returned to the calling application. A web service can be written in any language and can run on any platform and the application that uses the service can be written in another language and run in another platform without problems. XML-RPC and SOAP are two of the most commonly used protocols for web services.

XML-RPC

It's a spec and a set of implementations that allow software running on disparate operating systems, running in different environments to make procedure calls over the Internet (from the XML-RPC homepage).

Usage

XML-RPC is used for:

❑ Programming distributed applications
❑ Accessing or deploying web services
❑ Defining remote APIs for applications

Description

XML-RPC is a protocol designed to allow remote procedure calls from clients to servers using XML to encode the procedure calls and responses, and HTTP as its transport protocol. The goal of XML-RPC is to allow any application written in any language and running on any platform to call a service on any other computer or platform, in any language.

XML-RPC defines several data types that can be mapped to native data types of some languages by the XML-RPC specifications. When a procedure is called, the client indicates the method and the parameters properly encoded as XML-RPC data types. The server parses the request, calls the function that implements the method, then packs the result as XML-RPC and sends it back to the client.

Example

This example shows an XML-RPC request that calls a procedure to add two numbers:

```
POST /RPC2 HTTP/1.0
User-Agent: FooClient/5.1.2 (Unix)
Host: foo.mysite.com
Content-Type: text/xml
Content-length:

<?xml version="1.0"?>
<methodCall>
  <methodName>add</methodName>
  <params>
    <param>
      <value><i4>15</i4></value>
    </param>
    <param>
      <value><i4>98</i4></value>
    </param>
  </params>
</methodCall>
```

Resources

❑   The XML-RPC homepage at http://www.xmlrpc.com/

❑   The XML-RPC function list available at http://www.php.net/manual/en/ref.xmlrpc.php

SOAP

SOAP (Simple Object Access Protocol) provides a simple and lightweight mechanism for exchanging structured and typed information between peers in a decentralized, distributed environment using XML. SOAP does not itself define any application semantics such as a programming model or implementation-specific semantics; rather it defines a simple mechanism for expressing application semantics by providing a modular packaging model and encoding mechanisms for encoding data within modules. This allows SOAP to be used in a large variety of systems ranging from messaging systems to RPC.

Usage

SOAP is used for:

❑ Programming distributed applications

❑ Accessing or deploying web services

❑ Defining remote APIs for applications

Description

SOAP is another protocol to implement and use web services. It is a little bit more complex than XML-RPC and has some extended functionality. It can be transported over several protocols such as HTTP, FTP, or POP (Post Office Protocol). There are a lot of web services using SOAP and many implementations of SOAP for different programming languages already running. For example, we can mention the SOAP API for Google as one of the useful web services implemented using SOAP. Using this service you can query the Google search engine and display the results as you want.

Example

This example shows a SOAP request to call a method that retrieves the information for a stock quote:

```
POST /StockQuote HTTP/1.1
Host: www.stockquoteserver.com
Content-Type: text/xml; charset="utf-8"
Content-Length:
SOAPAction: "Some URI"
```

```
<SOAP-ENV:Envelope
        xmlns:SOAP-ENV="http://schemas.xmlsoap.org/soap/envelope/">
  <SOAP-ENV:Body>
    <m:GetLastTradePrice xmlns:m="Some-URI">
    <symbol>DIS</symbol>
  </SOAP-ENV:Body>
</SOAP-ENV:Envelope>
```

Resources

❑ Chapter 14 shows how you can use SOAP or XML-RPC to call web services from PHP

❑ The SOAP specification at the W3C http://www.w3.org/TR/SOAP/

❑ The SOAP FAQ at http://www.develop.com/soap/soapfaq.htm

❑ The SOAP CVS directory available at http://cvs.php.net/cvs.php/pear/SOAP/

❑ The Google SOAP Web Service (Google API) at http://www.google.com/apis/

Summary

In this chapter we've seen an overview of very important XML derivatives. First we examined the core derivatives for XML programming: SAX, XPath, XSLT, and DOM. We showed some examples of each of these derivatives and mentioned how we can use them from PHP. There are separate chapters in the book on SAX, XPath, XSLT, and DOM and you can learn a lot about these core technologies there.

Next, we examined some presentation vocabularies. Presentation vocabularies are used to render XML in a way that is viewable by some application, for example a web browser (XHTML) or a cell phone (WML).

Then we explored the semantic web and some XML vocabularies designed to convey meta data; RSS and RDF are two good examples of meta data vocabularies, the latter being the generic standard by the W3C for meta data.

Finally we did a very brief overview of web services, examining XML-RPC and SOAP as two of the protocols used to deploy and use web services. There's a lot of information in this book about web services including a whole chapter dedicated to XML-RPC and one on PHP as a client, where we study SOAP among other technologies.

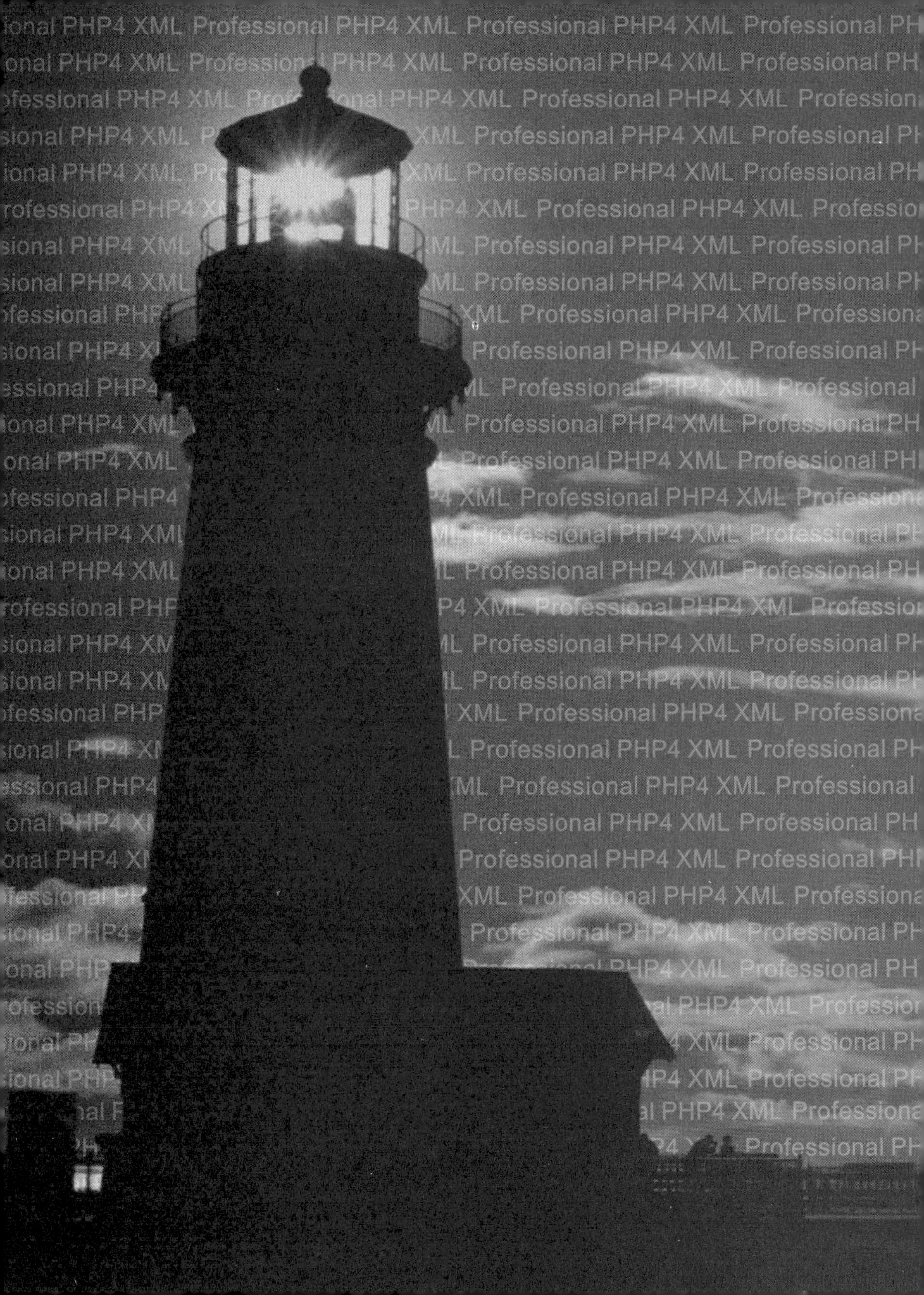
Professional PHP4 XML

5

SAX

In the previous two chapters, we learned about XML files, why they were developed and some current applications that use them. But how can we use XML content in our applications? The subsequent chapters will help us accomplish just that.

In this chapter, we'll learn how to read XML content using the Simple API for XML (**SAX**) interface using PHP. We'll cover:

- ❑ Parsing in general and SAX and Expat in particular
- ❑ Installing Expat with PHP on Windows and UNIX
- ❑ The SAX functions in Expat, with corresponding examples
- ❑ The eXtremePHP XML framework
- ❑ Tricks when parsing XML content

After reading this chapter, we'll have a solid understanding on how to integrate XML content into our new and existing web applications.

Parsing XML

While writing content in structured XML is fantastic, XML by itself won't do us any good. To actually make use of XML content in our applications, we have to read the content into memory where we can then examine and manipulate it. This scanning of content is called **parsing**.

The actual structure for any XML document is relatively simplistic, but it can often seem a lot more complicated if we are writing a custom parser. Let's say for the moment we are responsible for writing an application that parses a company's expense reports, which are stored as XML, to calculate the total amount owed for a given year.

At first look, we might open the file and start scanning character-by-character, looking for < and > characters, and commit the supplier names and price totals to memory. But what we might not realize is that we are about to be in store for more work than we had originally bargained for – some tags end in a special '/>' character sequences to indicate there is no character data. Another record might have the supplier name, 'Harry & Sons', which would force us to handle XML entities to process the replacements. Other times we might have to handle special CDATA blocks. Now with all this extra code, our program, which is simply supposed to add a few numbers together, has turned into several hundred lines of code, the majority of which is concerned with scanning the XML input.

Now, let's say the Human Resources department has now exported an employee contact list into an XML file and they would like to put this information on the company web site. Following the pattern above, we would start programming in exactly the same manner as before – open the file, read each of the tags, and look for special characters and sequences along the way. Notice that the program doesn't differ too much from the one before, but we have written several hundred lines of code for the simple task of displaying names and phone numbers.

Types of Parsers

Luckily, the programming community has realized this and developed APIs to handle all the grunt work automatically. These APIs are responsible for doing the scanning and recognizing for us, so all we have to do is write the application and not worry about the technical details.

All the APIs that are available today can be classified into two major categories:

❑ **Event-based parser**
This type of parser concentrates on reading the XML content in blocks and as each block is read, the parser calls several defined functions to handle the events. For instance, upon arriving at the start or the end of an element, or perhaps character data, the parser will call the appropriate function to handle these situations. These parsers are called SAX-based parsers, and are the main focus of this chapter.

❑ **DOM-based parser**
This type of parser reads in the entire XML document all at once and builds a tree representation of the document similar to a company organization chart. The tree consists of nodes where each node resembles an XML element, attributes, character data, or any other XML type. Once the tree has been read from memory, the programmer can traverse the tree using the API and parse its content or even manipulate the structure of the tree. These parsers are referred to as DOM-based because they build a representation of the Document Object Model defined by the W3C. This category of parsers is explained in the next chapter.

For now, let's take a detailed look at SAX.

What Is SAX?

Though SAX originally started out as a project for Java, it gained wide acceptance by everyone as a core framework for parsing XML documents and is considered to be a de facto standard today. SAX is an API that allows a programmer to interpret XML files. Though SAX can handle very large files, it has limited capabilities for manipulating the actual XML content because it only reads equal-length sections of the document at a time. Thus, it is impossible to add new nodes to the XML tree when the entire tree is not known.

SAX is different from most standards though, because it's not developed by an organization – it is an open standard. Unlike wire specifications like SMTP, SOAP, or TCP, SAX belongs to the public domain. This means that the software and standard belongs to everyone and no license is required to use it.

This was done for two reasons. Firstly, the founder of the SAX project, David Meggison, didn't want to burden developers and project managers from large organizations with legal issues over utilizing SAX within their applications. Secondly, the SAX project team had personal issues with other software that used licenses and decided to avoid the headaches.

What this means is that we can use, distribute, and tear apart anything to do with SAX and not worry about any negative after-effects – we can essentially do what we want with it.

This has helped the SAX framework and methodology to gain widespread use, allowing developers to freely implement it on any platform. However, this does lead to some drawbacks – because it is an open standard and the concept has been employed freely, its implementation is different in each programming language. The SAX project team has allowed other developers to discover the best way to implement SAX for any given language.

To read more about SAX, visit the official SAX web site at http://www.saxproject.org/.

How Does SAX Work?

No matter what language SAX is implemented in, the principles and concepts of SAX will always remain the same. SAX is an interesting parser in that it can parse the document without reading the document at once. Like traditional file parsing such as a document with a list of records, the SAX parser can read the document in equal-sized blocks and parse these blocks individually. This provides us with many advantages, as we will see later in the chapter, but most importantly we can parse very large files and conserve memory as we are only working with a small portion of the document at any given time. So now that we have a block of data, how does SAX parse the XML content?

Well, SAX is an **event-based** parser, meaning that when a specific event occurs, a callback function is invoked and its code is executed. These callback functions are called **handlers**. These events could be the start or the end of an XML tag, or perhaps the identification of an XML entity. As programmers who deal with XML, we no longer have to worry about the process of scanning the file ourselves; we simply create a set of event handlers specifying the actions the program is to take for any given event and execute the parser on that given file.

In event-based parsing, we have to get used to the idea that our application is not in control once things have been set in motion. We don't call the parser, the parser calls us. Since the events happen in a rather predictable manner, the XML elements have to be properly nested, so that we know every element that has been opened will sooner or later be closed.

To illustrate how this works, let's write three functions that will demonstrate event handlers for the expense report application mentioned earlier:

```php
$totalPrice = 0;

function HandleBeginTag()
{
    print ("New Price Encountered");
}

function HandleCharacterData($data)
{
    print ("The price is $" . $data);
    $GLOBALS['totalPrice'];
    $GLOBALS['totalPrice'] += $data;
}

function HandleEndTag()
{
    print ("Price added with total");
}
```

Now, let's see what would happen in this application when the parser comes across a `<price>` tag in the code above:

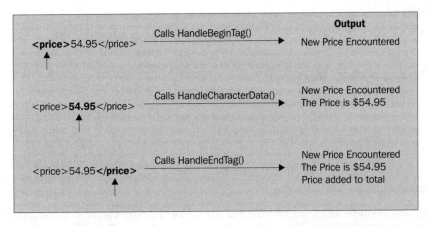

In this simplified example, we look at how the parser encounters events and how they are handled.

Firstly, when the parser arrives at the first `<price>` tag, it will call the `HandleBeginTag()` function, which outputs the message, '**New Price Encountered**'. The parser knows to call this function because `<price>` is of the proper form when starting a new tag.

Secondly, when `HandleBeginTag()` is finished executing, the parser continues to scan and recognizes the value '54.95', stopping just before the `<` character. Although this is a numeric value, to the parser's knowledge this is simply character data (a sequence of characters). Therefore, it calls the `HandleCharacterData()` function, which outputs the price and adds it to the total.

Lastly, the parser continues to scan and encounters the end tag, `</price>`. The parser will finally execute the `HandleEndTag()` function and output that the price has been added to the total. After execution, the parser is completely finished with this `<price>` tag and will continue scanning the XML file.

Although this example is unrealistically simplistic, it demonstrates exactly how a SAX parser behaves. As we can see, the programmer is no longer in control of the flow of the program; all the programmer does is tell the parser what to do when events happen, as seen in the three functions opposite. When we dive into actual examples, we'll see that developing parsers using SAX is exactly like this.

Let's now detail some inherent advantages and disadvantages of SAX.

Advantages

Let's look at the advantages:

❑ **Speed**
SAX is incredibly fast. Since it scans the file sequentially, the overhead of the program is the time to read in the block of data, scan each character, plus the amount of time for the code to execute. Although SAX offers fast parsing compared to other APIs, it is inherently slower than a database, thus it doesn't replace a database. In most cases, using a database leads to increased performance and scalability over XML.

However, in some instances, parsing content using XML can actually be faster than using a database. For instance, if we have a very complicated table structure, using an XML file with already un-normalized information can be much faster. Also, with an XML file, many records can be read and parsed with a single call whereas a database may need to make several calls over the network each time we fetch the results. This fetching process can also produce poorer performance. The last possibility where using SAX over a database might be beneficial is when a database is on another server and the XML file can be parsed locally. This can lead to increased performance as well.

In such situations, the programmer would have to think very carefully when architecting their application and in most situations, even though performance is key, spending too much time with these fine-grained details can be very cumbersome and not worth the time or effort.

With that said, even now, new XML content databases are emerging that solve issues concerning speed. These servers are not intended to replace current RDBMSs, but rather to provide a more preferable solution to using XML within our applications. These servers usually allow us to access XML content in a similar way but store the content in a binary form that provides concurrency, versioning, security, and many other features that one would expect from a RDBMS.

❑ **Parsable file size**
Unlike other XML parsers (such as DOM), SAX can theoretically parse a file of infinite size. In some applications, we may need to parse extremely large, shell-based applications. In many real-life examples, files of this nature are common and are necessary for large portals or document transportation applications. In these situations, SAX is our only option.

❑ **Low memory usage**
Because SAX reads XML files in blocks, it requires very low system memory. This makes it possible to have several scripts parsing XML files at the same time without burdening the server. As SAX reports parsing events by callbacks, it thus consumes less memory. As we will see in later chapters, other APIs are much more memory intensive compared to SAX – for example, DOM, builds an in-memory parse tree and thus needs more memory.

❑ **Increased control and flexibility**
Although the programmer is freed from the responsibility of scanning and recognizing symbols within the file, SAX parsers usually don't do much else. This gives us maximum control, efficiency, and flexibility over our application. On the other hand, this also means that we will have to write more code, leading to a decrease in productivity. It is possible, however, to construct an object-oriented SAX solution that solves this problem.

❑ **Ideal for web applications**
Because SAX is incredibly light, fast, flexible, and requires little memory, in most cases SAX is ideal for parsing XML content over the Web. This is why it is often referred to as the de facto standard whereas the recommended standard by the W3C is DOM. Although there is a need to generate and modify XML content online, it is often generated by databases or created by other sources.

It is sometimes noted that, since SAX was developed for the application needs of Java, its intention was not for web applications entirely. However, like most technologies, its real uses and benefits tend to make themselves known when the software is released to the public. At this time, we can see what developers are using the software for. Since web pages do not retain state without the aid of sessions, there is little need for keeping the document in memory. Thus, SAX usually provides a superior solution to DOM when parsing content.

Disadvantages

Though SAX gives the programmer maximum control and flexibility, it has some disadvantages:

❑ **Difficult to achieve structured or reusable code**
If we are required to carry out many tasks with the same XML data, it might be inconvenient to parse that data several times or complicate the application logic by placing it all in event handlers. If we accomplish these tasks in several different locations in our web application, this problem becomes even harder to manage because it may be necessary to repeat the code blocks. Although good design patterns and skill can help, this is one of the inherent problems with SAX.

❑ **Limited applicability**
Though SAX is very fast and flexible when parsing XML files, it is impossible to create or modify XML files with SAX. If we require the ability to generate or modify XML files, we will have to either generate the files ourselves, or consult with another API such as DOM. Also, SAX parsers are limited in that once they scan a line and call the necessary handler functions, they forget what they just did. Because SAX parsers cannot remember their actions or where they are in a file, some applications can be very difficult to write with a SAX-based parser.

Expat

As we have seen earlier, SAX is implemented in various languages.

For Microsoft systems, **MSXML 3.0** is used for unmanaged C++ and Visual Basic applications as a COM component. **Xerces, Lark**, and **Crimson** (soon to be Xerces2) are mainly used for parsing XML in Java. In fact there are so many parsers available for Java that a program called Java API for XML Processing (**JAXP**) has been developed by Sun to ensure that all parsers can be used in a driver-neutral way. Also, there is **Ælfred2**, a SAX parser which is used on small, embedded systems and it shows just how small SAX parsers can be.

Thus, it is no wonder why XML is taking the industry by storm, and PHP is no exception.

Expat is the PHP implementation developed by James Clark. Although it was originally written in C, PHP is able to use Expat either through Apache (if it's installed as a module) or built into PHP. If Expat is not installed, let's do that now.

> *More information on Expat can be found at http://www.jclark.com/xml/expat.html or http://sourceforge.net/projects/expat/.*

Installing Expat on Windows and UNIX

At the time of writing, the current version, PHP 4.2, contains Expat preinstalled. If you are running an old version, it is advisable to simply upgrade the version of PHP, as you will receive many bug fixes and additional features along with Expat.

> *Refer to Appendix B for detailed installation instructions.*

Verifying Expat

To verify that Expat is installed, point a browser at phpinfo(). After running this script, we should see the following section:

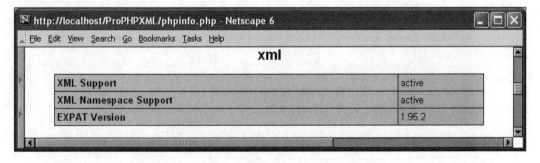

> If **XML Support** is not displayed as **active**, we will need to either enable Expat or install the latest release of PHP.

Parsing an XML Document with Expat

Once we have Expat working correctly with PHP, we are ready to parse our first XML document. For our first application, we are going to make a small web page to display a business article called 'Choosing a Business Partner'. The PHP script we are going to write will read the article from an XML file and display it to a browser as HTML. As far as SAX is concerned, this is a fairly simple application and will demonstrate the basic functions of Expat.

To start off, let's take a look at the source for the XML file:

```
<?xml version="1.0"?>
<!-- article.xml -->

<article>
  <name>Choosing A Business Partner</name>
  <author>Jon Doe</author>
  <email>jon@wrox.com</email>
  <date>January 25th, 2001</date>

  <intro>Well, this article is going to be short and informal. This is to all
those entrepreneurs that are having problems finding a suitable business partner
that is serious and ready to engage the public and carry out business activities
quickly and successfully. I speak sincerely and from experience.</intro>

  <section name="Attitudes and Behavior">
    <p>Where should I start? A good business partner needs all the behaviors as
well as a good attitude that suits the industry and management style that you are
trying to create for your new business venture. Behavior and Attitude? Yeah.
Behavior basically means that your business partner has to know how to do things,
and do them efficiently and effectively. Can that individual engage the public?
Can he be proactive and make decisions on his or her own? How well does their
underlying character scale up to meet the business needs for the next 5 years? If
your partner cannot decide what to do next, needs guidance and becomes frustrated
and weakened by the things around him/her, then that is a good indication that
they are not fit for the role...</p>

  </section>

  <!-- MORE SECTIONS WITH MULTIPLE PARAGRAPHS -->

  <outro>I hope you&apos;ve enjoyed this small, little article.</outro>
</article>
```

As we can see, the article tree is fairly simple. The XML structure contains a name, an author, an e-mail address, a date, and then the text of the article. The text structure is separated into three sections – the <intro>, various <section> tags containing a few paragraphs each, and an <outro>. Our goal is to parse this XML file and display it in the browser as it would normally appear on a news site.

To parse this file, we have to use the parser functions provided by Expat.

First, an XML application starts off by creating a new XML parser handle that is used by the other Expat functions. After the handle is created, we may want to set any options like the type of character encoding (if not selected already) or automatic case conversion (called **case folding**).

The next step is to define the event handlers. In a simple XML application, this is limited to defining a handler for the start and end elements, and a character data handler (the text in between XML start and end tags). In more complex applications, we may want to define handlers for processing instructions (PIs), entities, notation declarations, and namespaces.

Once the handlers have been defined and implemented, a file is opened and the data is parsed block-by-block using an XML parse function. During the parsing of each block, various events are triggered and the appropriate event handler is called. This process continues until there are no blocks left in the file, or an error has occurred. At this time, the parser is freed and the XML portion of the application is finished. Here is a model of this process:

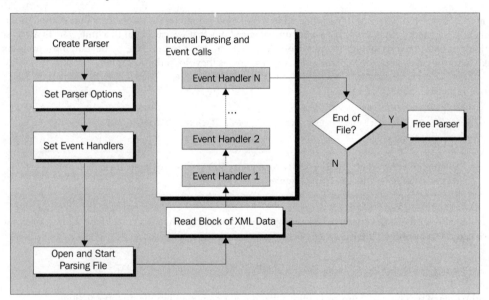

Expat Functions

Now that we know how a typical SAX application works, let's take a look at the functions used to make it all happen in the order we discussed.

xml_parser_create()

```
int xml_parser_create ([string encoding])
```

This function creates a new XML parser handle that is used by the other Expat functions. The handle stores all the parser options and event handlers so that when the parser is run, it knows how to behave and what functions to call when events fire.

This function takes an optional parameter that specifies the target character encoding. The values can be ISO-8859-1 (default), US-ASCII, UTF-8, and UTF-16, Any other value will invoke UnknownEncodingHandler. The character encoding is written in at the top of the XML file:

```
<?xml version="1.0" encoding="iso-8859-1"?>
```

If the character encoding is not specified, don't worry about it – just don't pass any parameters.

The following code will create an XML parser handle with the above character encoding:

```
$xmlParser = xml_parser_create("ISO-8859-1");
```

xml_parser_set_option()

```
int xml_parser_set_option (int parser, int option, mixed value)
```

This function sets a parser option, indicated in the second parameter, to a specific value. Although the function is generic, there are only two documented options that we can set at this time. The first is case folding, which converts all tags to uppercase. Although this is set to be TRUE by default, most programmers like to turn it off to keep the tag names looking exactly as they do in the XML file.

Here is the code to set case folding:

```
xml_parser_set_option($xmlParser, XML_OPTION_CASE_FOLDING, false);
```

> **A common error when parsing XML documents is that case folding is turned on and it appears that no events are being handled.**

We can also set the target character encoding if we did not set it when we created the XML parser handle. We can do so by adding the following code:

```
xml_parser_set_option($xmlParser, XML_OPTION_TARGET_ENCODING, "UTF-8");
```

At the time of writing, there are two options that are not mentioned in the documentation:

❑ **XML_OPTION_SKIP_WHITE**
This allows the parser to automatically skip whitespace characters such as a blank space, tabs, or new lines. This can save us a great deal of time since we won't have to provide any code to strip the whitespace manually.

❑ **XML_OPTION_SKIP_TAGSTART**
This is currently undefined and there is no information on the Web about what it does. It has been speculated that it skips a finite number of characters at the start of a tag name, but its usefulness is questioned.

Although they have been reported to be valid options on some OS installations, they will not work under Windows and in some cases on UNIX, such as FreeBSD. If these functions do happen to exist on a system (we'll know when we try them by not receiving any errors), one may still want to ignore them until they become apart of the documentation and are guaranteed to work on any PHP installation.

xml_parser_get_option()

```
mixed xml_parser_get_option (int parser, int option)
```

This function will return the current value for a given XML option. The second parameter, $option, takes in the same values as xml_parser_set_option(). Here is an example to find out what case folding is set to:

```
$caseFolding = xml_parser_get_option($xmlParser, XML_OPTION_CASE_FOLDING);

if ($caseFolding) {
    print ("Case folding is on");
} else {
    print ("Case folding is off");
}
```

In practical terms, this function isn't used for much more than debug information. It is better if we check an option before modifying it:

```
$caseFolding = xml_parser_get_option($xmlParser, XML_OPTION_CASE_FOLDING);

if ($caseFolding) {
    xml_parser_set_option($xmlParser, XML_OPTION_CASE_FOLDING, false);
    print ("Set case folding to off");
}
```

The above check implies that setting an option is an expensive operation. Although it might make sense to make this check in many scenarios, there is no noticeable penalty when setting an XML option. It is more efficient and less complicated to set the XML options without checking their existing values.

xml_set_element_handler()

```
int xml_set_element_handler (int parser, string startElementHandler,
                                string endElementHandler)
```

xml_set_element_handler() is used to let the parser know the functions to be called when a start and end tag is encountered while parsing the XML file. $startElementHandler and $endElementHandler are the names of the functions. The function only returns FALSE when $parser is not a proper handle.

To set the functions HandleBeginTag() and HandleEndTag(), write the following code:

```
xml_set_element_handler($xmlParser, 'HandleBeginTag', 'HandleEndTag');
```

Now whenever the parser finds the start or end of an element, it will call the respective function automatically. However, these functions cannot be of any arbitrary signature. They must contain a specific list of parameters.

To define the `HandleBeginTag()` function, the signature must look like this:

```
function HandleBeginTag($parser, $name, $attribs)
{
    ...
}
```

Similarly, to define the `HandleEndTag()` function, the signature is as follows:

```
function HandleEndTag($parser, $name)
{
    ...
}
```

In both of these examples, `$parser` is a reference to the `$xmlParser` handle returned by `xml_parser_create()`. Usually, we don't do anything with this variable. It is simply there to conform to the signature, but in rare cases we may want to set XML options.

The second parameter, `$name`, is the name of the XML tag currently being parsed when the event is fired. Thus, if we are currently parsing the `<section>` start tag defined in our XML document, `$name` will be equal to `section`. Likewise, when parsing the `</section>` end tag, `$name` will also contain `section`. If the case folding option is set to `TRUE`, `$name` will appear in all uppercase letters, such as `SECTION`.

The last parameter `$attribs`, only found in the `HandleBeginTag()` function, is an associative array containing all the attributes associated with that element. For instance, if we had the following tag:

```
<mytag name="Jon Doe" title="Chief Technology Officer" />
```

`$attribs` would contain the following:

```
array(2) {
    ["name"]=>
    string(12) "Jon Doe"
    ["title"]=>
    string(24) "Chief Technology Officer"
}
```

The common strategy employed by programmers is to `switch` the `$name` variable and perform various actions using `case` statements. Here is small example:

```
switch($name) {
case 'mytag':
    print ("I am at <mytag>");
    print ("This employee\'s name is $attribs[\'name\'] and ");
    print ("This title is $attribs[\'title\'] ");
    break;
default:
    print ("I am at a tag, other than <mytag>");
}
```

xml_set_character_data_handler()

```
int xml_set_character_data_handler (int parser, string handler)
```

This function is used to define the function handler for character data. When any character data is encountered, the parser calls this function. We can set the character data handler with the following code:

```
xml_set_character_data_handler($xmlParser, 'HandleCharacterData');
```

Like the start and end element handlers shown earlier, this handler must also have a specific signature. By following the code above, it is defined as:

```
function HandleCharacterData ($parser, $data)
{
    ...
}
```

Like previous functions, $parser is a reference to the $xmlParser variable returned by xml_parser_create(). The second parameter contains the character data that was parsed.

Unlike the start and end element handlers, the character data function does not pass the current element name in which the character data resides. For some reason, the PHP wrapper that calls the Expat functions does not contain this extra parameter, which may make simple applications easier to write. However, we frequently require the current tag name to decide what to do with the text. A common strategy is to store the character data into a global variable and let the HandleEndTag() function handle the data.

At first glance we might be tricked into thinking this function will return the entire set of characters between the start and end tags of an element. However, this is not the case. There are a few special exceptions where Expat will stop parsing, return a subset of these characters, and call the handler. This will happen when:

- The parser runs into an entity, such as & (&) or ' (')
- The parser finishes parsing an entity
- The parser runs into the new-line character (\n)
- The parser runs into a series of tab characters (\t)

For instance, consider the following element:

```
<mytag name="Jon Doe" title="Chief Technology Officer">
    Jon has been ABC&apos;s Chief Technology Officer for 2 years.
</mytag>
```

Once the parser scans the start tag, it will read the new-line (\n) character. At this point, it will stop and call the handler function, HandleCharacterData(). It is now up to our application to handle this piece of character data. After the function has finished executing, the parser will begin to scan and it will encounter a tab character (\t). Again, the parser stops and calls HandleCharacterData(). This time \t is passed into $data and our application processes this string.

Once the function has executed, the parser continues scanning until it reaches the entity, '. During this event, the parameter $data in HandleCharacterData() contains Jon has been ABC. In the next pass-through, $data will contain the apostrophe only, as the parser will convert the entity into its real character. This continues until the entire character data has been parsed. This is important to understand since we cannot assume that character data will always arrive in one 'chunk'. Be sure to keep this in mind.

To fully understand what is happening, let's look at a simple chart, which shows what $data will contain upon each pass with the previous tag:

Pass	$data
1	\n
2	\t
3	Jon has been ABC
4	'
5	s Chief Technology Officer for 2 years.
6	\n

Notice that if we had neglected to follow these exceptions, we might have ended up with a \n character instead of the entire sentence. It is up to our application to separate the meaningful character data from the whitespace. We will learn how to accomplish this later in the chapter.

> As programmers, we sometimes have no way of knowing the contents of the XML file and should develop the application with this in mind. Remember that new-line characters, tabs, and entity declarations cause the parser to halt and execute the character data handler. Handle these occurrences carefully and appropriately.

xml_parse()

```
int xml_parse (int parser, string data [, int isFinal])
```

This function parses the string, $data, that contains XML content and will process any events associated with $parser, as it recognizes them. If the parsing was successful, the function will return TRUE, else if there was an error, the function will return FALSE.

Sometimes an entire XML structure will be contained within a string, and other times it will come from a file. xml_parse() handles both situations adequately. If we wish to parse a string, we can do so with the following code:

```
$xmlString = '<employee><name>Jon Doe</name><title>CTO</title></employee>';
$parsedOkay = xml_parse($xmlParser, $xmlString);

if ($parsedOkay) {
    print ("Parsed successfully");
} else {
    print ("There was an error");
}
```

This will parse the content defined in $xmlString and call the appropriate handlers as they occur. Once the data has been parsed and is successful, $parsedOkay will contain TRUE.

If we are parsing XML content from a file, we should do this by setting up a while loop that reads one section of XML content at a time, and calls xml_parse() on each section:

```
if (!($fp = fopen('./article.xml', 'r'))) {
    die('Cannot open the XML file: ' . $fileName);
}

while ($data = fread($fp, 4096)) {
    $parsedOkay = xml_parse($xmlParser, $data, feof($fp));

    if (!$parsedOkay) {
        print ("There was an error or the parser was finished.");
        break;
    }
}
```

In this section of code, we begin to open a new file called article.xml. Once we receive a file pointer, we use fread() to retrieve a string containing a block of the XML file of up to 4096 bytes. The number 4096 is arbitrary; it bears no real significance other than that it is often used as the number of bytes to parse at once.

In each iteration of the loop, new blocks are read into $data, which is then parsed by the XML parser; the appropriate events are handled as often as necessary. Using the optional third Boolean parameter, $isFinal, we can make the parser stop by telling it which section is the last in the file. This is done by calling feof($fp), which returns TRUE when there are no more lines in the file to read. After the last section is parsed, xml_parse() will return FALSE, thus making the parser stop.

What happens if the content being parsed is cut off by the 4096 block size? For instance, what if the final 4 characters of a 4096 byte block are <myt and the starting 3 characters of the next block are ag>. If the parser is in the middle of a start or end tag like this situation, it remembers the remaining characters and returns TRUE. It does not parse these characters. In the next call to xml_parse() with a new block of data, it will append the previous string and continue to parse as normal. If the parser runs into character data at byte 4096, it will simply fire an event to the character data handler and return TRUE. The XML parser will continue to parse the additional characters once it is passed in the next iteration of the loop. If the parser reads <myt and there is no data left to parse in the next block, the parser will return an error as expected.

In a nutshell, Expat handles all these exceptions, so there is no reason to concern ourselves with them. However, it is a good idea to understand what is going on in the background.

xml_get_error_code(), xml_error_string(), and xml_get_current_line_number()

```
int xml_get_error_code (int parser)
string xml_error_string (int code)
int xml_get_current_line_number (int parser)
```

There is a possibility that all the XML might not be parsed correctly, so we need functions to identify errors. With these three functions, we can identify the type of the error, its error code, and the line in the XML file that it occurred. Firstly, given the XML parser handle, xml_get_error_code() can tell us the code of the error. Secondly, since it is difficult to remember what the error codes refer to, we can use the xml_error_string() function to convert the code into a message that will clearly tell us what is wrong. Lastly, we can use the xml_get_current_line_number() function, which gives us the line number where the error has occurred.

Here is some code, using similar variables to those defined earlier, that is often used to display an error if one occurred during parsing:

```
$parsedOkay = xml_parse($xmlParser, $data, feof($fp));

if (!$parsedOkay && xml_get_error_code($xmlParser) != XML_ERROR_NONE) {
    print (sprintf("XmlParse error: %s at line %d",
                   xml_error_string(xml_get_error_code ($xmlParser)),
                   xml_get_current_line_number ($xmlParser)));
    die();
}
```

When xml_parse() fails, it's not wise to continue parsing the file. Thus, it is recommended to kill the script or wrap this logic into a function and make it return appropriately to signal that an error has occurred. Remember, xml_parse() will return FALSE at the end of the file, so ensure that the error code does not equal XML_ERROR_NONE.

For a full list of error codes, visit http://www.php.net/manual/en/ref.xml.php#xml.error-codes.

> **On a production site, there should be absolutely no XML errors, so be sure to test any XML parsers with various sources of XML content before deploying them.**

xml_parser_free()

```
int xml_parser_free (int parser)
```

Lastly, we are going to talk about xml_parser_free(). This function simply frees the parser handle from memory, unsetting all the options and handlers defined on it. The function will return FALSE if $parser is not a valid handle. It can be used like this:

```
if (!xml_parser_free($xmlParser)) {
    die("Tried to free non-existent XML parser.");
}
```

There is no documentation on what will happen if we forget to free the parser from memory once we are finished with it, but the parser will indeed free itself from memory when the script has finished its execution, just as many other handles like mySQL free themselves after a script is finished executing. However, it's still a good idea to release the handle in the code as soon as we are done with it. Not only does this free up memory sooner, but it's one less thing that can potentially go wrong with our application if PHP would happen to crash before the script ends.

> Remember to free all XML parser handles when they are finished with.

Putting it Together

Now that we are familiar with the Expat functions and how they are to be used, writing an XML application won't be so difficult. This program uses all the functions described previously and demonstrates all the SAX fundamentals.

Unlike most HTML documents, we do not want to statically place the `<head>` tag in the file. We are going to define a header that contains the article name, so our header will be derived when the XML document is parsed.

First, to modularize our program, we are going to define functions for each of the steps. This makes our main parser program only a few lines long and easy to maintain.

> When writing parsers, be sure to modularize the steps as seen in the diagram at the beginning of the *Parsing an XML Document with Expat* section. In some cases, we will be able to reuse common XML functions to improve code productivity.

For our first step, we create a simple wrapper for creating the XML parser handle, which will terminate the script if there is not enough memory to create a new handle, or if there is some other error. The function returns the handle on success:

```
<html>
  <?php
  /* XML functions */
  function CreateParser()
  {
      $xmlParser = xml_parser_create();
      if ($xmlParser == false) {
          die('Cannot create an XML parser handle.');
      }
      return $xmlParser;
  }
```

To accomplish the second step, we create a `SetOptions()` function that takes in an XML parser handle and sets the case folding to `FALSE`. If we have to set any more options, this function provides a good base to add more without complicating the application:

```
  function SetOptions($xmlParser)
  {
      xml_parser_set_option($xmlParser, XML_OPTION_CASE_FOLDING, false);
  }
```

The third step is to use the `SetHandlers()` function that sets the start and end tag event handlers, as well as the character data handler. If our application needed any more handlers, they would also go here. We will define these `handle*` functions a bit later, but for now we will continue with the rest of the XML-based functions:

```
function SetHandlers($xmlParser)
{
    xml_set_element_handler($xmlParser, 'HandleBeginTag', 'HandleEndTag');
    xml_set_character_data_handler($xmlParser, 'HandleCharacterData');
}
```

In the fourth step, we have to prepare our XML source. Here we simply open a file with the given $fileName for read access and return its file pointer. Again, the script will die if the file is not found:

```
function OpenFile($fileName)
{
    if (!($fp = fopen($fileName, 'r'))) {
        die('Cannot open the XML file: ' . $fileName);
    }
    return $fp;
}
```

The Parse() function is the main parser engine for the application. As in xml_parse(), this function takes in an XML parser handle and a file pointer, and parses the entire contents, block-by-block. If the parser comes across an error in the document, it will be halted and the type and line number will be reported:

```
function Parse($xmlParser, $fp)
{
    while ($data = fread($fp, 4096)) {
        $parsedOkay = xml_parse($xmlParser, $data, feof($fp));

        if (!$parsedOkay &&
         xml_get_error_code($xmlParser) != XML_ERROR_NONE) {
            die('XmlParse error: ' .
            xml_error_string(xml_get_error_code($xmlParser)) .
            ' at line ' .
            xml_get_current_line_number($xmlParser));
        }
    }
}
```

In the last step, we must free the handle. As discussed previously, this will remove the event handler references, XML options, and any state information from memory:

```
function FreeParser($xmlParser)
{
    $freedOkay = xml_parser_free($xmlParser);
    if (!$freedOkay) {
        die('You did not pass a proper XML Parser to this function.');
    }
}
```

Now that our common code base has been laid down, let's begin defining the three event handlers: HandleBeginTag(), HandleEndTag(), and HandleCharacterData().

In `HandleBeginTag()`, we store the name of the tag to the global variable `$currentTag`. As mentioned before, the character data handler does not keep track of the current tag, so we are going to do this manually. Next, we enter a `switch` block that selects the appropriate HTML output given the name of the element the parser is currently processing:

```
/* Handler Functions */
function HandleBeginTag($parser, $name, $attribs)
{
    $GLOBALS['currentTag'] = $name;

    switch($name) {
    case "article":
        print ('<!DOCTYPE HTML PUBLIC "-//W3C//DTD HTML 4.0
Transitional//EN">');
        print ("<html>");
        break;
    case "name":
        print ("<head>");
        print ("<title>");
        break;
    case "intro":
        print ("<h4><i>");
        break;
    case "outro":
        print ("<i>");
        break;
    case "p":
        print ("<p>");
        break;
    case "section":
        print ('<b>' . $attribs['name'] . '</b><br />');
        break;
    }
}
```

Notice how each `case` is only a beginning HTML tag. As the parser finds future occurrences of character data and end tags, the closing HTML tags will be output to the browser.

In the character data handler, we also switch on the name of the tag it is currently parsing. In this code, we do two things – if the tag is `<name>`, `<intro>`, `<p>`, or `<outro>`, we want to print this data to the screen. As for the `<name>` tag only, we want to keep it in the memory for later use, so we will append the current `$data` string into the global variable `$name` using the `AppendToGlobal()` function.

In the next part, we simply save `<email>`, `<author>`, and `<date>` to memory. We do not want to display this on screen because the formatting is a bit more complicated. When we arrive at the `</date>` end element, the program will output the contents of all the variables into the HTML document:

```
function HandleCharacterData($parser, $data)
{
    switch($GLOBALS['currentTag']) {
    case "name":
        AppendToGlobal($currentTag, $data);
    case "intro":
    case "p" :
    case "outro":
        print ($data);
        break;
```

```
        case "email":
        case "author":
        case "date":
            AppendToGlobal($currentTag, $data);
            break;
        }
    }
```

The end tag handler behaves in the same manner as the start tag handler; whenever we encounter an end element, we simply display the corresponding HTML end tags. In the case of date, we simply get the three variables we committed and display it like this:

Written by Jon Doe (jon@wrox.com) on January 25th, 2001

Here is the `HandlEndTag()` function:

```
function HandleEndTag($parser, $name)
{
    switch($name) {
    case "article":
        print ("</html>");
        break;
    case "name":
        print ("</title>");
        print ("</head>");
        print ("<body>");
        print ("<h1>" . $GLOBALS["name"] . "</h1>");
        break;
    case "intro":
        print ("</i></h4>");
        break;
    case "outro":
        print ("</i>");
        print ("</body>");
        break;
    case "p":
        print ("</p>");
        break;
    case "date":
        print ('Written by ' . $GLOBALS["author"] .
        ' (<a href="mailto:' . $GLOBALS['email'] . '">' .
        $GLOBALS['email'] . '</a>) on ' . $GLOBALS['date']);
        break;
    }
}
```

Our last function is a support function. It simply takes the name of a global variable and value, and appends it to the global variable's current value. To accomplish this, we use variables. This minimizes the code we have to write in various locations in our handlers:

```
function AppendToGlobal($variableName, $value)
{
    global ${$variableName};
    ${$variableName} .= $value;
    ${$variableName} = trim(${$variableName});
}
```

The reason why we append it to the global variable is to solve those character data exceptions with new-line characters, tabs, and special entities that the parser comes across. Although this article may not have these exceptions during the <name>, <author>, <email>, and <date> tags, we can never be too sure when we parse other articles of the same format.

Once our program is modularized in this fashion, the main program is very short indeed. In fact, it follows the exact steps we outlined earlier in the flow diagram when we discussed parsing the XML document with Expat functions. Notice now that the details of handlers, options, and the parsing loop are hidden away. This is the ideal solution when writing a procedural parser. Lastly, the script drops out of PHP mode and displays the corresponding end tags that the parser did not echo:

```
/* MAIN APPLICATION */
$xmlParser = CreateParser();
SetOptions($xmlParser);
SetHandlers($xmlParser);
$fp = OpenFile('./article.xml');
Parse($xmlParser, $fp);
FreeParser($xmlParser);

?>
</body>
</html>
```

It may be convenient to place the OpenFile() function inside the Parse() function. After applying this refactoring, we would get the following code:

```
Parse($xmlParser, './article.xml');
```

After executing the PHP script, we should see the following article in our web browser:

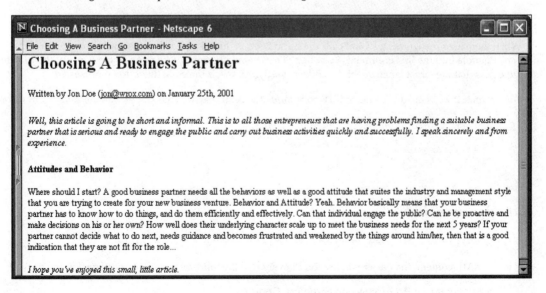

Additional Expat Functions

In the previous example, many advanced and optional functions were not introduced to avoid any premature complications. We will now learn how to handle special cases in XML, such as PIs, entities, and notation declarations.

xml_set_processing_instruction_handler()

```
int xml_set_processing_instruction_handler (int parser, string handler)
```

The xml_set_processing_instruction_handler() function sets the function handler for when the parser encounters a PI. The functions returns TRUE if the function handler's name is not empty and FALSE otherwise. The function will return FALSE if $parser is not a valid XML parser handle.

A **processing instruction** is a switch that tells the XML parser that there is a code here that needs to be processed, and the end result will be generated XML content. Here is an example:

```
<?php print ("Hello World"); ?>
```

The characters <? and ?> embody a PI. In this case, the characters php are the name of the PI and the code for the PI is in between the text php and the ending delimiter (?>).

To set the function handler for PIs, use the following code:

```
xml_set_processing_instruction_handler($xmlParser, 'handlePi');
```

Like all the Expat handlers, the PI handler function requires a special signature. The function is defined as:

```
function HandlePi($parser, $target, $data)
{
    ...
}
```

When the parser recognizes a PI and calls the handlePi() function, it will place a reference to the XML parser handle into the first argument, $parser. The second argument, $target, is the name of the PI. This indicates what the target language of the code is. Lastly, $data is the code that is to be processed.

For instance, if we wanted to evaluate PHP code inside the XML file, we could do so with the eval() function:

```
function HandlePi($parser, $target, $data)
{
    if ($target == 'php') {
        eval($data);
    }
}
```

If the character sequence:

```
<?php print ("I'm Supposed To Be Processing Structure Code"); ?>
```

is in the XML content, the parser will fire the PI event and the following would be displayed in the browser:

I'm Supposed To Be Processing Structure Code

A PI is useful to either execute PHP code, or perhaps another language. The neat thing about PIs is that they do make it possible to treat XML documents just like HTML. Instead of the browser parsing the code and displaying multimedia and interface objects, Expat becomes the parser that generates the HTML, and our PIs can also either generate XML or HTML.

xml_set_notation_decl_handler()

```
int xml_set_notation_decl_handler (int parser, string handler)
```

This function sets the notation declaration handler function. As we know with notations, they define a specific application that can assist in processing non-XML content, referenced in external entities. Since one can't expect Expat or any other parser API to process an infinite amount of file types, it is up to the programmer to call the necessary functions or programs to process the content and these notation declarations tell us how to do so.

As we learned in Chapter 3, a notation declaration has the following form:

```
<!NOTATION name {systemId | publicId}>
```

Whenever the parser comes across a notation declaration, it calls a handler function defined by this function. To set this function, use the following code:

```
xml_set_notation_decl_handler($xmlParser, 'handleNotationDecl');
```

The next step is to declare the HandleNotationDecl() function like this:

```
function HandleNotationDecl($parser, $notationName, $base, $systemId,
  $publicId)
{
    // .. code
}
```

For instance, we can associate a GIF file type as follows on a Windows operating system as:

```
<?xml version="1.0" encoding="iso-8859-1"?>

<!DOCTYPE bob [
  <!NOTATION gif SYSTEM "mygifprogram.exe">
  ]>
<bob/>
```

When the parser invokes the HandleNotationDecl() function, $notationName will contain gif, $systemId will contain mygifprogram.exe, and $publicId will contain FALSE.

In case we use a public ID for PDF documents, like this:

```
<!NOTATION pdf PUBLIC
  "-//Adobe Inc.//NOTATION Portable Document Format//EN">
```

the variable $systemId will contain FALSE and $publicId will contain the string, -//Adobe Inc.//NOTATION Portable Document Format//EN.

As of right now, the $base variable means absolutely nothing. Expat acknowledges this value for future releases, but the XML standard by the W3C does not indicate so. This value will always return FALSE unlike an empty string; like the documentation suggests, just ignore it.

In most situations, we'll want to store the program to call for the specific notation name because we won't need to do much else with it now. We can do this with a simple associative array, or any other manner of our choosing. Here is an example of what we could do:

```
function HandleNotationDecl($parser, $notationName, $base, $systemId,
  $publicId)
{
    global $notations;

    if ($systemId) {
        $notations[$notationName]->type = 'systemId';
        $notations[$notationName]->value = $systemId;
    } else {
        $notations[$notationName]->type = 'publicId';
        $notations[$notationName]->value = $publicId;
    }
}
```

This little code fragment collects the type of notation and its value into an associative array where the notation name is the index. For instance, after running the notation example above for GIF documents, the $notations array will contain the following data:

```
array(1) {
    ["gif"]=>
    object(stdClass)(2) {
        ["type"]=>
        string(8) "systemId"
        ["value"]=>
        string(16) "mygifprogram.exe"
    }
}
```

xml_set_unparsed_entity_decl_handler()

```
int xml_set_unparsed_entity_decl_handler (int parser, string handler)
```

This function sets the unparsed entity declaration handler function. As we learned in Chapter 3, an unparsed entity is content that is not parsed by an XML processor like Expat, having the following XML declaration within a DTD:

```
<!ENTITY name {publicId | systemId} NDATA notationName>
```

The notationName is the exact name that should match a notation declaration, so it is only fitting that these two handlers should be used in the same application. Whenever the parser comes across an unparsed entity declaration like the one above, it calls a handler function. To set this function, use the following code:

```
xml_set_unparsed_entity_decl_handler ($xmlParser, 'HandleUnparsedEntity');
```

The next step is to declare the `HandleUnparsedEntity()` function that is being defined opposite, like this:

```
function HandleUnparsedEntity($parser, $entityName, $base, $systemId,
 $publicId, $notationName)
{
    // .. code
}
```

For instance, this is how we would declare a new unparsed entity, such as a GIF document:

```
<?xml version="1.0" encoding="iso-8859-1"?>

<!DOCTYPE bill [
    <!NOTATION gif SYSTEM "mygifprogram.exe">
    <!ENTITY ArticleGif SYSTEM "http://localhost/article.gif" NDATA gif >
]>
<bill />
```

and the handler function:

```
function HandleUnparsedEntity($parser, $entityName, $base, $systemId,
 $publicId, $notationName)
{
    global $notations;

    if (isset($notations[$notationName])) {
        if ($entityName == 'ArticleGif')
            print ("It is our gif file we defined");
        system($notations->value . " " . $systemId);
    }
}
```

The script would fork the notation's designated program (`mygifprogram.exe`) on the entity. Of course, what we do with the entities is entirely up to us. To be honest, most programmers rarely take advantage of notation declarations and unparsed entities. Also concerning the function arguments, the `$base` variable contains `FALSE` and either `$publicId` or `$systemId` will remain `FALSE` depending on which one is in use – just as with the notation declaration handler.

So what about parseable entities like the following?

```
<!ENTITY String "A Very Long String We Do Not Wish To Type">
```

Entities, which are internal strings, will be automatically replaced by the parser when the character data handler is called, so we need not worry about replacing the internal entity references ourselves. For instance, any occurrence of `&String;` will be recognized by the parser and it will look up the entity declaration for us and replace the reference with, 'A Very Long String We Do Not Wish To Type'.

For whatever reason we might want our program to read a list of entity declarations, there is no 'clean' way to do so. We will have to use the default handler to accomplish this task, and the solution is neither pretty nor practical. This is described later in this section.

153

What about external entity declarations? Expat does not report external entity declarations to the programmer. As with internal entities, it does not provide a handler to parse the declaration. However, it does remember the declaration and its content and whenever a reference to this entity occurs within the XML content, the `xml_set_external_entity_ref_handler()` is responsible to take action. Let us look at this handler now.

xml_set_external_entity_ref_handler()

```
int xml_set_external_entity_ref_handler (int parser, string handler)
```

Sometimes there are entities that contain content that is not within the XML file itself, which are called external entities. For the ones that are considered parseable, this external reference handler function is called. Like we saw in Chapter 3, an external entity is declared by the following XML entity declaration within the DTD portion of the XML document:

```
<!ENTITY name {publicId | systemId}>
```

It is referenced within the XML document using the following **entity reference**:

```
&name;
```

Whenever the parser comes across an unparsed entity reference, such as &name, it calls a handler function defined. To set this function, use the following code:

```
xml_set_external_entity_ref_handler($xmlParser, 'HandleExternalEntity');
```

The next step is to declare the `HandleExternalEntity()` function like this:

```
function HandleExternalEntity($parser, $openEntityNames, $base, $systemId,
  $publicId)
{
    // .. code
}
```

However, unlike any of the other handlers seen previously, this handler will 'only' be called when there is an error. The parser is responsible for adding any external content where the external entity reference is located. If there are no problems, the content will be inserted into the document and the handler will not be called. If there is a problem with the XML content, such that it is not well-formed, this function handler will be called and Expat will report an error immediately after, shutting down the parser. In a nutshell, this function may allow us to investigate the problem, such as determining if the file is absent before the parser stops.

> A common error is to include a complete XML file into the resultant document. However, this places an XML PI and several other elements that are only supposed to be defined once within the document. Be sure to include partial documents only.

For example, here is an XML document that defines two external entities and uses them in the XML content:

```
<?xml version="1.0" encoding="iso-8859-1"?>

<!DOCTYPE joe [
    <!ENTITY ExternalOne SYSTEM "http://localhost/externalone.xml">
    <!ENTITY ExternalTwo SYSTEM "http://localhost/externaltwo.xml">
]>

<joe>
  &ExternalOne;
  &ExternalTwo;
</joe>
```

Now let's define the two files – `externalone.xml` and `externaltwo.xml`:

```
<!-- externalone.xml -->
  <job>Joe works in a factory</job>
  <email>joe@joeisverycool.com</email>
```

```
<!-- externaltwo.xml -->
  <address>1234 Joeville</address>
  <friends>Bob &amp; Bill</friends>
```

Once the parser begins parsing the file (with no extra code by the programmer) the resultant document will become:

```
<joe>
  <!-- externalone.xml -->
    <job>Joe works in a factory</job>
    <email>joe@joeisverycool.com</email>
  <!-- externaltwo.xml -->
    <address>1234 Joeville</address>
    <friends>Bob &amp; Bill</friends>
</joe>
```

The parser does not replace these before parsing begins, because that would require more than one pass-over in the XML content (making it inefficient). The replacements occur as the entity references are encountered, completely transparent to our application. We can treat the content as one XML file and not even know what is going on.

This process can help us write and divide up our XML content to make it more manageable, but it will make our parsing applications slower. To our benefit, most XML files that are large come from databases and other generators, so we might not use this handler very often. However, it adds an element of power to our arsenal and it can be quite effective as well as productive not only to us, but also to our XML content writers.

xml_set_default_handler()

```
int xml_set_default_handler (int parser, string handler)
```

This function sets a default function handler that handles all the cases in which we have no handlers defined. The function returns FALSE if $parser is not a proper XML parser handle and TRUE otherwise.

To define HandleDefault() as the default handler, use the following code:

```
xml_set_default_handler($xmlParser, 'HandleDefault');
```

To define the HandleDefault() function, use the following signature:

```
function HandleDefault($parser, $string)
{
    ...
}
```

As always, the first argument is the XML parser handle. The second parameter is the entire string that the parser scanned but could not process because the proper event handler was undefined. For instance, if there was no PI handler defined, the parser would invoke the HandleDefault() function and place the entire processing instruction into $string – that is, <?target data ?>.

In practical terms, there isn't much use for defining this handler. If we are unsure what to do with the data, then is probably best to avoid defining a handler for it in the first place. We should only define handlers that we are sure we can handle.

An Object-Oriented Approach

PHP currently has no direct support for a pure object model using Expat. However, there are user-contributed libraries that are available online such as **Manuel Lemos' XML parser class**, **Metabase**, and **eXtremePHP**. These add-on class libraries can be found at the following locations:

❑ Manuel Lemos' generic XML parsing class
http://phpclasses.upperdesign.com/browse.html/package/4

❑ Metabase
http://phpclasses.upperdesign.com/browse.html/package/20

❑ eXtremePHP
http://www.extremephp.org/ or http://sourceforge.net/projects/extremephp/

In this chapter, we are going to build the article application using eXtremePHP. The program will not differ in functionality or output from the previous version. This program will simply demonstrate how to write an object-oriented parser with SAX using one of the frameworks in eXtremePHP.

Refer to Appendix G for a detailed introduction to object-oriented technology. This appendix describes the essential concepts to programming object-oriented code using PHP, thus providing a good footing to start with and understand this chapter as well as utilize object-oriented capabilities within our applications.

The eXtremePHP Framework

eXtremePHP (XPL) is a set of object-oriented class libraries and application frameworks for developing web applications easily using PHP. It provides tools from basic data structures to frameworks for data layers, XML applications, form and processing managers, and anything else related to developing dynamic web sites. The library offers a database access framework, extended form processing, and HTML tag classes. It also provides great XML capabilities. In this chapter, however, we are only going to see how to use the SaxParser framework.

At the time of writing, the current version of the eXtremePHP framework is 0.15a. The library is currently in alpha stage, but the XML framework is very stable. The library is distributed under the GNU Lesser Public License v2.1, which allows us to freely use the library on any of our projects.

Installation

To install the framework, go to http://sourceforge.net/projects/extremephp/ or http://www.extremephp.org/ and download the latest release. There is a ZIP version and a tar ball.

For Windows, download `eXtremePHP-0.15.zip` and unzip it into Apache's document root.

In a UNIX environment, fetch the `tar.gz` file and copy it to the document root:

```
$ cp eXtremePHP-0.15a.tar.gz /websites/docroot
```

Use the following commands to uncompress the package:

```
$ cd /websites/docroot
$ gunzip eXtremePHP-0.15a.tar.gz
$ tar xvf eXtremePHP-0.15a.tar
```

Here, `/websites/docroot` is the document root of Apache. This will create a directory called `/xpl` under the document root that contains all the class libraries and frameworks.

On either installation, we have to prepend an include file that is used by the rest of the eXtremePHP classes. The file is called `/xpl/common/common.inc.php`. This can be done in one of the three ways:

❏   Prepend the file using an `Apache .htaccess` file

❏   Modify `php.ini` to prepend the `include` file to each script

❏   Include the file manually in each of our scripts

In most circumstances if we intend to use the library throughout our entire application, any of the first two options are preferred. We will detail the first method in the next section. The second method is pretty much self-explanatory. And in the application, we are simply going to include the file manually.

Setting up eXtremePHP Using a .htaccess File

Setting up a `.htaccess` file is usually the preferred way to use the eXtremePHP framework. This is because it provides several advantages over editing the `php.ini` file; therefore we'll first see how to set up the framework in this manner.

The main advantage is that we can tell Apache to include the XPL startup script for specific directories rather than every web site. For instance, if we run a hosting company and do not want every customer to have access to eXtremePHP automatically (because they may not use it and it will slow their applications down a bit), then .htaccess files will help to do that.

Secondly, we might not have access to edit the php.ini file since we may not be the owner of the server. In this case, .htaccess files help us configure PHP for our own needs without having to affect any other customers on the same box.

In order to use .htaccess files, the owner of the server must allow us to use them. With the latest version of the Apache HTTP server at the time of this writing, the ability to use .htaccess files is turned off by default. This is done for security reasons and generally makes sense as an out-of-the-box setting. If the owner of the server or the customer wants the ability to use .htaccess files, the administrator must go into the section entitled Section 2: 'Main' server configuration and look up the following section:

```
# This controls which options the .htaccess files in directories can
# override. Can also be "All", or any combination of "Options", "FileInfo",
# "AuthConfig", and "Limit"
#
    AllowOverride None
```

To change this default behavior, you must change the bottom line to:

```
    AllowOverride All
```

So what is an .htaccess file anyway? Well, Apache allows us to configure a directory (usually a virtual host) that is hosted through Apache using separate configuration files called .htaccess. These files basically supersede any options set in the main Apache configuration files so that virtual hosts can configure the server for their needs. We can use this file to enforce logins/passwords, provide redirection, specify error documents like 404 (page not found), and even specify additional MIME types. In this section, however, we are going to look at changes to the PHP configuration for a virtual host, thus overriding the values set in php.ini for our web site only.

When a page request is sent to Apache, the software first checks the directory the page is from for an .htaccess file. If it finds one, it'll use those settings over the ones specified in httpd.conf and related files in the conf directory. If it cannot find an .htaccess file, it will continue to search up the directory tree until it reaches the document root. At each step, it will continue to search for .htaccess files and use those configurations. If one is not found, Apache will use the default settings supplied in the server's httpd.conf and related files. In most cases when using eXtremePHP, it is best to put the .htaccess file in our document root as the web site typically uses the library on every page.

Configuring PHP through the .htaccess file is quite simple. To change a PHP configuration option, use the php_value command followed by the option name and its corresponding value:

```
    php_value parameter "value"
```

This instructs Apache to override the php.ini file's options so it can ignore the ones set in this file.

To tell Apache to auto-prepend the `common.inc.php` script, place this following code in `.htaccess` using any editor. This is the file that sets XPL options, constants, and defines a few functions required by the rest of the library:

```
php_value auto_prepend_file "DOC_ROOT/xpl/common/common.inc.php"
```

The path will differ depending on individual eXtremePHP installation.

Once this line is added and the `.htaccess` file is saved, the next time anyone requests a page from our web site, the eXtremePHP library common files will be loaded on every page.

Now that we have set up eXtremePHP, let's learn how to parse XML files using the object-oriented paradigm using eXtremePHP's SaxParser framework.

The SaxParser Framework

The SaxParser framework is very closely related to Expat, however, it is more modular and easier to use. Unlike some frameworks that are only customizable, the eXtremePHP XML framework is extendable, thus it is a **white box** framework. This gives us great power and flexibility at a small cost of understanding a bit more about the classes. With this framework, the following code modules have been distinguished:

❑   A general parser object that is reused from project to project. This is customizable in a way similar to Expat's XML parser handle.

❑   An extended `SaxParser` object that contains application-specific code, separate from the parser.

❑   A generic `XmlInput` class to allow various sources such as strings, files, or future sources not yet determined. Due to the power of polymorphism, this can be accomplished in a generic manner.

❑   An `XmlTagHandler` class to extend sets or individual tags to describe how they are handled. Therefore, this separates the logic of handling tags from the parser explicitly.

The framework is very modular compared to Expat or other SAX frameworks, and makes our applications very maintainable and reusable. Here is a typical model of how SAX applications are usually constructed using the framework:

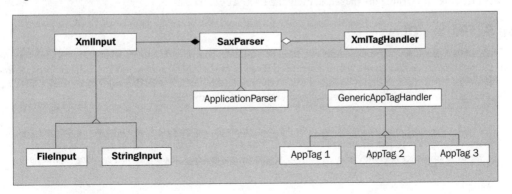

Here, the library provides the classes depicted in **bold**.

The first step to developing a parser is to make a new class that extends from SaxParser. In our example, we are going to make an ArticleParser class. This class will add all the tag handlers to the parser and provide any interfaces to global variables needed by the tag handlers. In more complex applications, the child class adds methods that contain application logic for the entire parser.

The next step is to code our custom handlers for the various events. Instead of having a generic handler that is responsible for providing the logic for all tags, in the object-oriented version, we have the concept of **handler objects**. Each object handles one tag, or possibly a set of tags, that achieve the same functionality. Each handler knows how to handle its start and end elements as well as character data.

The SaxParser class decides on which object to use when handling parsed data, just like Expat decides which function to call. The benefit of this approach is that tag-specific logic can now be grouped together in one component. We no longer have to maintain three functions to provide the logic for an XML element. This has tremendous maintenance advantages when parsing complex XML documents. Usually, as a good design practice, a base tag handler is created that the other application element handlers extend from. This base tag handler provides the base functionality and/or hook functions necessary to make the child classes easy to program.

Lastly, an XmlInput object must be chosen. Usually, this comes from a file, so logically we would instantiate a FileInput object with the source file name and pass it to our application-specific parser. This simple object conforms to a generic interface that the SaxParser understands. It has a simple read() method that sends data to the parser and has an isDone() method to let the parser know if the source has finished sending XML data.

By separating the input source from the parser we improve the maintenance of our application; we may change our application's XML source type many times. This makes it very easy to change sources without having to change any other class files. The secondary benefit is that we can create our own source or modify existing ones by using inheritance. We will see how to do so in a later section. For now, let's build the object-oriented parser.

Writing the Parser

Let's first look into writing the parser, namely the SaxParser class.

The SaxParser Class

The SaxParser class is unmistakably the bulk of the XML framework. Unlike many classes, SaxParser is not to be used as a standalone class or even used directly (most XML frameworks provide the programmer with one or two classes and they are used out-of-the-box). SaxParser was designed to be very different, because it follows a white box framework rather than a black box model.

Black box models have all the details hiding inside, only exposing an easy-to-use interface to interact with the object's services. These services shield us from the inner workings of the class and make it easy for us to customize the behavior of the object. However, in some cases we are limited to what we can do with that object.

White Box Framework

A white box framework is the opposite of a black box model. A white box framework expects the application programmer to understand the inner workings of the class to a certain extent. This is because white box classes or frameworks do not function without extra implementation. This doesn't mean that programmers need to know its member variables or private functions, but developers must have a good idea what the object's services are and what the designer meant to do with them.

Once programmers gain knowledge about these classes, they can utilize the white box framework by extending from the base classes and provide application-specific information. Knowing which functions to call as services and which ones to extend does this goal.

 The combination of the framework and the custom-built extensions is the complete program. This approach often provides ultimate flexibility and customizability compared to the black box approach, at the cost of having to invest time in understanding the services and its collaborations in greater detail.

To use the SaxParser class, we must extend it with an application-specific class. For our business article, we are going to call it ArticleParser.

SaxParser()

Usually, the programmer writes a new constructor to replace the SaxParser constructor. SaxParser() accepts any instance of the XmlInput class, which describes the input source of the XML content, but it is often easier to provide a simpler argument for the clients of the application-specific parser. This is done by the following code.

In this constructor, we receive the file name of the XML article and instantiate a FileInput object with the given filename. This FileInput is a subclass of XmlInput and it tells the parser that our XML content is coming from a file:

```
function ArticleParser($fileName)
{
    SaxParser::SaxParser(new FileInput($fileName));
}
```

The SaxParser also provides static factory methods to create these input classes. Here is an example on how to use them:

```
function ArticleParser($fileName)
{
    SaxParser::SaxParser(SaxParser::createFileInput($fileName));
}
```

Why doesn't the framework allow programmers to pass the file name without a padded object?

For one reason, it is difficult to distinguish if the argument is the name of the file, an XML string, or possibly any future source. Even if these types were parsed and identified, new types would have to be added to the SaxParser class and that would create greater maintenance issues for the library. The second issue is that parsing a string has different logic than parsing a file in the main engine. Therefore, two methods would have to be developed to handle both cases. To make matters worse, any future XML sources would also need their own parseXyz() method.

To solve these problems, the XmlInput class provides a generic interface for XML sources. The current two provided with the library are StringInput and FileInput. This also allows new sources to be added to the library in the future, and users can program their own if the library does not supply them at all. We will take a look at how to do this later in the chapter.

Setting Parser Options

Like Expat, SaxParser allows us to set the target encoding type or case folding. To set the parser's character encoding to ISO-8859-1 and case folding to TRUE, use the following code:

```
function ArticleParser($fileName)
{
    SaxParser::SaxParser(new FileInput($fileName));
    $this->useIsoEncoding();
    $this->setCaseFolding(true);
}
```

We can use useAsciiEncoding() and useUtfEncoding() to set the US-ASCII and UTF-8 characters types, respectively. By default, SaxParser automatically sets the ISO-8559-1 character encoding standard.

addHandlers() and addTagHandler()

The next major step to developing an application-specific parser using eXtremePHP is to specify our custom handler objects. We can specify them using the **hook method** called addHandlers().

> All methods that are overridden and are called by another method or constructor in the superclass(es) are called hook methods. The method or constructor that invokes the hook method is called a template method.

The reason addHandlers() is called a hook method is because it is meant to be overridden by the implementer. The template method executes this method automatically, so the implementer need not worry about invoking the method explicitly.

> We do not call addHandlers() explicitly. Since this is a hook method, the parser calls it automatically. Therefore, if the programmer were to call it explicitly, it would be called twice.

To assist the developer in adding a new handler object to the parser, the base parser object contains the addTagHandler() method. This method simply takes in an instantiated handler class and adds it to the list of handlers the parser is responsible for calling when events are fired. For example, if we wanted to add a new handler for the <name> tag, we would do so with the following code:

```
function AddHandlers()
{
    $this->addTagHandler(new NameTagHandler($this));
}
```

Once the parser is called, the `NameTagHandler` will be responsible for handling all begin element, end element, and character data events for the `<name>` tag. Although this particular example might suggest a relationship between the class name and the tag it handles, this most certainly may not be the case. However, like all well-written OO programs, naming the classes accurately is always recommended.

ArticleParser.class.php

Now that we understand how the `SaxParser` class works, we'll look at the OO implementation of the parser.

eXtremePHP provides a new `include()` function called `impxpl()`, which automatically includes a file from the `/xpl` directory under the document root. This makes it very easy to include files from the library into our scripts. Notice that, we need not put the `php` extension in the string that contains the file name.

The next `include()` incorporates a script which defines all the tag handlers used by the parser. We will take a look at these in more detail later in the chapter, but for right now assume that a handler class has been defined for each tag in our `article.xml` file:

```php
<?php

// ArticleParser.class.php

impxpl ('xml/SaxParser.class');
include ('./ArticleTagHandlers.php');
```

Next, we tell PHP that we want to define a new class called `ArticleParser` and that it will extend from the `SaxParser` object. By using the constructor of the parent class, we can initialize our parser object with a `FileInput` object as shown previously in our discussion about the `SaxParser()` constructor:

```php
class ArticleParser extends SaxParser
{
    function ArticleParser($fileName)
    {
        SaxParser::SaxParser(new FileInput($fileName));
    }
```

Next, we override the `addHandlers()` hook method and add our tag handlers to the parser:

```php
    function addHandlers()
    {
        $this->addTagHandler(new NameTagHandler($this));
        $this->addTagHandler(new AuthorTagHandler($this));
        $this->addTagHandler(new EmailTagHandler($this));
        $this->addTagHandler(new DateTagHandler($this));
        $this->addTagHandler(new IntroTagHandler($this));
        $this->addTagHandler(new SectionTagHandler($this));
        $this->addTagHandler(new PTagHandler($this));
        $this->addTagHandler(new OutroTagHandler($this));
    }
```

Notice that we pass the variable `$this` (which is passed by reference) into each handler. This establishes two-way communication between the parser and each handler. This is important because as the handlers are called, they will need to interact with the main parser in various situations. In most cases they set global state information, but in more complex applications, the parser is usually responsible for any logic that spans across the scope of one tag handler.

To complete our parser class, we provide two methods (not defined in the `SaxParser` interface) that keep track of the state. The function `AppendToVariable()` is precisely the same as `AppendToGlobal()` in the procedural version. It takes in a variable name and a value and appends the value to the current value of the global variable. However, this variable isn't in the global namespace. It is now a member variable in the main parser object, but for all intents and purposes it is global with respect to the parser and its handler objects:

```
function AppendToVariable($variableName, $value)
{
    $this->{$variableName} .= $value;
    $this->{$variableName} = trim($this->{$variableName});
}
```

The `GetVariable()` method returns the value of the member variable set by `AppendToVariable()`. Both these functions are used to store the name of the article, the author's name, the e-mail address, and the date the article was written. As we can see by comparing with the procedural version, this is almost identical:

```
function GetVariable($variableName)
{
    return $this->{$variableName};
}
}
?>
```

Now that parser class has been defined, programming the customized tag handlers is the next step to developing the parser.

The XmlTagHandler Class

The `XmlTagHandler` class is an abstract class. It provides absolutely no functionality whatsoever, but it does define the interface for a handler object. This means that all handlers must conform to this interface, or `SaxParser` will be unable to handle the events correctly.

To develop a new handler, it must extend from the `XmlTagHandler` class and overwrite and implement any of the abstract interface methods. There are three methods that handle the events for the start and end of an element along with its character data. These are called `HandleBeginElement()`, `HandleEndElement()`, and `HandleCharacterData()` respectively and are considered optional. There is a fourth method that must be implemented called `GetName()`. This method's responsibility is to return the name of the XML element this handler is responsible for. If this method is not overwritten, our parser will have problems. The `SaxParser` class requires the tag name because it uses the `GetName()` method for several of its operations. `GetName()` is intended to be abstract so if PHP supports proper enforcement of abstract methods, this wouldn't be a problem. However, since at the time of this writing PHP does not do this, it is up to the developer to remember.

> In PHP, it is up to the programmer to remember to override the `GetName()` method. Unlike many object-oriented languages, PHP has no support for the concept of abstract methods. Abstract methods force the implementer to define the method when creating a new child class.

ArticleTagHandler.class.php

As mentioned earlier, it is common to develop a base handler that the rest of our objects can extend from. We want to provide as much base functionality that is common to our handlers as we can, to reduce the amount of code in the subclasses. Build a few handlers and locate any common functionality if it is not clear what services should be in a base class. Any common functionality can then be refactored and placed in a common parent class.

There are three areas of functionality that our handlers share:

❑ All element handlers have the potential to output HTML tags during the begin and end element handlers. While not all handlers will display HTML, it makes sense to provide the base functionality so configuring the handlers that do have it will become easier.

❑ During the character data event, the data is either printed to the screen, saved to a variable, or both.

❑ All event handlers will have to communicate with the parser sometime or another, so we provide delegation methods to the parser's application logic.

As with `SaxParser`, we use eXtremePHP's import function to include the code for the `XmlTagHandler` class:

```php
<?php
// ArticleTagHandler.class.php

impxpl('xml/XmlTagHandler.class');
```

We define variables to store the HTML content that is displayed during the begin and end element events. Notice that these variables are initialized to an empty string, ensuring handlers that contain no HTML content will be handled correctly.

The next two variables are Booleans that indicate if the character data is to be displayed to the screen or is to be saved in the parser as a member variable. These variables will not be modified explicitly as services will be provided to set these variables:

```php
class ArticleTagHandler extends XmlTagHandler
{
    var $beginHtml = '';
    var $endHtml = '';

    var $isSaved = false;
    var $isPrintable = false;
```

For the constructor, we merely use `XmlTagHandler`'s constructor to initialize the event handler. We also add a call to a method called `SetOptions()`. Like the `addHandlers()` method in the `SaxParser` class, any child classes of `ArticleTagHandler` are expected to implement this method. This is also a hook method since no client is expected to invoke this method explicitly:

```php
function ArticleTagHandler(&$xmlDocument)
{
    XmlTagHandler::XmlTagHandler($xmlDocument);
    $this->SetOptions();
}

// abstract method
function SetOptions() {}
```

> Ensure that the subclasses of the `ArticleTagHandler` class implement the
> `SetOptions()` method. Do not forget to implement `GetName()` as well since any child
> of `ArticleTagHandler` is also a child of `XmlTagHandler`.

Now it is time to define our handler methods. Notice the parameter lists for these objects are much shorter than the Expat version. For instance, the `HandleBeginElement()` method has only one parameter `$attributes`, which is an associative array containing the attributes for the current tag:

```
// handler methods
function HandleBeginElement($attributes)
{
    print ($this->beginHtml);
}

function HandleEndElement()
{
    print ($this->endHtml);
}

function SetHtml($startHtml, $endHtml)
{
    $this->beginHtml = $startHtml;
    $this->endHtml = $endHtml;
}
```

When working with Expat, one may have noticed that the `$parser` parameter always stuck out like a sore thumb, but it didn't make a lot of sense when it was returned each time the parser called an event handler. To make the interface simpler, the SaxParser framework strips this parameter out altogether.

Since the document is contained with an `XmlTagHandler` class by default, if we really wanted to access the parser to set an option, we could do this:

```
$this->xmlDocument->setCaseFolding(true);
```

In most cases, we will not be using this reference to the parser to set up options, but rather to access global information of the document itself, such as its methods to retain state information. This is because once an `XmlTagHandler` object (any subclass) is released from memory, the data it parsed is essentially forgotten just like in a procedural Expat parser. Therefore, the `SaxParser` becomes a conduit to send information and requests to as the document is being parsed. We will see this idea in the example a little later.

> Although some may criticize the above violation of encapsulation, this provides the
> cleanest approach to retrieving the reference of the document without creating any copies
> by accident, and thus saves memory.

Unlike the Expat version, we are employing a default implementation that will display the HTML text when any handler fires the begin element and end element events in the `HandleBeginElement()` and `HandleEndElement()` methods, respectively. This ensures that once a child class sets its HTML text using `SetHtml()`, the handlers will already be defined, removing the burden of programming the begin and end methods from every handler object that is used in our program. In the case where these default implementations do not suffice, the child class can easily override the method and provide their own implementation.

> **If a handler displays HTML content in the begin and end events, the handler should call `SetHtml()` in its `SetOptions()` method to ensure the text is set prior to execution.**

The next set of methods deal with the handling of character data.

The `HandleCharacterData()` follows Expat's character data handler exactly. The only difference is that it only takes one parameter, `$data`. Like the other handle functions, a default implementation is provided for `HandleCharacterData()`. If the Boolean variable `$isPrintable` is set to TRUE, when the character data handle method is called, the character data will be displayed on the screen.

Likewise, if the `$isSaved` variable is `true`, it will instruct the handler to append the character data to the member within the main parser object. These variables are set by the `SetPrintable()` and `SetStore()` methods respectively. Like the `SetHtml()` method, these functions must be called using the hook method, `SetOptions()`:

```
function HandleCharacterData($data)
{
    if ($this->isPrintable) print ($data);
    if ($this->isSaved) $this->appendToVariable($data);
}

// property methods
function SetStore()
{
    $this->isSaved = true;
}

function SetPrintable()
{
    $this->isPrintable = true;
}
```

Lastly, we define methods to either append character data to a parser's member variable or retrieve it from the parser. These methods simply delegate to the ones defined in `ArticleParser`. Notice that `AppendToVariable()` does not take in the variable name in the parameter list. This is because the name will always be the name of the tag:

```
// methods to interact with 'global' data
function AppendToVariable($value)
{
    $this->xmlDocument->AppendToVariable($this->getName(), $value);
}

function GetVariable($variableName)
{
    return $this->xmlDocument->GetVariable($variableName);
}
}
?>
```

167

ArticleTagHandlers.php

The next step is to define our element handlers. Rather than creating a new file for each handler, we are going to place them all in the file `ArticleTagHandlers.php`. This makes it convenient to create and modify the handlers all at once. All our handlers will extend and use the core functionality of the class that was previously developed – the `ArticleTagHandler` class:

```php
<?php
// ArticleTagHandlers.php

include('./ArticleTagHandler.class.php');
```

The `NameTagHandler` is one of the most complex handlers in comparison to the others. First, we override the `SetOptions()` hook method and specify the course of action for the handle functions. Here, we are telling this handler to print `<head><title>` when the parser scans the start element `<name>` and to print `</title></head>` when the parser reaches `</name>`. The handler is also instructed to store the character data as a member variable within the `ArticleParser` object and to display any character data in the web browser:

```php
class NameTagHandler extends ArticleTagHandler
{
    function SetOptions()
    {
        $this->SetHtml('<head><title>', '</title></head>');
        $this->SetStore();
        $this->SetPrintable();
    }
```

The `NameTagHandler`'s end element event handler has been overridden. The default functionality does not suffice because the HTML body information must be displayed after the HTML header. This is done by first calling the parent `HandleEndElement()` method using the class' function call operator and displaying the HTML body information:

```php
    function HandleEndElement()
    {
        ArticleTagHandler::HandleEndElement();
```

Since we can assume that a `$name` member has been stored inside the `ArticleParser` object at the time the character data handler is called, we use the method `GetVariable()` to retrieve the contents of the article's name and display it between the `<h1>` tag:

```php
        print ('<body><h1>' . $this->GetVariable('name') . '</h1>';
    }
```

Lastly, we override the `GetName()` method and return the static string `name` to signify that this handler is for the `<name>` element with the XML content:

```php
    function GetName()
    {
        return 'name';
    }
}
```

The next few handlers are uneventful. Both the `AuthorTagHandler` and the `EmailTagHandler` store the character data as a member variable within the parser object. Notice that no HTML content was set, so the empty string will be displayed when the `HandleBeginElement()` and `HandleEndElement()` handlers are called:

```
class AuthorTagHandler extends ArticleTagHandler
{
    function SetOptions()
    {
        $this->SetStore();
    }

    function GetName()
    {
        return 'author';
    }
}

class EmailTagHandler extends ArticleTagHandler
{
    function SetOptions()
    {
        $this->SetStore();
    }

    function GetName()
    {
        return 'email';
    }
}
```

While the previous two handlers were unexciting, the `DateTagHandler` compensates. By the structure of the article, we are certain that `<date>` will be retrieved after the `<author>` and `<email>` elements. As soon as the parser executes `HandleEndElement()` on this handler, we can assume that all three values for author, e-mail, and date have been collected.

We use `GetVariable()` to obtain their values and display a formatted sentence underneath the title to specify the author of the article, a link to their e-mail, and the date the article has been written:

```
class DateTagHandler extends ArticleTagHandler
{
    function SetOptions()
    {
        $this->SetStore();
    }

    function HandleEndElement()
    {
        $author = $this->GetVariable('author');
        $email = $this->GetVariable('email');
        $date = $this->GetVariable('date');

        print ('Written by ' . $author . ' (<a href="mailto:' . $email . '">' .
$email . '</a>) on ' . $date);
    }
```

```
    function GetName()
    {
        return 'date';
    }
}
```

The next few event handlers work similarly to the others as they follow the basic formula of overriding
`SetOptions()` and `GetName()`, setting any properties desired to control the parser's reactions and output
during the events:

```
class IntroTagHandler extends ArticleTagHandler
{
    function SetOptions()
    {
        $this->SetHtml('<h4><i>', '</i></h4>');
        $this->SetPrintable();
    }

    function GetName()
    {
        return 'intro';
    }
}

class OutroTagHandler extends ArticleTagHandler
{
    function SetOptions()
    {
        $this->SetHtml('<i>', '</i>');
        $this->SetPrintable();
    }

    function GetName()
    {
        return 'outro';
    }
}

class PTagHandler extends ArticleTagHandler
{
    function SetOptions()
    {
        $this->SetHtml('<p>', '</p>');
        $this->SetPrintable();
    }

    function GetName()
    {
        return 'p';
    }
}
```

The last event handler, `SectionTagHandler`, deserves some attention. Unlike many of the other handlers, `SectionTagHandler` doesn't have any options to set. In fact, an empty `SetOptions()` method will do just fine. All this handler is concerned with is displaying a bolded title above the set of the section's paragraphs. This is done by overriding the `HandleBeginElement()` method; the HTML content displayed is the same from the Expat version. We have no need for setting the HTML content, so we do not bother calling the parent `HandleBeginElement()` method to display the HTML content for handling the start element event:

```
class SectionTagHandler extends ArticleTagHandler
{
    function HandleBeginElement($attribs)
    {
        print ("<b>" . $attribs["name"] . "</b><br />");
    }

    function GetName()
    {
        return 'section';
    }
}
?>
```

xmlarticleoo.php

This file is the main application. Like the procedural program, we start an HTML document and switch into PHP mode:

```
<!-- xmlarticleoo.php -->

<!DOCTYPE HTML PUBLIC "-//W3C//DTD HTML 4.0 Transitional//EN">
<html>
  <?php
```

Here we include the main file that is needed for all other eXtremePHP classes. It defines a few constants and functions that make the library easier to integrate into our applications. The library is also dependent on this file to operate correctly. Note, if we had configured the eXtremePHP library to use the `.htaccess` file or `php.ini`, we would remove this line from the code to prevent errors:

```
include('./xpl/common/common.inc.php');
```

Now we include the file containing the `ArticleParser` class and instantiate an instance of the parser with the `article.xml` file containing the business article content. Once a call to the `parse()` method has been made, the parser engine will start scanning the file and will execute any of the tag handlers as necessary:

```
include('./ArticleParser.class.php');

$parser = new ArticleParser('./article.xml');
$parser->parse();
```

Every child class will have a `parse()` method. It is a reusable method that contains the parser engine that reads the XML data from any instance of `XmlInput` and then processes that data. This alleviates us from programming the main parsing logic ourselves and lets us work on the handlers more closely:

```
    ?>

  </body>
</html>
```

After running the application in a web browser, the business article will be rendered exactly as the Expat version. Notice with the eXtremePHP version how clean the main application script is. In projects with a full-blown object-oriented library, single pages often become very short – maybe even two or three lines. This makes it very easy to maintain code and organize the various parts of the application.

Additional SaxParser Methods

In the eXtremePHP framework, the SaxParser class contains exactly the same functionality as Expat. In fact, the SaxParser framework is simply a complete object-oriented version of Expat, defining the relationships between data structures in the way OO principles would suggest.

handleProcessingInstruction()

To utilize any of the extra functionality, we have to override the base functionality provided in the SaxParser class with our own methods. For the ones that we don't override, nothing happens during those events. For example, to create a PI handler for a SaxParser object, we would do this:

```php
<?php
// TestParser.class.php

impxpl('xml/SaxParser.class');

class TestParser extends SaxParser
{
    function TestParser($fileName)
    {
        SaxParser::SaxParser(new FileInput($fileName));
    }

    function handleProcessingInstruction($parser, &$target, &$data)
    {
        if ($target == 'php') {
            eval($data);
        }
    }
}
?>
```

In this instance, we tell the parser to evaluate any code that is meant for PHP. Fortunately, eXtremePHP assumes this as a default option, since there really is no point to define this behavior for every application. We can define other handlers for processing instructions with the following code:

```php
    function handleProcessingInstruction($parser, &$target, &$data)
    {
        SaxParser::handleProcessingInstruction($parser, $target, $data);
        if ($target == 'ksp') {
            // code to execute ken's server page language
        }
    }
```

Here we simply call the parent function to handle the PHP code in the bolded portion of the above code.

The rest of the functions are handled similarly. They can be defined as follows within a derived `SaxParser` object:

```
function handleDefault($parser, $data) {}

function handleUnparsedEntityDecl($parser, $entityName, $base,
    $systemId, $publicId, $notationName) {}

function handleNotationDecl($parser, $notationName, $base, $systemId,
    $publicId) {}

function handleExternalEntityRef($parser, $openEntityNames, $base,
    $systemId, $publicId) {}
```

As far as the parameters go and how they function, it is identical to Expat. It would seem that even SAX has some room to grow in comparison to many of the C++ and Java parsers using the SAX interface. Until then, what we have seen is pretty much everything that can be done with Sax. The rest is up to our creative and specific needs.

Problem Data

Now that we know how to code both a procedural-based and an OO parser, it is time to improve these parsers to handle whitespace and potential XML syntax violations.

Handling Whitespace

When Expat parses character data, it returns absolutely everything in between the start and end elements. Sometimes this is inconvenient since we use whitespace to help format the XML content. Although the whitespace helps us visualize the structure of the document, Expat reads it as a flat file, treating those new-line characters and tabs as sequences that are apart of that character data. Therefore, it is the job of the programmer to eliminate the whitespace when it is necessary.

In the previous example, we did not remove the whitespace because HTML is much like XML – the browser does not display whitespace anywhere between the tags in most cases. However, when we need to parse XML content for more than HTML display, those extra characters can be quite a problem.

Imagine an XML file containing textual data on products that are to be e-mailed to prospective customers. Since some e-mail clients are text-based, those extra new-line characters and tabs would be shown visually within the e-mail, perhaps making the e-mail look unstructured, unpleasant, and difficult to follow. It is much better to strip the non-relevant whitespace from the character data before providing it to the application that requires it.

The Expat Solution

To modify our article example to take out whitespace, we must edit the `HandleCharacterData()` function. Our strategy is simple – because we know the parser returns the character data every time it scans a new-line character or a series of tab characters (more than one is the key here), we can simply check for these instances and decide not to process the character data normally. Here is a modification to our business article parser:

```
function HandleCharacterData($parser, $data)
{
    if ($data != "\n") {
        $data = ereg_replace("\t+", ' ', $data);
        global $currentTag;

        switch($currentTag) {
        case 'name':
            appendToGlobal($currentTag, $data);
        case 'intro':
        case 'p':
        case 'outro':
            print ($data);
            break;
        case 'email':
        case 'author':
        case 'date':
            appendToGlobal($currentTag, $data);
            break;
        }
    }
}
```

Notice that just before we carry out the switch logic, we test if $data is equal to the new-line character. Since Expat will only return one new-line character at a time, this will weed out every one of these in the file.

In the next statement, we trim out any series of tabs to a single space character. This is for a few reasons. For one, although this might render just fine in a browser (except for the <td> immediately followed by an <img> tag), if we were parsing the article.xml file to redistribute using text-based e-mail, the formatting would be absolutely unacceptable. Secondly, the extra whitespace at the beginning signals that we are writing on a new visual line according to this article.xml document. Let's take a look.

```
<intro>
    Well, this article is going to be short and informal.
    This is to all those entrepreneurs that are having
    problems finding a suitable business partner that is
    serious and ready to engage the public and carry out
    business activities quickly and successfully. I speak
    sincerely and from experience.
</intro>
```

Notice that after the word 'informal', we have a new-line character, followed by two tab characters, then the word 'This'. As humans read this document, it is very clear that the word, 'This' starts a new sentence. Even at a more abstract level, it is very clear that this is a new line in the document. If we were to strip the tabs with a $data = str_replace("\t", "", $data); function call, the result would be the following HTML:

```
<i>Well, this article is going to be short and informal.This is to all those
entrepreneurs that are havingproblems finding a suitable business partner that
isserious and ready to engage the public and carry outbusiness activities quickly
and successfully. I speaksincerely and from experience.</i>
```

As we can see by the highlighted portions of the document, in every occurrence where a new line was followed by a series of tabs, the words have been joined. This is because even though we humans can notice that those two words are separate, the computer read:

```
Informal.\n\t\tThis
```

Once the new lines and tabs were removed, we are left with just 'Informal.This'. Now, if all the characters were put onto one line, we wouldn't have this problem. But this wouldn't be a good chapter if it didn't talk about these rare exceptions would it?

The only way to correct this is by adding a space in-between the words. To add only 1 space instead of 2 (because there are two tab characters in this instance), we must use the power of regular expressions. Let's try `$data = ereg_replace("\t+", ' ', $data);` instead and see what happens:

```
<i> Well, this article is going to be short and informal. This is to all those
entrepreneurs that are having problems finding a suitable business partner that is
serious and ready to engage the public and carry out business activities quickly
and successfully. I speak sincerely and from experience. </i>
```

Notice that by using `ereg_replace()`, we have added a space in between all the words that contained tabs. We could have also used the following Perl type of regular expression to achieve the same result. Usually Perl expressions are much faster:

```
$data = preg_replace("/\t+/", ' ', $data);
```

Our work is nearly finished – the sentence is almost perfect. In the output above, there is still a single space before the word, 'Well' and after the word, 'experience.'. Although this will render just fine using HTML, this won't suffice for a pure text output. To fix this, we need to rely on the `trim()` function, in which we trim the whitespace characters from the output of the regular expression replace function. However, we can't just trim every time the character data parser handles the character data. We must only trim the first instance and the last instance. To do this easily, we must restructure our program a bit. Here is the replacement code:

```
function HandleCharacterData($parser, $data)
{
    if ($data != "\n") {
        $data = ereg_replace("\t+", ' ', $data);

        switch($GLOBALS['currentTag']) {
        case 'name':
        case 'intro':
        case 'p':
        case 'outro':
        case 'email':
        case 'author':
        case 'date':
            AppendToGlobal($GLOBALS['currentTag'], $data);
            break;
        }
    }
}
```

The file `xmlarticlews.php` contains the complete code with these modifications.

In the `HandleCharacterData()` function, we essentially combine all the possible element cases to append to its global variable. So in the case of 'intro', a new global variable $intro will be created using the `AppendToGlobal()` function. It is questionable that the `switch` statement is even needed now, but this still provides a filter to ensure any elements that do not conform to the article will not be processed (thus making the parser faster):

```
function HandleEndTag($parser, $name)
{
    switch($name) {
    case 'article':
        print ("</html>");
        break;
    case 'name':
        print ("</title>");
        print ("</head>");
        print ("<body>");
        print ("<h1>" . $GLOBALS["name"] . "</h1>");
        break;
    case 'intro':
        print ($GLOBALS['intro']);
        print ("</i></h4>");
        break;
    case 'outro':
        print ($GLOBALS['outro']);
        print ("</i>");
        print ("</body>");
        break;
    case 'p':
        print ($GLOBALS['p']);
        print ("</p>");
        break;
    case 'date':
        print ("Written by " . $GLOBALS["author;"] .
        ' (<a href="mailto:" . $GLOBALS["e-mail"] . '">' .
        $GLOBALS["email"] . "</a>) on " . $GLOBALS["date"];
        break;
    }
}
```

Not too much changed in the `HandleEngTag()` function since the `AppendToGlobal()` function automatically trims the entire variable for us automatically. Therefore, we just output the intro, paragraph, and outro text just before end tags. After these small changes have been made to the parser's handlers, we'll finally get the result that we want, which does not include any unnecessary whitespace.

```
<i>Well, this article is going to be short and informal. This is to all those
entrepreneurs that are having problems finding a suitable business partner that is
serious and ready to engage the public and carry out business activities quickly
and successfully. I speak sincerely and from experience.</i>
```

This approach will solve all the possible whitespace problems. There may be faster approaches if one is certain of the character data writing within the document, but this solution does not presume any assumptions.

The last thing to mention about this solution is that some people might bring up that a series of tabs can be negated in the `if` statement like this:

```
if (ereg('^\t+$', $data) || $data == "\n") {
```

Although this statement will remove several series of tabs, this condition will only remove the tabs before and after the character data. In other words, this will not remove the tabs that are in between the character data. Thus, it is important to make the application work in all cases. This is a problem with Expat return strings that start with tab characters that also contain a sequence of other meaningful characters. The `ereg_replace()` is the only quick way around it to form a solution.

The eXtremePHP Solution

To fix the whitespace problem in our object-oriented method, we have to modify the `HandleCharacterData()` method in the `ArticleTagHandler` class. The solution is actually identical to the procedural version once we locate the correct place to modify the logic. Here is the modified method:

```
function HandleCharacterData($data)
{
    if ($data != "\n") {
        $data = ereg_replace("\t+", ' ', $data);
        if ($this->isPrintable) echo $data;
            if ($this->isSaved) $this->AppendToVariable($data);
    }
}
```

Once this change is made, all the subclasses that extend from `ArticleTagHandler` will be changed and there will be no new lines or tabs displayed in the HTML output.

Non Well-Formed XML Content

Occasionally we have to deal with non well-formed XML content. In some situations the author of the XML content forgets certain syntax rules or fails to use the proper entity declarations when necessary. With small documents, the author of the content can easily rectify these errors and all is well. However, in many situations this isn't the case. A lot of XML content is also generated by databases or other software packages and the teams that wrote these packages didn't know XML as well as they thought.

Programmers who develop parsers for this poorly generated XML content become extremely frustrated because many SAX parsers will reject the content and shut down, and Expat is no exception. In these cases, it isn't so simple to modify the content because generated XML content can be quite large – so large in fact that the files may not fit in memory using any text editor. In these cases, the `vi` text editor is our best option, however, it will take some time to load the file and start making the necessary modifications. If we don't have enough RAM, it might even choke our system. In this case, it is impossible to modify the document.

Fortunately, there is a better way to manage non well-formed XML content. Every time we read a block of data before passing it to `xml_parse()` we can simply process it for corrections. Some corrections are difficult to make, such as the wrong placement of tags, but those errors usually don't occur when they are generated by another software package. The main issues are the following:

❏ Characters such as the apostrophe or quotation not being written as entities.

❏ Characters such as ^A through ^H, ^K through ^Z, and ^ [, ^\, ^], ^^, ^_. These are characters having ASCII character codes between 1 through 8 and 11 through 31.

❏ Rare occurrences of end tags with a missing greater than symbol (for example, </music).

These are just a few of the many things that make the XML file volatile. This is not the work of amateur programming teams; this has been taken from XML content of several large companies that use Texis or Oracle databases and several other popular products that generate XML.

If the programmers are not aware of these possibilities, they could be debugging for quite a long time without solving the problem. In most situations, programmers who work with small exports fix the problems as they come along, but this Band-Aid approach is inefficient for large scale projects that work with large XML content. Let us look at an example solution, using both Expat and eXtremePHP.

The Expat Solution

For Expat, the solution is rather simple. Once a block of data has been collected from the XML source, it can then be processed, making the necessary modifications, and then returned to xml_parse(). Let's take a look at a code snippet that solves a few of the problems mentioned earlier.

This is our fix function. It takes in a block of data and replaces any instances of apostrophes with the proper entity equivalent or remove any erroneous escape characters. It's not fast and sleek, but it does the job. Notice that str_replace() was used instead of one of the pattern matching functions, such as ereg_replace(). These functions tend to be slower and when parsing large XML content, it's important to produce a solution that processes as quickly as possible:

```
function FixData(&$data)
{
    // replace characters to entities
    $data = str_replace('\'', '&apos;', $data);

    // clear ^A through ^H
    $this->ClearCharacterSet($data, 1, 8);

    // clear ^K through ^Z and ^[, ^\, ^], ^^, ^_
    $this->clearCharacterSet($data, 11, 31);
}
```

One thing that needs mentioning is that the above string replace function will replace all apostrophes in the document. So if the XML document uses apostrophes for quoting attributes, then this will make the document's syntax incorrect. Thus, if we have a document that uses all apostrophes, we won't be able to use such a strategy. This is because even with a powerful regular expression to match the apostrophes we want, we might never get them all. The input source might give a chunked up block that is in the middle of the attribute, and thus our regular expression replacement might fail.

Usually if we are using a filter like this, there is a very good chance the XML content was generated by some software and used the double-quotes for XML attributes, so if the situation allows us to use this strategy, we should employ it. Otherwise we'll have to take a look at the document and decide if there is a better of way of generating the document or having the document fixed by the author in the first place as apostrophes were meant to be replaced with entity references for this reason.

The function `ClearCharacterSet()` is simply a support function that removes any characters that range from `$charStart` to `$charEnd`. This is a refactoring to clean up the code in `FixData()`:

```
function ClearCharacterSet(&$data, $charStart, $charEnd)
{
    for ($i = $charStart; $i <= $charEnd; $i++) {
        $data = str_replace(chr($i), '', $data);
    }
}
```

Lastly, to apply the patch to our procedural parser, we insert `FixData()` in between the reading of data from the file and the `xml_parse()` function:

```
function Parse($xmlParser, $fp)
{
    while ($data = fread($fp, 4096)) {
        FixData($data);
        $parsedOkay = xml_parse($xmlParser, $data, feof($fp));

        if (!$parsedOkay &&
         xml_get_error_code($xmlParser) != XML_ERROR_NONE) {
            die('There was an error');
        }
    }
}
```

The eXtremePHP Solution

The eXtremePHP solution relies on the programmer to have some knowledge on the collaborations of the classes. As an `XmlInput` class is contained within a `SaxParser` object, it provides all the methods the `SaxParser` needs to read the data, determine the block sizes, and find out if there is more information to parse, or to instruct the parser to shut down. The key to solving the problem is extending from a current `XmlInput` child class and modifying the `read()` method. Here the code for a `TexisFileInput` class solves the erroneous data that was generated by a Texis database:

```
<?php

impxpl('xml/FileInput.class');
```

Here we create a new class that extends from `FileInput`. We can safely assume that the other methods provided by the base class will work as they did before due to the properties of inheritance:

```
class TexisFileInput extends FileInput
{
```

As mentioned before, our job is to define a `Read()` method. To do this, we first read the data from the file using the `Read()` method in the `FileInput` class. This is done by calling the class function operation, `$data = FileInput::Read()`.

After we read in the data, we can make the exact changes as we did in the procedural version. However, as part of the `Read()` method's requirements, we must return the data in the same way `FileInput::Read()` does. This ensures that any clients to this object will not even know the difference. After changing our input source, our XML parser will begin to operate with the erroneous data:

```
function Read()
{
    if ($data = FileInput::Read()) {
        $data = str_replace('\'', '&apos;', $data);

        // clear ^A through ^H
        $this->ClearCharacterSet($data, 1, 8);

        // clear ^K through ^Z and ^[, ^\, ^], ^^, ^_
        $this->ClearCharacterSet($data, 11, 31);
    }

    return $data;
}

function ClearCharacterSet(&$data, $charStart, $charEnd)
{
    for ($i = $charStart; $i <= $charEnd; $i++) {
        $data = str_replace(chr($i), '', $data);
    }
}
}

?>
```

Here is the code to construct our `ArticleParser` class with the new `TexisFileInput` class:

```
...
function ArticleParser($fileName)
{
 SaxParser::SaxParser(new TexisFileInput($fileName));
}
...
```

After applying that change to the main application-specific parser object, we can safely test it and run it without affecting any other code. The key concept to take from this example is that `FixData()` was converted to a new class definition, meaning `TexisFileInput` is our fix for the original object itself.

The Ampersand

The ampersand is a unique character in that a simple parse and replace doesn't work effectively because the ampersand is contained within the entity syntax. The main problem is that if we replace the ampersands to &, we run the risk of creating the substring, "&amp; ". This is definitely not what we want to happen. The best and fastest solution is to replace all strings containing " & " with an ampersand, and then do the reverse. Here is the following code:

```
$xmlString = str_replace("&amp;", "&", $xmlString);
$xmlString = str_replace("&", "&amp;", $xmlString);
```

Are two string replaces inefficient? As mentioned before, str_replace() is quite fast. In fact, even 10 calls to str_replace() is faster than a single call to a pattern-matching function. Therefore, there is no need to whip up a fancy regular expression and make a call to ereg_replace() or preg_replace(). It is not the prettiest solution, but it will help repair ampersands that were not escaped using the entity notation.

Summary

In this chapter, we looked at the complications to writing XML parsers from scratch and where and how SAX was introduced as an open standard to help programmers parse XML content faster and in lesser time.

We have learned how to use SAX functions as an event-based parser and how it can be a fast, lightweight, and flexible solution, but can also take quite some time to code up applications. However, because of these reasons, SAX is extremely viable for web development and is considered the de facto standard.

We then learned that Expat, written by James Clark, is the implementation of SAX for PHP. After setting up Expat with the PHP installation, a model of the Expat process and a comprehensive introduction of the main functions were discussed.

After outlining each function in detail, we walked through a real example to display a business article titled, 'Choosing a Business Partner'. Although a procedural program was given, we also learned there were alternative methods to developing SAX-based parsers and learn how to do develop an object-oriented parser using the eXtremePHP XML framework, taken from a full-fledged library of web site development tools using PHP. Lastly, to close the section, a thorough discussion on the remaining Expat functions with examples was presented.

Next, we learned some tricks in parsing XML content such as eliminating whitespace and fixing non well-formed XML content generated by databases and other software packages.

The most important thing to take from this chapter is that many of our XML needs over the Web can be adequately handled with SAX. However, there are alternatives to parsing and doing even more with XML files, and the following chapters will explain processing XML.

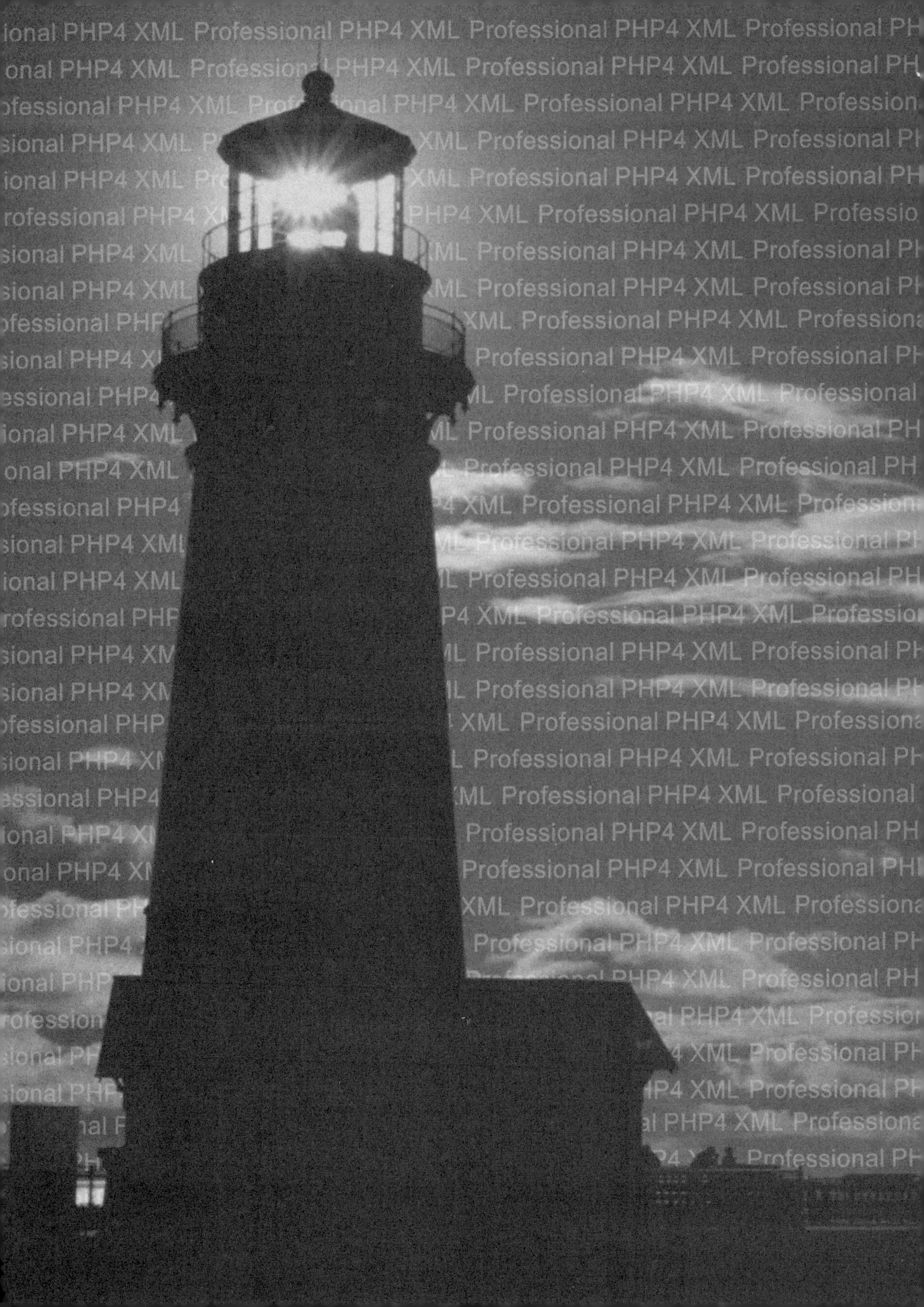
Professional PHP4 XML

6

DOM

In the last chapter we learned what a parser is and how to create PHP scripts that used the event-based parser, SAX. In this chapter we are going to take a look at an alternative method of parsing called the Document Object Model (DOM). Rather than view each interface as competing with each other, we will see how they are both used in different situations. We'll discover that DOM overcomes many of SAX's limitations and presents many advantages when solving specific XML problems.

In the course of this chapter, we will discuss:

- ❑   The DOM object-based parser
- ❑   How to compare SAX and DOM parsers
- ❑   How to parse XML content using a DOM interface
- ❑   How to add and modify XML content using DOM
- ❑   How to delete records from XML content

Once we have read this chapter, we should have a greater understanding of the DOM interface and its applicability to XML applications.

What is the Document Object Model (DOM)?

The Document Object Model, abbreviated as DOM, is a standard API, developed by the W3C that allows programs to access and manipulate markup documents. When DOM was first introduced, its main applicability was to dynamically alter HTML content and structure using an in-browser scripting language, like JavaScript. Later, a generic standard was created that could be used for XML documents as well. When parsing XML documents using DOM, we simply refer to this as **DOM XML**.

Unlike SAX or other event-based parsers, DOM is more intuitive to developers since the structure of the model is very much like the XML document itself. In an object-based parser, the application builds a resultant tree of the XML file in memory, breaking up the elements, attributes, comments, and any other components of the XML file into nodes. The tree consists of several of these nodes, where each node in the tree represents an XML component. For example, the business article structure (from the previous chapter) is represented by this DOM tree:

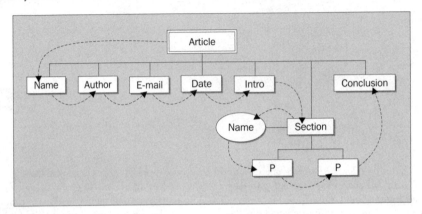

The arrows represent how a DOM parser traverses the XML content to construct the resultant tree.

And here is the same diagram in more detail:

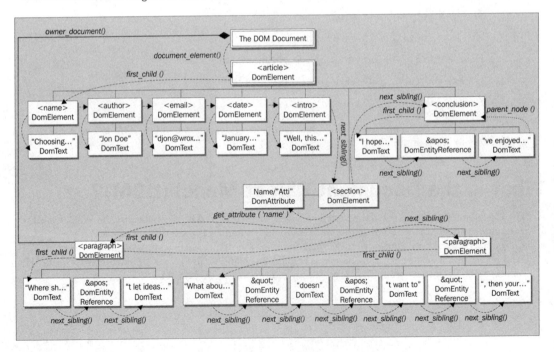

This detailed representation of the DOM tree depicts explicit parent-child relationships, as well as traversing the document using the `first_child()` and `last_child()`, and `first_sibling()` and `last_sibling()` methods. Thus it shows how the DOM tree is used for traversing/finding/removing elements to indicate how relationships between nodes in the tree are changed.

At this point, now that the tree is fully in memory, we can use the DOM XML API to interact with the tree to parse its data and, unlike a SAX interface, manipulate the tree. Let's say we wanted to create a second section to the `<article>` root node. With DOM, we could first select the `<article>` element and then add a new `<section>` element to it, like this:

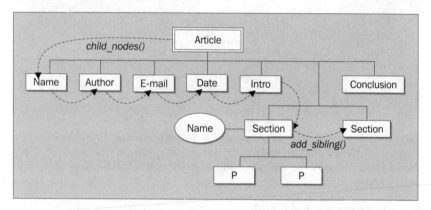

Here, we simply receive an array of children of the `<article>` node and traverse them until we arrive at the `<section>` element of the tree. Once there, we can create a new `<section>` element and add it to the tree by calling the `add_sibling()` method as seen in the diagram. With DOM, it is possible to update a node's content or attributes. So at the new `<section>` element that we just created, let's create a new `<p>` element and a `Name` attribute:

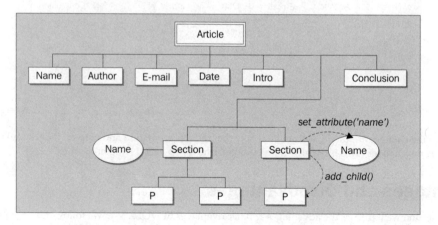

By calling the `set_attribute()` and `add_child()` methods on the current `<section>` node, we can create a new `Name` attribute and a `<p>` child element node.

With DOM, we can even delete nodes anywhere within the tree. For instance, let's delete the very first `<section>` element:

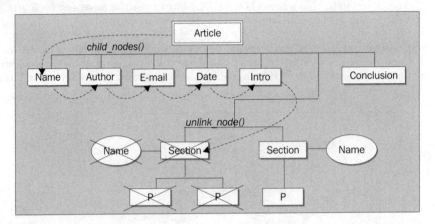

First we'd have to receive an array of child nodes from the article element. Once these are acquired, we can traverse the array one-by-one until we arrive at the `<section>` node, as depicted in the diagram. At this point, a call to the `unlink_node()` method on this node will remove it and all its children and associated attributes from the tree.

The final tree, after the deletion, looks like this:

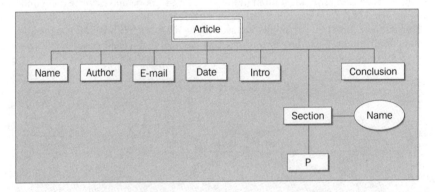

Once all the changes are made, we can then take the tree representation and convert it back into an XML file to persist the changes. This is usually done by calling the `dump_mem()` method.

Advantages and Disadvantages

In this section we'll discuss the advantages and disadvantages of DOM. We will follow this up with a comparison of SAX and DOM.

Advantages

Here are the advantages of using DOM:

❑ **Increased applicability**
DOM provides us with incredible flexibility since it can modify XML content. As of PHP 4.1.1, we are now able to add, modify, and delete nodes from an XML tree. In the event that we need to write an application to accomplish these tasks, DOM XML is the only viable solution.

❑ **More intuitive**
Due to the nature of DOM trees, programmers have an easier time getting familiar with the DOM API and can develop a program faster, which definitely makes it easier for newcomers and boosts project productivity. After learning how the API traverses the nodes, the programmer can (using skills already learnt) write programs traversing arrays and using objects.

❑ **Standard, platform-neutral API**
One of the benefits of DOM is that it is a definite standard so we can be assured that as long as an implementation adheres to the W3C standard, our work won't have to change. At the time of this writing, PHP 4.2.0's DOM XML API is getting closer to the standard and it is expected to be fully W3C-compliant by 4.3.0. Once this occurs, it will be assured that old code will not break on future versions of PHP.

Disadvantages

Essentially, DOM's disadvantages are because it accepts the whole XML file before it starts parsing. This puts undue pressure on the server. Some of the disadvantages of using DOM to parse XML documents are:

❑ **Limited file size**
Since DOM builds a complex tree of the entire XML file in memory, there is a limitation on the size of the XML content. DOM is limited by the RAM installed on the server. Remember, web servers must serve multiple users at once and a script that reads even a 200 kilobyte XML file could cause tremendous traffic problems. Caution must be maintained with the size of the XML content when using DOM parsers over the Web. SAX on the other hand can parse files of unlimited size; therefore it is often used when working with large files. However, large documents shouldn't be parsed on the Web at all unless users are willing to wait.

❑ **Increased memory usage**
DOM parsers utilize much more memory than SAX parsers. With a SAX parser, the script's memory usage is mostly determined by the memory used by the application logic rather than the parser overhead. SAX parsers use a constant chunk of memory no matter the size of the document, while the DOM parser's usage of memory is proportional to the size of the XML document. These trees usually consume between 3 to 30 times that of the stored XML content.

❑ **Insufficient for time-intensive applications**
DOM applications are usually slower than corresponding SAX programs. This is due to the time required to construct the DOM tree in memory. DOM traverses the entire XML file (once) when we create the parser, building the DOM tree. After the tree is built, any traversing that we do with application logic means that we are going over that data again. If the application traverses the entire file, we'll have looked at every node twice – once to build the tree and once to do what the application needs to do. This can be rather inefficient if the object we are looking for is located at a deep layer of the tree. Therefore, for sheer speed, SAX – and its linear, one-pass nature – is the best choice.

❏ **Increased code**
In comparison to SAX (Expat in particular), DOM programs require more lines of code. This is due to the extra code required to traverse and manipulate the DOM tree. Experienced SAX programmers tend to recognize this immediately, whereas newcomers feel familiar with the DOM API structure. As discussed in the previous chapter, SAX parsers handle the flow of the program automatically, relieving the programmer from having to write all of the iteration and traversal logic. This is often helpful when we want to parse a selected portion of a document, especially if the information is deeply nested within the document structure. With DOM XML, we are required to parse down to the leaf nodes at all times.

❏ **Not suitable for web applications**
Since DOM takes longer to parse XML content, SAX is a better option when writing a read-only application. Also, since DOM utilizes a great deal of memory, pages that receive many hits at once could possibly slow down the server by filling its memory. Of course, this also depends on the quality of the system hardware. Despite these issues DOM continues to be used since it is the only format that allows us to write and modify XML content.

SAX vs. DOM

Often, there is heated debate as to the 'best' API to use when parsing XML documents. The truth of the matter is that there is no single best solution. Though DOM is not a popular choice among PHP programmers, this should not be taken as a reason to avoid it. DOM has advantages over SAX in many situations and should be used when appropriate.

This table compares the most important parts of the SAX and DOM API:

	SAX	DOM
Model	Event-driven	Document tree
Installation	Installed by default	Requires installation
Document Size	Small to huge	Small to medium
Code Complexity	Moderate to complex	Moderate to complex
Supports Read, Write, Change	Only read	Yes
Best Fit Application	Machine readable and generated XML	Complex XML document
Maturity within PHP	Expat has been in PHP since Version 3.0 and it is quite mature and stable	Experimental
XML Format	XML 1.0, thus it can be used it for SML	XML 1.0, thus it can be used for SML

Getting Started

As with any standard, DOM has to be implemented on a specific platform and in a specific language. The W3C has provided recommended bindings for various languages such JavaScript, C++, CORBA, and Java. A binding is a recommended model for implementing the DOM standard. Anyone is able to implement the standard DOM API under these languages as long as it conforms to the recommended bindings. Anything else would be considered to deviate from the standard. Other languages that do not have a recommended binding are often built to exemplify the recommended bindings, but ultimately each platform or language implements DOM differently.

PHP has chosen to use a library called **libxml**, which is part of the GNOME project found at http://www.xmlsoft.org/. Unlike Java and many other implementations, the GNOME XML library, and PHP's extension that uses this library, is still in the experimental stage and is limited in comparison with others in C++ and Java.

However, libxml does not just provide an API for DOM. It is actually an all-out library for XML written entirely in C. It provides components for SAX as well as DOM, an HTML parser, a SAX tree module to build an in-memory DOM representation, a tree module to manipulate the DOM representation, a validation module using the DOM representation, an XPath module for global lookup in a DOM representation, and many more components. Although these features are available in libxml, PHP only utilizes the DOM portion of the library.

Let's now enable DOM XML with our PHP installation on both Windows and UNIX.

Installing DOM On Windows

Since DOM XML does not come enabled by default, we must configure PHP to use the correct dynamic link library (DLL). At the time of this writing, this library is distributed with PHP 4.2.0, making it very easy to configure PHP to use DOM XML. Make sure to use the ZIP version rather than the Windows Installer to ensure that we get the extensions.

The first step is to locate the php.ini file within the directory where we have PHP installed. Open this file and find the following block after the Paths and Directories section:

```
;;;;;;;;;;;;;;;;;;;;;;;;;;;;
; Paths and Directories ;
;;;;;;;;;;;;;;;;;;;;;;;;;;;;

; Directory in which the loadable extensions (modules) reside.
extension_dir = "C:\php\extensions"
```

Ensure that this directory contains the path of the PHP extensions (DLL files). On some installations, such as NuSphere, this directory is already set; on others, we must set it ourselves. With the current version of PHP, we must use the subdirectory extensions from our main PHP directory as shown above.

The next step is to add the php_domxml.dll to the list of loaded libraries for PHP to use. This can be accomplished by editing one line in the section titled Windows Extensions. Once this section has been located, find the following code:

```
;Windows Extensions
...
;extension=php_dbx.dll
;extension=php_domxml.dll
;extension=php_dotnet.dll
...
```

and uncomment the php_domxml.dll line as follows.

```
;extension=php_dbx.dll
extension=php_domxml.dll
;extension=php_dotnet.dll
```

Now, on older versions of PHP, this would normally be everything that we would have to do. As of PHP 4.2.0, we must copy the php_domxml.dll from the experimental subdirectory to the extensions subdirectory and overwrite the file if necessary. After these modifications, we will be able to use DOM XML inside our PHP scripts.

Installing DOM On UNIX

Enabling DOM XML on a UNIX machine is more difficult. libxml is not installed by default in UNIX. At the time of this writing, version 2.2.4.16 is the newest version, but any version of 2.2.4 or greater is all that is needed. It can be downloaded from http://www.xmlsoft.org/.

At the shell, the first step is to download the latest version from the xmlsoft.org FTP site. This can be accomplished by logging in as an anonymous user, switching to binary mode if required (since some FTP clients might have this turned on by default) and using the get command to download the file to the current directory, as seen with the following commands:

```
# ftp ftp.xmlsoft.org

Connected to ftp.xmlsoft.org.
220 ready, dude (vsFTPd 1.0.0: beat me, break me)
Name (ftp.xmlsoft.org:doe): anonymous
331 Please specify the password.
Password: jon@somewhere.com
230 Login successful. Have fun.
Remote system type is UNIX.
Using binary mode to transfer files.

ftp> binary
200 Binary it is, then.
ftp> get libxml2-2.4.15.tar.gz
local: libxml2-2.4.15.tar.gz remote: libxml2-2.4.15.tar.gz
200 PORT command successful. Consider using PASV.
150 Opening BINARY mode data connection for libxml2-2.4.15.tar.gz (1858216 bytes).
ftp> bye
```

Now the `libxml2-2.4.15.tar.gz` file is stored in the current directory:

```
# mv libxml2-2.4.15.tar.gz /usr/local
# cd /usr/local
```

From the current directory, move the file to the location where we normally install new programs. For the purposes of this chapter we will use the `/usr/local` directory. Once the file is moved, change to the current directory of the file:

```
# gunzip libxml2-2.4.15.tar.gz
# tar xf libxml2-2.4.15.tar
```

The next step is to uncompress the file using `gunzip` and `tar`. If it is needed to delete the file to conserve space, it can be deleted as follows:

```
# rm libxml2-2.4.15.tar
```

Once the archive has been uncompressed, we must change to the new libxml directory and build the program. This is done using the typical `configure`, `make`, and `make install` process:

```
# cd libxml2-2.4.15
# ./configure
# make
# make install
```

We should also verify that the library has been installed correctly and is working properly, by issuing the following command:

```
# make tests
```

There should be no errors since this library does not require any additional libraries that are not installed by default, but if some unexpected results crop up, consult the `INSTALL` file in the `libxml2-2.4.15` directory for more detailed instructions and possible solutions to any problem.

Lastly, we must rebuild PHP to include DOM support:

```
# ldconfig
# cd ../php/
# ./configure --with-dom --with-apxs=../apache/bin/apxs
# make
# make install
```

As indicated above, we will also have to supply any other parameters as we did before, such as building the Apache module or enabling MySQL support. On some operating systems, the `configure` script may not be able to search for the `zlib` directory. This library is required to use DOM XML. On some UNIX systems, such as FreeBSD, just supply `/usr/lib` and everything should work fine. If unsure as to where to find `zlib`, use the `locate` command, as follows:

```
# locate libz
/usr/lib/libz.a
/usr/lib/libz.so
/usr/lib/libz.so.2
/usr/lib/libz_p.a
/usr/src/gnu/usr.bin/gzip/zgrep.libz
...
```

Once we have located the proper directory that contains the zlib, we will execute a configure instruction similar to this in place of the previous one with the other instructions:

```
clients# ./configure --with-dom --with-zlib-dir=/usr/lib \
         --with-apxs=../apache/bin/apxs --with-mysql
```

After these instructions have been executed with no errors, we will have successfully enabled DOM with our PHP application. Now, the next step is to ensure it is working properly.

Verifying DOM XML

To ensure that DOM XML is enabled with the PHP installation, use the phpinfo() script.

After running this script, we will see the domxml section appear as shown:

If XML Support is not displayed as active, we will need to either enable Expat or install the latest release of PHP.

DOM Objects and Methods

Unlike many external libraries and functions in PHP, DOM XML has an object-oriented interface, meaning it takes advantage of OO technology. In this section, we will familiarize ourselves with the functions and classes in the DOM XML API. Because it is an object-oriented API and is the recommended method to using DOM XML, there will be no procedural examples.

Also, before we look at the objects and methods that make up the DOM XML API, it is worth mentioning that this interface is highly experimental. Over time, this extension has changed several times and will continue to change in the future. As of version 4.2.0, the extension is stabilizing closer to the standard set by the W3C, but there is still some work that needs to be done to follow the standard strictly. DOM XML has come a long way in PHP 4.2.0, and there will be even more changes in PHP 4.3.0 which will finally bring the API to be compliant with the standard binding set by the W3C.

So as one reads this chapter and learns the material, take caution since the examples and API descriptions may not be valid with future versions of PHP. Later in the chapter, we will see what to expect in version 4.3.0 and we will take a look at migrating our applications to use the library. We will also take a look at what to expect in the near future as well. Also, please check the Wrox web site for any updates to this chapter to receive the latest information when newer versions of PHP arrive.

In the following sections we will discuss:

❑   What classes describe the nodes within the DOM tree?

❑   How to create new DOM trees and how to extract trees from existing XML content from strings and files, using several factory methods

❑   How to parse, add root nodes, and save a DOM tree using the DomDocument class

❑   How to parse, add, update, and delete nodes within the tree using DomNode objects

❑   How to use other miscellaneous classes provided through the DOM interface

The DOM Architecture

DOM builds a tree of nodes that represents the XML content. There are three major node types with DOM XML:

❑   **DomDocument**
The DomDocument is the top-level node of the tree. It contains information about the XML file, the W3C DOM version in use, the character encoding type, and if the document is standalone.

It contains an instance of the root node (of the type DomNode). For example, in the business article shown in the previous chapter, the <article> element is described as a DomNode object, which is contained within the tree's DomDocument object. The DomDocument class also acts as a factory in that it is used to construct new elements that will be later added to the tree by other methods.

❑   **DomNode** (an abstract class)
DomNode objects are the actual nodes within the tree and they can contain a set of child DomNode objects. With the new version of DOM XML in PHP 4.2.0+, the DomNode class is abstract. This means that each different type of XML component is represented by a specialized class.

XML elements are represented by DomElement, comments are represented by DomComment, and blocks of text are represented by DomText. Some of the subclasses contain extra functionality. For instance, a DomElement can set and get attribute values and retrieve its tag name while DomProcessingInstruction can get extra info on its target and code to execute.

193

❑ **DomAttribute**
In DOM, attributes are also modeled as objects and are placed as nodes within the tree of type `DomAttribute`.

Here is a tree representing the inheritance hierarchy of the node classes:

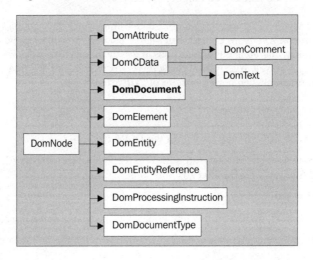

In the business article example, the `<article>` element has several child elements such as `<name>` and `<author>`. These elements are all represented as `DomElement` objects and are contained within the `<article>` `DomElement` as an array. In particular, the `<section>` child also has a series of children `<p>` tags. These are also represented as `DomElement` objects and are contained within each `<section>` `DomElement`. Unlike previous versions, each of these `DomElement` objects also contains `DomText` child nodes, which contain the actual character data inside the element. This is important to note since previous methods of setting and retrieving character data have been deprecated as they now work like any other node within the tree.

The `<section>` `DomElement` also contains an attribute labeled `Name`, which specifies the title of the section within the article. As mentioned earlier, attributes are modeled as objects and placed as nodes within the tree of type `DomAttribute`.

To illustrate this configuration, here is the model shown earlier with the types of objects representing each component within the XML file:

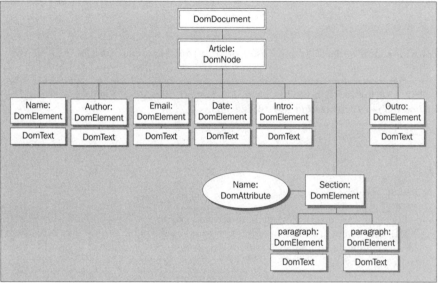

As can be seen in the illustration, the nodes within the tree mirror the structure of the XML. Once the tree is constructed, DOM parses these objects and manipulates the tree. In the next few sections, we will look at the different ways to create the trees and use the different classes.

Tree Construction Methods

Unlike most object-oriented components that require a class to be instantiated using the new operator, DOM XML provides several initial **factory** methods to build the object-based tree and create the initial DOM object for us. This object is an instance of the DomDocument class and it is the entry point to parsing and manipulating the XML content. The functions that construct this instance are new_xmldoc(), xmldoc(), xmldocfile(), and xmltree().

As of PHP 4.2.0, these functions have remained the same as earlier versions. However, the current documentation also suggests that these function names have been renamed but PHP 4.2.0 does not include these changes. For now, the old function names are the only ones available but it would be good to use the new function names in future releases of PHP.

new_xmldoc()

```
DomDocument new_xmldoc(string version)
```

The first of the tree construction methods is new_xmldoc(), which creates a new, empty DOM tree. The $version is supplied to indicate the version of XML used as a sting. For instance, to create a new document with XML version 1.0, execute the following line of code in a PHP script:

```
$doc = new_xmldoc('1.0');
```

Once this code is executed, `$doc` will contain a new instance of the `DomDocument` class, ready for adding new nodes to the DOM tree. If we were to convert this data structure to text, it would be equivalent to the following XML:

```
<?xml version="1.0"?>
```

We will provide a more in-depth example using `new_xmldoc()` when we discuss the `add_root()` method.

> **In PHP 4.3.0, this function will be renamed to `domxml_new_doc()` and the previous method will be deprecated but will still function.**

xmldoc()

```
DomDocument xmldoc(string XML)
```

The second of the four tree construction methods is called `xmldoc()`. This method takes in a string containing XML content and produces an object tree based on the input. Strings may come from alternative sources besides within the document, such as through a web service, a database, or possibly through another custom function call.

If something goes wrong, such as the XML content containing a syntax error, the function will return `FALSE`. Thus, strings passed to this function must be well-formed XML. With `new_xmldoc()` we had to pass in the version of the XML file as a string, while in this version we pass the string containing the XML content. A common mistake is to confuse this function with `new_xmldoc()` by supplying an empty string to imply the construction of a new file. Since an empty file is not a valid XML document according to DOM, the function will return `FALSE`.

> **In case of problems with poorly written XML content, use a program called `xmllint`, distributed with libxml, to verify the syntax and report any problems in an XML document.**

To create a DOM tree of some of the actors from a Star Trek movie, use the following code:

```
$xmlString =
  '<?xml version="1.0" encoding="iso-8859-1" ?' . '>' .
  '<movie name="Star Trek VII: First Contact">' .
  '<actor name="Patrick Stewart" role="Jean-Luc Picard" rank="Captain"/>' .
  '<actor name="Brent Spiner" role="Data" rank="Lt. Commander"/>' .
  '</movie>';

$doc = xmldoc($xmlString);
```

In this example, we have constructed a string containing XML content. Notice that in the XML processing instruction, the question mark (?) character has been separated from the greater-than (>) symbol and concatenated together. When these two characters are placed side-by-side, they trick many syntax highlighting IDEs (such as the popular EditPlus) to indicate that the script is exiting PHP mode – but in reality this is not the case.

> In PHP 4.3.0, this function will be renamed to domxml_open_mem() to better convey that a tree is constructed from XML content already in memory.

xmldocfile()

```
DomDocument xmldocfile(string filename)
```

In the case where the XML content is in an existing file, we can use the xmldocfile() function to build a DOM tree. This function takes in the filename and constructs a DOM tree from the file's content. The $filename variable being passed must be the complete path. Strings like ./file.xml or file.xml are not acceptable and the function will return FALSE. The correct syntax would be a string like C:\Apache Group\Apache\htdocs\bug_list.xml.

Specifying relative filenames is a common mistake because functions like fopen() can take relative paths. It must be remembered that the path is not in relation to the document root, it is in relation to the root (/) directory in an UNIX environment or the drive letter such as (C:\) on Microsoft Windows.

To create a DomDocument object using the xmldocfile() function, we can use the following code:

```
$doc = xmldocfile('DOC_ROOT\bug_list.xml');

if ($doc == false)
    print ("The file does not exist or the complete path has not been given");
else
    print ("The file has been parsed successfully.");
```

Notice here that xmldocfile() is being passed the absolute path and file name. The variable $doc will equal FALSE if and only if the file does not exist in this instance.

> In PHP 4.3.0, this function will be renamed to domxml_open_file() to convey that the tree will be constructed from a file.

xmltree()

```
DomDocument xmltree(string XML)
```

The last of the tree construction methods, xmltree(), is different from the previous two. Given a string containing XML content, this function returns an instance of the DomDocument class, but instead of utilizing the DOM XML interface (yet unexplored) to traverse the DOM nodes, we can access the nodes directly through the object's members. In other words, once an instance of this type of DomDocument has been returned, we will be unable to use any of the DOM XML methods on this object. In this case, the programmer is responsible for traversing the internal arrays of DomNode and DomAttribute objects within each object.

The following example displays the entire object tree for simple vendor XML content:

```
$xmlString =
    '<?xml version="1.0" encoding="iso-8859-1" ?' . '>' .
    '<vendors>' .
    '<name>Positive Edge</name>' .
    '</vendors>';

$doc = xmltree($xmlString);
print ("<pre>");
var_dump($doc);
print ("</pre>");
```

Once the tree has been constructed, we can parse the document at will. However, any changes to the nodes cannot be persisted and any modifications to the XML content are only temporary. According to the documentation on http://www.php.net/, this tree is for investigating the structure or the content quickly. This is the only method where a programmer can see the entire structure of the tree at a glance. Since using any of the previous functions to traverse the tree is no more difficult with this method, it is advisable to utilize this function when testing or perhaps parsing only.

> In PHP 4.3.0, this function will be renamed to `domxml_xmltree()` to add the domxml prefix to the function name for consistency.

The DomDocument Class

The `DomDocument` class is the heart of the DOM XML API. Not only is it the top source of the DOM tree where all the parsing or creation of XML content happens, but it also creates new elements that can be added to other levels within the tree by using factory methods. It is important to note that since `DomDocument` is a subclass of `DomNode`, it contains all the functionality of a `DomNode` object. Thus, it can contain and operate on child nodes.

As discussed in the previous section, the `DomDocument` object is created by any of the three tree construction methods (`xmltree()` is not strictly a tree construction method).

Node Creation Factory Methods

As mentioned at the beginning of this section, a `DomDocument` object functions as the center for creating all the objects that we can add to the DOM tree. So if we need to create a new XML element, a comment, or some character data, we must first ask the `DomDocument` object to construct the appropriate object for you before you can add it to the tree. This is quite different from previous versions, as `new_child()` was the only way that we could add new nodes to the tree, and we could only add XML elements with this method. Now it is possible to add any type of XML construct with DOM XML.

As of PHP 4.2.0, we can create elements, text nodes, comments, CDATA sections, processing instructions, and entity references. Although the API also contains a method for creating attributes, we do not know enough other topics in the API to cover it here. Therefore, we'll just set aside the `create_attribute()` factory method at this point.

Let's take a look at how to create and add some elements to the tree:

```php
<?php

$doc = new_xmldoc('1.0');
$comment =
 $doc->create_comment('A document that tests node creation methods');
$doc->add_child($comment);
```

After we create a new document using the `new_xmldoc()` method, we first create a comment as the first line of the document with the `create_comment()` method. This method takes in a string containing the contents of the comment and a `DomComment` object is returned into the variable `$comment`. `DomComment` objects aren't anything special; they simply contain the text of the comment and when asked to be dumped, the appropriate commenting syntax will surround the content. At this point, we can use the `add_child()` method of the `DomDocument` object – which is a method in the `DomNode` super class – to add it to the tree.

In general, the process of creating an element and then using `add_child()` is the way to append new nodes in DOM XML:

```php
$topElement = $doc->add_child($doc->create_element('top'));
```

An XML document wouldn't be a document without its root node. We use the `create_element()` factory method to create an element called `<top>` which is then added as the root XML element of the DOM tree. At this point, the `$doc` object contains two children – the `DomComment` objects and the `DomElement` object.

Let's say we wanted to include the following character data inside the `<top>` element:

```
Harry &amp; Sons <![CDATA[ is cool & stuff!]]>
```

This string contains 4 distinct pieces of information, as follows:

- The string – `'Harry'`
- The entity reference – `'&amp;'`
- The string – `' Sons'`
- The CDATA section containing – `' is cool & stuff!'`

Since these are viewed as 4 separate XML constructs, conceptually it only makes sense that these are represented by four nodes within the tree. The character data nodes can be constructed with the following code:

```php
$textNode1        = $doc->create_text_node('Harry ');
$entityReference = $doc->create_entity_reference('&amp;');
$textNode2        = $doc->create_text_node(' Sons');
$cDataNode        = $doc->create_cdata_section(' is cool & stuff!');
```

The `create_text_node()` method creates a `DomText` object containing the string, `'Harry'`. There isn't anything special about `DomText` nodes themselves; they are one of the simplest `DomNode` subclasses in the API, adding no extra functionality.

However, there are two interesting characteristics:

- ❑ If one does create a `DomText` object that contains a character that is a predefined entity (such as &), the character will automatically be converted to the entity reference

- ❑ If two or more `DomText` nodes are added to a tree right after each other, the DOM XML API will automatically merge them together

`DomEntityReference` objects can be created with the `create_entity_reference()` method. This method accepts only entity references such as `&amp;`, `&apos;`, or even custom entity references. A string missing either the ampersand or the ending semi-colon will be treated as an entity reference and the ampersand or the semi-colon will be added on automatically whenever either is missing.

The last factory method shown here is `create_cdata_section()`, which creates a `DomCData` object. This function doesn't different much from `create_comment()` in that it accepts any text supplied to the parameter. The reason they are so similar is because `DomComment` objects are actually a subclass of `DomCData`. The only difference is the text that surrounds the content. Whenever a `DomCData` object is finally dumped, it will surround the text with the special `<![CDATA[]]>` syntax. Notice in our example we used the ampersand within the content. This character will not be changed at all by the DOM API.

Earlier, we looked at a diagram of the architecture of DOM XML. If we look at `DomElement`, we'll see that it is also a subclass of `DomNode`, so it in turn has an `add_child()` method. Here we create a new `<element>` tag to contain the nodes we just created:

```
$myElement = $doc->create_element('element');
```

The next step is to add each of the nodes in the order they should appear using `$myElement->add_child()` and then add the `<element>` node to the tree itself by creating a link with the `<top>` node in the manner using `$topElement->add_child()`:

```
$myElement->add_child($textNode1);
$myElement->add_child($entityReference);
$myElement->add_child($textNode2);
$myElement->add_child($cDataNode);
$topElement->add_child($myElement);
```

The last method to check out is the `create_processing_instruction()`, which creates `DomProcessingInstruction` objects:

```
$pi = $doc->create_processing_instruction('php', 'print "Hello World";');
$topElement->add_child($pi);
?>
```

This method accepts two parameters:

- ❑ The first parameter is the target language or platform the code is to be run on. In this case, we pass in `php` as the target.

- ❑ The second parameter accepts the actual code to execute. In this case, a simple `Hello World` script is passed.

Once the object is constructed and stored in the variable $pi, we add it to the <top> element. Once all these have been added, we have successfully constructed the tree that represents this XML (visual new lines and tabs were added for clarity):

```
<?xml version="1.0"?>
<!--A document that tests node creation factory methods-->
<top>
    <element>Harry &amp; Sons <![CDATA[ is cool & stuff!]]></element>
    <?php print "Hello World";?>
</top>
```

> It is important to remember the call to add_child(). If we construct the element and fail to add it directly to some node that is connected to the tree, it will not be added. In future versions of PHP, this two-step process might be merged into one.

add_root()

```
DomElement add_root(string name)
```

The add_root() method constructs the top-level root element in the DOM tree with the given string titled $name. This string acts as the name of the root element and returns a DomElement object. We must be very careful when using this method because if the root already exists within the DOM tree, we might accidentally purge the old root node along with all its children, effectively destroying the document.

To create a new XML document with the root node 'vendors', execute the following code:

```
$doc = new_xmldoc('1.0');
$root = $doc->add_root('vendors');
```

At this time, it's difficult to explain what can be accomplished with $root since we need to first discuss the DomNode class. This will be explained in the next section.

> Currently, this method is considered deprecated in favor of using create_element() and add_child(). Use with caution.

document_element()

```
DomElement document_element()
```

The document_element() method returns an instance of DomElement, containing the top-level element of the DOM tree. This method is used when reading XML content that is either in memory or from a file. With this method, we are able to start parsing, traversing, and manipulating the document. If no top-level element exists, the function always returns FALSE. The function can simply be called from a DomDocument instance like this:

```
$root = $doc->document_element();
```

dump_mem()

```
string dump_mem()
```

> Older versions of DOM XML contained a dumpmem() method identical to this one. This method continues to work in PHP 4.2.0, but is considered deprecated and so it is best to migrate the code to use the new method.

The dump_mem() method converts the entire DOM tree to a string. At this point, we can either store the result in a database, send the result to another function, write the data to a file stream or echo it to the browser. The resultant DOM tree can be saved to a file, like this:

```
$doc = new_xmldoc('1.0');
$root = $doc->add_root('vendors');
$xmlString = $doc->dump_mem();

$fp = fopen('vendors.xml', 'w');
fwrite($fp, $xmlString, strlen($xmlString));
fclose($fp);
```

As explained earlier, a new instance of the DomDocument class is created using the new_xmldoc() function and 'vendors' is assigned to be the root element for the XML file. We use the dump_mem() method to convert the current tree in $doc to a string and begin to open a new file for writing.

Once the string has been written to vendors.xml, the file will have an opening XML processing instruction with a lone and empty <vendors> root tag, as shown below:

```
<?xml version="1.0"?>
<vendors/>
```

> As of PHP 4.3.0, the dump_mem() method will also contain an optional parameter called $format. This parameter tells the method to format the output with tabs and newline characters so it can be easily read by humans.

dump_mem_file()

```
string dump_mem_file(string filename)
```

Unlike older versions of DOM XML, the API also allows to dump the XML content to a file directly, saving us a few lines of code. This is similar to receiving a memory dump and writing it to a file manually. As with xmldocfile(), when using this method make sure that the file name is the complete path, or the file will not be written. Here is an example:

```
$doc = new_xmldoc('1.0');
$root = $doc->add_root('vendors');
$doc->dump_mem_file('C:\myfiles\vendors.xml');
```

After running this code, we'll notice that the exact same result as above is achieved.

In version PHP 4.3.0, this function will be renamed to `dump_file()` and will contain two additional optional parameters. The first parameter will be a Boolean value specifying if the file should be compressed XML and the second Boolean parameter will specify if the XML content should be neatly formatted with whitespace.

child_nodes()

```
DomNode[] child_nodes()
```

Unlike older versions of DOM XML, there is actually a legitimate reason for the DomDocument class to have a `child_nodes()` method. The `child_nodes()` method might seem like a strange function to be located within the DomDocument class because in most situations it has a single root node.

Since `document_element()` accomplishes this task of retrieving the top-level node nicely, one might question the design of DOM XML within PHP; however, all is well. Now that it is possible to add DomProcessingInstruction objects and DomComment objects, the DomDocument object can contain more than one node.

doctype()

```
Dtd doctype()
```

The last method within the DocDocument class is the `doctype()` method. This method will return an instance of the Dtd class if a DTD is defined and FALSE otherwise. The Dtd class is rather simple in that it only contains two members that are of any concern. These are $systemId and $name, respectively. The $systemId member will provide the name of the file containing the Document Type Definition. The $name variable will contain the name of the root-level element.

For example, assume we have the following code that creates a new XML file which declares a DTD:

```
$xmlString = '<?xml version="1.0" encoding="ISO-8859-1"?' . '>' .
'<!DOCTYPE xpl SYSTEM "xpl.dtd">' .
'<xpl />';

$doc = xmldoc($xmlString);
print ("<pre>");
var_dump($doc->doctype());
print ("</pre>");
```

Now that the document has a doctype specified, the program will produce the following output:

```
object(Dtd)(5) {
    ["type"]=>
    int(14)
    ["systemId"]=>
    string(7) "xpl.dtd"
    ["name"]=>
    string(3) "xpl"
    [0]=>
    int(2)
    [1]=>
    int(8374072)
}
```

Notice how $systemId is the file name indicated by SYSTEM in the DOCTYPE declaration and that $name identifies the top-level element. The fact this provides very little information suggests that this part of DOM XML is incomplete and that future releases should provide new features to the Dtd class.

> In PHP 4.3.0, it is expected that the Dtd class will in fact be renamed to
> DomDocumentType but the rest will function in the same manner. Also, calls to
> node_name() and node_value() will not return the expected result in PHP 4.2.0, so
> we will have to rely on the 'systemId' and 'name' member variables, which should be
> around for a long time.

DomDocument Members

The DomDocument also has many important members that describe the XML content that we can utilize in our programs.

Here is a table describing each of the members that may be useful when writing applications:

Member Name	Purpose
url	A string representing the absolute location of the file where the XML content originated. This member will contain an empty string if the xmldocfile() function was not used.
version	This member indicates the version of XML being used. This data is drawn from the XML processing instruction attribute, version.
encoding	A string containing the type of target character encoding indicated in the XML processing instruction. For instance, if the processing instruction is: `<?xml version="1.0" encoding="iso-8859-1"?>` the variable encoding would contain the string iso-8859-1.
standalone	This member contains an integer value indicating whether or not the file is standalone. A value of 1 is stored if the XML file is standalone and 0 if it is not. If this information is not present, the value will be -1.
type	This member contains an integer value to specify the type of content within the node. In most cases, this can be of several types (int, char, and so on) but a DomDocument object will always contain the integer 9 or the defined constant XML_DOCUMENT_NODE. This is because the DomDocument object may not contain data itself, but acts as a container for other nodes.
compressed	This member indicates that the XML content is compressed and will contain the value of 1 if it is so. If the XML content is not compressed, this member will contain the value of -1. Despite the existence of this variable, there is no known way to use compressed XML content with DOM, so this member can only offer the speculation that compressed documents will be allowed in the future.

The following code attempts to read these values in a PHP script. Make sure to change the file passed in the `xmldocfile()` function to one containing valid XML data:

```
// docmembers.php

$doc = xmldocfile('DOC_ROOT\bug_list.xml');

if ($doc != false) {
    print ('XML Version: ' . $doc->version . '<br />');
    print ('Character Encoding: ' . $doc->encoding . '<br />');

    if (!empty($doc->url))
        print ('XML url: ' . $doc->url . "<br />");

    if ($doc->standalone)
        print ('This document is standalone<br />');

    if ($doc->type == XML_DOCUMENT_NODE) {
        print ('This node type is a document node<br />');
    } else {
        print ('There is a serious problem with this document<br />');
    }
}
```

Upon executing this code, if a well-formed XML file is present, the version and character encoding are displayed to the browser. Since we are using `xmldocfile()`, the `$doc->url` member should not be empty and the string `DOC_ROOT\bug_list.xml` will also be displayed. If the document is standalone, this will also be indicated and the message specifying that the type is a `DocumentNode` will be displayed.

The DomNode Class

Now that we have learned how to construct `DomDocument` objects and can create and retrieve root nodes, it's time to learn about the `DomNode` class. The `DomNode` class is an extremely important class in the latest DOM XML API, as it is the cornerstone for every class that uses its functionality through inheritance. The `DomDocument` class we just looked at is also a `DomNode` object since it inherits from it, so all the functionality we see here is applied to `DomDocument` objects as well.

DOM trees consist of all `DomNode` objects so it might be safe to say that `DomNode` is the class that we have to deal with the most in our DOM work. The `DomNode` helps us accomplish many things from receiving information about the node such as its name, the node's content, or its type. So if we had a `DomElement` object, we'd be able to get its tag name as a string and the integer representation of its type telling us that it is an `XML_ELEMENT_NODE`.

The `DomNode` class allows us to manage the contents of the tree. For instance, we can add new children with the `add_child()`, `new_child()`, and `insert_before()` methods, and delete children and nodes with the `unlink_node()` method.

The DomNode class also provides us with ways of traversing the tree's children:

- With child_nodes(), we can retrieve an array of children under the current DomNode object and test if there are any children with has_child_nodes()
- With first_child() and last_child(), we can quickly go from the beginning to the end in the list of children
- With previous_sibling() and next_sibling(), we can traverse through the nodes on the same level of the tree without having to call a parent node to coordinate the effort
- With parent_node() and owner_document(), we can go up levels in the tree quickly, without having to keep a list of parents at each spot in the program

In this section, we are going to talk about all these functions of a DomNode object and more. First, let's talk about the set of functions where we can find out information on the name, value, and type of a DomNode object.

node_name()

```
string DomNode->node_name(void)
```

The node_name() method returns the name of a particular DomNode object. Unlike many methods within the DomNode interface, this method is abstract and is implemented in the various subclasses. For instance, if a DomElement or DomAttribute is asked for its name, it will return the name of the element that it represents. Some objects don't really have a name to identify the object, like DomComment or DomDocument, so in these cases a string beginning with a hash (#) is used.

Here is the complete table of return values for all the various DomNode subclasses within the API:

Class Type	Return Value
DomAttribute	Returns the name of the attribute.
	If the attribute is id='2', node_name() will return the string 'id'.
DomCDataSection	Returns the string, '#cdata-section'
DomComment	Returns the string, '#comment'
DomDocument	Returns the string, '#document'
Dtd/DomDocumentType	In PHP 4.2.0, the node_name() method of a Dtd object will return an empty string.

	To get the name of the document type, use the name member variable, as seen in the following code:
	
	```$doc = xmldocfile('C:\files\xpl.xml');```
	```$doctype = $doc->doctype();```
	```print ($doctype->name);```
	
	In PHP 4.3.0, the method of the DomDocumentType class will return the name of the document type.

Class Type	Return Value
DomElement	Returns the name of the tag. If the XML element is `<vendor>`, node_name () will return the string, 'vendor'.
DomEntity	Returns the name of the entity.

DomEntityReference	Returns the name of the entity reference.
	
	This code is a short example:
	
	`$doc = new_xmldoc();`
	`$ref =`
	`  $doc->create_entity_reference('&amp;');`
	`print $ref->node_name();`
	
	When this short script is run, the string 'amp' will be displayed in the browser. Notice that the ampersand and the semicolon are not present.

DomNotation	Returns the notation name.
DomProcessing Instruction	Returns the name of the target language. If `DomProcessingInstruction` contains the processing instruction: `<?php echo "hello world"; ?>` node_name () will return the string, 'php'.
DomText	Returns the string, '#text'.

node_value()

```
string DomNode->node_value(void)
```

The node_value () method returns the value associated with a DomNode object. Like the node_name () method, it too is abstract. Thus, each of the DomNode subclasses implements this method differently. Many of the classes that do not actually contain a value or content will return the null value, like DomElement or DomDocument. Others, like DomComment or DomText, return the content between their respective delimiters.

Here is a table containing the values returned and their meaning for each class in the DOM XML API:

Class Type	The Value Returned
DomAttribute	Returns the value of the attribute. If the attribute is id='2', then node_value () would return the string '2'.
DomCDataSection	Returns the content in the `<![CDATA[ ]]>` section.
DomComment	Returns the content in the `<!-- -->` comment section.
DomDocument	Returns the null value.

Table continued on following page

Class Type	The Value Returned
Dtd/DomDocumentType	Returns the null value.
DomElement	Returns the null value.
DomEntity	Returns the null value.
DomEntityReference	Returns the null value.
DomNotation	Returns the null value.
DomProcessingInstruction	The code to execute between the `<? target ?>` delimiters. If DomProcessingInstruction contains the processing instruction: `<?php echo "hello world"; ?>` node_value() will return the string, Hello World.
DomText	The content of the text.

In some cases, a content member variable will exist in a subclass of a DomNode object, such as DomText, DomCDataSection, or DomComment. The member variable still exists so it can help programmers migrate their older DOM XML code more easily, but for any new code it is recommended to use the node_value() method.

node_type() or type

```
DomNode->node_type
```

The node_type() method or the type member is an integer that describes the content within a DomNode object; that is, it returns the type of node. It is similar to the type member within the DomDocument class. However, instead of it being set to a static value all the time, this member is quite meaningful. Just by looking at the defined names, their uses are rather obvious since we have already familiarized ourselves with XML fundamentals. By using the type member to compare with the defined constants below, we can easily determine the appropriate action to take for a given node.

Here is a table of node types with their respective integer values:

Defined Constant	Integer Value
XML_ELEMENT_NODE	1
XML_ATTRIBUTE_NODE	2
XML_TEXT_NODE	3
XML_CDATA_SECTION_NODE	4
XML_ENTITY_REF_NODE	5
XML_ENTITY_NODE	6

Defined Constant	Integer Value
XML_PI_NODE	7
XML_COMMENT_NODE	8
XML_DOCUMENT_NODE	9
XML_DOCUMENT_TYPE_NODE	10
XML_DOCUMENT_FRAG_NODE	11
XML_NOTATION_NODE	12

For instance, if a node is of the XML_TEXT_NODE type, we might want to display the content to the screen. We can do this with the following code:

```
if ($node->node_type() == XML_TEXT_NODE) {
    print ($node->node_value());
}
```

Likewise, in the $child (PHP processing instruction), we may want to evaluate the content:

```
if ($child->node_type() == XML_PI_NODE && $child->name == 'php') {
    eval($child->node_value());
}
```

One thing to be noted is that DOM XML retains all character data. That means whitespace characters such as tabs and newline characters will also be included as nodes. These nodes are of the type XML_TEXT_NODE and to dismiss them, we will have to either skip text nodes entirely or parse them out in the same manner as a SAX parser. We have already seen this in the previous chapter.

> In all the DomNode subclasses, there will be type member variables indicating the type of the object. However, programmers should use the new node_type() method provided in PHP 4.2.0 and above to conform to the W3C coding standard. The type member is simply left there for convenience.

add_child()

```
DomNode add_child(DomNode $domNode)
```

The add_child() is new as of PHP 4.1.1 and continues to be used as the primary way for adding XML content in a DOM tree. As seen earlier, this function can take any instance of a DomNode object and add it as a child to the object invoking this function. A new DomNode object will be returned containing the same settings and values; however it will be connected to the actual tree.

In previous versions of DOM XML (pre-PHP 4.1.1), it only required one method to add a node to the tree. With the most recent version, we are required to make a call to the factory method in the DomDocument class to create the new DomNode object before it is added. Here is an example of how to add elements and text nodes to a new document:

```
<?php

$doc = new_xmldoc('1.0');
$employeesNode = $doc->add_child($doc->create_element('employeee'));
```

Here we construct a new <employee> element and use add_child() to add it as the root element of the tree. Since DomElement is an instance of DomNode, the add_child() method knows how to add it to the tree. The returned $employeesNode object is now connected to the tree with the $doc object as its parent:

```
$nameNode = $employeesNode->add_child($doc->create_element('name'));
$nameNode->add_child($doc->create_text_node('Jon Doe'));

$titleNode = $employeesNode->add_child($doc->create_element('title'));
$titleNode->add_child($doc->create_text_node('Chief Technology Officer'));
```

Further, we can create two child DomElement objects under the <employee> tag by calling the add_child() method on the $employeesNode object. The employee's name and title are stored in $nameNode and $titleNode elements, respectively. Once we have these new objects, we can use add_child() to add character data to the elements as well:

```
print (htmlentities($doc->dump_mem()));
?>
```

Lastly, we can see the created tree by using dump_mem(). The result has been formatted to make it easier to read:

```
<?xml version="1.0"?>
<employeee>
  <name>Jon Doe</name>
  <title>Chief Technology Officer</title>
</employeee>
```

Although any DomNode object can use add_child(), it is important to note that some combinations don't make sense, even though the API won't tell us that the methods are being used incorrectly. For instance, adding one DomDocument object into another will cause the program to crash while adding a DomAttribute object to a DomText class will cause an error. Keep in mind the integrity and robustness of the API is not perfect, but allows added flexibility and power.

> When PHP 4.3.0 is released, this method will be renamed to append_child() but add_child() will still function. At the time of writing, append_child() has some problems in PHP 4.2.0, so add_child() is currently the recommended method for adding children to the DOM tree.

new_child()

```
DomNode new_child(string name, string content)
```

The new_child() method creates a new DomElement child and adds it to the list of children for this DomNode object. The DomNode object is then returned so that it can be interfaced with. Although the new_child() method is considered deprecated, it does have the advantage that it saves a line of code every time that it is used. Therefore, since it is still around, the following code allows creating a new child under the root node:

```
$doc = new_xmldoc('1.0');
$employeesNode = $doc->add_child($doc->create_element('employees'));
$employeeNode = $employeesNode->new_child('employee');
```

This places a new <employee> element under the <employees> element of the XML file. Notice that the call to new_child() is cleaner than the add_child()/create_element() combination. The $employeeNode in turn could have several children like the name of the employee, the title, the office number, and an empty element to demonstrate how those are rendered within DOM:

```
$employeeNode->new_child('name', 'Jon Doe');
$employeeNode->new_child('title', 'Chief Technology Officer');
$employeeNode->new_child('office', '712');
$employeeNode->new_child('empty_element');
```

Once these lines have been executed, the <employee> tag will also have the 4 new elements within it. Here is the XML for all these operations:

```
<?xml version="1.0"?>
<employees>
  <employee>
    <name>Jon Doe</name>
      <title>Chief Technology Officer</title>
      <office>712</office>
      <empty_element/>
  </employee>
</employees>
```

Notice that we have formatted the XML with tabs and new lines to make it easier to read, but DOM XML will not do this in PHP 4.2.0.

There is a fairly large bug in DOM XML's new_child() method and it appears when entities are added in the $content argument. libxml behaves rather strangely since it applies the entity conversions prematurely, thus ensuring the resultant XML content will not be well-formed. For instance, in the following piece of code, we will add a new child that contains an ' entity:

```
$doc = new_xmldoc('1.0');
$root = $doc->add_root('bugs');
$root->new_child('bug', 'DOM XML&apos;s new_child() method is flawed.');
```

Now let's use the `$doc->dump_mem()` method. The `dump_mem()` method returns the tree in a string representation of the XML content:

```
$xmlOut = $doc->dump_mem();
print ($xmlOut);
```

This is the output:

DOM XML's new_child() method is flawed.

Notice that the resultant XML content contains an apostrophe since the entity, `&apos;`, has been converted to its equivalent form. This can be rather serious since the result may not be well-formed and any future parses may result in an error. It is best to use `create_text_node()` and `create_entity_reference()` instead to avoid these problems.

> Be extremely careful when setting XML content. If the data is intended to be parsed with SAX or another parser that does not tolerate non-conformance, DOM XML will most certainly give problems when entities exist in the content. We must be prepared to rewrite invalid XML prior to final processing.

insert_before()

```
DomNode DomNode->insert_before(DomNode newNode, DomNode nodeToInsertBefore)
```

The `insert_before()` method is much like `add_child()` in that it inserts any instance of `DomNode` in the tree. However, it is different in that given an additional `DomNode` reference that has already been created, it will place the new node as a sibling of that object just before it. If the reference provided in the second argument doesn't exist, then the object will not be added to the tree at all. The function returns a new object that is connected to the tree. It is important to realize that the node returned becomes a child to the parent of the node passed in the second parameter.

The `insert_before()` method is also very different from what most programmers would expect since it does not add an element before the `DomNode` object that invoked it. It is actually a method that can be called from any `DomNode` object within the entire tree. So a call to the `DomDocument` object or a `DomText` object will produce the same result.

Here is an example that first adds a `<title>` element as a child to the `<employee>` element, but later adds the `<name>` element before the `<title>` element. In this example, we use the `$doc` object to process the insertion, but ultimately it makes no difference:

```
$doc = new_xmldoc('1.0');
$employeesNode = $doc->add_child($doc->create_element('employee'));

$titleNode = $employeesNode->add_child($doc->create_element('title'));
$titleNode->add_child($doc->create_text_node('Chief Technology Officer'));

$nameNode = $doc->create_element('name');
$nameNode->add_child($doc->create_text_node('Jon Doe'));
$nameNode = $doc->insert_before($nameNode, $titleNode);

print (htmlentities($doc->dump_mem()));
```

This code produces the following XML:

```
<?xml version="1.0"?>
<employee>
  <name>Jon Doe</name>
  <title>Chief Technology Officer</title>
</employee>
```

Here, $nameNode was indeed inserted before $titleNode and has become a child of the <employee> element.

The last thing to mention is that the PHP 4.3.0 documentation says that any modifications done to the node after it has been inserted will not affect the end result of the tree. This may be true of PHP 4.3.0 but it currently has no effect in the current version 4.2.0. Here is an example demonstrating this:

```
$nameNode = $doc->create_element('name');
$connectedNameNode = $doc->insert_before($nameNode, $titleNode);

$nameNode->add_child($doc->create_text_node('Jon Doe'));
```

In this code, we add a new text node to the <name> element after it has been inserted. The documentation suggests that this text node addition will not take effect, however this is untrue when we make a call to dump_mem() – it returns the exact result as before. Even though this currently works in PHP 4.2.0, it is advised to make modifications to the connected node returned by insert_before() before the new node is inserted. In this case, the code would look like this:

```
$nameNode = $doc->create_element('name');
$connectedNameNode = $doc->insert_before($nameNode, $titleNode);
$connectedNameNode->add_child($doc->create_text_node('Jon Doe'));
```

> **To insert an element after a particular node, we must traverse to that node's sibling and use the `insert_before()` method.**

unlink_node()

```
DomNode unlink_node()
```

The unlink_node() function deletes this DomNode object from the tree and propagates the changes throughout the document (this is also a new addition since PHP 4.1.0). Once the node has been removed from the tree, the function returns a copy of the severed node, in case further processing is required, much like the pop() function's behavior within a typical stack.

To use unlink_node(), simply call the method with no parameters, like this:

```
$node->unlink_node();
```

> At the time of this writing, the function has been changed to `unlink_node()` as the old version was simply named as `unlink()`. However, as of PHP 4.2.0, both versions exist and accomplish the same task but it is advised to migrate all programs to use the new name.

In PHP 4.3.0, there will be a new method called `remove_child()` that removes a child `DomNode` object if it exists. Here is a short example on how it will operate:

```
$doc = new_xmldoc('1.0');
$employeeNode = $doc->add_child($doc->create_element('employee'));

$titleNode = $employeeNode->add_child($doc->create_element('title'));
$titleNode->add_child($doc->create_text_node('Chief Technology Officer'));

$employeeNode->remove_child($titleNode);
```

Although this method is currently part of the W3C standard, it will still be wiser to use `unlink()` since it is easier to use and it will not be taken away from the DOM XML in future versions.

clone_node()

```
DomNode DomNode->clone_node([bool $appendChildren])
```

The `clone_node()` makes it very easy to clone a part of the tree so that it can be used elsewhere. A call to this method will return an exact copy of the current node invoking the method that is unconnected to the tree itself. We can pass the value `true` as the first parameter to indicate that the clone should contain all the children as the current object. If this method is called with no parameters, the `DomNode` object returned will contain no children.

Here is an example that clones an experimental ant, named Bob, and adds it to the parent `<ants>` element:

```
<?php

$doc = new_xmldoc('1.0');
$antsNode = $doc->add_child($doc->create_element('ants'));

// add ant 1
$antNode1 = $antsNode->add_child($doc->create_element('ant'));
$antNode1->add_child($doc->create_text_node('Bob'));

// add ant 2 using clone_node()
$antNode2 = $antNode1->clone_node(true);
$antNode2 = $antsNode->add_child($antNode2);

print (htmlentities($doc->dump_mem()));
?>
```

The final XML looks like this (with formatting for easy viewing):

```
<?xml version="1.0"?>
<ants>
  <ant>Bob</ant>
  <ant>Bob</ant>
</ants>
```

child_nodes()

```
DomNode[] child_nodes()
```

The child_nodes() method returns an array of DomNode objects. If there are no children, the result will be an empty array. To illustrate how this method could be used, let's write a small snippet of code to count how many nodes within $children are character data and how many are element nodes. Assume that $node is an instance of DomElement and contains several children:

```
$textNodes = 0;
$elementNodes = 0;

$children = $node->child_nodes();
foreach ($children as $childNode) {
    if ($childNode->type == XML_TEXT_NODE) $textNodes++;
    if ($childNode->type == XML_ELEMENT_NODE) $textNodes++;
}

print ('The child set contained ' . $textNodes . ' text nodes and ' .
  $elementNodes . ' element nodes');
```

The foreach construct is often used to iterate through the list of children. Some examples also use array_shift() or array_pop() because removing the items from the array will not affect the tree in any way. This approach will also conserve memory; so ultimately, it is a question of what one is more comfortable with.

has_child_nodes()

```
bool DomNode->has_child_nodes()
```

This function makes it very easy to test if a DomNode contains any child or node, helping programmers avoid wasting CPU cycles on processing empty arrays or for making a call to the count() function on the array returned by child_nodes():

```
<?php

$doc = new_xmldoc('1.0');
$antsNode = $doc->add_child($doc->create_element('ants'));

// add ant 1
$antNode1 = $antsNode->add_child($doc->create_element('ant'));
$antNode1->add_child($doc->create_text_node('Bob'));
```

```
// add ant 2 using clone_node();
$antNode2 = $antNode1->clone_node(true);
$antNode2 = $antsNode->add_child($antNode2);
```

```
if ($antsNode->has_child_nodes()) {
    print ('This XML document has ant records');
} else {
    print ('This XML document does not have ant records');
}
?>
```

Since there are two <ant> records current in the $antsNode object, the script will output:

This XML document has ant records

first_child() and last_child()

```
DomNode first_child()
DomNode last_child()
```

These functions return either the first or last DomNode object within the children, respectively. If there are no children in this DomNode object, a value of FALSE is returned. Here is an example to retrieve the first and last child from a node and verify that they have been returned:

```
<?php

$doc = new_xmldoc('1.0');

$wordsNode = $doc->add_child($doc->create_element('Thing'));
$wordsNode->add_child($doc->create_element('Jon'));
$wordsNode->add_child($doc->create_element('Person'));
$wordsNode->add_child($doc->create_element('Thought'));
$wordsNode->add_child($doc->create_element('Peace'));
$wordsNode->add_child($doc->create_element('Rules'));

$firstWord = $wordsNode->first_child();
$lastWord = $wordsNode->last_child();

if ($firstWord != false || $lastWord != false) {
    print ($firstWord->node_name() . ' ' . $lastWord->node_name());
}
?>
```

As this script is run, it adds five elements under the <Thing> tag. Once the elements have been added to the tree, we call the first_child() to retrieve the <Jon> element and last_child() to retrieve the <Rules> element.

When the script is executed, this content is displayed in the browser:

Jon Rules

previous_sibling() and next_sibling()

`DomNode DomNode->previous_sibling()` and `DomNode DomNode->next_sibling()`

These methods allow the programmer to traverse the siblings of the current `DomNode` without having to talk with the parent function to coordinate the effort. Both functions will return `FALSE` when there are no siblings left to traverse. The `previous_sibling()` and `next_sibling()` methods, combined with `first_child()` and `last_child()`, present an alternative way to traverse the child of `DomNode`. Here is an example that creates a list of 5 children and traverses them forwards and backwards using all four methods:

```php
<?php

$doc = new_xmldoc('1.0');

$wordsNode = $doc->add_child($doc->create_element('Thing'));
$wordsNode->add_child($doc->create_element('Jon'));
$wordsNode->add_child($doc->create_element('Person'));
$wordsNode->add_child($doc->create_element('Thought'));
$wordsNode->add_child($doc->create_element('Peace'));
$wordsNode->add_child($doc->create_element('Rules'));

print ('<b>Words from first to last:</b><br />');
for ($word = $wordsNode->first_child();
    $word != false;
    $word = $word->next_sibling()) {
    print ($word->node_name() . '<br />');
}
```

Here we use the `first_child()` method to gather the first child of the five in the list and store it in `$word`. At the first iteration of the loop, `$word` doesn't contain `FALSE`, so the name of the element is displayed to the screen.

Next, the `$word` variable is replaced with its next sibling by making a call to `next_sibling()`. Since it contains the second word, it isn't `FALSE` and the word is also displayed to the screen. This continues until all five names of the elements are displayed to the screen. Once `next_sibling()` attempts to read a sixth word, the function will not find one and return `FALSE`:

```php
print ('<br /><b>Words from last to first:</b><br />');
for ($word = $wordsNode->last_child();
    $word != false;
    $word = $word->previous_sibling()) {
    print ($word->node_name() . '<br />');
}
?>
```

We can also traverse the child backwards by finding the last child and using `previous_sibling()` in the same manner. Here is the output when the script is run:

```
Words from first to last:
Jon
Person
Thought
Peace
Rules

Words from last to first:
Rules
Peace
Thought
Person
Jon
```

parent_node()

```
DomNode parent_node()
```

The parent_node() method is much like the last_child() method but it will return the parent node. If this DomNode object is the root node, expect the script to crash or the function to return false. At best, this function is highly experimental and volatile.

The following code snippet illustrates how to use the parent method correctly:

```
$doc = new_xmldoc('1.0');
$root = $doc->add_root('scratchy');
$sniffy = $root->new_child('sniffy', '');
$parent = $sniffy->parent_node();

if ($parent->tagname == $root->tagname) {
    print (('scratchy is the parent of sniffy'));
} else {
    print (('This will never happen.'));
}
```

> Running the parent_node() method on the root node may cause the system to crash PHP and the script to stop executing. Always perform a check for the root node first.

owner_document()

```
DomDocument DomNode->owner_document()
```

The owner_document() method provides a quick way for retrieving the original DomDocument element. This is helpful when we must create new elements inside a function but the $doc object is not available to us. When this function is called, we receive the exact reference of the DomDocument object first used to construct the tree.

To prove this, here is an example that shows that the element returned is not only equivalent member-by-member, but it also shares the same address in memory:

```php
<?php

$doc = new_xmldoc('1.0');
$thingNode = $doc->add_child($doc->create_element('Thing'));
$ownerDoc = $thingNode->owner_document();

if ($ownerDoc == $doc) {
    print ('These objects both have equivalent members.<br />');
}

if ($ownerDoc === $doc) {
    print ('Also, $ownerDoc is actually the same object in memory as $doc; thus it
is not a copy.');
}
?>
```

Here is the result of running this program:

These objects both have equivalent members.
Also, $ownerDoc is actually the same object in memory as $doc; thus it is not a copy.

set_content()

```
bool set_content(string content)
```

Introduced in PHP 4.1.0, this function takes a string and sets the content of the node. As we have seen, changing the internal member, content, manually does not signal to DOM that changes have been made. With this method, we are able to set a node's content after it has been created, allowing us to update content within nodes. If there is an error, the function will return FALSE.

As with the new_child() method, any content set here that contains entities will be transformed prematurely, resulting in non well-formed XML syntax when the tree is dumped to a string.

This code helps to update a node's content:

```
$doc = new_xmldoc('1.0');
$root = $doc->add_root('scratchy');
$root->set_content('This is text within the root node!');
```

It is not advisable to change content within a node that is complex, such as an element that contains several children (which may contain several other children and so on). This could damage the XML document. If specific leaf nodes need to be modified, we have to parse down the tree until we reach the proper node. This is one of the disadvantages to using DOM (as compared to SAX which reads the file in relatively small chunks and parses them).

> As of PHP 4.2.0, this method has been considered deprecated and should not be used. It is advised that DomText nodes are used in its place.

dump_node()

```
string DomNode->dump_node($domNode)   (PHP 4.2.0)
string DomNode->dump_node()           (PHP 4.3.0)
```

Sometimes it might be convenient to just dump the string contents of a single node in the tree rather than the entire tree. With the dump_node() method, we can do just that. Depending on the version that we are using, the method acts in different ways. In PHP 4.2.0, the method acts as a static method, but it cannot be called statically. Let's look at an example:

```
$doc = new_xmldoc('1.0');
$employeesNode = $doc->add_child($doc->create_element('employees'));

$employeeNode1 = $employeesNode->new_child('employee');
$employeeNode1->new_child('name', 'Jon Doe');
$employeeNode1->new_child('title', 'Chief Technology Officer');
$employeeNode1->new_child('office', '712');

$employeeNode2 = $employeesNode->new_child('employee');
$employeeNode2->new_child('name', 'Mary Smith');
$employeeNode2->new_child('title', 'Senior Technology Architect');
$employeeNode2->new_child('office', '713');
```

Here we created an XML tree that contains two employee records. Normally if we wanted to create an XML file, we would make a call to the $doc->dump_mem() function. But what if we want to store each record into separate files, a database, or display them separately to the screen. With PHP 4.2.0, we can do this by making a call using any DomNode object by passing in the DomNode object that we'd like to dump, like this:

```
print (htmlentities($employeesNode->dump_node($employeeNode1)));
print (htmlentities($employeeNode1->dump_node($employeeNode2)));
```

By making these calls to dump_node(), we will see the following XML displayed in the browser:

```
<employee>
  <name>Jon Doe</name>
  <title>Chief Technology Officer</title>
  <office>712</office>
</employee>
<employee>
  <name>Mary Smith</name>
  <title>Senior Technology Architect</title>
  <office>713</office>
</employee>
```

In this case, we managed to completely bypass the dump of the <employees> root node. Notice that we used the DomNode objects $employeesNode and $employeeNode1 to process the dumping. It didn't really matter which object was used. In object-oriented terminology, we say that we called this method statically since it doesn't operate on any of the member variables of the object it invoked. Although PHP supports the :: (static method function call) operator, this operator does not work with the DOM XML API.

When PHP 4.3.0 is released, this will be changed to an instance method and dump the node in which it was invoked. For instance, to dump both employee records, we can make two calls to dump_node() with zero parameters, like this:

```
print (htmlentities($employeeNode1->dump_node()));
print (htmlentities($employeeNode2->dump_node()));
```

The DomElement Class

The DomElement class is probably one of the most used classes in the DOM XML API. Since it contains all the functionality of the DomNode class, we'll be able to add child DomElement objects and character data as well. But XML elements need more functionality than the other nodes, so they are given additional functionality for handling all the needs of reading, setting, and removing attributes from the node as well as an alternative method for retrieving the name of the element. Let's take a look at the extra functionality of DomElement objects now.

> When PHP 4.3.0 is released, there will also be some new functions, namely has_attribute() which takes no parameters and tests if an object contains an attribute, and remove_attribute() which removes an attribute node from the DomElement given the string name of the attribute.

tagname, tagname(), or node_name()

```
string DomElement->tagname()
string DomElement->node_name()
```

Unlike other DomNode objects, the DomElement class contains a tagname member variable that is equivalent to the value returned by node_name(). The class also defines a method called tagname(), which essentially aliases node_name(). The tagname member and node_name() method are used to check the name of nodes that are XML elements. For instance, the name for the <stuff> element would be stuff.

set_attribute()

```
DomAttribute set_attribute(string name, string value)
```

The set_attribute() method sets an attribute to an XML element node using a name/value pair and returns TRUE. If the attribute $name has not been set, a DomAttribute object is constructed and a new attribute is added to the DOM tree. If the attribute with $name already exists, the attributes' value is updated.

We can set the attribute of a node using the following code:

```
$element->set_attribute('name', 'Sam');
$element->set_attribute('title', 'Chief Janitorial Engineer');
```

get_attribute()

```
object get_attribute(string name)
```

The get_attribute() method retrieves the value for an attribute identified by $name. The reason the result type is object is that the value can be of many types; that is, it is unpredictable until run-time. If the attribute does not exist, the function will return the Boolean value FALSE.

Assuming the attribute name has been defined as above, the following code can retrieve the value Bob:

```
$name = $node->get_attribute('name');
if ($name == 'Sam') print ('Everything is okay');
```

As mentioned in the paragraphs above, the function will return a FALSE value if the attribute does not exist. If error reporting is turned on, PHP will also elicit a warning message. In the case where name is not defined, the following message would appear as PHP output:

Warning: No such attribute 'name' in C:\'DOC_ROOT\Chapter06\attrdom.php on line X

attributes()

```
DomAttribute[] DomElement->attributes()
```

The DomNode object's last function, attributes(), returns an array of DomAttribute objects containing the name/value pairs for all the attributes associated with this DomNode. It contains two members – a $name member that indicates the unique name that identifies the attribute and an instance of DomNode that contains the value, and some other irrelevant information about the DomNode.

This code illustrates how to retrieve the name and value for each element:

```
$doc = new_xmldoc('1.0');
$root = $doc->add_root('scratchy');
$root->set_attribute('name', 'sam');
$root->set_attribute('title', 'chief janitorial engineer.');

$attributes = $root->attributes();

foreach ($attributes as $attributeNode) {
    $children = $attributeNode->children();
    $tempNode = $children[0];
    print ('Name: ' . $attributeNode->node_name());
    print (' & Content: ' . $tempNode->node_value() . '<br />');
}
```

This function isn't used frequently. It is more useful when converting all the attributes to a particular data structure, an HTML table, or possibly a file. In most cases, get_attribute() requires less code and is more efficient.

has_attributes()

```
bool DomElement->has_attributes()
```

The has_attributes() method is much like has_child_nodes() in the DomNode base class. This method tests the DomElement object to see if it contains any DomAttribute nodes contained within and simply returns a Boolean value TRUE or FALSE with the answer. Here is an example showing the method. Assume that $employeeNode is an instance of DomElement:

```
if ($employeeNode->has_attributes()) {
    print ('I have some attributes attached to me');
} else {
    print ('I have no attributes attached to me');
}
```

get_attribute_node() and set_attribute_node()

```
DomAttribute DomElement->get_attribute_node(DomAttribute attr)
bool DomElement->set_attribute_node(DomAttribute attr)
```

At the time of this writing, in PHP version 4.2.0, there exist two functions called set_attributenode() and get_attributenode(). However, both methods are not implemented and cannot be used. When PHP 4.3.0 is released, it will contain the set_attribute_node() and get_attribute_node() methods – notice with the added underscores – to provide an alternativee method for creating attributes. As mentioned earlier in the chapter, the DomDocument contained a method to create attribute nodes called create_attribute(). Although it's not usable in PHP 4.2.0, this method was created for use with these methods.

As it stands, even when these methods are implemented, it is better off using the older functions rather than these new, alternative implementations. For instance, to create two attributes on an <employee> element, it takes the following three lines (and five method calls) of code:

```
$employeeNode = $doc->add_child($doc->create_element('employee'));
$employeeNode->set_attribute_node($doc->create_attribute('name',
                                                 'Jon Doe'));
$employeeNode->set_attribute_node($doc->create_attribute('title',
                                      'Chief Executive Officer'));
```

Notice that we use the create_attribute() factory method to create the attribute nodes and then use set_attribute_node() to add them to the element. The equivalent code to create these attributes using the old method requires three lines of code and is much shorter and easier to read:

```
$employeeNode = $doc->add_child($doc->create_element('employee'));
$employeeNode->set_attribute('name', 'Jon Doe');
$employeeNode->set_attribute('title', 'Chief Executive Officer');
```

Since there are no plans to deprecate the set_attribute() and get_attribute() methods and since they are a part of the W3C standard, it is recommended to use the old methods; however, the choice is ultimately ours to make when the new version is released.

Now that we've learned the entire DOM API (except the specific XPath functions which are discussed in the next chapter), it is time to write our first DOM parser.

Parsing XML Documents

Now that we know how trees are constructed, the different classes that make up the trees and how to interface with these classes, it is time to write a parser.

Just to refresh, parsing involves extracting useful content from a well-formed XML document.

Chapter 5 includes a detailed explanation on parsing in general.

For our first example, we are going to parse an XML file that tracks bugs for various software systems in development. All the examples in this section will use `bug_list.xml`. It would be a good idea to note the exact path from C:\ in Windows and \ in UNIX. Here is its content:

```
<?xml version="1.0" encoding="iso-8859-1"?>
<bug_list>
<application name="sportran compiler" version="1.1">
  <bugs>
    <bug_item>
      <title>It crashes when a string with
             more than 256 bytes is declared</title>
      <report_date>2002-01-28T10:15:00</report_date>
      <reported-by>John Smith</reported-by>
      <status>Open</status>
      <last_update>2002-01-28T10:16:00</last_update>
      <description>...</description>
      <severity>3</severity>
    </bug_item>
    <bug_item>
      <title>String concatenation fails if a string contains a dot</title>
      <report_date>2002-01-14T14:30:00</report_date>
      <reported-by>Mike Brown</reported-by>
      <status>Closed</status>
      <last_update>2002-01-16T18:30:00</last_update>
      <description>...</description>
      <severity>5</severity>
    </bug_item>
    <bug_item>
      <title>Error when summing two integers</title>
      <report_date>2002-01-14T16:30:00</report_date>
      <reported-by>Mike Brown</reported-by>
      <status>Open</status>
      <last_update>2002-01-14T16:30:00</last_update>
      <description>...</description>
      <severity>4</severity>
    </bug_item>
  </bugs>
</application>

... other <application> elements ...

</bug_list>
```

As seen above in `<bug_list>`, the XML content contains a series of `<bug_item>` elements. The structure is almost self-explanatory. We are going to display the list of bug items in tabular format for each `<bug_item>` in a single HTML document.

As with the previous chapter, the program has been constructed in a modular manner. Each operation has been broken into a separate function. For DOM XML programs, this is most desirable as this keeps our code readable. Also there are many decisional and looping constructs, so the code can quickly become deeply nested – this is something we want to avoid.

The `ParseDocument()` function starts the parsing of the DOM tree by taking an instance of `DomDocument` as its argument:

```php
<?php
// buglist.php

function ParseDocument($doc)
{
    $root = $doc->document_element();               // gets <bug_list> element
    $applications = $root->child_nodes();
    foreach ($applications as $applicationNode) {
        ParseApplicationNode($applicationNode);
    }
}
```

Since there is nothing to do when the program arrives at the root node `<bug_list>`, the root node is retrieved from the document and the `ParseApplicationNode()` function is called on each child of the root. The array of children is retrieved using the `child_nodes()` method, which is found in all `DomNode` objects.

The `ParseApplicationNode()` function is responsible for displaying a title of the application to the screen and running `ParseBugsNode()` on the child node:

```php
function ParseApplicationNode($applicationNode)
{
    if ($applicationNode->node_name() == 'application') {
        DisplayApplicationTitle($applicationNode);

        $bugsNodes = $applicationNode->child_nodes();
        foreach ($bugsNodes as $bugsNode) {
            ParseBugsNode($bugsNode);
        }
    }
}
```

The program compares the node's name member with `application` to make certain the child is an `<application>` element node by using the `node_name()` method. Notice that the member variable `tagname` could have also been used to achieve the same effect here. Since DOM maintains the whitespace characters such as tabs and newline characters for visual formatting within the XML file, many nodes contain text. This condition ensures that only `application` elements are parsed in the future because the `DomText` objects are thrown away.

Before the child nodes are parsed, the function calls the `DisplayApplicationTitle()` function. This is seen here:

```
function DisplayApplicationTitle($applicationNode)
{
    if ($applicationNode->node_name() == 'application') {
        $appName    = $applicationNode->get_attribute('name');
        $appVersion = $applicationNode->get_attribute('version');

        print ('<h1>' . $appName . ' v' . $appVersion . '</h1>');
    }
}
```

This function retrieves the two attributes, name and version, from the `$applicationNode` object using the `get_attribute()` method and displays them to the screen using HTML. We also test to make sure that we have been passed an <application> node. In this particular application, we know this is the case, but including the test can help prevent errors when code is reused or built onto our application later.

The `ParseBugsNode()` function takes in a `DomNode` object that represents the <bugs> element and calls the `ParseBugItemNode()` function on its children:

```
function ParseBugsNode($bugsNode)
{
    if ($bugsNode->node_name() == 'bugs') {
        $bugItemNodes = $bugsNode->child_nodes();

        foreach ($bugItemNodes as $bugItemNode) {
        ParseBugItemNode($bugItemNode);
        }
    }
}
```

As with the other functions, this function blocks out other types of nodes from being parsed further. The function doesn't contain any other logic because there is nothing to do at this point other than go deeper within the XML file. As mentioned earlier in the chapter, DOM always requires code to dig into the leaf nodes, thus there is an increased amount of code within the application – it is a necessary evil.

The next function is for convenience and to shorten the rest of the program. With the new version of DOM XML, `get_content()` has been deprecated in favor of storing the character data as child nodes (`DomText` objects). So, to retrieve all the character data for an element, we must first retrieve an array of its children and cycle through each child and append the text only if it is of type `XML_TEXT_NODE`. This `GetTextFromElement()` function can be seen here:

```
function GetTextFromElement($element)
{
    $value = "";

    foreach ($element->child_nodes() as $child) {
        if ($child->node_type() == XML_TEXT_NODE) {
            $value .= $child->content;
        }
    }
    return $value;
}
```

In the future, a new method called get_cdata() *might be developed to provide this inherit functionality in all* DomElement *objects. This makes sense since by the rules of refactoring, this function should be moved into the* DomElement *class. This has not been done because the W3C standard does not currently specify it, so there are no plans right now that it will be included in PHP 4.3.0. So for now we must include a similar function in every program that parses character data from elements.*

Once we reach the `<bug_item>` node within the XML content, it is time to collect all the data about the node. This is accomplished by the `ParseBugItemNode()` function:

```
function ParseBugItemNode($bugItemNode)
{
    if ($bugItemNode->node_name() == 'bug_item') {
        $bugItemChildren = $bugItemNode->child_nodes();

        foreach ($bugItemChildren as $node) {
            switch($node->node_name()) {
            case "title":
                $title = GetTextFromElement($node);
                break;
            case "report_date":
                $date = GetTextFromElement($node);
                break;
            case "reported":
                $reportedBy = GetTextFromElement($node);
                break;
            case "status":
                $status = GetTextFromElement($node);
                break;
            case "last_update":
                $lastUpdate = GetTextFromElement($node);
                break;
            case "description":
                $description = GetTextFromElement($node);
                break;
            case "severity":
                $severity = GetTextFromElement($node);
                break;
            }
        }

        DisplayBugItemTable($title, $date, $reportedBy, $status,
            $lastUpdate, $description, $severity);
    }
}
```

First the function retrieves all the children DomNode objects from the bugItemNode object. By looking at the structure of the document, it can be seen that there are several distinct elements that describe the bug, such as a short description, the date, who reported the bug, and so on. We can test each child DomNode's name with each of these element names and store the value in a variable. Once all the data has been collected, the function displays the item to the screen in a table.

As a side note, this function can also be implemented using variable variables. This can ease up on the amount of code required to store the data from the individual children. This can be accomplished with the following code:

```
function ParseBugItemNode($bugItemNode)
{
    if ($bugItemNode->tagname == 'bug_item') {
        $bugItemChildren = $bugItemNode->child_nodes();

        foreach ($bugItemChildren as $node) {
            if ($node->node_type() == XML_ELEMENT_NODE) {
                ${ str_replace('-', '', $node->node_name()) } =
                    getTextFromElement($node);
            }
        }

        DisplayBugItemTable($title, $report_date, $reportedby,
            $status, $last_update, $description, $severity);
    }
}
```

By using variable variables, the case statements disappear and one line of code is put in its place. Since each child carries a specific, unique name that is a string, we can use this as the variable name and assign the node's character data to it. Notice that when DisplayBugItemTable() is invoked, we use the variable names exactly as they are in the XML content (without the dashes, since these need to be stripped). Although it may not follow variable naming standards, it's a quick and easy way to assign content from child nodes. This will also increase the maintainability of the application if the structure changes in the future, providing a very elegant solution to the problem.

The last function, DisplayBugItemTable(), accepts all the information on the bug item and displays the HTML table to the browser. Note that the xmldocfile() method accepts the absolute path of the bug_list.xml file as a parameter:

```
function DisplayBugItemTable($title, $date, $reportedBy, $status,
    $lastUpdate, $description, $severity)
{
    print ('<h3>' . $title . '</h3>');
    print ('<table border="0" cellpadding="2">');
    print ('<tr><td>Date:</td><td> ' . $date . '</td></tr>');
    print ('<tr><td>Reported By:</td><td> ' . $reportedBy .
            '</td></tr>');
    print ('<tr><td>Status:</td><td> ' . $status . '</td></tr>');
    print ('<tr><td>Last Updated:</td><td> ' . $lastUpdate .
            '</td></tr>');
    print ('<tr><td>Bug Description:</td><td> ' . $description .
            '</td></tr>');
    print ('<tr><td>Severity:</td><td> ' . $severity . '</td></tr>');

    print ('</table><br />');
}

$doc = xmldocfile('DOC_ROOT\bug_list.xml');
DisplayDocumentProperties($doc);
ParseDocument($doc);
?>
```

To execute the program, the ParseDocument() function must be called with an instance of DomDocument to start the chain of function calls that parse the DOM Tree.

Here is the output:

Adding XML Content

Next, let's take a look at how DOM XML handles the addition of new nodes to an existing tree. For this example, we are going to add a new application element and a bug to the existing bug_list.xml file used earlier. The program we are going to write will utilize HTML forms to input the new bug information. Upon submittal, PHP will retrieve the values entered in the form and will use DOM to append the new entries to the tree. After the tree has been updated, the program writes out a new bug_list.xml file with the added changes.

Here is the display of the application when it is executed in a web browser:

Once the user submits the application and bug information, the new XML file will contain the old content plus some new XML data describing a newly added application and bug to the bug list. Notice that the XML data has no whitespace, which makes it harder for humans to read:

```
. . .
<application name="eXtremePHP"
version="0.14"><bugs><bug_item><title>HtmlTagContainer's add()
method</title><report_date>200205161010</report_date><reported-by>Jon
Doe</reported-by><status>Open</status><last_update>200205101616</last_update><desc
ription>HtmlTagContainer's add() method does not accept strings as an
argument.</description><severity>5</severity></bug_item></bugs></application></bug
_list>
```

This is rather unfortunate because of the nature of DOM, but as long as we use parsers to read and edit the document, the appearance of the file is not much of a concern.

The model to this application is fairly simple. The entire program will be coded in a single file called `buglistadd.php`. When the program is first run, an HTML form will be displayed and the user must enter data into the form. When the form is submitted, a DOM tree will be constructed and the new application and bug item nodes will be added with the changes written. Here is an illustration of this model:

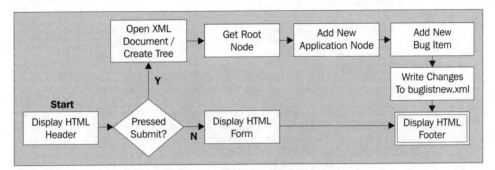

The first task is to display the HTML header for the page. Instead of placing the HTML in a function, it is better served at the top of the page where it can be used when the user is entering information into the form or when the result is written to the file and the results are displayed to the screen, as indicated in the decisional point (the diamond) in the diagram above:

```
<!-- buglistadd.php -->
<!DOCTYPE HTML PUBLIC "-//W3C//DTD HTML 4.0 Transitional//EN">
<html>
  <head><title> Adding XML Content </title></head>
  <body>
```

Next, we have to code functions that parse and manipulate the DOM tree:

```php
<?php

function AddApplicationNode($doc, $root, $applicationName,
  $applicationVersion)
{
    if ($root->tagname == 'bug_list') {
        $applicationNode = $doc->create_element('application');
        $applicationNode = $root->add_child($applicationNode);
        $applicationNode->set_attribute('name', trim($applicationName));
        $applicationNode->set_attribute('version',
                                        trim($applicationVersion));
    }

    return $applicationNode;
}
```

The first function is `AddApplicationNode()`, which takes in an instance of the `DomDocument` class, the root node, the name of the application, and its version number. Since PHP 4.2.0, we must use the `$doc` instance to create DOM objects using factory methods, so that is why we pass the `$doc` object as the first parameter. The only other option would be to make `$doc` a global variable, which is not advised in programming most of the time. This function will ensure that `$root` is the top-level node in the tree by comparing the `tagname` member to `'bug_list'`. Once this condition is met, a new application node is created using the `$doc` factory method, `create_element()`.

When the element is created, we add it to the list of children of the root element with the add_child() method and set two new attributes, name and version, to the node that is now connected to the tree. Lastly, the function returns the new node that was created or FALSE if $root was not the correct parent node.

The AddBugItem() function follows next:

```
function AddBugItem($doc, $bugsNode, $title, $reportDate, $reportedBy,
 $status, $lastUpdate, $description, $severity)
{
    if ($bugsNode->tagname = 'bugs') {
        $bugItemNode = $doc->create_element('bug_item');
        $bugItemNode = $bugsNode->add_child($bugItemNode);

        $titleNode = $doc->create_element('title');
        $titleTextNode = $doc->create_text_node($title);
        $titleNode->add_child($titleTextNode);
        $bugItemNode->add_child($titleNode);

        $bugItemNode->new_child('report_date', $reportDate);
        $bugItemNode->new_child('reported-by', $reportedBy);
        $bugItemNode->new_child('status', $status);
        $bugItemNode->new_child('last_update', $lastUpdate);
        $bugItemNode->new_child('description', $description);
        $bugItemNode->new_child('severity', $severity);

        return $bugItemNode;
    }

    return false;
}
```

This is very similar to the previous function, AddApplicationNode(). It anticipates a $bugsNode (containing the <bugs> element), and several properties (title, date, and so on) to describe a new bug item.

First, the function checks if $bugsNode is the correct element. If it is, a new <bug_item> element is created using the factory method in the $doc instance and add_child() is called to add the $bugItemNode that was constructed. Next, each of the arguments is added as a new child node to the bugitemNode object with $bugsNode being the exception since it is the container adding the elements.

Here, we add the <title> element to the <bug_item> element. We create a new DomText object using the create_text_node() factory method. Once the text node has been constructed with the text stored in the $title variable, we can add it to the list of children of the <title> element node. Once this is done, we can finally add the <title> element to <bug_item> node.

The next child nodes are created and added with the new_child() method. This essentially creates elements and adds them to the list of child with a corresponding DomText object all in a single line. Although new_child() is deprecated, the method isn't going to disappear from the API and this is still a desirable way to quickly add elements with character data due to its ease of use.

> In future versions of DOM XML, we might see factory methods in the DomNode class itself
> that function like new_child() but will be renamed to create_element(),
> create_text_node(), and so on. For now, we might do well to make our own
> convenience functions to simplify the coding of adding various nodes to the tree.

Like the previous function AddApplicationNode(), it returns FALSE if $bugsNode is different from the type of node expected. This next section writes the new content of <bug_list> into a file:

```
function WriteNewBugList($doc, $fileName)
{
    $xmlString = $doc->dump_mem();

    $fp = fopen($fileName, 'w+');
    fwrite($fp, $xmlString, strlen($xmlString));
    fclose($fp);
}
```

Recall that the dump_mem() method returns the DOM tree in a string representation of the XML content. To write to a file, it is necessary to call dump_mem() on the DomDocument object. By using standard PHP file functions, the WriteNewBugList() function opens $filename for writing, uses fwrite() to record the entire block of XML content into the file buffer, and closes the file.

Now that our convenience functions have been defined, let's take a look at the main script logic:

```
/* Main Program */
if ($_REQUEST['submit'] == 'submit') {
    $doc = xmldocfile('DOC_ROOT\bug_list.xml');
    $root = $doc->document_element();
```

When the script first executes, it checks the request variable $submit to see if the user has entered information in the form. We compare the variable to the 'submit' value because later in the program, this value is the caption on the button. This condition decides whether the program either displays the form or adds new content to the XML file.

In this case, if the form was submitted, we use DOM to open up the bug_list.xml file (using the full path to the file) and construct a new DOM tree and place it into the variable $doc. As with all DOM programs, we immediately retrieve the root node:

```
$applicationNode = AddApplicationNode($doc, $root,
 $_REQUEST['applicationName'],
 $_REQUEST['applicationVersion']);

$bugsNode = $doc->create_element('bugs');
$bugsNode = $applicationNode->add_child($bugsNode);
$bugItemNode = addBugItem($doc,
                          $bugsNode,
                          $_REQUEST['bugTitle'],
                          $_REQUEST['bugReportDate'],
                          $_REQUEST['bugReportedBy'],
                          $_REQUEST['bugStatus'],
                          $_REQUEST['bugLastUpdate'],
                          $_REQUEST['bugDescription'],
                          $_REQUEST['bugSeverity']
                          );

print ('Added new bug to the application bug list<br />');
```

As shown previously, we next call our user-defined function `AddApplicationNode()` on the `$root` node, with the first two form variables – `name` and `version` – and pass the `$doc` variable. This creates a new application `DomElement` object. According to the structure of the XML file, a `<bugs>` element must be created, so we accomplish this by first creating a `DomElement` object using the factory method contained in the `$doc` object and add the new element to the `$applicationNode`.

Now that we have a `DomElement` that contains the `<bugs>` element, our second user-defined function, `AddBugItem()`, can be called with the form variables to create the bug item to add the information input on the form to the XML tree:

```
WriteNewBugList($doc, './newbuglist.xml');
print ('Wrote XML content to the file "newbuglist.xml"');
```

Once both the application and bug item have been added to the tree, in order to persist the changes, we call `WriteNewBugList()` to write the changes to a new bug list file (in order to preserve the old file) and display a message indicating that the changes have been written.

In the case where the user calls the page for the first time and the form has not been submitted, the program exits out of PHP environment and displays the following form code in HTML. No matter what this script is called, the action attribute on the `<form>` tag uses a predefined variable, `$PHP_SELF`, that contains the URL for this page:

```
} else {
    ?>
    <form action="<?php print ($_SERVER["PHP_SELF"]); ?>" method="post">
      <h3>Input a New Application</h3>
      <table border="0" cellspacing="0" cellpadding="3">
      <tr>
        <td>Application Name:</td>
        <td><input type="text" name="applicationName" /></td>
      </tr>

      <tr>
        <td>Application Version: </td>
        <td><input type="text" name="applicationVersion" /></td>
      </tr>
    </table>
```

The last section and probably the easiest one is the construction of the HTML table:

```
      <h3>Input a New Bug</h3>
      <table border="0" cellspacing="0" cellpadding="3">
      <tr>
        <td>Bug Title: </td>
        <td><input type="text" name="bugTitle" size="60" /></td>
      </tr>
      <tr>
        <td>Report Date: </td>
        <td><input type="text" name="bugReportDate" /></td>
```

```
          </tr>
          <tr>
            <td>Reported By: </td>
            <td><input type="text" name="bugReportedBy" /></td>
          </tr>
          <tr>
            <td>Status: </td>
            <td><select name="bugStatus" >
              <option value="Open">Open</option>
              <option value="Closed">Closed</option>
            </select></td>
          </tr>
          <tr>
            <td>Last Update: </td>
            <td><input type="text" name="bugLastUpdate" /></td>
          </tr>
          <tr>
            <td>Description: </td>
              <td><textarea name="bugDescription" cols="40"
                        rows="3"></textarea></td>
          </tr>
          <tr>
            <td>Status: </td>
              <td><select name="bugSeverity" >
                <?php for ($i = 1; $i <= 10; $i++) { ?>
                <option value="<?php echo $i; ?>"><?php echo $i; ?></option>
                <?php } ?>
              </select></td>
            </tr>
            <tr>
              <td colspan="2"><input type="submit"
                                name="submit" value="submit" /></td>
            </tr>
          </table>
        </form>

        <?php
        }
        ?>
      </body>
    </html>
```

In the first table, there are only two inputs for the application name and its version. The second table contains the table and form code for the bug list-specific information.

Although this is a simple example on adding new XML elements, it demonstrates the principles in adding XML content from user input. Now other programs and scripts can use the resultant XML file in their applications, possibly on a bug list summary page or a bug search engine.

Deleting XML Content

As mentioned previously, with the new additions in DOM XML since PHP 4.1.0, we can now delete nodes from the tree without fear of dangling nodes. By being able to create, edit, and delete content as well as structure, DOM provides us with fairly comprehensive tools for file administration.

In this next example, we will demonstrate how DOM can delete nodes in the tree by deleting all the 'closed' or 'open' bug items (indicated by the status element) within one application. Specifically, we will delete all the closed bugs in the 'sportran compiler' application.

Here is a model of the program:

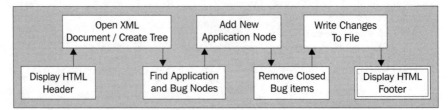

As with the previous example where we added new nodes, this program will use several functions to modularize the program. These functions allow traversing the tree to locate the <application> and <bugs> nodes, removing the closed <bug_item> nodes, and writing the changes to the file.

The top of the script contains the header HTML content as expected:

```
<!-- buglistdelete.php -->
<!DOCTYPE HTML PUBLIC "-//W3C//DTD HTML 4.0 Transitional//EN">
<html>
  <head><title> Deleting XML Content </title></head>
  <body>
```

Next, we define several functions.

Our first function is FindApplicationNode():

```php
<?php

function FindApplicationNode($root, $applicationName)
{
    $applications = $root->child_nodes();
    foreach ($applications as $applicationNode) {
        if ($applicationNode->tagname == 'application') {
            if ($applicationNode->get_attribute('name') ==
             $applicationName)
            {
                return $applicationNode;
            }
        }
    }

    die('Could not find application node with the name "' .
     $applicationName . '"');
}
```

Given the `$root` node and the name of the application, this function will parse and search the tree for `$applicationName`. If the application with the designated name does not exist, the script will end interrupted and die.

To accomplish this functionality, we retrieve the children from the `$root` node using the `child_nodes()` method, which contains several `<application>` nodes and character data. As the code suggests, we traverse the children with a `foreach` construct until a node's name is `'application'` and the name is equivalent to the argument `$applicationName`. If such a match is found, the node is returned.

The next function is simply a convenience method to dig deeper into the tree:

```
function FindBugsNode($applicationNode)
{
    if ($applicationNode->tagname == 'application') {
        $bugsNodes = $applicationNode->child_nodes();
        foreach ($bugsNodes as $bugsNode) {
            if ($bugsNode->type == XML_ELEMENT_NODE &&
            $bugsNode->tagname == 'bugs')
            {
                return $bugsNode;
            }
        }
    }

    die('Could not find a &lt;bugs&gt; node. The XML is not correct.');
}
```

Given an `$applicationNode`, the `FindBugsNode()` function attempts to find a `<bugs>` node and returns it. If one does not exist, the script will terminate with an error message.

The `RemoveBugItemsWithStatus()` function takes in a `$bugsNode`, containing the `<bugs>` element information, and a `$status` variable, indicating to delete either 'open' or 'closed' items. The `$status` string can be in any case. The function also keeps track of how many items the program deleted and returns the result:

```
function RemoveBugItemsWithStatus($bugsNode, $status)
{
    if ($bugsNode->tagname == 'bugs') {
        $bugItemNodes = $bugsNode->child_nodes();
        $deleted = 0;
        foreach ($bugItemNodes as $bugItemNode) {

            if ($bugItemNode->tagname == 'bug_item') {
                $bugItemChildren = $bugItemNode->children();

                foreach ($bugItemChildren as $node) {
                    if ($node->node_type() == XML_ELEMENT_NODE &&
                    $node->tagname == "status")
                    {
                        if (strtolower(getTextFromElement($node)) ==
                                                strtolower($status)) {
                            $bugItemNode->unlink_node();
                            $deleted++;
```

```
                    }
                }
            }
        }
    }

    return $deleted;
}
```

As one of the more complicated functions described in the chapter, RemoveBugItemsWithStatus() requires all the children of the $bugsNode. After traversing the list, each node is checked if it is a <bug_item> to avoid whitespace. Once the node has been proven to be a <bug_item>, its children are traversed to find the <status> node. If this node's character data is equal to the $status argument (with a case-insensitive match), then the unlink_node() method is called on the node to unlink the $bugItemNode from the tree.

Notice that we do not unlink_node() the $node, because that would only remove the <status> element from the XML file. This process is repeated for all children, incrementing the number of deletions from the tree for all bug items within the list.

Here is the GetTextFromElement() function:

```
function GetTextFromElement($element)
{
    $value = "";
    foreach ($element->child_nodes() as $child) {
        if ($child->node_type() == XML_TEXT_NODE) {
            $value .= $child->content;
        }
    }
    return trim($value);
}
```

With all our convenience functions defined, the main program is rather short, with only a few lines required to remove the nodes from the tree:

```
/* MAIN PROGRAM */
$doc = xmldocfile('DOC_ROOT\ProPHPXML\bug_list.xml');
$root = $doc->root();
```

The first few lines create a new tree from the original bug_list.xml file and retrieve the root node. Make sure that the absolute path to the bug_list.xml file is passed as a parameter to the xmldocfile() method.

The next series of lines are the bulk of the program. We use our custom-made FindApplicationNode() function to find the 'sportran compiler' node. With this node, we can sink into the tree one level deeper by calling FindBugsNode(). With the $bugsNode we then delete all the bug items within it that have the status, 'open' or 'Open'. This is accomplished through the user-defined function, RemoveBugItemsWithStatus(). After the nodes have been deleted from the tree, a message is displayed to the browser indicating how many records were deleted:

```
$applicationNode = FindApplicationNode($root, 'sportran compiler');
$bugsNode = FindBugsNode($applicationNode);
$numDeleted = RemoveBugItemsWithStatus($bugsNode, 'open');
print ($numDeleted . ' &lt;bug_item&gt; records have been deleted<br />');


$doc->dump_mem_file('DOC_ROOT\ProPHPXML\Chapter06\newbuglist.xml');
print ('Wrote XML content to the file "newbuglist.xml"');


?>
</body>
</html>
```

To make the changes persistent, a call to the dump_mem_file() method on the DomDocument object is made and the changes are saved. Note that this method must also take a full path or it will return false. The following output occurs when the script is run:

```
2 <bug_item> records have been deleted
'Wrote XML content to the file "newbuglist.xml"
```

Limitations

Although DOM XML within PHP allows us to parse, create, update, and delete XML content, it has many limitations. DOM XML is still in its infancy and there is much to be added until it is comparable to parsers from other platforms, such as Java or ASP. XML support is gradually integrating itself into PHP, but it may be several months before PHP matures its XML support.

In this section, we are going to talk about the following limitations:

❑   Incomplete DOM Level 1 and Level 2 standard

❑   Unsound architecture

❑   Limited object-oriented capability

Incomplete DOM Level 1 and Level 2 Standard

DOM XML should have evolved at the same rate as parsers from other platforms. But it clearly lacks some functionality. For instance, it is impossible to swap two nodes within the tree without a great deal of difficulty. Sure, it might be easy to swap and possibly sort leaf nodes, but swapping top-level elements is very difficult. This problem is due to an incomplete implementation of DOM.

As mentioned earlier, DOM is a W3C standard. In order to accommodate the future needs of the DOM standard, the W3C develops several **Levels**, where each level is built on the previous standard and new functionality is added. Currently, the W3C is working on DOM Level 3, but most parsers haven't evolved that far yet, albeit some have not evolved to Level 2. But what do Level 1 and Level 2 mean?

DOM Level 1

DOM Level 1 is the 'Core' standard. At this time, there are two sections to DOM Level 1 – HTML and XML. HTML DOM objects are referenced via a scripting language like JavaScript within a browser while XML documents possessed their own model that was slightly different. The XML specification describes the basic classes, their methods and properties, and how everything works in the abstract. All DOM standard implementations are supposed to follow the architecture laid out by the W3C, but the implementation details are left to the implementer.

In the case of PHP, it fails to implement this standard in several areas. There are several key members and methods that are not implemented at the time of this writing. For instance, a reference to the first child or the `replaceNode()` and `insertBefore()` methods are absent from the `DomNode` class.

For further information on this check out the W3C web page: http://www.w3.org/DOM/2000/12/dom2-javadoc/org/w3c/dom/package-summary.html.

DOM Level 2

DOM Level 2 is an extended standard that provides support for namespaces, stylesheets, filtering, event models, and other features. PHP currently has no real support for any of these features and it is unknown as to when they will be implemented.

This can be seen at the following web site: http://www.w3.org/DOM/2000/12/dom2-javadoc/.

Thus, PHP support for DOM is still in its infancy stage.

Unsound Architecture

Although DOM XML is taking steps forward to become DOM-compliant as set out by the W3C, it has taken many steps backwards as well. In this section we are going to be talking about the shortcomings and the problems with the new architecture and what measures might be taken by the PHP development community to address them.

We are going to talk about the following architectural shortcomings:

- ❑ The low-level nature of the API
- ❑ The improper distribution of logic
- ❑ The lack of power and convenience
- ❑ Lack of robustness

Low-Level API

In comparison to previous versions of DOM XML, the latest version requires a lot more code to produce the same results. This is attributed to its structured nature but there is a lack of support functions in the experimental API to make the work easy for the developer.

For instance, take these six lines of code which creates new levels to the `$root` of the tree where the second-level element contains a text node:

```
$someTagElement = $doc->create_element('sometag');
$connectedSomeTagElement = $root->add_child($someTagElement);
$anotherTagElement = $doc->create_element('anothertag');
$connectedAnotherTagElement = $doc->add_child($anotherTagElement);
$textNode = $doc->create_text_node('cdata');
$connectedAnotherTagElement->add_child($textNode);
```

In previous versions, this same functionality could have been accomplished with the deprecated methods in two lines, like this:

```
$someTagElement = $root->new_child('sometag');
$newChild = $someTagElement->new_child('anothertag', 'cdata');
```

So even though the DOM XML API has become highly structured and closer to the standard in its latest release, it has also become more tedious to work with, basically requiring a wrapper library to be developed to simplify these common operations to make it easier to write and test until there are new improved methods in future releases of the API.

There are few reasons why the API is harder to work with. One factor is that text nodes are now modeled as actual objects within the tree rather than as a member of the node's content. Although this has many advantages for implementation and abstraction, it causes the programmers to create additional nodes and makes it more difficult to parse character data from XML elements. Another factor is that the new API relies on a DomDocument instance to create the nodes to be added to the tree. For each node that we would like to create, there is at least 1 extra line of code and each text node that we need to add requires another two.

Improper Distribution of Logic

One of the current problems with the architecture is that the distribution of logic doesn't make sense to many object-oriented programmers. The main concern is dealing with the creation of new elements at the DomDocument level rather the DomNode level, which could be just 1 or even 10 levels apart to where we are currently editing the tree. Although the current setup emulates that of Java, PHP has many shortcomings with its extensions and its OO capabilities that make this setup fairly cumbersome. Like we saw earlier, this creates extra code when creating new elements, but it does much more than that.

In the Java programming language when using DOM, a program would normally contain the following code when adding a new element to a node within the tree:

```
node.appendChild(new Element(...));
```

Since the class is instantiated using the new operator and is then added to the tree, there isn't really a need for factory methods to create the objects – this is easily done by the new operator. However, in the PHP version, we are using $doc to make these classes. Due to limitations with PHP extensions, this setup is the closest solution to following the Java binding established by the W3C; however, it's not the most desirable.

If we write all our DOM code in a single function or the script itself, we wouldn't notice the subtle error with this design. However, if we need to modularize programs using many functions or use the object-oriented paradigm, the $doc requires us to add the $doc to the parameter list of each function within our program or contain an instance of the $doc object regardless of what level they are modifying in the tree.

In future versions of PHP, this will surely be added or improved by moving the factory methods into the DomNode object itself (perhaps having a type if it can add child elements or not). With this change, in the future the six-line program above would appear like this:

```
$someTagElement = $root->create_element('sometag');
$newChild = $someTagElement->create_element('anothertag', 'cdata');
```

As it currently stands, when programmers start writing extra code on how the tree is constructed and maintained, which should be contained within the API itself, they start doing things on the API's behalf and this can only produce excess code, repetition, increased bugs, and difficulty. As future versions of the API are released, DOM XML will be a very solid API to use.

Lack of Power and Convenience

Given that the API now has several subclasses of DomNode to take care of specific functionality of the different XML nodes, there is still much functionality missing from the API.

Take DomElement for example. When a programmer recalls what an XML element is, they mainly think about two things – attributes and character data. The API currently supports many functions for manipulating and receiving attribute data on DomElement objects, but there is nothing to interact and manipulate the character data of the DomElement itself. Although the character data has been moved to separate DomText nodes, there are currently no convenience methods for extracting character data from a node or setting simple one-line character data, having the API maintain the nodes internally.

For instance, let's assume $element is a DomElement object and we want to get all the character data associated with the element. This can be done with 5 lines of code:

```
$value = "";

foreach ($element->child_nodes() as $child) {
    if ($child->node_type() == XML_TEXT_NODE) {
        $value .= $child->content;
    }
}
```

Notice all the operations are being made on the contents of the $element object and its contained objects. Using the concepts of refactoring presented by Martin Fowler, the heuristics would suggest moving this method into the DomElement class itself. When, in the future, they are moved into the DOM XML API, a programmer would complete the same functionality with a single line of code:

```
$element->get_cdata();
```

Given that this is a common operation, this can save a programmer a lot of time. Also, it is sometimes convenient to have the DomText nodes intact, but weeding out the other types of nodes can lead to extra testing and longer code. Having a corresponding get_cdata_nodes() function will be a great addition as well when they are implemented in the future:

```
$textNodes = $element->get_cdata_nodes();
```

Instead of adding 'text' nodes with append_child(), a corresponding set_cdata() method is yet another possibility to simplify the logic used by the program.

Lack of Robustness

Due to the experimental nature of the API, there are also many cases where the functions and methods do not protect the programmer from wrongful behavior or the creation of non-standard XML 1.0. This is mainly due to the fact that the API is still in its experimental stage, so the API works but doesn't check for errors as yet.

Here are a few cases to look out for until newer versions provide internal error checking:

```php
<?php

$doc = new_xmldoc('1.0');
$root = $doc->add_child($doc->create_element('itchy'));
$root = $doc->add_child($doc->create_element('scratchy'));

print ($doc->dump_mem());
?>
```

Here, we simply create a new XML document and add two new children to the top-level DomDocument object. We know that XML documents can only have one root element or it is not a correct XML document. However, the code produces this document:

```
<?xml version="1.0"?>
<itchy/>
<scratchy/>
```

It is intended that programmers are smart enough not to add more than one root element, but the fact that it is possible suggests that we really have to check our code to ensure the results are exactly what we are looking for. The API does not protect us from these kinds of errors, mostly due to the fact that they should be handled by exceptions but that is not possible in PHP.

This problem results from the fact that DomDocument is a subclass of DomNode, which contains the add_child() method. As a result, the add_child() method was not overridden to either disallow more than one top-level element or possibly replace the old one as add_root() once did in PHP 4.1.0. In this case, we can still use the add_root() method or we'll have to be careful.

Creating Invalid Elements

The current version of the DOM XML API doesn't protect programmers from creating invalid XML elements. For instance, here is a script that creates an element that contains invalid characters:

```php
$doc = new_xmldoc('1.0');
$element = $doc->create_element('&~myelement;');
$doc->add_child($element);
print ($doc->dump_mem());
```

Although the API doesn't let us know that we have done anything wrong, the moment we parse the XML content using SAX, a browser, or any other parser of our choice, we will receive a lot of problems. When one creates the elements with hand-written code, this normally would not appear to be a large problem. However, if we are receiving programmatic, instructional data to create a DOM tree and the data being received is not valid, it is the programmer's responsibility to check this data first before passing it to any DOM XML functions and methods.

Adding One DomDocument Inside Another

Since all objects within DOM XML are DomNode objects (because they all inherit DomNode), each has an add_child() method. In most cases, this doesn't become too much of a problem but in some cases, it can crash the program. For instance, let's say we had two DomDocument trees and we wanted one tree to be added to the other. Someone might try out code like this:

```php
<?php

$doc = xmldocfile('DOC_ROOT\xpl.xml');

$doc2 = new_xmldoc('1.0');
$doc2->add_child($doc);

print ($doc2->dump_mem());
?>
```

To most people, they wouldn't even attempt this because they know that in the real world two XML documents can't be contained within each other. But once the script reaches $doc->add_child($doc);, the program will crash without any warning or error message stating that this operation cannot be done. These are just simple test cases which have not been tested as of yet, so cases like this prove that DOM XML is in its experimental stage and we should take care when writing our software.

Object-Oriented Capability

PHP has several limitations in its object-oriented nature. In most object-oriented programming languages, the classes are extendable, but in PHP, the developers have decided to hide these classes. For example, it should be impossible to extend from DomDocument and create a more object-oriented solution to these parsing problems.

Here is an example that might normally work in an object-oriented language:

```php
<?php
// testdomoo.php

class MyDocument extends DomDocument {}

$dom = new MyDocument();
$dom->add_root('stuff');
?>
```

In this test, we simply extend the DomDocument class and provide no new behavior. However, because DOM XML is so reliant on the tree construction methods, the DOM XML developers did not implement a constructor to this class. This means when the object is constructed using the new operator, none of its internal members are initialized. Because of this, there will be no parser handle initialized once the $dom object is constructed.

When executing this script, we receive the following error that indicates this:

Warning: add_root(): underlying object missing in DOC_ROOT\testdomoo.php on line 8

Warning: add_root(): cannot fetch DOM object in DOC_ROOT\testdomoo.php on line 8
object(mydocument)(0) { }

This is because there are zero members defined within the object – that's not supposed to happen. Classes, such as `DomElement`, `DomText`, and so on, also cannot be extended or instantiated with the `new` operator. This makes it impossible to extend DOM, meaning it isn't a framework that we can build from. This is a huge limitation for developers that like to use object-oriented processes in their PHP applications.

Summary

To summarize, we learned that DOM is an alternative API for parsing XML documents. Furthermore, we learnt that it can also manipulate XML because DOM possesses the ability to create, update, and delete content and structure. The architecture of DOM was discussed and several insights to the advantages and disadvantages were presented.

Later in the chapter, we discovered that DOM is a standard proposed by the standards organization, the W3C and that there are several different bindings available in different languages. DOM XML in PHP uses libxml from the GNOME project, which is not associated with the recommended bindings. After learning about libxml, we learned how to install it on the Windows and UNIX operating systems.

Once the API was installed, we went into great detail to learn the classes within the library and provided many examples. Once the chapter familiarized us with the API, we wrote applications that demonstrated parsing XML, adding XML content, and deleting nodes of an XML document.

Lastly, we spoke about DOM XML's infancy and the several limitations associated with the API. We covered a small overview of DOM Level 1 and Level 2, DOM XML's architectural shortcomings, and discussed why PHP does not currently fit these standards.

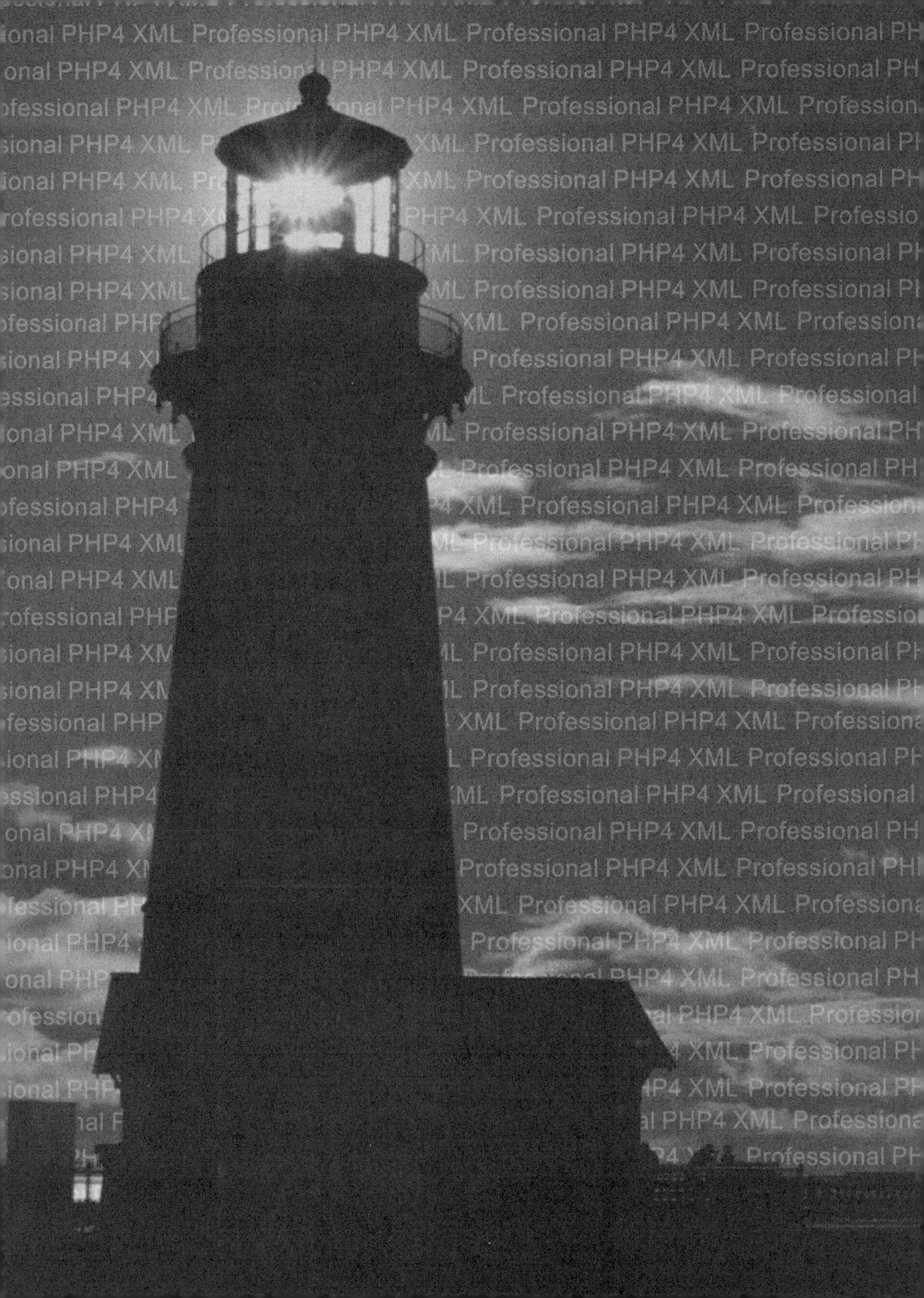
Professional PHP4 XML

7

XPath

There are times when we need a flexible way of pointing to different pieces of an XML document. XPath does exactly this – address sections of an XML document to allow us to get the exact pieces we need.

This chapter is a tutorial for learning and understanding XPath and a reference for programmers who are working with XPath.

In the course of this chapter we will look at:

❑   XPath syntax

❑   XPath expressions

❑   Axes

❑   Predicates

❑   XPath functions

❑   Predicates to manipulate bugs in the sample `bug_list.xml` file

Once we have gone through the essential XPath standards, we will detail how to use XPath from PHP:

❑   Using XPath from the DOM extension

❑   Using XPath from XSLT

XPath Defined

XPath is a syntax for selecting and accessing particular parts of an XML document. It can be used as an embedded syntax in other languages such as XSLT and as a standalone specification for XML querying.

The XML Path Language (XPath) is a standard recommendation of the World Wide Web Consortium (W3C). The W3C specification (http://www.w3.org/TR/XPath/) defines:

> *XPath is a language for addressing parts of an XML document, designed to be used both by XSL and XPointer.*

XSLT is a language for transforming XML documents. It relies on XPath to define templates that match against parts of XML documents. Chapter 8 details XSLT. The specification is available at http://www.w3.org/TR/xslt/.

XSLT uses XPath heavily as an internal way to select and process XML elements, and hence plays a vital role for every serious programmer who uses XML. Even without XSLT, XPath can be used as a powerful way to query XML documents. This is because we can perform a lot of simple queries using plain XPath expressions. Also, more sophisticated languages that are used to query documents, like XQuery, are based on XPath.

XPointer, which is based on XPath, is a language for addressing fragments of XML documents. It supports addressing into the internal structures of XML documents and allows for examination of the hierarchical document structure and choice of its internal parts based on various properties, such as element types, attribute values, character content, and relative position. See http://www.w3.org/TR/xptr/ for details about XPointer.

XQuery, a language for querying XML documents, uses XPath as its fundamental expression. Chapter 14 has a short introduction to XQuery. The specification is available at http://www.w3.org/TR/xquery/.

What XPath Can Do

Let's start with an overview of what XPath can do. As an example, we'll look at a snippet from the bug_list.xml document from Chapter 3:

```xml
<?xml version="1.0" encoding="iso-8859-1"?>
<bug_list>
  <application name="sportran compiler" version="1.1">
    <bugs>
      <bug_item>
        <title>
          It crashes when a string with more than 256 bytes is declared
        </title>
        <report_date>2002-01-28T10:15:00</report_date>
        <reported-by>John Smith</reported-by>
        <status>Open</status>
        <last_update>200201281016</last_update>
        <description>...</description>
        <severity>3</severity>
      </bug_item>
```

```
    </bugs>

    <!-- More bugs -->

  </application>
</bug_list>
```

This report can be used in several ways. For example, we can use it to solve questions that we may have about the bugs in the database:

❑ How many bugs do we have in the database?

❑ How many bugs are open and how many closed?

❑ Who are the programmers who reported bugs regarding string management?

❑ How many bugs have different reporting dates and last updated dates?

❑ Which applications have open bugs?

❑ What is the average severity of all the bugs?

❑ Which bugs were reported in the first 2 weeks of January 2002?

All these questions can be solved by an XPath expression; we only have to store, display, or manipulate the result. We will look into solving them in the *Useful Predicates* section later on in the chapter. For now let's look into some more initial concepts.

What XPath Can't Do

XPath has some limitations:

❑ **XPath is not designed for processing XML**
We can use XPath for some basic processing tasks such as computations and counting. However, using XPath as a processing tool would sooner or later lead to a problem.

❑ **XPath cannot process regular expressions**
It is best to use a parser to select tags or text from an XML document based on regular expressions.

❑ **XPath cannot perform complex mathematical operations like trigonometric functions**
We can use an XML parser or XSLT with an extension function for such tasks.

❑ **XPath cannot change an XML document**
We can use a DOM-based parser or XSLT to transform or alter a document.

❑ **XPath cannot process queries joining two or more XML documents**

How XPath Works

XPath selects elements and applies filters on them over the parsed XML document. This means that the document processed by the XPath processor will be different from the file we can see with a text editor. The entity references and CDATA sections will already be replaced in the parsed representation of the document.

Let's look at the following XML document:

```
<?xml version="1.0"?>
<foo>
  <comment><![CDATA[This is a comment]]></comment>
  <company>Johnson &amp; Johnson</company>
</foo>
```

The parsed representation is as follows:

```
<?xml version="1.0"?>
<foo>
  <comment>This is a comment</comment>
  <company>Johnson & Johnson</company>
</foo>
```

XPath Syntax

XPath uses compact non-XML syntax, so that it can be used from URIs and XML element attributes. XPath is based on a tree representation of the XML document, very similar to DOM. Here is a simple XPath tree representation:

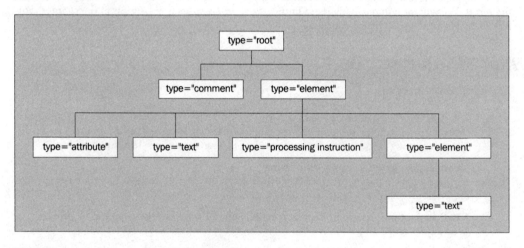

The XPath tree represents the XML root element as the root node of the tree. Subelements, comments, namespaces, Processing Instructions (PIs), and text inside the elements are represented as children of element nodes.

We can select the tree elements using access paths (similar to the paths used in the UNIX filesystem) and predicates. For example, this expression selects all the children elements (data) of the <foo> root element, in the XML document:

```
/foo/data
```

We will talk more about predicates in the *Predicates* section.

Attributes are represented in an exceptional way. Though an element node is a parent of its attribute node, the attribute node is not treated as a child of that element node. For example:

```
<foo name="smith" />
```

In this example, the element node `<foo>` is the parent of its `name` attribute. However, the `name` attribute is not a child of `<foo>`. This means that if we want the attributes of any element, we must ask for them. We don't get them as children of the element.

Nodes

In the earlier section we saw that documents can be viewed as a tree, with parents and children. We also saw that it is not just elements that form this tree; the comments, attributes, PIs, and anything else in the document also form part of the tree. For this reason, it is often useful to work with the parent/child relationships of an XML document without having to worry about whether the branches and leaves are elements, attributes, pieces of text, or anything else.

XPath uses the term **node** to refer to any part of a document, whether it be element, attribute, or otherwise.

There are seven node types in XPath:

❑ Root

❑ Element

❑ Attribute

❑ Text

❑ Processing Instruction

❑ Comment

❑ Namespace

Root

The root node contains the whole XML document, and is represented as `/`. It is the only node that doesn't have a parent but it has at least one child – the XML document element. All the comments and PIs outside the document node are also represented as its children.

> **Don't assume that `/` and `/name` (the name of the document element) are equivalent.**
> **The first one will also contain all the comments and PIs outside the document element.**
> **If we convert `/` to a string in XPath we get a string representation of all the nodes**
> **descendant from the root node.**

Element

An element node in XPath represents an XML element in the document. The element node contains all the children of the element such as text, subelements, PIs, and comments. For example:

```
<foo>Hello</foo>
```

and:

```
<foo method="one" />
```

are element nodes.

If we convert an element node to a string, we get a text representation of the text in the element, and all its subelements. We can view it as a hierarchical serialization of the element.

Attribute

Each element node has an associated set of attribute nodes, which may be empty. An attribute's parent is its containing element (even though the attribute is not considered to be a child of its parent). Therefore, we have to ask for the attribute node. Their value can be obtained by accessing them by name. For example:

```
<foo name="smith" />
```

Here, if we ask for the name attribute of this <foo> element, we get the string smith as its value.

Text

Text elements are all the text within an element. This implies that a text element can't have a preceding or following sibling that is also a text element:

```
<foo>Hello world</foo>
```

Here, Hello world is a text node, which is a child of the <foo> element node.

Processing Instruction

A PI node has two parts – a **name** and a **string value**. The string value is everything after the name, including whitespace (of course, excluding the closing ?>).

In the following example, the name node will return action and the string node will return do-something():

```
<?action do-something()?>
```

The PI node here is action.

Comment

A comment node is very simple; it contains comment text, without the opening `<!--` and closing `-->` comment declarations. For example:

```
<MyComment>
  <!--this works never touch it, never!-->
</MyComment>
```

In this example, the `<MyComment>` element node has a child comment node with a string value this works never touch it, never!.

Namespace

Namespace nodes represent the available namespaces at the element level. All namespace nodes have the element as its parent but they are not children of their parent.

Namespaces have an expanded name containing the namespace prefix. The string value of a namespace node is the URI corresponding to the namespace prefix. For example:

```
<foo xmlns:z="http://some.com">
  <z:hey>Hey</z:hey>
</foo>
```

The `<z:hey>` element will have at least two namespace nodes, one for the xml default prefix and the other for the z prefix. The namespace node for the z prefix will have z as its expanded name and if converted to string will yield http://some.com.

Namespace nodes are almost never used to query a document or an XSLT stylesheet, though they are one of the valid node types.

The XPath Representation of a Document

Having gone through the initial concepts, let's see the XPath representation of an XML document. First, the document itself:

```
<?xml version="1.0"?>
<!-- this document describes my house -->
<house>
  <bedroom name="bed1">
    This is a bedroom
    <?show src="bed1.jpg"?>
    <comment>
        This is the main bedroom
    </comment>
  </bedroom>
</house>
```

Now the XPath representation:

```
<NODE type="root" value="/">
<NODE type="comment" value="this document describes my house" />
<NODE type="element" name="house">
  <NODE type="element" name="bedroom">
    <NODE type="attribute" name="name" value="bed1" />
    <NODE type="text" value="This is a bedroom" />
    <NODE type="processing-instruction"
          name="show" value='src="bed1.jpg"' />
    <NODE type="element" name="comment">
      <NODE type="text" value="This is the main bedroom" />
    </NODE>
  </NODE>
</NODE>
```

Note that the XML syntax we used to describe the XPath view of our XML document is not standard; we used it here just for clarity.

We can also view the same representation as a tree:

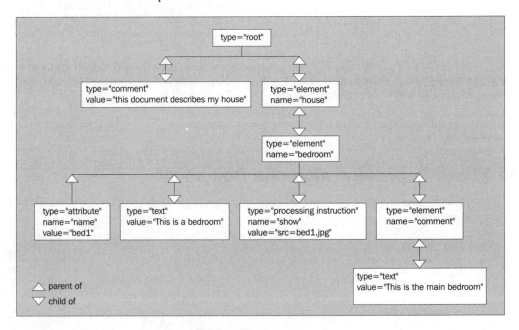

Here we have presented parent-child relationships between elements. Once again we see that attributes have a parent but they are not children of their parent. There is a 'parent' relationship between the attribute name "bed1" and the element "bedroom" but no 'child' relationship between the "bedroom" element and the "bed1" attribute.

XPath Expressions

An expression is the basic XPath construct. It is formed by a location path and a predicate (optionally). For instance, a basic location path can be:

```
/foo/name
```

The expression selects children elements (`<name>`) of the root element (`<foo>`).

An XPath expression is evaluated to yield an object, where the resultant object can be any of the following XPath data types:

❏   **Node-set**
A node-set is an unordered collection of nodes.

❏   **Boolean**
A Boolean can be TRUE or FALSE.

❏   **Number**
Numbers are expressed as floating point numbers. A number can have any double-precision 64-bit format IEEE754 value. These include a special 'Not-a-Number' (NaN) value, positive and negative infinity, and positive and negative zero.

❏   **String**
Strings are defined by a sequence of zero or more characters where characters are defined as in the XML specification.

Writing XPath Expressions

Now let's see how to write XPath expressions.

Location Paths

Location paths are used to select a node-set from an XML document. They can be written using /, which is very similar to the one we use to access files on a UNIX filesystem (we use \ on a Windows filesystem).

As with the filesystem, we can use absolute or relative paths in XPath. Absolute paths start with /, and refer to elements starting at the root of the XML document. Relative paths start without a /, and refer to the node which is the actual context of the XPath expression.

Context

XPath expressions are evaluated in a given **context**. For example, the whole XML document can be the context and then a relative path is equal to an absolute path.

The context can also be some other node of the document and in that case the relative expressions will be evaluated starting from that particular node. This often applies to expressions using predicates where first nodes are matched and then each node is evaluated against the predicate, for the predicate the node being evaluated will be the context node. We'll see more about predicates in the *Predicates* section.

For example:

```
<foo>
  <name>My files</name>
  <person>
    <name>Peter</name>
    <age>19</age>
  </person>
</foo>
```

Here:

- ❑ If <foo> is the context then the name relative path matches the <name>My files</name> element

- ❑ If <person> is the context then the name relative path matches the <name>Peter</name> element

- ❑ If the context is the whole document the name relative path returns no results since it should have been /foo/name to match the <name> element of the <foo> element

Selecting Elements

We can select elements from an XML document using location paths that can be written like this:

XPath Expression	Description
/	Matches the document
/foo	Selects the root element <foo>
/foo/data	Selects all <data> elements that descend from <foo>
/foo/*/data	Selects all <data> elements that descend from children elements of <foo> (grandchildren of <foo>)
/foo//data	Selects all data elements that descend from <foo> (children, grandchildren, grand-grand-children, and so on)
.	Selects the current node (the context node)
..	Selects the parent of the context node
../data	Selects <data> elements that descend from the parent of the context node (siblings of the context node)
application	Selects <application> elements that descend from the context node

All these expressions return node-sets. The first XPath expression in this table always returns a set of exactly one node, since we can't have more than one root element in an XML document. The rest of them can return an arbitrary number of zero or more nodes.

Selecting Text

If we select /foo/data, we will obtain a node-set containing all the <data> elements which are children of <foo> nodes. Often we may not want the <data> element, but its content; then we need to select the text() that descends from the node we are interested in. In this case, we can use the text() function:

```
/foo/data/text()
```

This selects the text of the <data> elements.

Selecting Processing Instructions

Like text, PI nodes are represented as descendants of the element where the PI is found. We access the PIs of an element using:

```
/some/data/processing-instruction()
```

If <data> has more than one PI, the result of the XPath expression will be a node-set, where each PI is a node:

```
<foo>
  <?too tool?>
    example
  <?boo bool?>
</foo>
```

The XPath expression would be:

```
/foo/processing-instruction()
```

This example returns a node-set with two nodes, one for each PI.

Selecting Comments

Comments are also represented in the XPath tree as children of the element that contains them. Comments can be obtained by using the comment() function. For example:

```
/some/data/comment()
```

This returns all the comments found in those <data> elements that are descendants of <some>.

Selecting Attributes

As mentioned earlier, attributes are not represented as descending from the element that contains them. To access attributes of a particular element, we have to use the XPath @ operator. This example selects the name attribute of all the <data> elements that are children of <foo>:

```
/foo/data/@name
```

Wildcards

XPath also provides a set of wildcards that we can use.

The * wildcard selects all children element nodes in the given context. This example selects all children element nodes of <foo>:

```
/foo/*
```

> The * wildcard selects only element nodes; comments, text, and processing
> instructions won't be selected.

The @* wildcard selects all the attributes in the given context. This will select all the attributes of the <data> element children of <foo>:

```
/foo/data/@*
```

We can select attributes for a given namespace (for example, in <foo name:pid="3" name:val="20" />) using @name:*.

The node() function selects all the nodes – elements, text, comments, and PIs – in the given context. This will select all the child nodes of <data> that are children of <foo>, regardless of their type:

```
/foo/data/node()
```

The double slash operator (//) indicates that zero or more elements may occur between the slashes. For example, /foo//data will select all <data> elements descending, directly or indirectly, from <foo>. Consider the following:

```
<foo>
  <data>some data</data>
  <other>
    <data>more text</data>
  </other>
</foo>
```

In this example, /foo//data will return both <data> elements, regardless of whether they are children, grandchildren, or great-great grandchildren of <foo>.

The // operator is very often found in expressions such as //title. This expression selects all the <title> elements in the document regardless of where they are found. This is a very simple and easy way to remember to pull all the elements with a given name.

> The // operator is usually very time consuming for the XPath processor, so use it only
> when it is really necessary.

Extended Syntax

We are now familiar with what is known as the abbreviated syntax for location paths. We'll find ourselves comfortable with the abbreviated syntax for most of our problems. However, we can also use the unabbreviated syntax that offers more power for selecting nodes. In the unabbreviated syntax, we use a combination of axes to select nodes from an XML document.

For example, this selects all the `<data>` elements that are children of the context node:

```
child::data
```

Here `child` is the axis.

Axes notation is as follows:

```
axis::name
```

There are several axes available to us, and we'll look at them in the next section.

> The samples in the following pages can be tested using the XML Cooktop tool, a freeware XML editor, which is described in the *XML Cooktop* section at the end of this chapter.

Axes

As we said before, an XPath expression is formed from a location path and a predicate; location paths are formed as sequences of **axes** used to traverse the XML document. XPath has 13 axes. Let's take a close look at what these axes are and what can they do for us.

child

The `child` axis selects all the children of the given context. For example:

```
/foo/child::data/child::name
```

is equivalent to:

```
/foo/data/name
```

Children nodes include PIs and comments. Namespaces and attributes are not selected by the child axis.

Let's consider the following XML document:

```
<doc>
<div>
  <data version="1">
```

```
      This is some text.
      <foo>bar</foo>
      <goo>other</goo>
      <obs>Yes</obs>
    </data>
    <obs>None</obs>
  </div>

  <some>
    <form>this one</form>
  </some>

  <data version="2">
    <anode>this is a node</anode>
    <!-- here's more data -->
    <bnode>Hey this is another node</bnode>
    <obs>Someone</obs>
  </data>
  </doc>
```

The child axis `//data/child::*` will result in the children of `<data>`:

```
<XPath-query query="//data/child::*">
  <foo>bar</foo>
  <goo>other</goo>
  <obs>Yes</obs>
  <anode>this is a node</anode>
  <bnode>Hey this is another node</bnode>
  <obs>Someone</obs>
</XPath-query>
```

Note that the result is presented as XML only to illustrate the example. Each element in this XML result is a node of the resultant node-set.

In this example, we select all children of all `<data>` elements in the document; the result is a node-set of 6 nodes. Note that the text child `This is some text` wasn't selected by the child axis.

parent

The parent axis selects the parent node of a given context. For example, `parent::data` selects all `<data>` elements that are descendants of the parent of the current context. The parent axis can be abbreviated as `..`, so `../data` and `parent::data` are equivalent expressions. Remember that in XML, a node can have only one parent, and the root element has no parent.

For the above XML document, the parent axis `//foo/parent::*` will result in:

```
<XPath-query query="//foo/parent::*">
  <data version="1">
    This is some text.
    <foo>bar</foo>
    <goo>other</goo>
```

```
    <obs>Yes</obs>
  </data>
</XPath-query>
```

In this case, we obtained only 1 node, the `<data>` element that is the only parent of the `<foo>` element in the document.

descendant

The `descendant` axis matches all the descendants, directly or indirectly, of the given context.

For example, `/foo/data/descendant` will return all the elements descending from `/foo/data`. This is equivalent to `/foo/data//*`. If we use `descendant` followed by a name we will match all the descendant elements with that name. So, `/foo/data/descendant::name` will match all the `<name>` elements descendant of `/foo/data`.

Note that `descendant` never returns attribute or namespace nodes since they are not children to their parent in the XPath representation of a document.

With our XML document, `/doc/div/descendant::*` will result in:

```
<XPath-query query="/doc/div/descendant::*">
  <data version="1">
    This is some text.
    <foo>bar</foo>
    <goo>other</goo>
    <obs>Yes</obs>
  </data>

  <foo>bar</foo>
  <goo>other</goo>
  <obs>Yes</obs>
  <obs>None</obs>
</XPath-query>
```

Note that as a descendant of `<div>`, we obtained the `<data>` element and all its children. This example shows the difference between the `child` and the `descendant` axis.

descendant-or-self

This behaves in the same manner as the `descendent` axis, but it also contains the context node.

ancestor

The `ancestor` axis returns the parent of the context node, the parent of the parent, and so on. This axis always returns the root node unless the context node is the root node itself. If we follow the axis with a name, then it will return all the ancestor elements with the given name. For instance, `ancestor::foo` will return all the `<foo>` ancestors of the current node; we should remember that this doesn't return all the ancestors of `<foo>`.

With the same XML document, `/doc/div/data/ancestor::*` will result in:

```
<!-- XPATH:/doc/div/data/ancestor::* -->
<XPath-query query="/doc/div/data/ancestor::*">

<doc>

<div>
  <data version="1">
    This is some text.
    <foo>bar</foo>
    <goo>other</goo>
    <obs>Yes</obs>
  </data>
  <obs>None</obs>
</div>
<some>
  <form>this one</form>
</some>
<data version="2">
  <anode>this is a node</anode>
  <!-- here's more data -->
  <bnode>Hey this is another node</bnode>
  <obs>Someone</obs>
</data>
</doc>

<div>
  <data version="1">
    This is some text.
    <foo>bar</foo>
    <goo>other</goo>
    <obs>Yes</obs>
  </data>
  <obs>None</obs>
</div>

</XPath-query>
```

In this example, we obtained 2 nodes, the root element <doc> and the <div> element, as the ancestors of the /doc/div/data element.

> **If we need ancestors, but want to skip processing the root element, we can use a predicate such as `/doc/div/data/ancestor[position()>1]`.**

ancestor-or-self

The same as the `ancestor` axis, but also includes the context node. That is, it returns all ancestors and the context node itself.

preceding

The `preceding` axis returns all the nodes that are not ancestors of the context node, and appear before the context node in the XML document.

With our XML document, `/doc/div/data/obs/preceding::*` will result in:

```
<XPath-query query="/doc/div/data/obs/preceding::*">
  <foo>bar</foo>
  <goo>other</goo>
</XPath-query>
```

following

The `following` axis returns all the nodes that are not descendants of the context node, and appear after the node in the XML document. `following` never returns attribute or namespace nodes.

With our XML document, `/doc/div/data/following::*` will result in:

```
<XPath-query query="/doc/div/data/following::*">

<obs>None</obs>

<some>
  <form>this one</form>
</some>

<form>this one</form>

<data version="2">
  <anode>this is a node</anode>
  <!-- here's more data -->
  <bnode>Hey this is another node</bnode>
  <obs>Someone</obs>
</data>

<anode>this is a node</anode>

<bnode>Hey this is another node</bnode>

<obs>Someone</obs>

</XPath-query>
```

following-sibling

This axis matches all the nodes with the same parent as the current node and which appear after the node in the XML document. If we use this axis followed by a name, it will return all the following sibling elements with that name.

With our XML file, `//goo/following-sibling::*` will result in:

```
XPath-query query="//goo/following-sibling::*">
```

```
<obs>Yes</obs>
</XPath-query>
```

preceding-sibling

The same as `following-sibling`, but all the siblings that appear before the context in the XML document are returned.

With our XML file, `//goo/preceding-sibling::*` will result in:

```
<XPath-query query="//goo/preceding-sibling::*">
<foo>bar</foo>
</XPath-query>
```

Note how the result differs from the `following-sibling` example.

self

The `self` axis matches the current context. Its equivalence in the shorter notation is a period (`.`).

For example, `//obs/` will result in:

```
<!-- XPATH://obs/. -->
<XPath-query query="//obs/.">
<obs>Yes</obs>
<obs>None</obs>
<obs>Someone</obs>
</XPath-query>
```

attribute

The `attribute` axis selects all the attributes of the context. `attribute::name` selects all the name attributes of the context. This axis is abbreviated as `@`, hence `@foo` and `attribute::foo` are equivalent. This axis will be empty unless the context node is an element.

For example, `//data/attribute::*` returns:

```
<!-- XPATH://data/attribute::* -->
results:
1
2
```

Predicates

We have looked at how to select particular elements from the XML document using location paths. However, we can't test elements to match some condition to be returned; this is what a predicate does.

> We can think about predicates as if they were the WHERE clause of a SELECT statement in SQL.

Predicates are written between square brackets following a location path. The XPath processor obtains a node-set by processing the location paths, and then each node of the node-set is tested against the predicate. If the predicate returns TRUE, then the node is passed to the resultant node-set, otherwise it is discarded. When checking nodes, the node being checked is the context node for the XPath processor. Hence, predicates normally use relative paths to test for certain conditions.

A predicate is a combination of Boolean expressions AND, OR, and NOT. We can use parentheses to group expressions, to enforce order of operations:

```
/foo/data[name/text()='smith']
```

This selects all the <data> elements that are the children of <foo>, and have a child element <name> with the text value Smith:

```
<foo>
  <data>
    <name>Smith</name>
  </data>
</foo>
```

Attributes in Predicates

The following expression selects all the <data> elements that descend from <foo>, and have a version attribute equal to the string 1.0:

```
/foo/data[@version='1.0']
```

The following example selects elements with value of version attribute as 1.0 or 1.1:

```
/foo/data[@version='1.0' OR @version='1.1']
```

When we use AND and OR expressions we may use any kind of expressions, so we need to know what is TRUE and what is FALSE for the XPath processor:

❑ **String**
A string with zero length is FALSE; a string whose length is not zero is TRUE.

❑ **Number**
Zero (positive and negative zero) and a NaN is FALSE; any other value is TRUE. A number is NaN when we try to convert hello into a number, or a number divided by 0, for example.

❑ **Node-set**
An empty node-set is FALSE while a non-empty node-set is TRUE.

To check for <data> elements that descend from <foo> that have a <b> element, we can use:

```
/foo/data[b]
```

We can use a predicate to select a particular node of a node-set. For example:

```
/foo/data[position()=1]
```

or:

```
/foo/data[1]
```

This will select the first `<data>` element child of `<foo>`. The expression will return a node-set with only one node or an empty node-set.

The following expression will return the first `<data>` element child of `<foo>`, regardless of its content, or all data elements child of `<foo>` that have a child element name with text value equal to `john`:

```
/foo/data[position()=1 or name/text()='john']
```

We have a lot of querying power by using XPath but let's add even more power by using XPath functions.

XPath Functions

The XPath standard defines a collection of functions that we can use in predicates. These XPath functions can deal with numbers, strings, and node-sets, and perform a nice collection of things we may want to do. We are going to see these functions grouped by the data type they manipulate.

Boolean Functions

Here is a list of the XPath Boolean functions:

❑ `boolean(object)` – This function converts the argument into a Boolean value. The conversion rules are:

   ❑ A number is TRUE if and only if it is not zero (positive zero or negative zero)

   ❑ A node set is TRUE if it is non-empty

   ❑ A string is TRUE if its length is greater than zero

❑ `not()` – This function will negate the Boolean expression passed as an argument

❑ `true()` – This function returns the Boolean value TRUE

❑ `false()` – This function returns FALSE

❑ `lang(string)` – This function returns TRUE or FALSE depending on whether the language of the context node specified by the `xml:lang` attribute is the same as, or is a sublanguage of, the language passed as the argument string.

Number Functions

This is a list of the XPath number functions:

❑ `number()` – This function tries to convert an XPath object to a number:

   ❑ If the argument is a Boolean value, TRUE is converted to 1 and FALSE to 0

❑ If the argument is a string, it will be converted to the number it represents, if possible; or to NaN, if the string can't be recognized as a number

❑ If the argument is a node-set, it will be converted to a string, and then the string will be converted to a number following the preceding rules

❑ `sum(nodeset)` – This function returns the sum of the nodes in the node-set. The nodes are converted to string values, and then to numbers to perform the operation.

❑ `floor(number)` – This function will return the largest integer number less than or equal to the argument; non-integer numbers will be rounded down.

❑ `ceiling(number)` – This function will return the smallest integer value which is equal to or greater than the argument. Non-integer numbers will be rounded up.

❑ `round(number)` – This function rounds a floating point number to the closest integer.

Arithmetic Operations

We can use numbers to perform basic arithmetic operations. We can use +, -, *, mod, and `div` between two numbers or the unary operation (-) to negate a number.

Comparing Numbers

We can compare numbers using =, !=, $<$, $>$, $>=$, and $<=$ operators.

Comparing Strings

We can compare strings using <, >, <=, = , and != operators.

String Functions

Let's take a look at the XPath string functions:

❑ `string()` – This function converts an object of any type to a string. It is important to understand how XPath deals with some objects when we treat them as strings:

❑ If the argument is a node-set, it will be converted to a string by returning the string value of the first node in the node-set. If the node-set is empty then an empty string, which is `false`, is returned.

❑ Numbers are converted to the string representation of the number; certain special numbers may generate special strings such as NaN, Infinity, -Infinity.

❑ If the argument is a Boolean, FALSE is converted to the string `false` and TRUE is converted to `true`.

❑ `concat(string, string, string*)` – This function returns a string with the concatenation of all the arguments. Note that the function may receive an arbitrary number of arguments.

❑ `starts-with(string_source, string)` – This function returns TRUE, if the source string (the first argument) starts with the string passed as the second argument, otherwise it returns FALSE.

❑ `substring-before(string, string)` – This function returns the substring of the first argument that can be found before the second string appears in the first one. It will return an empty string if the first argument doesn't contain the second one, or if the first argument starts with the second argument (then there's nothing before). For example:

```
substring-before('hey this is a test!','this')
```

This will return: 'hey ', including the whitespace before 'this'.

We can use single quotes or double quotes for strings in XPath. However, in the XML Cooktop tool we must use single quotes. Hence, we'll be using single quotes in the examples dealing with strings.

❑   substring-after(string, string) – This function will return the string that can be found in the first argument, after the second one appears in it. For example:

```
substring-after('hey this is a test!','this')
```

will return: is a test!.

❑   substring(string, number, number) – This function returns the substring of the first argument starting at the position indicated in the second argument. If the third argument is present, it will return that number of characters. Positions in a string are numbered starting with 1 in XPath, so the first character of a string can be extracted with substring(string,1,1).

> **Characters in XPath strings are numbered starting with 1; this differs from PHP, Java, Perl, and many programming languages.**

This example:

```
substring('hey his is a test!',3,4)
```

will return: y th.

❑   string-length(string) – This will return the number of characters in a string. If the argument is omitted, it defaults to the string representation of the context node.

❑   normalize-space(string) – This useful function returns the result of trimming leading and trailing whitespace from the string, and replacing sequences of whitespace characters by a single space.

Consider this:

```
<foo>This is the value of foo</foo>
```

If we get the text element inside <foo>, the result will have line breaks and spaces. If we only want the non-whitespace text in the string, we can use normalize-space(/foo/text()).

> **When the result of an XPath expression or a portion of the result of an XSLT transformation has a lot of unwanted whitespace, tabulations, and line breaks, we will use the normalize-space() function to remove it.**

❑ translate(string, string, string) – This function will make a character-by-character translation of the string passed as the first argument. The translation is defined by the second and third string. If the second and third arguments have equal length then the mapping will replace each character of the second argument with the character in the same position in the third argument. If the third string doesn't have a character for a character in the second argument, that character will be removed from the original string. For example:

```
translate('hey this is a test','aeiou','AEIOU')
```

This will result in: hEy thIs Is A tEst.

The translate() function cannot perform case conversion for all the languages.

Node-Set Functions

Here is a list of the node-set functions:

❑ last() – Returns a number equal to the context size from the expression evaluation context. In other words, if our location path matches 10 nodes, it will return 10.

❑ number() – Returns a number equal to the context position of the node being processed.

❑ number(nodeset) – Returns the number of nodes in the given node-set, the node-set can be any expression returning a node-set (including any kind of XPath expression).

❑ id(object) – This function selects elements by their unique ID. When the argument is of type nodeset, then the result is the union of the result of applying id() to the string value of each node in the node-set. When the argument is any other type, it is converted to a string, and the string is split into a whitespace-separated list of tokens. The result is a node-set containing the elements in the same document as the context node that have a unique ID equal to any of the tokens in the list.

❑ local-name() – The function returns the local part of the expanded name of the first node in the node-set. If the node-set is omitted then the context node becomes the node-set.

❑ namespace-uri() – This function returns the local part of the expanded name of the node in the argument node-set that is first in document order. If the argument node-set is empty, or the first node has no expanded name, an empty string is returned. If the argument is omitted, it defaults to a node-set with the context node as its only member.

❑ count() – This function returns the number of nodes in the given node-set, or in the current context if the argument is omitted.

Applying a Function to an XPath Expression

As we've seen until now, XPath expressions return a node-set. We can apply a function to the XPath expression to return a string, or a number.

This example:

```
count(/foo/data)
```

counts all the <data> elements that descend from <foo>.

> If the XML document we are processing uses namespaces, we have a `<xxx:foo>` tag, and we want to access it as `<foo>`, the `local-name()` function can be used to get the `foo` part of the tag.

Useful Predicates

Let's use this XML report to solve some questions that we may have about the bugs in the database we saw earlier:

- ❑ How many bugs do we have in the database?
- ❑ How many bugs are open and how many are closed?
- ❑ Which programmers reported bugs regarding string management?
- ❑ How many bugs have different reporting date and last updated date?
- ❑ Which applications have open bugs?
- ❑ What is the average severity of all the bugs?
- ❑ Which bugs were reported in the first 2 weeks of January 2002?

All these questions can be responded to by an XPath expression. We will now solve each of the questions using what we have learned about XPath.

How Many Bugs Do We Have in the Database?

To solve this question, we'll use the XPath `count()` function on a node-set that represents each bug in the database as a node. Hence, each `<bug_item>` will become a node in the node-set:

```
/bug_list/application/bugs/bug_item
```

Since we are counting `<bug_item>` elements regardless of where they occur in the document, the following also works:

```
//bug_item
```

Thus, our expression can be:

```
count(/bug_list/application/bugs/bug_item)
```

or:

```
count(//bug_item)
```

Both will return 7, which is the number of bugs we currently have in our sample XML document.

If we use the unabbreviated notation, the same expression will look like this:

```
count(/child::bug_list/child::application/child::bugs/child::bug_item)
```

This is why we normally use the abbreviated syntax, unless we need a specific axis that cannot be represented in the abbreviated notation.

How Many Bugs Are Open and How Many Are Closed?

This question is very similar to the first one, but we need to filter bugs depending on their status, so that the expression we built for the first question can be used by applying a predicate:

```
count(//bug_item[status/text()='Open' or status/text()='open'])
count(//bug_item[status/text()='Closed' or status/text()='closed'])
```

This is almost right, if the XML writer application always writes the `<status>` elements as `<status>Open</status>`. In this case the expression works, but if the XML has something like:

```
<status>
    closed
</status>
```

it won't match, because it has whitespace around, and the strings won't be equal. We can use the `normalize-space()` function to handle this problem:

```
count(//bug_item[normalize-space(status/text())='Open'
                or normalize-space(status/text())='open'])
count(//bug_item[normalize-space(status/text())='Closed'
                or normalize-space(status/text())='closed'])
```

This will show that we have 4 open bugs and 3 closed bugs. Here, we checked for both `Open` and `open`, since the application is case-sensitive, with XPath and XML being case-sensitive.

> If we are comparing `something/text()` with a literal, we must use `normalize-space()` to prevent elements with whitespace decorations not being matched by the expression.

Which Programmers Reported Bugs Regarding String Management?

We need to find bugs that have the word `string` in their title, and then list the programmers who have reported that bug. Since the result will be a node-set of programmers, our location path can be written as follows:

```
/bug_list/application/bugs/bug_item/reported-by
```

Now, we have to add a predicate to filter only those authors reporting bugs dealing with string management. We can use the `contains()` function, to find if the title of the bug has the word `string`. The expression would be:

```
/bug_list/application/bugs/bug_item/reported-
by[contains(../title/text(),'string')]
```

271

The result:

```
<XPath-query query="/bug_list/application/bugs/bug_item/reported-
by[contains(../title/text(),'string')]">
  <reported-by>John Smith</reported-by>
  <reported-by>Mike Brown</reported-by>
</XPath-query>
```

is a node-set with two nodes containing `<reported-by>` elements.

Here we referred to the title of the bug that is relative to the `<reported-by>` element, using `../title/text()`. We didn't need to use the `normalize-space()` function here, since we are using `contains()`. Hence, if there's a whitespace in the string, we search with `contains()`.

> In most of the expressions we write, predicates should use relative paths to filter information based on the context node being processed.

If a programmer reports more than one bug with the word `string` in the title, XPath will return the number of times the word appears in separate reports. If we want to obtain unique author names, we'll have to filter the result in the language where we used XPath, for example, PHP or XSLT.

How Many Bugs Have a Different Reporting Date and Last Update Date?

This will also use the `count()` function, and we have to select bugs so we can use the expression:

```
//bug_item
```

Now, we have to write a predicate that filters only those bugs with different `<report_date>` and `<last_update>`:

```
count(//bug_item[normalize-space(report_date/text()) != normalize-
space(last_update/text())])
```

The result will be a node-set with just one node that is a number indicating the number of bugs that match the condition. For example:

```
<!-- XPATH:count(//bug_item[normalize-space(report_date/text()) != normalize-
space(last_update/text())]) -->
result: 5
```

In XML Cooktop use:
s:count(//bug_item[normalize-space(report_date/text()) !=
normalize-space(last_update/text())]) since we want the expression to return a
value.

Which Applications Have Open Bugs?

In this query, we need the names of applications; therefore, we need a node-set with attribute names. The location path would be like this:

```
/bug_list/application/@name
```

This XPath expression returns all the values of the attribute names. Note that the node-set contains strings with the values of the name attribute, not elements.

The predicate needs to filter applications with open bugs:

```
/bug_list/application/@name[
                    normalize-space(../bugs/bug_item/status/text())='open'
             or normalize-space(../bugs/bug_item/status/text()='Open')]
```

Note how we accessed the <application> element with '..' and then moved to the status of bugs for the application. The XPath processor will analyze all the <bug_item> elements of the application. If one of them has the open status, then the predicate will be TRUE and the name of the application will be passed to the resultant node-set.

Note that the last text() component of each path is not needed, since the string value of the <status> element will be its text content. However, when an element may contain text() and subelements, like this:

```
<foo>
  <data>
  This is some text
  <obs>Yes</obs>
  </data>
</foo>
```

then those values differ.

In the example, string(/foo/data) and string(/foo/data/text()) are different. Therefore:

```
string(/foo/data)
```

will result in:

This is some text

while:

```
string(/foo/data/text())
```

will result in:

This is some text
Yes

273

> We can often omit the use of the `text()` function relying on the string value of the element. If the element contains subelements then the `text()` and the `string-value()` of the element can be different. We'll use `text()` if we need to compare the text content of an element that admits subelements.

What Is the Average Severity of All the Bugs?

Here, a computation needs to be performed in XPath to find the average. We need to sum all the severities and divide by the number of severity element, like this:

```
sum(//severity/text()) div count(//severity)
```

The result will again be a number. We could have divided by the number of bugs, but the presented expression is clearer.

Which Bugs Were Reported in the First Two Weeks of January 2002?

This query will make us operate with dates. If we take a close look at the XML document, we'll notice that the dates are written in ISO format, that is, YYYYMMDDHHMM. Therefore, finding bugs reported in the first 2 weeks of January means that the <report_date> of the bug has to be less than 200201160000 and greater than 200112310000. We'll list the bug titles for those matching these criteria:

```
//bug_item/title[normalize-space(../report_date/text()) < '2002-01-16T00:00:00']
```

Now, we'll have the titles of the bugs:

```
//bug_item/title[normalize-space(../report_date/text()) &lt; '2002-01-
16T00:00:00']
```

> If we use this expression inside an XSLT stylesheet, we must write the < character as an XML entity, since the XSLT stylesheet is a valid XML document. Many XPath processors use XSLT, so we may also need to escape the < sign.

Now that we have gone through the XPath standards, let's look into using XPath from PHP.

Using XPath from PHP

We can use XPath from a PHP script in two ways:

❑ Use XPath directly using the DOM extension and the `xpath_eval()` function of PHP

❑ Process an XSLT stylesheet with PHP

First, we'll look at the `xpath_eval()` function, and then we'll describe how to use XPath from XSLT stylesheets.

> We need PHP compiled with `--with-dom` for the DOM extension for `xpath_eval()` function to work. See Chapter 6 for more details.

Using XPath from the DOM Extension

> Examples in this section were done with PHP 4.2.0. These examples won't work with previous versions of PHP since the DOM extension has been changed for PHP 4.2. The DOM extension is experimental and may yet change in future versions.

To use XPath from PHP we first need to parse the XML document into a DOM tree using the DOM functions:

❑ `domxml_open_mem()` which parses an XML document from a PHP string

❑ `domxml_open_file()` which parses an XML document from a file

> The `domxml_open_mem()` function is a replacement for the `xmldoc()` function while `domxml_open_file()` is a replacement for `xmldocfile()`. If the PHP installation doesn't have these functions we can use the old ones instead, taking into account that they will be deprecated in a future PHP release.

We'll see an example step-by-step. First, we define an example XML document:

```php
<?php
$xml='
<foo>
  <person>
    <name>A</name>
    <age>10</age>
  </person>
  <person>
    <name>B</name>
    <age>15</age>
  </person>
  <person>
    <name>C</name>
    <age>16</age>
  </person>
</foo>';
?>
```

We'll execute the XPath `//name` expression and return the list of names from this document.

Now we parse the document using DOM:

```php
$doc = domxml_open_mem($xml);
```

We use `domxml_open_mem()` since we are parsing the XML document from the `$xml` string.

Then we have to initialize the XPath engine and create an XPath context object:

```
$xpath = $doc->xpath_init();
$ctx = $doc->xpath_new_context();
```

`$ctx` is now an object from the `XPathContext` class. The class provides a method to evaluate XPath expressions – the `xpath_eval()` method. So our next step will be executing the XPath query:

```
$result = $ctx->xpath_eval("//name");
```

The `xpath_eval()` method returns an XPath object, the object contains a `nodeset` property with the result of the query. So we get the node-set:

```
$nodes = $result->nodeset;
```

Here, `$nodes` is an array of `DomXMLNode` objects.

That's all from XPath, from now on we have to process the `DomNodes` using the DOM extension methods and manipulate them to render/find the appropriate result. As an example we'll see how to iterate through the node-set and show the text value of each `<name>` element in the node-set:

```
foreach ($nodes as $node) {
  $children = $node->child_nodes();
  foreach ($children as $child) {
    $cosa = $child->node_type();
    if ($child->node_type() == XML_TEXT_NODE) {
      $data = $child->get_content();
      print ("Name: $data <br />");
    }
  }
}
?>
```

Here we use the `child_nodes()` method to get the children of each node in the node-set, then we can traverse the children and if the node is a text node we get the content and output it to the browser.

This is the output:

Evaluating Expressions with Namespaces

What happens if we have a document that uses namespaces and we want to evaluate an XPath expression on the document? For example:

```
<foo xmlns:z="http://localhost">
  <person>
    <z:name>A</z:name>
    <age>10</age>
  </person>

  <person>
    <z:name>B</z:name>
    <age>15</age>
  </person>

  <person>
    <z:name>C</z:name>
    <age>16</age>
  </person>
</foo>
```

If we want to evaluate //z:name we can't use the expression as-is or we will get an error. To make the expression work we have to 'register' the z namespace first.

To register a namespace we use the XPathContext method register_ns(). The method takes two arguments – the namespace prefix and the namespace URI. For example:

```
$ctx->xpath_register_ns("z", "http://localhost");
```

Once the namespace is registered we can query //z:name normally.

This example shows a query using namespaces:

```
<?php
$xml = '
<foo xmlns:z="http://localhost">
<person>
  <z:name>A</z:name>
  <age>10</age>
</person>

<person>
  <z:name>B</z:name>
  <age>15</age>
</person>

<person>
  <z:name>C</z:name>
  <age>16</age>
</person>
</foo>';

$doc = domxml_open_mem($xml);

$xpath = $doc->xpath_init();
$ctx = $doc->xpath_new_context();
$ctx->xpath_register_ns("z", "http://localhost");
$result = $ctx->xpath_eval("//z:name");
$nodes = $result->nodeset;
foreach ($nodes as $node) {
```

```
      $children = $node->child_nodes();
      foreach ($children as $child) {
        $cosa = $child->node_type();
        if ($child->node_type() == XML_TEXT_NODE) {
          $data = $child->get_content();
          print ("Name: $data <br />");
        }
      }
  }
  ?>
```

Thus we evaluate an XPath expression and get an array of DomNode objects.

Chapter 6 details what we can do with DomNode objects and how to manipulate them. It covers the new DOM extension in PHP 4.2 describing the classes and methods that we can use.

Using XPath from XSLT

XSLT is an extremely powerful language used to process, validate, and transform an XML document. Many XSLT attributes accept an XPath expression as an argument.

Though we'll be covering XSLT in detail in the next chapter, let's take a look at the very basic XSLT we may need to process XPath queries.

Here, we have a basic XSLT stylesheet:

```
<xsl:stylesheet version="1.0"
              xmlns:xsl="http://www.w3.org/1999/XSL/Transform">
  <xsl:output method="text" />
  <xsl:template match="/bug_list/application/bugs/bug_item">
    Title: <xsl:value-of select="normalize-space(title)" />
  </xsl:template>
</xsl:stylesheet>
```

The first line declares the XML as a stylesheet, and declares the namespace, xsl, to be used in the stylesheet. The second line tells the XSLT processor that the output will be plaintext, other options are XML or HTML. Then we declare a template.

In this case, the template will match all the <bug_item> elements in the XML document. The XSLT processor parses the XML document and applies the template that best matches the element being processed. For XPath processing, we only need one template, and we put the XPath expression in the match attribute.

Inside the template, we can write the code necessary to process the node-set returned by the XPath expression. In this case, we use the <xsl:value-of> instruction to write the content of the <title> child of each node in the node-set. Note that the <xsl:value-of> instruction also uses an XPath expression in the select attribute, and that expression is relative to each node in the node-set being processed by the template.

For now, we will simply use our template XSLT for testing XPath expressions.

XML Cooktop

XML Cooktop is a freeware XML editor with many features, such as XML validating and editing, XSLT processing, and XSLT editing with snippets of code. One of its features is an **XPath console**. We only have to edit or load an XML document, and we can test XPath expressions for that document on the console. If we want to develop XSLT stylesheets, the XPath console is very useful to test and debug XPath expressions.

To use the XPath console in XML Cooktop, we have to type an XPath expression in one of the following ways:

- ❑ n:EXPRESSION – when we want the processor to return a node-set
- ❑ s:EXPRESSION – when we want the processor to return a single string/numeric value
- ❑ v:EXPRESSION – when we want the processor to return several string/numeric values

Let's consider the following example:

```
n:/foo/data
```

This returns a node-set with all <data> elements that descend from <foo>.

The following screenshot shows two XPath queries we performed using XML Cooktop on our sample XML document with the list of bugs. In the first one, we get a node-set for all the <title> elements in the document; and in the second one, we get all the titles in a string form:

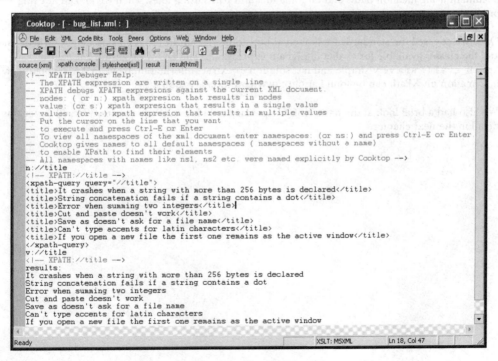

XML Cooktop is available for download at http://www.xmlcooktop.com/.

Xalan

Xalan is an XSLT processor developed by the Apache Software Foundation (ASF). We can obtain Xalan in Java or C++; the latter can be used from a Perl extension. If we want to use Xalan for PHP, we'll need to interface with Xalan Java, Xalan C++, or Xalan Perl.

There are several ways to use Xalan from PHP. We can create an XSLT TCP/IP server in Java, C++, or Perl, and use it from PHP by passing the XML and XSL data. We can also build an XSLT web service – for example, using XML-RPC – and use it from PHP.

Xalan is a very powerful processor, and supports the whole XSLT specification. It runs well in most UNIX environments. More information about Xalan can be found at http://xml.apache.org/.

Summary

XPath is a standard syntax for querying and accessing elements of an XML document. While it has some limitations it can be successfully applied to many of the queries we need to make on an XML document. When used from XSLT it can be a great way to extract or transform information from an XML document.

In this chapter we have learned the fundamentals of the XPath language and how to use XPath expressions to query XML documents. We looked at writing simple expressions to address parts of the document using location paths and building location paths using axes. Then we looked at using predicates to filter results and query documents for specific information.

Once we covered the standards we looked at how to use XPath from PHP using the DOM extension and the classes available for evaluating XPath expressions. The DOM extension lets us use xpath_eval() as a very simple and fast solution to extract information from an XML document. More information on XPath can be found at http://www.w3.org/TR/xpath/.

We also had a brief look at the basic XSLT necessary to process XPath queries. We will cover this in detail in the next chapter.

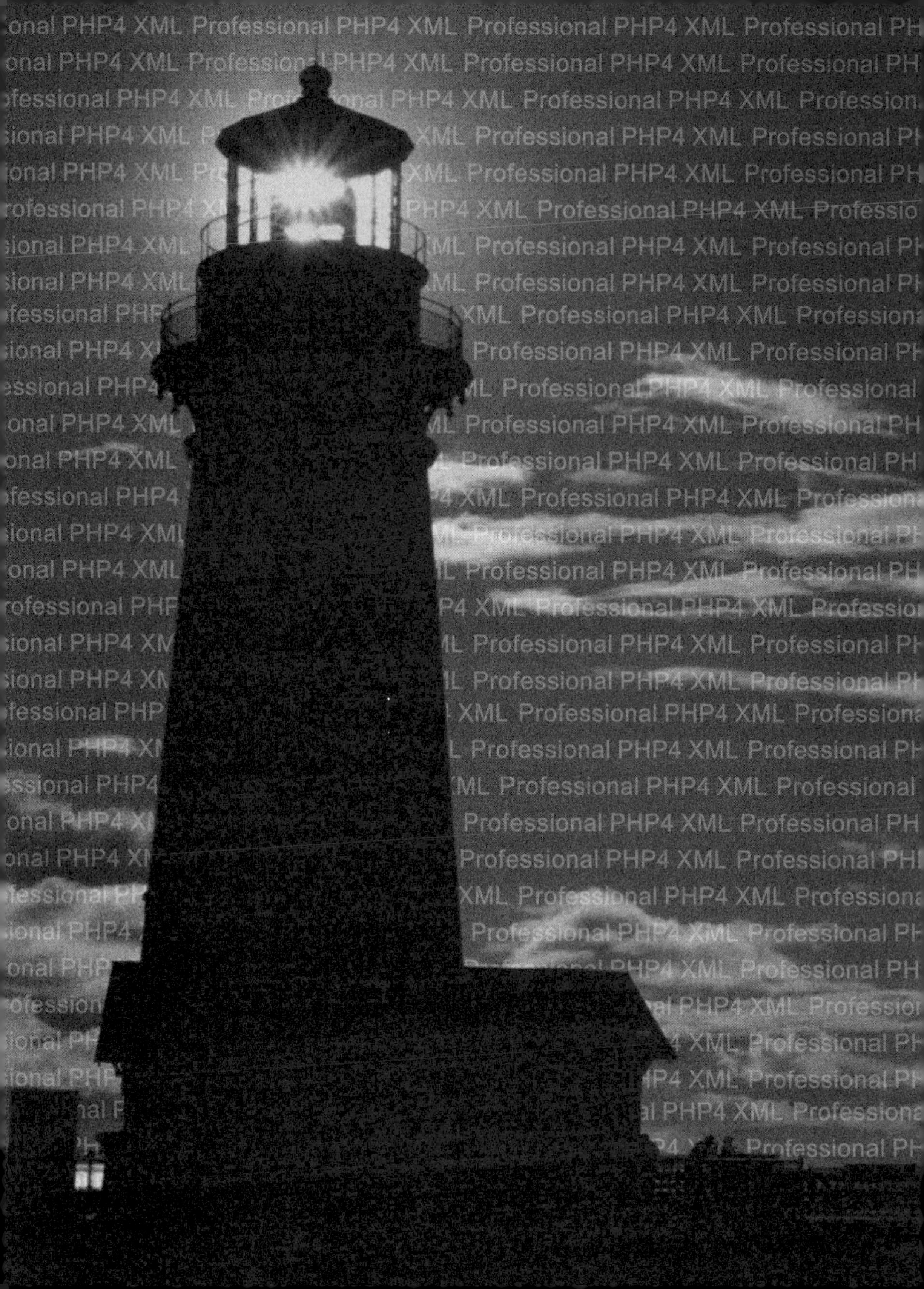
Professional PHP4 XML

8

XSL

In previous chapters, we used parsers to accomplish several tasks, such as computing the average amount of money allocated to a list of vendors, maintaining a set of bugs in an XML bug database, and displaying article content in HTML. In fact, since XML is actually data in a hierarchical format, we can interpret the data any way we like. This is why XML has gained popularity in the enterprise application field.

Another advantage is that it is a third-party standard that two companies can use to exchange information without controlling the standard. For instance, we might want to convert one XML document structure to a more widely accepted vocabulary, or perhaps one of our own. As in the past, we might take the XML data and provide an XHTML representation for it. Rather than using parsers to solve all these XML-related problems, there is another way to solve this small subset of XML-related issues – the **Extensible Stylesheet Language** (XSL).

In the last chapter, we learned that XPath is a language to query structure and content in an XML document. It is very useful because a simple series of characters can replace several lines of PHP code. In the case of DOM, xpath_eval() was used to retrieve DomElement sets without having to iterate through the entire document, thus removing one of DOM's extreme disadvantages of writing lots of code. XPath is a standard used with XSL documents and in this chapter we will learn XSL in great detail.

In the course of the chapter we will look at:

- ❑ XSL documents and XSLT (Extensible Stylesheet Language Transformations)
- ❑ Advantages of incorporating XSL into our web applications
- ❑ Applications using XSL

❑   Structure of an XSL document

❑   Examples illustrating XSL features:

   ❑   Creating HTML representations of XML content

   ❑   Creating static PHP scripts

   ❑   Transforming one XML document into another XML vocabulary

❑   Using XSL documents in PHP with Sablotron:

   ❑   Installing Sablotron on Windows and UNIX

   ❑   Transforming XSL documents using Sablotron

   ❑   Sablotron functions

❑   Using an object-oriented XSLT processor

❑   Creating a web site using XSL

This chapter will bring us up to speed on how to incorporate basic XML building blocks into our web applications using PHP. XPath and XSL are considered to be the core technologies when working with XML documents.

Transforming vs. Parsing

Oftentimes when a project is using XML documents, or when the developers are debating to use more XML on the project, the topic of transforming vs. parsing comes up. Take for example parsing an XML document to generate an XHTML representation. In the previous chapters, many of the examples discussed did exactly that. However, we can as easily transform an XML document into XHTML using XSLT. What are the benefits and disadvantages with either technique? That is what we are going to discuss in this section.

Presentation Transformations

A parser like SAX or DOM is probably too complicated for simple operations and sometimes chaotic for document translation or document generation applications (like converting XML to an HTML or WML document). This is because SAX parsers require more overhead to specify the function definitions and switch statements, and DOM parsers require even more to do the actual traversals within the program.

Therefore, XSL is a tool that can be used to deal with many XML problems – not as many as SAX and most certainly not as many as DOM – but it is much easier and more productive to construct XSL documents than it is to construct hand-coded parsers. Since markup documents are usually very small, there is not a strong need to use SAX for its ability to parse documents of a large size.

When Portability Is a Concern

XSL provides a completely portable, declarative solution for a very small set of XML-related applications, making it easy to use and maintain when it can be exploited. In the SAX chapter, we processed XML content and converted it into HTML. This approach is often very unclean because the mixture of HTML and PHP code can become extremely obfuscated. XSL provides a solution that is very clean and easy to maintain and is preferred over SAX.

Complex Computations

Unlike the complexities of choosing between SAX and DOM (with the XPath functions), the choice is very simple when we are required to deal with programs that require complex computations. As we learned in the last chapter, although XPath is a very expressive and powerful language when referencing XML structure and content, it cannot solve every problem like a programming language can. Its usefulness runs out when the calculations are extremely complicated, the token recognizing on the target XML document is not sophisticated enough, or XPath does not provide the necessary functions for complex computations.

XSL cannot solve large computational problems and cannot interface with programming languages like PHP. For instance, it would be impossible to generate user-defined PHP objects using XSLT or selecting nodes using regular expressions (because XPATH cannot select nodes based on regular expressions whereas PHP can within a SAX event handler). SAX can be used to allow complete control over how XML is structured and how content is interpreted using functions, classes, and constructs provided by a programming language. Therefore, it is suggested that SAX be used alone or DOM be used with XPath for these.

Document Size

For huge XML documents that have to be processed online (and offline), we need to use SAX due to its fast, single-pass nature and low overhead. Using DOM or XSLT can be very slow for such documents because the software for these services is often very complicated, conserves more memory, and has a high overhead.

For medium-sized documents or small documents, XSLT can usually be the best approach because of its elegance of language definitions, maintenance, and portability benefits. DOM and SAX can also be used if the application is very simple, or if you need to integrate with program code of your application inside the SAX event handlers, or when working with DOM.

Creating New Documents

If you have to generate new documents, your options are limited to SAX and DOM. Although XSLT can create XML documents, it can only use content that is already provided in XML form. DOM is your number one choice for creating new XML content because the API allows you to do so easily and fluently due to its tree-like nature. The SAX API doesn't have any mechanism for creating documents, but as you parse the content, it is possible to create your own library to construct XML documents within the event handlers. Although this is much harder than using DOM, you can still do it.

In a nutshell, the answer to our original question of whether to use XSL instead of a parser isn't extremely complicated if you take all these issues into consideration. Usually, just pick the simplest tool for the job. If the problem can be solved with XSL and we don't see any possibility of the application increasing in complexity, then XSL is the way to go. Otherwise, we must use either a SAX or DOM parser for increased programmatic control and extra functionality. Remember that XSL documents are portable whereas hand-coded parsers are not.

XSL

XSL is a specification proposed by the W3C that describes how XML documents can be recognized, styled, and transformed. This is similar to Cascading Style Sheets (CSS) used on HTML documents but is much more powerful. In fact, CSS is just one of the many technologies that can be used to style XML documents, but there are many more technologies that encompass XSL.

XSL is made of up of several components:

❑ XSLT (XSL Transformations)

❑ XPath (Querying)

❑ XSL-FO (XSL Formatting Objects)

The last technology, XSL-FO, is very similar to CSS but the language embeds itself into XSL documents. However, this technology is not very common and has not gained widespread use. PHP has not adopted this specification as of yet, but XSLT and XPath are currently supported by PHP 4.1.2. Since we have already covered XPath in Chapter 7, in this chapter we concentrate on XSLT – the specification for transforming XML documents. To learn XSLT, it is important that you first understand XPath before taking on XSLT.

XSL is a type of XML that can be looked upon as a complete language that describes several rules on how a source document can be transformed into a target document. This means that one XML document can be converted into another XML document like XHTML or WML, an HTML document, or simply plain text. Although these inputs and outputs can be defined as documents, they may be strings that contain XML content as well. An XSLT processor conducts the transformation of the XML document. Here is an illustration of the process:

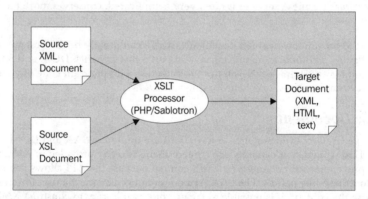

The XSLT Processor

The XSLT processor uses a high-level declarative language that follows the W3C specifications. These specifications dictate how the processor is supposed to behave, given an XSL and XML document, to generate the proper target document, regardless of programming language or platform.

In this chapter we shall use the **Sablotron** processor, developed by Gingerall (http://www.gingerall.com/charlie/ga/act/index.act). The implementation of this processor is almost XSLT 1.0 compliant (the working draft). Since the processor was written for C++ applications, to use it within PHP requires an extension. For both Windows and UNIX releases, the latest Sablotron extension is distributed with PHP 4.1.0 and higher. If you are using PHP with Windows, you have the added bonus of receiving the Sablotron processor DLLs as well. Although the W3C has developed XSLT 1.1 (abandoned) and XSLT 2.0 (in production), these new specifications are not implemented in PHP as of yet.

The latest version of Sablotron (0.81) has undergone many revisions. The entire API is completely remodeled from the ground up from the one introduced in PHP 4.0.6 to allow for more extensibility and flexibility.

Enabling Sablotron

In this section we will see how to install Sablotron on both UNIX and Windows environments.

Enabling Sablotron On Windows

Installing Sablotron is a fairly simple task on a Windows machine. The first step is to find and open the `php.ini` file. Search for the section labeled `Windows Extensions` and locate the following lines in the file under this section:

```
;Windows Extensions

;extension=php_iconv.dll
;extension=php_xslt.dll
```

These lines will be located in different positions, listed in alphabetical order. Uncomment them by deleting the beginning semi-colon (;).

For these PHP wrapper libraries to work correctly, some DLL files must be located within the Windows PATH. To get the latest versions, go to the Ginger Alliance web site (http://www.gingerall.com/charlie/ga/xml/d_sab.xml), and download the latest Sablotron 0.81 FullPack (Sablotron, iconv, JavaScript). Unzip the binary to a temporary location and copy the files to the Windows `system` directory (this directory is called `c:\windows\system32` for Windows 9x, ME, and XP systems, and `c:\winnt\system32` for Windows NT and 2000).

This can be done by executing the following command:

```
cd C:\tempxslt\
copy js-1.5rc4\js32.dll libiconv-1.7\iconv.dll sablot-0.81\sablot.dll
C:\WINDOWS\system32
```

Also, make sure that the following `.dll` files from the PHP directory are copied to the system directory:

```
cd C:\php\dlls
copy libxml2.dll xmltok.dll xmlparse.dll c:\windows\system32
```

After these files have been copied, it may be necessary to reboot the web server and possibly the system itself for everything to run correctly. Now, Sablotron should be installed and operating correctly with the PHP installation.

Enabling Sablotron On UNIX

To install Sablotron on UNIX, we must have **Expat** installed on our system. Most distributions of Linux (RedHat, Mandrake, and Debian) have these packages available. However, FreeBSD does not come with the Expat C libraries preinstalled, hence the Sablotron sources cannot compile. To download the latest version of Expat, go to the project's web site on SourceForge (http://sourceforge.net/projects/expat/), and download the latest compressed `.tar` file. At the time of writing, the latest version is 1.95.2.

After the download is complete, copy the file to the location where the sources are stored (usually /usr/local/src) and execute the following commands to uncompress the files:

```
# gunzip expat-1.95.2.tar.gz
# tar xf expat-1.95.2.tar
# rm expat-1.95.2.tar
```

Once the package has been uncompressed, we can install the package using a typical configure, make, and make install process:

```
# cd expat-1.95.2/
# ./configure
# make
# make install
```

The next step is to download and install the latest version of Sablotron. The files can be found at http://www.gingerall.com/charlie/ga/xml/d_sab.xml. Download the file from the link called Sablotron 0.81 – sources. Once the file is downloaded, execute the following commands to uncompress the file and install the Sablotron sources:

```
# gunzip Sablot-0.82.tar.gz
# tar xf Sablot-0.82.tar
# rm Sablot-0.82.tar

# cd Sablot-0.82/
# ./configure
# make
# make install
```

If there are any problems with the install, such as the configure program not being able to find certain files, resort to the INSTALL file as it has several alternatives for different operating systems. Most of the solutions entail setting up environment variables containing paths to Expat to help the configure program run correctly. Once Sablotron has been added to the system, we can reconfigure PHP to use Sablotron like this:

```
# cd ../php-4.1.1/
# ./configure --with-dom --with-zlib-dir=/usr/lib --with-
apxs=../apache/bin/apxs --enable-xslt --with-xslt-sablot --with-sablot-js
```

Testing the Installation

Assuming all goes smoothly, we can verify that Sablotron has been installed correctly by looking at phpinfo.php:

Internal Working of an XSL Processor

At the abstract level, when dealing with XSL, every component within the source XML document is viewed as a **node**, similar to how a document is modeled in DOM. Thus elements, attributes, character data, and processing instructions are all viewed as nodes within the source XML document. Using an XSL document, we can define several rules that tell the XSLT processor what to do when it comes across a node, or a set of nodes. For instance, we can say within the XSL document that for every `<application>` node we'd like to display the following HTML:

```
<h2>Application Node</h2>
```

If the source XML document contained four instances of the `<application>` element, the HTML document produced would contain the HTML code 4 times. So how do we specify these rules? XSL documents use XPath as a recognition mechanism for each rule within the XSL document. For instance, to say "For all `<application>` elements", we would define a rule with the following XPath expression:

```
/bug_list/application
```

This would instruct the XSLT processor to call this rule on every `<application>` element node that is a child of the `<bug_list>` root element, within the XML document. When the processor calls this rule, it is referred to as matching the source document with a rule from the XSL document. Now that a rule has been matched with content from the file, the HTML content `<h2>Application Node</h2>`, would be added to the target XML file.

Here is a diagram that shows how this works in general:

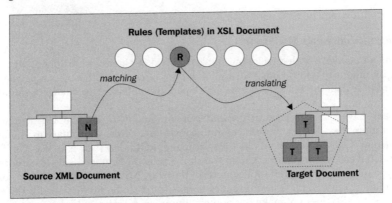

Here we have seven rules (represented as circles) defined by XPath expressions in the XSL document, a source, and a target XML document depicted as a tree. This diagram shows just one match and one transformation in an arbitrary position in the document.

First, the XSLT processor scans the source document in a serial manner. After arriving at each node within the document, the processor checks all the rules defined and tries to pick the one that best matches that particular node. If the processor does find a match, then the node N is matched with rule R. Once the matching takes place, the processor looks at the rule and processes any instructions within it, much like a programming language that executes sourcecode in a function or method.

The result will be from zero-to-many new nodes, which are added to the correct position in the resultant tree. These nodes have been identified as upside down Ts in the diagram, surrounded by a pentagon. Collectively, they are the direct translation of N using R. If the node N does not match an XSL rule within the XSL document, the processor matches the empty rule and continues scanning the remainder of the source XML document in the same manner until there are no nodes left in the source document to process.

The rules within an XSL document are actually called **templates** inside the XSL language. The term template comes from concepts like template methods in objected-oriented terminology or Microsoft Word Document Templates. Templates in XSL define a preset format or interpretation (in either XML, HTML, or plain text) for a single node or a group of nodes. These templates allow the programmer to declaratively say what happens when the XSLT processor parses various nodes, but the programmer doesn't control how the XSLT processor calls the nodes, or the matches that occur once the processor is set in motion.

Benefits

XSL is a technology that handles or provides an alternative solution to small subsets of XML-related issues. There are several benefits that come with this approach – why invent a new technology if it doesn't offer anything new? In this section, we are going to discuss the benefits of using XSL over a programming language-specific parser:

- ❑ Increases maintainability and modularity
- ❑ Use of many presentation languages
- ❑ Faster deployment and increased productivity
- ❑ Less new code is written
- ❑ Increases portability
- ❑ Legacy browser support

Increased Maintainability and Modularity

One of the major concerns with developing software is making it easy to maintain. Since the advent of enterprise applications that may consist of a million lines of code, and businesses developing new requirements faster than the software can be developed, the potential for change is immense.

XSL documents have a very clean structure that is easy to maintain, and the XSL source is contained within one or more files. XSL can also be used to convert one XML vocabulary to another, so we can transform current XML content to an old XML structure, SQL, or a flat file to use with legacy applications. Conversely, we can use XSL to transform older XML documents to conform to a newer document type to work with newer applications. In this way, XSL encourages support for new and old XML vocabularies. With all these opportunities to save sourcecode, there is hardly any arguable evidence that says XSL does not make our applications more maintainable.

Use of Many Presentation Languages

With businesses providing wire services in addition to traditional browser support, there was an increased need to provide the same data and applications to several different types of clients. Before XSL, if any organization wanted to adopt these different technologies and modify their current web sites, they would have to either code an entirely new application or rewrite several fragments of code to provide output for the various presentation languages, thus putting the program through a great deal of refactoring. In today's applications, XSL can be used to transform a generic page object to the appropriate language. Here is an illustration of this process:

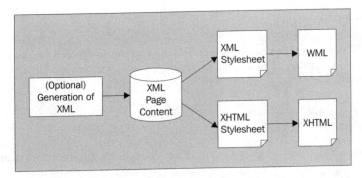

In the above diagram, the XML content for the pages is either handwritten or generated by some other program; perhaps the data was retrieved from a database or other XML sources. Either way, once the XML content that describes all the pages on the web site is retrieved, we can use XSLT to translate the XML content into any presentation language that we want. In this case, the document can be either transformed into a WML or an XHTML representation. This greatly increases the maintainability of the application since all the application logic occurs before the generation of the XML document, thus completely separating the application logic from presentation logic, achieving application-presentation independence.

Faster Deployment and Increased Productivity

Another benefit of using XSL is that we can develop solutions more quickly. For instance, the code to change one XML document to an alternative vocabulary could be quite time consuming using a DOM parser. The programmer would have to instantiate two DOM documents and write code to traverse the source document at each level and then create the new DOM structure using the second document instance at each pass. Considering that several loops, if/switch statements, and function definitions can take up several hundred lines, this can take many hours developing the translator and even more time for the programmer when he has to go back and maintain the application. By using XSLT, it may take less than thirty minutes for a seasoned XSL developer. Thus, XSL helps to develop and deploy applications more quickly.

Coding Reduction

This one isn't really a new benefit, but a consequence of the others. When software becomes more maintainable, can be developed faster, or can push application logic to its own tier, there has to be less code being written as a logical consequence.

Increased Portability

One of greatest advantages of using XSL is that no code has to be written within a target programming language. All the code that describes the translation is contained within a standard XSL document and the code to process documents is limited to a few function calls. This means that we can physically take all our XML files and XSL documents and move them into another environment (Java for example) and not have to write any new code to make the transformations work correctly. Since all XSLT 1.0-compliant processors generate equivalent resultant documents, this mass portability amongst languages and platforms is possible.

Legacy Browser Support

XML documents that specify an external XSL stylesheet (much like a CSS stylesheet can be embedded within an HTML document) can be displayed, with the applied transformations, automatically in Microsoft's IE 5.0 and greater. This is done by adding an additional processing instruction at the top of the XML document, like this:

```
<?xml version="1.0" encoding="iso-8859-1"?>
<?xml-stylesheet href="mystylesheet.xsl" type="text/xsl"?>
```

There is also some XSLT support in Netscape 6.2 and Mozilla 0.9.9, but it hasn't matured yet.

This approach is not recommended for Internet-scale sites because there are several other versions of IE and Netscape that do not support client-side XSL transformations at all, thus browsers won't know how to deal with the content – a loss in potential customers for sure. If client XSLT processing was available, it would definitely be the preferred technique for content rendering, just as you rely on the browser to render HTML properly. With the release of Mozilla 1.0 on the way very soon and Netscape 6.5, there are high hopes for XSLT to be supported in all browsers. While we wait until browser support for XSLT becomes mature (perhaps in late 2002), we have to rely on server-side XSLT processors and this utilizes extra resources on the server.

> Although XSLT support might be underway, it is usually recommended for Internet-scale development that you do not use any client-side technologies until 2 years after they are fully supported (as suggested by many usability analysts). This is because many users do not upgrade their browsers on a regular basis and you cannot expect the entire Internet population to be up-to-date. So if you do plan to use XSLT on the client-side for developing your web sites, it is recommended to hold out until late 2004.

In the case where we are developing Intranet or web applications that run in a controlled environment, using XSLT on the client-side is acceptable and can make the response times of the applications much faster for your users. The only choices at the time of this writing are IE, and to a lesser extent Mozilla, which allows you to do XSLT transformations on the client side properly. Since most company environments use Microsoft Windows for the OS of their workstations and the IT departments can upgrade the browsers internally, it is acceptable to develop XSLT solutions in these cases.

So why all this negative talk in the *Benefits* section?

The answer to that question is that processing the transformations on a server guarantees that any client, no matter if it is IE 3.0, Netscape 2.0, or Netscape 6.2, will see the exact same web site (browser HTML rendering differences aside). Therefore, processing XSL using PHP/Sablotron is the preferred method for styling and transforming documents at this time.

The XSL Language

In this section, we are going to talk about the structure of an XSL document. Here is a diagram of the stylesheet document:

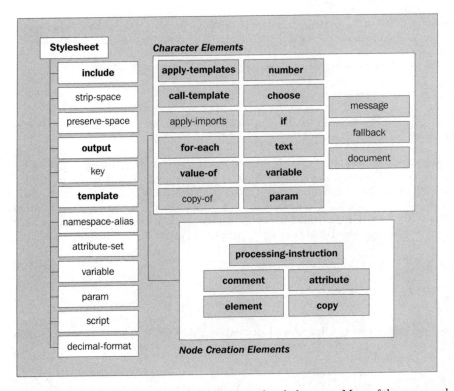

The elements that are in white boxes are considered top-level elements. Most of these can only be placed under the `<xsl:stylesheet>` element, else the XSLT processor will make a fuss. The `<xsl:template>` element is the only element that can have children, and they can be categorized in the two large groups:

- **Character elements**
  Character elements can encapsulate either user-defined nodes or character data. Generally, the main use for these elements is to instruct the XSLT processor on how to create the resultant content.

- **Node creation elements**
  Node creation elements are similar to character elements, but they instruct the XSLT processor to create actual XML constructs that create the nodes in the resultant tree.

In this chapter, we will discuss all the elements where the text is bolded, since these are the most widely used constructs (around 80% of them).

Creating XSL Documents

The simplest XSL document is an empty `<stylesheet>` element:

```
<?xml version="1.0" encoding="iso-8859-1"?>

<xsl:stylesheet version="1.0"
            xmlns:xsl="http://www.w3.org/1999/XSL/Transform" />
```

Notice the qualified `xsl:` namespace before the element name. To assign a namespace to an element (and all its children), we use the `xmlns:xsl` attribute. This attribute is shared with all XML documents.

In general, to define a namespace, add the following attribute to any element:

```
<mytag xmlns:mynamespace="url" />
```

Now, any tag or attribute at this level or any child level can use the namespace to qualify its elements and attributes.

In our case, the stylesheet element is qualified as `<xsl:stylesheet>` where `xsl` is the name of the namespace. All XSL elements must be qualified in a similar manner. At the time of this writing, the current URL to use for the namespace is http://www.w3.org/1999/XSL/Transform/. If this URL is slightly different then the XSLT processor will not work correctly. However, we are not required to use the string `xsl` – we can use anything we want. The relation of the name to the URL is what is important. For instance, we could have easily defined the above code like this:

```
<?xml version="1.0" encoding="iso-8859-1"?>

<xyz:stylesheet version="1.0"
                xmlns:xyz="http://www.w3.org/1999/XSL/Transform" />
```

Here we make a relationship that says all elements qualified by the `xyz` namespace are XSL elements. Although it is possible to title the namespace however we like, it is a de facto standard that the XSL namespace be called `xsl`.

What happens if we don't use the namespace? Well, the answer to this question is why namespaces came about. Suppose the XSL document is generating an XML vocabulary that has the element `<stylesheet>` in the resultant document. Namespaces allow us to distinguish the XSL stylesheet element from the user-defined stylesheet element. When the XSLT processor encounters `<stylesheet>`, it will not recognize this element as an XSL instruction. This helps prevent any ambiguities. In the case of most XSLT processors, the namespace is required. If it is absent, none of the XSL instructions will be recognized.

The next part of the stylesheet element is the `version` attribute. Since Sablotron is nearly XSLT 1.0-compliant, XSL documents usually will have a version with 1.0. However, there are XSLT 1.1 and 2.0 documents available as well. As far as Sablotron is concerned, we can leave the version number out or put anything we want because Sablotron currently only supports version 1.0 and it doesn't deal with forward compatibility issues. Although it is possible to leave the value out when dealing with Sablotron, keep it in mind that it is not very advisable if you plan to move these XSL documents to other platforms that use other processors, or you would like to maintain forward compatibility for future releases.

A Simple Example

For most of the examples in this chapter, we will be using the communal `bug_list.xml` file employed in other chapters. For reference, the content of this XML file is included in Chapter 3.

In this first example, let's develop a stylesheet that demonstrates how to define our own templates (or rules) that generates an HTML document given the `bug_list.xml` file. The output to the browser will consist of large, bold titles for the application names with an unordered list of the bug titles associated with each application. Here is the entire XSL document to provide such a translation:

```
<?xml version="1.0" encoding="iso-8859-1"?>
<!-- bltemplate.xsl -->

<xsl:stylesheet version="1.0"
                xmlns:xsl="http://www.w3.org/1999/XSL/Transform">

<xsl:output method="html" indent="yes" />

<xsl:template match="/">
  <html>
    <head>
      <title>Status Bug Report</title>
    </head>
    <body>
      <h1>Applications</h1>
      <xsl:apply-templates />
    </body>
  </html>
</xsl:template>

<xsl:template match="application">
  <h2><xsl:value-of select="@name" /></h2>
  <ul>
    <xsl:apply-templates select="bugs/bug_item/title" />
  </ul>
  <br />
</xsl:template>

<xsl:template match="title">
  <li><xsl:value-of select="text()" /></li>
</xsl:template>

</xsl:stylesheet>
```

The highlighted portions are the most important, and we will look at each of them in turn.

As mentioned earlier, XSLT can be used to convert XML content to XML, HTML, or plaintext. To instruct the XSLT processor to generate HTML content, we need to use the <xsl:output> instruction. As the name suggests, we can control the format of the output, its indentation, its encoding, and the MIME type (if the document is XML). In this example, the method attribute is used to tell the XSLT processor the format of the document. In this case, it is HTML:

```
<xsl:output method="html" indent="yes" />
```

The <xsl:output> instruction also allows the programmer to specify how the output is indented, with the indent attribute. We can pass either yes or no values. The string yes is the default value, but in this example it is explicitly stated for demonstration purposes. The XSLT processor will use spaces to control the indentation of the resultant document if it is turned on, otherwise the document will not contain any whitespace in between the elements. Later on, we will look at how indentation could lead to problems when very complex HTML is used.

295

The next three sections of the XSL document are template definitions, or rather rules, that describe how the bug list nodes are translated to HTML.

The first rule matches the root node of the document, as shown with this code:

```
<xsl:template match="/">
  <html>
    <head>
      <title>Status Bug Report</title>
    </head>
    <body>
      <h1>Applications</h1>
      <xsl:apply-templates />
    </body>
  </html>
</xsl:template>
```

The root node will only be matched once by the XSLT processor, so it is only fitting that the beginning and ending of the HTML content is located here. As explained in the previous chapter, the root node is not the <bug_list>, but rather the document root of the entire XML file. When the processor starts reading the source document and arrives before the root node, it will match the above template definition. The XSLT processor copies the character data (in this case, the HTML content) within the template into the target document.

Here is an illustration of the two files once the processing is complete:

Source Document	Target Document
`<?xml version="1.0" encoding="iso-8859-1"?>`	`<html>`
	`<head>`
	`<title>`
`<bug_list>`	`Status Bug Report`
`<application name="sportran compiler" version="1.1">`	`</title>`
	`</head>`
`...`	`<body>`
	`<h1>Applications</h1>`
	`<xsl:apply-templates />`
	`</body>`
	`</html>`

The process then advances to the next line in the source document (the <bug_list> element) and moves to the position of the <xsl:apply-templates> element in the target document. So what does <xsl:apply-templates> do? This XSL instruction orders the XSLT processor to continue matching nodes in the source document that are children of the XPath expression. In this example, the template uses the / XPath expression – the root element of the source document – thus the XSLT process will scan all the children of the bug list XML file and continue to match nodes with any templates defined. Whenever a new rule is matched, content will be added to the target document within the <body> tag. More content will be added to the document shortly.

> If the `<xsl:apply-templates>` element is not specified, the XSLT processor will stop processing the source content under the current node (the root node in this case).

The second template defines the translation for the `<application>` element in the source document.

```
<xsl:template match="application">
  <h2><xsl:value-of select="@name" /></h2>
  <ul>
    <xsl:apply-templates select="bugs/bug_item/title" />
  </ul>
  <br />
</xsl:template>
```

In this case, the XPath expression matches all `application` nodes, regardless of where they exist within the document. Since we know there is only one type of application node in the bug list document, we do not need to specify an absolute path from the root node. We could have used the following template definition to specify an absolute path:

```
<xsl:template match="/bug_list/application">
```

or an XPath expression to match any `application` node that is a child of the `<bug_list>` element:

```
<xsl:template match="bug_list/application">
```

In all cases, the processor will match the `<application>` elements in the source document. In this template, there is a new XSL instruction – `<xsl:value-of select="@name" />`. The `<xsl:value-of>` instruction tells the processor to put a string into the resultant document at this location.

The `select` attribute contains an XPath expression specifying where to grab the text. In this case, the expression is `@name`. Recall from the last chapter that the `@` symbol followed by a title indicates that the result will be the text value of an attribute at the current node. The bug list file has a `name` attribute attached to the `<application>` element, so the value at the current application node will be inserted into the resultant document in between the `<h2>` begin and end tags.

After the first `<application>` element has been processed, here is the current state of the target HTML document:

Source Document	Target Document
`<?xml version="1.0"` `encoding="iso-8859-1"?>` `<bug_list>` `<application name="sportran compiler"` `version="1.1">` `...`	`<html>` `<head>` `<title>` `Status Bug Report` `</title>` `</head>` `<body>` `<h1>Applications</h1>` `<h2>sportran compiler</h2>` `<ul>` `<xsl:apply-templates` `select="bugs/bug_item/title" />` `</ul>` ` ` `<xsl:apply-templates />` `</body>` `</html>`

Notice the new HTML code positioned within the target HTML document. Also, the string, `sportran compiler`, is in between the `<h2>` tags. This is the result of the `<xsl:value-of>` instruction.

Like the previous template definition, the `<xsl:apply-templates>` instruction is also employed, but this time we are refining what elements can be matched in the source document. The `select` attribute on the `<xsl:apply-templates>` instruction tells the XSLT processor to match only future `<title>` elements that occur as children of the `<bug_item>` element. Also, remember that the XPath expression, `bugs/bug_item/title`, is relative to the current node and not the root node of the document. This is because XSLT expects all expressions within a template to be defined according to the current node and not the root document, making our XPath expressions shorter. Now the XSLT processor will skip every node in the source document except for these `<title>` elements.

The third template in the XSL document is to match the `<title>` element itself. As with the previous template, this rule will match all `<title>` elements within the document, regardless of where they are located:

```
<xsl:template match="title">
  <li><xsl:value-of select="text()" /></li>
</xsl:template>
```

Once the `<title>` element is matched, a list item is put in its place. By using `<xsl:value-of>`, we can insert the character data of the `<title>` element from the source document. This is accomplished by the `text()` function in XPath. Since the current node is the `<title>` element, there is no need to specify the absolute path. The XSLT processor knows to place the character data for the current element. Here is the result of the target document after the first `<title>` element has been processed in the source document:

Source Document	Target Document
`...` `<bug_item>` `  <title>It crashes when a string with more than 256 bytes is declared</title>` `<report_date>200201281015</report_date>` `  <reported-by>John Smith</reported-by>` `  <status>Open</status>` `<last_update>200201281016</last_update>` `  <description>...</description>` `  <severity>3</severity>` `</bug_item>` `...`	`...` `  <body>` `    <h1>Applications</h1>` `    <h2>sportran compiler</h2>` `  <ul>` `    <li>It crashes when a string with more than 256 bytes is declared</li>` `      <xsl:apply-templates` `      select="bugs/bug_item/title" />` `    </ul>` `     ` `    <xsl:apply-templates />` `    </body>` `    ...`

The XSLT processor grabbed the string, `<li>It crashes when a string with more than 256 bytes is declared</li>`, and placed this character data between the list item code.

Since there is no `<xsl:apply-templates>` instruction within the recently inserted code, the XSLT processor stops processing any potential children of the `<title>` element and continues to the previous position where new content needs to be added. This application will match two more list items upon completing the unordered list.

Here is the target document after the new list items have been inserted into the resultant HTML document:

Source Document:	Target Document:
. . .	. . .
`</bug_item>`	`<body>`
`</bugs>`	`<h1>Applications</h1>`
`</application>`	`<h2>sportran compiler</h2>`
`<application name="SportyEditor" version="1.0">`	`<ul>`
	`<li>It crashes when a string with more than 256 bytes is declared</li>`
`<bugs>`	`<li>String concatenation fails if a string contains a dot</li>`
`<bug_item>`	`<li>Error when summing two integers</li>`
. . .	`</ul>`
	` `
	`<xsl:apply-templates />`
	`</body>`
	. . .

Now the XSLT processor is finished with the first application node, it will repeat the exact steps for every application node within the document. The code to actually process this file and see these results using PHP is actually very simple.

Using the XSLT PHP Extension

To simplify the code (and reuse for other examples), let's create a function called `transform()`. This function takes in two arguments – the source XML file and the XSL file to translate the document. The function returns a string of the constructed XML content by the processor. Here is the code for this function:

```php
<?php

function transform ($sourceXml, $sourceXsl)
{
    $sourceXml = 'file://' . $sourceXml;
    $sourceXsl = 'file://' . $sourceXsl;
```

The first step is to concatenate the string `file://` to the beginning of both file names. As we will see later, the processor requires that any content that is given using a file must have this before the full path of the file name, otherwise the parser will return a parsing error. The PHP function documentation fails to mention this minor detail (although the Sablotron documentation includes it), so if you miss the prefix, you could run into a lot of problems in which the error messages do not help you very much.

```php
    $xslt = xslt_create();
```

The next step is to create a new handle to an XSLT processor using the `xslt_create()` function. The function takes in no arguments and simply returns a handle into the variable $xslt:

```
// Process the document
if (!$result = @xslt_process($xslt, $sourceXml, $sourceXsl)) {
  print ("Error: <b>" . xslt_error($xslt) . "</b><br />" .
    "Code: <b>" . xslt_errno($xslt) . "</b>");
  die();
}
```

Once the handle has been created, we can use it to call other Sablotron functions (we will be discussing Sablotron functions later in this chapter). To process the document, we call the `xslt_process()` function. This function takes three parameters.

The first parameter takes the handle of the processor and the second and third arguments are the file names passed in earlier. After the processing is finished, the function can either return FALSE or a string containing the content of the resultant document. In this case, if the value is FALSE we display an error on the screen, letting the programmer know what went wrong by showing them the error message and the line number in the XSL document.

Once the processor is finished we have to free it. This can executed by invoking the `xslt_free()` function with the handle:

```
xslt_free($xslt);
```

At this point, the PHP script can no longer use the handle:

```
return $result;
}
```

The function finally returns the result if the processor did not run into any errors and contains the actual content. At this point, we can use PHP's `print()` statement to display it to the screen or write it out to a file. There are other ways to use these functions; we will look at these details in the *An Object-Oriented Approach* section:

```
$sourceXml = 'c:\Apache\htdocs\prophpxml\bug_list.xml';
$sourceXsl = 'c:\Apache\htdocs\prophpxml\chapter08\bltemplate.xsl';

print (transform($sourceXml, $sourceXsl));
?>
```

To use this function, we simply pass the location of the bug list XML source document and the XSL file we developed earlier into the `transform()` function, and if everything checks out okay, we'll get the new HTML document. Since the solution to translating XSL documents is generic, almost all XSL applications will look something like this. In fact, most of the examples in this chapter can use this code. If this XSL stylesheet was processed, the result would look like this:

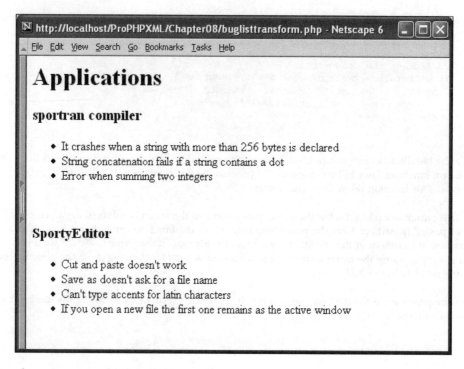

Before discussing more about the Sablotron functions, this section will continue with the tutorial on designing and writing XSL documents.

Precedence Rules and Predefined Templates

What happens when the XSLT processor encounters nodes that have no templates defined within the XSL document? In these cases, the XSLT processor uses predefined templates. Like CSS, rules can take precedence over other rules. Without getting into too much detail about how precedence is calculated by the XSLT processor, this section will discuss enough material to give a good understanding of the predefined templates.

Precedence is determined by three factors:

❑ **The position of the template within the XSL file**
The lower an XSL template appears in the file, the higher the priority the XSLT processor gives it. For instance, from the following two templates, the second has a higher priority than the first:

```
<xsl:template match="xyz">I will not get used.</xsl:template>
...
<xsl:template match="xyz">I will get used </xsl:template>
```

In this example, even though we have two templates defined to match the expression xyz, whenever an <xyz> element is encountered by the processor, the second template will be the one that is matched.

❏ **The specificity of the XPath expression**

Sometimes in a document we may have some conflicts where multiple XPath expressions are all possible matches. For the processor to determine which one to use, there is a method of analyzing the pattern within the expression and grading its priority. When the expression is very generic (meaning it can be applied to many nodes in the source tree), it is given a lower priority. Consequently, when an expression matches a very specific node, it is given higher priority. Take the following three templates for example:

```
<xsl:template match="*" />
<xsl:template match="xyz" />
<xsl:template match="ken/abc/xyz" />
```

The wildcard expression to match all elements is given the lower priority because it applies to a wide set of matches. All nodes that are not defined will be matched by this expression. The second expression matches any element with the name <xyz>, regardless of where it appears within the XML source file. For instance, if <xyz> were a top-level node and a leaf, in both cases the processor would execute the matching and transformation process. Since this expression is more specific than the wildcard example, this template overrides it. The third example is the most specific, thus gaining the highest priority, because it expects the <xyz> element to have the parent <abc> and the grandparent <ken>. As long as this condition is TRUE, the processor will use this template, otherwise the second template will be used.

❏ **The priority assigned to the template**

The last method to increase the precedence of a template is setting its priority. Setting the priority attribute can do this:

```
<xsl:template match="xyz" priority="1" />
```

Priority values can be either positive or negative. Positive values are given the highest precedence and lower values are given lower precedence. If a priority is not specified, the previous two methods are used to implicitly compute the priority value. These implicit values vary from -0.5 to 0.5. If you want something to have a low priority, use below -0.5 and if you want something to have a priority, use anything greater than 0.5.

Now that priorities are out of the way, the declaration of the predefined elements will make more sense. The first predefined template matches all XML element nodes within the source tree, including the root node:

```
<xsl:template match="*|/">
  <xsl:apply-templates/>
</xsl:template>
```

When the processor encounters an element or root node that is not defined anywhere in the XSL document, this default template is used to instruct the XSLT processor to continue processing the document. As indicated, no new nodes are constructed and added to the target tree. As with all the predefined templates, this one is defined at the top of the document, allowing the XSL writer to override it:

```
<xsl:template match="text()|@*">
  <xsl:value-of select="."/>
</xsl:template>
```

The next predefined template matches any character data and attribute values. Since character data and attributes do not have children to process, the `<xsl:apply-templates>` instruction is not required.

However, each time this template is used, a text node will be added to the target tree with either the character data or the assigned value of the attribute. In many situations this is undesirable, so to avoid this default behavior, simply replace it with the following template, preferably at the top of the file:

```
<xsl:template match="text()|@*" />
```

This replacement template instructs the XSLT processor to do nothing when character data or attributes are encountered. When this is defined, it is our responsibility to ensure that we explicitly select content and attribute values within the other definitions.

The last predefined template matches processing instructions and comments:

```
<xsl:template match="processing-instruction()|comment()"/>
```

This instruction is simply left blank, ready for us to override if necessary. Later on in the chapter, examples of using processing instructions in XSL documents will be discussed.

Named Templates

In addition to having the XSLT processing matching templates, it is possible to invoke a template explicitly in the same manner we would call a function in PHP. In XSL terms, these functions are called **named templates**. These can be extremely useful as they allow us to modularize our XSL code like we would refactor a program. Often the output of a single template can reach over a 100 lines, so splitting up the template into several smaller ones is an excellent strategy.

Here is a short example that prints out the applications within the bug list file using named templates:

```
<?xml version="1.0" encoding="iso-8859-1"?>
<!-- blnamedtemplate.xsl -->

<xsl:stylesheet version="1.0"
  xmlns:xsl="http://www.w3.org/1999/XSL/Transform">

<xsl:output method="html" indent="yes" />

<xsl:template match="/">
  <html>
    <head>
      <title>Status Bug Report</title>
  </head>
    <body>
      <xsl:call-template name="begin" />
    </body>
  </html>
</xsl:template>

<xsl:template name="begin">
  <h2>Application Names</h2>
```

```
    <xsl:apply-templates select="bug_list/application" />
  </xsl:template>

  <xsl:template match="application">
    <xsl:value-of select="@name" /><br />
  </xsl:template>

</xsl:stylesheet>
```

This example is very similar to the first one introduced in the chapter, but the portion that displays the list elements has been removed.

To define a named template, the `<xsl:template>` instruction must have a value set for the `name` attribute. Just as with functions in PHP, a string identifier is used in the `name` attribute and the processor will return an error if two or more templates have the same name. Other than this minor difference, the content within a named template is exactly as before. We can put any valid XSL instructions as well as character data inside the template.

Here is the template definition for this example:

```
<xsl:template name="begin">
  <h2>Application Names</h2>
  <xsl:apply-templates select="bug_list/application" />
</xsl:template>
```

This template has the name `begin`. Its contents were cut from the root node and placed into this template from the previous example. So why does the `<xsl:apply-templates>` instruction have the relative expression, `bug_list/application`? What is it relative to? Whenever a template is called, its current node is the same as the calling template. In this case, the root node of the source document is the current node.

To invoke the template, we have to use the `<xsl:call-template>` instruction within another template instruction, like this:

```
<xsl:call-template name="begin" />
```

This instruction takes a single attribute, `name`, which specifies the name of the template to execute.

The output of this example is:

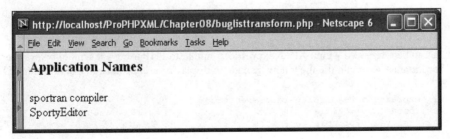

305

One thing to be aware of when using named templates is to avoid infinite recursion. As our XSL documents increase in size, one template might call another and back again without us noticing. For example, consider the following XSL code:

```
<xsl:template name="begin">
  <xsl:call-template name="end" />
</xsl:template>

<xsl:template name="end">
  <xsl:call-template name="begin" />
</xsl:template>
```

If the begin template is invoked, the XSLT processor will execute the end and begin templates indefinitely. These errors can be difficult to track since the XSLT processor will not report a formal error, but rather Apache will eventually report an internal server error (error code 500). Although these occurrences are rare, it's wise to be aware of them.

Using Parameters

Like functions in PHP, we can also call templates with arguments called parameters. To define a parameter in a template definition, we must use the <xsl:param> instruction. Any parameters that we define must be located at the top of the template. If they contain any character data external to the <xsl:param> elements, or the construction of new nodes or XSL instructions, the XSL processor will report an error.

Here is an example on how to define a parameterized template:

```
<xsl:template name="template-name">
  <xsl:param name="parameter-name1" />
  <xsl:param name="parameter-name2" />

  <!-- More param definitions -->
  <!-- Code Goes Here -->
</xsl:template>
```

Here the <xsl:param> instruction takes an attribute name that specifies the name of the parameter. We can have many parameters defined within the template, but each one must have a unique name. With parameters, we can also specify a default value by using the character data portion of the element, like this:

```
<xsl:param name="parameter-name">Default value</xsl:param>
```

Thus, if an argument is not passed to the template, the parameter will contain the string Default value. Either way, a new variable is created with the exact name as the name attribute.

Variables can be referenced within XPath expressions similar to PHP using a $ symbol before the variable name. For instance, we could use the following code to display a variable in large letters within HTML:

```
<xsl:template name="display-large-letters">
  <xsl:param name="title" />
  <h1><xsl:value-of select="$title" /></h1>
</xsl:template>
```

Now that the template is defined with the use of parameters, to call the template the `<xsl:with-param>` element should be added inside the `<xsl:call-template>` instruction. There are two ways to pass a value with this instruction:

❑ Use XPath to select a string or node-set (an unordered collection of nodes within the source document) to compute the result

❑ Use XSL instructions and character data

Here is an example that demonstrates several approaches:

```
<xsl:call-template name="template-name">
  <xsl:with-param name="parameter-name1" select="XPath-expression" />
  <xsl:with-param name="parameter-name2">Value</xsl:with-param>
  <xsl:with-param name="parameter-name3">
    <xsl:value-of select="XPath-expression" />
  </xsl:with-param>
  <!-- Code Goes Here -->
</xsl:template>
```

In this template call we pass three parameters (expected to be used in the target template definition):

❑ In the first example, we use the `select` attribute to acquire a string or a node-set to be passed. The XSLT processor will compute the XPath expression and store the result in a variable that can be accessed within the called template. In this case, the variable name will be `$parameter-name1`. This variable can contain strings, Boolean values, numbers, or node-sets since XPath expressions can return a variety of types of values.

❑ We might want to adopt the tactic given by `parameter-name2` if we do not want to use XPath. In this approach, we provide a string, in this case `Value`, in the form of character data of the `<xsl:with-param>` element. A variable called `$parameter-name2` will contain the character data.

In combination with the second approach, we can add any XSL instructions anywhere between the `<xsl:with-param>` instruction. All of the nodes constructed and character data returned will be stored in the argument.

❑ With `parameter-name3`, a combination of the `<xsl:value-of>` instruction with the second approach essentially achieves the same thing as using the `select` attribute.

> Unlike functions in PHP, when a template is called with multiple parameters, the parameters need not appear in the same order as they were defined. This is because the name and the value are sent as a pair. However, take caution when manipulating the order since this may make the XSL file hard to follow, thus thwarting maintainability.

Using Variables

XSLT also allows us to define variables that store the complex XPath expressions for later use. Like parameters, variables must be defined within a template, but are not limited to being defined before any new nodes are constructed in the resultant tree; that is, they can be placed anywhere. To create a variable we use the XSL instruction `<xsl:variable>`, like this:

```
<xsl:variable name="some-variable" select="XPath-expression" />
<xsl:variable name="another-variable">A Value</xsl:variable>
```

Like parameters, variables are given a unique identification using the `name` attribute. In the first example, `$some-variable` uses the `select` attribute to retrieve a value, which may be later retrieved in an XPath expression. The second example stores the string A Value, into `$another-variable`.

We could make a mistake when passing a variable that contains an XPath expression into any instruction that can accept these expressions, such as `<xsl:value-of>`. For instance, if the variable `$number-of-titles` contained the XPath expression `count(//title)`, a call to

```
<xsl:value-of select="$number-of-titles" />
```

might provide the impression that the XSLT processor will evaluate the XPath expression and return a number, such as 17. Here is a step-by-step view of what we think will happen:

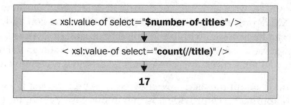

It is easy to make this mistake because, after all, this is how PHP and other programming languages behave. However, this is simply not the case with XSLT – XPath expressions only get evaluated once. This means that the variable itself is actually considered an XPath expression and will get converted into the string `count(//title)`. Therefore, a new text node containing this value will be added to the resultant tree instead of the numeric value.

Here is the actual result:

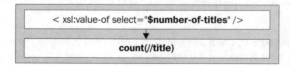

To avoid this common mistake and evaluate the XPath expression accurately, we must evaluate the result prior to the usage of the variable, like this:

```
<xsl:variable name="number-of-titles">
  <xsl:value-of select="count(//title)" />
</xsl:variable>
<xsl:value-of select="$number-of-titles" />
```

If we use the same code as earlier, the variable $number-of-titles already contains the result 17, thus when the <xsl:value-of> instruction is executed using the variable, 17 will be returned and added to the resultant XML tree. With this method, you only have to assign a value to the variable once, and it can be reused over and over again through out the template or stylesheet that provides the scope of the variable.

Using XPath for Calculations

Although XSL is used for transformations, as mentioned earlier, it is possible to manufacture answers for a small set of computational problems using XPath. It can't solve every computational problem, but it might be advisable to avoid a programming language as discussed in the *Portability* section of the chapter. Thus, at times, it is appropriate for XSL to act like a small program.

XPath's ability to provide computations is still very useful and it is possible to write semi-complex programs within an XSL document. Should you write the calculations in XSL or write them in your native language? The trade-off is rather simple: portability vs. functionality. Depending on what your goals are for the application will determine which route you take when developing your application.

With the knowledge gained in this section about templates, parameters, and variables, let's write an XSL document to answer the following questions (discussed in the last chapter) and display the results on the screen in HTML. For review, here are the questions asked in the last chapter:

❑   How many bugs do we have in the database?

❑   How many bugs are open?

❑   Who are the programmers who reported bugs regarding string management?

❑   How many bugs have different reporting dates and last updated dates?

❑   Which applications have open bugs?

❑   Which is the average severity of all the bugs?

❑   Which bugs were reported in the first 2 weeks of January 2002?

The output will consist of a question number in bold, the question itself, and finally the answer in bold/italic, all in a single line. Since all seven questions will be displayed in this way, our strategy will be to encapsulate the presentation logic for each question and to use templates calls with the appropriate values. If, in the future, we need to make changes (like making all the questions appear in italic and the colour red), we will only need to change one spot in the XSL document rather than 7 (or possibly more in larger documents) throughout the entire file.

In this example, we are going to take several approaches to demonstrating the full use of the defined named template:

```
<?xml version="1.0" encoding="iso-8859-1"?>
<!-- expressions.xsl -->

<xsl:stylesheet version="1.0"
  xmlns:xsl="http://www.w3.org/1999/XSL/Transform">
<xsl:output method="html" indent="yes" />
```

As with all our examples so far, we begin the XSL document by defining the top-level
`<xsl:stylesheet>` and `<xsl:output>` elements. This example will feature two templates. The first
one acts as a function for displaying the question and answer pair in HTML, labeled `display-question`. The second one displays the entire HTML page.

Here is the first template:

```
<!-- DISPLAY QUESTION TEMPLATE -->
<xsl:template name="display-question">
  <xsl:param name="num" />  <!-- A string rep. of the question -->
  <xsl:param name="text" /> <!-- The question text -->
  <xsl:param name="answer"> <!-- An evaluated XPath expression -->
    <xsl:value-of select="count(//bug_item)" />
  </xsl:param>

  <b><xsl:value-of select="$num" /></b>
  <xsl:text>. </xsl:text>
  <xsl:value-of select="$text" />
  <strong><i><xsl:value-of select="$answer" /></i></strong><br />
</xsl:template>
```

The `display-question` template is instructed to take in three parameters, two of which are
mandatory.

The `num` parameter expects a string representation of the question's number. We'll be passing the values
1 through 7 each time this template is called. The second parameter is the question text. Neither of
these two parameters has a default value, therefore if one is not supplied, the variable will simply
contain an empty string. We'll learn how these expressions are checked later, but for now we'll have to
remember to pass a value. The last parameter expects an evaluated XPath expression. In this case, it'll
be an XPath string result. Unlike the previous two, this parameter contains a default value – it counts all
the bug items within the XML file (using `//bug_item`) and stores the result in `$answer`.

In any real-life program, this default result would be unacceptable, but, for demonstration purposes, this
is the answer to the first question – how many bugs do we have in the database?

At this point, three variables have been constructed by the XSLT processor containing the question
number, its text, and the answer. The template displays the question number in bold, followed by a
period and a space using a new instruction, `<xsl:text>`. This instruction creates a text node within the
result tree. In this case, the text node contains two characters, `". "` (a period and a space). Next, the
question's text is displayed precisely after the space with a bold/italic answer afterwards. In effect, this
function creates the following result tree to be attached to the final target XML file:

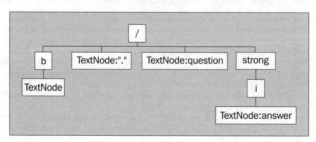

Although no actual root node will be inserted into the resultant tree, it has been added here to make the diagram look like a tree. In effect, these four newly constructed nodes (and their respective children) will find a place in the target XML structure each time this template is called. Now that we have an idea what this functionalized template does, let's see how it is used in the main template:

```
<!-- HTML OUTPUT -->
<xsl:template match="/">
  <html>
    <head>
      <title>Bug Report</title>
    </head>
    <body>
      <xsl:variable name="q3" select="/bug_list/application/bugs/bug_item/
        reported-by[contains(../title/text(),'string')]" />

      <xsl:variable name="q4" select="count(//bug_item[normalize-space
        (report_date/text()) != normalize-space(last_update/text())])" />

      <xsl:variable name="q5" select="/bug_list/application/@name
        [normalize-space(../bugs/bug_item/status/text())='open' or
         normalize-space(../bugs/bug_item/status/text()='Open')]" />

      <xsl:variable name="q6" select="sum(//severity/text()) div
        count(//severity)" />

      <xsl:variable name="q7" select="//bug_item/title[normalize-space
        (../report_date/text())&lt; '2002-01-16T00:00:00']" />
```

Since the answers to most of the questions have relatively long XPath expressions, it makes sense to put each answer into its own variable to clean up the rest of the file. As indicated by the code above, the first thing we do is select the expressions and store them into variables named q3 to q7 for questions 3 through 7. To see how these XPath functions were derived, please revert back to the previous chapter.

This section of the XSL document instructs the XSLT processor to add the header, Bug Report, in large letters and invokes the display-question template for the first time. The first parameter that is passed is num, containing the number of the question – in this case it is the static value 1. The next parameter indicates the question text. Notice with this template, the answer parameter has not been provided within the parameter list, thus forcing the processor to use the default answer, evaluating count(//bug_item) and placing 7 into the $answer variable:

```
<h1>Bug Report</h1>

<xsl:call-template name="display-question">
  <xsl:with-param name="num">1</xsl:with-param>
  <xsl:with-param name="text">
    How many bugs do we have in the database?
  </xsl:with-param>
</xsl:call-template>
```

Here is the result of this segment of code after the template has been fully executed:

```
<h1>Bug Report</h1>
<b>1. </b>
How many bugs do we have in the database?
<strong>
  <i>7</i>
</strong>
<br>
```

The second question works in the same way, but instead we pass an expression to the answer parameter manually (highlighted in the code below):

```
<xsl:call-template name="display-question">
  <xsl:with-param name="num">2</xsl:with-param>
  <xsl:with-param name="text">
      How many bugs are open?
  </xsl:with-param>
  <xsl:with-param name="answer">
    <xsl:value-of select="count(//bug_item[status/text()='Open' or
                                  status/text()='open'])" />
  </xsl:with-param>
</xsl:call-template>
```

This overrides the default value and retrieves the answer from the provided XPath expression. In this case, it tries to find all the bug items with an Open or open string contained within the <status> element's character data. Using the bug list XML file, the answer returned will be value 4.

The next calls to the display-question template use the variables defined above and are essentially all the same:

```
<xsl:call-template name="display-question">
  <xsl:with-param name="num">3</xsl:with-param>
  <xsl:with-param name="text">
    Who are the programmers who reported bugs regarding string
    management?
  </xsl:with-param>
  <xsl:with-param name="answer">
    <xsl:value-of select="$q3" />
  </xsl:with-param>
</xsl:call-template>
```

In this template call, $q3 has already been evaluated to the value John Smith, so it is placed into the $answer variable, local to the invoked template. The remainder of the template calls operate in the same manner:

```
<xsl:call-template name="display-question">
  <xsl:with-param name="num">4</xsl:with-param>
  <xsl:with-param name="text">
    How many bugs have different reporting date and last updated date?
```

```
        </xsl:with-param>
        <xsl:with-param name="answer">
        <xsl:value-of select="$q4" />
        </xsl:with-param>
      </xsl:call-template>

      <xsl:call-template name="display-question">
        <xsl:with-param name="num">5</xsl:with-param>
        <xsl:with-param name="text">
          Which applications have open bugs?
        </xsl:with-param>
        <xsl:with-param name="answer">
          <xsl:value-of select="$q5" />
        </xsl:with-param>
      </xsl:call-template>

      <xsl:call-template name="display-question">
        <xsl:with-param name="num">6</xsl:with-param>
        <xsl:with-param name="text">
          Which is the average severity of all the bugs?
        </xsl:with-param>
        <xsl:with-param name="answer">
          <xsl:value-of select="$q6" />
        </xsl:with-param>
      </xsl:call-template>

        <xsl:with-param name="num">7</xsl:with-param>
        <xsl:with-param name="text">
          Which bugs were reported in the first 2 weeks of January 2002?
        </xsl:with-param>
        <xsl:with-param name="answer">
          <xsl:value-of select="$q7" />
        </xsl:with-param>
      </xsl:call-template>
    </body>
  </html>
</xsl:template>

</xsl:stylesheet>
```

If this example were run on the bug_list.xml file, the following result would appear in the web browser:

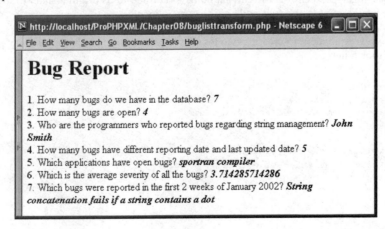

One very interesting consequence of creating the XSL document this way is that the template calls actually model the data of the question entity. Picture the template call being a `<question>` top-level element and the `number`, `text`, and `answer` parameters being children of this element. There is a striking resemblance when the presentation information has been pushed into another part of the XSL document.

XSL Instructions

This section details the various XSL instructions.

Repetition – xsl:for-each

As mentioned in the XPath chapter, expressions can be evaluated to several types of data. At this point, we've mainly looked at expressions returning strings, such as the expressions to calculate the answers to the questions in the previous example. We also have seen some examples where XPath expressions return a node-set. For instance, when we execute `//bug_item`, the XSLT processor creates a list of `<bug_item>` elements that is of the node-set type. XSLT allows us to iterate over node-set types just as PHP lets us iterate over arrays with the `foreach` construct. At this point, the only method known to iterate over a series of nodes was to scan and match nodes within the source XML tree using templates.

Using the `<xsl:for-each>` instruction, we can iterate over a node-set within a template. Using the `select` attribute, we can use XPath to gather the list of nodes. Here is an example:

```
<xsl:template match="/">
  <h2>Bug Item List</h2>
  <xsl:for-each select="//bug_item">
    <xsl:value-of select="title/text()" /><br />
  </xsl:for-each>
</xsl:template>
```

This code iterates a collection of `<bug_item>` elements and displays each one in a single line. What is rather interesting about the `<xsl:for-each>` instruction is that anywhere within it, the **current node** (the one where all XPath expressions are relative to) is replaced with the node currently being supplied by the `<xsl:for-each>` instruction. Thus, `title/text()` resolves to `../bug_item/title/text()` and we avoid having to specify the absolute path using the root node. After the `<xsl:for-each>` instruction has finished executing, the current node is returned to its original state. In this case, the current node would point to the root node of the source document.

The above code is equivalent to creating two templates and matching only the root and `<bug_item>` elements, as shown here:

```
<xsl:template match="/">
  <h2>Bug Item List</h2>
  <xsl:apply-templates select="bug_item" />
</xsl:template>

<xsl:template match="bug_item">
  <xsl:value-of select="title/text()" /><br />
</xsl:template>
```

There are many useful applications for the `<xsl:for-each>` instruction. For instance, we can minimize the use of templates. Using many templates in an XSL document can cause clutter, but using the `<xsl:for-each>` instruction can clean up a few of them to leave the meaningful matches in place. As we will see in the next section, it is possible to have an XSL document contain one implicit template, thus eliminating all template definitions and top-level XSL instructions. In these instances, the `<xsl:for-each>` instruction is one of the prime ways of navigating the source document.

Here is a complete example that creates a table of bug items for each application within the `bug_list.xml` file:

```
<?xml version="1.0" encoding="iso-8859-1"?>
<!-- bldisplay.xsl -->

<xsl:stylesheet version="1.0"
  xmlns:xsl="http://www.w3.org/1999/XSL/Transform">

<xsl:output method="html" indent="yes" />

<xsl:template match="/">
  <html>
    <head>
      <title>Bug Report</title>
    </head>
    <body>
      <h1>Bug Report</h1>
      <xsl:apply-templates />
    </body>
  </html>

</xsl:template>

<xsl:template match="application">
  <h2><xsl:value-of select="@name" /></h2>
  <xsl:apply-templates />
</xsl:template>

<xsl:template match="bugs">
  <table border="0" cellspacing="0" cellpadding="5">
    <xsl:for-each select="bug_item">
    <tr>
      <td><xsl:value-of select="title/text()" /></td>
    </tr>
    </xsl:for-each>
  </table>
</xsl:template>

</xsl:stylesheet>
```

Looking at just the bugs template, let's see how each `<bug_item>` is constructed in the target XML tree. When the bugs template is first invoked, it adds the `<table>` element to the target document. At this point, the `<xsl:for-each>` instruction is called and a temporary node-set is constructed with the entire set of bug items that are the children of the `<bugs>` element. In the first bugs node, there are three bug items, thus the code within the `<xsl:for-each>` block will be executed three times. Here is an illustration of what happens after the iteration on the first bug item node:

Source Document	Target Document
`<bug_item>`	`...`
`<title>It crashes when a string with more than 256 bytes is declared</title>`	`<table border="0" cellspacing="0"` `cellpadding="5">`
`<report_date>200201281015</report_date>`	`<tr>`
`<reported-by>John Smith</reported-by>`	`<td>It crashes when a string with more than 256 bytes is declared</td>`
`<status>Open</status>`	`</tr>`
`<last_update>`	`<xsl:for-each ... >`
`200201281016</last_update>`	`</table>`
`<description>...</description>`	`...`
`<severity>3</severity>`	
`</bug_item>`	
`...`	

As we can see, a new row with one column has been added into the HTML `<table>` tag with the title of the first `<bug_item>`. At this point, the XSLT processor knows there are additional nodes to traverse, so it moves to the next item and repeats the same process until all the elements have been added to the table.

The final result after all the nodes have been processed for this application produces the following HTML:

```
...
<h2>sportran compiler</h2>
<table border="0" cellspacing="0" cellpadding="5">
  <tr>
    <td>It crashes when a string with more than 256 bytes is declared</td>
  </tr>
  <tr>
    <td>String concatenation fails if a string contains a dot</td>
  </tr>
  <tr>
    <td>Error when summing two integers</td>
  </tr>
</table>
...
```

If we run this example with the `bug_list.xml` file, the following result would appear in the web browser:

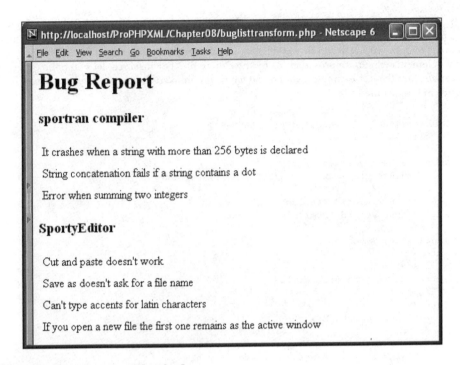

Including XSL Files – xsl:include

XSL documents can get quite large and moreover they can become quite difficult to maintain as the translations become more complex. To allow us to modularize our work, we can use `<xsl:include>`, which is an instruction to include other stylesheets.

Not only does this allow us to manage our templates more effectively, but we can also group templates based on their reusability. What if we wanted to reuse the bugs template in the previous section to generated the table of bug items? To maintain our stylesheets and avoid duplication, we could place it in its own stylesheet, like this:

```xml
<?xml version="1.0" encoding="iso-8859-1"?>
<!-- blincluded.xsl -->

<xsl:stylesheet version="1.0"
  xmlns:xsl="http://www.w3.org/1999/XSL/Transform">

<xsl:template match="bugs">
  <table border="0" cellspacing="0" cellpadding="5">
    <xsl:for-each select="bug_item">
      <tr>
        <td><xsl:value-of select="title" /></td>
      </tr>
    </xsl:for-each>
  </table>
</xsl:template>

</xsl:stylesheet>
```

Generally, there is nothing new here. A new stylesheet was constructed with the bugs template, and added as the only template within the file. As with some template strategies, this one is not meant to be used on its own but rather with other stylesheets, so it doesn't contain any HTML <html>, <head>, or <body> elements which are provided for by the calling file. For instance, let's take the other half of the application from the last example. Notice that we have removed the bugs template in anticipation of its presence in the included file:

```
<?xml version="1.0" encoding="iso-8859-1"?>
<!-- blinclude.xsl -->

<xsl:stylesheet version="1.0"
  xmlns:xsl="http://www.w3.org/1999/XSL/Transform">

  <xsl:include href="blincluded.xsl" />
  <xsl:output method="html" indent="yes" />

<xsl:template match="/">
  <html>
    <head>
      <title>Bug Report</title>
    </head>
    <body>
      <h1>Bug Report</h1>
    </body>
    <xsl:for-each select="bug_list/application">
      <h2><xsl:value-of select="@name" /></h2>
      <xsl:apply-templates />
    </xsl:for-each>
  </html>
</xsl:template>
</xsl:stylesheet>
```

In the gray portion of the XSL document, the first stylesheet is included into the main stylesheet. This is included at the top as the first top-level element for a good reason – the processor will return errors if documents are included after other instructions are defined. The <xsl:include> instruction only takes one attribute called href that describes the location or URI of the XSL document (similar to an <link/> in HTML).

At the time the XSLT processor arrives and executes this instruction, many things happen. First, the processor scans the stylesheet document and includes all the top-level elements that are placed under its <xsl:stylesheet> root node. This means that all the elements that are defined in the included stylesheet are defined before the instructions and templates of the main stylesheet. This is very important because, as the priority rules suggests, any rule that has the same priority value and exact XPath expression precedence will not be used if a similar template rule is defined afterwards. Although this is not a problem with our current example, if a bugs template was defined in the main stylesheet, it will nullify the contents of the included template. For instance, take this new bugs template:

```
<xsl:template match="bugs" />
```

If this template was defined, it would inhibit the bug items from being displayed under its application title. In fact, no HTML table code would appear at all.

If we run this example, the results would be identical to those opposite. The only real difference is that if we wanted the bug items to be displayed within a table in another stylesheet, we could include this XSL document once again to take advantage of reusability.

The XSLT specification also mentions a slightly more powerful inclusive strategy called **importing**, but unfortunately it is not implemented and so the processor skips it. Thus, this section will not discuss it. Let us move our attention to writing XSL documents using a new simplified syntax.

The Literal Result Element

If the XSL document is quite small and we only require (or prefer) to have one template, it is possible to remove all the XSL template definitions and top-level instructions, and have the transformation instructions contained within a single result. When this is done, the code within the XSL document will be matched with the root node of the source document and nothing more. This effectively makes the XSL document look a lot more like the exact resultant document – hence the name **literal** result. This feature allows us to create simple documents very quickly.

Here is a small example that demonstrates the literal result element:

```
<html xsl:version="1.0" xmlns:xsl="http://www.w3.org/1999/XSL/Transform">
<!-- blliteralresult.xsl -->

  <head>
    <title>Status Bug Report</title>
  </head>
  <body>
    <h2>Application Names</h2>
    1. <xsl:value-of select="/bug_list/application[1]/@name" /><br />
    2. <xsl:value-of select="/bug_list/application[2]/@name" /><br />
    <br />
  </body>
</html>
```

This closely resembles the target document. This definition is equivalent to the following XSL document:

```
<?xml version="1.0" encoding="iso-8859-1"?>

<xsl:stylesheet version="1.0"
  xmlns:xsl="http://www.w3.org/1999/XSL/Transform">

<xsl:output method="html" indent="yes" />

<xsl:template match="/">
  <html>
    <head>
      <title>Status Bug Report</title>
    </head>
    <body>
      <h2>Application Names</h2>
      1. <xsl:value-of select="/bug_list/application[1]/@name" /><br />
      2. <xsl:value-of select="/bug_list/application[2]/@name" /><br />
```

```
        <br />
      </body>
    </html>
  </xsl:template>
</xsl:stylesheet>
```

Although this example uses HTML, we can use literal result documents for any root node from an XML document.

To create a literal result document, the root node must contain two items:

- ❑ The XSL document version
- ❑ The namespace declaration

These items appear exactly as they would appear in the `<xsl:stylesheet>` element. While Sablotron will not complain if the `xsl:version` attribute is omitted, it would be best to include it as other processors from other platforms may require it.

To close this section, there are a few drawbacks to using literal result elements:

- ❑ We will not be able to use any top-level XSL elements. Although the chapter has not discussed many top-level instructions at this point, this might inhibit us from taking advantage of this shortcut method. As the complexity of our XSL documents increases, we'll most likely be using the XSL `include` function as well as customizing the output of the resultant document. These instructions will be impossible to execute using the literal result element.

- ❑ We will not be able to use any other templates. An offset of this limitation is that many of our XPath expressions will be larger because the current node will always be the root node (except for some exceptions like the `<xsl:for-each>` instruction). Thus, we will have to provide the full XML source path at all times.

Single Conditional Element – xsl:if

In all our examples thus far, we've been matching the entire set of nodes that exist within the source document. For instance, when we used `<xsl:for-each>`, we traversed through the entire list of bug items under an application tree. However, if we only wanted to display the open bug items or display bug items with a specific date, it has been impossible up to this point.

XSL includes an `<xsl:if>` instruction that allows us to test for these conditions in order to refine our output result. The `<xsl:if>` instruction says, "if this XPath condition is TRUE, then I want the XSLT processor to add these nodes to the resultant tree".

With the combination of `<xsl:for-each>` and `<xsl:if>`, XSL does behave much like a programming language, but although it might have similar constructs, its behavior is quite different. A programming language controls the flow of the data and its I/O. If we want something displayed to the browser in PHP, we utilize `printf()` or similar functions, or use `echo` statements. To have some input read in from a file, we have to explicitly program all the actions.

In XSL, we have little control on how the source document is read and how the target document is written. The best we can do is provide instructions, using XSL documents, to generate the expected result. With XSL documents, we must declare rules that define what is to happen if this happens, but ultimately we have little control on how the XSLT processor handles these situations. This is the true difference between a programming language and XSLT, which is a declarative language. We can think of XSL like SQL, since SQL is also a declarative language. With SQL, we specify the result we want (similar to a target transformation), but we don't specify how it is done (equivalent to the XSLT processor).

Nonetheless, procedural constructs in a language like XSL are very useful. Let's say we want to list all the bug items that have an open status, regardless of where they reside within the XML file. We can do this by testing if the `<status>` element contains either the values open or Open.

```
<h2>Open Bugs</h2>
<xsl:for-each select=".//bug_item">
  <xsl:if test="status = 'open' or status = 'Open'">
    <xsl:value-of select="title/text()" />
  </xsl:if>
</xsl:for-each>
```

The `<xsl:if>` instruction takes a `test` attribute that contains an XPath expression expected to evaluate to either TRUE or FALSE. All bug items in the source file are tested with this expression and only the ones that are open will have their `<title>` elements copied to the resultant XML tree. Using this idea, it is possible to display a list of open bugs and a list of closed bugs separately:

```
<html version="1.0" xmlns:xsl="http://www.w3.org/1999/XSL/Transform">
<!-- blif.xsl -->
  <head>
    <title>Status Bug Report</title>
  </head>
  <body>
    <h1>Status Bug Report</h1>

    <h2>Open Bugs</h2>
    <xsl:for-each select=".//bug_item">
      <xsl:if test="status = 'open' or status = 'Open'">
        <xsl:value-of select="title" /><br />
      </xsl:if>
    </xsl:for-each>

    <h2>Closed Bugs</h2>
    <xsl:for-each select=".//bug_item">
      <xsl:if test="status = 'closed' or status = 'Closed'">
      <xsl:value-of select="title" /><br />
      </xsl:if>
    </xsl:for-each>
  </body>
</html>
```

This example uses the two similar `<xsl:for-each>` blocks as seen earlier, where the XSLT processor scans all the open bug items first, and then the closed ones.

This is the result:

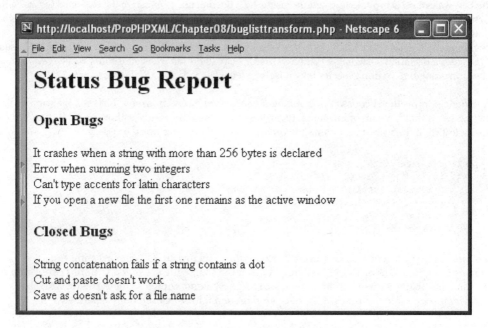

We should make a note to check the actual data of the XML content so that when we write the test conditions, we can make sure the test case works for all items. In this instance, the integrity of the XML file is somewhat questionable because the status is either open or Open. Did this come from a software package? Was this from a data entry person? What will happen if future bug items have an o or O for their character data? In such cases, we might want to pose a suggestion and make a change, solving the chronic problem rather than patching the XSL document with Band-Aids.

Multiple Conditional Element – xsl:choose

There is also an equivalent instruction to PHP's multi-conditional if...else constructs called <xsl:choose>. It might also be described as a switch block with implicit break statements. With this instruction, we can test many conditions one after the other, but once a conditional is evaluated to FALSE (or no conditions are met), the XSLT processor will break out of the instruction and resume executing XSL instructions. In effect, the processor chooses one of the following conditions and executes the code assigned within it.

A <xsl:choose> instruction consists of one or more <xsl:when> statements. Each one can test a different condition by using a test attribute, exactly as the <xsl:if> instruction shown earlier. Within the <xsl:when> test blocks, there can be XSL instructions and character data to describe how the target XML tree is constructed when it's been selected by the XSLT processor. It is also possible to specify an else clause called <xsl:otherwise>. If none of the <xsl:when> conditions are satisfied, the processor will use the <xsl:otherwise> block.

Here is the element structure for a multi-conditional instruction as discussed:

```
<xsl:choose>
  <xsl:when test="expression1">…</xsl:when>
  <xsl:when test="expression2">…</xsl:when>
  <xsl:when test="expression3">…</xsl:when>
  <xsl:otherwise>…</xsl:otherwise>
</xsl:choose>
```

Let's take a look at an example that uses the `<xsl:choose>` instruction. In this example, we are going to display a table of all the bug items in the XML database. In this table, there will be three columns describing what application the bug belongs to, the nature of the bug, and who it was reported by. To take advantage of the `<xsl:choose>` instruction, we are going to test each bug item in the loop for its current status and display it in bold or in italics depending on if it is open or closed, respectively.

Here is the sourcecode for the XSL document. Notice that this example takes advantage of the literal result syntax:

```
<html version="1.0" xmlns:xsl="http://www.w3.org/1999/XSL/Transform">
<!-- blchoose.xsl -->

  <head>
    <title>Status Bug Report</title>
  </head>
  <body>
    <h1>Status Bug Report</h1>

    <table border="2" cellpadding="2">
      <tr>
        <th>Application</th>
        <th>Title</th>
        <th>Reported By</th>
      </tr>
      <xsl:for-each select=".//bug_item">
        <tr>
          <td><xsl:value-of select="../../@name" /></td>
            <xsl:choose>
              <xsl:when test="status = 'closed' or status = 'Closed'">
                <td>
                    <i><xsl:value-of select="title" /></i>
                </td>
              </xsl:when>
              <xsl:otherwise>
                <td>
                    <b><xsl:value-of select="title" /><b/>
                </td>
              </xsl:otherwise>
            </xsl:choose>
          <td><xsl:value-of select="reported-by/text()" /></td>
        </tr>
      </xsl:for-each>
    </table>
  </body>
</html>
```

323

The XSLT processor looks at every bug item using a `<xsl:for-each>` construct and executes a `<xsl:choose>` block. Let's take the first bug item, for instance:

```
<xsl:when test="status = 'closed' or status = 'Closed'">
  <td>
  <i><xsl:value-of select="title" /></i>
  </td>
</xsl:when>
```

The processor tests its status to see if it has been closed. If we refer to our source document, we can see that this bug item is in fact open, thus the test will fail and return `false`. Since this statement has failed, none of the statements within this `<xsl:when>` block will be executing and no new content will be added to the resultant XML document.

However, there is a new test that will execute because it uses the `<xsl:otherwise>` instruction. Since `<xsl:otherwise>` is called when all of the preceding tests have failed, a new `<td>` element is added to the HTML table in the resultant code, like this:

```
<td><b>It crashes when a string with more than 256 bytes is declared</b></td>
```

When the first iteration of the `<xsl:for-each>` is finished, a new bug item will be tested. In this case, the bug item is closed. When the processor arrives at the `<xsl:choose>` block and tests the first `<xsl:when>` condition, the first test will evaluate as `FALSE`. In this case, the result will appear in italics. Here is the result of applying this stylesheet if displayed in a browser:

Sorting – xsl:sort

Although the last example makes it very clear which bugs are open and which ones are closed, the organization of the display is still not quite up to par. It might have been better to sort the results so that the open bugs (the ones people might want to see first) are displayed at the top. More so, it would be good to display the more severe bugs first so we can prioritize and tackle the most detrimental bugs in the program we are trying to build. With XSLT's `<xsl:sort>` instruction, we can do just that.

Let's build a sorting mechanism into our previous example:

```
<html version="1.0" xmlns:xsl="http://www.w3.org/1999/XSL/Transform">
<!-- blsort.xsl -->

  <head>
    <title>Status Bug Report</title>
  </head>
  <body>
    <h1>Status Bug Report</h1>

    <table border="2" cellpadding="2">
      <tr>
        <th>Application</th>
        <th>Title</th>
        <th>Reported By</th>
      </tr>
      <xsl:for-each select=".//bug_item">
        <xsl:sort select="status" order="descending" />
        <xsl:sort select="severity" order="descending" data-type="number" />
        <xsl:sort select="title" order="ascending" data-type="text" />
        <tr>
          <td><xsl:value-of select="../../@name" /></td>
          <td>
            <xsl:choose>
              <xsl:when test="status = 'closed' or status = 'Closed'">
                <i>
                  <xsl:value-of select="title" />
                </i>
              </xsl:when>
              <xsl:otherwise>
                <b>
                  <xsl:choose>
                    <xsl:when test="severity &gt; 3">
                      * <xsl:value-of select="title" /> *
                    </xsl:when>
                    <xsl:otherwise>
                      <xsl:value-of select="title" />
                    </xsl:otherwise>
                  </xsl:choose>
                </b>
              </xsl:otherwise>
            </xsl:choose>
          </td>
          <td><xsl:value-of select="reported-by/text()" /></td>
        </tr>
      </xsl:for-each>
    </table>
  </body>
</html>
```

When sorting a list of nodes, there are only two ways to do it:

❑ By calling a sort within the `<xsl:apply-templates>` instruction

❑ By using an `<xsl:for-each>` construct

325

Anywhere else, the sort just doesn't make any sense. In this example, we use a sort when we traverse all the bug items within the document. When sorting the list of elements within a `<xsl:for-each>` block, the `<xsl:sort>` commands must be issued as the first instructions within the block, or the processor will return an error. Here is the portion of code:

```
<xsl:for-each select=".//bug_item">
    <xsl:sort select="status" order="descending" />
    <xsl:sort select="severity" order="descending" data-type="number" />
    <xsl:sort select="title" order="ascending" data-type="text" />
    <tr>
```

In this example, we use three `<xsl:sort>` instructions. Before any output nodes in the resultant tree are constructed, the parser first looks at contents of the `<xsl:for-each>` block for `<xsl:sort>` instructions. It will scan one instruction after another until it finds an instruction other than a `<xsl:sort>` instruction. This is precisely the reason why the `<xsl:sort>` elements need to appear within the `<xsl:for-each>` block first.

Also, the order of the instructions is very important since it identifies to the processor the order in which the keys are sorted. In this case, the `status` key is sorted first, thus all the open bug items are separated from the closed items. Next, `severity` is the second `<xsl:sort>` key. This means that the first bug item in the list should have the highest severity, and it will gradually decrease for all open bugs. The same will occur for closed bug items. Lastly, any remaining unsorted nodes with equal severity will be sorted by their `title`.

There is also a twist added to the document, that if a bug was open and it was really crucial, it should probably stand out from the rest. Since the severity values ranged from 1 to 6, the value of 4 and above seem like good values to indicate bugs that needed to be fixed immediately. Hence, we have another `<xsl:choose>`. The titles that are in bold within the table will now have asterisks around them if the severity is greater than 3:

```
<b>
  <xsl:choose>
    <xsl:when test="severity > 3">
      * <xsl:value-of select="title" /> *
    </xsl:when>
    <xsl:otherwise>
      <xsl:value-of select="title" />
    </xsl:otherwise>
  </xsl:choose>
</b>
```

select

The `<xsl:sort>` instruction takes one mandatory attribute called `select`, which is an XPath expression that normally returns a string or a number. This describes the particular characteristic that we want to sort on. In the first instruction, we desire to have the status sorted first, separating the open bug items from the closed ones. When referring to XML elements, the processor automatically appends the `text()` function to the element, to select the character data. This short form is not just for sorting, but for any other XSL instructions that expect a value other than a node-set.

case-order

What about the different cases? Normally, XSL provides a way to deal with sorting letters of different cases. By default, the processor treats the letter 'c' the same as the letter 'C'. However, these characters are not exactly the same. Normally the processor treats lowercase letters with lower numeric weight than their capitalized counterparts, but we use a case-order attribute that can be equal to upper-first to reverse them. However, in the current version of Sablotron, this feature is unsupported. This really isn't that big of deal though as in most cases we will never require this function.

order

The <xsl:sort> instruction also contains an order attribute that specifies ascending or descending order. As we can see from the code in this example, the values ascending and descending are the proper values. In this example, we want the status to be sorted in descending order since open bugs should appear first. Severity should also be in descending order since we want to see the most severe bugs first, allowing the reader to understand the priority. Lastly, the bug item's title will be sorted in ascending order.

data-type

The last attribute to mention is data-type parameter. This attribute tells the XSLT processor what type of key it is sorting on. For instance, the values 10 and 2 can be sorted in two ways: by default, the processor sorts the data as strings, thus 10 would come before the value 2. Since these are numeric values, this is obviously incorrect. To fix this, the data-type attribute is used to tell the processor these are numeric values, using the number value as seen above.

Running the Example

Once this example is run in a browser, we will see a table with the sorted bug items that we indicated above:

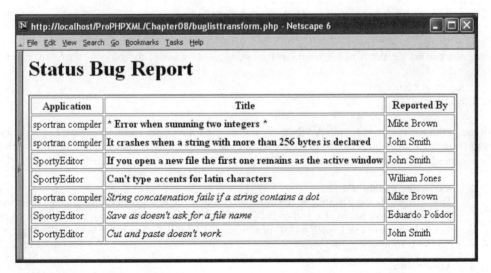

Earlier, this section mentioned that the <xsl:sort> instruction could be used with apply-templates. Here is a quick snippet of code that demonstrates this feature:

```
<xsl:apply-templates select="//bug_items">
  <xsl:sort select="status" order="descending" />
  <xsl:sort select="severity" order="descending" data-type="number" />
  <xsl:sort select="title" order="ascending" data-type="text" />
</xsl:apply-templates>
```

If this code was placed in a root template and a new bug_item template was defined, the processor would first gather the node-set of bug items and sort the results before matching each item in the list. In essence, this approach would achieve the same effect as the above.

Numbering – xsl:number

The last of the character instructions is <xsl:number>, which allows us to automatically number a series of nodes in a variety of formats. This instruction is far more powerful than any ordered list in HTML. Not only does it pre-render the numbers, it works with any target document type.

So, how does it work? When the XSLT processor evaluates an <xsl:apply-templates> instruction or an <xsl:for-each> block, it assigns a numeric value to every node in the tree. The number is calculated on the type and position of the node in the result set. For instance, if an <xsl:for-each> instruction iterates through a list of bug items for the Sportran compiler application, the numbers would read 1 through 3. Also, if a template matches all the bug items within the bug list document, the numbers would range from 1 to 7.

Now that we have an idea how numbers are assigned, let's look at using the instruction.

As the simplest form, the <xsl:number> element can be used like this:

```
<xsl:template match="application">
  <xsl:number /> <xsl:value-of select="@name" /><br />
</xsl:template>
```

Using our bug list file, this template would match two application nodes and generate the following HTML:

1 sportran compiler
2 SportyEditor

Although the template has numbered them, it has not used the power of this element. For instance, the <xsl:number> instruction can be given a format attribute to specify the type of numbering. Here are the accepted values for this attribute:

❑ **Any string ending in 1**
   This string tells the counting mechanism to count in the decimal number system. If set to 1, the counting will begin at 1 and count upwards. It is also possible to put any number of zero values in front of the 1, such as '01' producing '01 02 03…'. Any other value will simply resort to count from 1.

❑ **Alphabetical**
   The string a or A can be passed to indicate an alphabetical counting mechanism. In the first case, the sequence 'a b c … aa ab ac …' is produced. A similar sequence is produced for A, but the characters are all uppercase.

❑ **Roman numerals**

It is also possible to count with roman numerals. Supply the string I, and the `<xsl:number>` instruction will produce the following sequence – 'i ii iii ...'. Like alphabetical counting, it is possible to supply a capital letter to produce uppercase Roman numerals.

For example, to specify alphabetical counting, the following value is used:

```
<xsl:template match="application">
  <xsl:number format="a. " /><xsl:value-of select="@name" /><br />
</xsl:template>
```

This format also includes a period with an extra space. The XSLT processor knows that these are part of the display after the number, and will be included in the target tree as text nodes. The following is the HTML output:

a. sportran compiler
b. SportyEditor

The XSLT processor calculates the numeric value of the node based on its location in the current list. In this case, there are only two application nodes being matched, so the processor assigns the values 1 and 2 to these nodes. It is also possible to assign our own values by using the value attribute, overriding the XSLT processor's pre-made calculations.

Here is an example to make the `<xsl:number>` instruction skip every 3 numbers:

```
<xsl:template match="application">
  <xsl:number format="a. " value="position() * 3" />
  <xsl:value-of select="@name" />
  <br />
</xsl:template>
```

This will output the values d. and h., assuming that the application node type is the only one being matched (through the use of `<xsl:apply-templates>`). Otherwise the position() function will return different results. If no value attribute is specified, then the `<xsl:number>` element inserts a number based on the position of the current node in the source tree.

> At the time of this writing, there is a bug in the XSLT Sablotron extension. The position() function sometimes doesn't return the correct result. For instance, in the above example, the code will return f and l and this is incorrect. In PHP 4.1.1, this worked fine but as of PHP 4.1.2, this stopped working correctly. By the time you read this book, this problem should be fixed.

Using our knowledge of the `<xsl:number>` instruction, here is an example that numbers the bug list's applications and subnumbers their respective bug items. We accomplish this by matching the application and bug list elements:

```
<?xml version="1.0" encoding="iso-8859-1"?>
<!-- blnumber.xsl -->

<xsl:stylesheet version="1.0"
  xmlns:xsl="http://www.w3.org/1999/XSL/Transform">

<xsl:output method="html" indent="yes" />

<xsl:template match="/">
  <html>
    <head>
      <title>Bug Report</title>
      </head>
    <body>
      <h1>Bug Report</h1>
      <xsl:apply-templates />
    </body>
  </html>
</xsl:template>

<xsl:template match="application">
  <h2>
    <xsl:number format="1. " />
    <xsl:value-of select="@name" />
  </h2>
  <xsl:apply-templates />
</xsl:template>

<xsl:template match="bugs">
  <xsl:for-each select="bug_item">
    <xsl:number format="1" count="application" />.<xsl:number format="1"/>.
    <xsl:value-of select="title" /><br />
  </xsl:for-each>
</xsl:template>

</xsl:stylesheet>
```

In the `application` template, we use the `<xsl:number>` instruction in a similar way to our previous short examples. The applications' name will be placed between an `<h2>` tag with a numeric value starting at 1 instead of starting from the alphabetic character 'a'.

The second template is a bit trickier since it uses two `<xsl:number>` instructions to form the complete two-digit reference number:

```
<xsl:number format="1" count="application" />.<xsl:number format="1"/>.
<xsl:value-of select="title" /><br />
```

The first instruction uses an attribute we haven't discussed previously – the `count` attribute. This attribute tells the processor to count from somewhere other than the current node. In this case, we are telling the processor to count from the current `application` node. The first time this template is called, the `sportran compiler` application would be the `<application>` element for all the bug items traversed. Therefore, the number '1' is added to the resultant tree because it is the first application node the processor has come across. It is possible to obtain a formatted number sequence for a node from anywhere within the document.

The second `<xsl:number>` instruction is similar to the first example in that it derives the number from the current node. In this case, it is the `<bug_item>` element because `<xsl:for-each>` blocks establish a new current node `temporary`, as stated previously in the chapter. Here is the result of this example:

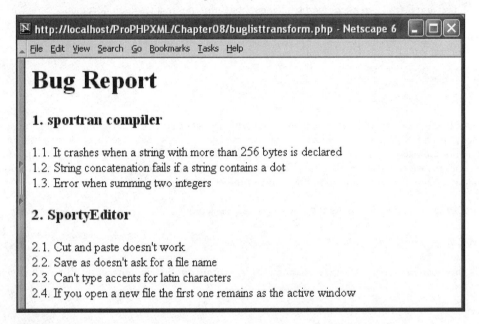

Creating Resultant XML Documents

XSLT also offers a way to create new nodes in the target tree explicitly by using XSL commands. These are most helpful when we want to transform the XML document into a new vocabulary, create static PHP scripts, or clean up the construction on target elements.

In this section we will look at:

❏   How to create elements and attributes.

❏   How to create comments in the target document.

❏   How to copy elements, attributes, and character data from one document to another. This section will look at converting the bug list XML document into a much more desirable format.

❏   How to create PHP scripts by creating processing instructions.

By the end of the section we will have an excellent appreciation of what we can do with XSL documents.

xsl:element and xsl:attribute

The first two elements that construct nodes in the resultant tree are the most common – **elements** and **attributes**. These are useful in many different situations.

For instance, there are times where specifying an attribute is not practical because there is a lot of data to be set for its value or it contains too many forbidden characters to conform to the XML syntax, making it difficult to convert. These situations can be solved by using the `<xsl:attribute>` instruction. This instruction also helps to create or modify elements and attributes in a resultant document.

Here is a short example:

```
<xsl:element name="img">
  <xsl:attribute name="src">/graphics/stuff.jpg</xsl:attribute>
</xsl:element>
```

The following code models an `<img>` attribute with a single `src` attribute; similar to a meta data description for XML tags. The `<xsl:element>` tag contains zero or more `<xsl:attribute>` elements and each `<xsl:attribute>` contains character data containing the value for that attribute. In the example we can also see that the XSL `<xsl:element>` and `<xsl:attribute>` instructions contain a `name` attribute containing the name of the element or attribute.

Here is the resultant XML generated by this small example:

```
<img src="/graphics/stuff.jpg" />
```

It is also possible to combine these instructions by writing out the elements explicitly as character data, like this:

```
<img>
  <xsl:attribute name="src">/graphics/stuff.jpg</xsl:attribute>
</img>
```

This will output the same HTML code as before. In some situations, using one or two `<xsl:attribute>` instructions is preferable over writing the entire element using these new commands.

Lastly, character data can be added to the target element, just as it can be added to any other element – it is added within the `<xsl:element>` instruction.

Here is a short example that defines a few attributes and character data:

```
<xsl:element name="bug-item">
  <xsl:attribute name="severity">
    <xsl:value-of select="severity/text()" />
  </xsl:attribute>
  <xsl:value-of select="description" />
</xsl:element>
```

The highlighted code will construct a text node in the new element in the XML tree. Here is the final element assuming the severity is 4 and the description contained the string, "...":

```
<bug-item severity="4">...</bug-item>
```

xsl:comment

Since XSL documents are XML files, any comments put within the document will not be copied over to the target document. In most cases, this is desirable and makes sense; however, there are times when we really want comments to be placed in the resultant document. Usually, they are not placed for commenting the structure and meaning of the target document, but rather to aid in the use of scripts, and in embedding stylesheets that are required for HTML pages.

The `<xsl:comment>` instruction is as simple as writing comments in a document. To create a comment, we must use the `<xsl:comment>` element and enter character data to indicate the text of the comment. For example:

```
<xsl:comment>This is a comment</xsl:comment>
```

will produce the comment:

```
<!-- This is a comment -->
```

More complicated XSL instructions can also be placed between the `<xsl:comment>` elements. Doing this will put all the resultant XML content within a comment.

xsl:copy

The `<xsl:copy>` element provides an easy way of copying the current node to the resultant XML tree. Using this instruction we can copy elements, attributes, and character data – anything that constitutes a node. The namespace nodes associated with the current node are also automatically copied, but the attributes and children of the node are not automatically copied, hence, these must be copied individually.

Here is an example that is considered to be the identity rule, meaning, "what comes in must go out". In other words, this rule matches all nodes (for example, elements, comments, and PIs), including attributes, and copies them to the resultant tree, which will then be identical to the source document. To match all of these XML constructs, we must use the XPath `@*|node()` expression, like this:

```
<xsl:template match="@*|node()">
  <xsl:copy>
    <xsl:apply-templates select="@*|node()"/>
  </xsl:copy>
</xsl:template>
```

Since the `<xsl:apply-templates>` instruction tells the processor to keep handling the children of the current node, it must be placed within the `<xsl:copy>` instruction. Once this is set, every node within the tree will be matched with this rule. This is often useful when we want to change the rules for a few instructions, but do not want to provide rules for others, thus saving some time writing an XSL file to convert one XML vocabulary to another. In fact, that is our next example.

At times we may find a need to redesign XML files. Luckily for us, it is possible to change the structure of the file using XSLT. A programmer has the ability to make changes and that is what this section is going to discuss.

For instance, let's take a look at changing the structure of the bug_list.xml document:

❑ **The XML Element Names**
Like most things, when dealing with programming, consistency should come before anything else. In a development environment, we want all our XML files to have the same format if possible. For instance, our document contains the node bug_item and reported-by. If we weren't too familiar with this distinction, we could have written code that was buggy and it might have taken a long time to figure out the quirks. Common naming strategies help reduce bugs, hence, care should be taken when designing an XML vocabulary.

❑ **Unnecessary \<bugs\> element**
If we recall, there was a \<bugs\> element under the application node. Since we are using this XML document for just a bug list for several applications, any children under the \<application\> element should be bug items; as far as our application is concerned, we don't plan on adding anything else, so why an extra node to group them? We do this to make the document less confusing when we parse it, since we reduce the parsing and transforming efforts on the programmer.

❑ **Structure of the bug items**
Now we know how to model and design XML documents. While doing this, the distinction between attributes and elements is always a major issue. In this case, all the information describing a bug item is constructed using elements. It would be a wise idea to describe all this information as attributes except for the description because all of these describe the auxiliary information of the bug item. They are also easier to parse this way. The real bug information is the description and that should be represented as character data.

❑ **Inconsistent values for \<status\> element**
The last thing to notice is that the file contains different values that mean the exact same thing. For instance, 'Closed' and 'closed' are read very differently by programs and the XSLT processor but to humans they are the same. This can be caused by different people when they add new content to the document. To overcome this problem, the strings must be changed to common literal values that will set the standard. In this case, the lowercased versions of closed and open will suit just fine, so it is imperative that these be changed. The result will make XPath expressions and parsers easy to write.

Our challenge is to use XSLT to convert the old document to one with these changes. Here is a diagram describing the structure of the new target XML document:

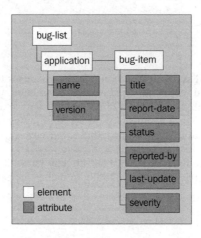

Notice that this representation removes the <bugs> element, renames any elements and attributes to a more consistent scheme, and moves most of the bug item children to attributes. The status change cannot be seen in this diagram, but let's see how this is done using XSL code:

```
<?xml version="1.0" encoding="iso-8859-1"?>
<!-- blnewresultant.xsl -->

<xsl:stylesheet version="1.0"
  xmlns:xsl="http://www.w3.org/1999/XSL/Transform">
<xsl:output method="xml" indent="yes" />

<xsl:template match="bug_list">
  <xsl:element name="bug-list">
    <xsl:apply-templates select="application" />
  </xsl:element>
</xsl:template>
```

The first template matches the <bug_list> element.

Remember that we wanted to rename this element? To do this, we use the <xsl:element> instruction and tell the processor to keep creating new nodes under the new <bug-list> element. We only apply the application node to ignore any processing of whitespace or misplaced character data:

```
<xsl:template match="bugs">
  <xsl:apply-templates select="bug_item" />
</xsl:template>
```

The next element processes the <bugs> element. Since we want to strip this element out of the target document, we do not add any nodes to the target XML tree. In this case, we simply tell the processor to keep going, only processing the <bug_item> elements:

```
<xsl:template match="bug_item">
  <xsl:element name="bug-item">
    <xsl:attribute name="title">
      <xsl:value-of select="title" />
    </xsl:attribute>
    <xsl:attribute name="report-date">
      <xsl:value-of select="report_date" />
    </xsl:attribute>
    <xsl:attribute name="reported-by">
      <xsl:value-of select="reported-by" />
    </xsl:attribute>
```

The bug-list template is the largest portion of the document. In the first portion, we create a new <bug-item> element and start adding its attributes. Notice that as we add the element and attributes we make the naming format consistent with what we've chosen. By selecting the attribute in the source file, we can add the content:

```
<xsl:attribute name="status">
  <xsl:choose>
    <xsl:when test="status = 'Open'">open</xsl:when>
```

```
            <xsl:when test="status = 'Closed'">closed</xsl:when>
            <xsl:otherwise><xsl:value-of select="status" /></xsl:otherwise>
        </xsl:choose>
    </xsl:attribute>
```

The `<status>` element needs to be converted in a more complicated manner because we have to rename the capitalized values back to lowercase. This is done by a small `<xsl:choose>` block. If the value is not one of the capitalized forms, then we resort to the one in the source document and use that. No matter what condition is chosen, the result will be added to the attribute as character data, setting the value of the `status` attribute.

The remaining attributes work in a similar manner as the first ones by obtaining their values using XPath and adding the attributes nodes. The description field is not added as an attribute, but rather as character data, just before the element is closed off with the ending `<xsl:element>` tag:

```
    <xsl:attribute name="last-update">
      <xsl:value-of select="last_update" />
    </xsl:attribute>
    <xsl:attribute name="severity">
      <xsl:value-of select="severity" />
    </xsl:attribute>
    <xsl:value-of select="description" />
  </xsl:element>
</xsl:template>
```

Finally, this function is the identity element and it will be used on any of the elements and attributes in the source document that do not have templates defined. In our example, this means the `<application>` node. In most cases, we may not want to use the identity template where this matches only one occurrence in the source file, but in many other examples we might only want to convert one or two elements in a 20-element XML document. This of course will save us time:

```
<xsl:template match="@*|node()">
 <xsl:copy>
  <xsl:apply-templates select="@*|node()"/>
 </xsl:copy>
</xsl:template>

</xsl:stylesheet>
```

So why does this not match any of the other elements and attributes? XSL precedence rules say that the XPath expression implicitly calculates a priority for each template. In this case, the template is of the lowest priority since the XPath expression is very generic. Thus, every element and attribute will be matched by the defined templates before it is matched by this one – except for the `application` node of course.

Once this XSL document is run through an XSL processor, the following document will be produced. The structure is much cleaner, the document size has decreased, and programming efforts will also be minimized when working with this document as compared to the previous version:

```xml
<?xml version="1.0" encoding="UTF-8"?>
<bug-list>
  <application name="sportran compiler" version="1.1">
    <bug-item title="It crashes when a string with more than 256 bytes is
                     declared"
              report-date="200201281015" reported-by="John Smith"
              status="open" last-update="200201281016"
              severity="3">
    </bug-item>

    <bug-item title="String concatenation fails if a string contains a dot"
              report-date="200201141430" reported-by="Mike Brown"
              status="closed" last-update="200201161830"
              severity="5">
    </bug-item>

    <bug-item title="Error when summing two integers"
              report-date="200201141630" reported-by="Mike Brown"
              status="open" last-update="200201141630"
              severity="4">
    </bug-item>
  </application>

  <application name="SportyEditor" version="1.0">
    <bug-item title="Cut and paste doesn't work"
              report-date="200201051725" reported-by="John Smith"
              status="closed" last-update="200201091015"
              severity="5">
    </bug-item>

    <bug-item title="Save as doesn't ask for a file name"
              report-date="200201271839" reported-by="Eduardo Polidor"
              status="closed" last-update="200201271839"
              severity="6">
    </bug-item>

    <bug-item title="Can't type accents for latin characters"
              report-date="200201011415" reported-by="William Jones"
              status="open" last-update="200201271839"
              severity="1">
    </bug-item>

    <bug-item title="If you open a new file the first one remains as the
                     active window"
              report-date="200201211041" reported-by="John Smith"
              status="open" last-update="200201271839"
              severity="2">
    </bug-item>
  </application>
</bug-list>
```

xsl:processing-instruction

This XSL instruction deals with creating processing instructions within the target document. This can be accomplished by using the `<xsl:processing-instruction>` element. Much like the other node creation instructions, this element takes a `name` attribute, signifying the target application to use to process its contents, and character data containing the code to execute.

In many cases, this instruction is called with a CDATA block. Often, programming languages contain many characters that violate the XML syntax. So, to create a processing instruction node with PHP sourcecode, we can use the following XSL instruction:

```
<xsl:processing-instruction name="php">
  <![CDATA[
    print ("Sourcecode goes here");
]]>
</xsl:processing-instruction>
```

Remember, the XSLT processor doesn't execute this code – it just copies this code into the target document. Hence, we can generate PHP scripts from XML files if need be, or any other processing language for that matter. Here is an example that generates a PHP script that statically displays an HTML table of all the bugs in the source document with the bug item title, its status, and who it was reported by. The information is statically issued into an array and will be read by the PHP interpreter to display the table:

```
<?xml version="1.0" encoding="iso-8859-1"?>
<!-- blphp.xsl -->

<xsl:stylesheet version="1.0"
             xmlns:xsl="http://www.w3.org/1999/XSL/Transform">

<xsl:output method="xml"
            indent="yes"
            media-type="text/xhtml"
            encoding="utf-8"
            omit-xml-declaration="yes" />
```

The first difference from the other examples is that in this one we need to highly customize the type of output. For flavor, this example will use XHTML 1.0, rather than using the normal HTML 4.01 specification.

Issuing a `method` attribute describing the format does this. The `media-type` attribute is also used to specify the MIME-type of the target document. In this case we are explicitly saying XHTML. Whenever the method is using the XML format, it is best to specify a `media-type` with it.

The last attribute is the `omit-xml-declaration` attribute. Whenever a traditional XML declaration is included in an unprocessed portion of a PHP script, the processor won't know what to do with it and will complain with a fatal error. Therefore, it's important to make sure this is removed from the target document so PHP won't complain. Normally, the default value is set to `no`:

```
<xsl:template match="/">
  <html>
    <head><title>Buglist using PHP</title></head>
```

```
<body>
  <xsl:processing-instruction name="php">
    $bugItems = array();
      <xsl:for-each select="bug_list/application/bugs/bug_item">
        $bugItems[<xsl:value-of select="position()" />]->title =
          &quot;<xsl:value-of select="title" />&quot;;
        $bugItems[<xsl:value-of select="position()" />]->reportedBy =
          &quot;<xsl:value-of select="reported-by" />&quot;;
        $bugItems[<xsl:value-of select="position()" />]->status =
          &quot;<xsl:value-of select="status" />&quot;;
      </xsl:for-each>
  </xsl:processing-instruction>
```

Our first goal is to create the PHP code that assigns all the bug item data to an array. We do this by looping through all the bug items using the `<xsl:for-each>` instruction and creating each element within the array. Because XSLT maintains the numeric value of each bug item in the `<xsl:for-each>` list, we can use the `position()` function of XPath to assign each index of the array. Instead of creating three arrays for the three pieces of information, we dynamically create a record for each one, create each variable of the array one at a time, and get the value through XPath.

Remember that bit about PHP using many characters that are not valid in XML files?

```
$bugItems[<xsl:value-of select="position()" />]->title = &quot;<xsl:value-of
    select="title" />&quot;;
```

We will have to manually convert all these characters to the entity reference equivalent and this can take some time. We just coded it this way to see how obfuscated the XSL document can look if CDATA blocks are not used when they should be. Now an array of bug items has been constructed, we have to create the HTML table and iterate through the array to display the table rows:

```
<table border="2" cellpadding="5">
  <tr>
    <th>Title</th>
    <th>Reported By</th>
    <th>Status</th>
  </tr>
  <xsl:processing-instruction name="php">
    <![CDATA[
      foreach ($bugItems as $bugItem) {
          print ('<tr>');
          print ('<td>' . $bugItem->title . '</td>');
          print ('<td>' . $bugItem->reportedBy . '</td>');
          print ('<td>' . $bugItem->status . '</td>');
          print ('</tr>');
      }
    ]]>
  </xsl:processing-instruction>
```

By escaping the processing instruction, we can be assured that any new elements will be unprocessed HTML. At this point we start making the HTML table and display the headers for each column. To display the actual bug items, we have to go back into the processing instruction mode. This time, for ease of writing the PHP code, a CDATA block is used. Since the target document has the array initialized with data, we can write the PHP code to read the data from the array and display the rows as seen above:

```
          </table>
        </body>
      </html>
    </xsl:template>

  </xsl:stylesheet>
```

At this point, the table is closed and the XSLT processor stops making the XHTML/PHP document. Once this XSL file has been used by XSLT, a target document will be generated and can be stored into a file. Now a web server running PHP statically without the XML source file can read this file. Here is the content of this generated file:

```
<html>
  <head>
    <title>Buglist using PHP</title>
  </head>
  <body>
    <?php
    $bugItems = array();

    $bugItems[1]->title = "It crashes when a string with more than 256
                          bytes is declared";
    $bugItems[1]->reportedBy = "John Smith";
    $bugItems[1]->status = "Open";

    $bugItems[2]->title = "String concatenation fails if a string
                          contains a dot";
    $bugItems[2]->reportedBy = "Mike Brown";
    $bugItems[2]->status = "Closed";

    $bugItems[3]->title = "Error when summing two integers";
    $bugItems[3]->reportedBy = "Mike Brown";
    $bugItems[3]->status = "Open";

    $bugItems[4]->title = "Cut and paste doesn't work";
    $bugItems[4]->reportedBy = "John Smith";
    $bugItems[4]->status = "closed";

    $bugItems[5]->title = "Save as doesn't ask for a file name";
    $bugItems[5]->reportedBy = "Eduardo Polidor";
    $bugItems[5]->status = "closed";

    $bugItems[6]->title = "Can't type accents for latin characters";
    $bugItems[6]->reportedBy = "William Jones";
    $bugItems[6]->status = "open";

    $bugItems[7]->title = "If you open a new file the first one remains
                          as the active window";
    $bugItems[7]->reportedBy = "John Smith";
    $bugItems[7]->status = "open";
    ?>
    <table border="2" cellpadding="5">
      <tr>
```

```
        <th>Title</th>
        <th>Reported By</th>
        <th>Status</th>
      </tr>
    <?php
    foreach ($bugItems as $bugItem) {
        print ("<tr>");
        print ("<td>" . $bugItem->title . "</td>");
        print ("<td>" . $bugItem->reportedBy . "</td>");
        print ("<td>" . $bugItem->status . "</td>");
        print ("</tr>");
    }
    ?>
    </table>
  </body>
</html>
```

In most cases, if we want to generate PHP scripts, they will probably be more complicated than this example. However, this gives us a pretty good idea of how to create PHP scripts from XML documents and allows us to expand our possibilities with XML.

Now that we have looked at all the XSL instructions in this chapter, let's take a look at processing them by using PHP.

Sablotron Functions

Although there isn't much platform-specific functionality using XSLT, there are several ways to process documents through variables and generating physical files. We can also use Sablotron in an object-oriented fashion.

At the time of this writing, many of the Sablotron functions are undocumented, are experimental, and often do not behave as the documentation suggests. For instance, the documentation suggests that no `file://` prefix be used when passing files to the `xslt_process()` function. If we fail to provide details like these, the process will return unexpected errors. Another instance is where variables containing XML should be parsed, but instead the server crashes on some operating systems, such as Windows. Nonetheless, that doesn't mean this processor does not work – we just have to learn to use it correctly.

Output the Target Document to a File

At this point, all of our examples have been displaying the contents of the resultant document to the screen using a `print()` statement. It is possible to instruct Sablotron to write the contents of the translation to a file directly; perhaps for generating static PHP documents as discussed earlier, or generating static HTML pages in a Content Management System.

Let's develop the code to process the `<xsl:processing-instruction>` example shown earlier:

```
<!-- xsltoutput.php -->
<?php

$sourceXml = 'file://C:\Apache\htdocs\prophpxml\bug_list.xml';
```

```
$sourceXsl = 'file://C:\Apache\htdocs\prophpxml\Chapter08\blphp.xsl';
$targetXml = 'file://C:\Apache\htdocs\prophpxml\Chapter08\mynewfile.php';

$xslt = xslt_create();

// Process the document
if (!$result = @xslt_process($xslt, $sourceXml, $sourceXsl, $targetXml)) {
    print ("Error: <b>" . xslt_error($xslt) . "</b><br />" .
        " Code: <b>" . xslt_errno($xslt) . "</b>");
}

xslt_free($xslt);
return $result;
?>
```

To generate a PHP script using XSLT, we first have to define the full path to the target file name when assigning the $targetXml variable. Notice that the prefix must also be maintained. To tell the processor to generate a file instead of returning the resultant content as a string, all we need to add is an extra parameter after the XSL source file argument. In this case, the xslt_process() function will still return a value, but it will now be either TRUE or FALSE. In either case, the remaining code needs no change from the examples shown earlier in the chapter.

Using Variables Instead of Files

In many situations, the XML content is generated through DOM or some other custom API because the actual data is retrieved from another source, such as a database. In these cases, it is often inefficient and wasteful to write the XML content to a file every time the page is run to simply read it over again. This can also introduce many problems since two people cannot write to the same file at once.

To resolve this problem, Sablotron allows us to supply a list of arguments containing the XML and XSL content as strings. As long as any XML retrieval API allows us to generate a string representation of the XML content, we can use it with Sablotron. This approach is much faster than the previous approach and it does not introduce any shared access problems.

This example will input the XML source document and the XSL document as variables to the XSLT processor rather than files and the processor will return a string representation of the translated document:

```
<!-- xsltargument.php -->
<?php

// assume $xml and $xsl contain string of XML content

$arguments = array('/_xml' => $xml, '/_xsl' => $xsl);

$xslt = xslt_create();

// Process the document
if(!$result = @xslt_process($xslt, 'arg:/_xml', 'arg:/_xsl',
                            NULL, $arguments)) {
    print ("Error: <b>" . xslt_error($xslt) . "</b><br />" .
```

```
        " Code: <b>" . xslt_errno($xslt) . "</b>");
}

xslt_free($xslt);

print ($result);
?>
```

XSLT uses this concept of arguments to pass string representations to the processor. Normally, in the second and third arguments to `xslt_process()`, files would be passed. These files require a prefix (`file://`) to let the processor know that it needs to open the files to retrieve the content. With arguments, this works in a similar manner.

When using arguments, we must create an associative array containing the XML and/or XSL content. There are two special arguments called `/_xml` and `/_xsl`. These indicate to the processor what content is stored at that particular index. In this example we created the following array using both these indexes. Thus, the XML and XSL content is now stored in the array, ready for the XSLT processor to retrieve the data.

So how do we tell the processor to read these arguments instead of files? Like files, we must use a different prefix when passing the XML and XSL arguments. In this case, the prefix `arg:/` instructs the processor to look up an item in the argument array and retrieve its value. For instance, to reference the `/_xml` argument in the array, we would use `arg:/_xml`. This string would be passed into the second parameter of the `xslt_process()` function. Likewise, we could also use the `arg:/_xsl` string value in the third parameter to the `xslt_process()` function to tell the processor to retrieve the XSL content as string as well.

For the processor to retrieve the content from the `$arguments` array, it must be passed to the `xslt_process()` function. Therefore, the fifth argument has been reserved for this purpose.

```
$result = @xslt_process($xslt, 'arg:/_xml', 'arg:/_xsl', NULL, $arguments);
```

As discussed earlier, the fourth argument expresses the file name of the target physical document. If we do not want to output the result to a document and would rather have the function return a string, we can pass the `NULL` value in its place as indicated above.

Once this line has been executed, the processor will fetch the content from the `$arguments` array and will apply the transformations as before. In many situations, the XSL content will not be contained within a string as it is practical to store this information in a physical file. With Sablotron, we are not restricted to use arguments entirely. For instance, our argument list could contain a single XML element:

```
$arguments = array('/_xml' => $xml);
```

and the `xslt_process()` function can just use one `arg:/` parameter, like this:

```
$result = @xslt_process($xslt, 'arg:/_xml', 'file://c:\blah\blah.xsl',
                        NULL, $arguments);
```

Sablotron is fairly flexible, allowing us to achieve any combination of input and output as desired. One of its flaws is the inconsistency of providing full paths to files and providing prefixes to the arguments in the `xslt_process()` function, but once we become familiar with the API we will enjoy its flexibility.

An Object-Oriented Approach

It is also possible to create an object-oriented version to process XSL documents. The idea is to abstract the processor itself and develop methods that the processor can perform. For instance, an XSLT processor in the simplest sense can transform documents or variables. The key to designing a well-made object is to allow for all the cases to be considered.

For instance, the XML content might come from a variable and the XSL document may come from a physical file. We need to be able to handle all these cases in a generic way. Secondly, we might want to display the results to the screen, contain them in a variable, or store them in a target file.

This does not mean that previous methods were difficult, but the process could be streamlined, so we will take that into consideration while designing this small class:

```
<!-- xsltoo.php -->
<?php

define("XSLT_FILE", 1);
define("XSLT_VALUE", 2);
```

To distinguish the type of files given to the class in the constructor and various functions, there must be a `type` field and a set of values that define the types. Here we define the constants for the physical files as well as content contained within a variable, called `value` for short:

```
class XsltProcessor
{
    var $xslt;
    var $sourceXsl = '';
    var $sourceXslType = XSLT_FILE;
    var $arguments = array();
```

Since the processor needs a handler for all the functions within the Sablotron API, it makes sense to store the handler's state within the processor object, encapsulated away from any clients. **Wraps** like this can save a considerable amount of time since the attention to detail is minimized, allowing our mind to focus on the problem at hand.

The next two variables store the XSL document's content and type, being a file or the actual string of XSL content. In most situations we'll be using a file since storing the actual stylesheets in a database is often not required. The last variable stores any permanent or temporary parameters used by the processor such as the content for XSL or XML as discussed earlier:

```
function XsltProcessor($sourceXsl, $type = XSLT_FILE)
{
    if($type == XSLT_FILE) {
        $this->setSourceXslDocument($sourceXsl);
    } else {
```

```
                    $this->setSourceXslValue($sourceXsl);
        }
        $this->xslt = xslt_create();
    }
```

The constructor is rather simple in design – for each processor object there must be an XSL file defined for it. Thus the processor object is responsible for translating one type of document. If another type of document needs to be translated, a new object should be created. This is to allow multiple translations without the burden of specifying the source document over and over again. In this case we can just supply a list of the XML sources one after the other and all will be well.

The code within the constructor is pretty self explanatory. Depending on what type the source XSL content is, we'll need to set it up in different ways, so we test the type and call the appropriate function. The next step is to create a new handler and store it within the object so all the calls to the Sablotron API functions can be called internally throughout the other members:

```
function setSourceXslDocument($sourceXsl)
{
    $this->sourceXsl     = 'file://' . $sourceXsl;
    $this->sourceXslType = XSLT_FILE;
}

function setSourceXslValue($sourceXsl)
{
    $this->sourceXsl             = NULL;
    $this->arguments['/_xsl'] = $sourceXsl;
    $this->sourceXslType         = XSLT_VALUE;
}
```

These functions to set the XSL source content are meant to be private. They have been refactored out of the constructor to clean up code, following the rule that each function should do one thing and do it well. Notice that we add prefixes like `file://` so the client code using this class need not worry about this Sablotron detail.

This is a very flexible transform method, but it is not made to be called explicitly, although it can be. The function can take an XML document, either a file or a variable (defined by the first parameter), and apply the internal XSL document on that XML source document. The function will return a string containing the results of the applied transformations. An optional third parameter exists for users who want to write out the resultant document to a physical file. In these situations, the function will return a Boolean value where TRUE is returned on success and FALSE on failure:

```
function transform($type = XSLT_FILE, $xmlDocument,
                    $targetDocument = NULL)
{
    if ($type == XSLT_VALUE) {
        $this->arguments['/_xml'] = $xmlDocument;
    }

    $inst = $this->getXsltProcessLine($type, $targetDocument);
```

When the function calls the `xslt_process()` function, instead of testing all the combinations of XML and XSL source files, as well as what type of output (which could lead to 8 possible combinations), it would be better to construct a string of the function call dynamically. We can do this with the `eval()` function that allows us to execute PHP code contained in a string. As long as the syntax is valid, we can use any of the local variables in the functional namespace. All the functions and classes are available to us, and any new variable we make can be accessed after `eval()` has finished executing all the statements:

```php
eval($inst);

if (!$result) {
    print ("Error: <b>" . xslt_error($this->xslt) . "</b><br/>"
            " Code: <b>" . xslt_errno($this->xslt) . "</b>");
}

unset($this->arguments['/_xml']);

return $result;
}
```

To make the arguments transparent, we can test if the incoming XML content is a value and add its content to the argument array. Since we can be dealing with multiple files, and they could be of both types, it makes sense to clear the `xml` argument before the function returns the result.

> The `eval()` function can make our code more dynamic in more ways than generating a function. We can use it to instantiate classes that would otherwise be impossible to instantiate normally. Although many would say a call to this function is poor programming, this function is easier to maintain and is much smaller than an 8-condition `switch` or `if` block.

Let's now look at how the `getXsltProcessLine()` works:

```php
function getXsltProcessLine($type, $targetDocument)
{
    $inst = '$result = @xslt_process($this->xslt, ';

    if($type == XSLT_FILE) {
        $inst .= '"file://" . $xmlDocument, ';
    } else {
        $inst .= "'arg:/_xml', ";
    }

    if($this->sourceXslType == XSLT_FILE) {
        $inst .= '$this->sourceXsl, ';
    } else {
        $inst .= "'arg:/_xsl', ";
    }

    if($targetDocument != NULL) {
        $inst .= '"file://" . $targetDocument, ';
    } else {
```

```
        $inst .= 'NULL, ';
        }

        $inst .= '$this->arguments);';

        return $inst;
    }
```

This function tests several of the internal members as well as the XML source type and the possibility of creating a target document. Based on the state of the object and the file to transform, it can create the correct call to `xslt_process()`. For instance, if we were doing a simple transformation where the XSL and XML documents were both files, and the function was to return a string output, the following line would be generated by this function:

```
$result = @xslt_process($this->xslt, "file://" . $xmlDocument,
                        $this->sourceXsl, NULL, $this->arguments);
```

The function doesn't actually replace the variables with their contained values. It simply constructs the line that we might have coded ourselves. The best way to visualize what is happening is to place this line of code where the call to `getXsltProcessLine()` is made.

The next two functions make it very easy to transform the XML content because we no longer have to supply the first type parameter – it is implicit in the name of the function. Thus, to transform a file, we only have to pass one or two arguments for each transformation:

```
    function transformDocument($xmlDocument, $targetDocument = NULL)
    {
        return $this->transform(XSLT_FILE, $xmlDocument, $targetDocument);
    }

    function transformValue($xmlString, $targetDocument = NULL)
    {
        return $this->transform(XSLT_VALUE, $xmlString, $targetDocument);
    }
```

That last function is to free the handler from memory, destroying the parser. This method should be called somewhere within our script to ensure the memory is released. PHP does not support destructors or guaranteed resource collection once the script is finished:

```
    function free()
    {
        xslt_free($this->xslt);
    }
}
?>
```

In future versions of PHP, we will be able to specify destructors. When this new version of PHP comes out, you can place this code within the destructor instead, to remove the burden from the programmer writing the calling code.

To test out the new class, let's provide several ways to use it. Assuming the xsltoo.php file is included in these examples, the first way we might want to use it is to supply two physical files and display the translated result to the standard output:

```
$xslt = new XsltProcessor('C:\Apache\htdocs\prophpxml\Chapter08\bltemplate.xsl');
print ($xslt->transformDocument('C:\Apache\htdocs\prophpxml\bug_list.xml');
$xslt->free());
```

A new processor object is constructed using the XSL file name. Since XSLT_FILE is the expected type by default, the end result is a very clean call to instantiate the object. To display the translated bug list document to the screen, we have to make a call to the transformDocument() method with just a single parameter. The transformations will then be applied and the result will be displayed to the browser. Finally, the object is freed and the program is finished.

To translate a variable containing XML content and writing the resultant document to a file, we must use the following code. In this case we can output the results to a file, newbuglist.php:

```
$xml = getXml(); // assume this method is defined and returns a string
                 // containing XML content (that is, your own implementation)
$xslt = new XsltProcessor('C:\Apache\htdocs\prophpxml\Chapter08\blphp.xsl');
$xslt->transformValue($xml,
                      'C:\Apache\htdocs\prophpxml\Chapter08\newbuglist.php');
$xslt->free();
```

In this case, we use the transformValue() method with 2 parameters. The first must be the variable containing the XML. We have assumed that a function getXml() exists, and will return a string of XML. This could be collected from a database or perhaps read from a file. The next parameter contains the target file. At this point, the Sablotron process will be called to transform the content and a new file will be generated containing the resultant document.

One last combination we are going to see is how to use a variable containing the XSL information:

```
$xsl = getXslSource(); // Again, assume this function returns the XSL
                       // document as a string. (that is, your own implementation)
$xslt = new XsltProcessor($xsl, XSLT_VALUE);
$xslt->transformDocument('C:\Apache\htdocs\prophpxml\bug_list.xml',
                         'C:\Apache\htdocs\prophpxml\Chapter08\newbuglist.php');
$xslt->free();
```

The only element new to this example is that a variable is supplied containing a string of the XSL information. To tell the object that this is a value, we must also pass the XSLT_VALUE parameter explicitly since the default assumes a file (mentioned earlier). Now that the object has been instantiated, we can go about transforming files exactly as before.

Although this object makes it easy to transform files, it is by no means finished. For instance, we can expand on this object and make several useful functions such as transforming a list of XML content all at once or provide extensions to future Sablotron functionality as the library grows and allows object-based references.

Ensuring Forward Compatibility

As new standards are defined and implemented in the popular XSLT processors, it is desirable to ensure that older processors will not process newer versions of the XSL document. As mentioned before, Sablotron does not require the version attribute on the `<xsl:stylesheet>` root node.

For example, let's take this XSL document:

```
<?xml version="1.0" encoding="iso-8859-1"?>

<xsl:stylesheet version="3.0"
  xmlns:xsl="http://www.w3.org/1999/XSL/Transform">

<xsl:output method="html" indent="yes" />

<xsl:template match="/">
  <xsl:if test="system-property('xsl:version') >= 3">
    <xsl:new-xsl-tag />
  </xsl:if>
</xsl:template>

</xsl:stylesheet>
```

Most XSLT processors have hard-coded system properties like the version of the standard it used (usually 1.0, 1.1, and 2.0), the vendor who developed the processor, and the corresponding company's web site to download or purchase it. By using the `system-property()` function in XPath, we can get at these property values.

For instance, here is an `<xsl:if>` statement that checks the `xsl:version` property to ensure that the processor can handle XSLT 3.0 documents:

```
<xsl:if test="system-property('xsl:version') >= 3">
  <xsl:new-xsl-tag />
</xsl:if>
```

This instruction would ensure that the instruction was installed in the XSLT processor and would only use it if available. However, XSLT has a design flaw that fails to let this type of code be used. Sablotron does an XSLT syntax check on the entire document before it processes it, so once it scans the `<xsl:new-xsl-tag />` instruction, it will report an error before the transformation can begin. This makes it impossible to attempt a transformation of forward-compatible documents.

Although this is a small limitation, there are very few 2.0 processors and individuals developing 2.0 documents, but as time passes we can count on them being adopted. However, until that time we will not be able to check for forward compatibility and must edit the documents manually to make them work as expected.

Useful XSL Applications

In this section we are going to take a look at how the technology lends itself to applications that include:

❑ Multi-tiered applications

❑ Introduction of new languages

❑ Document conversion

❑ Publishing

Multi-Tiered Applications

Although building multi-tiered applications is largely out of scope of this chapter, ignoring it completely would be a crime. With the addition of XSL, we can transform XML pages to the appropriate presentation language (or the dialect of one), thus separating the application logic from the presentation logic.

Before XSL, it was extremely difficult to develop 3-tiered applications using PHP. In most cases, programmers would settle for one-tier, or an effective two-tier design separating the database retrieval calls from the application logic. There has always been the problem of removing the HTML or other presentation content from PHP code.

Now, as explained in the *Benefits* section, these two components can be separated. Here is a typical design for a large PHP application:

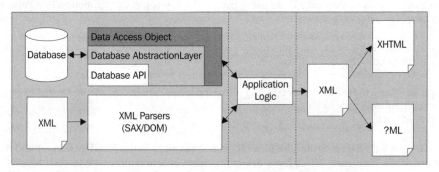

In most cases, when a page is requested from the browser or some other device, the application logic requests data, either from a call to several data access objects or perhaps using a parser on an XML file. In case of the XML content, there might be some application logic present, but this logic is de-coupled from the rest of the application, making it easy to maintain in the future. Once the data required for the page is retrieved, any computations can be executed and a generic XML document is spawned, either using DOM or a specific API internally developed by the organization. At this point, depending on the type of client we need to serve the content to, we can use XSLT to derive the appropriate presentation language to display to the user.

In this manner, XSLT helps to build easily maintainable 3-tiered applications. Some may argue that when generating XML, the result may be as cryptic as deriving HTML. At least in this case once the generation is finished, the odds are greatly in our favor that changes will not be needed in the future unless new features are added to the web site. If we encapsulate the document generation code into a class called `MyXmlPageBuilder` and provide an easy-to-use interface to build the XML document, we can avoid the problem of obfuscated code within the application altogether.

A design such as this makes the presentation of the web site very easy to maintain because any changes to the XHTML or other stylesheets will not require changes to any other layers. Thus, this design of separating the various layers can save you a great deal of time in the future when you need to make changes.

Introduction of New Languages

Although the very nature of XML is to develop new languages, the birth of XSL provided us with many concepts for new languages. For instance, we might like to write HTML in a certain way. Over the years, we might have grown accustomed to a specific style when writing HTML content and there are times where we would like the default settings to be different than the browser's settings. In other cases we might like to see new tags implemented in the XHTML recommended standard. Well, we can use XSL to satisfy all these needs by creating a new markup language. For instance, we can add:

- A `<flash>` tag to display flash animations in a single line without resorting to Macromedia examples
- A `<dynamic-menu>` tag to create highlighted horizontal and vertical menus without calling JavaScript directly
- A new attribute for HTML tables to implement alternating row colors (without using PHP)
- A new `<flow-layout>` tag to construct content within a table similar to Java's `FlowLayout` class

We can derive new default settings to many tags (such as `<img>` and `<table>`) and other useful features. To accomplish this, we need to create a new document type called **DML** (Doe's Mark-up Language), and develop the XSL document to translate DML to XHTML. Here is an illustration on how it can be used:

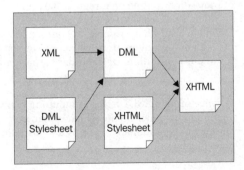

Here we have an XML document that first becomes styled using the DML stylesheet. This stylesheet is always custom developed per application, just like an XML-to-XHTML translation would be. The resultant document is a DML document. Next, another translation is applied to the DML document, converting it to XHTML using the DML-to-XHTML stylesheet. This stylesheet is always reused from application-to-application. At this point, the result is sent to the browser in XHTML.

This gives the programmer the ability to code the resultant markup quicker with an added execution time required for the second translation. Is it worth it? That depends on the speed of the hardware, the number of clients, and how often the DML-to-XHTML stylesheet needs to be used. The key here is ROI (return on investment). It is good to develop our own languages when other languages out there are not available. The cost and time savings can be quite remarkable.

Although this example talks about a new presentation language, we can develop many other languages that act as tools to help us work faster.

Document Conversion

One of the most obvious applications for XSL is converting one document type into another. Technically, this is what XSL does all the time, but developing an application to convert one XML vocabulary into another for the sole purpose of converting its structure falls under this category.

We will look at some of the reasons for converting one XML document to another.

One reason may be to support legacy applications. If we suppose that XSLT 2.0 stylesheets were not backward compatible, then the W3C could provide an XSLT document to convert XSLT 1.0 documents to XSLT 2.0 documents since they are all XML-to-XML translations, or given knowledge of the new standard we could create our own. In another instance, before parsing a document, we may want to convert it to a document type that our application accepts by using XSLT. This can save time since we won't have to rewrite the SAX or DOM parsing code to work with the newest document type. In other cases, we might want to convert a document to rename the elements and attributes to another language, such as French, Russian, or Japanese. This strategy could be employed when HTML content authors would rather write HTML in their native language and then later transform their content to the English representation of HTML.

Sometimes we might want to change the underlying structure of the document to one that is more maintainable and fixes errors in the design of the content. In this chapter, we take a look at using XSLT to correct the fundamental design problems while preserving the content of the XML file.

If we need to call a document translation routine on a regular basis in a time-intensive application, we should have a good reason for doing so. If we want to save ourselves the trouble of working with a poorly generated document, then we would have to bear the burden and skip the extra translation step. However, if time requirements are not a problem, or if we can prove that stripping XML structure and content can increase the speed of our application, we should incorporate XSL into our real-time application by all means.

Let's now look at a specific instance of how XSLT helps in inputting many site-specific, proprietary XML document types into a common document type, which is then converted to SQL. The XSL application relies on the technology unconditionally. Here is an illustration of how the content for the portal is inserted into the Oracle database:

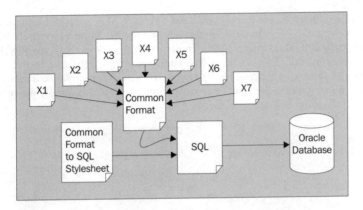

In this example, several proprietary documents (labeled X1 through X7) are converted to a common XML format using XSL. Since each of these documents has a different format, a different stylesheet is developed for each proprietary document type. The next step is to translate the 7 common documents into actual SQL INSERT statements. This is done using the common format-to-SQL stylesheet. Once the SQL is generated, the data is manually inserted into the database.

Here we used two transformations instead of one. We could have developed a transformation for each proprietary document type to SQL directly, but the advantage of possessing a common format is tremendous. For starters, the common document can be used to convert the data into the original proprietary formats, but with combined data from all the sites. Thus, the document type could be adopted as a standard for other sites within the industry. Let's explore this possibility further.

If you have N vocabularies on the left and M vocabularies on the right, you need N by M transformations. If the vocabularies on the left are the same as on the right, the total number of translations decreases to N by (M-1). This can take a lot of development time, where the developers might even lose morale by carrying out a lot of this monotonous work. In this example we have 5 vocabularies, so we need to develop 4 different XSL transformations for each vocabulary, totalling 20 distinct XSL files using the N by (M-1) formula. If we look at the following diagram, it looks very complicated indeed:

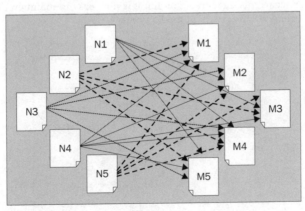

If you use a common intermediate format you need only $N + M + 1$ transformations and that is always better. In the case where the vocabularies on the left side are the same as vocabularies on the right, the formula requires only $N + M$ transformations. In the example below, there are only 10 transformations, reducing the number by half. This is because the common format only introduces 2 transformation instead of 4. As you can see, when you have to convert many different vocabularies of formats into many different representations, the use of a middle common format is usually the best strategy, as you can see from the following diagram:

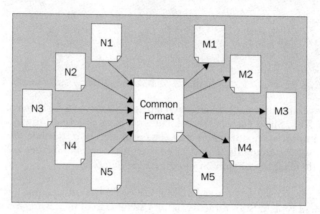

Here instead of keeping the data in XML we used a database. This is to illustrate the possibility that at times the documents we need to convert may contain as much as 400 megabytes to 2 gigabytes of information. Parsing this content at the web-site level is essentially unrealistic, thus, a relational database becomes mandatory to perform data accesses quickly.

Publishing

Since XML can be used to describe data without presentation information, publishers can now utilize XML to store the structure and content for their books. Since publishers are trying to sell their books in various formats, such as in written book form, e-Books, HTML files, styles for hardcover and paperback editions, and in some occurrences generated audio, it is now easy to maintain the published work in one file and use XSLT to generate the resultant media types:

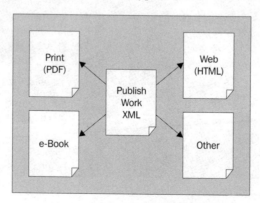

XSLT As a Functional Language

By now we all know that XSLT is a declarative language, which allows us to transform a source document or an XML data structure into a result tree for a new XML document.

XSLT, however, can also be looked at as a functional language, as it supports programming constructs like `if` conditionals, `for` loops, and XPath functions. XSLT can replace your programming language, as it is powerful enough to do simple computations and formatting that can help you make your applications more portable. This is because you can write the computations within the stylesheet rather than using a SAX or DOM parser that is specific to the native language that the application uses.

In the following example, we are going to demonstrate two concepts: recursion and string manipulation. Suppose we had a list of phone numbers in XML and we would like to strip out the dashes in between the numbers before we sent the XML file to another business partner. Although we could use SAX to use the `str_replace()` method to remove the dashes within the phone number string, generating the XML file will prove to be quite difficult, thus we would use a combination of SAX and DOM. Furthermore, maintaining the state of two DOM trees can lead to many traversals, which can lead to confusing and somewhat obfuscated sourcecode. Using a nice elegant language such as XSLT, we can perform these functions quickly and even gain a boost that the code is portable with other technologies such as Java and .Net, if we decide to migrate our code in the future.

Here is the `phone.xml` file that contains a list of phone numbers that we want to remove the dashes from:

```
<?xml version="1.0" encoding="iso-8859-1"?>

<phone-numbers>
   <phone-number>519-332-3233</phone-number>
   <phone-number>416-323-1344</phone-number>
   <phone-number>444-574-7544</phone-number>
</phone-numbers>
```

The file is very simple and straight-forward. Let's see what the document is expected to look like after we run the stylesheet, which we are going to write in this section.

```
<?xml version="1.0" encoding="UTF-8"?>
<phone-numbers>
   <phone-number>5193323233</phone-number>
   <phone-number>4163231344</phone-number>
   <phone-number>4445747544</phone-number>
</phone-numbers>
```

With all the knowledge that you've gained up to this point, you might still be wondering, "How do I do this?". Since XSLT uses XPath, you can take advantage of the functions in the XPath Core Function Set. Every API that implements the XPath 1.0 standard contains functions for concatenating strings, doing string replacements, finding substrings, and getting the number of nodes within a node-set. By using some of these functions, we can split the string up into chunks to get rid of the dashes.

Using these functions alone, however, will not completely solve our problem. We have to use recursion to break up the string until no existing dashes remain. Recursion within XSLT is exactly the same as in a programming language. Like recursion within programming, you must make sure there is a break-out point so the recursion stops. In our case, the program should break when no more chunks contain dashes. Here is a diagram illustrating the split/recursion process:

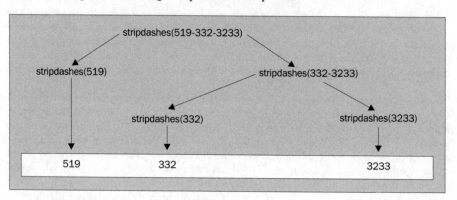

As you can see from the diagram, our template recurses, splitting the phone number one section at a time, until there are no numbers that contain dashes. Let's have a look at the code that accomplishes this functionality:

```xml
<?xml version="1.0" encoding="iso-8859-1"?>

<xsl:stylesheet version="1.0"
                xmlns:xsl="http://www.w3.org/1999/XSL/Transform">

<xsl:output method="xml" indent="yes" />
```

Because we are converting one document to another, we specify the format with indenting turned on. This will provide us with an identical looking document as the source XML document:

```xml
<xsl:template match="phone-numbers">
  <phone-numbers>
    <xsl:apply-templates select="phone-number" />
  </phone-numbers>
</xsl:template>
```

This template simply recreates itself in the target document. Notice that we could have used `<xsl:copy>` here, but it would not have saved us any coding effort for this example:

```xml
<xsl:template match="phone-number">
  <phone-number>
    <xsl:call-template name="stripdashes">
      <xsl:with-param name="phone-number" select="text()" />
    </xsl:call-template>
  </phone-number>
</xsl:template>
```

The `phone-number` template creates a new `<phone-number>` element within the XML document and calls the `stripdashes` named template (yet to be defined). Here we simply pass the phone number as a parameter. Assuming the `stripdashes` template works, it will output string of the new, un-dashed phone number as character data between the `<phone-number>` element. Now, let's define the `stripdashes` template:

```
<xsl:template name="stripdashes">
  <xsl:param name="phone-number" />
  <xsl:choose>
    <xsl:when test="contains($phone-number, &apos;-&apos;)">
```

When the program is first executed on a phone number, it tests to see if a dash character is contained within the phone number string. We can use the `contains()` function to test if a given string contains a substring. Recall that variables and parameters are referenced with a $ sign in front of them to indicate that they are variables, like in PHP. We also use the `&apos;` entity reference to quote the dash character to ensure the XSL document is well-formed:

```
<xsl:call-template name="stripdashes">
  <xsl:with-param name="phone-number"
              select="substring-before($phone-number,
                                     &apos;-&apos;)" />
</xsl:call-template>
<xsl:call-template name="stripdashes">
  <xsl:with-param name="phone-number"
              select="substring-after($phone-number,
                                     &apos;-&apos;)" />
</xsl:call-template>
</xsl:when>
```

If this test is TRUE, then that means the phone number contains at least one dash character. We can use the `substring-before()` to split the string at the first occurrence of a dash character. The `substring-before()` function returns the substring before the character put in the second argument. So for the number `519-332-3233`, the string `"519"` is returned. We can then use this new string and call the `stripdashes` template on it. Note that we are counting on the function to stop the recursion.

Next, we use the `substring-after()` function to obtain a string that contains the numbers on the right-hand side of the first dash. In the first iteration of the recursion, the number will be `332-3233`. This value is also put into a parameter when the `stripdashes` named method is executed. As you can see with this call, the function will split the string into the values `332` and `3233` in the next pass through:

```
    <xsl:otherwise>
      <xsl:value-of select="$phone-number" />
    </xsl:otherwise>
  </xsl:choose>
</xsl:template>
```

We tested if the string contained a dash character above. When the template receives a string such as 519, 332, or 3233, the `contains()` test will return FALSE. In these cases, we execute the `<xsl:otherwise>` block and simply add the result to the resultant tree. Notice that no whitespace characters are added, so any subsequent additions will appear right beside each other. After each segment of the phone number has been stopped, the function will finally stop running and the next phone number will be stripped of its dashes until no more phone numbers exist in the list:

```
</xsl:stylesheet>
```

Many computational problems use this recursive technique shown here. In fact, the recursive technique is essentially to solve many XSLT computational-related problems. If things get too rough, you might want to look at SAX or DOM as an alternative, because those methods are more suited for these kinds of problems. However, using XSLT does give you another option and if it suits the problem well, by all means use it.

Supporting Legacy Applications

With everyone using XML content in their applications, it's extremely difficult to keep our legacy applications up-to-date so that they can utilize XML. In most cases, the systems are so old that it would take a lot of work to retrofit the application to utilize XML, or in many other cases the APIs are not even available. XSLT can help in this area by transforming the data to a format that the legacy application does understand. These types of translations could be done with a parser, but in many cases if the data is small to medium-size, XSLT works wonderfully well due to its elegant and easy-to-write syntax.

Let's say our legacy application stores lists of people with their names and age. In some cases, a particular person might not have his name and age in the database, but we'd like to add them to the database anyway. Now a customer provides us with an XML file (legacy.xml) containing a list of people that they would like to add to the legacy application, as follows:

```
<?xml version="1.0" encoding="iso-8859-1"?>

<people>
  <person>
    <name>Bob Jones</name>
    <age>42</age>
  </person>
  <person>
    <name>Susan Shears</name>
  </person>
  <person>
    <name>Betty Sue</name>
    <age>22</age>
  </person>
</people>
```

Since the application doesn't understand XML, we must convert the XML to a representation that the application can understand. For this example, we are going to serialize the XML content into a flat file that has the following format:

```
name1,age1|name2,age2|...|nameN,ageN
```

So for the above example, the resultant text file would appear like this:

```
Bob Jones,42|Susan Shears|Betty Sue,22
```

Let's take a look at the XSL document (legacy.xsl) to achieve this result:

```
<?xml version="1.0" encoding="iso-8859-1"?>

<xsl:stylesheet version="1.0"
                xmlns:xsl="http://www.w3.org/1999/XSL/Transform">
<xsl:output method="text" indent="no" />
```

Since we are creating a text-based document, we need to supply the value text into the method attribute of the `<xsl:output>` element. This prevents the XSLT processor from adding a DOCTYPE declaration at the top of the file or any XML-specific declarations:

```
<xsl:template match="text()">
  <xsl:apply-templates select="person" />
</xsl:template>
```

Since XSLT automatically outputs any character data that it comes across, the whitespace in between the `<people>` root element automatically is included in the resultant document. To prevent this from happening, we re-match the character data with the `text()` function and tell the processor to simply carry on with the `<person>` elements only, if any exist as child to the current node:

```
<xsl:template match="person">
  <xsl:value-of select="name/text()" />
```

When we match the `<person>` element, we want to immediately grab the name and add it to the resultant text file. Since we know the incoming XML file contains all names (let's suppose we were told by the author of the document), we can make this assumption:

```
<xsl:if test="age/text() != &apos;&apos;" >
  <xsl:text>,</xsl:text>
  <xsl:value-of select="age/text()" />
</xsl:if>
```

Since all people in the XML file do not have to have an age defined, we must first test if the `age/text()` contains any data. If so, we can add a comma and the age to the result:

```
<xsl:if test="position() div 2 != count(//person)">
  <xsl:text>|</xsl:text>
</xsl:if>
</xsl:template>
</xsl:stylesheet>
```

The last part is fairly tricky, as the record separator (the | character) must not appear after the last entry. Since XSL is a declarative language, we can't strip away the | character afterwards, because it will already be added to the document. To remove it, we must use many functions that are available through XPath. Since the `count()` function returns the number of elements within a node-set, we can count the number of people contained within the XML document. For this small example, the total number is 3. If we take the current position and compare the values, we can avoid printing the | character at the last entry as seen in the test condition above.

Interoperating with legacy applications can be difficult, but with XSLT to help you along with many other technologies such as web services, the task of connecting new applications with legacy systems can be rather painless.

Summary

In this chapter we have concentrated on XSL, one of the more innovative technologies developed using the XML specification, and we learned more than just the syntax.

Firstly, we looked at the topic of traditional parsing. We learned that XSL cannot solve as many problems as DOM or SAX parsers, but XSL provides a clean and portable method to solving XML-related problems and provides an excellent alternative when the technology can be utilized.

Secondly, we looked at several benefits that XSL can provide to us, such as portability, faster deployment, and the use of multiple presentation languages. After learning all about the usefulness of XSL, it was necessary to take a look at how the magic happened, so the section looked at XSL templates. Later we learned how to create XSL documents. We discussed how to build the basic template matches using `<xsl:for-each>`, `<xsl:sort>`, and `<xsl:if>` constructs.

We discussed several key concepts of how XSL documents are scanned and matched by analyzing precedence rules and how to modularize our XSL documents by creating named templates and using variables. Later we discussed creating new nodes using the element creation instructions to help generate and convert other XML documents. We also learned how these templates are defined, and in what manner they are matched by an XSLT processor.

We then dove into Sablotron, the XSLT processor that is bundled with PHP. Furthermore, we looked at several applications in which XSL can be used, such as multi-tiered enterprise applications, publishing, document generation applications, and other new applications inspired by XSL itself. We took a look at Sablotron bit by bit to run these XSL files through PHP to see the results along the way.

Lastly, we looked at XSLT as a functional language, and how it supports programming constructs like `if` conditionals, `for` loops, and XPath functions. In the end we learned how difficult interoperating with legacy applications can be, and how XSLT can help us along with many other technologies such as web services, making the task of connecting new applications with legacy systems rather painless.

To learn about XSL beyond this chapter, consult the W3C web site at http://www.w3.org/TR/xslt10/. It's an excellent resource to learning XSLT with over 100 pages of material.

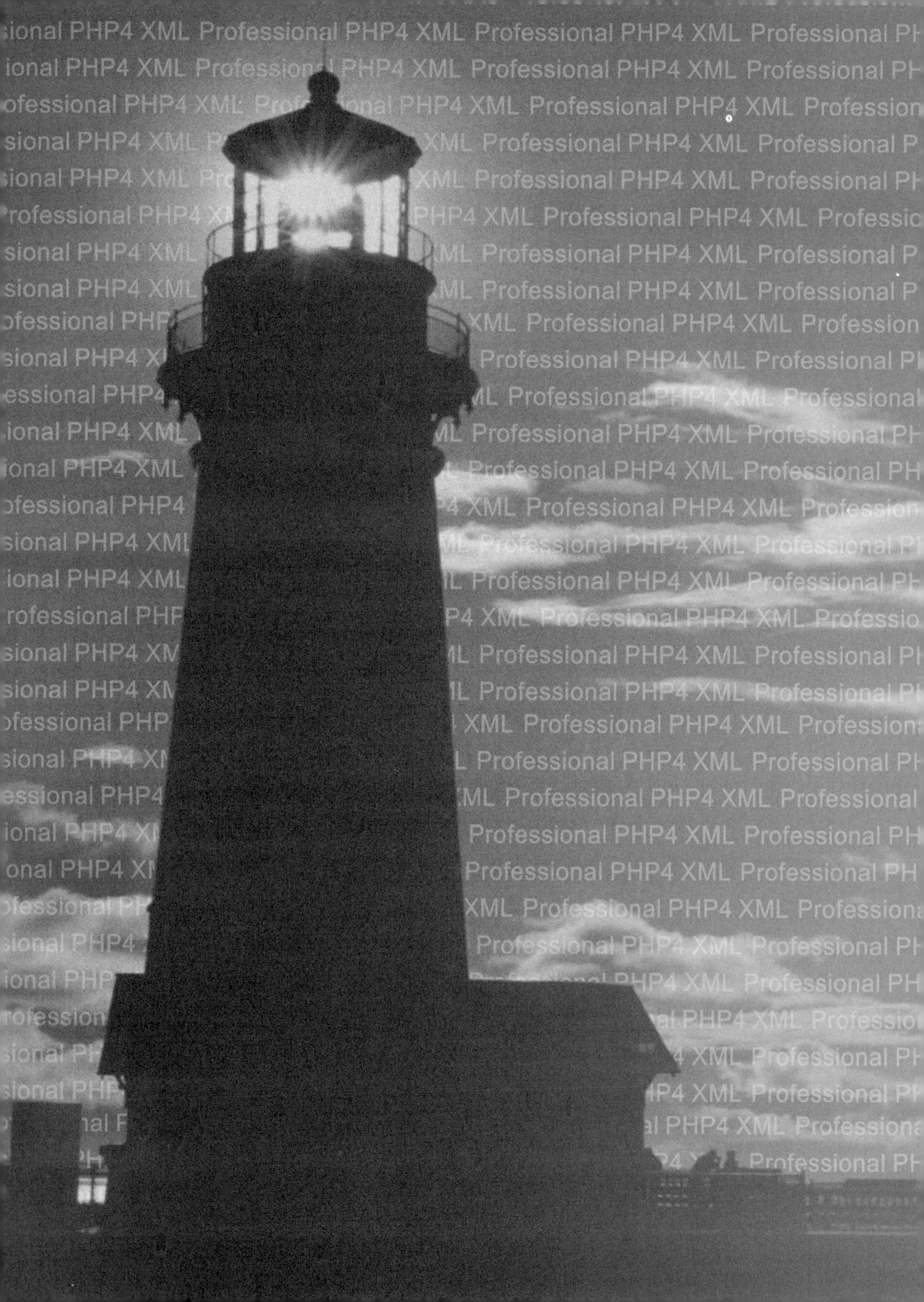
Professional PHP4 XML

9
XML Classes

In Chapter 2, we saw how classes can be created and used within the context of PHP. They provide powerful methods to attack various problems and have the useful feature of being extensible. That is to say, we can take a PHP class that has already been written and give it some new functionality without having to rewrite all that has been done. This is an example of how code can be reused efficiently through the use of object-oriented programming (OOP). However, often the term "code reuse" simply means that we use code libraries that other people have already coded. In an effort not to reinvent the wheel we are going to use pre-existing classes to look at our example XML file.

In the course of this chapter we will:

❑ Become more comfortable using third-party classes in general

❑ Use several different techniques to parse an XML document and manipulate data

❑ Learn to appreciate the benefits of using existing code

To begin with, let's look at a class that handles the parsing of XML files in a very generic way. It is useful as an 'all-purpose' tool, and provides an excellent introduction to the topic at hand.

Generic XML Parser Class

The first example is a generic XML parser class written by Manuel Lemos and available at http://phpclass.kiffer.idv.tw/browse.html/package/4.html. To get to the code we will have to go through a free registration.

This class provides a wrapper around the SAX API provided with PHP. This is principally useful for stream-based parsing of documents and has the advantage of being extremely fast while not being memory intensive on the machine. Here the class takes care of a good number of things for us, such as error handling and setting up callback functions. The parsed data is stored in a fairly complicated array holding the structure of all the tag and data elements.

> This distribution is a bit different from the usual kind of class distribution because the functions provided go into the global namespace. Typically, in class-file distributions there are only classes in the included files so there are no potential namespace conflicts.

We will need to download the `xml_parser.php` file. It provides classes and some utility functions for using them. Create a directory called `classes` under the document root and store the `xml_parser.php` file in it.

As a first example, we will simply recreate the XML file that we read in. While not the most interesting application, this is the easiest way to provide some insight into other ways we could use this class.

To begin with, let's create a file called `reprint_file.php`. The first two lines just include the class and define our XML file:

```php
<?php
require_once "../classes/xml_parser.php";
$xml_file = "../bug_list.xml";
```

Parsing the File

Now, we'll make use of the `XMLParseFile()` function that is defined for us in the `xml_parser.php` file. There are many arguments that can be passed to the `XMLParseFile()`, but most have default values. Refer to the function definition in the class file for a list of all the options available.

The next line of our example is this:

```php
$xml_error = XMLParseFile(&$parser, $xml_file, 0);
```

We've passed three arguments to this function:

❑   The first is a reference to a currently undefined parser object

❑   The second is the file name we wish to look at

❑   The third tells the function that it doesn't need to keep track of the physical positions of all the elements in the file (we won't need to do that for this example)

When `XMLParseFile()` runs, it first checks for an error and if it encounters one, then it will return that error into the `$xml_error` variable. We can then check this and act accordingly.

Second, and more importantly, a new object called `$parser` is created. We must understand that we are not talking about creating an XML parser and assigning it to `$parser`. We are creating an object of type `xml_parser_class` that is defined in the `xml_parser.php` file.

Once `XMLParseFile()` is run, the data is parsed and the data held within it is stored in variables contained in `$parser`. At this point we have already parsed the XML file and stored the data for our use.

This brings up another one of the great effects of using well-written classes. We don't have to know how they accomplish everything that they do. As a programmer, all that's required is that we know what to give them and what they give us back. When we ran `XMLParseFile()` a bunch of error checking was done for us, callbacks were defined and implemented, and results were stored in array structures. But we don't have to know the nitty-gritty of this; we just need to know that we now have our data waiting for us.

We should pause for a moment to examine how our freshly parsed data will be presented to us. Now, there is an array available that we will need to understand to get to our data. It can be referenced through the `$parser` object by using:

```
$structure = $parser->structure;
```

`$structure` is an array whose first key is a comma-delimited set of integers corresponding to the location of data in the file. The value for any given key could be the character data for an element or an array (of the same structure) containing the data for elements deeper in the tree. There are also entries for:

- ❑ `$structure[$location]["Tag"]` which gives the name of the Tag represented at `$location`

- ❑ `$structure[$location]["Elements"]` which gives the number of elements down the tree from `$location`

- ❑ `structure[$level]["Attributes"]` which is an array containing any attributes for the current tag

With this in mind, it is not too difficult to create a function that will reconstruct our original XML data. The clear choice is to use a recursive function that will keep calling itself at any point until the entire tree has been handled. It starts like this:

```
function ShowStructure($structure, $level)
{
    // if we're at an array node, then check for tag attributes and use recursion
    if (is_array($structure[$level])) {
```

Here, we check to see if the point we are at in the `$structure` array is data, or an array that digs deeper into the tree.

We are looking at the case where it's an array. Now we'll print out the upcoming tag along with any attributes it might contain:

```
    print ("&lt;" . $structure[$level]["Tag"]);
    // include attributes if there are any
    if (count($structure[$level]["Attributes"])) {
        foreach ($structure[$level]["Attributes"] as $k => $v) {
            print (" $k=\"$v\"");
        }
    }
    // don't forget to close the tag!
    print ("&gt;");
```

Next, we call the ShowStructure() function again after determining what level it should start on. We can tell where to start next from the Elements stored for us:

```
        for ($element = 0 ; $element < $structure[$level]["Elements"] ;
                         ++$element) {
            ShowStructure($structure, $level . ",$element");
        }
        print ("&lt;/" . $structure[$level]["Tag"] . "&gt;");
    }
```

And don't forget to close the tag when it's done.

Finally, for the case where we have some data to print out, let's do so, like this:

```
    else {                          // else print out the character data
        print $structure[$level];   // for toplevel
    }
}                                   // end of function
?>
```

Displaying the Results

The HTML needed for the display is very simple. It comes immediately after the application code we have just finished writing. The chunk of HTML code given below immediately follows the PHP code given above:

```
<html>
  <head>
    <title>Reprint File</title>
  </head>
  <body>

    <h2>Behold, the XML file!</h2>
    <br />

    <?php
    // make sure we didn't get some error parsing the file
    if (0 != strcmp($xml_error, "")) {
        print ($xml_error . "<br />\n");
        exit();
    }

    print ("<pre>\n");

    ShowStructure($parser->structure, 0);

    print ("</pre>\n");

    ?>

  </body>
</html>
```

First, we check to make sure that the initial parsing didn't generate any kind of error. If some problem shows up, we can quit the application with the error message. Next, we call our ShowStructure() function with the $parser->structure argument for the array, and 0 as the starting place in the structure. That is, we'll start at the root of the document and reprint all of the data. The output should look just like the original file:

```
http://localhost/ProPHPXML/Chapter09/reprint_file.php - Netscape 6
File  Edit  View  Search  Go  Bookmarks  Tasks  Help

Behold, the XML file!


<bug_list>
<application name="sportran compiler" version="1.1">
        <bugs>
                <bug_item>
                        <title>It crashes when a string with more than 256 bytes is declared</title>
                        <report_date>20020128015</report_date>
                        <reported-by>John Smith</reported-by>
                        <status>Open</status>
                        <last_update>20020128016</last_update>
                        <description>...</description>
                        <severity>3</severity>
                </bug_item>
                <bug_item>
```

A Trimmed Down Bug List

Now let's look at a slightly more practical example using the same technology. Let's assume that our manager needs to see what applications have bugs, but is not interested in who reported the bug or the severity and simply wants a display of the applications and the titles of the bugs associated with them.

We will use the same basic strategy. That is, we'll use a recursive function that will help us traverse through the available XML data. However, this time we'll just add in some checks to see where we are and record appropriate data into global storage when we need to.

The first three lines are exactly the same as in the last example:

```php
<?php
require_once("../classes/xml_parser.php");
$xml_file = "../bug_list.xml";

$xml_error = XMLParseFile(&$parser, $xml_file, 0);
```

This time, let's check right away to see if there was a problem, and get out of it (if there was one):

```php
// get out of here if there was an error
if (0 != strcmp($xml_error, "")) {
    print ($xml_error);
    exit();
}
```

Now, as noted, our plan is to store the data we want into global variables. Let's initialize the two variables necessary for this example to work:

```
// globals that we'll need
$app_data = array();
$app_counter = 0;
```

This time, we are particularly interested in the contents of the `<title>` tag in the XML file, because we need that data for our output.

Therefore, we'll include an extra argument in our function declaration so that we can tell which tag we are looking at as the function proceeds recursively. Also, we'll need to have our global variables handy from within this function:

```
// recursive function TraverseXml
// gets through all the data
function TraverseXml($structure, $level, $tag)
{
    global $app_data;
    global $app_counter;
```

The next part should be familiar. We check to see if we are at an array node or a data node.

First, examine the case where we are at an array:

```
if (is_array($structure[$level])) {
    // keep track of where we are
    $newtag = $structure[$level]["Tag"];
```

Note that we're using the variable `$newtag` to keep track of where we are since we just passed into some new node within the XML document.

Next, we need to check and see if the current tag is the `<application>` tag, because the name of the application is stored as one of its attributes. If we're in the right place, we need to grab the name of the application and put it into global storage:

```
if (0 == strcmp($structure[$level]["Tag"], "application")) {
    $app_data[$app_counter]["name"] =
                        $structure[$level]["Attributes"]["name"];
    ++$app_counter;
}
```

We've incremented `$app_counter` because we've already got the name of the current application.

Let's look at the recursive part of the function. This time, we're going to feed it `$newtag` as the third argument, so that the next run-through knows where it is:

```
for ($element=0 ; $element < $structure[$level]["Elements"] ;
                                            ++$element) {
    TraverseXml($structure, $level . ", $element", $newtag);
}
}
```

Finally, we'll look to see if we're in the `<title>` element. If so, we take the title and append it to `$app_data`:

```
    if (0 == strcmp($tag, "title")) {
        $app_data[$app_counter-1]["title"][] = $structure[$level];
    }
}
?>
```

Note that we have to reference `$app_counter-1` in the first part of the array. This is because we incremented `$app_counter` earlier in the routine, so we need to go one back in the index to make sure that we're in the right place.

When we run `TraverseXml()` we'll get all of the data we want stored neatly in our `$app_data` array. An application referenced by `$index` will have the following structure:

```
$app_data[$index]["name"] => The name of the application
$app_data[$index]["title"] => An array holding all the corresponding bugs
```

With a little bit of display code our example is now finished:

```
<html>
  <head>
    <title>Print Out Bug List</title>

  </head>
  <body>

    <pre>
      <?php
      TraverseXml($parser->structure, "0", "");
      for ($i=0 ; $i < $app_counter ; ++$i) {
          print ("Application: " . $app_data[$i]["name"] . "\n");
          foreach ($app_data[$i]["title"] as $v) {
              print ("    $v\n");
          }
          print ("\n"); // formatting
      }
      ?>

    </pre>
  </body>
</html>
```

If everything is done correctly, then the output looks like this:

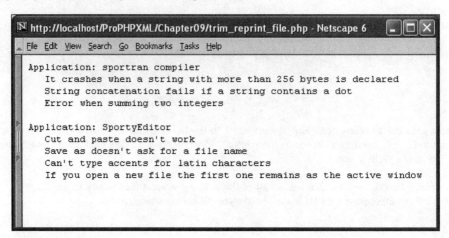

```
Application: sportran compiler
    It crashes when a string with more than 256 bytes is declared
    String concatenation fails if a string contains a dot
    Error when summing two integers

Application: SportyEditor
    Cut and paste doesn't work
    Save as doesn't ask for a file name
    Can't type accents for latin characters
    If you open a new file the first one remains as the active window
```

This class has several features that we have not covered here. In particular, it is possible to make the class cache the contents of the XML file that we are using, so that it doesn't have to be re-parsed every time the application is run. Remember to explore the xml_parser_class to look into these options.

XMLFile

Next, we will look at reading and writing data using the XMLFile class written by Chris Monson. It is available at: http://phpclasses.upperdesign.com/browse.html/package/79. For this class to work properly, the php.ini file must be set to allow call time pass by reference. The specific line in the file should therefore look like this:

```
allow_call_time_pass_reference = On
```

Additionally, you'll want to make sure that your error reporting is set to the following in php.ini:

```
error_reporting = E_ALL & ~E_NOTICE
```

These are the standard settings for PHP4 on a Linux (or other UNIX) type of installation.

There is only one file included in the package called xmlfile.php. As before, download this file and put it in the classes directory. This file defines two classes – XMLFile and XMLTag.

XMLFile makes it easy to parse and traverse the data in a given XML file. Additionally, it simplifies the process of writing any data we already have to a well-formed XML file.

The inclusion of the xmlfile.php file in our code will cause the global variable $XMLFile_Included to be set to 1, so be aware that we are introducing this into our global namespace.

Another point to make is that the XMLFile class is best used to handle small to medium-sized XML files. When we use this kind of object to parse a file, the entire content is stored in memory. Thus, the application could become a serious resource hog if the file in question was particularly large. The maximum length of a file can be around 100k or so. Our example bug_list.xml file is quite small so it shouldn't be a problem. Let's start examining how to use this object.

We'll first include the xmlfile.php file into our program, and then instantiate an object of type XMLFile like this:

```php
<?php
require_once("../classes/xmlfile.php");
$xmlFile = new XMLFile();
```

Now we will need to read and parse the file. The class doesn't provide a method that will let us access the file directly (although we could easily add such a method by extending the class). Instead, we use the read_file_handle() method that, as the name suggests, requires a file handle. It might be worthwhile noting that we have invoked read_file_handle(), which is a method of the class XMLFile. This is not to be confused with readfile(), which is a PHP method.

The code that will read and parse the file is:

```php
// name our file
$xml_file = "../bug_list.xml";

// create a read-only file handle
$fh = fopen($xml_file, "r");

// read and parse the file
$xmlFile->read_file_handle($fh);

// close our file handle
fclose($fh);
```

Now, as before, the file has already been read and parsed for use by our handy class, saving us all the work of doing it ourselves. Again, this is one of the nicest things about using classes when embarking on these sorts of projects.

Before we can continue, we'll need to understand what XMLFile classes do to the XML data once it's been parsed. There are two important predefined member variables – $roottag and $curtag. As the name implies, $roottag refers to the root of the XML document, and $curtag refers to whatever the current tag is. They are both instances of the XMLTag class, meaning that they have their own XMLTag properties. These are listed here, assuming that $xmlTag is an instance of the XMLTag class:

Attribute	Meaning
$xmlTag->name	The name of the tag
$xmlTag->cdata	The character data for the tag
$xmlTag->attributes	An array containing key/value pairs for the tag attributes
$xmlTag->tags	An ordered (not associative) array that has the tags contained within the tag

A Trimmed-Down List Revisited

For this example, let's try to recreate the list that we did in the previous section. We will print out a list of the applications in our `bug_list` file along with the bugs pertaining to each application.

To begin with, let's create a new file called `test_xmlfile.php` above the `classes` directory, where the class definition file is stored. As before, we'll use a recursive function to go through all of our data. Also, we'll make use of two global variables to keep track of and hold our data.

However, this function is a fair bit simpler due to the convenient access syntax that the class makes available to us. First we'll define global variables and start the function:

```
// global variables for data
$app_data = array();
$app_counter = 0;

function FindBugs($tag)
{
    global $app_data;
    global $app_counter;
```

Now, we'll go through all the tags contained in our current tag using the `$xmlTag->tags` array and a `foreach` statement. If we are in an `<APPLICATION>` tag, then we'll grab the `NAME` attribute to get the name of the application:

```
    foreach ($tag->tags as $k => $v) {
        if (0 == strcmp($v->name, "APPLICATION")) {
            // we are in the application tag!
            // grab the NAME attribute
            foreach ($v->attributes as $attname => $attval) {
                if (0 == strcmp($attname, "NAME")) {
                    $app_data[$app_counter]["name"] = $attval;
                    ++$app_counter;
                }
            }
        }
```

Next, if we are in a `<TITLE>` tag then we need the CDATA from the tag since that's the title of the bug:

```
        // show the CDATA if we're in a TITLE tag
        if (0 == strcmp($v->name, "TITLE")) {
            $app_data[$app_counter - 1]["title"][] = $v->cdata;
        }
```

And finally, we do the recursion and close the function:

```
        // do recursion
        FindBugs($v);
    }
}
?>
```

As can be seen, it is not really necessary to store the data in our $app_data array. It would be quite simple to have the FindBugs() function print the data out for us. However, we'll have use for the array in the next section, so we've implemented things this way.

The rest of the application looks effectively the same as in the previous example:

```
<html>
  <head>
    <title>Test Of XMLFile</title>
  </head>
  <body>
    <pre>

      <?php
      FindBugs($xmlFile->roottag);
      for ($i=0 ; $i < $app_counter ; ++$i) {
          print ("Application: " . $app_data[$i]["name"] . "\n");
          foreach ($app_data[$i]["title"] as $v) {
              print ("    $v\n");
          }
          print ("\n"); // formatting
      }

      // we're done with this, so let it go!
      $xmlFile->cleanup();
      ?>

    </pre>
  </body>
</html>
```

At the very end, we called the cleanup() method of the XMLFile class. Because PHP does not currently support destructors, this is necessary to make sure that all the object references are cleared out.

If we have done everything correctly, then the output will be identical to that of the previous example:

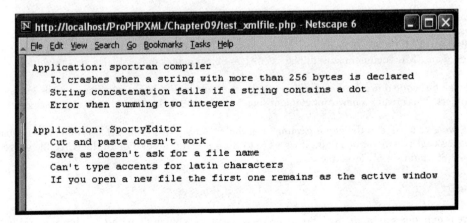

373

A Simplified XML File

Now we'll take our example one step further. Our manager is no longer content with just looking at the list output and now wants to be able to syndicate this slimmed-down version of the bug database so that other people connected to the network can get to it. This means creating a new, simpler XML file from the data. The XMLFile class has some convenient methods that make this possible.

We will put this program in a file called write_simple_xmlfile.php alongside our recently finished test_xmlfile.php.

From the beginning of the file to the end of the function FindBugs(), the two files are identical, so we will start from that point in the write_simple_xmlfile.php file. The first thing we will do is call our FindBugs() function. After that, we won't need our XMLFile object anymore, so we'll clean it up right away:

```
// put the data in the array, and free the memory from $xmlFile
FindBugs($xmlFile->roottag);
$xmlFile->cleanup();
```

We've cleared out our original $xmlFile object. Now, we'll create a brand-new XMLFile object that we'll use to write out XML data (not to read it in). We'll also create a root node in this new object, and give it an appropriate name:

```
// make a new instance for writing
$simpleXmlFile = new XMLFile();
$simpleXmlFile->create_root(); // required, no root exists at first

// set name of root tag
$simpleXmlFile->roottag->name = "BUG_LIST";
```

We used BUG_LIST here as opposed to something with lowercase letters. This is because the XMLFile class has case folding turned on by default, that is, it converts all tag names to uppercase automatically when it uses them. We will see this trend in all of the XMLFile examples.

What's happening above is that we are directly modifying the DOM of the XML data in $simpleXmlFile. Of course, when it's first created, there is no data in the object, so we are actually modifying the DOM by putting a root element into it. The ability to directly access and modify the pieces of an XML document stored in an XMLFile object makes these objects very powerful.

To break this code down further, we first use the method create_root() after we have instantiated our object. This creates a new root element since none existed when the object was initialized.

Next, we give a value to the name parameter of the roottag, this is an XMLTag object contained in our $simpleXmlFile. So at this point if we were to see a text representation of the XML file we've created, it would simply look like this:

```
<BUG_LIST />
```

There is only one root node, with no attributes or elements contained within it. However, we will now fill it up with elements based on the data in our $app_data array:

```
for ($i=0 ; $i < count($app_data) ; ++$i) {
    $simpleXmlFile->roottag->add_subtag("APPLICATION",
                                array("NAME" => $app_data[$i]["name"]));
    for ($j=0 ; $j < count($app_data[$i]["title"]) ; ++$j) {
        // IMPORTANT: APPLICATION is the current tag in this loop!
        $simpleXmlFile->roottag->curtag->add_subtag("BUG");
        $simpleXmlFile->roottag->curtag->tags[$j]->cdata =
                                $app_data[$i]["title"][$j];
    }
}
```

Each time the outer `for` loop executes, it adds a new subtag of type `APPLICATION` to the root tag. This tag has a `NAME` attribute that will contain the name of the application that is stored in `$app_data`.

The inner `for` loop is just a little bit more complicated. First, for each bug title stored in `$app_data`, it adds a new subtag to the current tag, where `curtag` is defined by the `XMLFile` as the tag added most recently. The important thing to understand here is that because of the way loops are executed in PHP, the `<APPLICATION>` tag is the current tag everywhere within the code block of the loop. Therefore, the appropriate way to assign the value of the `cdata` for the `<BUG>` tag we've just added is by going through the `tags` array (which is a member of every `XMLTag` object). The `curtag` referenced in this line is still referring to the `<APPLICATION>` tag, not the `<BUG>` tag that was added just above.

Now that we've added all of our data, let's create a new file with a well-formed XML structure that could be used for syndication as our manager wanted. This is exceedingly easy with the `XMLFile` class:

```
$output_file = "./simplebuglist.xml";
$fh = fopen($output_file, "w");

$simpleXmlFile->write_file_handle($fh);
fclose($fh);

$simpleXmlFile->cleanup();
?>
```

The `write_file_handle()` method will output all the XML data stored in the `XMLFile` object that calls it in a nice, well-formed document.

> **For this example to work, make sure that your web server process has permission to write to the directory that the script is executing in.**

Let's add a little more code and check the file we created to make sure everything worked properly:

```
<html>
  <head>
    <title>write simple xmlfile</title>
  </head>

  <body>
    <pre>
```

```
    <?php
    $fh = fopen($output_file, "r");
    $contents = fread($fh, filesize($output_file));
    fclose($fh);
    print (htmlspecialchars($contents));
    ?>

  </pre>
 </body>
</html>
```

If everything was done correctly, then this should appear in our web browser:

And there we have it: a stripped-down version of our original information written out in a brand-new XML document.

At this point, we might ask ourselves as to why we bothered to create two different XMLFile objects for this example. We could have simply taken the original object and started removing nodes and modifying the names of the ones we kept, until we arrived at the same ending XML document. This would have been a perfectly valid way to approach the problem. The reason that we took this approach is that we were able to leverage the code we had already written where we extracted the specific data we were looking for into an array. Having already accomplished that task in previous examples, it was only sensible to make use of the results here.

XML Transformer

In a previous example, we produced some simple output that just listed each application and its bugs for our manager. But managers will be managers, and their demands keep increasing. Now she's going to do a presentation and she needs a nicer looking display of that same data.

We are going to accomplish this with some help from the PEAR XML_Transformer class, available for download at http://pear.php.net/package-info.php?pacid=37.

Extract the `Transformer.php` file and put it into the `classes` directory under the document root.

Using the XML Transformer Class

This class allows us to assign PHP callback functions to specific elements in our XML document. This effectively transforms our document into a different kind of SGML file without the use of something like XSLT. When the parser gets to a particular element, a function that we define can manipulate the attributes and character data for that element on the fly as the parser gets to the opening and closing tags. This may seem confusing at the moment, but will make much more sense once we get into the code. First, we will look at the methods of the class that we will make use of for our example:

Function	Usage
Void XML_Transformer::XML_Transformer (array parameters)	Constructor that takes an array of predefined parameters discussed below
string XML_Transformer::transform (string xml)	Performs the transformation on the XML document provided as the argument

The array that we pass to the constructor may contain several predefined parameters. The ones we will need for this example are:

Parameter	Value
overloadedElements	Array that tells the class what callbacks to assign to individual elements
startup	Boolean that tells the class whether to try and parse data immediately or not

Again, the `overloadedElements` parameter may seem a bit obtuse right now, but it will be much more easily understood with some actual code to look at, so we'll save a full explanation until then.

An overview of the process though, is in order. When the parser gets to the beginning of an element we are interested in, a callback function that we define and write gets any attributes contained in that element as an argument. It can generate whatever output we desire, and use the attribute data if wanted. When the parser gets to the end of that element, another callback is called. This "end element" callback gets any character data that the element contained as an argument, and can produce output accordingly.

With this in mind, let's start writing some code.

A Nice Buglist Presentation

If we visually scan down the `bug_list.xml` file, we notice a few things that are convenient for what we want to do. Namely, all the bugs come in order under the applications they pertain to. This makes perfect sense given the structured nature of XML.

What we should do is simply take the elements we want, specifically the ones that define the application names and bug titles, and transform these from XML tags to HTML table tags that we can use to make a nice looking output. Since this is precisely what XML_Transformer does for us, it's a good choice for the job. Create a file called transformer_demo.php in the web server's document root. The first lines of code are:

```php
<?php
require_once("../classes/Transformer.php");
$input = "../bug_list.xml";
```

This just includes our Transformer class and defines the input file. Next, let's get the data for our XML document and put that into a variable we can use later:

```php
// read in the XML data and put it into
// our $contents variable
$fh = fopen($input, "r");
$contents = fread($fh, filesize($input));
fclose($fh);
```

Now we are going to define that seemingly confusing array that we will need to pass to the constructor method. Go ahead and type this in and then we'll examine what's happened:

```php
// set up the elements that we are going to tie to
// callback functions. callbacks don't need to be
// defined yet
$overload_array = array ('overloadedElements' =>
                array ('application' =>
                   array ('start' => 'startApp',
                          'end' => 'endApp'),
                          'title' => array ('start' => 'startRow',
                                             'end' => 'endRow'), ),
                          'startup' => FALSE
             );
```

There are two keys for $overload_array, namely overloadedElements and startup. The second of these is easy. It just tells the constructor not to try and parse any data until we ask it to do so explicitly.

The first key, overloadedElements, is a little more complicated. overloadedElements is itself an array with two keys application and title. These keys correspond to the elements that we want the class to pay attention to, since they contain data we want. And, each of these keys is yet again an array. Both have the keys start and end, which have values that correspond to the callback functions that we will define shortly.

This is a little messy, but it's really not too complicated. An examination of the code should clear things out.

The next thing to do is to write those callback functions. Remember, these happen at the beginning and end of the elements we've designated. So we're going to have them output some HTML that will draw tables for us:

```
// startApp function begins our table
// and prints out the name of the app
// into the first row
function startApp($attributes)
{
    print ("<table cellpadding=\"3\" cellspacing=\"1\"
                    border=\"0\" width=\"60%\">\n");
    print ("<tr>\n");
    print ("  <td class=\"dark\">");
    print ("<b>" . $attributes["name"] . "</b>");
    print ("</td>\n");
    print ("</tr>\n");
}

// the endApp function closes out
// our table
function endApp($cdata)
{
    print ("</table>\n");
    print ("<br />\n");
}

// startRow really does just start a table row
function startRow($attributes)
{
    print ("<tr>\n");
}

// endRow prints out the character data for
// the element and then closes out the row
function endRow($cdata)
{
    print ("  <td class=\"light\">" . $cdata . "</td>\n");
    print ("</tr>\n");
}
```

We have defined table elements here with CSS classes that we'll put in the HTML in just a little bit. The last thing to do is to instantiate an XML_Transformer object using the $overload_array as an argument:

```
// instantiate our object
$transformer = new XML_Transformer($overload_array);
?>
```

What's left is really very, very simple. It's some very basic HTML and CSS, with just one line of PHP to output the XML that we've transformed into HTML:

```
<html>
  <head>
    <title>Demo of XML_Transformer</title>
    <style type="text/css">
      <!--
        body {
          margin-top: 40px;
          margin-left: 55px;
          background: #ffffff;
          font-family: verdana, arial, helvetica, sans-serif;
```

```
        }

        td {
          color: #eeeee;
        }

        .dark {
           background-color: #cccccc;
           color: #222222;
        }

        .light {
           background-color: #ddddee;
           color: #222222;
        }

      -->
   </style>
  <head>

  <body>
    <h2>The Buglist</h2>

    <?php

    // now, we just run the transform method
    // on the contents of our XML file
    print ($transformer->transform($contents));
    ?>

  </body>
</html>
```

The output of the program should look like this:

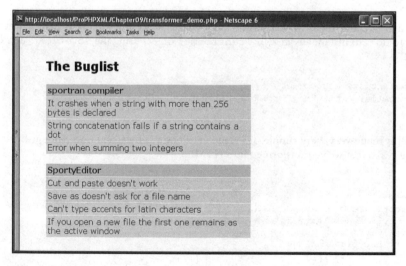

So we have succeeded in our goal and our manager has some nice output for her presentation. There's more documentation on how to use this class at the PEAR web site: http://pear.php.net/.

XPath with phpXML

The last class that we are going to look at in this chapter is **phpXML** from Michael Mehl. It is available for download at http://phpclasses.upperdesign.com/browse.html/package/180. It would be a good idea to check if php.ini is configured with the same settings as was used in the *XMLFile* section.

The distribution comes with a number of files, but the one we'll need to make the examples work is called xml.php. Let's put this into the classes directory.

The purpose of the XML class defined in this file is to allow use of the powerful XPath language. This allows us to get to various pieces of information in a given XML document, and can be a tremendous timesaver when combined with technologies such as XSLT.

> *We have covered XPath in detail in Chapter 7. Good online resources are available at*
> *http://www.w3.org/TR/xpath/ and*
> *http://www.zvon.org/xxl/XPathTutorial/General/examples.html.*

One Last Trimmed-Down List

The first thing we'll do is to once again write out a simplified version of our bug_list.xml file. XPath provides us with a convenient way to get to the data.

We will need to know about a few of the methods available to us to get this job done:

Method	Implementation
void XML($filename)	Constructor takes the file name of the file we'll use
array XML->evaluate($path)	Returns an array of the paths of the nodes that match the evaluated XPath $path
array XML->get_attributes($path)	Returns a key/value array corresponding to the attributes at the node designated by $path
string XML->get_content($path)	Returns the character data at the node designated by $path

Let's start by creating a new test_phpxml.php file and including the needed class definition file. We will also go ahead and instantiate an object to use and initialize some handy global variables:

```php
<?php
require_once("../classes/xml.php");

// instantiate our XML object
$phpxml = new XML("../bug_list.xml");

// our global variables
$app_data = array();
$app_counter = 0;
```

Next, we'll get an array with the paths to the `application` nodes. We'll need these because we have to extract data held in the attributes of the `<application>` tags:

```
// apps is an array with paths to the application tags
$apps = $phpxml->evaluate("//application");
```

Now, we will go ahead and loop through these paths and grab the names of the application, similar to how we've worked the previous examples:

```
foreach ($apps as $app) {
    //get attributes for this application
    $attributes = $phpxml->get_attributes($app);

    // put name attribute in storage
    $app_data[$app_counter]["name"] = $attributes["name"];
```

Now the real joy of using XPath will become apparent. Using the `descendant` function, we can jump right to the `title` nodes that we're interested in and store the data. This is accomplished easily, once we have the paths to the `title` nodes, by using the `get_content()` method on each node:

```
    // get path to the title tag for this app
    $title_path = $app . "/descendant::title[1]";

    // $title_nodes has paths to the title tags
    $title_nodes = $phpxml->evaluate($title_path);
    foreach ($title_nodes as $node) {
        // store title info
        $app_data[$app_counter]["title"][] = $phpxml->get_content($node);
    }
    ++$app_counter;
}
?>
```

And that's really it. We've done all of the actual work at this point. The display HTML and PHP code is identical to what we've used before:

```
<html>
  <head>
    <title>test of phpxml xpath</title>
  </head>

  <body>
    <pre>

    <?php
    for ($i=0 ; $i < $app_counter ; ++$i) {
        print ("Application: " . $app_data[$i]["name"] . "\n");
        foreach ($app_data[$i]["title"] as $v) {
            print ("   $v\n");
        }
        print ("\n"); // formatting
```

```
      }
      ?>

    </pre>
  </body>
</html>
```

The result looks just the same:

```
N  http://localhost/ProPHPXML/Chapter09/test_phpxml.php - Netscape 6    _ □ X
   File  Edit  View  Search  Go  Bookmarks  Tasks  Help

   Application: sportran compiler
       It crashes when a string with more than 256 bytes is declared
       String concatenation fails if a string contains a dot
       Error when summing two integers

   Application: SportyEditor
       Cut and paste doesn't work
       Save as doesn't ask for a file name
       Can't type accents for latin characters
       If you open a new file the first one remains as the active window
```

A Searchable Bug List

By now our manager is probably rather bored of looking at five different versions of the same simplified list. Let's do something really nice and build a simple search mechanism that can be used to hunt for bugs. Our goals will be to allow a search for words in the titles of the bugs, and a provision to filter the results based on whether or not the bugs are open or closed (or no filter at all). The output should be a list of any application(s) that have matching bugs and the entire title of the bugs.

To begin with, let's create a simple form that can be used as an interface. The HTML (with a little PHP thrown in) should look like the following when saved in a file called search_buglist.php:

```
<html>
  <head>
    <title>search through buglist</title>
  </head>

  <body>
    <h2>Use the Form Below to Query the Buglist</h2>

    <form name="searchxml" action="<?php print ($_SERVER['PHP_SELF']); ?>"
          method="post">
      <table border="0" cellpadding="3" cellspacing="1">
        <tr>
          <td align="left">Open/Closed</td>
          <td align="left">Keyword Search</td>
        </tr>
        <tr>
```

```
            <td align="left">
              <select name="open_status">
                <option value="NA"
                  <?php if (0 == strcmp($_POST["open_status"], "NA"))
                            print (" selected"); ?>>Doesn't Matter
                </option>
                <option value="Open"
                  <?php if (0 == strcmp($_POST["open_status"], "Open"))
                            print (" selected"); ?>>Open
                </option>
                <option value="Closed"
                  <?php if (0 == strcmp($_POST["open_status"], "Closed"))
                            print (" selected"); ?>>Closed
                </option>
              </select>
            </td>
            <td align="left">
              <input type="text" name="keyword" size="40"
                    value="<?php print ($_POST['keyword']); ?>">
            </td>
          </tr>
          <tr>
            <td align="left"><input type="submit" value="Submit"></td>
            <td align="left"> </td>
          </tr>
        </table>
      </form>

      <pre>
      </pre>

    </body>
</html>
```

On the desktop, a browser shows this:

The first lines of our code for this application, which should go into PHP tags above the beginning of the HTML, will be used to include our class file. Also, it will be used to define base XPath expressions for the applications and for the search based on the presence of a keyword:

```php
<?php
require_once("../classes/xml.php");

// base path to get app names
$path = "//application";

// create a search path based on the presence
// of a keyword search
if (0 == strcmp($_POST['keyword'], "")) {
    $xpath_search = "/descendant::title[1]/..";
} else {
    $xpath_search = "/descendant::title[1]/[contains(., " .
    $_POST['keyword'] . ")]/..";
}
```

Here, we are making use of the XPath `contains()` function as well as the `descendant` structure to get to the data that we want. Also, note that we have a trailing `..` at the end of each expression. This is a standard trick that will make the path completions work more easily later on.

Next, we'll instantiate the object, evaluate the base XPath expression, and initialize the global storage variables:

```php
// instantiate new object
$phpxml = new XML("../bug_list.xml");

// evaluate the base path
$paths = $phpxml->evaluate($path);

// handy global variables
$app_counter = 0;
$bug_list = array();
```

It's once again time for our primary loop, where all of the real work happens. This is fairly simple, as in our previous XPath example. We will first store the name of the application. Then we will construct XPath expressions for the bug titles we are interested in and use `get_content()` to retrieve those titles for storage. This time, we are also going to store the status (open or `closed`) of the bug since we will be interested in that data later on:

```php
foreach ($paths as $app) {
    // get attributes for each application tag and store name
    $attributes = $phpxml->get_attributes($app);
    $bug_list[$app_counter]["name"] = $attributes["name"];

    // create XPath search path and evaluate
    $search_path = $app . $xpath_search;
    $match_paths = $phpxml->evaluate($search_path);

    foreach ($match_paths as $match) {
        // store the bug titles that matched and their open
        // or closed status
        $bug_list[$app_counter]["bugs"][] =
                        $phpxml->get_content($match . "/title[1]");
```

```
              $bug_list[$app_counter]["status"][] =
                     strtoupper($phpxml->get_content($match . "/status[1]"));
     }
     // don't forget to increment counter!
     ++$app_counter;
}
?>
```

The values of the <status> tag have all been made uppercase with PHP's strtoupper() function. This is because we are going to check for a value using the in_array() function a little later, and this function is case-sensitive.

All that's left is to display the results. The filtering will be done based on the open or closed status of the bugs here, as opposed to using the XPath search. There are two reasons for this. First, it's a little easier to do it this way. Second, it is possible that we might want to display the filtered results in such a way that we would need all matching titles. For example, if our manager was looking for closed bugs, we might want to show all of them but make the closed ones appear in bold text. However, in this example, we are going to omit any bugs that do not make it through the open/closed filter.

The following PHP code should be placed in between the <pre></pre> tags in our HTML:

```
<?php
// give a little message about whether they
// cared if the bug was open or closed
if (0 != strcmp($_POST["open_status"], "NA") &&
      isset($_POST["open_status"])) {
   print ("You searched for <b>" . $_POST["open_status"] .
         "</b> bugs.\n\n");
}
```

Obviously, this is just a little reminder in case our manager forgot the requirement:

```
// do nothing if we have no bugs
if (count($bug_list)) {
   for ($i=0 ; $i < $app_counter ; ++$i) {
      // if this isn't an array, we have nothing, so jump
      // to next loop
      if (!is_array($bug_list[$i]["status"])) {
         continue;
      }
```

These first few lines just make sure that we have some actual bugs to work with. Otherwise, we'll just jump to the next loop iteration. Next, if there are any bugs that meet our open/closed requirements, we'll print out the application name:

```
         // if the status is okay, get the app name
         if (0 == strcmp($_POST["open_status"], "NA") ||
            in_array(strtoupper($_POST["open_status"]),
                  $bug_list[$i]["status"])) {
            $found = TRUE;
            print ("Application :: " . $bug_list[$i]["name"] . "\n");
```

Finally, we'll loop through the actual bugs and pick out the ones that individually match the open/closed requirements. Remember that the only bugs we'll have in our array have already matched the keyword entered from our XPath expression:

```
                // now go through the bugs and print them out IF
                // they have the correct open/closed status
                for ($j = 0 ; $j < count($bug_list[$i]["bugs"]) ; ++$j) {
                    if (0 == strcmp($bug_list[$i]["status"][$j],
                                    strtoupper($_POST["open_status"])) ||
                        (0 == strcmp(strtoupper($_POST["open_status"]), "NA"))) {

                        print ("     " . $bug_list[$i]["bugs"][$j] ."\n");
                    }
                }
            }
            // if we've found a match we want to separate this
            // application from the next one
            if ($found == TRUE) print ("\n\n"); // formatting
        }
    }
    // If the form has been submitted and we've not found a match, print
    // a message to that effect.
    if (isset($_POST["open_status"]) and $found != TRUE) {
        print ("Sorry, no bugs were found");
    }
?>
```

A sample result from this program looks like this:

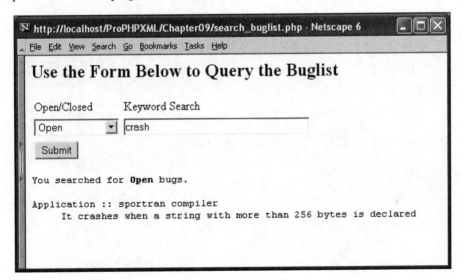

387

Summary

In this chapter we focused on using a few of the many available XML-based classes for PHP.

We have deconstructed and taken output from the bug_list.xml file in four completely different ways:

❑   By parsing it with a generic parser

❑   By taking the XML data into an in-memory tree structure

❑   By transforming it into an HTML table for presentation

❑   By using it with the XPath query language

Furthermore, we used the in-memory structures available in the XMLFile class to generate a simplified XML buglist file, and we used the features of XPath to easily create a simple bug query application.

Even with all of this, each of the classes we looked at has abilities that were not covered here. Also, these are only four of a great many classes available for use by developers. Two excellent resources are the Upperdesign class repository and the PHP PEAR repository. These are located at: http://phpclasses.upperdesign.com/ and http://pear.php.net/ respectively.

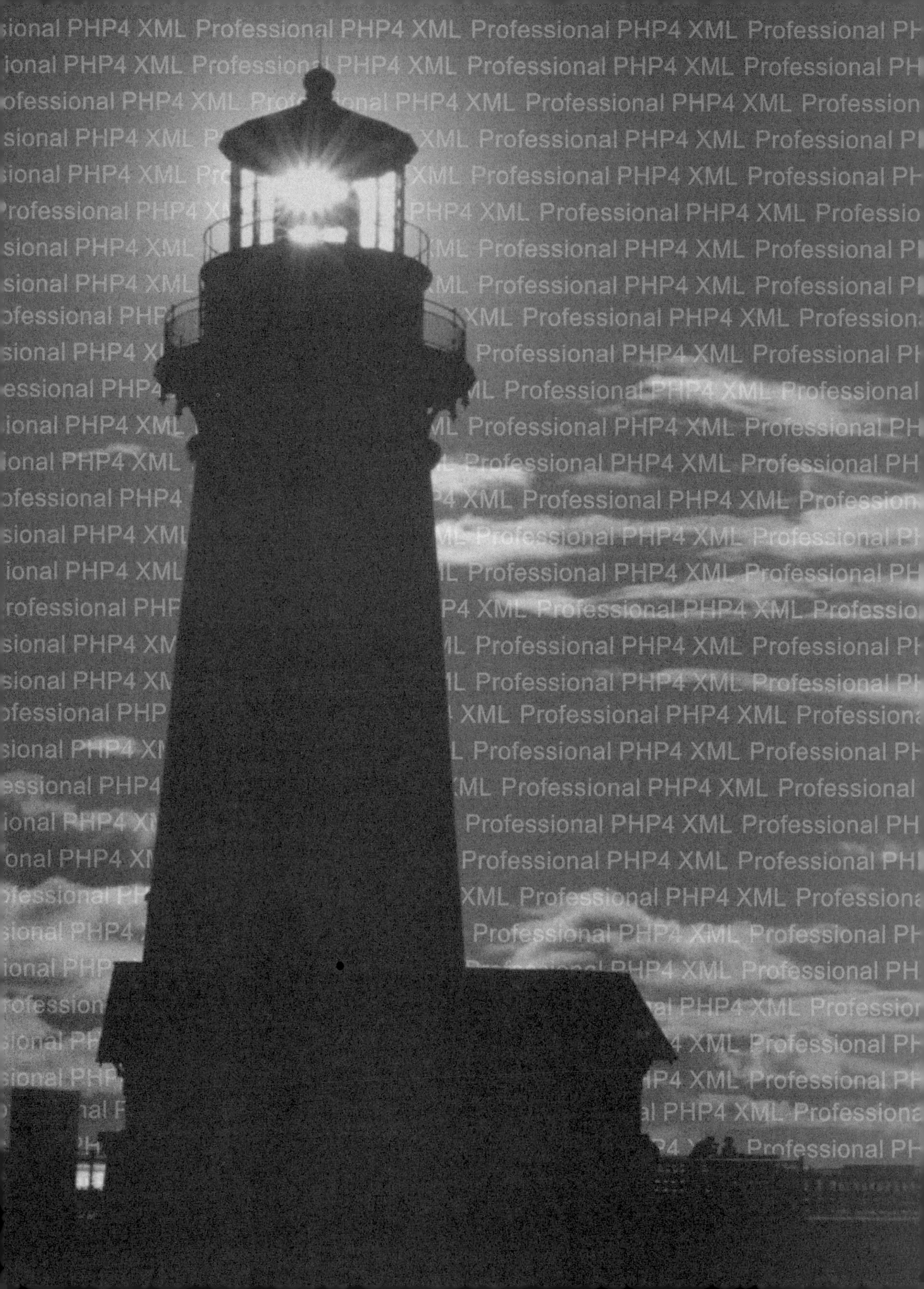
Professional PHP4 XML

10

Putting It Together

In the preceding chapters we have taken a detailed look at XML, SAX, DOM, XPath, and XSL. We have also looked at some XML technologies – XHTML, WML, SVG, VXML, RSS, RDF, XML-RPC, and SOAP. Finally, we looked at four XML classes that share one major common feature – they allow us to interact with an XML document.

XML is used for:

❑ Storing data – XML documents

❑ Describing data – RDF, RSS

❑ Querying and Parsing – DOM, SAX, XSLT

❑ Presentation – XHTML, WML, SVG, VXML

❑ Services – XML-RPC, SOAP

Finding the right mix of XML to use in a project is sometimes a challenging task. This chapter does just that, it describes how to put these different technologies to work.

Here's is a brief summary of what we have learned so far:

❑ The basics of XML

❑ What is SAX and when and how to use it

❑ What is DOM and when and how to use it

❑ What is XPath and when and how to use it

❑ What XSLT is and when and how to use it

In this chapter we'll be putting what we've learned in the previous chapters into practice to see different solutions to the same problem using different technologies. By the end of this chapter we'll have learned:

❑   How to abstract different XML processing problems

❑   How to transform XML documents using XSLT or SAX

❑   A way to implement SAX filters, and examples of SAX filter chains

❑   What can be done to speed up XSLT transformations

❑   How to modify XML documents using DOM

❑   How to modify XML documents using SAX filters

❑   How to modify XML documents using XSLT

❑   How to transform XML data into PHP objects

❑   How to write XML data from non-XML data using DOM

❑   How to write a SAX parser for non-XML data

Programming XML Applications

With a very broad vision we may classify programming tasks using XML into two major categories:

❑   Storing and retrieving XML

❑   Processing XML

Storing and retrieving XML is detailed in Chapter 13.

Up till now in this book we've covered the core standards for XML processing – XPath, SAX, DOM, and XSLT. In this chapter we are going to study different XML processing problems and study different solutions to these problems using the tools we've mastered in the previous chapters.

We need to process XML data from some source since it is useful to our application. We are going to study some very common problems that arise when processing an XML document. For each problem we'll discuss different options to solve the problem and the scenarios where each solution is better than the others.

The assumption here is that we are in the middle of a large application, and maintaining it is an important issue, hence, we'll be focusing on OOP solutions most of the time. We'll also observe some patterns of OOP that can be applied to programs that process XML.

Transforming XML

When it comes to transforming XML, we have an XML file or XML data source that we need to transform. This can be achieved in many different ways, for example:

- ❑ Transform XML into HTML to be displayed in a browser
- ❑ Transform XML into a PDF file and store it on the disk
- ❑ Transform XML into objects that are going to be stored in an OO database
- ❑ Transform XML into SQL scripts to insert data in a relational database
- ❑ Transform an XML file from a given vocabulary to a different vocabulary
- ❑ Transform XML into proprietary message syntax to be sent over some communication network
- ❑ Transform XML into a text report that will be sent by e-mail
- ❑ Transform XML into an SVG chart to be used in a presentation
- ❑ Transform XML into an XSLT stylesheet that will be used to perform a transformation or validation of another XML document

Transforming implies reading XML, peeking at the content, and writing something that may or may not be XML.

Example

To illustrate different solutions, we'll work with a very simple example. Let's use the following XML file describing some applications coded by a software company:

```
<?xml version="1.0" ?>
<!-- This XML file is an example -->
<apps>
<application id="1">
  <name>Editor</name>
  <author>John</author>
  <bugs>
    <bug>
      <!-- This is one bug -->
      <desc>Foo</desc>
      <sev>2</sev>
    </bug>
    <bug>
      <desc>Bar</desc>
      <sev>3</sev>
    </bug>
  </bugs>
</application>
<application id="2">
  <name>Compiler</name>
```

```
  <author>Peter</author>
  <bugs>
    <bug>
    <desc>Foo Bar</desc>
    <sev>5</sev>
    </bug>
  </bugs>
</application>
</apps>
```

Our transformation task will be to transform all the `<name>` elements to a `<name><b>text</b></name>` format where all the text is uppercase. After transformation, the sample file would look like this:

```xml
<?xml version="1.0" ?>
<!-- This XML file is an example -->
<apps>
<application id="1">
  <name><b>EDITOR</b></name>
  <author>John</author>
  <bugs>
    <bug>
      <!-- This is one bug -->
      <desc>Foo</desc>
      <sev>2</sev>
    </bug>
    <bug>
      <desc>Bar</desc>
      <sev>3</sev>
    </bug>
  </bugs>
</application>
<application id="2">
  <name><b>COMPILER</b></name>
  <author>Peter</author>
  <bugs>
    <bug>
    <desc>Foo Bar</desc>
    <sev>5</sev>
    </bug>
  </bugs>
</application>
</apps>
```

We can transform XML documents using:

❑   DOM

❑   XSLT

❑   SAX

Using DOM for XML Transforming

It is possible to use the DOM standard to transform an XML file. We can parse the XML file into the DOM tree and then perform different operations on the tree to transform the source XML file into a different XML file. This is useful only in limited situations, where the result is also XML and the file is small and the transformation simple. Since using the DOM standard for transformation is restricted to very specific situations we shall not look into a detailed example in this chapter.

Here are some of the advantages and disadvantages of using DOM for XML transformations:

Advantages	Disadvantages
Based on a solid standard by the W3C.	Uses a lot of resources. Not good for transforming medium- to large-sized documents.
Easy for removing/adding elements from a document.	Makes sense if the transformation implies modifying a document, very hard if the transformation result is not XML.
	Scales badly, not suitable for online processing unless the document size is known and small.

Using XSLT for XML Transforming

XSLT is the de facto standard for transforming XML content. This language was created to define XML transformations. We write an XSLT stylesheet and then use an XSLT processor to transform the XML file using the XSLT stylesheet, the result can be XML, HTML, a binary format, or some text.

Chapter 8 covers XSLT support in PHP.

We can easily write an XSLT stylesheet to perform our sample transformation. Here is the `tr1.xsl` XSLT stylesheet:

```
<?xml version="1.0" encoding="utf-8"?>
<xsl:stylesheet xmlns:xsl="http://www.w3.org/1999/XSL/Transform" version="1.0">
  <xsl:output method="xml" encoding="utf-8" />
  <xsl:template match="name/text()">
    <b>
      <xsl:value-of select='translate(string(.),
                  "abcdefghijklmnopqrstuvwxyz",
                  "ABCDEFGHIJKLMNOPQRSTUVWXYZ")' />
      <xsl:apply-templates />
    </b>
  </xsl:template>

  <xsl:template match="@*|node()">
    <xsl:copy>
      <xsl:apply-templates select="@*|node()" />
    </xsl:copy>
  </xsl:template>
</xsl:stylesheet>
```

The source XML file is transformed using the above stylesheet and the output redirected to a new XML file. Once it is done, we can see that just the text contents of the <name> element are matched, and the output displays the text in uppercase because of the translate() function enclosed in a <b> tag in the above stylesheet. We also used a 'match anything else' template to copy the rest of the XML document without modifications to the result.

> The presented stylesheet is useful as a base template for changing XML documents since it copies everything that is not matched as-is to the output document.

This is the PHP code used to perform the transformation:

```php
<?php
include_once("class_xslt.php");
$xslt = new Xslt();
$xslt->SetXml("applications.xml");
$xslt->SetXsl("tr1.xsl");
if ($xslt->Transform()) {
    $ret = $xslt->GetOutput();
    print ($ret);
} else {
    print ("Error:".$xslt->GetError());
}
?>
```

And this is the class_xslt.php abstraction that we used:

```php
<?php
class Xslt
{
    var $xsl, $xml, $output, $error ;

    /* Constructor */
    function Xslt()
    {
        $this->processor = xslt_create();
    }

    /* Destructor */
    function Destroy()
    {
        xslt_free($this->processor);
    }

    /* output methods */
    function SetOutput($string)
    {
        $this->output = $string;
    }
    function GetOutput()
    {
        return $this->output;
```

```
}

/* set methods */
function SetXmlString($xml)
{
    $this->xml = $xml;
    return true;
}

function SetXslString($xsl)
{
    $this->xsl = $xsl;
    return true;
}

function SetXml($uri)
{
    if ($doc = new DocReader($uri)) {
        $this->xml = $doc->GetString();
        return true;
    } else {
        $this->SetError("Could not open $xml");
        return false;
    }
}

function SetXsl($uri)
{
    if ($doc = new DocReader($uri)) {
        $this->xsl = $doc->GetString();
        return true;
    } else {
        $this->SetError("Could not open $uri");
        return false;
    }
}

/* transform method */
function Transform()
{
    $arguments = array('/_xml' => $this->xml,
                       '/_xsl' => $this->xsl
                      );
    $ret = xslt_process($this->processor, 'arg:/_xml', 'arg:/_xsl',
                        NULL, $arguments);
    if (!$ret) {
        $this->SetError(xslt_error($this->processor));
        return false;
    } else {
        $this->SetOutput($ret);
        return true;
    }
}
```

397

```
    /* Error Handling */
    function SetError($string)
    {
        $this->error = $string;
    }
    function GetError()
    {
        return $this->error;
    }
}

/* DocReader -- read a file or URL as a string */
/* test */
/*
   $docUri = new DocReader('http://www.someurl.com/doc.html');
   print ($docUri->GetString());
*/
class DocReader
{
    var $string; // public string representation of file
    var $type;   // private URI type: 'file', 'url'
    var $bignum = 1000000;
    var $uri;

    /* public constructor */
    function DocReader($uri)
    {                                               // returns integer
        $this->SetUri($uri);
        $this->uri = $uri;
        $this->SetType();

        $fp = fopen($this->GetUri(), "r");
        if ($fp) {                                  // get length
            if ($this->GetType() == 'file') {
                $length = filesize($this->GetUri());
            } else {
                $length = $this->bignum;
            }
            $this->SetString(fread($fp, $length));
            return 1;
        } else {
            return 0;
        }
    }

    /* determine if a URI is a filename or URL */
    function IsFile($uri)
    {                                               // returns boolean
        if (strstr($uri, 'http://') == $uri) {
            return false;
        } else {
            return true;
        }
    }
```

```
/* set and get methods */
function SetUri($string)
{
    $this->uri = $string;
}
function GetUri()
{
    return $this->uri;
}
function SetString($string)
{
    $this->string = $string;
}
function GetString()
{
  return $this->string;
}
function SetType()
{
    if ($this->IsFile($this->uri)) {
        $this->type = 'file';
    } else {
        $this->type = 'url';
    }
}
function GetType()
{
    return $this->type;
}
}
?>
```

Here we used a PHP class to hide the XSLT processor from the application. This is a key recommendation if we use XSLT. Separating the XSLT implementation from its use has the following advantages:

❑   We can change the XSLT processor without changing the code that uses it. For example, we can write a wrapper class for Xalan C and test if Xalan performs worst, better, or equal as compared to Sablotron.

❑   If the PHP XSLT extension API changes we won't need to modify all the sources.

❑   We can use the class to abstract different sources of XML data for the XSLT transformation. In our class we can pass an XML document as a string or as a file, and by adding some more code, we could have passed a SAX parser, a DOM tree, or a handler to an XML database and performed the transformation there.

❑   We can add a caching mechanism to the XSLT class making it transparent to applications. We can write the class to use/not use the caching mechanism according to the user preferences. This allows us to use caching at the level we want if some other class also caches.

> It may sound trivial, but abstracting the XML processing tools from the application is a key design decision in a large project. The SAX parser, DOM extension, or XSLT processor should be encapsulated in wrapper classes to ease software maintenance. The PEAR project will surely provide such abstractions in the near future. Stay tuned to http://pear.php.net/.

What Happens If the Transformation Is Complex?

If the transformation we need to perform is really complex, then using XSLT is the best option as it can handle complex transformations without any problem. XSLT is rich with features such as the document() function, sort capabilities, and features related to writing templates. We can use <xsl:include> to modularize our stylesheets, if they get very large. Thus, it is beneficial to use XSLT when we are dealing with large and complex transformations.

What Happens If the XML Document Is Large?

The Sablotron XSLT processor used by PHP parses the whole XML document into memory, as well as the XSLT stylesheet, for processing. This means that the larger the document to transform, the larger will be the memory consumed by the application, and the time that is needed to transform the document.

If the XSLT stylesheet is well-written (XSLT does some things faster than others, for example, expressions tend to be slow) we'll be able to handle transformation of middle- to large-sized documents without much trouble, and we could even do it online.

However, if the documents get really big and the time consumed by the transformation is not acceptable, we can try some of these workarounds:

- Use a caching mechanism for XSLT transformations
- Use batch transformations
- Use SAX

Using a Caching Mechanism for XSLT Transformations

Many times we'll be transforming the same XML document with the same XSLT stylesheet. This is very common, for example, if we use XSLT to create an HTML representation of an XML document for web presentation. It is clear that after the first transformation is done all the others are a waste of resources. Caching implies making the result of XSLT transformations persistent and outputting that result if the same transformation is requested. A caching mechanism can be used in:

- The XSLT wrapper class used for the XSLT processor
- A transformation class used to abstract XML transformations
- The application level

It is advisable that we implement caching at the XSLT processor abstraction level or at the transformation abstraction level, because at the application level our code will be harder to maintain.

A caching mechanism must remember the XML source and the XSLT stylesheet used (storing MD5 checksums is generally a good way to do it), and store the result of the transformation along with the checksums. It also has to decide what policy will be used to prevent the cache from growing ad infinitum – keeping a maximum cache size and cleaning, for example, the 'n' least used transformations, when the cache is full.

With this in mind it will be easy for us to add caching to our transformation classes using, for example, a MySQL database to store the results. Since MySQL is fast, it is a good option for caching. Once caching is enabled we can check if the resources and time used for our transformations are down to acceptable levels. Even if we don't have a performance problem, caching is a good idea as it consumes fewer resources on the server; we don't need them but other processes may.

Using Batch Transformations

If caching is not enough, we must think about not transforming the documents online. We can write a batch transformation system to queue up the transformations and produce the outputs as they are processed.

If we are in an online system this may be difficult, but if we are at the backend of a system we will find that we can transform documents in the background while the application runs in the foreground. This is a very good alternative in the following situations, for example:

❑ Transforming XML documents into PDF files that may be downloaded later by the application

❑ Transforming XML documents to SQL data that the application may use later

❑ Transforming XML documents into reports that will be stored or sent later

However, if we need to use the result of the transformation immediately in the application then this approach is not very useful. Web publishing systems are a clear example of systems that can't benefit from batch transformations.

Batch transformations can be done in many different ways. What we need is a client-server model with a **transformation server**. We store the document and the XSLT stylesheet at some other location and the server does the transformation when available (when not doing other transformations), storing the result at a desired location. Another batch system can then pick up results and put them in the proper place for the application. A database, files, or TCP/IP can be used for communications between the transformation server, and the client application.

The following table shows some of the advantages and disadvantages of using XSLT:

Advantages	Disadvantages
Solid standard by the W3C	May scale badly if the XML documents are really huge
Eases maintainability and reuse of transformations	
Fast enough for online processing of small- to mid-sized documents	
Can be used to perform complex transformations	

Using SAX

If both the above options are not enough, then we can draw the conclusion that an XSLT transformation is not feasible in our application. Though this may happen, it is not a very common scenario. We must be making performing transformations of huge and mutable (non-cacheable) documents for this to happen. If it does happen it is best to use SAX, instead of XSLT, for our transformations. In the next section we will see how to use SAX.

Using SAX for XML Transforming

SAX is an event-driven parser for XML. PHP uses Expat which is a SAX parser written by Jim Clark. In this section we will see how to use SAX for XML transformations.

SAX is described in Chapter 5 of this book.

Why SAX?

SAX breaks the XML file into smaller chunks of data (buffers of raw data) and then parses them, so the amount of memory consumed by SAX is constant, no matter how big the XML file is. This also makes SAX faster than DOM or XSLT, and it scales better than these standards for large files, no matter what we are doing with the document.

How To Use SAX for Transformations

The first intuitive approach for using SAX to transform XML documents is to write handlers for the SAX events, and, keeping context between the handlers, perform the transformation inside them. In our example we can think about the following solution:

❑   Step 1 – Initialize a flag to 0

❑   Step 2 – Define the handlers for SAX events:

    ❑   StartElementHandler
       If the element is <name> turn a flag on (1)

    ❑   EndElementHandler
       If the element is <name> turn the flag off (0).

    ❑   CharacterDatahandler
       If the flag is on (1) then output uppercased data, else output data

❑   Step 3 – Parse the document

We are assuming that no subelements may appear inside a <name> tag (no mixed content). If subelements do appear then we can use an integer flag and increment or decrement it. This way we can keep track of the text of a <name> tag and not its subelement <name>.

We just wrote the sketch of a SAX parser that transforms our XML file. We can easily write this using the PHP XML parser functions, as we learned in Chapter 5, and the result will be the desired transformation. While this works, it is not a very good long-term solution.

After writing applications that use SAX we'll learn that complex processing becomes a nightmare due to the limitations of the SAX parser. We will not feel very comfortable if the parser only tells us when an element starts, or when an element ends. As processing becomes more complex we will have to write a lot of code to keep context using stacks, push and pull flags, use integer semaphores, and many other obscure programming techniques.

Imagine a situation where we have to perform a complex transformation. It may be the worst coding nightmare ever, and even if we succeed, it will still be difficult for us to understand the code after some weeks. Every programmer has to be extra careful when faced with such situations. As programmers we know that the best way to address a complex problem is to break it into pieces, solve each piece, and then unite all of them in the end. This is called **modularization** or factoring. Modularization of SAX driven applications is crucial whenever the task is complex. We can do this using **SAX filters**.

SAX Filters for XML Transformations

We have learnt a lot about SAX and filters in Chapter 5. In this chapter we touch on this concept of filters, and some techniques to use them. It is expected that PEAR will define a standard for SAX filters in PHP in the near future. In the meantime we can use the approach discussed in Chapter 5, or our own approach, provided we understand the concept well.

A SAX filter is a class that performs transforming from the output of a SAX parser or another SAX filter. A filter can encapsulate a simple transformation, so we can write many filters and **chain** them later. Passing the output of one filter as an input to another creates a complex transformation from simple ones.

We'll be building a very simple example to illustrate these concepts. Let's now write the class.

The `AbstractSAXParser` receives an XML file and produces SAX events that must be passed to a filter. The SAX parser alone is useless: it is used as a generator of SAX events for another class.

The abstract class is important as it helps us to understand the methods that implementations must have.

Here are some observations:

❑ **The class hides the SAX parser from the application**
If we change the parser from Expat to another one, nothing will have to be changed except this class.

❑ **The class allows parsing non-XML data**
We can write an `AbstractSAXParser` for non-XML data, parse the data with it, and produce SAX events. This way we can transform non-XML to XML.

❑ **The class can hide the XML source from its users**
We can write a SAX parser for XML files, XML strings, and for XML stored in a database.

The abstract class is as follows:

```
class AbstractSAXParser
{
    var $listener;

    function AbstractSAXParser() {}

    function ParserSetOption($opt, $val) {}

    function SetListener($obj)
    {
        $this->listener = $obj;
```

```
    }

    function StartElementHandler($parser, $name, $attribs)
    {
        $this->listener->StartElementHandler($name, $attribs);
    }

    function EndElementHandler($parser, $name)
    {
        $this->listener->EndElementHandler($name);
    }

    function CharacterDataHandler($parser, $data)
    {
        $this->listener->CharacterDataHandler($data);
    }

    function Parse() {}
}
```

The **listener** will be the object that will receive the SAX events produced by this class. As we can see, the handlers in this class are fixed, and they only call their brothers in the listener object. The **abstract parse method** will depend on the implementation, and is supposed to parse the XML data. It generates the events that are intercepted by the methods in this class and calls the same methods in the listener. Note that the listener methods don't receive a parser since they don't need it. The `SetListener()` method allows us to set the object that will be used as a listener for the events produced in this class. Finally the `ParserSetOption()` method is prepared to set options specific to the SAX parser, such as case folding.

> Note that for space-saving reasons only `startElement`, `endElement`, and `characterData` events are considered. It is easy to extend the example to the full range of SAX events with very minor changes.

We can write a class for the Expat parser, as follows:

```
class ExpatParser extends AbstractSAXParser
{
    var $parser;
    var $filename;
    var $buffer;
    var $error_string;
    var $line;

    function ExpatParser($xmlfile)
    {
        $this->filename = $xmlfile;
        $this->parser = xml_parser_create();
        $this->buffer = 4096;
        xml_set_object($this->parser, &$this);
        xml_set_element_handler($this->parser, "StartElementHandler",
```

```
                                      "EndElementHandler");
        xml_set_character_data_handler($this->parser,
                                       "CharacterDataHandler");
    }

    function ParserSetOption($opt, $val)
    {
        return xml_parser_set_option($this->parser, $opt, $val);
    }

    function Parse()
    {
        if (!($fp = fopen($this->filename, "r"))) {
            return 0;
        }

        while ($data = fread($fp, $this->buffer)) {
            if (!xml_parse($this->parser, $data, feof($fp))) {
                $this->error_string =
                        xml_error_string(xml_get_error_code($xml_parser));
                $this->line = xml_get_current_line_number($xml_parser);
                die("Error: ".$this->error_string." on ".$this->line);
            }
        }
        xml_parser_free($this->parser);
        return 1;
    }
}
```

This class is just an implementation of the abstract class using the Expat parser. Some methods such as `getErrorString()` and `getErrorLineNumber()` are missing, but we won't need them for our examples.

Now we define an `AbstractFilter` class. The abstract filter receives SAX events, manipulates them, and re-transmits the events to a listener. Also, the filter can change tag names, modify the content of elements, add elements by generating events, and so on.

Here is the abstract class:

```
class AbstractFilter
{
    var $listener;

    //to set the listener of the filter and handlers for the events
    function SetListener($obj)
    {
        $this->listener = $obj;
    }

    function StartElementHandler($name, $attribs) {}

    function EndElementHandler($name) {}

    function CharacterDataHandler($data) {}
}
```

The `SetListener()` method sets the listener of the filter and the handlers for the events. In the handlers we have to perform a task and then pass the event to the next listener.

We will use the same example that we used earlier in this chapter, and write a filter to convert the text inside <name> tags to uppercase:

```php
class FilterName extends AbstractFilter
{
    var $flag = 0;

    function StartElementHandler($name, $attribs)
    {
        if (strtolower($name) == "name") {
            $this->flag = 1;
        } else {
            $this->flag = 0;
        }
        $this->listener->StartElementHandler($name, $attribs);
    }

    function EndElementHandler($name)
    {
        if (strtolower($name) == "name") {
            $this->flag = 0;
        }
        $this->listener->EndElementHandler($name);
    }

    function CharacterDataHandler($data)
    {
        if ($this->flag) {
            $data = strtoupper($data);
        }
        $this->listener->CharacterDataHandler($data);
    }
}
```

Note that we used the simple approach we described before, that is, using a `flag` to track when we are inside a <name> element and when we are not. Also notice how the listener is passed the events immediately after the modification is done. The listener will receive the same events as this filter but it will receive uppercased text for <name> elements.

Finally we can write a filter that doesn't produce events but outputs the XML for testing:

```php
class FilterOutput extends AbstractFilter
{

    function StartElementHandler($name, $attribs)
    {
        print ("&lt;$name");
        foreach ($attribs as $key => $val) {
            print (" $key = '$val'");
        }
        print ("&gt;<br />");
    }

    function EndElementHandler($name)
```

```
    {
        print ("&lt;/$name&gt;<br />");
    }

    function CharacterDataHandler($data)
    {
        print ("$data");
    }
}
```

As we can see this filter can't be used in the middle of a chain because it consumes all the SAX events. It just outputs the XML data (the `print()` statements where it used to just write a short example).

This is the way we can use them:

```
$f1 = new ExpatParser("applications.xml");
$f1->ParserSetOption(XML_OPTION_CASE_FOLDING, 0);
$f2 = new FilterName();
$f3 = new FilterOutput();

$f2->SetListener($f3);
$f1->SetListener($f2);

$f1->Parse();
```

It is very important to build the chain in the proper order. We first have to set the listener of the `$f2` filter as `$f3` and then the listener of `$f1` as `$f2`. The following figure shows what will happen:

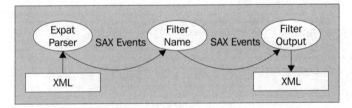

If we remember correctly, our transformation not only asked us to uppercase the <name> tags but also to place them in a <b> tag. We can write a filter that converts <name>some</name> elements into <name><b>some</b></name> elements as follows:

```
class FilterNameBold extends AbstractFilter
{
    var $flag = 0;

    function StartElementHandler($name, $attribs)
    {
        if (strtolower($name) == "name") {
            $this->flag = 1;
        } else {
            $this->flag = 0;
        }
        $this->listener->StartElementHandler($name, $attribs);
```

If we are in a <name> element (flag = 1) then we generate an artificial startElement event with a b tagname by calling the StartElementHandler() method in the listener:

```
        if ($this->flag) {$this->listener->
                        StartElementHandler("b", array());}
    }

    function EndElementHandler($name)
    {
        if (strtolower($name) == "name") {
            $this->flag = 0;
            $this->listener->EndElementHandler("b");
        }
        $this->listener->EndElementHandler($name);
    }

    function CharacterDataHandler($data)
    {
        if ($this->flag) {
            $data = strtoupper($data);
        }
        $this->listener->CharacterDataHandler($data);
    }
}
```

This is a nice example because it uses a common trick in SAX filters. To add an element we just invent an event for that element by passing it to the next filter. We can run the example instantiating the new chain of filters as follows:

```
$f1 = new ExpatParser("applications.xml");
$f1->ParserSetOption(XML_OPTION_CASE_FOLDING, 0);
$f2 = new FilterNameBold();
$f2b = new FilterName();
$f3 = new FilterOutput();

$f2b->SetListener($f3);
$f2->SetListener($f2b);
$f1->SetListener($f2);

$f1->Parse();
```

The result of this will be the XML file with composite transformation applied.

Streaming

One good characteristic of SAX filters is that as the SAX parser parses the XML chunks, SAX events are propagated for the chunk. So the last filter in the chain can stream the result of the composite transformation step-by-step without having to concatenate or wait for the whole result to arrive. This allows streaming the result to the disk, database, or whatever its destination is without delays.

To stream the result we need to have a streaming filter as the last link in the chain that, instead of calling the print() statements in our example, calls a Stream() method in another object. That object can save the results chunk by chunk to a file, database, or send them to the browser:

```
class FilterStreamer extends AbstractFilter
{
    var $stream;

    function FilterStreamer($obj)
    {
        $this->stream = $obj;
    }

    function StartElementHandler($name, $attribs)
    {
        $this->stream->Stream("<$name");
        foreach ($attribs as $key => $val) {
            $this->stream->Stream(" $key='$val'");
        }
        $this->stream->stream(">");
    }

    function EndElementHandler($name)
    {
        $this->stream->Stream("</$name>");
    }

    function CharacterDataHandler($data)
    {
        $this->stream->Stream("$data");
    }
}
```

This filter expects to receive an object in its constructor, and that object must implement a `Stream()` method capable of receiving the result of the filter chain as chunks. For example:

```
class SimpleStreamer extends AbstractStreamer
{
    function Stream($data)
    {
        print ($data);
    }
}
```

We can build the filter chain as follows:

```
$ss = new SimpleStreamer();

$f1 = new ExpatParser("applications.xml");
$f1->ParserSetOption(XML_OPTION_CASE_FOLDING, 0);
$f2 = new FilterNameBold();
$f3 = new FilterStreamer($ss);
$f2b = new FilterName();

$f2b->SetListener($f3);
$f2->SetListener($f2b);
$f1->SetListener($f2);

$f1->Parse();
```

The following table shows some of the advantages and disadvantages of using SAX:

Advantages	Disadvantages
Scales very well for huge documents	Transformations can be complex
Resource consumption is constant for documents of any size	Harder to use if the result is not XML
It is fast	Requires a lot of coding for even simple transformations
Allows streaming	

Choosing a Transformation Strategy

So far in this chapter we've seen how DOM, XSLT, and SAX can be used to perform transformations. The question is when to use each approach, and as we can imagine there's no definite answer. The best recommendation, however, seems to be to use XSLT whenever we can and SAX only when XSLT can't be used. DOM could be an alternative only for very simple transformations.

This table describes the best possible approach in each situation:

Document Type	Simple Transformations	Medium Complexity Transformations	Complex Transformations
Small	DOM or XSLT	XSLT	XSLT
Mid-sized	XSLT or DOM (if the transformation is very simple)	XSLT	XSLT
Large	XSLT or SAX	XSLT (preferred) or SAX	XSLT
Very large	SAX	SAX or XSLT	Try to use XSLT or SAX (if XSLT is impossible)

If transformations are almost always the same, we may want to use XSLT and caching no matter how big the documents are, since we'll only waste time and resources once in a while.

> If the result of the transformation is not XML, XSLT is the best alternative and we should try to evade DOM or SAX unless there's no escape.

Abstracting XML Transformations

As we can see, sometimes the choice between SAX and XSLT can be difficult, and at times we may start using XSLT and then need to prepare a SAX alternative for huge documents. Taking this into consideration we recommend abstract transformations by defining transformation classes that implement a given transformation, for example, RSS to HTML. We then can implement that transformation class using XSLT or SAX without changing the application. The class is also a good place to put a caching mechanism if necessary. Abstraction is always worth the effort.

Modifying XML

Modifying XML is a problem where we have an XML data source and need to modify it. We may want to change some text, add an attribute, add an element, or remove a subtree of the document.

Modifying is a subset of the transforming problem since the output is always XML, and belongs to the same vocabulary as the original file.

Here are some situations where we might find instances of this problem:

❑   Using XML data as a catalog and then having to add/modify/remove items from the catalog

❑   Using XML to keep statistics that need to be updated

❑   Using XML for logging and having to add data

Example

For example, let's imagine we use XML to keep track of a shopping cart in some online store application. We may face a simple XML such as:

```
<cart>
  <user uid="382378">
    <name>John Smith</name>
  </user>
  <products>
    <product pid="12">
      <name>ACMEPencilHB</name>
      <desc>Soft Pencil by ACME</desc>
      <quantity>2</quantity>
      <unit_price>0.50</unit_price>
    </product>

    <product pid="13">
      <name>ACMEPen089</name>
      <desc>Rollerball pen</desc>
      <quantity>1</quantity>
      <unit_price>1</unit_price>
    </product>

  </products>
</cart>
```

411

Customers will use an interface to add/remove products from the shopping cart, and we have to reflect those changes to the XML file. Therefore, we'll need a way to:

❑ **Add a product**
Given the pid (product ID), <name>, <desc>, <quantity>, and <unit_price>. We'll add the product to the cart; if the product already exists in the cart we don't change it, we add it to the end.

❑ **Remove a product**
Given the pid, we remove all instances of the product from the cart.

Of course we should need more functions for our shopping cart to be usable, but let's use only these three for our examples.

When modifying XML is our task, the options are:

❑ DOM

❑ SAX

❑ XSLT

Using DOM To Modify XML Files

DOM is a good tool to modify XML files since it represents the XML document as an object and has all the methods we need to modify the object. We have methods to add/remove elements, add/remove attributes, move subtrees, and many other tasks. All this would be hard to code using XSLT or SAX.

While DOM eases the process, we have to remember that it consumes a lot of resources and that sometimes, if the documents are really big, it won't perform well enough. Only when the DOM approach is failing due to the size of the XML file, we'll have to look for an XSLT- or SAX-based solution.

For our example we have to write a function to add a product to the XML shopping cart and a function to remove a product from the cart. This is the addProduct() function:

```
function AddProduct($xml, $id, $name, $desc, $quantity, $unit_price)
{
    $doc = xmldoc($xml);
    //$doc = domxml_open_mem($xml);

    $root = $doc->document_element();
    $children = $root->child_nodes();
    foreach ($children as $child) {
        if ($child->node_type() == XML_ELEMENT_NODE){
            if ($child->tagname() == "products") {
                $newpro = $doc->create_element("product");
                $newpro->set_attribute("pid", $id);

                $newname = $doc->create_element("name");
                $newname_text = $doc->create_text_node($name);
                $newname->add_child($newname_text);
```

```
                $newprice = $doc->create_element("unit_price");
                $newprice_text = $doc->create_text_node($unit_price);
                $newprice->add_child($newprice_text);

                $newdesc = $doc->create_element("desc");
                $newdesc_text = $doc->create_text_node($desc);
                $newdesc->add_child($newdesc_text);

                $newquan = $doc->create_element("quantity");
                $newquan_text = $doc->create_text_node($quantity);
                $newquan->add_child($newquan_text);

                $newpro->add_child($newname);
                $newpro->add_child($newprice);
                $newpro->add_child($newdesc);
                $newpro->add_child($newquan);

                $child->add_child($newpro);

            }
        }
    }
    $xml = $doc->dump_mem();

    return $xml;
}
```

Note how the DOM tree is traversed looking for the `<products>` element, and then the `add_child()`, `create_text_node()`, and `create_element()` methods are used to create a `<product>` element and its subelements. The `set_attribute()` method is also used to set an attribute for the `<product>` element. This mechanism of navigation and insertions is very common when using DOM.

> `add_child()` is an alias of `append_child()`. `append_child()` is the proper function to use and works in PHP 4.2.1 and above. So use `append_child()` instead of `add_child()` with newer versions of PHP.

To remove all the instances of a product we can use this function:

```
function RemoveProduct($xml, $id)
{
    $doc = xmldoc($xml);
    //$doc = domxml_open_mem($xml);

    $root = $doc->root();
    $children = $root->child_nodes();
    foreach ($children as $child) {
        if ($child->node_type() == XML_ELEMENT_NODE){
            if ($child->tagname() == "products") {
                $products = $child->child_nodes();
```

```
                    foreach ($products as $product) {
                        if ($product->node_type() == XML_ELEMENT_NODE) {
                            // $product_children = $product->child_nodes();
                            $ats = $product->get_attribute("pid");
                            if ($ats == $id) {
                                $product->unlink_node();
                            }
                        }
                    }
                }
            }
        }
    }
    $xml = $doc->dumpmem();
    return $xml;
}
```

The function shows how to iterate the DOM tree looking for `<product>` tags, and how to check for an attribute of an element to see if we did find a product with the ID that we passed to the function.

To be more efficient we may write functions to add/remove elements from the DOM tree, thus parsing the document only once even if we want to add and remove many products. We didn't use this approach on other examples, but it is usually recommended if possible.

DOM is a solid standard for XML modification with methods to add/remove and change nodes. However, it is still not scalable in PHP, and especially scales badly for large XML documents. It also consumes lots of resources.

> If you get an errror such as 'undefined function xxx' when trying to test the examples in this chapter, you are probably using an old version of PHP. Examples in this section have been produced from the new DOM extension in PHP 4.2. If you have an earlier version you may want to check the following list of deprecated methods and their replacements in 4.2.

From the PHP documentation:

Deprecated Function	Replacement Function
DomDocument_dtd()	DomDocument_doctype()
DomDocument_root()	DomDocument_document_element()
DomDocument_children()	DomNode_child_nodes()
DomDocument_imported_node()	No replacement
DomNode_add_child()	Create a new node with, for example, DomDocument_create_element() and add it with DomNode_append_child()
DomNode_children()	DomNode_child_nodes()

Deprecated Function	Replacement Function
DomNode_parent()	DomNode_parent_node()
DomNode_new_child()	Create a new node with, for example, DomDocument_create_element() and add it with DomNode_append_child()
DomNode_set_content()	Create a new node with, for example, DomDocument_create_text_node() and add it with DomNode_append_child().
DomNode_get_content()	Content is just a text node and can be accessed with DomNode_child_nodes()
DomNode_set_content()	Content is just a text node and can be added with DomNode_append_child()

Using SAX To Modify a Document

If we could use SAX to transform a document we can surely use it to modify it. In fact, the approach used to modify a document with SAX should be the same as used when transforming the document – write filters that perform some basic transformations, and then chain the filters if needed, to perform a more complex modification. When modifying a document, chaining will be less frequent but the filter approach is good because each transformation is a separate class that can be maintained and updated easily.

Using SAX filters we can write the following filter to add a product to our XML cart example:

```
class FilterAddProduct extends AbstractFilter
{
    var $products = Array();

    function AddProduct($id, $name, $desc, $quantity, $unit_price)
    {
        $elem = Array();
        $elem["pid"] = $id;
        $elem["name"] = $name;
        $elem["desc"] = $desc;
        $elem["quantity"] = $quantity;
        $elem["unit_price"] = $unit_price;
        $this->products[] = $elem;
    }

    function StartElementHandler($name, $attribs)
    {
        $this->listener->StartElementHandler($name, $attribs);
        if ($name == "products") {
            // Perform insertions
            foreach ($this->products as $product) {
                $this->listener->StartElementHandler("product",
                                        Array("pid" => $product["pid"]));
```

```
                    // Name
                    $this->listener->StartElementHandler("name", Array());
                    $this->listener->CharacterDataHandler($product["name"]);
                    $this->listener->EndElementHandler("name");

                    // Desc
                    $this->listener->StartElementHandler("desc", Array());
                    $this->listener->CharacterDataHandler($product["desc"]);
                    $this->listener->EndElementHandler("desc");

                    // Quantity
                    $this->listener->StartElementHandler("quantity", Array());
                    $this->listener->CharacterDataHandler($product["quantity"]);
                    $this->listener->EndElementHandler("quantity");

                    // Unit_price
                    $this->listener->StartElementHandler("unit_price", Array());
                    $this->->
                         listener->characterDataHandler($product["unit_price"]);
                    $this->listener->EndElementHandler("unit_price");

                    $this->listener->EndElementHandler("product");
                }
            }
        }

    function EndElementHandler($name)
    {
        $this->listener->EndElementHandler($name);
    }

    function CharacterDataHandler($data)
    {
        $this->listener->CharacterDataHandler($data);
    }
}
```

This filter lets us prepare the filter to add many products when parsing the document; we store the products to be added in a member array of the filter. When parsing the document, if the filter sees that a `<products>` element has started, it traverses the list of products to be added, generating the events needed to insert the elements on the XML file.

We can use the filter this way:

```
$f1 = new ExpatParser("cart.xml");
$f1->ParserSetOption(XML_OPTION_CASE_FOLDING, 0);

$f2 = new FilterAddProduct();
$f2->AddProduct("15", "foo", "foo bar", "1", "6");
$f2->AddProduct("17", "Goo", "GOO", "2", "16");

$f3 = new FilterOutput();
$f2->SetListener($f3);
$f1->SetListener($f2);

$f1->Parse();
```

To remove elements from an XML document using SAX, we can use the following filter:

```
class FilterRemoveProduct extends AbstractFilter
{
    var $products = Array();
    var $ignore = 0;

    function RemoveProduct($id)
    {
        $this->products[] = $id;
    }

    function StartElementHandler($name, $attribs)
    {
        if ($name == "product") {
            if (in_array($attribs["pid"], $this->products)) {
                $this->ignore = 1;
            } else {
                $this->listener->StartElementHandler($name, $attribs);
            }
        }
        if (!$this->ignore) {
            $this->listener->StartElementHandler($name, $attribs);
        }
    }

    function EndElementHandler($name)
    {
        if (!$this->ignore) {
            $this->listener->EndElementHandler($name);
        } else {
            if ($name == "product") {
                $this->ignore = 0;
            }
        }
    }

    function CharacterDataHandler($data)
    {
        if (!$this->ignore) {
            $this->listener->CharacterDataHandler($data);
        }
    }
}
```

This filter can also store IDs of products to be deleted; we can use the removeProduct() method as many times as we want before parsing the document, preparing our chain to remove as many elements as we want.

We use a flag in the filter, and we turn the flag on each time a <product> element with an ID to be deleted starts. While the flag is on, we don't propagate events to the following filter, thus eliminating the element's text and subelements. When a <product> element ends, we turn the flag off (if it was on), to let further products pass to the filter. Ignoring SAX event propagation is a common way to eliminate elements from an XML document using SAX.

In the following example we add some products to the cart and then remove some others:

```
$f1 = new ExpatParser("cart.xml");
$f1->ParserSetOption(XML_OPTION_CASE_FOLDING, 0);
$f2 = new FilterAddProduct();
$f2->AddProduct("15", "foo", "foo bar", "1", "6");
$f2->AddProduct("17", "Goo", "GOO", "2", "16");

$f3 = new FilterRemoveProduct();
$f3->RemoveProduct("13");
$f3->RemoveProduct("15");

$f4 = new FilterOutput();

$f3->SetListener($f4);
$f2->SetListener($f3);
$f1->SetListener($f2);

$f1->Parse();
```

SAX scales very well for huge documents. Its resource consumption is constant for documents of any size, and it is fast. However, every modification needs coding, and at times it is complex. The same modifications are easy using DOM.

Using XSLT To Modify a Document

XSLT can also be used to modify an XML document; we need to write stylesheets to perform the transformations, receiving parameters about what to do.

For example, we can write the following XSLT file to add a product to a shopping cart:

```
<?xml version="1.0" encoding="utf-8"?>
<xsl:stylesheet xmlns:xsl="http://www.w3.org/1999/XSL/Transform" version="1.0">
<xsl:output method="xml" encoding="utf-8" />

<xsl:param name="pid" />
<xsl:param name="name" />
<xsl:param name="desc" />
<xsl:param name="quantity" />
<xsl:param name="unit_price" />

  <xsl:template match="/cart/products">
    <xsl:element name="product">
      <xsl:attribute name="pid">
        <xsl:value-of select="$pid" />
      </xsl:attribute>
      <xsl:element name="name"><xsl:value-of select="$name" /></xsl:element>
      <xsl:element name="desc"><xsl:value-of select="$desc" /></xsl:element>
      <xsl:element name="quantity">
        <xsl:value-of select="$quantity"/>
      </xsl:element>
      <xsl:element name="unit_price">
        <xsl:value-of select="$unit_price"/>
      </xsl:element>
    </xsl:element>
    <xsl:apply-templates />
```

```
      </xsl:template>

    <xsl:template match="@*|node()">
      <xsl:copy>
        <xsl:apply-templates select="@*|node()" />
      </xsl:copy>
    </xsl:template>

  </xsl:stylesheet>
```

The interesting issue here is that the XSLT stylesheet receives parameters with the information of the product to be added. The parameters declared at the beginning of the stylesheet show the parameters that the stylesheet is expecting to receive.

This PHP file shows how to pass parameters to an XSLT stylesheet using Sablotron:

```
// Allocate a new XSLT processor
$xh = xslt_create();

$new_prod = Array("pid" => "19",
                  "name" => "Newby",
                  "desc" => "A new product",
                  "quantity" => "1",
                  "unit_price" => "19"
              );

$result = xslt_process($xh, 'cart.xml',
                       'addProduct.xsl', NULL, Array(), $new_prod);
if ($result) {
    print ($result);
} else {
    print ("Sorry, cart.xml could not be transformed by ");
    print ("addProduct.xsl into the \$result variable. ");
    print ("The reason is that " . xslt_error($xh));
    print (" and the error code is " . xslt_errno($xh));
}

xslt_free($xh);
```

We are not using an XSLT abstraction class here to show how to pass parameters to Sablotron.

And the following XSLT stylesheet removes products from the cart:

```
<?xml version="1.0" encoding="utf-8"?>
<xsl:stylesheet xmlns:xsl="http://www.w3.org/1999/XSL/Transform" version="1.0">
<xsl:output method="xml" encoding="utf-8" />
<xsl:param name="pid" />
  <xsl:template match="/cart/products/product[@pid=$pid]">
  </xsl:template>

  <xsl:template match="@*|node()">
    <xsl:copy>
      <xsl:apply-templates select="@*|node()" />
    </xsl:copy>
  </xsl:template>

</xsl:stylesheet>
```

This is a simple stylesheet where, if the product with the ID passed as a parameter is found, then nothing is sent and everything else is copied.

This PHP code tests the stylesheet:

```
// Allocate a new XSLT processor
$xh = xslt_create();

$new_prod = Array("pid" => "13");

$result = xslt_process($xh, 'cart.xml',
                        'removeProduct.xsl', NULL, Array(), $new_prod);
if ($result) {
    print $result;
} else {
    print ("Sorry, cart.xml could not be transformed by ");
    print ("removeProduct.xsl into the \$result variable. ");
    print ("The reason is that " . xslt_error($xh));
    print (" and the error code is " . xslt_errno($xh));
}
xslt_free($xh);
```

If the DOM approach is too slow or uses a lot of resources, or we find it hard to write SAX filters for some modifications, it is good to use an XSLT stylesheet.

The main advantage of using XSLT is that powerful and complex modifications can be performed. However, it uses more resources than SAX, and passing parameters is not so easy if we have to perform complex transformations. One more problem with XSLT is that it does not have a caching option as yet.

Abstracting the Modifications To an XML Document

As with transformations, we may implement modifications to an XML document in many different ways – using XSLT, SAX filters, or the DOM approach as per the circumstances. Then it's logical to think that abstracting the modifications can be a good idea. We have several ways to abstract transformations to an XML document – the command pattern of OOP can be used to implement a command processor that can perform/undo commands from an XML document.

We can find a good description of the command pattern in this article from http://www.xml.com/pub/a/2000/01/19/feature/index.html.

Creating Objects from XML Files

This problem is stated as follows – we have an XML document and we want to create PHP objects from the information in the document. These objects can then be used for different tasks depending on the application that needs them. This is known as the **XMLable** pattern.

Example

We may have an XML file describing books, and we may want to create book objects from our XML document. This is a simplified representation of the XML document:

```xml
<?xml version="1.0"?>
<books>
  <book>
    <title>The Two Tours</title>
    <author>J.R.R Tolkien</author>
  </book>

  <book>
    <title>Second Foundation</title>
    <author>I.Asimov</author>
  </book>

  <book>
    <title>Foundation and Empire</title>
    <author>I.Asimov</author>
  </book>
</books>
```

And this can be the Book class:

```php
class Book
{
    var $title;
    var $author;

    function GetTitle()
    {
        return $this->title;
    }

    function GetAuthor()
    {
        return $this->author;
    }

    function SetTitle($title)
    {
        $this->title = $title;
    }

    function SetAuthor($author)
    {
        $this->author = $author;
    }
}
```

As usual we may think about DOM, XSLT, or SAX, but in this problem we don't have choices, let's see why.

Firstly, DOM is unacceptable in this case. We parse the XML document into the DOM tree, and then we'll be facing the same problem we had before – how to convert the DOM tree to many book objects. XSLT is too exotic for this problem; we may write an XSLT transformation that creates PHP code that creates the objects, and then `eval()` the transformation result.

So the obvious solution is to use SAX, where we parse the XML document and we create the objects as we collect enough information for each one of them.

Using SAX To Create PHP Objects from XML

Here we build a SAX filter that can be used to create the book objects from our document. We store references to the objects in an array to keep track of the objects in memory. This is the strategy used to create objects:

Whenever a <book> tag is found, create a new book object and store the reference in the array. Whenever an <author> or a <title> tag is found, store the content in the object property with the same name.

Here is the code:

```php
class FilterBuildBooks extends AbstractFilter
{
    var $oneBook = 0;
    var $book;
    var $property = 0;
    var $books = Array();

    function GetBooks()
    {
        return $this->books;
    }

    function StartElementHandler($name, $attribs)
    {
        if ($name == "book") {
            $this->books[] = new Book();
            $this->oneBook = 1;
        } else {
            if ($this->oneBook) {
                $this->property = $name;
            }
        }
        $this->listener->StartElementHandler($name, $attribs);
    }

    function EndElementHandler($name)
    {
        $this->property = 0;
        if ($name == "book") {
            $this->oneBook = 0;
        }
        $this->listener->EndElementHandler($name);
```

```
        }

        function CharacterDataHandler($data)
        {
            if ($this->oneBook && $this->property) {
                // Here we construct the name of the method to be called.
                $method_get = "get".strtoupper(substr($this->property, 0, 1)) .
                                            substr($this->property, 1);
                $method_set = "set".strtoupper(substr($this->property, 0, 1)) .
                                            substr($this->property, 1);
                $prop = $this->books[count($this->books)-1]->$method_get();
                $this->books[count($this->books)-1]->$method_set($prop.$data);
            }
            $this->listener->CharacterDataHandler($data);
        }
    }
}
```

This PHP code parses the XML file that creates the book objects:

```
$f1 = new ExpatParser("books.xml");
$f1->ParserSetOption(XML_OPTION_CASE_FOLDING, 0);
$f2 = new FilterBuildBooks();
$f3 = new FilterNull();

$f2->SetListener($f3);
$f1->SetListener($f2);
$f1->Parse();
$books = $f1->listener->GetBooks();
```

We can make two observations about this piece of code:

❑   A NULL filter was used at the end of the chain since we neither want any output nor want to store the XML. Once parsed this design is better than making the FilterBuildBooks object a FilterNull because with this schema we can do something with the parsed XML document besides creating the objects. All our filters should pass events to a listener and we can use a NULL filter at the end.

❑   The books are obtained calling the getBooks() method of the FilterBuildBooks object through the parser; because the FilterBuildBooks is a member (listener) of the parser. If we try to obtain the books using $f2->getBooks() we will get an empty array.

The Flyweight Pattern

There's an interesting application of the **Flyweight** pattern in this example. Imagine we are processing a very large XML document where we create objects from the document. Many objects created from the document may have the same content for some of their properties if the elements repeat in the XML document. For instance, in our example, we may have many books from the same author.

In such cases we can use the Flyweight pattern to use an object that resolves the properties of the book objects.

Instead of storing the value of each property, we ask a `Flyweightfactory` object to return an object representing the property. We won't know if many objects share this object and the functionality of the object can be the same. The factorizing object can use a hashtable, or something similar, to store and retrieve properties reusing the same value for as many objects as it can, thus reducing the amount of memory consumed by the objects.

The flyweight pattern is an optimization pattern. It can be used when we are creating a very large number of objects and those objects may have properties with a long value that may be the same value for a big number of objects.

We can read about this pattern in the article at
http://www.xml.com/pub/a/2000/01/19/feature/index.html.

Querying XML

If our data model is based on XML we'll be querying documents very often. Some examples of the need to query XML are:

- ❏ We have an XML file describing products and we want to find a price
- ❏ We have an XML file with a shopping cart and we want to calculate the total price
- ❏ We have an XML file with a log and we want to find some statistic
- ❏ We have an XML file for cars and we want to find cars below 20,000 USD, and with three doors

Querying an XML document means that we should traverse the XML document looking for particular information; what we do with the information once it is found is beyond the scope of the problem.

Example

Here we'll present a simple example to check how to solve the same problem using different approaches. In this case our example will show an XML file describing cars. This is the XML document:

```
<cars>
  <car>
    <type>F1</type>
    <brand>Ferrari</brand>
    <model>X1</model>
    <maxspeed>305</maxspeed>
    <hp>800</hp>
  </car>

  <car>
    <type>F1</type>
    <brand>Williams</brand>
    <model>W89</model>
    <maxspeed>298</maxspeed>
    <hp>1000</hp>
  </car>
```

```
  <car>
    <type>F1</type>
    <brand>Brabham</brand>
    <model>B01</model>
    <maxspeed>311</maxspeed>
    <hp>1020</hp>
  </car>
</cars>
```

And the query will be: "Find brand and model of F1 cars that can run at more than 300 kmh".

We have the following options to query an XML document:

❑   DOM

❑   XPath

❑   XSLT

❑   SAX

Using DOM To Query an XML Document

Using DOM to query an XML document is rather weird. Once we parse the document we obtain the DOM tree. Then we'll have to parse the tree to perform the query, and we don't have any useful querying feature in the DOM objects that may lead to such a strategy. We won't say that we can't use DOM to query a document, but we'll say that such a solution is uncommon.

If we do decide to use DOM for our query we can use the following code:

```php
<?php
function GetContent($domnode)
{
    $content = '';
    foreach ($domnode->child_nodes() as $child) {
        if ($child->node_type() == XML_TEXT_NODE) {
            $content .= $child->content;
        }
    }
    return $content;
}

//$doc = xmldocfile("cars.xml");
$doc = domxml_open_file("cars.xml");

$root = $doc->document_element();
foreach ($root->child_nodes() as $element) {
    if ($element->node_type() == XML_ELEMENT_NODE and
                              $element->tagname() == "car") {
        $cond1 = false;
        $cond2 = false;
        foreach ($element->child_nodes() as $car_element) {
```

```
            if ($car_element->node_type() == XML_ELEMENT_NODE and
                            $car_element->tagname() == "type") {
                if (($type = getContent($car_element)) == "F1") {
                    $cond1 = true;
                }
            }
            if ($car_element->node_type() == XML_ELEMENT_NODE and
                            $car_element->tagname() == "maxspeed") {
                if (($maxspeed = getContent($car_element))>300) {
                    $cond2 = true;
                }
            }
            if ($car_element->node_type() == XML_ELEMENT_NODE and
                            $car_element->tagname() == "brand") {
                $brand = getContent($car_element);
            }
            if ($car_element->node_type() == XML_ELEMENT_NODE and
                            $car_element->tagname() == "model") {
                $model = getContent($car_element);
            }
        }
        if ($cond1 && $cond2) {
            print ("Brand: $brand Model:$model<br />");
        }
    }
}
?>
```

The code shows a typical approach to using DOM for querying. Traversing the DOM tree and finding the nodes that match some conditions is not that simple, and it isn't short either.

Using XPath To Query a Document

We haven't considered XPath so far in the chapter because XPath is a standard that is only useful to query an XML document and that's why it makes its stellar appearance in this section.

XPath is a standard to identify and retrieve portions of an XML document using location paths and predicates to filter the results. Many extremists say that XPath is the SQL of XML, but the truth is that many queries and computations can be solved easily using an XPath expression.

We have discussed XPath in detail in Chapter 7.

For our example we could have used the following XPath expression to solve the query:

```
/cars/car[normalize-space(maxspeed/text())>300 and normalize-
space(type/text())='F1']
```

The expression will return all the cars that match the criteria. We can then use the following PHP code to execute the XPath query, and extract the brand and model from the result:

```php
<?php
//$doc = xmldocfile("cars.xml");
$doc = domxml_open_file("cars.xml");

$xpath = $doc->xpath_init();

$ctx = $doc->xpath_new_context();

$result = $ctx->xpath_eval("/cars/car[normalize-space(maxspeed/text())>300
                        and normalize-space(type/text())='F1']");

$nodes = $result->nodeset;

foreach ($nodes as $node) {
    foreach ($node->child_nodes() as $child) {
        if ($child->node_type() == XML_ELEMENT_NODE) {
            if ($child->tagname() == "brand") {
                print ("Brand:");
                foreach ($child->child_nodes() as $sub) {
                    if ($sub->node_type() == XML_TEXT_NODE) {
                        print ($sub->content);
                    }
                }
                print (" / ");
            }
            if ($child->tagname() == "model") {
                print ("Model:");
                foreach ($child->child_nodes() as $sub) {
                    if ($sub->node_type() == XML_TEXT_NODE) {
                        print ($sub->content);
                    }
                }
                print ("<br />");
            }
        }
    }
}
?>
```

The above code produces this simple output for our sampled XML document:

In PHP, the `xpath_eval()` function is part of the DOM extension, so using XPath implies parsing the XML document into a DOM tree. That's why the XPath function in PHP faces the same problems that we have found when using DOM in the previous example – it can be very resource-consuming or slow for larger documents.

If the document is small- to medium-sized then XPath is usually a very good alternative to query a document, since the query can usually be expressed with a simple expression minimizing the amount of code that we have to write for the query.

If the PHP XPath implementation is slow for large documents we can't blame XPath. It's easy to imagine that a SAX-based XPath processor will be faster than the DOM version, and we may also find an ad-hoc XPath processor, which will be even better.

> *At the time this book was written the only XPath implementation available for PHP was the* `xpath_eval()` *function in the DOM extension. It's logical to see new XPath processors emerging in the near future for PHP.*

Here are some of the advantages and disadvantages of XPath:

Advantages	Disadvantages
A simple expression can solve many queries and computations.	Based on DOM, it inherits DOM's disadvantages – slow for large documents and uses a lot of resources. Thus, it can be unfeasible for huge documents.
Very easy to use.	Some complex queries or computations may not be solved with XPath.
Solid standard by the W3C.	

Using XSLT To Query a Document

XSLT is a very good tool to query a document. Whenever XPath is not enough to query a document we may think of using XSLT.

The same XSLT that is normally used to transform a document can be used to query it, obtaining a result instead of a transformation.

> *A query can be seen as a transformation where the document is transformed in the query result.*

When using XSLT we can isolate each query into an XSLT stylesheet and write composite queries using `<xsl:include>`.

For example, the following XSLT stylesheet solves the query of our example:

```
<?xml version="1.0" encoding="utf-8"?>
<xsl:stylesheet xmlns:xsl="http://www.w3.org/1999/XSL/Transform" version="1.0">
  <xsl:output method="text" />

  <xsl:template match="/cars/car">
    <xsl:if test="normalize-space(maxspeed/text())>300 and
```

```
                     normalize-space(type/text())='F1'">
        Brand: <xsl:value-of select="brand" />
        Model: <xsl:value-of select="model" />
        <br />
    </xsl:if>
  </xsl:template>
</xsl:stylesheet>
```

The output after processing the XML file with the above XSLT would have been the same as the PHP script using XPath.

Here are the advantages of XSLT:

Advantages	Disadvantages
More powerful than XPath, can perform very complex queries or computations	Can be slow for huge documents
Fast enough for online processing of small- to mid-size documents	

Using SAX To Query a Document

When dealing with huge documents SAX is the only way out. The approach used to query a document is the same as when we transform or modify the document using SAX filters. We can write a filter for each query, and a combination of filters can be used for complex queries.

This SAX filter can be used to perform the query of our example:

```
class FilterQueryCars extends AbstractFilter
{
    var $results = Array();
    var $oneCar = Array();
    var $prop;

    function GetResults()
    {
        return $this->results;
    }

    function StartElementHandler($name, $attribs)
    {
        $this->prop = '';
        if ($name <> "cars" && $name <> "car") {
            $this->prop = $name;
            $this->oneCar[$this->prop] = '';
        }
    }

    function EndElementHandler($name)
```

```
    {
        if ($name == "car") {
            if (((trim($this->oneCar["type"])) == "F1") &&
                (trim($this->oneCar["maxspeed"])>300)) {
                $this->results[] = $this->oneCar;
            }
            $this->oneCar = Array();
        }
    }


    function CharacterDataHandler($data)
    {
        if ($this->prop) {
            if (!empty($data)) {
                $this->oneCar[$this->prop] .= $data;
            }
        }
    }
}
```

Note that the filter doesn't propagate events to a listener, so this filter has to be used at the end of the chain; query filters are usually placed at the end of the chain. For complex queries we may want to try to build the query using more than one filter. Chaining them reduces the complexity of each filter, and makes it easy to maintain them as well.

Here are some of the advantages and disadvantages of using SAX:

Advantages	Disadvantages
Scales very well for huge documents	No querying features, everything must be hand-made
Resource consumption is constant for documents of any size	Some complex queries may require a lot of code
It is fast	
Allows streaming	

Other Querying Alternatives

There are other querying alternatives for XML such as XQL and XQuery. We didn't cover them in this chapter since there isn't a PHP implementation of these alternatives. As they evolve and become stable we may find PHP extensions that support them.

Chapter 14 has a short introduction to XQuery. The specification is available at http://www.w3.org/TR/xquery/.

Abstraction Again

Querying an XML document is the problem where more solutions can be applied – XQL, XQuery, XSLT, XPath, DOM, SAX, and others can be used to query a document. So it's useful to have a query class abstracting queries. Also, it is almost always good to separate what the application needs from how it is done.

Caching Strikes Back

As with transformations, we might cache query results to reuse the result if the same query is applied to an unchanged document. The same considerations we made about caching transformations apply here.

Choosing a Querying Strategy

With so many options, choosing a querying strategy can sometimes be hard. We recommend the following strategy:

- ❏ If the documents are really huge then use SAX.
- ❏ If there are medium-sized documents then try using XPath. If performance is not satisfactory, or the query can't be solved, use XSLT.

Writing XML

Writing XML is a problem where an XML file has to be generated from a non-XML source (or it will be a transformation). For example, we may have some data in a database, a file, or objects, and we have to write an XML document. What we do with the XML document later is beyond the scope of the problem. Following are some instances of this problem:

- ❏ We have data in a relational database and want to produce an XML representation of the data
- ❏ We have data in a plaintext file that describes news and want to produce an XML RSS file
- ❏ We have some PHP objects and want to produce an XML file describing object properties
- ❏ We have a file in a proprietary format and want to convert it to XML for processing

We won't cover in this problem parsing the non-XML data, which is usually harder than writing the XML document.

Example

In this example we have the following text file describing a to-do list for some people:

```
Jim Smith, Go to the library and pick up books
Sidney, Make 13 copies of memo no:19
Kelly, Distribute memo no:5 by email
Sidney, Arrange meeting with foo managers
Kelly, Write a draft of the technical document for project X
Jim Smith, Distribute books to team members
Sidney, Record book loans in HR software
```

Our task is to generate a representation such as the following:

```
<to-do>
  <person>
    <name>Jim Smith</name>
    <tasks>
      <task>Go to the library and pick up books</task>
      <task>Distribute books to team members</task>
    </tasks>
  </person>

  <person>
    <name>Sidney</name>
    <tasks>
      <task>Make 13 copies of memo no:19</task>
      <task>Arrange meeting with foo&amp;foo managers</task>
      <task>Record book loans in HR software</task>
    </tasks>
  </person>

  <person>
    <name>Kelly</name>
    <tasks>
      <task>Distribute memo no:5 by email</task>
      <task>Write a draft of the technical document for project X</task>
    </tasks>
  </person>
</to-do>
```

We can use the following tools to write XML documents:

❑ Manual writing

❑ DOM

❑ SAX

Manual Writing

Manual writing is a simple and intuitive way of writing XML documents – create a string with the desired XML. Simple PHP string management is used to generate the XML file. Generating the XML manually implies that the writing function must generate well-formed XML data. We will have to parse the strings and convert special characters such as & to the proper XML entities that represent them.

For our example we'll be using the following class that parses the .txt file with the to-do list to generate an array:

```
class ParseToDoTxt
{
    var $persons = Array();

    function ParseFile($filename)
    {
        $f = fopen($filename, "r");
```

```
        if (!$f) {
            return 0;
        }
        $txt = fread($f, filesize($filename));
        return $this->ParseString($txt);
    }

    function GetPersons()
    {
        return $this->persons;
    }

    function ParseString($txt)
    {
        $lines = Array();
        $line = Array();
        $lines = explode("\n", $txt);
        foreach ($lines as $line) {
            $line = chop($line);
            $line = explode(",", $line);
            if (!isset($this->persons[$line[0]])) {
                $this->persons[$line[0]] = Array();
            }
            $this->persons[$line[0]][] = $line[1];
        }
        return 1;
    }
}
```

The following bit of code generates the XML file:

```
$parser = new ParseToDoTxt();
$parser->ParseFile("todo.txt");
$persons = $parser->GetPersons();
$xml = '<?xml version="1.0"?>';
$xml .= '<to-do>';
foreach ($persons as $person => $tasks) {
    $xml .= '<person>';
    $xml .= '<name>'.XmlEntities($person).'</name>';
    $xml .= '<tasks>';
    foreach ($tasks as $task) {
        $xml .= '<task>';
        $xml .= XmlEntities($task);
        $xml .= '</task>';
    }
    $xml .= '</tasks>';
    $xml .= '</person>';
}

$xml .= '</to-do>';
print ($xml);
```

The `XmlEntities()` function replaces special characters with their corresponding XML entities:

```
function XmlEntities($data)
{
    $position = 0;
    $length = strlen($data);
    $escapeddata = "";
    for(;$position<$length;) {
        $character = substr($data, $position, 1);
        $code = Ord($character);
        switch($code) {
            case 34:
            $character = "&quot;";
            break;

            case 38:
            $character = "&amp;";
            break;

            case 39:
            $character = "&apos;";
            break;

            case 60:
            $character = "&lt;";
            break;

            case 62:
            $character = "&gt;";
            break;

            default:
            if ($code<32)
                $character = ("&#".strval($code).";");
            break;
        }
        $escapeddata .= $character;
        $position++;
    }
    return $escapeddata;
}
```

We can use this code as a method of the parsing class, or build a new `XmlWriter` class that uses the parsing class and constructs an XML string storing it as a property of the object. Without worrying about where we use the code we can see that the code is easy to understand and fairly easy to write too.

Manual writing is a simple and flexible way to write XML, however, such documents are difficult to maintain as encoding entities and producing well-formed XML documents is 100% the responsibility of the program.

Using DOM To Write XML Data

The DOM extension is usually used to parse an XML document to the DOM representation, but it can also be used to begin an empty document and add children, sub-children, and sub-sub-children until an XML document is constructed. The dump_mem() method then allows us to recover the XML document from the DOM tree.

The methods used to insert elements and attributes to the DOM tree are very useful when constructing XML documents.

This is the same code we used in the manual writing approach, but here we use DOM calls to generate the XML file:

```
$parser = new ParseToDoTxt();
$parser->ParseFile("todo.txt");
$persons = $parser->GetPersons();

//$doc = domxml_new_doc("1.0");
$doc = new_xmldoc("1.0");

$node = $doc->create_element("to-do");
$root = $doc->add_child($node);

foreach ($persons as $person => $tasks) {
    $node_person = $doc->create_element("person");

    $node_name = $doc->create_element("name");
    $node_name_text = $doc->create_text_node($person);
    $node_name->add_child($node_name_text);

    $node_tasks = $doc->create_element("tasks");

    foreach ($tasks as $task) {
        $node_task = $doc->create_element("task");
        $node_task_text = $doc->create_text_node($task);
        $node_task->add_child($node_task_text);
        $node_tasks->add_child($node_task);
    }

    $node_person->add_child($node_name);
    $node_person->add_child($node_tasks);

    $root->add_child($node_person);
}

$xml = $doc->dump_mem();
print ($xml);
```

Using DOM we may skip calling the XmlEntities() function, since the DOM class is supposed to construct valid well-formed XML documents from our text.

In many ways using DOM is the best way to generate an XML file. The only problem we may face is that the PHP DOM extension is not very stable and changes to the extension may require changing programs that use it if we want to update our PHP installation.

Here are some of the advantages and disadvantages of using DOM:

Advantages	Disadvantages
Entities are generated by the DOM extension	Sometimes just manual writing is easier
Methods to ease the creation of complex XML documents	Programs depend on the unstable DOM extension of PHP
Code is easier to maintain	

Using SAX To Write XML Data

SAX can be used to generate XML documents. This is a use of SAX that is not seen very often and can lead to some good ideas once understood.

The idea is to write a SAX parser for non-XML data. We will use the examples of SAX filters we've already seen, write a new parser, and then apply all the filters we want to the new parser.

This is a parser that extends the AbstractSAXParser class, but parses a to-do plaintext file using the parsing class we used before:

```
class ToDoTxtParser extends AbstractSAXParser
{
    var $persons = Array();

    function ToDoTxtParser($txt)
    {
        $parser = new ParseToDoTxt();
        $parser->ParseFile($txt);
        $this->persons = $parser->GetPersons();
    }

    function Parse()
    {
        $this->StartElementHandler($this, "to-do", Array());
        foreach ($this->persons as $person => $tasks) {
            $this->StartElementHandler($this, "person", Array());
            $this->StartElementHandler($this, "name", Array());
            $this->CharacterDataHandler($this, XmlEntities($person));
            $this->EndElementHandler($this, "name");
            $this->StartElementHandler($this, "tasks", Array());

            foreach ($tasks as $task) {
                $this->StartElementHandler($this, "task", Array());
                $this->CharacterDataHandler($this, XmlEntities($task));
                $this->EndElementHandler($this, "task");
            }
            $this->EndElementHandler($this, "tasks");
            $this->EndElementHandler($this, "person");
        }
        $this->EndElementHandler($this, "to-do");
    }
}
```

As we can see, we parse the plaintext file and then traverse the array generating events for the XML elements that we want to produce. As we did with the manual writing approach, special characters must be converted to XML entities.

It would have been more efficient to make this class parse the plaintext file, but since we had little space we decided to reuse the parsing class we had. If we are parsing large non-XML files we should try to parse the file on-the-fly, that is, generate the proper SAX events as we read the non-XML file.

This is the PHP code used to generate an XML representation of the to-do plaintext file:

```php
$f1 = new ToDoTxtParser("todo.txt");
$f2 = new FilterOutput();
$f1->SetListener($f2);
$f1->Parse();
```

Here are some of the advantages and disadvantages of using SAX:

Advantages	Disadvantages
Can be used as the start of a filter chain for many processing tasks	The parser is responsible for generating well-formed XML data converting special characters to entities
Allows streaming – we can generate the XML file as we read the non-XML data	

Summary

In most cases, the DOM approach uses more resources and is the slowest one too. DOM is a good solution to modify and write small- to medium-sized documents from non-XML data. DOM is not recommended for querying and transforming documents.

XSLT is the most interesting solution for modifying, transforming, or querying documents, unless the documents are so big that XSLT can't process them and we have to use SAX instead. Our XSLT stylesheets can perform complex queries or transformations with just a few lines of XSLT code, so if the size of the documents allows us to use XSLT, then it should surely be one of our primary weapons.

SAX is the only solution for processing really large files and it is also a good solution for a fast implementation of other processing problems. SAX filters and filter chains are the tools we should be constructing when SAX is our selected tool for a problem.

XPath, as we've seen in this chapter and in Chapter 7, is a good solution for not very complex queries since it requires just an XPath expression and a few lines of code. Since the XPath implementation of PHP is part of the DOM extension, it is not recommended for big files. SAX-based XPath implementations can be used to query large documents.

In this chapter we have seen examples that provide a good base, examples that use DOM, SAX, and XSLT for XML processing, and seen how to use these standards from PHP. After reading and practicing these examples we'll be able to select the best approach to a given problem and that's a key skill for any programmer dealing with XML data in the enormous ocean of derivatives available.

11

Syndicated Content

Syndicated content is fast becoming a popular and convenient way for people to provide easy access to news and important information about ongoing events on the World Wide Web. Simply put, when somebody syndicates a piece of content, they make it available to some, or possibly any, network resource that can read and parse the content. The resource is then able to incorporate that data into its own operations.

In practice this is generally used to provide information and links to data that is updated on a fairly regular basis. News story headlines, financial data such as stock quotes, sports scores, and weather immediately come to mind, since the data describing these events is constantly changing. As one would imagine, XML is a terrific way to provide syndicated content. It is easy for network-enabled programs to read and parse XML data and XML is designed to be a flexible format that can describe different types of events. Also the files are portable since XML is essentially a flat text format.

One of the most common ways to syndicate content is within **RDF Site Summary** (RSS) files. RDF, in turn, stands for Resource Description Framework. RSS is a lightweight meta data description format that uses XML. It was originally developed by Netscape for use in their web site. The specification can currently be found at http://www.purl.org/rss/1.0/.

In this chapter we will:

❑ Learn the basics of the PEAR RSS parser class

❑ Use this class to parse an external data file in an application

❑ Extend the application to cache the data from the external files locally

❑ Create a simple RSS syndication class

❑ Use the syndication class to generate a well-formed RSS file viewable by others

RSS

An RSS file is a description of a web site's contents called a **channel**. Other sites then subscribe to this channel and acquire its contents. As this file is XML it can be converted into HTML and displayed as part of a headlines service, for example. Alternatively, it can be modified to reflect the interests of the site's users. For example, we might only want to display sports headlines on a sports web site.

The channel is further split into **items** that describe the articles available on the channel. These are the individual links that will be displayed to the users of the syndicated content web site.

RSS Structure

An RSS document should begin with an XML declaration. Though RSS 1.0 doesn't require this (as RSS files are XML-compliant), RSS 0.9 did and backward compatibility should be maintained:

```
<?xml version="1.0"?>
```

The root element of every RSS file is the <RDF> element. It associates the rdf: namespace prefix with the RDF Schema and makes this Schema the default for this document:

```
<rdf:RDF xmlns:rdf="http://www.w3.org/1999/02/22-rdf-syntax-ns#"
         xmlns="http://purl.org/rss/1.0/">
```

The <channel> Element

The <channel> element comes next. It contains the meta data about the channel described in this RSS file, which includes a title, a URL that typically links to the channel's provider, and a short description. The <channel> element's about attribute acts as a URI for this channel:

```
<channel rdf:about="http://slashdot.org/slashdot.rdf">
  <title>Slashdot: News for nerds, stuff that matters</title>
  <link>http://slashdot.org/</link>
  <description>
    News for nerds, stuff that matters
  </description>
```

This <image> subelement establishes an association between the optional <image> element (described later) and this channel. Its resource attribute must be the same as the main <image> element's about attribute:

```
<image rdf:resource=
               "http://images.slashdot.org/topics/topicslashdot.gif"/>
```

The <items> subelement acts as a table of contents for this channel. Each resource attribute must match with its corresponding item's about attribute. Note that any <item> elements that appear in the document and not in the <items> element may be discarded by RDF parsers:

```
<items>
  <rdf:Seq>
    <rdf:li
       resource="http://slashdot.org/article.pl?sid=02/05/06/0139258" />
    <rdf:li
       resource="http://slashdot.org/article.pl?sid=02/05/05/2351237" />
  </rdf:Seq>
</items>
```

The `<textinput>` subelement associates the optional `<textinput>` element (described below) with this channel. A text input usually represents a search box for searching the provider of the channel. The `resource` element must be the same as the `about` attribute of the `<textinput>` and represents the target of the search query:

```
<textinput rdf:resource="http://slashdot.org/search.pl" />
</channel>
```

The `<image>` Element

The main `<image>` element represents an image to be associated with an HTML rendering of the channel. This can then be displayed at the top of any listings as a link to the homepage of the channel's provider. The `about` attribute is the URL of the image file:

```
<image rdf:about="http://images.slashdot.org/topics/topicslashdot.gif">
```

The `<title>` subelement is the alt text to be associated with this image when it is rendered as HTML:

```
<title>Slashdot: News for nerds, stuff that matters</title>
```

The `<link>` element is the link that will be associated with the image when it is rendered as HTML. This usually points to the site's homepage:

```
<link>http://slashdot.org/</link>
```

The `<url>` subelement is the value of the `src` attribute when the image appears in HTML:

```
<url>http://images.slashdot.org/topics/topicslashdot.gif</url>
</image>
```

The `<item>` Element

Items are the content from the channel that is of interest to the visitors of the web site that displays them. These are usually headlines from a news site, but can be pretty much anything with a URI. Our examples later will begin by rendering news headlines from various news sites before we create our own items for a fictional band's performance schedule.

The `about` attribute must be unique among all other `rdf:about` attributes in this channel. This attribute acts as a URI and should be the same as the value of the `<link>` subelement:

```
<item rdf:about="http://slashdot.org/article.pl?sid=02/05/06/0139258">
```

441

The `<title>`, `<link>`, and `<description>` subelements of `<item>` are self-explanatory and function in the same way as their namesakes above:

```
<title>Community Networks and Websites?</title>
<link>http://slashdot.org/article.pl?sid=02/05/06/0139258</link>
<description>
  Can real-life communities succeed in the online environment as well?
  How so?"
</description>
</item>
```

The `<textinput>` Element

The final element we shall look at is the `<textinput>` subelement. It describes the data to construct a search box for rendering along with the items in this channel. The target is usually the search engine or subscription manager on the syndicated web site and is assumed to handle at least the GET HTTP method. All its subelements are similar to those already discussed and so do not warrant an explanation. However, the about attribute of `<textinput>` should match the value of the `<link>` subelement:

```
<textinput rdf:about="http://slashdot.org/search.pl">
  <title>Search Slashdot</title>
  <description>Search Slashdot's archives</description>
  <name>s</name>
  <link>http://slashdot.org/search.pl </link>
</textinput>
```

The PEAR RSS Parser Class

The PHP Extension and Application Repository (PEAR) is a repository for PHP code and PHP extensions written in C. One of the objectives of the PEAR project was to create a tool similar to that of the Perl CPAN archive. The project tries to define standards that can help developers write portable and reusable code. Initial documentation for the project can be found at http://pear.php.net/manual/.

For the first example we will rely heavily on the excellent RSS parser class that is part of the PHP PEAR repository. It is available from the PEAR web site at: http://pear.php.net/package-info.php?pacid=22.

Download the package and extract the files. Create a directory classes directory under the web directory and then another directory under classes called pear. We can then put the RSS.php file into the pear directory.

The RSS.php file provides our application with an **XML_RSS class** that makes parsing and displaying data from RSS files very easy. It is an extension of the base XML_Parser class that is part of the standard PEAR installation, so we automatically have all of the methods available from XML_Parser as well. The XML_Parser class provides functionality to set up a SAX style parser for an XML document. That is to say, it sets up the needed callback functions for all the elements for us. It also provides a parse() method that actually parses the document.

> One caveat is that this class does not degrade gracefully if `error_reporting` is set to `E_ALL` in `php.ini`. The correct line to have in `php.ini` is: `error_reporting = E_ALL & ~E_NOTICE`, which is the typical setup.

For our first application, we will only need a few methods from `XML_RSS`:

Function	Description
`void XML_RSS(string filename)`	Constructor for the class that sets up our data source
`void parse()`	Inherited from the base `XML_Parser` class
`array getItems()`	Returns an array with the items from the data source
`array getImages()`	Returns an array with the data for any images defined in the source
`array getTextinputs()`	Returns an array with the data for any text input defined in the source

A Simple RSS Application

In this application, we are going to get the headlines from http://slashdot.org/. The Slashdot team provides information about their stories in an RSS file that we can read and parse with our `XML_RSS` class. We begin by creating a file called `slashdot_headlines.php`:

```php
<?php
// include our class definition file
require_once ('../classes/pear/RSS.php');
```

Next, we will instantiate an instance of the `XML_RSS` object we now have available:

```php
// instantiate new XML_RSS object with slashdot RSS file
$rss =& new XML_RSS("http://slashdot.org/slashdot.rdf");
```

This highlights one of the great things about PHP. The `fopen()` function is 'network transparent' in the sense that it understands how to open files using the HTTP and FTP protocols. So we can 'open' a file on a remote server just as easily as reading a file on our local machine. The `XML_RSS` constructor makes use of this transparency when it gets the `slashdot.rdf` file from the Slashdot server. However be careful that the `fopen()` wrappers are enabled. This can be easily accomplished by checking `php.ini` for the line:

```
allow_url_fopen = On
```

If this line points to `Off`, change it to `On`. The program may not work as intended if this is not the case.

Now that we have an `XML_RSS` object complete with data from the server, we'll parse it as follows:

```php
// parse the file
$rss->parse();
```

The XML_RSS class extends the base XML_Parser class from the PEAR repository and parse() is an XML_Parser method. We have access to it in the $rss object since we extend a class and thus inherit all of its methods. This method takes care of setting up our event handler functions for SAX-style parsing, creating a parser, and actually parsing the file. Fortunately for us, all of that work is hidden from us and we can be content just calling parse() without being concerned about all the details going on behind the scenes.

At this point, we have done all the real work needed for our application. The data from the RSS file has been parsed and stored in our object, and all we have to do is extract it. Fortunately, the XML_RSS class provides methods that make this easy. We will also write a quick function that will be useful for displaying the data:

```php
// grab this array
$headline_items = $rss->getItems();

// grab any images
$images = $rss->getImages();

// grab textinputs
$textinput = $rss->getTextinputs();

// this will be useful in a moment
function PrintLink($link , $title)
{
    return "<a href=\"$link\" target=\"_blank\">$title</a>";
}
```

The variable $headline_items is an array of arrays. Each array contained within $headline_items is itself an associative array, with key/value pairs corresponding to the data type and data from the items in the RSS file. The structure of $images is exactly the same. It is an array of arrays, with the inner arrays containing key/value pairs for the image data in the RSS file.

However, the $textinput variable is a little different. It is a simple associative array with the key/value pairs corresponding to the elements nested in a text input element from the RSS file.

Remember that the RSS file contains a number of <item> tags. Each <item> tag encloses <title> and <link> tags that contain the syndicated content links which the web site intends to distribute. We will see this once more when we see how to use $headline_items to display our results.

Let's start with the HTML header:

```html
<html>
  <head>
    <title>Simple Slashdot Headlines</title>

    <link rel="stylesheet" type="text/css" href="sd.css"
          title="slashdot example stylesheet" />

  </head>
  <body>

    <h2>Simple Slashdot Headlines</h2>
```

Note that we use the CSS file sd.css. This is a file with some CSS declarations that make the output look better. It is available for download from the book's page on http://www.wrox.com/.

In the body of our HTML file, we loop through each index of $images and $headline_items and put the resultant arrays into our associative $image and $items arrays. Then we use the PrintLink() function to output the data for the headlines:

```php
<?php
// output any images

foreach($images as $image_info) {
    // put data from $image_info into easier variables
    $url = $image_info["url"];
    $link = $image_info["link"];
    $title = $image_info["title"];

    // print results
    print ("<a href=\"$link\" title=\"$title\">
            <img src=\"$url\" border=\"0\"></a>\n");
}
?>

<ul>

<?php
foreach($headline_items as $items) {
    print ("<li>" . PrintLink($items['link'] , $items['title']) . "</li>\n";
}
?>
</ul>
```

Last but not least, we include the output from any text input that was defined in the file:

```php
<?php
// print out textinputs

$title = $textinput["title"];
$description = $textinput["description"];
$name = $textinput["name"];
$link = $textinput["link"];
print ("$description<br />\n");
print ("<form name=\"queryform\" action=\"$link\" method=\"post\">\n");
print ("<input type=\"text\" name=\"$name\"><br />\n");
print ("<input type=\"submit\" value=\"Submit\"><br />\n");
?>
```

Sample output looks like this:

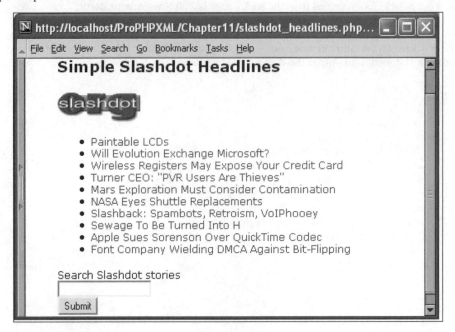

This display should show and link to the current **slashdot.org** headlines. Also, the associated image is displayed and we can use the text input to directly search the site.

Multiple Sources and Cached Content

Now that we've seen how to use XML_RSS in a simple example, we will graduate to a more real-world application. We will extend the previous logic in two ways. First, as with most services on the Web, there are many RSS sources on the Internet. We will create an application that lets us choose headlines from a variety of different sites. Next, instead of getting the data over the network every time, we are going to cache the content in a local file. Many sites (Slashdot included) request that we should check for updates every half hour or so to reduce the load on their servers. We will respect this by caching the data locally and getting new data only if the cache is old.

Application Logic

The application will have a <select> form element that will allow the users to choose the site they want to see the headlines from. Once selected, the form will set a variable that will be used by PHP to identify the appropriate data source.

Once the data source is chosen, our application will check if there is a cache file for that source, and if there is, it will check for the age of the file. If the cache is 'young' enough, meaning that it has been updated within the last thirty minutes, then the application will use data from the cache. However, if the cache file doesn't exist or if it is 'stale' (which means that it is over thirty minutes old) then data will be read from the RSS file available on the network. Also, the cache will be refreshed or a new cache will be created (in the event that it is our first attempt) which will contain new freshly parsed content.

Finally, the news items from the chosen source will be displayed in the browser in much the same way as in the previous example.

Application Code

This time, let us start with the HTML section of our application, so that we can see how the `<form>` element is to be employed. Create a new file in the web server document root called `show_cache_headlines.php`:

```html
<html>
  <head>
    <title>Simple Headlines With Cache</title>

    <link rel="stylesheet" type="text/css" href="grabber.css"
          title="stylesheet" />

  </head>
  <body>

    <h2>Headlines Grabber</h2>

    <form name="grabber" action="<?php print $_SERVER['PHP_SELF']; ?>"
          method="post">
      <select name="rss_source" onchange="window.document.grabber.submit()">

        <option value="1"<?php if(1 == $_POST['rss_source'])
                                 print ("selected"); ?>>
          Slashdot
        </option>

        <option value="2"<?php if(2 == $_POST['rss_source'])
                                 print ("selected"); ?>>
          Freshmeat
        </option>

        <option value="3"<?php if(3 == $_POST['rss_source'])
                                 print ("selected"); ?>>
          Linux.com
        </option>

      </select>
    </form>

  </body>
</html>
```

Here, we are again using an external CSS file called `grabber.css`, which can also be downloaded from the book's page on http://www.wrox.com/.

We are creating a small form on the page with one `<select>` element. This element will be used by the user to choose the news source they are interested in. There is a little bit of PHP in the form that causes the currently selected element to be displayed when the page loads. There is also a small bit of JavaScript that causes the form to be submitted automatically when the user changes the `<select>` element (as opposed to using a submit button).

447

With this section of HTML and PHP, the browser looks like this when we open the file:

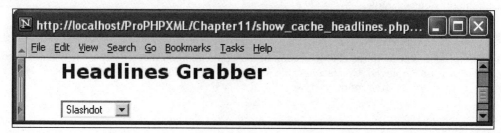

Now it's time to begin the application logic. Keep in mind that the application logic should come before the display code we just wrote in our `show_cache_headlines.php` file. We start with the `require_once()` statement and the declaration of a few global variables:

```php
<?php

require_once ('../classes/pear/RSS.php');

// our global variables
$read_from_cache = FALSE;
$cache_file = '';
$cache_age = 0;
$headline_items = array();
$images = array();
$textinput = array();
```

Here we are initializing $read_from_cache. This will be actively set later on.

We now write a function to determine if our cache file is 'young' or not. It makes use of our global variables $cache_file and $cache_age.

An important thing to note is that this function does not check to make sure if the cache file actually exists. It is generally better to have functions for specific operations, and descriptive function names to define what those operations are. Later we will look at a `file_exists()` function that checks the file's existence.

We start by defining the function and referencing the global variables it will use:

```php
// see if the cache file is current
function CacheCurrent($filename , $minutes)
{
    global $cache_file, $cache_age;
```

Next, we will get the last modified time of the cache file using the PHP `filemtime()` function. We also get the current system time with the `time()` function. These functions are invoked by the following section of code:

```php
    if(!($mtime_timestamp = filemtime($cache_file)))
        die("Couldn't get mtime for $cache_file!\n");
    $current_timestamp = time();
```

We are now computing the time since the cache was last refreshed. Both `filemtime()` and `time()` return UNIX-style timestamps, which is measured in seconds relative to a specific reference date called the UNIX Epoch (January 1 1970 00:00:00 GMT). This means that `$mtime_timestamp` and `$current_timestamp` are both referenced in seconds. The difference is computed as follows:

```
$diff = $current_timestamp - $mtime_timestamp;
```

This yields the number of seconds between the current system time and the time when the cache file was last modified. With this information available, we will first set the global variable `$cache_age`:

```
// formatted age in minutes for printing later
$cache_age = (int) sprintf("%.0f" , $diff / 60);
```

and then return TRUE or FALSE based on the age of the cached file:

```
// return true if mtime is within $minutes min. of current time
if(($diff / 60) < $minutes) {
    return TRUE;
} else {
    return FALSE;
}
}
```

Now it is time to write the `GetRssContent()` function. This is a fairly large function that is at the heart of the application. It checks to see whether there is an appropriate cache file to use for the requested data. If yes, then that data is read from the local file. If not, then the function instantiates an XML_RSS object, gets the data from the network, puts the data into our global variable `$headline_data`, and finally writes a cache file for future reference.

> For this to work, we must ensure that the web server process is allowed to write to the directory where the **show_cache_headlines.php** file exists. Also, the **allow_url_fopen** line in the **php.ini** file must be On.

We start with the function definition and referencing of global variables that we will use:

```
// function to grab content from cache or network
// depending on age of cache file
function GetRssContent()
{
    global $cache_file, $headline_items, $images,
            $textinput, $read_from_cache, $source_file;
```

Then we see if there is a cache file available that is suitable (meaning young enough) to use:

```
// see if we have a current cache file available
if(file_exists($cache_file) && CacheCurrent($cache_file , 30)) {
```

As can be seen, we are using the `CacheCurrent()` function we just wrote. Also, this is the point where we use PHP's `file_exists()` function to make sure that the appropriate cache file is actually available on the server.

449

Moving on, we now deal with the case where there is a cache file that is less than thirty minutes old. So we will open a file-handle to that file:

```
// open cache file for reading
$fh = fopen($cache_file , "r");

// get content or die if we can't
if(!($cache_content = fread($fh , filesize($cache_file))))
    die("Couldn't get cache content!\n");
```

Here, we create a filehandle for reading the cache file, and put the contents of that file into a $cache_content variable. The program dies with an error message if, for whatever reason, the fread() function fails.

Chapter 2 has a brief refresher on the file access functions.

Next, we populate the $headline_items array with the data that we put into $cache_content. Also, we will finish off this case by setting the $read_from_cache variable and closing the filehandle:

```
// unserialize the array in the file and get data
$rss_data = unserialize($cache_content);
$headline_items = $rss_data["headline_items"];
$images = $rss_data["images"];
$textinput = $rss_data["textinput"];
$read_from_cache = TRUE;

// clear this up
fclose($fh);
}
```

As can be seen in the code above, we have used the PHP unserialize() function on the $cache_content variable.

PHP provides two functions – serialize() and unserialize() – that make it easy to store complex data structures such as arrays. The serialize() function takes a PHP value and creates a single string that stores all the information for that value. This will work for any type of PHP variable except for the resource type. For example, if we have an array called $a and we want to create a single, storable value that contains all the information in $a, we could do it with $storable = serialize($a). Then we could pass or store the $storable variable for use later. Finally, we could recreate $a by using $a = unserialize($storable).

In a moment, when we move to the next case, it will become apparent that we use serialize() to store the data into the array, which is why we must unserialize() it when we get it out.

> **When unserializing the object, make sure that the class that defines the object has already been included somewhere in the code. Otherwise errors will be generated.**

Moving on to the next part of code, we will deal with the case where there is no cache file or the cache file is stale. In this instance, we first need to create an XML_RSS object and use it to get the data from the network:

```
    else { // get file from network and process, write cache

        // instantiate new XML_RSS object with slashdot RSS file
        $rss =& new XML_RSS($source_file);
```

As before, we parse the data and put the results into the $headline_items array:

```
        // parse the file
        $rss->parse();

        // grab this array
        $headline_items = $rss->getItems();

        // grab images
        $images = $rss->getImages();

        // grab textinput
        $textinput = $rss->getTextinputs();
```

To finish up the function we serialize the data in $headline_items, $images, and $textinput and write that data out to a cache file for future use. We do this by wrapping each of the three arrays in a 'higher-level' array called $rss_data so that everything is in one place and we can use serialize():

```
        // now we have to write the cache file...
        // start by putting our needed data into a big array
        $rss_data["headline_items"] = $headline_items;
        $rss_data["images"] = $images;
        $rss_data["textinput"] = $textinput;

        // serialize and store
        $cache_data = serialize($rss_data);

        // write serialized data out to file
        $fh = fopen($cache_file , "w");
        if(!(fwrite( $fh , $cache_data )))
            die("Couldn't write cache data!");

        fclose($fh);

    }
}
```

We now create the same PrintLink() function that we had used before:

```
function PrintLink($link , $title)
{
    return "<a href=\"$link\" target=\"_blank\">$title</a>";
}
```

And finally, this last section checks the value of the $rss_source variable. This value will depend on the user's selection in the select box. It then assigns values to the $source_file and $cache_file global variables that our functions make use of:

```
// first things first, identify rss file
if(isset($rss_source)) {
    switch ($rss_source) {
    case "1" :
        $source_file = "http://slashdot.org/slashdot.rdf";
        $cache_file = "slashdot.rdf.cache";
        break;
    case "2" :
        $source_file = "http://freshmeat.net/backend/fm.rdf";
        $cache_file = "freshmeat.rdf.cache";
        break;
    case "3" :
        $source_file = "http://www.linux.com/linuxcom.rss";
        $cache_file = "linux.rdf.cache";
        break;
    }
}
```

Again, it is important to make sure we use the isset() function to see if we should do anything at all. This is to make sure the application behaves correctly when we initially go to the web page and the form has not yet been used to select a data source.

Now, we will write the code that actually displays our results on the screen. This code should start directly below the end of the form on the page. To begin with, we check to see if our $rss_source variable has been set to see if we should do anything at all. Assuming we should, we call our GetRssContent() function:

```
<?php

if(isset($_POST['rss_source'])) {

    // grab content
    GetRssContent();
```

Next we will loop through any items in our $image_array and generate the HTML needed to display the images in question:

```
foreach($images as $image_info) {
    // put data from $image_info into easier variables
    $url = $image_info["url"];
    $link = $image_info["link"];
    $title = $image_info["title"];

    // print results
    print ("<a href=\"$link\" title=\"$title\">
            <img src=\"$url\" border=\"0\"></a>\n");
}
```

The all important headlines come next. Since `$headline_items` is also a nested array, we loop through it as well, making use of our `PrintLink()` function from before:

```
// start outputting the headline info
print ("<ul>\n");

foreach($headline_items as $items) {
    print ("<li>" . PrintLink($items['link'] ,
                              $items['title']) . "</li>\n");
}

print ("</ul>\n");
```

And finally, we will create a form for the text input and use the information from `$textinput` to make it actually useful:

```
// print out textinputs

$title = $textinput["title"];
$description = $textinput["description"];
$name = $textinput["name"];
$link = $textinput["link"];
print ("$description<br />\n");
print ("<form name=\"queryform\" action=\"$link\" method=\"post\">\n");
print ("<input type=\"text\" name=\"$name\"><br />\n");
print ("<input type=\"submit\" value=\"Submit\"><br />\n");
}
?>
```

As a last little inclusion, let's give the user some idea of how old the data they are looking at is:

```
<?php
if($read_from_cache) { ?>
    <br />
    <div class="smalltext">
      Read from cache: <?php print ($cache_age); ?> minutes old
    </div>
<?php } ?>
```

Thus, the application tells us if we are looking at cached data that might be interesting. A sample output of the Slashdot headlines looks like this:

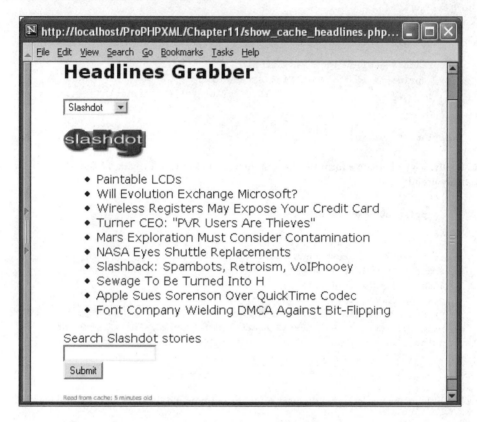

There are several ways that we can extend the functionality of the program to make it more useful. For example, we could add a checkbox to the form that would allow the user to bypass the caching, meaning that the data would be read directly from the network each time. We could even add a textfield that would allow the user to put in a URI to a different data source than the three in the select box.

There is a large listing of available newsfeeds at http://www.webreference.com/services/news/.

A Simple RSS Generation Class

We have now looked at several examples of how to read external syndicated data from web sites. However, reading other peoples' data is only half the story. Generating and distributing content that we ourselves have created is the other half. In that case we will need to create an RSS file from data that resides within our system. In this section, we are going to write our own class that will help us generate such a file.

Design Goals

Before we start coding, we will enunciate some design goals for our new class. The example we are going to execute is about an imaginary band called 'The Swell Mob'. We will syndicate some data about the dates of the shows it is performing. We don't need to use all of the meta data features available in the RSS specification to do this.

For example, we don't need to include images if we are just talking about show dates. Therefore, in the interest of keeping this example simple and concise, the class we intend to develop will not be 'feature complete' in terms of allowing us to use all the functionality built into the RSS specifications. It will just include the parts that we need for the job at hand. Of course, if we need to add in more functionality, it is not a complicated task to extend our class.

Another of our design goals is to make maintaince of the RSS class easy. We may need to add or change content, thus, simplifying this process should be one of our design priorities.

Application Code

We will call our class `RSS_Simple`, and begin it by declaring our member variables. Here we create a file called `rss_simple.php`:

```php
<?php

// a very simple class to write an rss file
// for ourselves.
// is not complete with the RSS specification

class RSSSimple
{
    // member variables
    var $mChannel;
    var $mItems;
    var $mEncoding;
    var $mCurrentItem;
```

As can be seen above, we haven't provided any initial values for the member variables. This is considered good practice, as we are supposed to initialize these with a constructor or initialization function. We will write these next:

```php
    // never do anything important in a constructor
    function RSSSimple()
    {
        $this->Init();
    }

    // initial values
    function Init()
    {
        $this->mChannel = array();
        $this->mItems = array();
        $this->mEncoding = 'ISO-8859-1';
        $this->mCurrentItem = 0;
    }
```

We set up our member variables in the Init() function. The $mChannel and $mItems variables are both arrays which are empty to begin with. $mEncoding and $mCurrentItem are fairly obvious variables that are given reasonable initial values.

The next function will give the user a way to change the encoding for the XML file we will create:

```
// just in case you want something else
// like UTF-8 for example
function SetEncoding($encoding)
{
    $this->mEncoding = $encoding;
}
```

The $mEncoding variable is initially set to ISO-8859-1. However, there are other encodings that are commonly used (UTF-8 in particular). The method just described will allow a developer using the class to change the encoding if desired.

Next, there will be two simple functions that generate the very beginning and end of our XML file:

```
// beginning of XML output
function WriteHeader()
{
    $header .= "<?xml version=\"1.0\" encoding=\"" .
               $this->mEncoding . "\"?>\n";
    $header .= "<rdf:RDF\n";
    $header .= "  xmlns:rdf=
                  \"http://www.w3.org/1999/02/22-rdf-syntax-ns#\"\n";
    $header .= "  xmlns=\"http://purl.org/rss/1.0/\"\n";
    $header .= ">\n";

    return $header;
}

// end of XML output
function WriteClose()
{
    return '</rdf:RDF>\n';
}
```

This might not be a very interesting section of code, but it will be convenient later on.

We now approach a very important function that is often left out of these types of classes:

```
// fix bad characters that mess up our XML
function FixEntities($s)
{
    $s = str_replace("<" , "&lt;" , $s);
    $s = str_replace(">" , "&gt;" , $s);
    $s = str_replace("&" , "&amp;" , $s);

    return $s;
}
```

In well-formed XML files, the characters <, >, and & are not allowed since they are in conflict with the naming conventions in other XML structures. We must always be careful to replace these with the proper SGML entities. Failure to do so will result in an XML file that is not considered valid. And, if an XML file is not valid, then there are a large number of parsers in use that will simply choke on the file and not process it, which basically makes our file useless.

Now we can get into the heart of the class. As stated earlier, we are going to make this RSS file as simple as we can. The minimal set of elements that we will need is a channel (allows the RSS file to adhere to the corresponding DTD), and a sequence of items that hold links to the band's show date information. To start off with, we will provide methods to put in the data needed in the channel element:

```
// set title
function SetChannelTitle($s)
{
    $this->mChannel["title"] = $this->FixEntities($s);
}


// set link
function SetChannelLink($s)
{
    $this->mChannel["link"] = $this->FixEntities($s);
}


// set description
function SetChannelDescription($s)
{
    $this->mChannel["description"] = $this->FixEntities($s);
}


// set rdf:about attribute
function setChannelAbout($s)
{
    $this->mChannel["about"] = $this->FixEntities($s);
}
```

These are all simple functions that populate the associative array $mChannel with the desired data. We will use this data when we generate the file later. Note that in every case, we use FixEntities() to make sure that no bad characters sneak into our file and make the resulting XML invalid.

Next, we will start adding <item> elements. Since it is not possible to put a finger on the exact number of items we will need, our class should be able to handle the addition of an arbitrary number of items. We accomplish this by creating the StartItem() and EndItem() methods that we use to manipulate the $mCurrentItem member variable. This can then assist us in populating the $mItems array with item data:

```
    // returns the current id, in case your app needs it
    function StartItem()
    {
        return $this->mCurrentItem;
    }

    // set title
    function AddItemTitle($s)
    {
        $this->mItems[$this->mCurrentItem]["title"] =
                                        $this->FixEntities($s);
    }

    // set link
    function AddItemLink($s)
    {
        $this->mItems[$this->mCurrentItem]["link"] = $this->FixEntities($s);
    }

    function AddItemDescription($s)
    {
        $this->mItems[$this->mCurrentItem]["description"] =
                                        $this->FixEntities($s);
    }

    // increment mCurrentItem at end of item
    function EndItem()
    {
        $this->mCurrentItem++;
    }
```

With these methods, a developer using this class can add as many items as desired without having to worry about keeping track of how many there are.

The final part of our class is a method that will actually output the RSS file with the data that we have populated it with. It is the largest method in the class, but it is not very complicated. When called, it will return an RSS file that can be parsed by others who have access to it:

```
function GetRssContent()
{
    // get the header info
    $rss = $this->WriteHeader();
```

After the header, we generate the `<channel>` element and the elements contained within it:

```
    // write out channel info
    $rss .=
        "  <channel rdf:about=\"" . $this->mChannel["about"] .  "\">\n";
    foreach ($this->mChannel as $k => $v) {
        // "about" is an attribute, not an element
        if(0 != strcmp($k , "about")) {
            $rss .= "    <$k>$v</$k>\n";
        }
    }
    $rss .= "  </channel>\n";
```

Next, we loop through the $mItems array to generate the <item> elements contained in the file:

```
        //write out all of our items
        for($i=0 ; $i < count($this->mItems) ; ++$i) {
            $rss .=
                "  <item rdf:about=\"" . $this->mItems[$i]["link"] . "\">\n";
            foreach($this->mItems[$i] as $k => $v) {
                $rss .= "    <$k>$v</$k>\n";
            }
            $rss .= "  </item>\n";
        }
```

To finish up, we get to the end of the XML document and return the result:

```
        // get close
        $rss .= $this->WriteClose();

        return $rss;
    }
} // end class RSSSimple
?>
```

With this class, it should be very easy to create some syndicated content for the band.

Generating an RSS File

Creating an appropriate file with our new class is a simple exercise. This, of course, is by design, since one of our basic goals for the class was 'ease-of-use'. So let us create a sample driver file called simple_rss_syndication.php:

```
<?php

require_once ('/rss_simple.php');

header("Content-type: text/xml");

$rss = new RSSSimple;

// dummy data. this would be taken from some other
// source like a database in practice

$rss->SetChannelTitle("Swell Mob Show Dates");
$rss->SetChannelLink("http://www.swellmobband.com");
$rss->SetChannelDescription("All about our band, the Swell Mob!");
$rss->SetChannelAbout("http://www.swellmobband.com/");

$rss->StartItem();
$rss->AddItemTitle("The Roxy");
$rss->AddItemLink("http://www.swellmobband.com/roxy");
$rss->AddItemDescription("June 5th 2002");
$rss->EndItem();

$rss->StartItem();
$rss->AddItemTitle("The Troubador");
$rss->AddItemLink("http://www.swellmobband.com/troubador");
$rss->AddItemDescription("August 25th 2002");
```

```
$rss->EndItem();

$rss->StartItem();
$rss->AddItemTitle("The Whiskey");
$rss->AddItemLink("http://www.swellmobband.com/whiskey");
$rss->AddItemDescription("November 1st 2002");
$rss->EndItem();

$rss->StartItem();
$rss->AddItemTitle("The Eagle & Child");
$rss->AddItemLink("http://www.swellmobband.com/eagle");
$rss->AddItemDescription("December 24th 2002");

$rss->EndItem();

print ($rss->GetRssContent());
?>
```

It might be interesting to note that we used PHP's header() function to set the Content-type of the output to text/xml. This is because XML is a text format (HTML is not), so we want other network-enabled applications to see the output as text. This is the output from the driver file:

This is a perfectly well-formed RSS file that can be used by others to get the desired syndicated content. Here we have used 'dummy data'. In practice, we could get data from a resource on the system such as a database. We could also modify the caching headline grabber from the previous example to include the news headlines from the band (though it's doubtful if any band changes its performance dates on an hourly basis) and so on.

Now let's look into parsing this RDF file. Save the above file as `swellmob.rdf`. We can create a `swellmob.php` file that can be used to parse the RDF file. This PHP file would be very similar to the `slashdot_headlines.php` file we wrote earlier. The first thing to do would be to point the `require_once()` method in the beginning of the program to `swellmob.rdf`. We should change the HTML display section too. The `swellmob.php` screen displays this:

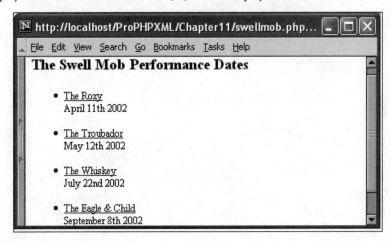

Summary

We have covered some basic techniques for getting and generating syndicated RSS content in this chapter. The PEAR RSS class was used extensively for the task of reading and parsing content. The PEAR repository, online at http://pear.php.net/, is always an excellent resource to tap into since they may have classes available for the task we are working on.

After creating a basic headline grabber, we developed a more complicated example that included two new pieces of functionality. First, it was able to get headlines from multiple sources. Second, and more importantly, it cached the data locally for thirty minutes thus reducing network load.

After these examples, we moved on to the task of generating our own data. This required writing a custom class making it easy to generate the simple RSS file needed. As we noted, this class does not offer the ability to tap into the complete range of features in the RSS specification. However, it could be extended to do so. Some sample data was used in conjunction with this class and an appropriate RSS file was subsequently created and parsed.

Syndicated data is likely to become more abundant as applications become increasingly network aware, and XML is the format of choice for this kind of content. PHP is a good language to use for looking at remote network resources, because reading external data is often no different than reading local data. So the XML functionality available with PHP provides a good way to examine syndicated content. The examples in this chapter offer insight into the techniques that can be used to get this content to users.

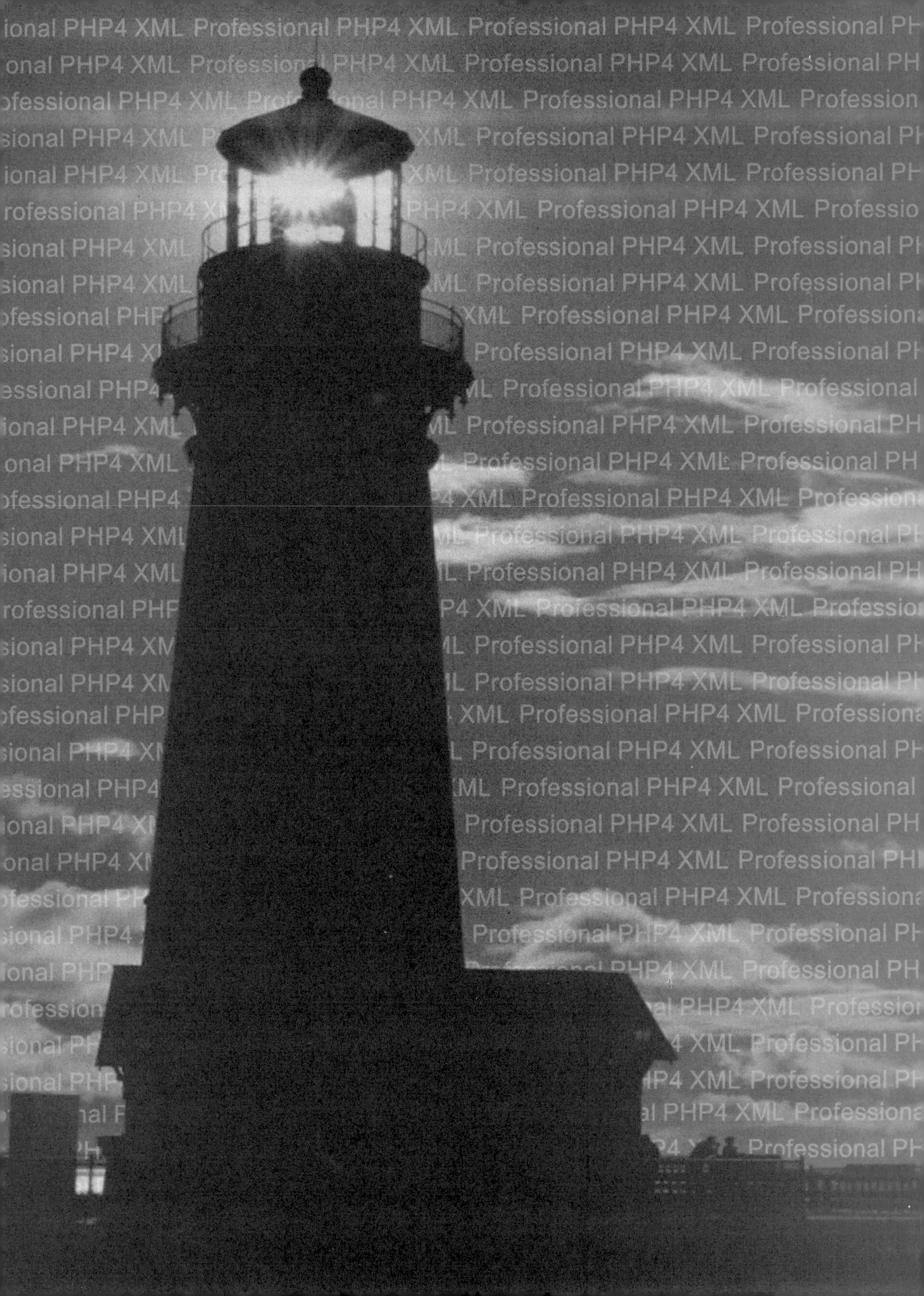
Professional PHP4 XML

12

XML to DB, DB to XML

As we develop increasingly complex PHP XML applications, we will run into the problem of selecting the best way to store all of our data. It's certainly possible to handle data storage through methods such as writing it to flat files. The fact is, this is by far the most commonly used method. However, this becomes horribly unruly as the number and size of the files increases. Also, the process of opening a file handle, doing a linear scan through the file's data to find what we want, and then closing the file handle is more complicated than we would like. As our applications grow more complex, developers have to adopt new and more advanced techniques for storage.

This typically means the use of a Relational Database Management System (RDBMS). These allow us to store our data in a highly structured manner and at a central location. Furthermore, with the SQL query language, we are provided with an easy and efficient way to access the specific data that we need.

These are obvious advantages that an RDBMS gives to us. However, many of these statements are true for XML documents as well. In both cases, we are given a well-defined, open, and structured way to store our data. In the case of a database, we can get to the data we want using SQL statements. With an XML document, we can get to what we want by using XPath, or by using a prebuilt class that makes searching through nodes easy for us.

With all these similarities, it only makes sense to talk about the ways that we can get databases and XML to interact. There are only two directions that this can go:

❑ We have some XML data, and we wish to store part or all of it in an RDBMS

❑ We have a database full of data, and we want to put some or all of that data into an XML document format

The first of these can be a little more complicated than the second. We have seen in previous chapters how to ferret out the portions of an XML document that we're interested in. We will take the same approach here, and once we've collected the data we want it's a fairly simple jump to put the data into a database.

Arguably the more interesting case is the second one, where we have a database populated with data and we want to get that information into an XML document. There are several reasons for this. There are an enormous number of things that we can do with an XML document, enough to warrant this entire book on the subject. At the same time, there is also an enormous amount of data currently being stored in databases. So, having an easy way to get from a database storage format to XML is a valuable asset.

Basic XML Storage

First we'll have a quick look at the two main ways of storing XML: as flat text files and using a database. We'll look at these options in more detail in the next chapter. A short discussion here is enough for now.

Flat Files

The simplest way to store XML documents is just to save flat files to our computer's filesystem. This is by far the most common method of archiving XML data in use today. The technique has both strong advantages and disadvantages.

On the positive side, the most valuable feature of this method is simplicity. Flat files are usually in ready-to-use self-contained units. There is no complexity in the storage format; the chances of making code-based errors while getting the data are very small. This is very convenient for developers. We saw in Chapter 9 how to use the XMLFile class to capture the data from a flat XML file. The beauty of simply having flat text files in the filesystem is that we can get the data with a few short and simple lines of code:

```
$xmlFile = new XMLFile();
$fh = fopen($my_xml_file_name, "r");
$xmlFile->read_file_handle($fh);
fclose($fh);
```

This does what we need, and is bulletproof in terms of not having any errors. Of course, there are other ways that we could read in the data from our file, but this demonstrates that in any case it will not be hard to retrieve what we need.

The downside of this technique becomes apparent when we have a very large number of XML files to be stored and called up. For example, if we have 10,000 files in our repository directory, then searching for any one of them is quite CPU intensive. And that's making the assumption that we know the name of the file we are looking for *a priori*, which may not always be the case.

Furthermore, if we are in a situation where we have hundreds or thousands of files to keep track of, we will almost certainly want a way to look for files based on information other than just the file's name. We may want to examine files written by a particular author, or posted before or after a specific date. This type of meta data is not available to PHP through a typical file-system structure. It's possible to avoid the issue to some degree with clever naming schemes for the files, but ultimately meta data-based file lookups will become a necessity.

Finally, there is the issue of portability as well. Different file systems support different features, and these may not be the same if we take our application from one platform to another. As noted, people often use detailed naming schemes for files to make finding a particular file a more algorithmic process. This can often result in fairly long file names. Imagine if we were using such a scheme, and then moved to a file system that couldn't support very long file names (they do exist). Our storage technique in that case would be brutally crippled. Fortunately, databases offer methods that tend to be much more machine-independent.

Simple Database Storage

The next method up in terms of complexity is to simply store the entire file in a field in our database. A typical table (xml_files) for such a storage container might look like:

```
+--------------+--------------+------+-----+---------+----------------+
| Field        | Type         | Null | Key | Default | Extra          |
+--------------+--------------+------+-----+---------+----------------+
| file_id      | int(11)      |      | PRI | NULL    | auto_increment |
| time_posted  | timestamp(14)| YES  |     | NULL    |                |
| xml_data     | blob         |      |     |         |                |
+--------------+--------------+------+-----+---------+----------------+
```

Using this database schema, we are almost in the same position we were in before. Instead of a unique file name on the file system, we have a unique file_id column in the database. But there are two critical differences that give this approach some advantage over flat files. The first is that it is much easier for the database to search for the data based on the file_id than it is for the computer to read through a great many filenames in the file system. Of course, this now requires that we know the file_id of the file in question; a problem analogous to needing to know the actual file name in the case of plaintext files. The seek functionality in a modern RDBMS is highly optimized, so something like:

```
SELECT xml_data FROM xml_files WHERE file_id = 18;
```

is very efficient compared to a linear scan over a number of files.

The second advantage is that we have a time_posted column. This allows us to use SQL to select documents based on when they were added to the database. It is of course easy to see how this idea can be extended. If we added a field to the above schema for the author's name, then that information could be used to pick out specific files. Naturally, any number of fields could be included that would allow us to harness SQL queries for our purposes.

> The reason for selecting xml_data as blob type is it would be useful when we want to use full-text searching. This approach works out quite well for documents that do not change frequently.

Extending this, we get into issues where we want to be able to query based on some piece of information that is in the XML file itself. For example, looking at our bug_list.xml file, we might want to query based on the name of the application. In an upcoming section, we will do exactly this sort of thing.

XML to Database

In this section we will look at how we can store an XML document in a database. We will look at some simple examples that deal with this problem. But first, since we are going to be interacting with the database a good deal, we will review the use of the DB.php class that is part of the PEAR libraries.

Using DB.php

In the next section we will start interacting with the database. To achieve this, we will make use of the excellent database access class that is included in the PEAR class libraries: DB.php. Since you may not have used this class before, we will go over a brief primer here to get us ready.

Using the PEAR database class gives us several immediate advantages compared to directly using the database connection functions in PHP:

❏ A uniform API covering many different RDBMS systems

❏ An object-oriented approach

❏ The common PEAR error handling system

If you are used to the Perl language, it may help to think of the PEAR database access class as something that gives Perl DBI-type functionality to PHP.

The full documentation for this and other PEAR classes is available online at http://pear.php.net/. We will review a few of the conventions and functions that we will be employing later in the examples.

To begin with, any application that makes use of this class should include the line:

```
require_once("DB.php");
```

Of course, the PEAR libraries must be in PHP's include_path for this to work. Otherwise we will need to include the full path name.

The DSN

The next thing to turn our attention to is the creation of a DSN (**Data Source Name**). In reality, this is just a string that contains the information needed to create a database connection. There are several formats allowed for a DSN. The most commonly used is:

```
$dbtype://$user:$pass@$host/$db_name
```

The value of $dbtype corresponds to one of the supported RDBMS systems. Currently these are the ones that are supported:

$dbtype	RDBMS
mysql	MySQL
pgsql	PostgreSQL
ibase	InterBase
msql	Mini SQL
mssql	Microsoft SQL Server
oci8	Oracle 7/8/8i
odbc	ODBC (Open Database Connectivity)
sybase	SyBase
ifx	Informix
fbsql	FrontBase

The meanings for $user, $pass, $host, and $db_name are shown below:

Variable	Meaning
$user	The username to connect to the database
$pass	The password for database user $user
$host	The name of the machine where the database resides
$db_name	The name of the database to connect to

The Connection

Once we have created a properly formed DSN string, it's time to establish a connection to the database. This is accomplished with the connect() function:

```
$db = DB::connect($dsn, TRUE);
```

Here, $dsn is the DSN string we constructed and TRUE requests a persistent connection. If this function succeeds, the variable $db is a PEAR database object. If not, then $db is a PEAR Error object. This is very useful, since we can (and should) always make the following error check after attempting a connection:

```
if (DB::isError($db)) {
    die ($db->getMessage());
}
```

After we are done with our database object, we should always remember to disconnect from the database server with the disconnect() method:

```
$db->disconnect();
```

Query and Fetch

With our database connection established, it's time to get on to the business of querying the database and getting data out of it. Once again, the class provides methods that make everything easy to handle.

Queries are handled with the `query()` method. So a typical implementation might look like this:

```
// once we have a $db database object
$sql = "SELECT * FROM tablename";

$result = $db->query($sql);

// make sure $result isn't an error message
if (DB::isError($result)) {
    die ($result->getMessage());
}
```

Again, the common PEAR `Error` handling comes in handy here, giving us a uniform way to check for errors. Now that we have a valid result object in `$result`, we can use the `fetchRow()` method to actually get at the data:

```
while ($row = $result->fetchRow()) {
    $id = $row[0];
    $name = $row[1];
    // and so on
}
```

Here we are assuming that there's an ID of some kind in the first column of the table, and a `name` in the second. Calling `fetchRow()` with no arguments results in a return value that is an ordered array.

There are actually three constants that can be passed as an argument to `fetchRow()` that can be used to control this behavior:

Argument	Meaning
DB_FETCHMODE_ORDERED	Default, returns an ordered array
DB_FETCHMODE_ASSOC	Returns an associative array, with keys equal to the column names
DB_FETCHMODE_OBJECT	Returns an object with column names as properties

There is a wealth of other functionality in this class. However, what we've covered here is sufficient to get us through our example applications. We will start with a simple example designed just to get our feet wet with `DB.php`.

RSS from a Database

You may recall that in Chapter 11 we created a class to help us generate an RSS file. This helped us syndicate some information about the upcoming shows for a band. However, we put all of the show information into the class manually. As we noted then, that is not typically how we would do such an operation, because normally that information would already be stored somewhere else.

In this section, we are going to recreate that example, but we are going to pull the show information from a database using the DB.php class, which will help us to avoid unneeded labor. The first step is to set up a new database band_db with a single table called shows that has the following very simple schema:

```
+------------+----------+------+-----+---------+----------------+
| Field      | Type     | Null | Key | Default | Extra          |
+------------+----------+------+-----+---------+----------------+
| show_id    | int(11)  |      | PRI | NULL    | auto_increment |
| show_venue | text     |      |     |         |                |
| show_url   | text     |      |     |         |                |
+------------+----------+------+-----+---------+----------------+
```

All we really need for the <item> elements in our RSS file are the show's venue and the corresponding URL link. Populate the shows table with the following data:

```
+---------+-------------------+-------------------------------------------+
| show_id | show_venue        | show_url                                  |
+---------+-------------------+-------------------------------------------+
|       1 | The Roxy          | http://www.swellmobband.com/roxy/         |
|       2 | The Troubador     | http://www.swellmobband.com/troubador/    |
|       3 | The Whiskey       | http://www.swellmobband.com/whiskey/      |
|       4 | The Eagle & Child | http://www.swellmobband.com/eagle/        |
+---------+-------------------+-------------------------------------------+
```

This, you will note, is exactly the same data that we put in manually before. But this time we're going to use DB.php to automate that process for us.

Now that we have all of our data ready to go, create a new file called rss_from_db.php. Since we are going to make use of the RSSSimple class that we developed in Chapter 11, you'll want to copy the rss_simple.php file into the classes directory under the server's root.

The first lines of the file as usual just include the appropriate classes. We also put a line in to force the output to plaintext. This keeps XML-aware browsers such as Netscape 6 from trying to interpret the data, and instead makes them simply display it for us to see:

```php
<?php
require_once("../classes/rss_simple.php");
require_once("DB.php");
header("Content-type: text/plain");
```

The next step is to set up variables that we need to access our database, and define the DSN connection string that we'll be using:

```php
// database variables
$dbname = "band_db";
$dbuser = "root";
$dbpass = "";
$dbserver = "localhost";
$tablename = "shows";

// create our dsn
$dsn = "mysql://$dbuser:$dbpass@$dbserver/$dbname";
```

Obviously, you'll want to change the variable names to ones that suit your system.

We're going to tackle the database part of this application first, since that's the focus of the example. So the next thing to do is to define a variable that contains our SQL query:

```
// define our SQL query
$sql = "SELECT show_venue,show_url FROM $tablename";
```

Everything is now set up, so we will use the `connect()` method to connect to the database. Also, we will use the handy PEAR error handling mechanism to make sure that everything worked properly:

```
// connect to the database and check for any errors
$db = DB::connect($dsn);
if (DB::isError($db)) {
    die ($db->getMessage());
}
```

If the connection succeeded, then we can perform the query and get a result variable to use. Again, we check for errors with the PEAR handling routines:

```
// perform the query and check for any errors
$result = $db->query($sql);
if (DB::isError($result)) {
    die ($result->getMessage());
}
```

The query has been successful, so we now have a resultset in `$result` that we can loop through to get our data. What remains is to set up an `RSSSimple` object to use and fill it with the needed data:

```
// now we'll create our RSSSimple object
// and get it ready.

$rss = new RSSSimple;

// set the channel information manually, since
// we only have to do it once.
$rss->SetChannelTitle("Swell Mob Show Dates");
$rss->SetChannelLink("http://www.swellmobband.com");
$rss->SetChannelDescription("All about our band, the Swell Mob!");
$rss->SetChannelAbout("http://www.swellmobband.com/");
```

Since the channel information only needs to be entered once, it's not too troublesome to do it manually here. However, since there could be many items to be added, it is simpler to loop through a database resultset to get the information, which is our next step:

```
// now, loop through our resultset and get all of
// the show information

while ($row = $result->fetchRow(DB_FETCHMODE_ASSOC)) {
    $rss->StartItem();
```

```
        $rss->AddItemTitle($row["show_venue"]);
        $rss->AddItemLink($row["show_url"]);
        $rss->EndItem();
    }
```

We set the flag `DB_FETCHMODE_ASSOC` in the `fetchRow()` method. This makes `fetchRow()` return an associative array where the keys are equal to the column names in the database table. That in turn makes the code a little more readable when we actually use the data in the `AddItemTitle()` and `AddItemLink()` methods.

All that's left is to output the result to the browser:

```
// print out the RSS file
print ($rss->GetRssContent());
?>
```

The resulting output should look like this:

```
N Netscape 6                                                                    _ □ ✕

  File  Edit  View  Search  Go  Bookmarks  Tasks  Help

  <?xml version="1.0" encoding="ISO-8859-1"?>
  <rdf:RDF
    xmlns:rdf="http://www.w3.org/1999/02/22-rdf-syntax-ns#"
    xmlns="http://purl.org/rss/1.0/"
  >
    <channel rdf:about="http://www.swellmobband.com/">
      <title>Swell Mob Show Dates</title>
      <link>http://www.swellmobband.com</link>
      <description>All about our band, the Swell Mob!</description>
    </channel>
    <item rdf:about="http://www.swellmobband.com/roxy/">
      <title>The Roxy</title>
      <link>http://www.swellmobband.com/roxy/</link>
    </item>
    <item rdf:about="http://www.swellmobband.com/troubador/">
      <title>The Troubador</title>
      <link>http://www.swellmobband.com/troubador/</link>
    </item>
    <item rdf:about="http://www.swellmobband.com/whiskey/">
      <title>The Whiskey</title>
      <link>http://www.swellmobband.com/whiskey/</link>
    </item>
    <item rdf:about="http://www.swellmobband.com/eagle/">
      <title>The Eagle &amp; Child</title>
      <link>http://www.swellmobband.com/eagle/</link>
    </item>
  </rdf:RDF>
```

So we accomplished our task of using `DB.php` to do the repetitive task of adding our `<item>` elements to the RSS file.

In the next example, we will again use `DB.php`, both to put data into a database and extract data from it while we create a search interface for our `bug_list.xml` file.

Dissecting an XML File

In Chapter 9, we built a simple search interface to our `bug_list.xml` file. In this example, we will again assume that we are interested in having a web interface that lets us see the status of various bugs. But this time, we are going to go a few steps further in the application. The basic plan of attack is as follows:

- ❏ Create a table in a MySQL database to hold our data
- ❏ Use `XMLFile` to extract the parts of the XML document we are interested in
- ❏ Insert this into the table
- ❏ Build a SQL-based query interface that lets us search for different bugs

We'll start by examining what we need in our MySQL table. Looking at `bug_list.xml`, we see that we really should store all the elements within the `<bug_item>` elements, as well as the name of the application that the bug relates to.

Create a table in MySQL called `buglist` with the following structure:

```
+-----------------+------------+------+-----+---------+----------------+
| Field           | Type       | Null | Key | Default | Extra          |
+-----------------+------------+------+-----+---------+----------------+
| bug_id          | int(11)    |      | PRI | NULL    | auto_increment |
| bug_app_name    | tinytext   |      |     |         |                |
| bug_title       | tinytext   |      |     |         |                |
| bug_report_date | tinytext   |      |     |         |                |
| bug_reported_by | tinytext   |      |     |         |                |
| bug_status      | tinytext   |      |     |         |                |
| bug_last_update | tinytext   |      |     |         |                |
| bug_description | text       |      |     |         |                |
| bug_severity    | int(11)    |      |     | 0       |                |
+-----------------+------------+------+-----+---------+----------------+
```

> *If you haven't already discovered it, there is an excellent web-based MySQL administration tool called phpMyAdmin. It greatly simplifies the process of creating databases and tables, and is available for free at http://phpmyadmin.sourceforge.net/.*

Now it's time to use the `XMLFile` class to extract the data we want from the `bug_list.xml` file. Create a file called `bugs_to_db.php`.

The beginning lines are quite obvious and should be mostly familiar if you've gone through Chapter 9:

```php
<?php
header("Content-type: text/plain");

require_once("../classes/xmlfile.php");

require_once("DB.php");


// our global variables
$bug_data = array();
$bug_counter = 0;
```

Here, we're setting the content type to text/plain to keep our fancy modern browsers from doing any 'interpretation' of the data.

Notice that we remembered to require the DB.php file. Next we set up a few variables and create our DSN string:

```
// database variables
$dbname = "buglist";
$dbuser = "root";
$dbpass = "";
$dbserver = "localhost";
$tablename = "buglist";

// create our dsn
$dsn = "mysql://$dbuser:$dbpass@$dbserver/$dbname";
```

After that's done we name the XML file that we'll be reading, and instantiate an XMLFile object called $xmlFile:

```
// xml file to be read
$xml_data_file = "../bug_list.xml";

// instantiate our XMLFile object
$xmlFile = new XMLFile();
```

As before, we will now open up a file handle to the XML file on our filesystem. Then we will use the read_file_handle() method of the XMLFile class to read and parse the data. Then we close the file handle, and assign the root tag to our $xmlFile object:

```
// open a file handle to the file and read in the data
if (FALSE == ($fh = fopen($xml_data_file, "r"))) {
    die ("Couldn't open $xml_data_file for reading.");
}

$xmlFile->read_file_handle($fh);

fclose($fh);

// assign the root node
$roottag = &$xmlFile->roottag;
```

Now comes the most important part. The XMLFile class gives us the ability to examine our XML data on a tag-by-tag basis. Therefore, since we want to go through the entire file and get all of the bug data, we will need to define a recursive function to take us through all the tags.

The information we are principally interested in is contained in elements whose parent tag is <bug_items>. However, we will also want to attach the application's name to each bug record that we store. Since that is not included with the rest of the bug information, but rather as an attribute of the <application> tag, we'll want to pass the current application name along every time the function is called again. Let's start in with the following code:

```
function parse_bug_list($tag, $app_name)
{
    global $bug_counter, $bug_data;
```

Here, we have to remember to register the global variables needed. Next is the main `foreach()` loop that takes us through the nodes immediately under our current position in the file. We'll start out by checking to see if we need to increment the `$bug_counter` variable:

```
foreach ($tag->tags as $k => $v) {

    // increment bug counter if parent is "BUGS" tag
    if (0 == strcmp($v->parent->name, "BUGS")) {
        $bug_data[$bug_counter]["APPNAME"] = $app_name;
        ++$bug_counter;
    }
```

Remember that `XMLFile` has case folding enabled by default, so the names of tags and attributes are all in uppercase. Next, let's see if we are in the `<application>` tag, and get the application name if we are:

```
    // grab application name if we're at an "APPLICATION" tag
    if (0 == strcmp($v->name, "APPLICATION")) {
        foreach ($v->attributes as $attname => $attval) {
            if (0 == strcmp($attname, "NAME")) {
                $app_name = $attval;
            }
        }
    }
```

The final check we make is to see if we are at one of the elements that describe the bug. We can tell if we are by looking to see if the parent of the current tag is `<bug_item>`. If it is, then we store the CDATA for the element:

```
    // grab cdata if we're in the bug description
    if (0 == strcmp($v->parent->name, "BUG_ITEM")) {
        $bug_data[$bug_counter-1][$v->name] = $v->cdata;
    }
```

Lastly, we recurse the function:

```
    // do recursion
    parse_bug_list($v, $app_name);
    }
}
```

Now that our function is written, we run it. After it has executed, don't forget to run the `cleanup()` method of `$xmlFile` to free the memory that was used:

```
// run the function
parse_bug_list($roottag, "");

// clean up memory from $xmlFile object
$xmlFile->cleanup();
```

Excellent, now our `$bug_data` array is nicely arranged so that it's very easy to loop through on a per-bug basis. This will make it easy to insert the array's data into the database.

Now that we're on the actual database part, we need to establish a connection:

```
$db = DB::connect($dsn, true);
```

We'll want to make sure that the table is clear before we put anything into it:

```
// clear out table
$sql = "DELETE FROM $tablename";

$result = $db->query($sql);
// Always check that $result is not an error
if (DB::isError($result)) {
    die ($result->getMessage());
}
```

As we saw in the explanation, the PEAR DB access class has some nice built-in error checking functionality – be sure to make use of it as it is good practice and is very helpful in debugging.

Now, we'll loop through each of the bugs in $bug_data and do an INSERT query for each one. Therefore, we must construct an appropriate SQL statement for each bug:

```
for ($i=0 ; $i < count($bug_data) ; ++$i) {
    // create SQL statement
    $sql = "INSERT INTO $tablename (bug_app_name, bug_title,
                                    bug_report_date, bug_reported_by,
                                    bug_status, bug_last_update,
                                    bug_description, bug_severity)
            VALUES (" . $db->quote($bug_data[$i]["APPNAME"]) . ",
                    " . $db->quote($bug_data[$i]["TITLE"]) . ",
                    " . $db->quote($bug_data[$i]["REPORT_DATE"]) . ",
                    " . $db->quote($bug_data[$i]["REPORTED-BY"]) . ",
                    " . $db->quote($bug_data[$i]["STATUS"]) . ",
                    " . $db->quote($bug_data[$i]["LAST_UPDATE"]) . ",
                    " . $db->quote($bug_data[$i]["DESCRIPTION"]) . ",
                    " . $db->quote($bug_data[$i]["SEVERITY"]) . ")";

    // perform query
    $result = $db->query($sql);
    if (DB::isError($result)) {
        die ($result->getMessage());
    }

    // quick message for success
    print ("Put bug \"" . $bug_data[$i]["TITLE"] . "\" into database\n");
}
```

Again, doing the query is very simple, and we've added a little output to make sure that everything went according to plan.

All that remains now is to disconnect from the database:

```
// be sure to disconnect
$db->disconnect();
?>
```

We're done now.

We have now accomplished our goal of taking data from our XML document and planting it in a SQL database. Now that the hard work is done, let's build a quick query form that uses SQL to query the database for the appropriate bugs.

Create a new file called query_db.php. We'll start out by just putting in the HTML segment of the application, which should need no explanation:

```html
<html>
  <head>
    <title>query bug db</title>
    <style type="text/css">
      <!--
      body {
        margin-top: 40px;
        margin-left: 90px;
      }
      -->
    </style>
  </head>

  <body>

    <h2>Bug Database Query Form</h2>
    <form name="queryform" method="post"
          action="<?php print ($_SERVER["PHP_SELF"]); ?>">
      Find bugs with status
      <select name="bugstatus">
        <option value="0">Doesn't matter</option>
        <option value="1">Open</option>
        <option value="2">Closed</option>
      </select> and severity
      <select name="severity_comparison">
        <option value="0">Equal to</option>
        <option value="1">Greater than</option>
        <option value="2">Less than</option>
      </select>
      <select name="severity">
        <option value="1">1</option>
        <option value="2">2</option>
        <option value="3">3</option>
        <option value="4">4</option>
        <option value="5">5</option>
        <option value="6">6</option>
      </select>
      <br/><br/>
      <input type="submit" value="Submit">
```

```
    </form>
    <br/><br/>

  </body>
</html>
```

When opened in a browser, this page should closely resemble the following:

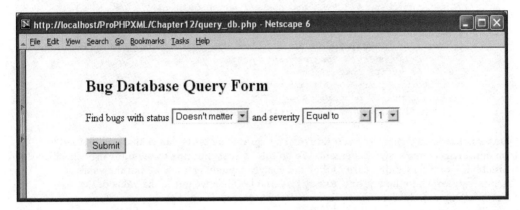

Now we'll start in with PHP. Keep in mind that this should all come before the HTML we just entered. The start should look quite familiar after the last bit of coding:

```
<?php
require_once("DB.php");

// database variables
$dbname = "buglist";
$dbuser = "root";
$dbpass = "";
$dbserver = "localhost";
$tablename = "buglist";

// create our dsn
$dsn = "mysql://$dbuser:$dbpass@$dbserver/$dbname";
```

We will also register any variables that were submitted by the form and are therefore held in the superglobal $_POST array:

```
// variables from the form
$bugstatus = $_POST["bugstatus"];
$severity_comparison = $_POST["severity_comparison"];
$severity = $_POST["severity"];
```

Next, we'll check on the status of the variables that get set from within the form. We wrap everything in a quick check to make sure that the form was actually submitted:

```
if (isset($bugstatus)) {

    // status
    if ($bugstatus == 0)
        $status_query = "";
    elseif ($bugstatus == 1)
        $status_query = "UPPER(bug_status) = \"OPEN\"";
    elseif ($bugstatus == 2)
        $status_query = "UPPER(bug_status) = \"CLOSED\"";

    // severity
    if ($severity_comparison == 0)
        $severity_query = "bug_severity = $severity";
    elseif ($severity_comparison == 1)
        $severity_query = "bug_severity > $severity";
    elseif ($severity_comparison == 2)
        $severity_query = "bug_severity < $severity";
```

The variables $status_query and $severity_query are set to values that will be used to dynamically generate a SQL statement. We do this by first checking to see if the user specified open or closed bugs, or if they didn't care. If they did specify something, then we put the value of $status_query into the $query_array[] variable. Then we put in the value of the $severity_query. Finally, we join these with the SQL AND keyword:

```
if (strlen($status_query) > 0) {
    $query_array[] = $status_query;
}
$query_array[] = $severity_query;

$query = join(" AND ", $query_array);
$sql = "SELECT * FROM $tablename WHERE $query";
```

So, the $query variable might contain a string such as UPPER(bug_status) == "CLOSED" AND bug_severity < 4 if the user had entered the corresponding inputs. This would come after the WHERE keyword in the actual SQL query defined by the $sql variable.

Finally, we connect to the database and perform the query. Again, don't forget to check the connection and result:

```
$db = DB::connect($dsn, true);
// Make sure we got a connection
if (DB::isError($db)) {
    die ($db->getMessage());
}

$result = $db->query($sql);
// Always check that $result is not an error
if (DB::isError($result)) {
    die ($result->getMessage());
}
}
?>
```

All that's left now is to display whatever our results are. The following code should be inserted in the file after the two <br/> tags:

```php
<?php

if (isset($bugstatus)) {
    while ($bug_data = $result->FetchRow(DB_FETCHMODE_ASSOC)) {
```

We use the `while()` control structure to loop through our resultset. Note that we set the `DB_FETCHMODE_ASSOC` flag for the `FetchRow()` function. As in the previous example, this makes `$bug_data` an associative array with the key values being equal to the appropriate column names in the MySQL table.

Next we will print out an HTML table for each bug found:

```php
        print ("<table border=\"1\" cellpadding=\"3\">\n");
        print ("  <tr>\n");
        print ("    <td><b>Application Name</b></td>\n");
        print ("    <td>" . $bug_data["bug_app_name"] . "</td>\n");
        print ("  </tr>\n");
        print ("  <tr>\n");
        print ("    <td><b>Bug Title</b></td>\n");
        print ("    <td>" . $bug_data["bug_title"] . "</td>\n");
        print ("  </tr>\n");
        print ("  <tr>\n");
        print ("    <td><b>Bug Status</b></td>\n");
        print ("    <td>" . $bug_data["bug_status"] . "</td>\n");
        print ("  </tr>\n");
        print ("  <tr>\n");
        print ("    <td><b>Bug Severity</b></td>\n");
        print ("    <td>" . $bug_data["bug_severity"] . "</td>\n");
        print ("  </tr>\n");
        print ("</table>\n\n");
        print ("<br/>\n");
    }
```

We are only displaying four of the pieces of data we have for each bug, though we could display any that we choose easily enough. A little cleanup and we are done:

```php
    // always disconnect!
    $db->disconnect();
}
?>
```

A sample output corresponding to just hitting the Submit button without touching the selectboxes looks like the following:

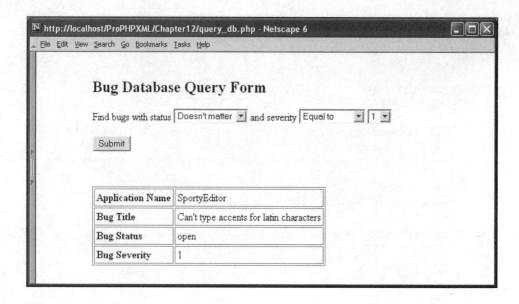

Database to XML

We have gone through an example where we have XML data that we wish to have in a database storage format. The other case of interest is the reverse situation. Namely, where we have data in a database and we want to put that into an XML format. Many databases such as Oracle, SQL Server, and Virtuoso can do this by themselves. However, we are using MySQL here, so we'll need some help from PHP to get the job done.

Fortunately for us, there's a PEAR class that does exactly what we want. The xml_sql2xml package can be downloaded from http://php.chregu.tv/sql2xml/.

This is a fairly large and complicated class, but we are going to go over some of its basic functionality. In a nutshell, it transforms SQL queries into well-formed XML documents. Of course, to take information from a database and put it into XML, we must first have a database of information. We'll create two new tables for this example, the first of which, authors, should contain the following:

```
+-----------+-------------------+---------------+---------------------+
| author_id | author_name       | year_of_birth | place_of_residence  |
+-----------+-------------------+---------------+---------------------+
|         1 | Natasha Roseberry |          1980 | San Francisco       |
|         2 | Chris Maier       |          1974 | Tokyo               |
|         3 | Ann Moreno        |          1980 | Santa Barbara       |
|         4 | Chris Lea         |          1975 | Los Angeles         |
+-----------+-------------------+---------------+---------------------+
```

Next create a table called `books` and put the following into it:

```
+---------+-----------+----------------------------------+------------------+
| book_id | author_id | book_name                        | publication_year |
+---------+-----------+----------------------------------+------------------+
|       1 |         4 | Beginning PHP4                   |             2000 |
|       2 |         3 | Party Girls Rule                 |             2001 |
|       3 |         1 | Everyday People                  |             1998 |
|       4 |         2 | How to Eat Sushi                 |             1997 |
|       5 |         1 | Working Women                    |             1999 |
|       6 |         3 | Ann's Guide to Santa Barbara     |             1999 |
+---------+-----------+----------------------------------+------------------+
```

Now we have two tables that are linked by means of the `author_id` attribute. The reason that we've set this up this way will become apparent when we get to a more complicated example.

Non-Nested Query

For the moment, however, we will just do a very simple example. Despite its lack of complexity, it does nicely illustrate how powerful the `xml_sql2xml` class is. We'll only need two methods from the class for this example:

Method	Description
`object xml_sql2xml($dsn)`	Constructor. Takes a DSN in the same format as the PEAR database class.
`string getxml($sql)`	Public method that takes a SQL query, and returns XML data that is based on the results.

To begin with, put the `sql2xml.php` file in the `classes` directory. Then, create a new file called `simple_sql2xml.php`. The start of the file is straightforward:

```php
<?php
header("Content-type: text/plain");
require_once("classes/sql2xml.php");
// database variables
$dbname = "book_db";
$dbuser = "root";
$dbpass = "";
$dbserver = "localhost";

// create our dsn
$dsn = "mysql://$dbuser:$dbpass@$dbserver/$dbname";
```

Again, we're setting the content type to `text/plain` to avoid nasty interpretation.

Next, we instantiate our object and perform the query using the `getxml()` method. This will give us the XML data that we are looking for:

```
// instantiate new object
$sql2xml = new xml_sql2xml($dsn);

// perform query and get XML data
$xml_data = $sql2xml->getxml("SELECT * FROM books");
```

The variable $xml_data is now a string containing an XML document. Unfortunately, the xml_sql2xml class does not do a very good job of adding things like line breaks and indentation to make the XML easily readable. Let's do a little regular expression magic to help ourselves out in this regard:

```
// need to clean up the XML so that we can read it easily
$replace_tags = array("/<root>/", "/<result>/",
                      "/<row>/", "/(<\/\w+>)/");
$replace_with = array("$0\n", "$0\n", "$0\n", "$0\n");
$xml_data = preg_replace($replace_tags, $replace_with, $xml_data);
```

All we are doing here is introducing linefeeds after the tags <root>, <result>, <row>, and after any closing tag. Now that it's presentable, we will print out the corrected output:

```
// see what we got
print ($xml_data);
?>
```

If everything worked properly, then the output should look like this:

```
<?xml version="1.0"?>
<root>
<result>
<row>
<book_id>1</book_id>
<author_id>4</author_id>
<book_name>Beginning PHP4</book_name>
<publication_year>2000</publication_year>
</row>
<row>
<book_id>2</book_id>
<author_id>3</author_id>
<book_name>Party Girls Rule</book_name>
<publication_year>2001</publication_year>
</row>
<row>
<book_id>3</book_id>
<author_id>1</author_id>
<book_name>Everyday People</book_name>
<publication_year>1998</publication_year>
</row>
<row>
<book_id>4</book_id>
<author_id>2</author_id>
<book_name>How to Eat Sushi</book_name>
<publication_year>1997</publication_year>
```

```
    </row>
    <row>
    <book_id>5</book_id>
    <author_id>1</author_id>
    <book_name>Working Women</book_name>
    <publication_year>1999</publication_year>
    </row>
    <row>
    <book_id>6</book_id>
    <author_id>3</author_id>
    <book_name>Ann's Guide to Santa Barbara</book_name>
    <publication_year>1999</publication_year>
    </row>
    </result>
    </root>
```

Quite an impressive result considering how little work was involved. With a small amount of setup and a simple query, we have a nicely made XML document from our database query.

Notice that the root element of the document is called `<root>`, and that the `<result>` and `<row>` tags were generated without us specifying them. Fortunately, xml_sql2xml does provide a way to adjust these. In the case of the `<root>` element, the xml_sql2xml() constructor method takes an optional second argument that sets the value. Also, the class provides a SetOptions() method that takes an array as its argument and can be used to change the names of the `<result>` and `<row>` elements.

Try changing the line with the constructor to:

```
// instantiate new object
$sql2xml = new xml_sql2xml($dsn, "books_table");
```

Immediately underneath this, add the following lines:

```
// options for <result> and <row> elements
$options = array(tagNameResult => "books", tagNameRow => "book_entry");
$sql2xml->SetOptions($options);
```

Then rerun the script and examine the output to see that the appropriate element names have been changed.

A Nested Query

Recall that we originally set up two distinct tables, and for good reason. When using MySQL, the xml_sql2xml class is smart enough to know how to nest the resulting XML document when performing operations such as a left join. Based on this, we should be able to construct a SQL query that will give us each author, and then within that author's data the data for each of the books they have written. Let's try it out.

Copy the original `simple_sql2xml.php` file to a new file called `nested_sql2xml.php`. We'll only need to change one line to get this example to work. Find the line that contains the SQL query and change it to the following:

```
// perform query and get XML data
$xml_data = $sql2xml->getxml("SELECT * FROM authors LEFT JOIN books
                             ON authors.author_id =
                             books.author_id");
```

That's it. Run the script and examine the output. We'll show it here with some nice indenting to see what we've come up with:

```xml
<?xml version="1.0"?>
<root>
  <result>
    <row>
      <author_id>1</author_id>
      <author_name>Natasha Roseberry</author_name>
      <year_of_birth>1970</year_of_birth>
      <place_of_residence>San Fransicso</place_of_residence>
      <row>
        <book_id>3</book_id>
        <author_id>1</author_id>
        <book_name>Everyday People</book_name>
        <publication_year>1998</publication_year>
      </row>
      <row>
        <book_id>5</book_id>
        <author_id>1</author_id>
        <book_name>Working Women</book_name>
        <publication_year>1999</publication_year>
      </row>
    </row>
    <row>
      <author_id>2</author_id>
      <author_name>Chris Maier</author_name>
      <year_of_birth>1974</year_of_birth>
      <place_of_residence>Tokyo</place_of_residence>
      <row>
        <book_id>4</book_id>
        <author_id>2</author_id>
        <book_name>How to Eat Sushi</book_name>
        <publication_year>1997</publication_year>
      </row>
    </row>
    <row>
      <author_id>3</author_id>
      <author_name>Ann Moreno</author_name>
      <year_of_birth>1980</year_of_birth>
      <place_of_residence>Santa Barbara</place_of_residence>
      <row>
        <book_id>2</book_id>
        <author_id>3</author_id>
        <book_name>Party Girls Rule</book_name>
        <publication_year>2001</publication_year>
      </row>
      <row>
```

```
          <book_id>6</book_id>
          <author_id>3</author_id>
          <book_name>Ann's Guide to Santa Barbara</book_name>
          <publication_year>1999</publication_year>
        </row>
      </row>
      <row>
        <author_id>4</author_id>
        <author_name>Chris Lea</author_name>
        <year_of_birth>1975</year_of_birth>
        <place_of_residence>Los Angeles</place_of_residence>
        <row>
          <book_id>1</book_id>
          <author_id>4</author_id>
          <book_name>Beginning PHP4</book_name>
          <publication_year>2000</publication_year>
        </row>
      </row>
    </result>
</root>
```

So the result is exactly as we had hoped. We have an XML document where the data for each of the books an author has written is nested under the data for the author. Now, let's ask the question, "what if I didn't want the data to be nested?". Well, we can use the SetOptions() method again to tell the object what we want. Add the following lines before the line where we call the getxml() method:

```
$options = array(nested => FALSE);
$sql2xml->SetOptions($options);
```

After rerunning the script, the start of the output will now look like this (indentation added again):

```
<?xml version="1.0"?>
<root>
  <result>
    <row>
      <author_id>1</author_id>
      <author_name>Natasha Roseberry</author_name>
      <year_of_birth>1970</year_of_birth>
      <place_of_residence>San Fransicso</place_of_residence>
      <book_id>3</book_id>
      <author_id>1</author_id>
      <book_name>Everyday People</book_name>
      <publication_year>1998</publication_year>
    </row>
    <row>
      <author_id>1</author_id>
      <author_name>Natasha Roseberry</author_name>
      <year_of_birth>1970</year_of_birth>
      <place_of_residence>San Fransicso</place_of_residence>
      <book_id>5</book_id>
      <author_id>1</author_id>
      <book_name>Working Women</book_name>
```

```
        <publication_year>1999</publication_year>
    </row>
    ...
```

The xml_sql2xml class has a number of other methods that give it more advanced functionality. However, these examples cover the most commonly used implementations.

Summary

We've looked at methods for getting XML data into and out of databases. To start off, we talked about some common ways that XML is stored in RDBMS systems. Then we examined and employed a technique for extracting XML data from our bug_list.xml document. Once we had it, we put this data into a MySQL table, and built a lightweight query application that lets us search for various kinds of bugs.

Moving to the flip side of the coin, we started to work with the powerful xml_sql2xml class that is part of the PHP PEAR libraries. This made it fairly simple to take data from our database and generate XML documents. In fact, we saw a variety of examples that let us choose the structure of the resulting XML. This should set you well on your way in terms of building applications where it is necessary to take legacy data from a database and publish it as XML. In the next chapter, we'll look at different options for storing XML.

13

XML Storage

In the previous chapters of the book we covered XML fundamentals, derivatives, and the various XML APIs. We have learned how to parse XML documents (DOM and SAX), how to modify them (DOM), how to query them (XPath), and how to transform them (XSLT).

In this chapter we will detail how to store the documents and how to search/retrieve the documents to be processed.

Analysis of an XML Storage Solution

An XML storage solution must provide methods to store and retrieve XML documents. It could also provide functions to organize documents, search for documents, and search for text in documents.

The store/retrieve and the optional organizational features form the core of an XML storage solution. Also, a storage solution can implement one or several APIs to access and process the documents that can be used to query, modify, or transform the document from the repository without needing to retrieve the document and process it in memory. This has two clear advantages:

❑ Since the storage solution provides the API, we don't need an implementation of the API in the application

❑ In case of huge XML documents, it would be better to use APIs based on secondary storage than resident-memory solutions, since we may not have enough resources to process the whole document in memory

Some of the APIs that might be implemented by XML storage solutions are:

- XPath –http://www.w3.org/TR/xpath/
- DOM – http://www.w3.org/DOM/
- SAX –http://www.saxproject.org/
- XSLT – http://www.w3.org/Style/XSL/
- XQuery – http://www.w3.org/XML/Query/
- XMLDB:XUpdate – http://www.xmldb.org/xupdate/index.html
- XQL – http://ibiblio.org/xql/xql-tutorial.html

> *When choosing an XML storage product, verify which APIs are implemented by the product and check that it can be used for the application.*

Another feature to consider for an XML storage solution is how the database/repository is accessed. For instance, can we use HTTP to access the repository or does it provide a way to access the database using XML-RPC or SOAP, and so on.

Since XML is a standard that can be used from any programming language and since it is great for data exchange, it is probable that the XML storage solution is going to be accessed from several different programming languages; the more access methods the better the solution will be. It is best to use SOAP or XML-RPC and HTTP as ways to access the repository. ODBC and WebDAV are other common interfaces that may be nice to have in an XML repository.

A XML storage solution can be implemented in two ways:

- We can build our own storage solution
- We can use a product (examples include the Apache Foundation's Xindice and MS Access)

Since the status of the market in XML storage products is still nascent it makes sense to study how to build such a product. We'll cover both alternatives in this chapter.

Building our Own Storage Solution

It makes sense to build our own storage solution when we can't find a product with the features which are needed for our application or if our storage problem is simple and we need a customized approach.

Building a complete storage solution for XML documents can be broken down into:

- Storage of XML documents
- Organization of XML documents
- Implementation of APIs to access and query documents

Storing XML Documents

The first decision we have to make, when building an XML storage solution, is to decide how XML documents will be stored in our repository. We need to design a persistent representation of an XML document. The options are:

❑   Using text files to store documents

❑   Using a relational database to store documents

❑   Using special file structures to store documents

Using Text Files to Store Documents

This is the simplest approach and one that we have been using so far to store our XML documents. With this approach the implementation of store/retrieve mechanisms is trivial since we only need to read/write files from the file system.

The advantages of this approach are obvious – the solution is simple and the implementation is very easy. The big disadvantage is that this method doesn't provide any help to implement APIs since it doesn't organize XML content at all. We can implement or use a SAX parser if we want but other APIs must be handled at the application level by retrieving the whole document in memory and processing it there. Thus this method is not very useful when dealing with very large documents or if we want to provide a storage solution with a variety of APIs as choices for the processing application.

Text files however are useful in solutions specially designed to handle a large number of documents. Here the focus is on finding documents instead of processing them.

Using a Relational Database to Store Documents

The second approach is to use a relational database to store XML documents. RDBMSs provide a lot of features that can be useful to our implementation. The first advantage of using a relational database to store XML documents is that we immediately inherit DBMS features like:

❑   Replication

❑   Backup and recovery

❑   Indexes

❑   SQL language for querying

❑   Administration tools

XML also allows us to feature meta data tags. When using an RDBMS to store XML documents we have several options depending on how we represent the XML document using relational tables:

❑   **Mapping at document level** (XML documents as Blobs)
    Mapping at the document level means storing XML documents as BLOBs (Binary Large Objects) in the relational database. A BLOB is an opaque collection of bytes containing data. It is unstructured information and can be manipulated as an opaque object, but cannot be inspected, queried, and so on. From a practical standpoint, a file in a file system is a BLOB. In fact, any storage mechanism that treats XML data as a single, large entity and does not expose the XML at a greater level of detail fits the category. This is very similar to using text files with the difference that an RDBMS is used instead of the file system to store and retrieve files.

For example we can map the XML documents to the following relational table:

Column Name	Type	Description
DocumentId	int(11) (PRI)	ID of the document
Filename	varchar(200)	Filename of the XML document
Data	longblob	XML data

This is the simplest structure we can use. We may add meta data such as a timestamp, author, and so on.

Storing a document implies issuing a SQL INSERT statement to the DBMS while retrieving a document is achieved using a SELECT statement. Indexes can be used to speed up the storing and retrieving processes. We can have similar functionality in the file system. In addition to this we can add resources to undo (rollback) the insertion or deletion of a document or add meta data in a separate column of the table.

The 'documents as BLOBS' approach has the same disadvantages as the text files mode – we don't have a useful structure to implement APIs. The APIs can only be implemented at the application level by parsing the documents in memory.

❑ **Mapping at element level** (the Edge table approach)
Mapping at the element level is another way of using a DBMS to store XML documents. What we require is a relational representation of an XML document. This should allow us to implement queries and process APIs. API methods can then be implemented using SQL statements to traverse and use the relational representation of the document.

Since XML documents are hierarchical, mapping them to a relational structure is no trivial task. There are many mappings but we'll look at one of them to see how hierarchical data can be mapped onto a relational structure – the Edge table approach.

The Edge Table Approach

Daniela Florescu and Donald Kossman first described the Edge table approach in a paper titled *A Performance Evaluation of Alternative Mapping Schemes for Storing XML Data in a Relational Database*. This paper can be viewed at ftp://ftp.inria.fr/INRIA/publication/publi-pdf/RR/RR-3680.pdf. The idea is to view the XML document as a directed graph and represent graph edges as rows in a relational table. The best way to understand this idea is by an example.

Let's use the following XML document as an example:

```
<staff>
  <person ssn='1'>
    <name>John</name>
    <age>27</age>
  </person>
  <person ssn='2'>
    <name>Peter</name>
    <age>28</age>
  </person>
</staff>
```

We can represent the XML file as a directed graph where nodes represent XML elements and edges represent relationships between the elements. For example:

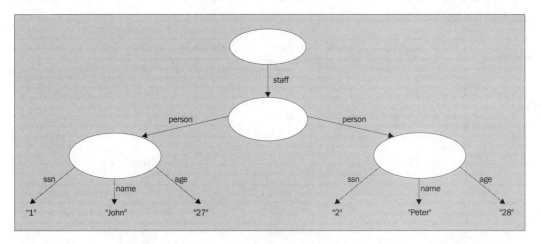

If we assign an id to each node we can represent the graph using the following table called the Edge table:

Source	Order	Tag	TargetId	Data
1	1	staff	2	
2	1	person	3	
2	2	person	4	
3	0	ssn	5	
3	1	name	6	
3	2	age	7	
4	0	ssn	8	
4	1	name	9	
4	2	age	10	
5	0	NULL	0	1
6	0	NULL	0	John
7	0	NULL	0	27
8	0	NULL	0	2
9	0	NULL	0	Peter
10	0	NULL	0	28

If we **inline** (a simple lookup on the edge) the nodes that only have text data as the data element of their parents, and if we represent attribute values as the data of attribute nodes, we get this representation (that is shorter than the previous one):

Source	Order	Tag	TargetId	Data
1	1	staff	2	
2	1	person	3	
2	2	person	4	
3	0	ssn	0	1
3	1	name	0	John
3	2	age	0	27
4	0	ssn	0	2
4	1	name	0	Peter
4	2	age	0	28

The primary key for this table is (source, order).

Elements that contain only text are inlined in the parent node. This means that they don't have a source node in the Edge table. We save rows with this technique.

For elements with mixed content, a special tag __TEXT__ can be used to store the text content for the element. Attributes are stored as order 0 tags where the attribute name is the tag name and the attribute value is the data. An **order 0 tag** is a tag that's not in the ordered list of child nodes for a given node (children are numbered starting from 1).

The order column in the Edge table is important as it preserves the document order of the XML document so we can reconstruct the XML document as it was inserted. Several XML documents can be stored in the same Edge table. A separate table can be used to link the document name and other meta data with the document source node (1 in this example).

The authors of the Edge table structure recommend indexing the table by the tag name to speed up queries that select elements from the table looking for an element by name.

We can use the structure to store XML documents and re-generate the original documents from the structure. We can also use the structure to implement any querying and modification APIs that we may need. For example we can implement a persistent DOM structure or XPath. If performance is an issue we may build indexes or secondary tables to help the job that the APIs need to be done.

> **When representing XML documents on disk, keep in mind that document order should be remembered so we can reconstruct the document as it was inserted. In XML, the order of elements does matter.**

Object Relational Mapping

Many mappings used to store XML documents in a database are based on objects. In order to represent objects in a relational database we use an **object relational** mapping.

In an object relational mapping each object will be assigned a unique id and be represented using relational tables. The most standard way to produce an object relational mapping is the following:

❑ Each class will be represented as a table. We use a table column for each property an object of the given class may have.

❑ Each object will receive a unique id. All the tables will have the id as a column.

❑ Objects will be mapped as rows in the table. The value of object properties will be the value of the table column.

❑ Inheritance is represented storing the object in two tables – one for the base class and one for the derived class. Since the object will have the same id in both tables we can recover base properties easily from the derived class.

For example, let's use the following classes:

```
class Person
{
    var $name;
    var $age1;
}

class Employee extends Person
{
    var $employee_number;
}
```

We can map the classes to relational tables as follows:

Person Table	
Column Name	**Description**
id	Unique id of the object
name	Name property for the object
age	Age property for the object

Employee Table	
Column Name	**Description**
id	Unique id of the object (person object)
employee number	Employee number

Instances are mapped as rows in the tables, for example:

```
//constructor receives name, age and employee number)
$e1 = new Employee("John", 27, 99817);

$e2 = new Employee("Peter", 28, 99818);
```

is represented as:

Person Table

id	name	age
0	John	27
1	Peter	28

Employee Table

id	employee_number
0	99817
1	99818

Object relational mappings for XML storage must be based in an object model of the XML document. For example, we can get the DOM model to represent XML documents using object relational mapping.

We'll look at an example of mapping DOM objects to relational tables using the same XML document that we used in the Edge table example:

```
<staff>
  <person ssn='1'>
    <name>John</name>
    <age>27</age>
  </person>
  <person ssn='2'>
    <name>Peter</name>
    <age>28</age>
  </person>
</staff>
```

Using the DOM standard the document would be represented as the following tree of objects:

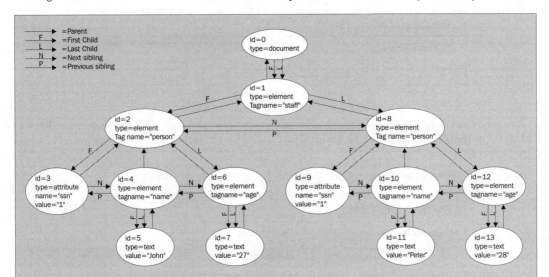

To store the objects in a database each object must receive a unique id, that's why we added an id property to the objects in the diagram.

If we decide to use DOM as our object model we'll have to map each DOM class into a relational table. The DOM standard defines several classes, and we'll use just a few in our example, a complete DOM mapping must consider implementing all the classes as tables.

These are some of the tables used to map DOM classes to a relational database:

The Nodes Table	
Column Name	**Description**
id	Unique id of the object (node)
type	Type of node (Document, Element, Text, Comment, CData_section, Processing_Instruction, Entity_reference, Notation, Attribute)
parent	Id of the parent node, can be null only for document nodes
first_child	First child node id or NULL
next_child	Next child node id or NULL
previous_sibling	Previous sibling node id or NULL
next_sibling	Next sibling node id or NULL

The Nodes table represents DOM nodes and the tree. Note how the pointers in the diagram are represented as references to object ids in this mapping.

The following classes/tables are derived from the node class. This table represents element nodes in DOM:

The Element Nodes Table	
Column Name	**Description**
id	Node id
tagname	Tagname

Element nodes have a `tagname` associated, some mappings might implement the `tagname` inlined as a column in the nodes table but since not all DOM nodes have a `tagname` this is the pure implementation.

This table represents DOM documents:

The Document Table	
Column Name	**Description**
id	Node id
Filename	Filename of the document
DocType	DTD of the document
Other meta data	Other meta data that may be interesting for the storage application

We'll have a row in this table for every document stored in the database. Note that since documents are also nodes we can get the root of a document by selecting the `first_child` or `last_child` column from nodes where the node id is equal to the document id.

This table represents attributes; we store the node id, the name of the attribute, and the value:

The Attribute Nodes Table	
Column Name	**Description**
id	Node id
name	Name of the attribute
value	Attribute value

Text nodes table will store DOM text nodes:

The Text Nodes table	
Column Name	**Description**
id	Node id
data	Text value

The following DOM classes, among others, were not mapped in the example but should be mapped in a complete mapping – DOM processing instruction, DOM CDATA section, DOM comment, DOM entity reference, DOM notation, and so on.

We stated before that many variants are admissible; many implementations tend to unnormalize some of the tables adding extra information that can be NULL to reduce the number of tables that have to be accessed or joined for a query. For example, we can add tagname to the Nodes table and avoid using an Element nodes table.

In our example the tables would be populated like this:

Nodes						
id	type	parent	first_child	last_child	previous_sibling	next_sibling
0	Document	NULL	1	1	NULL	NULL
1	Element	0	2	8	NULL	NULL
2	Element	1	3	6	NULL	8
3	Attribute	2	NULL	NULL	NULL	4
4	Element	2	5	5	3	6
5	Text	4	NULL	NULL	NULL	NULL
6	Element	2	7	7	4	NULL
7	Text	6	NULL	NULL	NULL	NULL
8	Element	1	9	12	2	NULL
9	Attribute	8	NULL	NULL	NULL	10
10	Element	8	11	11	9	12
11	Text	10	NULL	NULL	NULL	NULL
12	Element	8	13	13	10	NULL
13	Text	12	NULL	NULL	NULL	NULL

Element Nodes	
id	tagname
1	staff
2	person
4	name
6	age
8	person
10	name
12	age

Document Nodes		
id	filename	(other meta data)
0	staff.xml	Other meta data here (not relevant for the example, for example DTD, etc)

Attribute Nodes		
id	name	value
3	ssn	1
9	ssn	2

Text Nodes	
id	data
5	John
7	27
11	Peter
13	28

With this mapping many APIs can be implemented. For instance, a persistent DOM API will be very simple to implement by coding DOM methods as stored procedures or functions using SQL queries.

Using Special File Structures to Store Documents

Since text files are meant to store text and relational databases to store relational data, we may think about creating a special file structure designed for XML files. Many native XML databases use this **model-based** approach.

What is a Special File Structure?

A special file structure is a proprietary file format designed to store XML documents. These formats use b- trees, b+ trees, hash tables, or proprietary data structures that are mapped to disk thus creating what is called a file structure. Normally, XML documents are represented in a tree format.

Let's look at an example of a special file structure that can be used to store XML files. We'll represent each XML document using a binary file with variable-length registers. Each register will represent an element of the XML document. Elements will be stored one after the other in a binary file. Text nodes and attributes will be inlined in their parent element nodes.

Each element will have the following structure:

Length	Length of the record representing the element
Data	Data representing the element, a list of comma separated items
Structure:	tag = name (name of the element's tag)
	parent = offset (offset of the parent element)
	prev = offset (offset of the preceding sibling)
	next = offset (offset of the following sibling)
	firstchild = offset (offset of the first child of the document)
	lastchild = offset (offset of the last child of the document)
	att = attribute list (list of attributes in the format – "key"="value", "key2"="value")
	text = text data (if the element has text content)

We'll keep a doubly-linked list of siblings, and we'll also double link parent-child relationships. This will be the structure that can be used to traverse the file. We'll use the offsets in the binary file as keys. Let's work again with our sample document:

```
<staff>
  <person ssn='1'>
    <name>John</name>
    <age>27</age>
  </person>
  <person ssn='2'>
    <name>Peter</name>
    <age>28</age>
  </person>
</staff>
```

Our example document can be represented as shown below:

```
Offset: 0
length=75,staff,parent=null,prev=null,next=null,firstchild=75,lastchild=125
Offset: 75
length=50,person,parent=0,prev=null,next=125,firstchild=177,lastchild=217,
att=("ssn"="1")
Offset: 125
length=52,person,parent=0,prev=75,next=null,firstchild=247,lastchild=282,
att=("ssn"="2")
Offset: 177
length=40,name,parent=75,prev=null,next=null,firstchild=null,lastchild=null,
text=John
Offset: 217
length=30,age,parent=75,prev=null,next=null,firstchild=null,lastchild=null,
text=27
Offset: 247
length=35,name,parent=125,prev=null,next=null,firstchild=null,
lastchild=null,text=Peter
Offset: 282
length=30,age,parent=125,prev=null,next=null,firstchild=null,lastchild=null,
text=28
```

Note that the lengths and offsets aren't real, just created for the example.

This is similar to object relational mapping. We store objects in a file writing one object after the other. The object id is the offset where the object can be found on the file. Each object has a defined structure that allows us to retrieve the object from the file, given its id.

For example, if we want to retrieve the object at offset 177, we should read 40 bytes since the length is 40. We read the 40 bytes and parse them knowing how objects were stored on the file, to discover that this is a <name> element whose parent is the node at offset 75 – the element has a text node with value John, but it has no child elements or siblings.

The binary file representing the XML document is the concatenation of all the records. We can traverse the document starting from the root element at register 0 and then jump to the proper offsets following the links. In this structure parent-child relationships as well as sibling relationships are doubly-linked.

It is easy to traverse a document with this structure. Also, elements can be easily inserted by adding a register and then changing the pointers as needed. Modifications and deletions can be harder since the whole file may have to be rewritten to reflect the proper changes. This structure is a good way to map documents for queries but it isn't as good for modifications.

When using a proprietary representation, storing a document implies parsing it and writing it to disk with the selected structure. Reading implies reading the structure and regenerating the XML document. One should remember to follow the document order as explained earlier. Querying and modification APIs can be built on top of this structure since we have a way to traverse the document without reading it into memory.

This example introduced a simple way to store XML documents using a proprietary format and many improvements can be made. We may use b- trees, b+ trees, and hash tables to construct complex and powerful representations of documents and indexes can be added to speed up queries and processing depending on the APIs that will be implemented on top of the structure.

Implementing XML Storage

We've seen how XML documents can be stored as text files, relational information in RDBMSs, or as a special file structure. Once a storage strategy is decided it will be necessary to implement a way to parse documents from files or memory to the storage media and APIs, allowing us to manipulate the documents from the disk.

Parsing usually implies using SAX parsers because XML storage solutions are specially useful or necessary for processing very large documents. A SAX parser can parse an XML file without needing many resources since the file is processed using sequential reads of fixed-length buffers. As SAX events are generated we should collect and store the proper information for our storage solution.

APIs such as DOM, XSLT, XPath, and XQuery can be implemented directly over the storage solution giving persistent APIs for XML processing. Documents are never retrieved as a whole into memory; instead they are accessed and modified from the storage media. This is particularly useful for very large and huge documents where a memory-based query or modification would be very difficult since there might not be enough memory/processing resources to handle such a big document.

Organizing XML Documents

We've seen several approaches to store XML documents in a repository; the next question is how to organize the repository. The simplest approach is to use a single repository without any organization to store all the documents. This may have some appeal for the sake of simplicity but it leads to a very heterogeneous and unclean storage solution (a bag of documents as opposed to a filing cabinet). We won't be able to classify or organize our XML documents and performance of the repository will deteriorate each time a new document is added. Imagine a large number of short documents describing user accounts mixed with huge XML files describing database dumps. If we want to locate one of the big documents we will have to scan through a large number of other documents that don't have any relationship with the document we intend to view. A bag of documents is certainly not very good as a structure for our storage solution.

So we need to give the repository some structure. The most accepted approach is to use **collections** as a hierarchical method to organize documents. A **root** collection is the starting point of the repository. The root collection may contain XML documents as well as other collections. Collections can then contain documents or sub-collections and so on. This organization can be viewed as similar to the organization of the file system where directories can contain files or sub-directories allowing us to hierarchically organize our files:

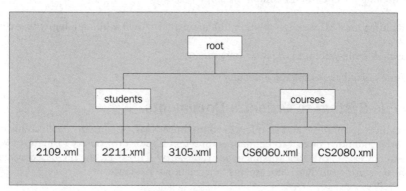

Here we have a repository organized using 3 collections – the root collection, a students collection, and a courses collection. Documents are stored in their respective collections.

When properly organized, documents can be indexed, which allows the user to retrieve documents faster from the repository. The most common indexing strategy is **full text indexing** where documents are indexed using the terms found in the document as index keys. If documents are full text indexed we can retrieve, for instance, all the documents containing the word 'tree' or a combination of words. Many RDBMSs support full text indexing.

Other indexes can be built as well, for example we may associate each document in the repository with a **key** and index documents by key, thus allowing us to make a quick retrieval of a document given its key.

A good organization of documents should allow us to locate documents by a given key, to search for documents that contain some particular text, provide quick access to a document, and so on.

> *The XMLDB API, used by the Xindice XML database, (http://www.xmldb.org/xapi/index.html) is a standard API for accessing XML repositories and is based on collections.*

This is a list of the features that we can add to our repository using collections and eventually indexes:

- ❑ Creating a collection
- ❑ Listing collections
- ❑ Removing a collection (recursively or not)
- ❑ Listing documents in a collection
- ❑ Counting number of documents in a collection
- ❑ Retrieving a document from a particular collection
- ❑ Storing a document in a collection
- ❑ Storing a document with a given key in some collection
- ❑ Retrieving a document by key from a collection
- ❑ Creating an index on a set of documents using an XML element as key
- ❑ Searching for documents containing some text

If we are building an XML storage solution, the main alternatives while implementing collections are:

- ❑ Using the file system to organize documents
- ❑ Using a database to organize documents

Using the File System to Organize Documents

The file system is an intuitive and simple way to organize XML documents. Collections can be mapped into directories and documents can be mapped into text files or proprietary formats (or whatever format we choose to represent XML documents in our repository). However, the file-based system is not very useful if we are storing our XML documents in a relational database.

The only important implementation detail when using the file system is to abstract file system functions in a way that allows us to easily adapt the repository to work on other operating systems. In the event that we directly tie our code to the file system functions we may have portability issues under different operating systems and that is undesirable.

It might be worthwhile to take note of the limitations of the file system during the design process itself:

- ❑ File system constraints can affect the XML storage solution (for instance, maximum number of files in a directory or the size of individual files)

- ❑ Security and access control will depend on the file system

- ❑ If we don't use an index, performance may depend on the file system

- ❑ If we don't use indexes, the level of meta data that we can use for each document would depend on the file system

Xindice is an example of a native XML database that uses directories to organize XML documents (documents are stored in a proprietary format).

Using a Database to Organize Documents

A database can be used to organize documents into collections. This allows us to use as much meta data as we need to organize documents. We can also define indexes without special implementations using RDBMS index creation features such as the CREATE INDEX statement.

> **Indexes can greatly increase performance when searching for documents from a particular collection or by a given key especially if we manage a huge number of documents in our repository.**

While a database can be used to organize documents stored as text files or using proprietary formats it sounds comical to use an RDBMS to just organize documents. Frequently we'll see that databases are used only when XML documents are also stored in a relational database. If documents are stored using text files or proprietary formats we may not want to use a database to organize documents.

As an example we can use the following relational structure to implement collections. First, the Collections table:

Collection Id	Collection Name	Parent Collection
1	root	NULL
2	students	1
3	courses	1

Now the `Documents` table where each document must belong to a collection indicated with the `CollectionId` field:

DocumentId	CollectionId	Filename	Key (opt)	Timestamp (opt)	Other meta data (opt)
1	2	7506.xml	7506		
2	2	php_course .xml	php4		
3	1	jwilliams. xml	John Williams		

Functions to store, retrieve, and search for documents will be implemented as SQL queries, and indexes can be used to optimize those queries. Sometimes XML querying APIs can be combined with SQL queries to retrieve data from XML documents.

APIs

Selection of the right API is of prime importance regardless of whether we use a product for our XML storage solution or if we are building our own solution. The API must provide suitable access and processing functionality to our solution. The APIs will define what we can and can't do with our stored XML documents. The greater the number of APIs implemented by our solution, the greater the flexibility to query and modify the documents stored in the repository.

These are some of the APIs that can be found on XML storage solutions:

❑ XPath

❑ DOM

❑ SAX

❑ XSLT

❑ XQuery

❑ XMLDB:XUpdate

XPath

XPath is a standard from the W3C to select and access parts of XML documents. XPath is the result of an effort to provide a common syntax and semantics for functionality shared between XSLT and XPointer. Storage solutions implement XPath as a query mechanism for documents. There are a lot of new languages emerging for queries but XPath is still one of the most accepted languages so it is present as a basic tool in many products.

Chapter 7 explains the XPath standard in detail.

DOM

DOM is a standard from the W3C to parse and process XML documents. It is based on the DOM representation of an XML document – a tree of objects defined by the standard.

DOM is a good way to modify XML documents in a repository. Persistent DOM implementations are especially useful when dealing with large documents since in-memory DOM parsing can be a heavy resource-consuming task.

Chapter 6 covers the DOM standard in detail.

SAX

Though SAX originally started out as a project for Java, it has gained wide acceptance as a core framework for parsing XML documents. SAX is an event-driven parser that allows a programmer to interpret XML files. Though SAX can handle very large files, it has limited capabilities for manipulating the actual content of the XML content because it only reads equal-length sections of the document at a time. Thus, it is impossible to add new nodes to the XML tree when the entire structure of the tree is not known.

Chapter 5 details SAX.

XSLT

XSLT is a standard from the W3C to transform XML documents. It can be used to query, modify, and transform XML documents into arbitrary formats. XSLT also uses XPath, which has a natural subset that can be used for matching (testing whether or not a node matches a pattern).

An XSLT API can be very powerful in a repository since XSLT can be used to query, update, or transform XML documents. If a solution has to implement only one API, XSLT would be a good choice. It is worthwhile to check that the repository implements disk-based or memory-based XSLT processing, since the memory-based approach can take a lot of resources for very large documents.

Chapter 8 covers XSLT in detail.

XQuery

XQuery is the proposal from the W3C for querying XML documents. XQuery is a declarative language based on XPath and XML schema data types. XQuery is still emerging as a query language for XML documents but being a W3C specification it will probably be used in many applications.

We'll make a short introduction to XQuery in this chapter.

Basic XQuery Expressions

XQuery is based on expressions. The simplest XQuery expression is a simple XPath expression, for example:

```
//name
```

This is a valid XPath expression and as such it is a valid and complete XQuery expression. It will return all <name> elements in a context that is defined by the querying engine. For example, in a certain context it would return an XML document, a collection of documents, or part of a document depending on the engine.

XQuery implements the document() function as an extension to XPath, to allow us to point to a specific XML document in case we need it for the query engine:

```
document("persons.xml")     //name
```

This will make the query engine return all <name> elements from persons.xml.

The results can be returned in any format that the query engine defines. Typically some form of XML is returned enclosing DOM nodes or something similar.

An XQuery expression can also be used to construct XML documents, for example:

```
<qualified-persons>
  {//person[age>25]}
</qualified-persons>
```

We can use variables bounded to XQuery expressions or XQuery expressions between { }.

FLWR Expressions

The really interesting part of XQuery is the use of **FLWR** (pronounced 'flower') expressions. FLWR is an acronym for 'For, Let, Where, Return' being a similar concept to 'SELECT, FROM, HAVING, WHERE' in SQL.

Here is the formal definition of a FLWR expression (from the W3C working draft):

```
FlwrExpr    ::= (ForClause | letClause)+ whereClause? returnClause
  ForClause    ::= 'FOR' Variable 'IN Expr (',' Variable IN Expr)*
  LetClause    ::= 'LET' Variable ':=' Expr (',' Variable := Expr)*
  WhereClause  ::= 'WHERE' Expr
  ReturnClause ::= 'RETURN' Expr
```

Using LET

The LET construction allows us to bind an XQuery expression to a variable. For example, our previous query (written using plain XPath) could be written as:

```
LET $result := //name
  RETURN
    $result
```

We assign a node-set containing all <name> elements to the $result variable and then return the variable as the result of the XQuery expression.

Using FOR

The FOR statement iterates through each node in a resulting node-set, binding each node to a variable, so we can get all the <name> elements in a document using the following XQuery expression:

```
FOR $result IN      //name
   return $result
```

Complete FLWR Expressions (Using Where and Return)

Let's analyze the following XQuery expression:

```
FOR $p IN document("bib.xml")     //publisher
LET $b := document("bib.xml")     //book[publisher = $p]
   WHERE count($b) > 100
      RETURN $p
```

The FOR statement generates a binding to $p of all the publishers in the bib.xml document, then for each $p:

❏   The LET statement selects all the books that where published for the $p publisher

❏   The WHERE statement filters the publisher if there are more than 100 books ($b)

So the expression will return a list of publishers (concatenation of $p variables) that have published more than 100 books.

We can use the distinct keyword to eliminate duplicates:

```
FOR $p IN distinct document("bib.xml")    //publisher
   LET $b := document("bib.xml)           //book[publisher = $p]
      WHERE count($b) > 100
         RETURN $p
```

FLWR expressions can also be used to compute joins of XML documents. Imagine we have an XML document called persons.xml with the following format:

```
<persons>
  <person>
    <name></name>
    <ssn></ssn>
    <address></address>
  </person>
  ...
</persons>
```

And we have a document called loans.xml where we register loans that were made:

```
<loans>
  <loan>
    <ssn></ssn>
    <amount><amount>
    ...
  </loan>
  ...
</loans>
```

We can use the following XQuery expression to list persons with loans of more than $100:

```
FOR $1 IN document("loans.xml")        //loan[amount > 100]
   FOR $p IN document("persons.xml")   //person[ssn = $1/ssn]
      RETURN
         <person>
            <ssn> { $p/ssn } </ssn>
            <name> { $p/name } </name>
            <amount> { $1/amount } </amount>
         </person>
```

The first FOR selects all the loans with amounts greater than $100, the second FOR selects persons matching the SSN of the first FOR, and then we just return a <person> element with the information we want from the persons.xml and loans.xml documents. Using nested FORs we can join as many documents as required.

This was just an introduction to XQuery. Since the standard is currently a working draft many things may change but FLWR expressions should remain as the fundamentals of the language. The available working draft describes more interesting features of XQuery such as lists, conditional statements (IFs), and data types.

XQuery Implementations

This is a list of available XQuery implementations taken from the W3C XQuery specification:

- **Cognetic Systems** – http://www.cogneticsystems.com/xquery/xquery.html

- **Enosys Markets** – http://www.enosysmarkets.com/products/xq.html

- **Fatdog** – http://www.fatdog.com/

- **Ipedo's XML Database v3.0** – http://www.ipedo.com/

- **IPSI-XQ** – http://xml.darmstadt.gmd.de/xquerydemo/

- **Lucent** – http://db.bell-labs.com/galax/

- **Microsoft** – http://xqueryservices.com/

- **OpenLink Software (Virtuoso Universal Server)** – http://demo.openlinksw.com:8890/xqdemo/

- **Oracle** – http://otn.oracle.com/tech/xml/xmldb/htdocs/xquery.html

- **Software AG** – http://developer.softwareag.com/tamino/quip/

- **X-Hive** – http://217.77.130.189/demos/xquery/index.html

- **XML Global** – http://www.xmlglobal.com/

- **SourceForge's Kweelt** – http://kweelt.sourceforge.net/ (open source)

- **SourceForge's XQuench** – http://xquench.sourceforge.net/ (open source)

- **Qexo (Kawa-Query)** – http://www.gnu.org/software/qexo/
  This open source tool compiles XQuery on-the-fly to Java byte codes; it is based on and is part of the Kawa framework

From the list presented above, there are a couple of interesting free implementations that can be used to test XQuery expressions and learn the XQuery standard.

Quip

Quip is a free program by Software AG, the creators of Tamino – a native XML database. This tool can be downloaded from Software AG's web site at http://developer.softwareag.com/tamino/quip/.

It is a Java application that can run on Windows or UNIX machines and allows us to test XQuery expressions against a list of sample XML documents or our own documents.

Kweelt

Kweelt is an open source implementation of the XQuery standard in Java (with some slight variations). It can be downloaded from http://kweelt.sourceforge.net/.

Once downloaded, we'll have a Java command-line application that can receive an XQuery query from a text file returning the result of the query to the standard output. For example, if we want to test the following query (from the W3C use-cases):

```
/*
List books published by Wrox Press after 1995, including their
year and title.
*/

<bib>
  FOR $book IN document("bib.xml")//book[ @year .>=. 1995 AND
                                publisher = "Wrox Press" ]
  RETURN <book year=$book/@year>$book/title</book>
</bib>
```

The bib.xml document must be found in the same directory where Kweelt is run.

We'd need to use the following command:

```
java xacute.quilt.Main Q1.qlt
```

and the result would be like this:

```
melpomenia:~/kwelt$ java xacute.quilt.Main Q1.qlt
<?xml version="1.0"?>
<bib>
  <book year="1999">
    <title>
      Professional PHP Programming
    </title>
  </book>
  <book year="2002">
    <title>
      Professional PHP4
    </title>
  </book>
</bib>
<!-- end of document -->
```

Further Information

Check the following resources to learn more about XQuery:

❑ The XQuery page at the W3C – http://www.w3.org/TR/xquery/

❑ An XQuery tutorial – http://www.brics.dk/~amoeller/XML/querying/languages.html

❑ A short introduction to XQuery – http://www.fatdog.com/XQuery_Intro.html

❑ XQuery use-cases – http://www.w3.org/TR/xmlquery-use-cases/
The use-cases are particularly useful since they show common XML querying problems and how they can be solved using XQuery.

XMLDB:XUpdate

XUpdate is also presented as a working draft. It is an initiative from the XMLDB group (http://www.xmldb.org/) to define modifications of XML documents.

It is useful to learn about XUpdate since the XML native database from the Apache software foundation (Xindice) uses XUpdate as its mechanism to modify XML documents. The working draft of the XUpdate specifications can be found at http://www.xmldb.org/xupdate/xupdate-wd.html.

Using XUpdate we define a modification to an XML document using, what else, XML. XUpdate uses XPath to locate sections of XML documents to be changed and supports the following operations:

❑ `<xupdate:insert-before>`
Creates an element before elements selected by an XPath expression

❑ `<xupdate:insert-after>`
Creates a child element after elements selected by an XPath expression

❑ `<xupdate:append>`
Adds a child after a list of elements selected by an XPath expression

❑ `<xupdate:remove>`
Removes elements selected by an XPath expression

❑ `<xupdate:rename>`
Renames elements selected by an XPath expression

XUpdate also has conditional statements (`IFs`), variables, and a `value-of` expression that can be used in XUpdate expressions.

Insert

XUpdate defines a syntax to create XML elements and attributes that can be added to XML documents. For example, we can generate an XML element as follows:

```
<xupdate:element name="foo">
  <name>Peter</name>
</xupdate:element>
```

This will create the element:

```
<foo>
  <name>Peter</name>
</foo>
```

Attributes can be created using a similar syntax:

```
<xupdate:element name="foo">
  <xupdate:attribute name="fid">2</xupdate:attribute>
</xupdate:element>
```

The expression will create:

```
<foo fid="2" />
```

We can also use `<xupdate:text>` to create text nodes, `<xupdate:comment>` to insert comments, and `<xupdate:processing-instruction>` to create processing instructions.

`<xupdate:insert-after>`, `<xupdate:insert-before>`, or `<xupdate-append>` can be used to add elements to an XML document. An XPath expression is used to locate the place where the new node will be added.

For example, if we have an XML document with a list of `<address>` elements we may add an address using the following expression:

```
<xupdate:append select="/addresses">
  <xupdate:element name="address">
    <city>Lyon</city>
    <street>...</street>
    <number>...</number>
    <zip>...</zip>
  </xupdate:element>
</xupdate:append>
```

The `<xupdate:append>` element is used to append an element to a node-set. There's a mandatory `select` attribute that must select a list of nodes where the new element will be added.

Update

The `<xupdate:update>` element can be used to change an existing node, for example:

```
<xupdate:update select="/foo[1]/name">
  John
</xupdate:update>
```

This expression will change the name of the first `<foo>` element in the document to John.

Remove

`<xupdate:remove>` can be used to remove nodes from a document. A `select` attribute indicates the nodes should be removed using XPath. For example:

```
<xupdate:remove select="/foo[2]" />
```

This will remove the second `<foo>` element of the document.

513

A Complete Example

This is an example of updating some data represented in XML using different XUpdate modifications. This example shows how XUpdate expressions are used to insert an element into a document.

The input data is:

```
<?xml version="1.0"?>
 <addresses version="1.0">
   <address id="1">
     <fullname>John Doe</fullname>
     <born day='01' month='01' year='1980'/>
     <town>California</town>
     <country>United States Of America</country>
   </address>
 </addresses>
```

Note that the XUpdate expressions given below must always be enclosed in an <xupdate:modifications> element that must indicate the version of XUpdate to be used and the namespace for XUpdate elements:

```
<?xml version="1.0"?>
<xupdate:modifications version="1.0"
 xmlns:xupdate="http://www.xmldb.org/xupdate/">

  <xupdate:insert-after select="/addresses/address[1]" >

    <xupdate:element name="address">
      <xupdate:attribute name="id">2</xupdate:attribute>
      <fullname>Bat Masterson</fullname>
      <born day='6' month='12' year='1974'/>
      <town>Tombstone</town>
      <country>UnitedStates</country>
    </xupdate:element>
  </xupdate:insert-after>
</xupdate:modifications>
```

The XML output should be:

```
<?xml version="1.0"?>
  <addresses version="1.0">
    <address id="1">
      <fullname>Matthew Moodie</fullname>
      <born day='13' month='06' year='1978'/>
      <town>Glasgow</town>
      <country>Scotland</country>
    </address>

    <address id="2">
      <fullname>Bat Masterson</fullname>
      <born day='6' month='12' year='1974'/>
      <town>Tombstone</town>
      <country>UnitedStates</country>
    </address>
  </addresses>
```

More information on XUpdate and the XUpdate working draft can be found at http://www.xmldb.org/xupdate/xupdate-wd.html.

SiXDML

SiXDML is a proposed language for XML repositories; it is interesting since the Xindice project is considering adopting this approach as an API for the Xindice database.

What is SiXDML?

From http://www.sixdml.org/:

> *SiXDML was designed to create a common syntax and semantics for performing tasks most often required of XML repositories. SiXDML consists of two parts; a data definition and manipulation language inspired by SQL and an API based on the XML:DB Database API.*

The following functions can be expressed using SiXDML

- Create collection
- Show collection
- Drop collection
- Insert into collection
- Drop from collection
- Constrain collection
- Show constraints
- Drop constraint
- Create index
- Show index
- Drop index
- Select
- Insert before
- Insert into
- Insert after
- Insert attribute
- Delete
- Replace
- Rename

More information about SiXDML is available from the official web site at http://www.sixdml.org/.

Proprietary APIs

In this section we looked at the most standard APIs used to query and modify XML documents. Many products define their own APIs as variations of existing APIs, extensions, or completely new languages. While some of the proprietary APIs may be very useful when using a product, many developers prefer standard APIs in order to have flexibility for application development. It is important to have applications that work even if we decide to change the way in which documents are stored. That's why SAX, DOM, XPath, XUpdate, and eventually XQuery (when stable) will be the preferred APIs for accessing XML storage solutions.

Using a Product for XML Storage

Often an existing product can be used as our XML storage solution. The variety of products available keeps increasing and the number of options available right now makes it likely that we would find a product that suits our requirements. In this section we'll analyze some commercial and free products that support XML as a storage format.

A good compilation of these products is available at the following site: http://www.rpbourret.com/xml/XMLDatabaseProds.htm#xmlenabled.

Relational Databases

Many relational databases offer some degree of support for XML storage:

Microsoft Access

Developer: Microsoft
Web Site: http://msdn.microsoft.com/library/default.asp?url=/library/en-us/dnacc2k2/html/odc_acxmllnk.asp
License: Commercial

Access provides functions to store and retrieve XML documents from tables in a very limited way. Documents can't have attributes and the document structure must be suitable for the conversion to a relational table.

DB2

Developer: IBM
Web Site: http://www-3.ibm.com/software/data/db2/extenders/text.htm
License: Commercial

IBM provides XML functionality for its relational DB2 database where documents are mapped from its DTD to a relational mapping using a language called DAD (Document Access Definition). Once stored in the DB2 database there is a good selection of search technologies to retrieve the documents.

Oracle

Developer: Oracle
Web Site: http://otn.oracle.com/tech/xml/xmldb/content.html
License: Commercial

Oracle has implemented support for XML data in its RDBMS since version 8i. It has an XML datatype that can be used as a column type in a relational table and native storage of XML documents is supported too. A huge variety of XML related functionality can be found in Oracle 8 and Oracle 9 databases.

Microsoft SQL Server 2000

Developer: Microsoft
Web Site: http://msdn.microsoft.com/library/default.asp?url=/library/en-us/dnmag00/html/sql2000.asp
License: Commercial

SQL Server 2000 supports three mechanisms to use XML documents. The first form allows manipulating XML from SQL SELECT statements. The second way is by using XPath queries and the third mechanism is the OpenXML function that can be used in stored procedures.

Native XML Databases

The term **native XML database** is confusing. Tamino first introduced it and then the use of the term extended to other products. According to the XML:DB Initiative, a native database has the following characteristics:

❑ It has an XML document as its fundamental unit of storage, just as a relational database has a row in a table as its fundamental unit of storage.

❑ It defines a model for an XML document and stores and retrieves documents according to that model. At a minimum the model must include elements, attributes, PCDATA, and a document order. Examples of such models are the XPath data model, the XML Infoset, and the models implied by DOM and the events in SAX.

❑ It is not required to have any particular underlying physical storage model. A native XML database can be built using text files, a relational database, an object-oriented database, or a proprietary format.

The concept of native XML databases is explained in this article available at http://www.xml.com/pub/a/2001/10/31/nativexmldb.html.

Now let's look at some commercial and free native XML databases that can be used from our applications.

Coherity XML Database (CXD)

Developer: Coherity
Web site: http://www.coherity.com/
License: Commercial

This is a native XML database based on a proprietary XML format. The database runs in several platforms and provides the following APIs:

❑ XPath
❑ XSL
❑ XML/HTTP
❑ XSQL
❑ DOM

517

Support for XQuery is planned in the next version of Coherity.

An HTTP interface allows us to use this product from PHP – the query can be sent to the Coherity server as an HTTP POST request and the answer will be an XML format. This method can be used to issue queries directly from the application (dynamic queries) or to execute server-side queries (queries that are stored on the CXD server).

DBDOM

Developer: K. Ari Krupnikov
Web Site: http://dbdom.sourceforge.net/
License: Open Source

DBDOM is a persistent DOM implementation. It is free and open source and is written in Java. This project uses an object relational mapping to represent XML documents as DOM trees storing the trees in a relational database. The project is in its initial stage and supports Oracle and PostgresSQL. DOM methods are implemented as stored procedures that access the relational mapping of the XML documents.

Infonyte DB

Developer: Infonyte
Web Site: http://www.infonyte.com/en/index.html
License: Commercial

The Infonyte DB is a native XML database based on a proprietary format. Infonyte's product supports the following APIs:

❑   DOM (Level 2)

❑   XQL'99

❑   XSLT

❑   XPath

The database can store documents of up to 1 terabyte in size. The database can be accessed using a Java API so the PHP Java extension must be used to access the product from PHP applications.

Ipedo XML Database

Developer: Ipedo
Web Site: http://www.ipedo.com/html/products_xml_dat.html
License: Commercial

The Ipedo XML databases stores documents in a proprietary format. The database offers the following APIs to manipulate documents:

❑   XPath

❑   XSLT

❑   XQuery

The APIs can be used through COM, .NET, SOAP, and other interfaces. In particular, SOAP can be used from PHP to access the database.

Virtuoso Universal Server

Developer: OpenLink Software
Web Site: http://www.openlinksw.com/virtuoso/
License: Commercial

Virtuoso is a cross-platform multi-purpose server that has native XML storage among a large number of other features. Regarding XML processing the virtuoso server provides the following APIs:

❑ XPath

❑ XSLT

❑ XQuery

The server can be accessed using HTTP, SOAP, WebDAV and ODBC. The server is a traditional RDBMS, a virtual DBMS (linking multiple databases), and a native XML database.

It has a built-in hook to store PHP documents and execute them from the database serving them up directly from a built-in HTTP server.

We can test XQuery expressions at the XQuery demo page at:
http://demo.openlinksw.com:8890/xqdemo/demo.vsp

Tamino

Developer: Software AG
Web Site: http://www.softwareag.com/tamino/
License: Commercial

Tamino was one of the first native XML servers in the market and certainly one of the most advanced products available for XML storage. It uses a proprietary format based on an ADABAS database to store XML documents.

Tamino supports the following APIs:

❑ XPath (functionality extended)

❑ XSLT

❑ DOM

❑ SAX

❑ XQuery (planned)

The Tamino database can be accessed using SOAP and several HTTP-based mechanisms. Other features include full text indexing, storing of non-XML objects, and many features related to integration between the Tamino database and other systems and architectures.

X-Hive/DB

Developer: X-Hive
Web Site: http://www.x-hive.com/
License: Commercial

This is an XML database written in Java, documents are stored in an object-oriented database accessed using JDBC. The following standards are supported in X-Hive:

❑ XPath

❑ XLink/XPointer

❑ XQuery (preview)

❑ DOM (Level 2)

❑ XUpdate

❑ XSLT

❑ WebDAV

Additional features include full text indexing of XML documents and version control of documents in the database. To use X-Hive from PHP, we have to use the PHP Java extension to access the X-Hive Java API.

Xindice (formerly dbXML)

Developer: Apache Software Foundation (ASF)
Web Site: http://xml.apache.org/xindice/
License: Open Source

Xindice (pronounced 'zeen-dee-chay') is a native XML database by the ASF.

Xindice is a native database written in Java that uses a proprietary binary format to store XML documents. Currently the database is recommended for collections of small to medium-sized XML documents. Support for large XML documents is planned for a near future.

Xindice supports the following APIs

❑ XPath

❑ XMLDB:XUpdate

There are plans to add XQuery and SiXDML to this list.

Xindice works on any platform with a Java Runtime Environment (JRE). The Xindice server uses port 4080 by default but this can be changed if needed.

Xindice can be accessed using the Java API or an XML-RPC plugin that allows the developer to use the Xindice API from any programming language. It makes sense to use Xindice from PHP using the XML-RPC plugin. The next section discusses this.

XML-RPC Access

Once the XML-RPC plugin is added to Xindice, we can use the following methods to access the Xindice database:

Method Name	Parameters (XMLRPC type)	Description	Example
createCollection	parentCollection (string) name (string)	Creates a new collection with the given name under a parent collection	createCollection("/db/foo", "mycol")
createIndexer	collection (string) indexName (string) pattern (string)	Creates an index on the collection for a given pattern	createIndexer("/db/foo", "nameIndex","//name")
dropCollection	collection (string)	Drops the collection	dropCollection("/db/foo")
dropIndexer	collection (string) indexName (string)	Drops an index	dropIndexer("/db/foo", "nameIndex")
getDocument	collection(string) documentId (string)	Retrieves a document	getDocument("/db/foo", "adoc")
getDocumentCount	collection(string)	Returns the number of documents in a collection	getDocumentCount("/db/foo")
insertDocument	collection (string) id (string) data (string)	Inserts a document in the database	insertDocument("/db/foo", "adoc", "<foo>hi</foo>")
listCollections	parentCollection (string)	Returns a list of subcollections	listCollections("/db/foo")
listDocuments	collection (string)	Returns a list of documents in a collection	listDocuments("/db/foo")
listIndexers	collection (string)	Returns a list of indexes in a collection	listIndexers("/db/foo")

Table continued on following page

521

Method Name	Parameters (XMLRPC type)	Description	Example
queryCollection	collection (string) type (string) [Xpath or Xupdate] query (string) namespaces (struct)	Queries a collection using XPath or XUpdate	queryCollection(" /db/foo", "Xpath", "//name",Array())
queryDocument	collection (string) type (string) (see prev) query (string) namespaces (struct) Id (string)	Queries a document	queryDocument("/db/foo", "Xpath", "//name", Array(),"adoc")
removeDocument	collection (string) id (string)	Removes a document	removeDocument("/db/foo", "adoc")
setDocument	collection(string) id (string) data (string)	Updates the content of a document	setDocument("/db/foo", "adoc", "<hi>Hi</hi>")

Using Xindice from PHP

To use Xindice from PHP we need a library implementing the listed methods and call these methods using XML-RPC in the server accordingly. A library maintained by Kurt Ward at http://sourceforge.net/projects/phpxindice/ implements a PHP class to access Xindice as well as a web-based admin interface in PHP for Xindice (check for frequent updates).

An Example of Xindice from PHP

To detail an instance of working with a native XML database we'll look at how to use the Xindice XML-RPC interface to run an example on Xindice.

> *It might be worthwhile to refer Chapter 16 to learn about XML-RPC before going on with this chapter.*

Requirements

We need:

- ❏ A PHP installation (UNIX or Windows).

- ❏ The XML-RPC library from Usefulinc (https://sourceforge.net/projects/phpxmlrpc/). We learn about it in Chapter 16.

- ❏ Xindice for UNIX or Windows (http://xml.apache.org/xindice/#Releases).

- ❏ A Java Development Kit (JDK) to run Xindice.

- ❏ The Xindice XML-RPC plugin (http://xindice-xmlrpc.sourceforge.net/).

Installing the Xindice XML Server

The installation process of the Xindice XML Server is straightforward. Just follow the steps and Xindice should be running,

This is the installation procedure for Xindice 1.0:

Step	Windows Instructions	UNIX Instructions
1	Unzip the Xindice distribution to `c:\Xindice`.	Extract the Xindice tarball to a directory.
2	Set the `JAVA_HOME` environment variable to point to the JDK. This may already been done by your JDK.	Set the `JAVA_HOME` environment variable to the location of your JDK. This may already been done by your JDK.
3	Set the `XINDICE_HOME` environment variable to the location where you extracted the Xindice distribution. For example, `C:\Xindice`.	Set the `XINDICE_HOME` environment variable to the location where you extracted the Xindice distribution. For example, `/usr/local/Xindice`.
4	Add the `%XINDICE_HOME%\bin` directory to the `PATH` environment variable.	Add the `$XINDICE_HOME/bin` directory to the `PATH` environment variable.
5	Add the `Xindice.jar` file to the `CLASSPATH` environment variable. For instance, `%XINDICE_HOME%\java\lib\Xindice.jar`	Add the `Xindice.jar` file to the `CLASSPATH` environment variable. For instance, `$XINDICE_HOME/java/lib/Xindice.jar`
6	Make sure the JDK `bin` directory is in the `PATH`.	Start the server typing cd `$XINDICE_HOME ;./start`. If everything went well, Xindice should be running.
7	Start the server using the `startup.bat` batch file. If everything went well, Xindice should be running.	

Try pointing a browser to http:\\localhost:4080 to see if Xindice is running on the machine.

Installation instructions can also be found at:

❑   Installing Xindice on UNIX: http://xml.apache.org/xindice/INSTALL

❑   Installing Xindice on Windows: http://xml.apache.org/xindice/INSTALL.windows

Installing the Xindice XML-RPC plugin

Once we have Xindice running we need to install the XML-RPC plugin for Xindice.

These are the instructions to install the plugin:

❑   Go to http://xindice-xmlrpc.sourceforge.net/ and get the .zip or .tgz distribution of the plugin.

❑   Unzip/untar the package to a directory.

❑   Copy the apache-xmlrpc.jar and xindice-xmlrpc-0.6.jar files from the distribution's lib directory to XINDICE_HOME/java/lib.

❑   Edit the XINDICE_HOME/config/system.xml file to add the XMLRPCHandler to the Xindice configuration. Right after the line in the file that reads:

```
<components class="org.apache.xindice.server.standard.StdComponentManager">
```

add:

```
<component class="org.xmldatabases.xmlrpc.XMLRPCHandler" name="XMLRPCHandler"/>
```

❑   Start Xindice as usual. We should see a message saying, XMLRPCHandler added to filter chain, indicating that Xindice is ready to receive XML-RPC requests.

Now let's test the Xindice XML-RPC API from PHP using a class to abstract the XML-RPC interface from the PHP application. The application can call methods on the class to add documents, query documents, and modify them without worrying about XML-RPC.

> Please note that this examples work for Xindice 1.0. If you have a newer release the XML-RPC API might have changed and you may need to change the Xindice class used here.

The Xindice Class

This is a PHP class implementing the XML-RPC interface of Xindice as class methods, the class uses the XML-RPC library from Usefulinc that will be explained in Chapter 16.

This is the class:

```php
<?php
include_once("/xmlrpc/xmlrpc.inc");

class Xindice
```

```
{
    var $client;
    var $error;

    function GetError()
    {
        return $this->error;
    }

    function SetXmlRpcDebug($debug)
    {
        $this->client->setDebug($debug);
    }

    function Xindice($server_uri, $server_port = 4080)
    {
        $this->client = new xmlrpc_client("/", $server_uri, $server_port);
    }

    // Collection management functions
    function listCollections($collection)
    {
        $paths = split('/', $collection);
        $method = $paths[1].'.'."listCollections";
        $msg = new xmlrpcmsg($method,
                            array(new xmlrpcval($collection, "string")));
        return $this->sendMsg($msg);
    }

    function getDocumentCount($collectionPath)
    {
        $paths = split('/', $collectionPath);
        $method = $paths[1].'.'."getDocumentCount";
        $msg = new xmlrpcmsg($method,
                            array(new xmlrpcval($collectionPath,
                                                "string")));
        return $this->sendMsg($msg);
    }

    function createCollection($base, $collectionName)
    {
        $paths = split('/', $base);
        $method = $paths[1].'.'."createCollection";
        $msg = new xmlrpcmsg($method, array(new xmlrpcval($base, "string"),
                            new xmlrpcval($collectionName, "string")));
        return $this->sendMsg($msg);
    }

    function dropCollection($collectionPath)
    {
        $paths = split('/', $collectionPath);
        $method = $paths[1].'.'."dropCollection";
        $msg = new xmlrpcmsg($method,
                            array(new xmlrpcval($collectionPath)));
```

```
            return $this->sendMsg($msg);
    }

// Document management functions

    function insertDocument($collection, $id, $content)
    {
        $paths = split('/', $collection);
        $method = $paths[1].'.'."insertDocument";
        $msg = new xmlrpcmsg($method,
                            array(new xmlrpcval($collection, "string"),
                                    new xmlrpcval($id, "string"),
                                    new xmlrpcval($content, "string")));
        return $this->sendMsg($msg);
    }

    function setDocument($collection, $id, $content) {}

    function getDocument($collection, $id)
    {
        $paths = split('/', $collection);
        $method = $paths[1].'.'."getDocument";
        $msg = new xmlrpcmsg($method,
                            array(new xmlrpcval($collection, "string"),
                                    new xmlrpcval($id, "string")));
        return $this->sendMsg($msg);
    }

    function listDocuments($collection)
    {
        $paths = split('/', $collection);
        $method = $paths[1].'.'."listDocuments";
        $msg = new xmlrpcmsg($method,
                            array(new xmlrpcval($collection, "string")));
        return $this->sendMsg($msg);
    }

    function removeDocument($collection, $id)
    {
        $paths = split('/', $collection);
        $method = $paths[1].'.'."removeDocument";
        $msg = new xmlrpcmsg($method,
                            array(new xmlrpcval($collection, "string"),
                                    new xmlrpcval($id, "string")));
        return $this->sendMsg($msg);
    }

// Index management functions

    function createIndexer($collection, $indexName, $pattern)
    {
        $paths = split('/', $collection);
        $method = $paths[1].'.'."createIndexer";
        $msg = new xmlrpcmsg($method,
```

```php
                                array(new xmlrpcval($collection, "string"),
                                new xmlrpcval($indexName, "string"),
                                new xmlrpcval($pattern, "string")));
        return $this->sendMsg($msg);
    }

    function dropIndexer($collection, $indexName)
    {
        $paths = split('/', $collection);
        $method = $paths[1].'.'."dropIndexer";
        $msg = new xmlrpcmsg($method,
                            array(new xmlrpcval($collection, "string"),
                                new xmlrpcval($indexName, "string")));
        return $this->sendMsg($msg);
    }

    function listIndexers($collection)
    {
        $paths = split('/', $collection);
        $method = $paths[1].'.'."listIndexer";
        $msg = new xmlrpcmsg($method,
                            array(new xmlrpcval($collection, "string")));
        return $this->sendMsg($msg);
    }

    // Query functions

    function queryDocument($collection, $type, $query, $id)
    {
        $paths = split('/', $collection);
        $method = $paths[1].'.'."queryDocument";
        $msg = new xmlrpcmsg($method,
                                array(new xmlrpcval($collection, "string"),
                                    new xmlrpcval($type, "string"),
                                    new xmlrpcval($query),
                                    new xmlrpcval(Array(), "struct"),
                                    new xmlrpcval($id, "string")));
        return $this->sendMsg($msg);
    }
}

    function queryCollection($collection, $type, $query)
    {
        $paths = split('/', $collection);
        $method = $paths[1].'.'."queryCollection";
        $msg = new xmlrpcmsg($method,
                                array(new xmlrpcval($collection, "string"),
                                    new xmlrpcval($type, "string"),
                                    new xmlrpcval($query),
                                    new xmlrpcval(Array(), "struct")));
        return $this->sendMsg($msg);
    }

    // PRIVATE METHODS
    function getBase($collection)
```

```
        {
            $paths = split('/', $collection);
            return $paths[0];
        }

        function sendMsg($msg)
        {
            $result = $this->client->send($msg);
            if(!$result) {
                $this->error = 'Cannot send xmlrpc message to the server';
                return 0;
            }
            if($result->faultCode()) {
                $this->error = $result->faultString();
                return 0;
            }
            $ret = xmlrpc_decode($result->value());
            return $ret;
        }
    }
?>
```

The code is simple, for each Xindice XML-RPC method we provide a class method where the XML-RPC message is constructed and sent to the server, then the result is decoded to a PHP variable returned to the application or an error is set and FALSE is returned. If a method returns FALSE the application can use the getError() message to check for the error message.

The class constructor expects to receive the server URI and the port to be used defaulting the port to 4080 (Xindice's default) in case it is not received.

The Test Program

The test program will show Xindice features and how to use them from PHP using the Xindice class that was just presented above. We will go through the test script step-by-step.

This is the initialization bit:

```
// PLEASE CHANGE THIS TO POINT TO YOUR XINDICE SERVER
$server = "localhost";
$port = 4080;
$base = "/db";

include_once("xindice.php");

print ("<table width='600' bgcolor='#9999cc' border='1'
bordercolor='#000000'><tr><td><h3>Testing Xindice</h3></td></tr></table><br />");

// Create the Xindice access object
$xi = new Xindice("$server", $port);
if (!$xi) {
    die("Cannot create Xindice object, check servername and port<br />");
}
$xi->SetXmlRpcDebug(0);
```

528

In the initialization we set the server URI and port and the base collection to be used. In this example we use the /db default base collection from Xindice. We create the Xindice access object and check for errors. There's also some HTML to provide a neat presentation.

Now let's create a collection:

```
// Create a collection "my_test" under db
$xi->createCollection($base, "my_test");
```

As we can see creating a collection is a trivial task – we just indicate the base collection (/db) and the name of the collection to be created (my_test).

Here we insert a document:

```
// Insert a sample document there
$a_doc = '
<people>
  <person>
    <name>Foo</name>
    <age>10</age>
  </person>
  <person>
    <name>Goo</name>
    <age>83</age>
  </person>
</people>';

$xi->insertDocument("$base/my_test", "people", $a_doc);
```

We create an example document and insert it into the repository using the insertDocument() method. Note that the collection, a key, and the document are passed to the method. The key is people in this case and will be used to find/retrieve the inserted document from the Xindice server.

Next we list the collections:

```
// List collections under base, should be an Array with "system"
// and "my_test"

$cols = $xi->listCollections($base);

print ("<table width='600' bgcolor='#ccccff' border='1'
bordercolor='#000000'><tr><td colspan='2' bgcolor='#9999cc'>Collections under
$base:</td></tr>");

foreach ($cols as $col) {
    print ("<tr><td>Collection</td><td>$col</td></tr>");
}

print ("</table><br />");
```

The snippet presented above gets all the collections present from /db and lists them as an HTML table.

Here we count the documents:

```
// List number of documents under base/my_test should be 1
// (the inserted doc)

$tot = $xi->getDocumentCount ($base."/my_test");

print ("<table width='600' bgcolor='#ccccff' border='1'
bordercolor='#000000'><tr><td bgcolor='#9999cc'>Documents in $base/my_test:
$tot</td></tr>");

if ($tot == 1) {
    print ("<tr><td>Test passed ok</td></tr></table>");
}

print ("<br />");
```

This part shows the getDocumentCount () method that returns the number of documents present under the collection. Since we just created the collection the number of documents must be 1.

Now comes listing the documents:

```
// List the documents under base/my_test should be "people"

$docs = $xi->listDocuments ($base."/my_test");

print ("<table width='600' bgcolor='#ccccff' border='1'
bordercolor='#000000'><tr><td colspan='2' bgcolor='#9999cc'>Documents in
$base/my_test: $tot</td></tr>");

foreach ($docs as $doc) {
    print ("<tr><td>Document</td><td>$doc</td></tr></table>");
}

print ("<br />");
```

Now documents under /db/my_test are listed using the listDocuments () method.

Here we retrieve the document:

```
// Retrieve the "people" document

$people = $xi->getDocument ($base."/my_test", "people");

print ("<table width='600' bgcolor='#ccccff' border='1'
bordercolor='#000000'><tr><td bgcolor='#9999cc'>Document  people:</td></tr>");

print ("<tr><td><textarea rows='11'
cols='40'>$people</textarea></td></tr></table>");

print ("<br />");
```

The getDocument () method is used to retrieve a document from a collection. Note how the key people is used to retrieve the document we inserted before, since we gave that document the people key.

This is an XPath query:

```
// And the document

$query = $xi->queryDocument($base."/my_test", "XPath", "//name", "people");

print ("<table width='600' bgcolor='#ccccff' border='1'
bordercolor='#000000'><tr><td bgcolor='#9999cc'>Query result
(queryDocument):</td></tr>");

print ("<tr><td><textarea rows='11'
cols='40'>$query</textarea></td></tr></table>");

print ("<br />");
```

This shows how easy it is to query a document using the `queryDocument()` method: the method receives the collection, the type of query (XPath), the query and the document key. In this example we are querying for the `<name>` elements.

The result will be an XML fragment as the following:

```
<?xml version="1.0"?>
<result count="2">
  <name xmlns:src="http://xml.apache.org/xindice/Query"
        src:col="/db/my_test" src:key="people">Foo</name>
  <name xmlns:src="http://xml.apache.org/xindice/Query"
        src:col="/db/my_test" src:key="people">Goo</name>
</result>
```

We can see how the XPath node-set is wrapped between result tags where the `count` attribute of the `<result>` tag indicates the number of nodes in the node-set. We can also see how Xindice adds some extra attributes, like the `src:col` attribute indicating the collection where the document was found and the `src:key` attribute indicating the key of the document.

This is an XUpdate modification:

```
// An XUpdate modification
$modification='
<?xml version="1.0"?>
<xupdate:modifications version="1.0"
xmlns:xupdate="http://www.xmldb.org/xupdate/">
  <xupdate:insert-after select="/people/person[1]" >
    <xupdate:element name="person">
      <name>Pirincho</name>
      <age>2</age>
    </xupdate:element>
  </xupdate:insert-after>
</xupdate:modifications>
';

$query = $xi->queryDocument($base."/my_test", "XUpdate",
                            "$modification", "people");
```

The example shows how to add a `<person>` element to the `people` document using XUpdate. We use `<xupdate:insert-before>` to insert the `person` before the first person in the document (see how XPath is used to indicate that). Issuing the query is very easy using the `queryDocument()` method in this case selecting XUpdate as the type of query to be executed.

Now we remove the document:

```
// Remove the document
$xi->removeDocument($base."/my_test", "people");
```

This simple fragment shows how to use the `removeDocument()` method to remove a document.

Finally, we remove the collection:

```
// Drop the test collection
$xi->dropCollection($base."/my_test");
```

The `dropCollection()` method shows how to remove a collection.

This is the output on a Netscape browser:

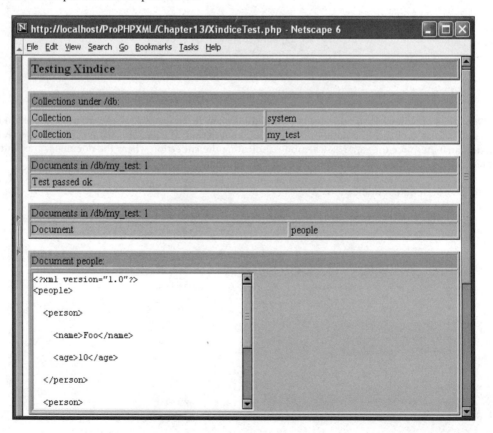

Note that the methods for index creation and removal where not shown in the example but are very useful when querying a collection with a large number of documents.

Command-Line Tools

Xindice can be used from a command-line interface. We can list collections, add and remove collections, add and remove documents, or query documents using the command-line interface.

For example:

```
xindiceadmin add_collection /db foo
```

adds a collection named foo to the /db collection.

This statement:

```
xindice add_document /db/foo -f doc.xml
```

adds a document doc.xml to the /db/foo collection on the server.

We can also give each inserted document a key, allowing document retrieval by key later:

```
xindice add_document /db/foo -f doc.xml -n adoc
```

The result is the same as before but the document is added with the adoc key.

Documents can be retrieved using:

```
xindice retrieve_document -c /db/foo -n adoc -f sample.xml
```

In this case the document with the adoc key is retrieved from /db/foo and stored in the sample.xml file.

We can also query documents, remove them, import multiple documents, work with XML objects, create indexes, and more using the command-line interface. See a pointer to the command-line interface later in the next section for a URI detailing the command-line interface.

HTTP Access

The HTTP plugin can be used to retrieve documents from the Xindice server using HTTP. For example, http://loclahost:4080/db/students/2080.xml.

Resources

- ❑ The PHP library to use Xindice – http://sourceforge.net/projects/phpxindice/
- ❑ The Xindice project home – http://xml.apache.org/xindice/
- ❑ XML-RPC plugin for Xindice – http://xindice-xmlrpc.sourceforge.net/
- ❑ XML-RPC documentation for Xindice – http://xindice-xmlrpc.sourceforge.net/
- ❑ The HTTP plugin – http://www.xmldatabases.org/radio/xmlDatabases/projects/Xindice-HTTP/
- ❑ The command-line reference – http://xml.apache.org/xindice/ToolsReference.html

Summary

This chapter introduced the world of XML storage solutions, as it is highly probable that we will need to find or use some kind of XML storage solution for projects using XML.

We started this chapter by analyzing the different ways to go if we want to implement our own storage solution. We covered different alternatives to store XML documents – plaintext files, relational databases, and proprietary formats.

Then we described APIs that we may need to access the XML repository if we are using a product or need to implement in our own solution. We mentioned DOM, XPath, SAX, and XSLT that were covered in specific chapters of this book and some new APIs specific for accessing XML repositories – XQuery, XMLDB:XUpdate, and SiXDML.

XQuery is an interesting standard since it is a project by the W3C that can be easily adopted by a lot of products as an XML querying API. We did a quick review of XQuery in this chapter and pointed to some tools and implementations that can be used to learn this language.

Later in the chapter we covered commercial and free products that offer native XML storage; we described the most important features of these products with links to their developers/companies. This can be a good place to start if one decides to use a product for XML storage.

Finally we covered Xindice in some detail. This is an open source native XML database by the ASF. Xindice uses XPath and XMLDB:XUpdate as its main APIs in version 1.0. Since Xindice can be accessed using an XML-RPC interface we covered how to use this interface from PHP and provided an abstraction class and some test snippets to test Xindice features.

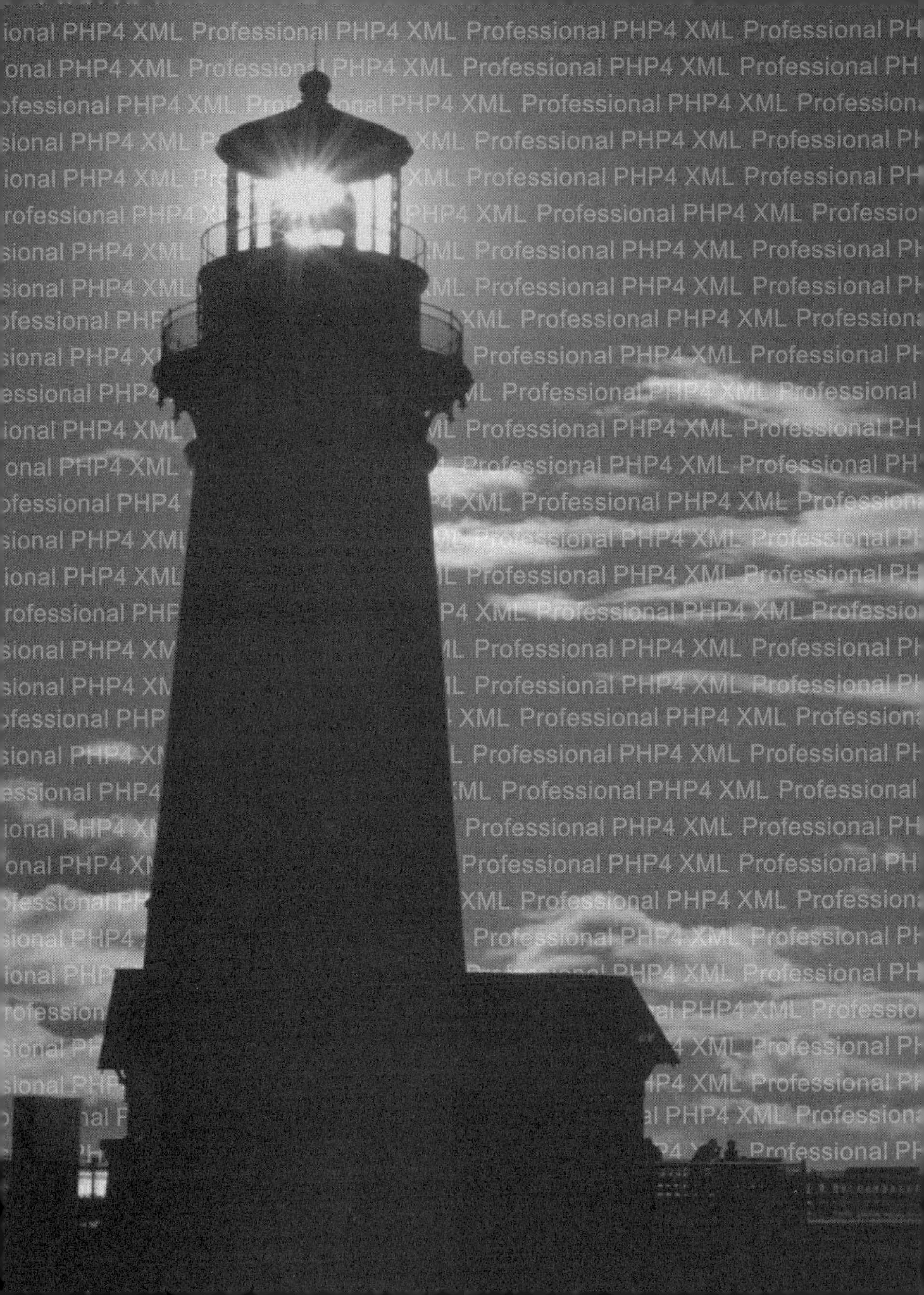
Professional PHP4 XML

14

PHP As a Client

Every PHP programmer should have in their toolkit a variety of methods with which to approach the development of client applications. In this chapter we will review a mixture of techniques for connecting, messaging, and integrating with XML-based client-server technologies and protocols. The chapter also spends some time in reviewing the fundamentals of **SOAP** (Simple Object Access Protocol) and general issues that are related to Service Orientated Architectures (SOA).

We will cover:

- ❑ WDDX
- ❑ TCP/IP
- ❑ Jabber
- ❑ SOAP and web services

WDDX

The **WDDX** (Web Distributed Data eXchange) is an XML-based technology designed for exchanging complex data structures between application environments. Initially, WDDX was created by **Allaire** (now taken over by Macromedia Inc.), the makers of ColdFusion, to solve the key problems in exchanging data between web applications. Later, this work was generalized into a cross-language framework, and resulted in the creation of the **WDDX SDK**. We might want to use WDDX, if we need to transfer textual data between:

- ❑ Two different computing languages
- ❑ A client and a server
- ❑ A client using one language and a server using another language

Description

WDDX is not a formal standard, but it's based on standards-based technologies like XML 1.0, and is free for use and redistribution. WDDX consists of a language-independent representation of data based on an XML 1.0 DTD, and a set of modules for a wide variety of languages that use it. WDDX can be used with HTTP, SMTP, POP, FTP, and other Internet protocols that support transferring textual data.

> **WDDX is a language-independent method for exchanging structured data from one processing environment to another using XML as an intermediate, serialized format that encodes textual information.**

We can see many examples that use XML as a transport format between application environments, peers, or servers. However, transporting to another peer or server is not specified within the WDDX specification, as there are many existing ways of sending data; for example, through a form field sent by HTML POST. Specifically, WDDX may be considered as a form of marshaling of data structures, without specification of the message transport between two endpoints.

A typical WDDX process involves two clear steps:

❑ **Serialization**
Create an XML representation of our data

❑ **Deserialization**
Instantiate the application data from its XML representation into the native structure of the receiving environment or language

We may use WDDX as an interchange mechanism between a client and a server, instead of using other XML-based methods such as XML-RPC or SOAP. Some of the languages/interfaces that support WDDX are COM, Java, Perl, Python, ColdFusion, JavaScript, and ASP. WDDX may be natively supported within a language, if not we require the WDDX SDK (http://www.openwddx.org/) as a prerequisite for usage.

Let's consider a typical WDDX XML document:

```
<wddxPacket version='1.0'>
<header/>

<data>
  <struct>
    <var name='favoritebeer'><string>Radagast</string></var>
  </struct>
</data>

</wddxPacket>
```

Notice that there are reserved keywords like, <header>, <data>, <struct>, <string>, <var>, and <wddxPacket>, that are used in describing the data structures and their values. WDDX, being an XML-based technology, has a related DTD that determines all the allowed elements and attributes allowed within a WDDX document.

Here is another example of a serialized WDDX document:

```
<wddxPacket version='1.0'>
<header>
  <comment>Results of Geophysics Database Search</comment>
</header>

<data>
  <struct>
    <var name='one_var'>
      <string>Geoelectrical Analysis of Rte6</string>
    </var>
  </struct>
</data>

</wddxPacket>
```

The `<header>` element contains some meta data about the first `<struct>` element. We will use the `wddx_packet_start()` and `wddx_serialize_value()` commands in our example to demonstrate how to specify header meta data in our example. The `<data>` element contains a `<struct>` element that defines a string variable of the name `one_var`. The `one_var` variable contains a string value of 'Geoelectrical Analysis of Rte 6'.

WDDX takes care of handling the data type of a particular variable in the target language. The data type is encoded within the WDDX packet above, using a `<string>` element. Upon deserialization, the particular target language will use the element to 'know' how to type a variable.

Now we can easily interchange data from a set of variables in one language to another set of variables in another, without having to do any additional coding. Much more complex data structures are allowed, which will be demonstrated in our example.

WDDX is extremely simple to use, and PHP provides 6 functions for handling the typical WDDX processes. WDDX is supported natively in PHP 4.2.0.

Code Example

Our first example will demonstrate how to generate a WDDX packet with a fairly simple data structure. This packet will then be transported via a form field, then deserialized into a data structure:

❏ `serialize.php` will serialize a WDDX packet with a header comment

❏ `deserialize.php` will use the WDDX packet generated by `serialize.php` and create a data structure from this packet

We would use this technique when we want a simple time-saving method of transporting data structures between different local PHP pages, without having to declare the variables in the target page. This is also the primary technique of sharing data structures between two remote PHP servers.

Here is our page that generates the WDDX packet:

```php
<?php

// Initiate a few simple variables to serialise
$myvar = "just a simple variable to transfer";
$myinteger = "1";
$mybooks = array("PHP Programming", "PHP and XML",
                 "XSLT Programmers Reference");

// Create a WDDX packet
$packet_id = wddx_packet_start("my header comment");

// Add myvar to the packet
wddx_add_vars($packet_id, "myvar");

// Add myinteger to the packet
wddx_add_vars($packet_id, "myinteger");

// Cast myinteger as a proper integer
$myinteger = (int)$myinteger;

// Now add myinteger again
wddx_add_vars($packet_id, "myinteger");

// Now add mybooks array
wddx_add_vars($packet_id, "mybooks");

// Mark the end of the packet
$stringwddxpacket = wddx_packet_end($packet_id);

// Print out WDDX XML representation to output
print ($stringwddxpacket);
?>
```

The above code declares a variety of variables; myvar, myinteger, and mybooks. These variables could be generated prior to processing the WDDX packet, or could be declared **during** the processing of the packet. This on-the-fly processing is illustrated by the casting of the myinteger variable from a string to an integer, before including it again using the wddx_add_vars() command. We could perform all sorts of processing and continue appending the results to the WDDX packet, but once we invoke the wddx_packet_end($packetid) command, the packet creation process halts. The wddx_packet_end() command returns a string (held by our $stringwddxpacket), which holds the entire WDDX packet, which will be used by our deserialized page.

Here is the result of running serialize.php:

```xml
<wddxPacket version='1.0'>

<header>
  <comment>my header comment</comment>
</header>
```

```
<data>
  <struct>

    <var name='myvar'>
      <string>just a simple variable to transfer</string>
    </var>

    <var name='myinteger'>
      <string>1</string>
    </var>

    <var name='myinteger'>
      <number>1</number>
    </var>

    <var name='mybooks'>
      <array length='3'>
        <string>PHP Programming</string>
        <string>PHP and XML</string>
        <string>XSLT Programmers Reference</string>
      </array>
    </var>

  </struct>
</data>
```

Notice that there is a `<header>` element that is defined with the PHP `wddx_packet_start()` command. All the variables are contained within the `<struct>` element and each have a `<var>` element. Each type is declared by either a `<string>`, a `<number>`, or an `<array>` element, with the array element having an additional `length` attribute. The array contains the additional `<string>` type for each `<array>` element, with an implied ordering of elements reflecting array order.

Now let's use this WDDX packet from the serialized PHP page to illustrate how the serialized packet is taken and then deserialized into an associative array on a separate PHP page (`deserialize.php`):

```php
<?php

// Get data from serialize.php which generates the WDDX packet
// Please amend URL path to actual location
$url_gen = "http://example.com/wddx/serialize.php";

$packet_in = join("", file($url_gen));

// Deserialize the values
$values = wddx_deserialize($packet_in);

// Dumping the deserialized variables
print (var_dump($values));
?>
```

We have to make sure that our URL reflects the location where we have placed the `serialize.php` page. We could use any valid WDDX packet; even the result of XSLT processing could generate a WDDX packet that could be used by `deserialize.php`.

541

Here is the result of running `deserialize.php`:

```
array(3) {
  ["myvar"]=>
  string(34) "just a simple variable to transfer"
  ["myinteger"]=>
  int(1)
  ["mybooks"]=>
  array(3) {
    [0]=>
    string(15) "PHP Programming"
    [1]=>
    string(11) "PHP and XML"
    [2]=>
    string(26) "XSLT Programmers Reference"
  }
}
```

Wow, a WDDX packet was generated on one page, and then deciphered into an array on another page! Since the `deserialize.php` page uses a valid URL, there is no reason why the WDDX packet could not have originated from a remote server.

WDDX is generally a great time-saver, as we don't have to worry about declaring variables, or doing any kind of special data handling, other than the requirements enforced by the WDDX DTD and the general rules of XML. We could just as easily use JavaScript or another processing language to take the WDDX packet and deserialize it into a native data structure. In fact, to prove that WDDX is language neutral, let's make a JavaScript example that takes in a message, serializes it, and then pushes it out to a slightly changed deserialized PHP page.

Our 2nd example will need the WDDX JavaScript library. This can be downloaded for free at the official WDDX site at http://www.openwddx.org/.

Instead of hard-coding our variables in the page (as in `serialize.php`), we will use an HTML form field to allow for a user to input a string message. The form page will then use the JavaScript `WDDXSerializer` object to serialise the form field input and place the WDDX packet result in another form field. The form will then be POSTed to a PHP page, `jsdeserialize.php`, for deserializing, as in our first example.

The page contains the HTML form, a reference to external JavaScript library, and the custom `SerializeMessage()` function:

```html
<html>
  <head>
    <title>WDDX Message Test</title>

    <!-- Include WDDX JavaScript library -->
    <script language="JavaScript" SRC="original/Wddx.js"></script>

    <!--- use to create custom  function --->
    <script language="JavaScript">

      function SerializeMessage() {

        // Create a new serializer object
        MySer = new WddxSerializer;

        // Serialize the Message variable value into WDDX Packet
```

```
            MyWDDXPacket = MySer.serialize(document.sendmessage.Message.value);

            // Place result into textarea form field
            document.sendmessage.wddxPacket.value = MyWDDXPacket;

        }
    </script>

</head>

<body>

    <h2>WDDX Message test: Javascript to PHP</h2>

    <form name="sendmessage" method="post" action="jsdeserialize.php">
        <b>Message:</b>
        <br /><br />

        type in message<br />
        <textarea name="Message" rows="4" cols="60"></textarea>

        <input type="button" value="Serialize Message"
                onClick="SerializeMessage()"/>

        <br /><br />
        WDDX encoding to be sent for processing<br/>
        <textarea name="wddxPacket" rows="4" cols="60"></textarea>
        <input type="submit" value="Submit WDDX Packet"
                onClick="SerializeMessage();return true;"/>

    </form>
</body>
</html>
```

The WDDX packet that is generated and placed in the form field contains only one `<string>` result within a `<data>` element. This essentially means that upon deserialization there will be only one string variable instantiation and is a valid WDDX, even without a `<var>` element.

One important configuration that may affect the processing of POST forms (including GET and Cookies) is the magic_quotes_gpc setting. This entry may be found in our PHP configuration file. The jsdeserialize.php page will have to apply the stripslashes() command if magic_quotes_gpc is enabled for the WDDX XML to be processed correctly, otherwise our XML will be interpreted as badly-formed XML:

```php
<?php

// Check to see if our PHP configuration has magic quotes enabled
if (!get_magic_quotes_gpc()){
    // Deserialize the values
    $values = wddx_deserialize($wddxPacket);

} else {
    // Deserialize the values, and stripslashes as magic_quotes is on
    $values = wddx_deserialize(stripslashes($wddxPacket));
}
// Dumping the deserialized variables
print (var_dump($values));
?>
```

We should now see the deserialized result as a variable dump, with the message placed in a string variable.

> Use the PHP `stripslashes()` function to handle escaped quotes, when `magic_quotes_gpc` (`GET`, `POST`, Cookies) configuration is enabled. The WDDX packet must be valid XML to be deserialized properly, and since a packet may have attributes which use quotes, this is something to be aware of.

Let's overview the situations where WDDX can be applied with PHP:

❑ When transferring data structures and values between local and remote PHP clients and servers.

❑ When transferring data structures and values between two processing environments, one of which is PHP.

❑ When transferring client HTML form, data structure, and values into a PHP server.

❑ By first applying an XSLT transformation (XML2WDDX), we could convert any internal XML DOM into a native PHP data structure for further processing, instead of using memory intensive DOM methods.

❑ Using WDDX as an interchange format for XML formats, such as RSS or DOCBOOK, which are cumbersome, can vastly reduce the time to develop and maintain, instead of hard coding. This is especially compelling when the format's schema is unknown, but is still required for native PHP processing

Using WDDX as a serialized format for data promotes the overall interoperability of our application, as it is ready to receive and marshal data from nearly every common programming language. In addition, WDDX is an excellent method for transporting data between programming environments, and in situations where XML-RPC or SOAP are either non-existent or too overblown a technical solution.

> WDDX is not confined to use on the Web. If our specific processing environment or programming language supports it, we may pipe (like in UNIX) the serialized WDDX result into another process, essentially creating a pipeline of processing.

Reference

Remember to review the WDDX DTD and free WDDX libraries at the official site (http://www.openwddx.org/).

The following lists PHP WDDX commands with examples of common usage:

PHP Function Prototype	Description

`wddx_serialize_vars(variable, variable ...)`	Generates a WDDX packet containing values of the supplied variables. This is useful when dealing with serializing variables or a list of variables, and encapsulates the `wddx_packet_start()`, `wddx_add_vars()`, and `wddx_packet_end()` all into one function call.
	
	Example:
	
	`$favoritebeer = "Radagast";`
	`$name = array (`
	`        "firstname"=>"James",`
	`        "lastname"=>"Fuller"`
	`        );`
	`print (wddx_serialize_vars("name", "favoritebeer"));`
	
	The above will return the following WDDX packet:
	
	`<wddxPacket version='1.0'>`
	`<header/>`
	
	`<data>`
	`<struct>`
	
	`<var name='name'>`
	`  <struct>`
	`    <varname='firstname'>`
	`      <string>James</string>`
	`    </var>`
	`    <var name='lastname'>`
	`      <string>Fuller</string>`
	`    </var>`
	`  </struct>`
	`</var>`
	
	`<var name='favoritebeer'>`
	`    <string>Radagast</string>`
	`</var>`
	
	`</struct>`
	`</data>`
	`</wddxPacket>`

Table continued on following page

545

PHP Function Prototype	Description
`wddx_packet_start (comment)`	Returns a packet identifier to be used with `wddx_packet_end()` and `wddx_add_vars()` when serializing a number of variables. This function takes an optional parameter to be used as comment in the packet header.
`wddx_packet_end ($packet_id)`	Used to identify the end of a WDDX packet creation and returns the string representation of the packet for transport.

`wddx_serialize_value ($variable , comment)`	Instead of using `wddx_packet_start()` and `wddx_packet_end()`, we may simply use this one command to create a WDDX serialized packet with an optional header comment.
	
	Example:
	
	`$myvar = "testing the serialize value function";`
	
	`print (wddx_serialize_value($myvar, "header comment"));`

`wddx_add_vars ($packet_id)`	Used in conjunction with `wddx_packet_end()` and `wddx_packet_start()` for adding a large number of variables. Use `$packet_id` to append to correct `wddxPacket`.
`wddx_deserialize ($string)`	Takes a WDDX packet as a string argument, and creates a corresponding data structure, usually as an associative array, with language-specific syntax to access.

PHP and TCP/IP

TCP/IP (Transmission Control Protocol/Internet Protocol) is one of the protocols used for communicating between computers on a network, and is predominantly used on the Internet. Its transport mechanism is used by many protocols like HTTP, SMTP, FTP, POP3, and telnet, which are used in client/server technology. In fact, all of the current XML technologies have been designed to include TCP/IP binding, which is why we review TCP/IP in some detail here.

The TCP/IP protocol is a suite comprising several protocols like TCP, IP, UDP, and ICMP. IP handles the movement of data between host computers, whereas TCP manages the movement of data between applications. UDP also manages the movement of data between applications, but is less complex and reliable than TCP. ICMP on the other hand transmits error messages and network traffic statistics.

One of the advantages of using TCP/IP is that the details of what is happening on a lower or higher network level may be abstracted, or hidden for us, to focus on the particular layer that we are interested in.

Description

A typical TCP/IP client may want to send a request for a particular resource, or a result of some processing, to the server. Luckily enough, PHP has a built-in functionality via an access to a Berkeley sockets implementation, which provides a generic interface for creating sockets. Sockets are the endpoints of the communication. In other words, a socket is opened on the client, and a corresponding socket is opened on the server. These two sockets represent the communication endpoints through which data may be sent or received.

We will create a generic socket scanner which will scan a range of sockets, otherwise known as ports. It is important to note that there are some sockets or ports that have been specifically identified to be used for certain protocols. For example, HTTP is normally port 80, and there is no technical reason for this (we may run it under port 663, as with HTTPS), but if all web servers used different ports, then it would be difficult for us to know which port to use for this service.

Code Example

It is always good practice to separate client-side code (classes and methods) from server-side code. In this example, we create a client that interrogates a host server's TCP/IP ports.

We will create a TCP/IP scanner class which will encapsulate:

❑   Opening a socket to query the host server socket

❑   Looping through a range of sockets

❑   Printing success or failure, if the server was listening on the corresponding socket for requests

```
// scanner.php
<?php

class Scanner
{

    // Our main method for this class
    function ScanPorts($host, $port_begin, $port_end, $timeout = 30)
    {
        // Sets how long the program will run for, regardless of number of
        // scanned ports
        set_time_limit($timeout);

        // Verbose message
        print ("begin scanning\r\n");
        print ("host:$host\r\n");
        print ("begin port:$port_begin\r\n");
        print ("end port:$port_end\r\n");
        print ("\r\n");

        // Seed port_range with beginning port to scan
        $port_range = $port_begin;

        // While loop through port range
        while ($port_range >= $port_begin and $port_range <= $port_end) {
```

```
                // Opens a tcp/ip socket on the client and attempts to connect
                // to the server socket, if successful $socket becomes a pointer
                // for use with standard I/O
                # functions
                $socket = fsockopen($host, $port_range);

                // Tests to see if server socket was listening, print
                // corresponding success or # failure message
                if (!$socket){
                    print ("port closed:$port_range\r\n");
                } else {
                    print ("port open:$port_range\r\n");
                }
                fclose($socket);
                # iterate the port range to the next port
                $port_range++;


            }

            // The ScanPorts function has completely executed, reset default
            // timeout
            set_time_limit(30);

            return true;
        }
    }
?>
```

In the above class, function ScanPorts() accepts four parameters – a host (for example, 127.0.0.1), start and end values specifying the range of ports to scan, and an option to set the timeout in seconds that defines how long the program is allowed to process. If the port responds, that is if the connection is established, then it is open, and a simple message is printed.

The PHP function fsockopen() is the central statement in our Scanner class. Upon successful connection the $socket becomes a pointer which can be used with PHP's standard I/O functions such as fread(), fgets(), fwrite(), fpassthru, and feof().

Here is the PHP script that instantiates our scanner class:

```
//index.php
<?php
// Include the scanner class file
require("scanner.php");

// Instantiate scanner class
$scanner = new Scanner;

// Invoke ScanPorts method
$fp = $scanner->ScanPorts("127.0.0.1",78,85,60);
?>
```

We have supplied the class with a host of 127.0.0.1 and a port range of 78 to 85, with a timeout of 60 seconds. Since 127.0.0.1, is our loopback (localhost) address, the client and server happen to be on the same machine; this is useful for testing applications that use TCP/IP ports for communications.

In our Scanner class, we could have used fsockopen() to set a timeout, which would have applied to each socket call. Instead, we opted for a global timeout using the set_timout_limit() function.

Here are some ways in which we could expand our scanner class:

- A single ScanPort() method
- A looping method that requests ScanPort()
- A method that reads the result (connecting to the port) using possibly fgets(), fread(), or fpassthru()
- A method that writes to the opened port with fwrite() or fputs()
- A method that tries to identify the port with a particular web protocol
- A method that places the scan result into an array, with the array being referenced as a public class variable, instead of verbose printing

Reference

Our main functions to open a socket and related standard I/O operations with descriptions as they relate to TCP/IP are:

PHP Function Prototype	Description
fsockopen(host, port, errno, errstr, timeout)	Attempts to open communication with a port on the host with an optional timeout and error responses. If successful, the variable that instantiated the call can now be used as a pointer with respect to standard I/O operations. Example: `$socket = fsockopen('127.0.0.1', 80);` Will attempt to connect to common HTTP port 80 on host 127.0.0.1. If successful $socket is returned as a file pointer handle.
fread($socket, length)	Reads from $socket pointer up to length characters.
fwrite($socket, string, length)	Writes the string up to length to $socket (opened server socket).
fgets($socket, length)	Reads a line up to length-1 from the socket. Example: `$Result = fgets($socket, 128);` Will read in 128 characters from $socket (server response) and place them in $Result variable.

Table continued on following page

PHP Function Prototype	Description

`feof( $socket )`	Returns TRUE if end of file is reached from `$socket`.
	
	Example:
	
	`$idx = 0`
	
	`while(!feof($socket))`
	
	`    $Result[$idx++] = fgets($socket,`
	
	`                          128);`
	
	This code snippet will place in the `$Result` array socket response until end-of-file condition is true.

`fpassthru($socket)`	Will send the entire contents of socket response to an output stream.

We already know that most of PHP's standard I/O functions can be used whenever we are specifically dealing with native HTTP or FTP:

Resource	Description
http://www.ipprimer.com/overview.cfm	TCP/IP Primer
http://www.php.net/manual/ref.sockets.php	Raw Sockets in PHP
http://www.itprc.com/tcpipfaq/default.htm	TCP/IP FAQ

Jabber

Jabber is an instant messaging protocol based on XML. Jabber-based software is currently being used on several computers across the world. The protocol is managed by Jabber Software Foundation.

Description

Jabber is a free-for-use XML-based messaging system for instant messaging. It is open-standards based, and supports many existing server and client implementations that allow for a message to be sent between two registered clients. Other popular instant messaging services are also supported by Jabber, which eases development of a PHP-based IM solution that can access a variety of clients.

Luckily, there exists an open-source development effort that has an experimental Jabber PHP class, which we will use to connect to a live Jabber server.

> The PHP class is available from JabberStudio (www.jabberstudio.org) or at:
> http://www.jabberstudio.org/cgi-bin/viewcvs.cgi/phpjabberclass/PHPJabberClass/.

Code Example

We would like to use PHP to connect to a Jabber server so that we may:

- Have a gateway to all popular Instant Messaging clients (AOL, ICQ, MSN IM, SMS gateways) instead of writing a PHP handler for each service
- Use Jabber as an interim messaging protocol instead of XML-RPC or SOAP
- Create richer instant groupware applications such as White Board on top of Jabber

As with many of the popular instant messaging system we have to log on with a username and password from a particular server. We would suggest finding a public Jabber server, or install your own for testing (server implementations can be downloaded from www.jabber.org).

> **We can find a list of public Jabber servers at http://www.jabbercentral.org/.**

Let's first take a look at the Jabber test page that instantiates the class. Remember that we must put in our Jabber username and password.

```php
<?php
include("jabber/jabber.php");

// Details that we set up with either a public jabber server or our own
// local server
$loginusername = "phpbrowser" ;
$loginpassword = "password" ;
$loginserver   = "example.com" ;

// Instantiate class and fetch the data from the server.
$jabber = new Jabber;
$jabber->server($loginserver);
$jabber->auth($loginusername, $loginpassword);
if ($dest == "") {
    $dest = $loginserver;
}
$browsed = $jabber->say('<iq id="browse_1" type="get" to="' .
                   htmlentities($dest) . '">
                   <query xmlns="jabber:iq:browse"/></iq>', "browse_1");
$jabber->close();

// Let's use the data as we see fit.
header ("Content-Type: text/xml");
print ("<?xml version='1.0'?>");
print ("<?xml-stylesheet href='browser.xsl' type='text/xsl'?>");
print ("$browsed");
?>
```

As we can see, the Jabber class can be supplied with logon credentials to access a Jabber server.

Our actual viewer is created using XSLT, which performs a transform on XML data generated by the PHP Jabber class, and ultimately data is sent from the Jabber server. Here's `browser.xsl`:

```xml
<?xml version="1.0"?>
<xsl:stylesheet xmlns:xsl="http://www.w3.org/1999/XSL/Transform"
version="1.0">
  <xsl:output method="html" encoding="iso-8859-1" />

  <xsl:template match="/">
    <html>
    <head>
      <title>PHP Jabber Browser -demo</title>
      <script language="Javascript1.2" type="text/javascript">
        <xsl:text>
          function browseto(destination) {
          var myurl;
          myurl = document.location + "";
          myurl = myurl.split('?')[0];
          document.location = myurl + "?dest=" + destination;
          }
        </xsl:text>
      </script>
    </head>
    <body>
      <xsl:apply-templates select="/IQ"/>
    </body>
    </html>
  </xsl:template>
  <xsl:template match="/IQ/SERVICE/CONFERENCE">
    groupchat: <xsl:call-template name="linkit">
      <xsl:with-param name="dest"><xsl:value-of
                  select="@JID"/></xsl:with-param>
      <xsl:with-param name="name"><xsl:value-of
                  select="@NAME"/></xsl:with-param>
    </xsl:call-template><br/>
  </xsl:template>
  <xsl:template match="/IQ/SERVICE/SERVICE">
    Child: <xsl:call-template name="linkit">

      <xsl:with-param name="dest"><xsl:value-of
                  select="@JID"/></xsl:with-param>
      <xsl:with-param name="name"><xsl:value-of
                  select="@NAME"/></xsl:with-param>
    </xsl:call-template><br/>
  </xsl:template>
  <xsl:template match="/IQ/SERVICE/*" priority='0'>
    Unknown element <xsl:value-of select="name()"/>
  </xsl:template>
  <xsl:template match="/IQ">
    <h1>Jabber Browser, browsing
      <xsl:value-of select="@FROM" />
    </h1>
    <xsl:apply-templates/>
  </xsl:template>
```

```
  <xsl:template name="linkit">
    <xsl:param name="dest"/>
    <xsl:param name="name"/>
    <xsl:element name="span">
      <xsl:attribute name="onclick">browseto('<xsl:value-of
                     select="$dest"/>')</xsl:attribute>
      <xsl:value-of select="$name"/>
    </xsl:element>
  </xsl:template>

  <xsl:template match="/IQ/SERVICE">
    Parent:
      <xsl:call-template name="linkit">
        <xsl:with-param name="dest"><xsl:value-of
                        select="@JID"/></xsl:with-param>
        <xsl:with-param name="name"><xsl:value-of
                        select="@NAME"/></xsl:with-param>
      </xsl:call-template>
    <br/>
    <xsl:apply-templates/>
  </xsl:template>
</xsl:stylesheet>
```

We must make sure that XSLT processing is available in our web browser (most likely IE), or we could use PHP to parse the result by performing the transform on the server, which would ensure that all browsers would be able to use this.

Here is the code to be replaced:

```
// Let's use the data as we see fit.
header ("Content-Type: text/xml");
print ("<?xml version='1.0'?>");
print ("<?xml-stylesheet href='browser.xsl' type='text/xsl'?>");
print ("$browsed");
```

Replace the above snippet from jabber.php with the following common bit of transform code.

XSLT code to perform transformation on the server:

```
// Place $browsed in an array
$arguments = array('/_xml' => $browsed);
// instantiate a new XSLT processor
$x = xslt_create();

// Transform browsed with browser.xsl
$result = xslt_process($xh, 'arg:/_xml', 'browser.xsl', NULL, $arguments);
if ($result) {
    print ($result);
} else {
    print ("supplied XML did not transform properly ");
    print (" the \$result variable the reason is that " . xslt_error($x))
    print (" and the error code is " . xslt_errno($x));
}

  // Destroy XSLT processor
  xslt_free($x);
```

> **We must have XSLT processing enabled for our amended example to work.**

We now have an implemented instant messenger service built using Jabber, XML, and PHP. There is no reason why we could not extend this to include more sophisticated activities, for example, in/out message board, telephone message, whiteboard, and to browse and talk.

Reference

Resource	Description
http://www.jabber.org/	Official Jabber site which has many lists and links to client/server implementations
http://www.jabberstudio.org/	Open Jabber development site
http://www.jabberstudio.org/projects/view.php?id=9	Direct link to Jabber PHP classes

PHP and Web Services

Now, we'll stitch together many of the PHP XML concepts we've learned, in building our understanding of connecting to web service-type applications. Web services are a key component of the future of the Web as a medium of automated transactions and applications created from building blocks that we can compose.

In this section we will review:

❑ Current status and definition of web services

❑ Service-orientated architectures

❑ General security issues

❑ SOAP request-response MEP with various examples

❑ Changes in SOAP versions

Current State of Web Services

If this book was to be written a year from now then there will exist a well-defined characterization of web services. Here are some current conceptions of what web services are from the various standards organizations:

❑ Web services are Internet-friendly distributed applications that use XML

❑ Web services are distributed, transport-neutral application building blocks that can be discovered and composed into larger applications

❑ Web services are a method of performing RPC operations over TCP/IP

❑ Web service is an XML document-centric messaging system

❑ Web services are a major component of the proposed Semantic Web

In the recent past, we would assess DCOM, RMI, CORBA, or a variety of other network technologies to fulfil our messaging and RPC requirements. These technologies tend to be over-qualified when doing something simple, such as implementing a stateless client/server situation, but are well-suited to the complex requirements of a full-fledged distributed enterprise application. Web services can loosely be considered as a distant lightweight cousin to these heavy weight protocols. Web services make it easy to create client/server applications.

Who's Defining Web Services?

The key participants in specifying the architecture of web services are:

❑ World Wide Web Consortium (W3C): a more in-depth discussion later on in this section.

❑ Organization for the Advancement of Structured Information Standards (OASIS): relevant efforts are RELAX NG (a simpler alternative to XML schema), DOCBOOK, eBXML initiatives.

❑ Internet Engineering Task Force (IETF): the fundamental standards organization for the Internet.

❑ Microsoft: SOAP, .NET strategy, and various standards efforts.

❑ Sun Microsystems: a raft of standards and XML processor implementations, including XML pipeline.

❑ IBM: XML encryption and various implementations.

❑ Web Services Interoperability Organization (WS-I:): supported by industry. Set up by industry giants to promote standard conventions and adoption of web services as a whole.

The history of any standards effort can be interesting in interpreting the standard's intended use – especially in vendor lock-in implications. An appropriate example is the development of SOAP. SOAP was originally cooked up by DevelopMentor, Microsoft, and Userland Software and the SOAP specification was then submitted to the IETF. Though a quick check on the W3C web site will show that SOAP resides there in its current SOAP v1.2 version.

Let's quickly take a look at the W3C efforts, as many of the underlying technologies that web service architectures propose and implement are specified here.

Efforts At W3C

The W3C has a large number of Working Groups that have some impact on web services:

❑ XMLP – the XML protocol working group

❑ SOAP

❑ Web Services WG

❑ TAG

❑ XML Schemas

❑ The suite of XML technologies, for example, XQuery, XPath, XSLT, XPointer, XInclude, and XLink

The W3C has published a Web Services Architecture Requirements document (http://www.w3.org/TR/2002/WD-wsa-reqs-20020429/) that succinctly characterizes a web service:

> *A web service is a software application identified by a URI, whose interfaces and binding are capable of being defined, described, and discovered by XML artifacts and supports direct interactions with other software applications using XML-based messages via Internet-based protocols.*

In addition, the WG has identified some standard web services user scenarios:

- One-way message with guaranteed delivery
- Document-centric computing
- Remote procedure call
- Request with acknowledgement
- Third-party intermediary
- Communication via multiple intermediaries
- Asynchronous messaging
- Events and events notification
- Versioning

Probably the most important recent event at the W3C is the creation of TAG (Technical Architecture Group), which attempts to focus and build consensus throughout all of the W3C's efforts. The TAG e-mail discussion list is particularly active in issues that affect web services (http://www.w3.org/2001/tag/).

References

Resource	Description
http://www.ws-i.org	WS-I
http://www.w3.org/2002/ws/	W3C
http://www.w3.org/2001/03/wsws-popa/paper51	IBM & Microsoft
http://www.oasis-open.org	OASIS
http:// www.ietf.org	IETF
http://wwws.sun.com/software/xml/developers/	SUN Microsystems
http://www.microsoft.com/webservices	Microsoft
http://xml.apache.org	Apache XML Site
http://www.xml.com	O'Reilly XML Site
http://www.xmlhack.com	Up to the Minute XML news

Service-Orientated Architecture (SOA)

PHP is commonly found within a complicated processing stream with respect to integrating data from disparate sources or interfacing with multiple programming environments. For example, a PHP-powered web site may be required to bridge data from an IBM 3270 mainframe and cross-correlate with data from an RDBMS database. This dataset may then require query forms for searching, and possibly for editing, the data. There may be an additional requirement to push the data out in an RSS format for external consumption. In addition, we will most certainly want to present the data in compelling experiences, possibly repurposing the data for use in other applications.

These scenarios reinforce the use of PHP as the glue framework between various systems. Historically, the programmer has had to manually discover integration methods between programming environments and create one-off architectures that are hard to maintain and scale. Web services propose a general simplification of disparate architectures by exposing functionality in discrete units, which are self-describing about their functions and interfaces.

Casting web services within a Service Orientated Architecture creates a powerful marketplace where consumers discover and contract only desired services. A PHP programmer may then create applications that discover and choose web services (based upon inference rules) without ever having to know specific programmatic or operating environment details.

An architecture that is built up of disparate services promotes interoperability between all the different applications that exist today. Current software architectures may be replaced over time, and can be built again with web services. Service-orientated architecture may aggregate many services into composite packages. This ability to build up or break down services is known as decomposability:

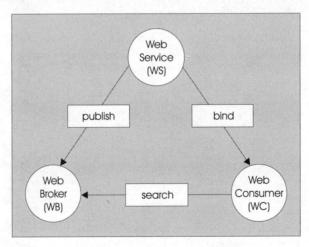

The above diagram delineates the relationship between:

❑ **Web Services** (WS):
A discrete unit of functionality which may bind (create a contract for use and provision a particular user) with a consumer. In addition, the service exposes meta data for description and discovery.

❑ **Web Consumers** (WC):
An application and/or a user may search for an appropriate service for use. When a desired service is found, a contract is negotiated between the web service provider and the consumer for usage.

❑ **Web Brokers** (WB):
Acts as a repository of information about published web service meta data, so that web consumers may search for an appropriate service based on inference rules. This may also provide mechanisms that assist contract negotiations, provisioning, and quality of services issues.

The following diagram characterizes a more complicated real-life situation, where there exists an internal corporate network and the public Internet:

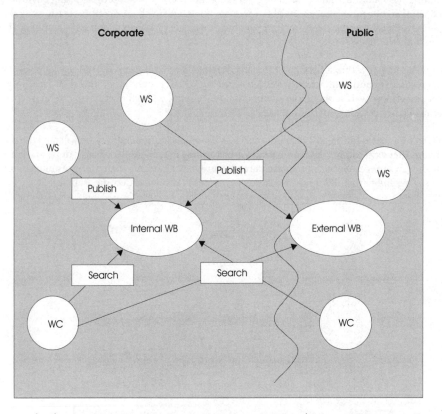

Web services (WS) can publish their information into internal **UDDI**s (Universal Description Discovery and Integration) (WB) for internal consumers (WC) to bind to, though it may be desirable to publish certain services for public consumption. The reverse is true, in that a composite internal service may use an external web service, which itself has been registered with an internal broker.

The implementation of programming environments and languages are abstracted behind common well-known interfaces and technologies that we will discuss later on in this section. The following abstract diagram illustrates the main components involved in a SOA with their most common technical counterparts (for example, SOAP, WSDL, and UDDI):

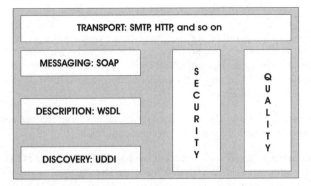

The diagram, however, does not address all the issues encountered in SOAs:

❑ **Provisioning**:
Currently there is a lack of conventions as regards handling the registration of a user to use a web service; either this is coupled with the web service as an additional interface or with some external mechanism.

❑ **Contract**
A contract between a consumer and service will require a mechanism for negotiating the terms and conditions of service usage.

❑ **Versioning**
With new versions a web service may fundamentally change its interfaces. This may cause a composite service to break, or a web consumer's existing contract to not be honored.

❑ **Security Credentials**:
Require a mechanism for exchanging security credentials and quality of service information.

There are higher order abstractions such as business orchestration or mechanisms assisting in real business supply chains and workflows that need to be addressed. In addition, the creation of intelligent agents that make decisions based on a set of static and dynamic inference rules will also require additional mechanisms and meta data.

We will now describe the SOA layers plus security issues in greater detail.

Messaging

Reliable messaging is essential for implementing decoupled web service architecture. It ensures that a message is delivered once and only once. An optional requirement may be placed on the receiving a confirmation or failure of delivery. This definition of reliability should also work when there are multiple nodes to be processed between the initial sender and receiver.

This strict transactional nature of messaging does not exist in pure TCP/IP, or HTTP, as they are stateless transport protocols. Reliable messaging may be implemented on top of these protocols, but there are other efforts that may augment TCP/IP and its specifications, such as IBM's proposed **HTTPR** (http://www-106.ibm.com/developerworks/webservices/library/ws-phtt/?dwzone=webservices).

A message system that is loosely coupled is another requirement of an SOA. When two systems are loosely coupled then the only requirement for messaging between them is to understand self-describing text-based messages. Since XML is text-based and self describing it is a natural choice for SOAP to fulfil some of these requirements.

Description

A service provides a description about itself in the form of meta data, which contains details about the interfaces a service has, its related schema, and data types of any input and output parameters. This meta data allows for the message to be processed independently without going back to where the message originated from. The service becomes self describing to the potential consumer of the web service and the programmer who may have to interface with the service.

A text description, version information, privacy policy, or qualities of service are additional meta data examples that could also be provided for the web service consumer.

Protocols which are concerned purely with transport, such as XML-RPC and SOAP, may be augmented to be fully descriptive and self contained. **WSDL** (Web Service Description Language) is an example of this, which we will discuss when we create some examples using WSDL with SOAP later in this chapter.

Discovery

Programmers or applications may search for services via specific directory engines and apply rules with which to choose them, based on the meta data that they expose. One may also search for composite services, or possibly decompose just part of the service to the desired set of services. There are already specific search engines and registries that specialize in web services. Various efforts are being made to organize a global directory of web services.

UDDI is probably the most popular of these initiatives. UDDI is a SOAP-based web service that uses a WSDL description of a web service. It is also a global registry for describing a business' service. Specifically, UDDI is a software concept and a business registry.

Security

There are difficulties in implementing encryption and access controls on a streams-based protocol on which web services are based.

Currently there are a few efforts that are addressing security issues, one of which is the XML Encryption effort, of which there is one excellent implementation by IBM.

> **IBM's Security Suite provides an implementation of the W3C's XML Encryption and Signature specification. Also, OASIS's XACML specification is implemented for handling information access policies.**

Here is a brief list of the most mature and important standards that relate to security processes within web services.

XML Encryption

The W3C's recommendation for capturing the results of an encryption process within XML allows for a partial encryption of XML data.

XML Signature

The W3C's proposed a recommendation that defines a schema for capturing the results of a digital signature operation. Typically, digital signatures assist in authentication, non-repudiation, and data integrity; all of which XML signature addresses, though the XML signature is specific to both the Internet and XML.

XACML (eXtensible Access Control Markup Language)

An OASIS specification in the form of a markup language which addresses the definition of fine-grained control mechanisms over authorized activities such as reading and writing to a file in a directory. Control is referenced by a user, a request protocol, and the authentication mechanism such as the presence of a particular signature ID.

SAML (Security Assertion Markup Language)

Defines a standard for exchanging authentication and authorization information between domains. SAML addresses single sign-on for users/machines, permission definition, and assertions of authentication.

P3P (Platform for Privacy Preferences Project)

This project is part of the W3C's effort for defining privacy policies for web sites. Here is an example of some P3P markup that describes a web site's privacy policy:

```
<POLICIES xmlns="http://www.w3.org/2002/01/P3Pv1">
<POLICY discuri="http://www.example.com/p3p.html">
  <ENTITY>
    <DATA-GROUP>
      <DATA ref="#business.name">example.com</DATA>
      <DATA ref="#business.contact-info.postal.street">34 Bedford Row</DATA>
    </DATA-GROUP>
  </ENTITY>
  <ACCESS><nonident/></ACCESS>
  <STATEMENT>
    <PURPOSE><admin/><develop/></PURPOSE>
    <RETENTION><stated-purpose/></RETENTION>
    <DATA-GROUP>
      <DATA ref="#dynamic.http"/>
    </DATA-GROUP>
  </STATEMENT>
</POLICY>
</POLICIES>
```

Essentially, this policy expresses that no user profile data is acquired by example.com, yet data on HTTP (such as a web server access log) transactions is stored and analyzed for development and administrative purposes (as indicated by the `<PURPOSE>` element).

> Microsoft Internet Explorer v6.0 includes P3P support for blocking functionality based on policy assertions.

WS-Security

Microsoft, IBM, and others describe a suite of enhancements to the SOAP specification that addresses authentication and integrity. It also provides a generic mechanism for associating security tokens.

> SAML has been chosen by the Liberty Alliance (a consortium of companies defining security standards and processes for identity), for defining authentication assertions from one business to another.

561

The PHP programmer has to be aware of the security implications of web service technologies. SOAP, UDDI, and the above security technologies require an investment in time and energy, and all have security pitfalls, which are characterized by the following paragraph.

> *The major problem of allowing a diverse range of clients performing complex operations, or invoking local methods, is that the responsibility of enforcing ACL's and general access is spread across many problem domains.*

A firewall, for example, is typically responsible for the blocking, non-blocking, or auditing of TCP/IP ports. As applications have grown and become Internet-enabled, the firewall starts enforcing application-level security requirements instead of its initial role as a gatekeeper. Web services, implemented over SOAP, bring unique problems, highlighting the inadequacy of HTTP headers and the lack of clear identifiers within the headers by telling the firewall that "hey, we're a SOAP RPC packet", that's going to activate some processes. Existing firewall solutions will have a problem with proposed SOA implementations:

- ❏ SOAP will tunnel through to internal enterprise
- ❏ Port 80 normally is monitored for HTTP web operations, not remote method invocation
- ❏ HTTP SOAP binding defines very little information in HTTP header for the firewall to analyze; in addition, the SOAPAction in HTTP header is not mandatory

References

Resource	Description
http://www.webservices.org/	Web Service Org
http://www.w3.org/2002/ws/	SOAP
http://www.w3.org/tr/wsdl	WSDL
http://www.w3.org/Encryption/2001/	W3C XML encryption effort
http://www.w3.org/P3P/	W3c Privacy Policy Effort
http://www.uddi.org/specification.html	UDDI
http://uddi.microsoft.com/default.aspx	Microsoft UDDI
http://www.systinet.com/	Sysinet UDDI v2 implementation
http://www.alphaworks.ibm.com/tech/xmlsecuritysuite	IBM Security Suite
http://www.xml.com/pub/a/2001/04/04/webservices/index.html	Web Service Overview
http://www.oasis-open.org/committees/xacml/	XACML
http://www.oasis-open.org/committees/security/	SAML

SOAP

Simple Object Access Protocol is a stateless, XML-based set of conventions that defines a method for exchanging textual and structured information in a distributed environment. More specifically, SOAP is used as an XML messaging framework between a SOAP sender and receiver. A SOAP conversation between nodes follows certain patterns, known within the SOAP specification as **MEP** (Message Exchange Patterns). A common message pattern is analogous to an HTTP client sending a request to a server, which then responds back to the client. This was formally known as a request-response MEP.

This section will take an in-depth look at SOAP. The typical scenarios where SOAP could be employed are:

- ❑ When sending XML documents between peers/nodes/client/server
- ❑ As a document-centric messaging framework
- ❑ As a method for exposing functionality via an RPC (Remote Procedure Call) style interface
- ❑ As a document-centric processing framework where there are multiple nodes which process the request or response

A SOAP client creates a request, and sends it to a SOAP server whereupon the server responds possibly with the result of some processing. Both the request and response SOAP messages are XML documents:

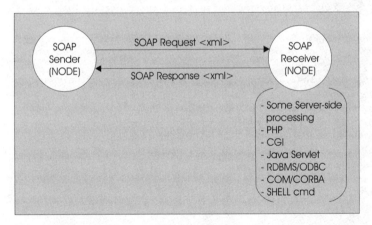

As illustrated, a SOAP server can perform various processes based on receiving a request, for instance, processing a PHP, shell, or CGI script, Java servlets, a COM or CORBA call, or possibly generating an XForms document. It will return the results of any of these processing as an XML document within an HTTP payload.

SOAP defines two recognized styles:

- ❑ An XML messaging system (document style) – the SOAP body carries a generic XML document of our own definition
- ❑ A method invocation mechanism (RPC style) – the SOAP body conforms to a specific convention, as specified in the SOAP specification

In our major example, throughout this section, we will be employing the RPC style.

SOAP currently has two major versions, v1.1 and v1.2. Where appropriate, use of a specific version will be explicitly flagged. Otherwise v1.1 will be used. There are few non-trivial changes, and these are listed at the end of this section.

SOAP is self-contained and has been designed to be accessed in a generic way. It has many client- and server-side implementations in many different languages like C, C++, C#, Java, JavaScript, Perl, Tcl, Python, Ruby, Smalltalk, and VB.

SOAP Over Different Transport Protocols

SOAP is agnostic to transport protocol. This is great advantage for application developers, as it gives a wide range of choices, and makes interoperability easier to implement.

Here is an example of a SOAP message using SMTP as its transport:

```
From:jim@on-idle.com
To: reservations@example.com
Subject: Travel to Providence, RI
Date: Thu, 29 Mar 2002 12:00:00 GMT
Message-id:<EE492E16A0B8D311AC490090276D208424960C0C@on-idle.com>

<?xml version='1.0' ?>
<env:Envelope xmlns:env=" http://schemas.xmlsoap.org/soap/envelope/" >
<env:Body>
  <p:itinerary xmlns:p="http://www.example.com/reservation/travel">
    <p:departure>
       <p:departing>London</p:departing>
       <p:arriving>Providence</p:arriving>
       <p:departureDate>2002-04-15</p:departureDate>
       <p:departureTime>early morning</p:departureTime>
    </p:departure>
  </p:itinerary>
</env:Body>
</env:Envelope>
```

The SMTP header is used by the SOAP processor, which in turn must be aware of the application-specific details of how to process such a header. Otherwise the key message is contained within the XML document, so any transport environment that can handle text-based XML markup, in theory could have SOAP implemented over it.

Protocol Examination

Let's study the components of SOAP in some detail.

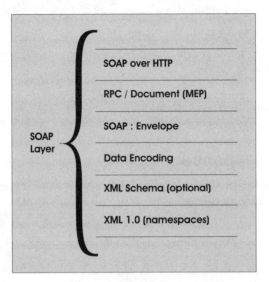

The above diagram shows the relationships of technologies and SOAP conventions. Let's now decompose the protocol in some detail.

Encoding Data Structures

The SOAP encoding system is a generic type system modeled after common languages, databases, and structured data. Simple types and more complex types (called compound types), may be created out of simple types.

The SOAP `encodingStyle` attribute is used to indicate serialization rules (how data is formatted and typed) on either the entire XML document, or on specific elements:

- ❑   `SOAP-ENV:encodingStyle=http://schemas.xmlsoap.org/soap/encoding/` : SOAP v1.1
- ❑   `SOAP-ENV:encodingStyle=http://www.w3.org/2001/12/soap-encoding` : SOAP v1.2
- ❑   `SOAP-ENV:encodingStyle=http://www.myencoding.com/`
- ❑   `SOAP-ENV:encodingStyle=" "`

The final declaration declares that there is no statement made about the encoding of the message

> The default namespace for SOAP encoding and data types is
> **http://schemas.xmlsoap.org/soap/encoding/.**

The SOAP body contains textual values, and simple types like integers, strings, enumerations, and more complex types, like structs or arrays.

Don't get too caught up in data types at the moment, just keep in mind that SOAP provides a out-of-the-box rich set of mechanisms for which we may type and format data. Here are some more salient points:

❏   We can use data types built-in with a Schema, for example, `integer`, `float`, and `date`

❏   SOAP encoding uses XML Schema types

❏   SOAP has built-ins for `<arrays>` & `<structs>` in an external Schema document directly in our message using `xsi:type`

> **SOAP must not have a DTD embedded within any part of the message.**

SOAP Request-Response

In this section we will review in detail a message exchange pattern which is described in detail within the SOAP specification, and is known as Request-Response. A SOAP node acts as sender and creates a request, a SOAP node receiver then processes and returns a **response**, as illustrated in the previous diagram.

Since SOAP can send messages in the form of an XML document, it may be used as a mechanism to invoke RPCs. SOAP has no specifications for dealing with RPC, but instead has a set of conventions that describe the use of RPC in a SOAP message. Let's take a look at the details of a SOAP request and subsequent SOAP response.

Request

The request part of SOAP is initiated by the SOAP client in the form of an HTTP-formatted message sent to the server. Since we are interested in SOAP as it pertains to PHP, HTTP is going to be one of our main usages, so, for our purposes, we will use the SOAP HTTP binding in our examples.

HTTP Request Header

First is our HTTP request header used for a SOAP request:

```
POST /soap/servlet/rpcrouter HTTP/1.1
Host: services.xmethods.net:80
SOAPAction:
Content-Type: text/xml ; charset="utf-8"
Content-Length: 516
```

The complete URL is http://services.xmethods.net:80/soap/servlet/rpcrouter for our HTTP POST.

The optional `SOAPAction` HTTP verb identifies the specific method requested via a URN, in the above case there is no `SOAPAction` value (as we mentioned in our discussion of security). It's always a good practice to include this (even if blank) as it is a mechanism for firewalls and proxies to detect that this is a SOAP request.

A `Content-Type` of `text/xml` (or `application/soap` for SOAP v1.2) is required for the message to be processed correctly by a SOAP server. Notice that the character encoding, as usual, can be appended for HTTP to interpret correctly. Setting this to UTF-8 ensures maximum interoperability.

It is always recommended to include a content length that must have the correct size for the entire message in bytes.

Following the HTTP header is the XML document known as the **SOAP envelope**.

SOAP Request Envelope

The main SOAP message is contained in a `<soap:Envelope>` element after the HTTP header, fully qualified by the correct namespace:

```
<SOAP-ENV:Envelope
  xmlns:SOAP-ENV="http://schemas.xmlsoap.org/soap/envelope/"
  xmlns:xsi="http://www.w3.org/1999/XMLSchema-instance"
  xmlns:xsd="http://www.w3.org/1999/XMLSchema">

  <SOAP-ENV:Body>
    <m:getTemp xmlns:m="urn:xmethods-Temperature"
    SOAP-ENV:encodingStyle="http://schemas.xmlsoap.org/soap/encoding/">
    <zipcode xsi:type="xsd:string">94041</zipcode>
    </m:getTemp>
  </SOAP-ENV:Body>
</SOAP-ENV:Envelope>
```

There are normally two children elements: `<Header>` (optional, used for generally extending the SOAP message), and `<Body>` (mandatory). Nothing can precede this `Envelope` element.

The `<Header>` element is responsible for containing meta data, or processing hints for a particular SOAP node, in addition to assisting in handling intermediate node processing. The `<Body>` element contains the RPC or document style XML message. We will talk about both of them more in detail now.

SOAP Request: <Header>

Header elements are the main extensibility mechanism in SOAP. They describe to a SOAP node, which headers are for processing, and which header elements are pure meta data, in no particular order. The header element could be optional in any situation.

Some typical scenarios of using headers are:

❑ Authenticate a user to access the SOAP method

❑ Contain data on a user's profile, which may assist in logging or processing of the SOAP body

❑ Contain important information for transactions, or purchasing

As per the SOAP specification, a header must have:

❑ A local name

❑ The typical SOAP namespace

❑ Zero or more children elements with a declared namespace

Each SOAP header element is known as a **SOAP header block** and must be namespace-qualified. Every SOAP header block may also have various attributes that determine how they are processed and by which SOAP nodes.

We have not used any header example in this chapter; it's just being presented here to illustrate what a typical SOAP header would look like:

```
<soap:Header>
  <p:Block xmlns:p="http://www.test.com"
    soap:actor="http://www.w3.org/2001/12/soap-envelope/actor/next">

  </p:Block>
  <p:Block xmlns:p="http://www.test.com"
    soap:actor="anonymous" soap:mustUnderstand="true">

  </p:Block>
</soap:Header>
```

There are two `<soap:Header>` elements, with each element being verbose with respect to namespace declaration. A classic problem with SOAP is the seemingly confusing amount of namespaces for both the SOAP-specific namespace and the particular children element namespaces (for example, `xmlns:p=` `http://www.test.com`). The `soap:Header` namespace could be declared here or in the parent `<Envelope>` element.

> We will see declared namespaces everywhere in SOAP; initially it could be a little confusing. In general, it makes a SOAP message a bit unreadable. It is therefore recommended that we review as many SOAP messages as possible, in the specs and repositories, until we feel more comfortable.

For now we may not even encounter headers in the current use of SOAP. Headers are a good place to put additional meta data about a service, and as their usage becomes more common it is expected that more complicated message patterns will arise, making full use of headers.

SOAP Request: <Body>

The body of the SOAP message carries the input to a particular method that is being invoked. In terms of an RPC, the `<SOAP-ENV:Body>` element will contain one child, and is modeled as a **struct** (for those who are familiar with C). More rigorously, the method invocation (`<struct>`) contains child elements, each an accessor for each parameter. The `<struct>` is typed and named exactly as the actual method's name as per the convention.

In the example below a SOAP v1.1 version shows a `<Body>` element, wrapped in an `<Envelope>` element:

```
<SOAP-ENV:Envelope
  xmlns:SOAP-ENV="http://schemas.xmlsoap.org/soap/envelope/"
  xmlns:xsi="http://www.w3.org/1999/XMLSchema-instance"
  xmlns:xsd="http://www.w3.org/1999/XMLSchema">

  <SOAP-ENV:Body>
    <m:getTemp xmlns:m="urn:xmethods-Temperature"
    SOAP-ENV:encodingStyle="http://schemas.xmlsoap.org/soap/encoding/">
    <zipcode xsi:type="xsd:string">94041</zipcode>
    </m:getTemp>
  </SOAP-ENV:Body>
</SOAP-ENV:Envelope>
```

Let's decipher the declared namespaces, elements, and attributes in this RPC-style body:

❑ `xmlns:SOAP-ENV`: is the SOAP namespace for using SOAP v1.1.

❑ `xmlns:xsi`: is the namespace associated with defining the parameter type attribute.

❑ `xmlns:xsd`: is the namespace that declares that this SOAP message uses XML schema for defining types.

❑ `getTemp`: is the method name that is being invoked.

❑ `xmlns:m`: is the namespace declared for the method and associated input parameters. This could be a reference to an external XML schema file. Remember that a namespace identifies uniqueness so we may use the URL format or a URN format. In this case, `urn:xmethods-Temperature`, is obviously the URN format.

❑ `SOAP:ENV attribute`: this defines that the method is using this encoding style.

❑ `xsi:type`: the input parameter `<zipcode>` is defined as a string, as per XML schema with a value of 94041.

This particular web service returns the temperature of a Postal Zip code (94041) region within the USA. We will use this web service throughout all our examples.

Now let's see what the SOAP server responds with.

Response

The SOAP request is processed by the **ultimate** SOAP receiver, which performs some processing and then generates either a SOAP response, or a SOAP fault. This XML document is then sent back to the original SOAP sender.

HTTP Response: <Header>

This is not any special SOAP HTTP header, but just a plain old HTTP header:

```
HTTP/1.0 200 OK
Date: Tue, 09 Apr 2002 16:50:42 GMT
Status: 200
Content-Type: text/xml; charset=utf-8
Servlet-Engine: Lutris Enhydra Application Server/3.5.2 (JSP 1.1; Servlet 2.2;
Java 1.3.0; Linux 2.4.7-10smp x86; java.vendor=IBM Corporation)
Content-Length: 465
Set-Cookie: JSESSIONID=NFn4wNTyBHTRXEBoXyGlXSWj;Path=/soap
Server: Enhydra-MultiServer/3.5.2
```

Obviously, the amount of information presented is based upon how a particular web server or SOAP server is set up. There really isn't any information here that is useful for processing, except of course that the `Content-Type` is `text/xml` and we have the `Content-Length`, which we will be using for client-side processing of the SOAP response.

We could also look for the typical HTTP errors (for example 401 and 500) and use this as a basis of some formatting. Though, if an error does occur, we will get much more information from the SOAP fault body.

SOAP Response: <Body>

The body will look quite similar to the SOAP request. This SOAP v1.1 response has returned a temperature of 55.0 degrees (Fahrenheit):

```
<?xml version='1.0' encoding='UTF-8'?>
  <SOAP-ENV:Envelope
    xmlns:SOAP-ENV="http://schemas.xmlsoap.org/soap/envelope/"
    xmlns:xsi="http://www.w3.org/1999/XMLSchema-instance"
    xmlns:xsd="http://www.w3.org/1999/XMLSchema">
    <SOAP-ENV:Body>
      <ns1:getTempResponse xmlns:ns1="urn:xmethods-Temperature"
      SOAP-ENV:encodingStyle="http://schemas.xmlsoap.org/soap/encoding/">
      <return xsi:type="xsd:float">55.0</return>
      </ns1:getTempResponse>
    </SOAP-ENV:Body>
  </SOAP-ENV:Envelope>
```

Notice that the original method name getTemp, has been appended with Response. This is one of the conventions specified when dealing with RPC-style messages. In addition, the SOAP response has its own namespace ns1, with the same unique namespace as declared in the SOAP request. The other difference to the SOAP request is that there is now a new output parameter called <return> and it has a floating point data type (this is a service that gets the temperature, so we need floating point).

So, our server responded with a return value of 55, which of course represents 55 degrees Fahrenheit in the specified postal code which was our input.

We have covered the actual SOAP specification in enough detail, however, there is one last detail that we need to cover: how SOAP handles fault and error conditions?

SOAP Faults

SOAP has a set of conventions for handling faults, and it's not surprising that a SOAP fault message looks very similar to all the other SOAP messages that we have reviewed. There are some non-trivial changes between the notation and number of fault codes between SOAP v1.1 and SOAP v1.2; be sure to know which version of SOAP server is generating the response, if we are a client of such a server.

When a SOAP receiver or SOAP node throws an error, a fault response will be sent, either to the SOAP sender or to the ultimate SOAP node, in a complex multi-node MEP. We will not be handling SOAP errors in our following examples; so, the SOAP fault response that you see is a fictitious response from a travel agency web service.

Following is a typical SOAP fault response:

```
<?xml version='1.0' ?>
<env:Envelope xmlns:env="http://www.w3.org/2001/12/soap-envelope"
              xmlns:f='http://www.w3.org/2001/12/soap-faults'>
  <env:Body>
    <env:Fault>
      <faultcode>env:Receiver</faultcode>
      <faultstring>Processing Error</faultstring>
      <detail>
```

```
            <e:myfaultdetails xmlns:e="http://travelcompany.example.org/faults">
              <message>Name does not match card number</message>
              <errorcode>999</errorcode>
            </e:myfaultdetails>
          </detail>
        </env:Fault>
      </env:Body>
    </env:Envelope>
```

All the fault information must be contained by a single <env:Fault> element, and can only appear once within the SOAP body element. In turn, there must exist at least two children elements, a <faultcode>, and <faultstring>. There can also be two child elements <faultactor> and <detail>.

❏ <faultcode>
   Contains a specific SOAP-defined error code, as defined in the following error code table

❏ <faultstring>
   Contains a short human understandable message of the fault in question

❏ <faultactor>
   In multi-stage processing, this contains the particular <actor> as referenced by a matching header entry, which ultimately caused the error

❏ <detail>
   Contains application-specific fault information, which is up to the application developer to supply

Fault Code	Description
VersionMatch	Invalid namespace for the SOAP Envelope element
MustUnderstand	A SOAP header element that had an attribute of MustUnderstand was not processed or understood by the SOAP node
DTDNotSupported	SOAP message contained a DTD
DataEncodingUnknown	A header or body element was scoped with a data encoding that the current SOAP node does not support
Sender	The message was not well-formed, or did not contain enough or the correct information, to be processed correctly
Receiver	The message was not processed because of problems with the current SOAP node, and not because of problems with the message contents or format

Simple PHP SOAP Client Example

We will now create an example of how to generate and send a SOAP request over HTTP. This will be achieved by having a manual input HTML form, with default values to a remote web service. Our remote web service provides the current temperature of an area in the USA, based on an input of a zip code. This was the same web service we used to demonstrate the structure of SOAP (previous section), but now we will use it in a real working example.

Remember, to use this service, we should be able to physically access it via the Internet, otherwise we will require a local web service implemented within our development environment, with the caveat that we must enter in the specific details of the web service. Also make sure that if we have a proxy or firewall, our efforts are not being blocked.

Specifically our first PHP SOAP example will demonstrate how to:

❑ Use PHP to create a SOAP request

❑ Use an HTML form with particular web services default values for testing purposes

❑ Use PHP to create and send a SOAP request

❑ Capture a SOAP response from the web service

This example will be useful in testing our own, or remote web services.

Simple Test Form

Initially, we will have to create a HTML form with the following form fields:

❑ `servicehost`
Contains IP or web address

❑ `serviceport`
Which port the service lives on

❑ `servicepath`
The rest of the URL, that is, `servicehost` plus the complete path that is an absolute endpoint to the service

❑ `soapaction`
The optional `SOAPAction`

❑ `contenttype`
Either `text/xml` or `application/soap`, depending on what version of SOAP is being accessed

❑ `charset`
Char encoding

❑ `soapbody`
Complete XML document

These form fields are everything that we need to construct a SOAP request:

```
<html>
  <head>
    <title>SOAP RPC Test</title>
  </head>

  <body>

    <h2>Simple SOAP RPC test</h2>
    <form name="sendrpc" method="post" action="sendsoapmessage.php">

      <table>
        <tr>
```

```
    <td>host:</td>
    <td>
      <input type="text" name="servicehost"
             value="services.xmethods.net"/>
    </td>
</tr>

<tr>
    <td>port:</td>
    <td>
      <input type="text" name="serviceport" value="80"/>
    </td>
</tr>

<tr>
    <td>path:</td>
    <td>
      <input type="text" name="servicepath"
             value="/soap/servlet/rpcrouter"/>
    </td>
</tr>
<tr>
    <td>SOAPAction:</td>
    <td>
      <input type="text" name="soapaction"/>
    </td>
</tr>

<tr>
    <td>Content-Type:</td>
    <td>
      <input type="text" name="contenttype" value="text/xml"/>
    </td>
</tr>

<tr>
    <td>charset:</td>
    <td>
      <input type="text" name="charset" value="UTF-8"/>
    </td>
</tr>

<tr>
    <td>SOAP Message:</td>
    <td>
      <textarea name="soapmessage" rows="20" nowrap cols="80">
        <SOAP-ENV:Envelope
          xmlns:SOAP-ENV="http://schemas.xmlsoap.org/soap/envelope/"
          xmlns:xsi="http://www.w3.org/1999/XMLSchema-instance"
          xmlns:xsd="http://www.w3.org/1999/XMLSchema">

          <SOAP-ENV:Body>
            <m:getTemp xmlns:m="urn:xmethods-Temperature"
              SOAP-ENV:encodingStyle="http:
              //schemas.xmlsoap.org/soap/encoding/">
              <zipcode xsi:type="xsd:string">94041</zipcode>
            </m:getTemp>

          </SOAP-ENV:Body>
        </SOAP-ENV:Envelope>
```

```
            </textarea>
          </td>
        </tr>

        <tr>
          <td>SOAP Message:</td>
          <td>
            <input type="submit" value="Make SOAP request"/>
          </td>
        </tr>
      </table>
    </form>
  </body>
</html>
```

The form contains default values to a temperature service offered by the **Xmethods** web site (**www.xmethods.net**), which is an Apache SOAP v1.1 web service.

Our form should look like the following:

Processing SOAP Message

We will now process the form's variables with PHP to create the SOAP request.

PHP can concatenate all the variables to create the HTTP header for our SOAP request, and simply appends the XML document which is our SOAP message. We then use the PHP `fsockopen()` to open up the correct socket (port) and send the XML data (our SOAP envelope), to the remote web service.

```php
<?php
# strip escape slashes to handle magic_quotes_gpc condition
$holdsoap=stripslashes($_REQUEST["soapmessage"]);
$messagesize=strlen($holdsoap);

# Create HTTP header
$query = "POST ". $_REQUEST["servicepath"]." HTTP/1.1\r\n".
  "Host: ".$_REQUEST["servicehost"].":".$_REQUEST["serviceport"]."\r\n".
  "Content-Type: ".$_REQUEST["contenttype"]." ; charset=".$_REQUEST["charset"]."
\r\n".
  "Content-Length: $messagesize\r\n".
  "SOAPAction:".$_REQUEST["soapaction"]."\r\n".
  "\r\n";

#open a tcp/ip port
$fp = fsockopen($_REQUEST["servicehost"],$_REQUEST["serviceport"]);

if (!$fp) {
    print ("failed to connect to web service !");
} else {
    # inject the header and the soap message which was supplied by the form
    fputs($fp, $query, strlen($query));
    fputs($fp, $query, "<?xml version='1.0'?>");
    fputs($fp, $holdsoap, $messagesize);
}

# print out SOAP server Response to a web form
print ("<html><body><form>");

print ("SOAP Response Message<br/><textarea name='resultmessage'
                                    rows='30' nowrap cols='80'>");

print (fpassthru($fp));
print ("</textarea></form></body></html>");
?>
```

Now we have a form that should contain the SOAP response message that is returned from the web service:

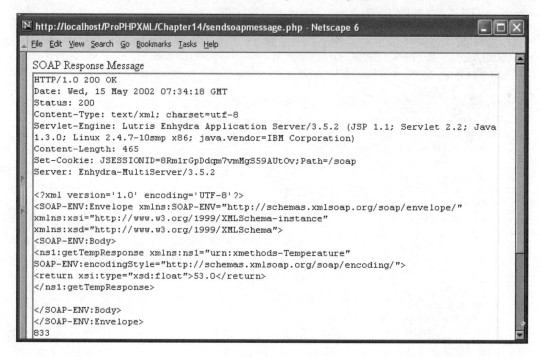

Admittedly, the processing page needs some work, and we will take what we've done here, and create a SOAP client class, and get a bit more sophisticated in the next example. But let's digress a little and discuss a little bit about how SOAP can be extended, now that we have reviewed an actual example.

How To Extend SOAP

Extensibility can be a difficult goal to achieve in any computing context. SOAP achieves a flexible mechanism for extending the original SOAP XML message format through the use of `<soap:Header>` elements.

SOAP header elements may contain information used for processing by the SOAP receiver, or by some intermediate SOAP node. In addition, header elements can contain plain meta data to assist in processing. Here is a SOAP v1.2 message:

```
<soap:Envelope xmlns:soap='http://www.w3.org/2001/10/soap-envelope'>
  <soap:Header>
    <p:data xmlns:p="http://www.test.com"
      soap:actor="http://www.w3.org/2001/12/soap-envelope/actor/none">

    </p:data>
    <p:Block xmlns:p="http://www.test.com"
      soap:actor="http://www.w3.org/2001/12/soap-envelope/actor/next">

    </p:Block>
    <p:Block xmlns:p="http://www.test.com"
```

```
      soap:actor="anonymous" soap:mustUnderstand="true">

    </p:Block>
  </soap:Header>
  <soap:Body>
    <!- payload of the soap message --!>
  </soap:Body>
</soap:Envelope>
```

Let's take a walk through some example header elements and discover the various options available.

Firstly, each header element may have an `actor` attribute. This `actor` attribute allows for more complicated multi-stage processing to occur. A SOAP message may pass through many different processing steps.

The `<p:data>` header declares which namespace it belongs to with the `<xmlns:p=http://www.test.com>` attribute. As mentioned earlier, SOAP elements are exceptionally descriptive in their declaration of namespaces. We need not be bothered with the standard namespaces, but must always remember to declare our own; this is required for RPC style and is a good habit to get into in any event. One of the reasons for this verbosity is that a SOAP message must be self-describing wherever they find themselves (which may mean it has no access to the SOAP node it came from).

`<p:data>` also has a `soap:actor` attribute value of `http://www.w3.org/2001/12/soap-envelope/actor/none`, which identifies this header element as an additional piece of information to assist in processing of the body or header. Consider any `<header>` element with an `actor` attribute of `none` as a place to put additional meta data. When SOAP throws a fault condition, the `actor` that was involved in the `<header>` is quoted, so that the ultimate SOAP receiver may know which SOAP node produced the error.

The next element, `<p:Block>`, is another SOAP header, with its own namespace and an `actor` attribute of `http://www.w3.org/2001/12/soap-envelope/actor/next`. This attribute is used by the next SOAP node.

The last `<p:Block>`, is a direct child of the `<soap:Header>` element, and has its namespace declared as usual. The `actor` attribute, `anonymous`, is another SOAP-defined standard `actor`, which declares that this header is to be processed at the ultimate SOAP node or final SOAP receiver.
The SOAP attribute called `mustunderstand` is set to `TRUE`; which means that that particular SOAP node, as defined by the `actor`, must understand or process the header. If a particular SOAP node, marked as `mustunderstand`, does not understand the header then an error or fault will be generated.

The following diagram shows a multi-stage SOAP MEP:

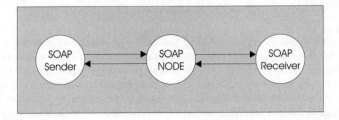

Header directives determine if an intermediary has any part to play with respect to processing of the SOAP message.

> **SOAP headers are processed by SOAP nodes, based upon their `actor` attribute. This allows for complex processing that may occur in multiple remote stages. The SOAP specification does not define how and in what order headers are processed, this is left to the SOAP processor.**

Reference

Resource	Description
http://www.xmethods.net/	A great site that lists publicly available SOAP web services of both RPC and document style. Also provides useful utilities based on web service WSDLs.
http://www.soapclient.com/SoapServices.html	A central repository for all SOAP related things, including a list of available web services.

Generating a SOAP Client Request with WSDL

Now that we have a good overview of SOAP and an example under our belt, let's create our second example of implementing a PHP SOAP client, but now we will use WSDL to assist in automatically creating the SOAP XML.

There are a few XML-based methods of generating a PHP SOAP client:

❑ Parse the WSDL file using SAX and create PHP code to be immediately evaluated

❑ Use XSLT to transform a WSDL file to create PHP client code

We will create an HTML-based SOAP client tool, which performs an XSLT transformation on a WSDL file and generates a valid SOAP client call. SOAP, all by itself, is not descriptive enough when trying to discover what methods are exposed, and that related input/output parameters are used. This is where WSDL, as the description part of the web services puzzle, is put into place.

WSDL (http://www.w3.org/TR/wsdl/) is used to define the service, for either the programmer wishing to write a client for a service, or for the user of that service.

WSDL is an XML format for describing network services as a set of endpoints operating on messages containing either document-oriented or procedure-oriented information. The operations and messages are described abstractly, and then bound to a concrete network protocol and message format to define an endpoint. Related concrete endpoints are combined into abstract endpoints (services). WSDL is extensible to allow description of endpoints and their messages regardless of what message formats or network protocols are used to communicate. However, the only bindings described in this document describe how to use WSDL in conjunction with SOAP 1.1, HTTP `GET`/`POST`, and MIME.

The SOAP header is processed by the SOAP node, based upon its `actor` attribute. This allows for WSDL to be simply a descriptive add-on that helps a web service client extract the necessary details to interact with the server. Here is the W3C abstract on WSDL:

> **WSDL is simply a description of a web service, in the form of a separate XML file. There are many technologies which use WSDL file; UDDI for example.**

WSDL describes important details which a client may use to enumerate methods, and the associated inputs, more specifically:

❑ The physical path or endpoint to a service

❑ The list of services or methods offered

❑ The list of inputs and outputs and what their types are

❑ Defines a variety of binding situations

Since we are focusing on being a consumer of web services we will not be creating WSDL, but using it as a basis to auto-generate a SOAP client request .

SOAP Client Class

We'll make things easier on ourselves, by creating one method of SOAP client class that takes in all the specific variables for creating the header, and takes in the SOAP body.

Here is our `soapclient` class:

```php
<?php

# Our class declaration
class Soapclient
{

    var $fp = 0;

    # SoapRequest function
    function SoapRequest($servicehost, $servicepath, $serviceport = 80,
                         $contenttype = "text/xml", $charset = "UTF-8",
                         $soapmessage, $soapaction )
    {

        # utility stuff handling magic_quotes_gpc condition
        $holdsoap = stripslashes($soapmessage);
        $messagesize = strlen($holdsoap);

        # build up the HTTP header
        $query = "POST $servicepath HTTP/1.1\r\n".
                "Host: $servicehost:$serviceport\r\n".
                "Content-Type: $contenttype; charset = $charset \r\n".
                "Content-Length: $messagesize\r\n".
```

```
                    "SOAPAction: $soapaction\r\n".
                    "\r\n";

        # Open up socket
        $fp = fsockopen($servicehost, $serviceport);

        if (!$fp) {
            # In case the port or server is not accessible
            print ("web service cannot be physically accessed");
        }else{
            # inject HTTP header and SOAP body
            fputs($fp, $query, strlen($query));
            fputs($fp, $query, "<?xml version='1.0'?>");
            fputs($fp, $holdsoap, $messagesize);
        }

        # just pass server response thru
        fpassthru($fp);

        return true;
    }
}
?>
```

OK, this will serve our purpose; it essentially encapsulates an entire SOAP request. We could obviously expand it greatly, here are some suggestions:

❑ Parse the SOAP response into a DOM

❑ Parse the SOAP response into an array

❑ Printing options

❑ SOAP fault handling

Parse the WSDL

Our next step is to use PHP to get the remote or local WSDL file and parse the important details for generating our SOAP request. We are simply going to use a few web services at Xmethods as our tests: remember this tool is currently configured for use with web services that expose only one method with one parameter. We will see how easy it will be to expand the work done here to suit our own purpose (not to mention that we could amend the XSLT to be more generic).

Here is our PHP page that performs an XSLT transform on a remote or local WSDL file:

```
<?php
// Instantiate a new XSLT processor
$x = xslt_create();

// Transform WSDL to SOAP, we may have to prepend file name with file://
$result = xslt_process($x, 'TemperatureService.wsdl', 'wsdl2soap.xsl');
if ($result) {
    print ($result);
} else {
    print ("supplied WSDL did not transform properly ");
```

```
        print ("  the \$result variable the reason is that " . xslt_error($x));
        print (" and the error code is " . xslt_errno($x));
}

// Destroy XSLT processor
xslt_free($x);
?>
```

This piece of PHP should look rather familiar; it's our standard code for performing an XSLT transformation. Here it is taking in a `TemperatureService.wsdl` and applying the `wsdl2soap.xsl` transform. Here are our processing steps:

❑ Select WSDL and input

❑ Transform WSDL to SOAP call

❑ Use `soapclient` PHP class to generate SOAP request and perform call

So let's select the WSDL:

```
<html>
  <head>
    <title>WSDL to SOAP RPC Test</title>
  </head>

  <body>

    <h2>WSDL to SOAP RPC test</h2>

    <form name="sendrpc" method="post" action="wsdlform2.php">

      <table>

        <tr>
          <td>WSDL:</td>
          <td>
            <textarea name="wsdl" rows="30" nowrap cols="100">
            </textarea>
          </td>
        </tr>

        <tr>
          <td></td>
          <td>
            <input type="submit" value="Parse WSDL into SOAP Body"/>
          </td>
        </tr>
      </table>

    </form>
  </body>
</html>
```

This simply takes in a WSDL file through an HTML form, and submits it to our next page for processing.

Generating the SOAP Request

Now we'll generate the SOAP request:

```html
<html>
  <head>
    <title>WSDL2SOAP RPC Test</title>
  </head>

  <body>

    <h2>WSDL2SOAP RPC test</h2>

    <form name="sendrpc" method="post" action="sendsoapmessage.php">

      <table>
        <tr>
          <td>
            host:
          </td>
          <td>
            <input type="text" name="servicehost"
                   value="services.xmethods.net"/>
          </td>
        </tr>

        <tr>
          <td>
            port:
          </td>
          <td>
            <input type="text" name="serviceport" value="80"/>
          </td>
        </tr>

        <tr>
          <td>
            path:
          </td>
          <td>
            <input type="text" name="servicepath"
                   value="/soap/servlet/rpcrouter"/>
          </td>
        </tr>

        <tr>
          <td>
            SOAPAction:
          </td>
          <td>
            <input type="text" name="soapaction"/>
          </td>
        </tr>

        <tr>
          <td>
            Content-Type:
          </td>
          <td>
            <input type="text" name="contenttype" value="text/xml"/>
```

```
          </td>
        </tr>

        <tr>
          <td>
            charset:
          </td>
          <td>
            <input type="text" name="charset" value="UTF-8"/>
          </td>
        </tr>

        <tr>
          <td>
            SOAP Message:
          </td>
          <td>
            <textarea name="soapmessage" rows="20" nowrap cols="80">
            <?php
            $xml = stripslashes($wsdl);

            $arguments = array('/_xml' => $xml);

            // Instantiate a new XSLT processor
            $x = xslt_create();

            // transform wsdl to SOAP
            $result = xslt_process($xh, 'arg:/_xml', 'wsdl2soap.xsl', NULL,
                                    $arguments);
            if ($result) {
                print ($result);
            } else {
                print ("supplied WSDL did not transform properly ");
                print ("  the \$result variable the reason is that " .
                        xslt_error($x));
                print (" and the error code is " . xslt_errno($x));
            }

            // Destroy XSLT processor
            xslt_free($x);

            ?>
            </textarea>
          </td>
        </tr>

        <tr>
          <td>
            SOAP Message:
          </td>
          <td>
            <input type="submit" value="Make SOAP request"/>
          </td>
        </tr>
      </table>
    </form>
  </body>
</html>
```

This form should look familiar from our last example, except that we now pipe in the WSDL and transform it within the `<textarea>` element. Now we are ready to make our SOAP call with our new `soapclient` PHP class.

The following XSLT is used to extract the relevant information from the WSDL XML document:

```
<?xml version="1.0"?>
<xsl:stylesheet
  version='1.0'
  xmlns:xsl="http://www.w3.org/1999/XSL/Transform"
  xmlns:wsdl="http://schemas.xmlsoap.org/wsdl/"
  xmlns:soap="http://schemas.xmlsoap.org/wsdl/soap/"
  xmlns:SOAP-ENV="http://schemas.xmlsoap.org/wsdl/soap/"
  xmlns:xsd="http://www.w3.org/1999/XMLSchema"
  xmlns:xsi="http://www.w3.org/1999/XMLSchema-instance"
  xmlns:SOAP-ENC="http://schemas.xmlsoap.org/wsdl/soap/"
>
  <xsl:output method='xml'/>

    <xsl:template match='/'>
      <SOAP-ENV:Envelope
        xmlns:xsi="http://www.w3.org/1999/XMLSchema-instance"
        xmlns:xsd="http://www.w3.org/1999/XMLSchema"
        xmlns:SOAP-ENV="http://schemas.xmlsoap.org/soap/envelope/"
        xmlns:SOAP-ENC="http://schemas.xmlsoap.org/soap/encoding/">
      <SOAP-ENV:Body SOAP-ENV:encodingStyle=
              "http://schemas.xmlsoap.org/soap/encoding/">

      <xsl:apply-templates select="wsdl:definitions/wsdl:binding"/>
      </SOAP-ENV:Body>
      </SOAP-ENV:Envelope>
      </xsl:template>

      <xsl:template match='wsdl:binding'>

        <xsl:for-each select='wsdl:operation'>
          <xsl:element name="{@name}" namespace="
                {wsdl:input/soap:body/@namespace}">
            <xsl:attribute name="SOAP-ENV:encodingStyle">
                http://schemas.xmlsoap.org/soap/encoding/</xsl:attribute>
              <xsl:element
                name="{//wsdl:message[contains(@name,'request')]
                /wsdl:part/@name}"
                namespace="{wsdl:input/soap:body/@namespace}">
                <xsl:attribute name="xsi:type">
                  <xsl:value-of
                    elect="//wsdl:message[contains(@name,'request')]
                    /wsdl:part/@type"/>
              </xsl:attribute>PLACE VALUE HERE</xsl:element>
            </xsl:element>
          </xsl:for-each>
        </xsl:template>
</xsl:stylesheet>
```

Remember to put in an actual value, which is a US zipcode, during step 2, so that we get a sensible answer (current temperature) from the remote web service.

> Our XSLT example `wsdl2soap.xsl` only handles a web service that has one method and one input value; we should be able to easily adjust the XSLT to fit other scenarios.

Now we will perform our final step, which imports our class definition so we can instantiate and use it:

```php
<?php
require("soapclient.php");

# instantiate the soapclient class
$soapclient = new soapclient;

print ("<html><body><form>");
print ("SOAP response message<br/><textarea name='resultmessage' rows='30'
                                    nowrap cols='80'>");

# supply the method with the correct variables from the input form
$result = $soapclient->SoapRequest($_REQUEST["servicehost"],
                                   $_REQUEST["servicepath"],
                                   $_REQUEST["serviceport"],
                                   $_REQUEST["contenttype"],
                                   $_REQUEST["charset"],
                                   $_REQUEST["soapmessage"],
                                   $_REQUEST["soapaction"]);

print ("</textarea></form></body></html>");
?>
```

And that's it, we've just created a PHP process that takes a WSDL file and creates the accompanying SOAP request message. It should be now apparent to us that SOAP and WSDL is a powerful combination, and drastically eases the time to develop clients to web services that are described with WSDL.

> Still a little confused about WSDL? Use the WSDL analyzer tool found at **www.xmethods.net** that takes in any WSDL file and generates a full readable report on it.

Changes from SOAP v1.1 To SOAP v1.2

The versions of SOAP that matter are version 1.1 and the current draft of version 1.2. Any draft always changes so it is recommended to always review working drafts with great scepticism.

Here is a list of major changes from SOAP version 1.1 and version 1.2:

❑ No elements are allowed after the `<soap:Body>` element. The version 1.1 Schema allows for this, so ensure that we use the most up-to-date schema.

❑ A `<misunderstood>` header element is added when a header is not understood or could not be processed.

❑ New header `actor` attributes of `none` and `anonymous` assist in how headers are processed by SOAP nodes.

❑ In the HTTP binding, a `SOAPAction` line is not required in the HTTP header.

❑ In the HTTP binding, the `Content-Type` line should be `application/soap` instead of `text/xml`.

❑ Fault response and codes have different notation and have many additions.

❑ The namespaces between versions are obviously different, developers, therefore, should always check them.

References

Resource	Description
http://www.w3.org/TR/wsdl/	WSDL Specification

We've gone through quite a lot of related topics in this chapter. Let's take a step back, and put all these technologies into perspective.

Future of Web Services and PHP

As with any crystal ball gazing activity, looking into the future is probably best exercised with one eyeball on the past. XML has had some successes and some clear failures, let's go through some and finally make some statements about how all this applies to PHP.

The following lists some of the technical and architectural issues that affect the development and implementation of web services:

❑ XML Infoset can be considered a success in terms of XSLT, RDF, and XPath and arguably XML Schema, as all have relatively high adoption rates including various heterogeneous parser/processor implementations.

❑ XML Schema has experienced modest adoption rates. This is probably due to the entrenchment of DTDs and the variety of alternative validation techniques. XPath 2.0 and SOAP's use of XML Schema data types will most likely drive future adoption.

❑ XHTML will undoubtedly have high adoption rates, due to the fact that it's simple refactorization of HTML 4.01. There also has been some success in mobile and PDA clients adopting XHTML subsets.

❑ XLink and XPointer have had poor adoption rates. This is an unusual situation, as the universal acceptance of hyperlinking is considered a key success factor for the Internet. Possibly URLs are still being considered in the evolving web architecture, read the discussion on REST in this section.

❑ As XML becomes a ubiquitous common data format, XML repositories will aggregate classical data sources, such as RDBMS, and also XML document collections. The querying power of XPath and XSLT is not robust enough for heavy-duty data situations; which is where XQuery is expected to undoubtedly have an impact.

❑ XML-RPC and SOAP have both experienced high adoption rates. Microsoft .NET has completely embraced this fact and has integrated SOAP (and WSDL) as a central strategy for exposing RPC and messaging functionality. One would hope that Microsoft has clearly analyzed their strategy.

❑ Second and third generation technologies such as UDDI depend on success of preceding technologies. There is an overall lack of commercial quality implementations for many of the above technologies. Many of the key processors and parsers are open source, which will require some maturity and larger developer communities to support.

❑ Lack of benchmarking for many of these technologies means the developer may encounter performance bottlenecks during development with no solution or fallback.

❑ DOM and SAX have a greater support in the developer community and are commonly understood within the PHP processing environment.

❑ Semantic Web: the W3C proposal for a machine processing architecture that defines an XML modeling of semantic meaning. Specifically, the Semantic Web will require a Services Orientated Architecture to allow for automatic machine based discovery, composing and modification of semantic services, and data.

❑ Representational State Transfer (REST) is an attempt at defining the current web architecture, (Roy Fielding: http://www.ics.uci.edu/~fielding/pubs/dissertation/top.htm). REST is nothing new, just a reiteration that the current Internet with XML can satisfy the requirements of a web service without defining new protocols such as SOAP.

❑ The Remote Procedure Call (RPC) models tend to make the local processing model available in a network context. There are many arguments over the usage of REST and RPC models for the Internet. It is probable that the introduction of XML-RPC and SOAP-RPC will promote further usage of RPC models, if not only because they are simple to implement. In any event, it is expected that an alternative to RPC-based web services will be put forward, and most likely this will be REST-type architecture.

PHP is in a great position to take advantage of the suite of XML technologies in creating superior client applications, though there is a lack of native SOAP support built into the language, which is a cause for some concern. In addition, complementary SOA technologies such as UDDI and WSDL still seem to yet have a large population of utility classes that would ease development.

Summary

This chapter went through a few fundamentals as a basis for understanding how and where to use XML-based technologies in PHP client development. We should feel comfortable in identifying what 'level and scope' of solution is required in our specific client development situation (for example, WDDX versus SOAP).

We also went into some detail as regards the SOAP specification and related SOA technologies, such as WSDL. Finally, a technique transforming WSDL, using XSLT, into a SOAP call was demonstrated, which should serve as a powerful reminder of how simple client development can become with interoperating XML technologies.

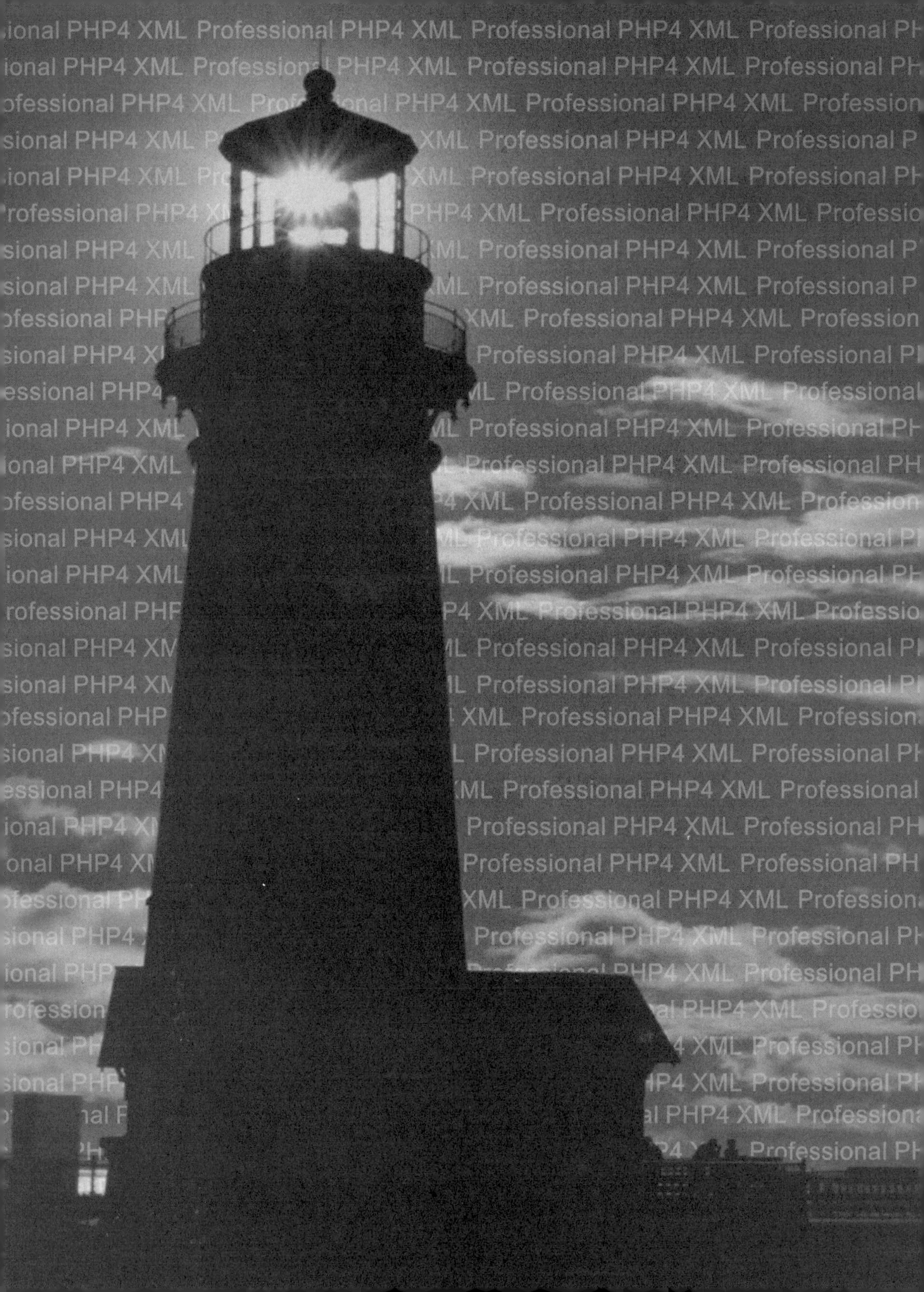
Professional PHP4 XML

15

SVG

In this chapter, we will look at how to create graphics and animation using **SVG** (Scalable Vector Graphics). We have divided this chapter in four different sections. The first section introduces SVG with a list of some of its important features. We will also look at the client-side requirements to view the SVG documents, and how SVG and PHP can be integrated. The second section talks about the basic structure of an SVG document and the syntax of basic SVG elements. The third section briefly describes a PHP and SVG base class and how it can be used to generate SVG documents. In the final section, an SVG animated bar chart is created, first by embedding PHP in SVG and then by using the SVG base class.

> In the examples in the chapter, we will only describe the code snippet relevant to the topic we are describing. The complete SVG files for this chapter can be downloaded from the book's page on the Wrox web site (**http://www.wrox.com/**).

SVG

SVG is the World Wide Web Consortium (W3C) standard for presenting and delivering vector-based 2-dimensional graphics on the Internet. The latest version of the specification can be found at http://www.w3.org/TR/SVG/. SVG can integrate with other XML technologies such as XSL, DOM, and SMIL (Synchronized Multimedia Integration Language). It can manipulate the SVG DOM on the client side and respond to events. It also has integrated CSS and ECMAScript support.

SVG has extensive graphic capabilities and can clip graphics, text, and animation to arbitrary paths. It also has anti-alias rendering, transparencies, patterns, and gradients capabilities. SVG source is viewable from the user agent. Also, because the files are text-based and not binary, they are search engine friendly and the graphic text is selectable and searchable. The files can also contain meta data.

Because SVG is vector-based it scales with no quality loss and the shapes can be independent from the colors, enabling stylesheets to render the same SVG file in different ways.

SVG is an extensive specification and there are whole books written about it. In this chapter we will look at the basic parts of the SVG specification. We will not be learning filter effects, gradients, advanced text rendering, ECMA scripting, advanced CCS properties, DOM, or advanced animation.

SVG User Agents

A user agent is an application that retrieves and displays web content, for example the web browser. Sometimes the user agent needs an additional plug-in to render some types of content. There are both native and plug-in SVG user agents that allow users to view SVG documents.

We will look at three of these user agents and provide references for other implementations:

❑ **Adobe SVG Viewer Plug-In**
Adobe is the most popular plug-in and works on Linux, Windows, and Macintosh platforms. It plugs in seamlessly with IE 4 and above, Real Player 8, Netscape 4.5-4.77, Mozilla, and Opera 5.x. The Adobe SVG Viewer is presently the closest to supporting the complete SVG specification. We can download the plug-in from http://www.adobe.com/svg/.

❑ **Mozilla Browser**
The Mozilla project is currently working on native support for the SVG specification. When complete the Mozilla browser will be able to handle compound documents that include SVG, MathML, XHTML, and XUL, by using XML namespaces. The browser will also be SVG content 'aware' and it will be able to modify the SVG DOM through the scripting engine.

The only drawback is that SVG is not currently supported in the official Mozilla builds, but unofficial builds can be downloaded. Visit http://www.mozilla.org/projects/svg/ for more information and a list of unofficial builds.

❑ **Batik Toolkit**
Part of the Apache XML Project, the **Batik** Toolkit is a Java-based SVG viewer, generator, manipulator, and toolkit. The project's ambition is to give developers a set of core modules that can be used together or individually to support specific SVG solutions. Batik is Java-based so it can be run on any operating system that is running a Java Virtual Machine (JVM). Visit http://xml.apache.org/batik/ for more information on the Batik Toolkit or to download the build.

❑ **Others**
New SVG implementations are continually appearing. They include viewers, editors, exporters, converters, generators, and validators for mobile and desktop devices. The official SVG implementation list is located at http://www.w3.org/Graphics/SVG/SVG-Implementations.htm8 – it lists the different SVG implementations along with their abilities.

There are currently no specific PHP APIs to create and manipulate SVG but all of the PHP XML APIs can be used because SVG is XML. However, the quick and dirty way to embed dynamic content into an SVG document is to embed PHP in SVG, just like embedding PHP in HTML.

SVG Basics

Before diving into all the examples in this chapter a few basics need to be sorted out. Just like any XML document, we need to know the DOCTYPE. Also, the MIME type needs to be specified in order for the user agent to recognize that SVG is being transmitted. All of the basic document type questions are answered in the first section. The second section describes the different ways to embed SVG into HTML to add SVG content to web pages. The third section addresses one of the problems with developing SVG with PHP and that is error messages. It describes several techniques to show the PHP error message from within an SVG document. After that it's all examples: how to create, group, style, and animate shapes and text:

- ❑ MIME types, file extensions, Prolog, DTD, namespace, and document structure
- ❑ Embedding SVG in HTML
- ❑ Errors
- ❑ Container elements
- ❑ Coordinate system
- ❑ Style
- ❑ Creating shapes
- ❑ Creating basic text
- ❑ Basic animation

MIME Type, File Extensions, Prolog, DTD, Namespace, and Document Structure

The SVG MIME type is image/svg+xml. If the web server isn't configured to automatically send the SVG MIME type or if we are serving up SVG files using a .php extension, we need to tell the user agent the correct type of the data it is receiving. To do this we include the Content-Type header, before outputting any text:

```php
<?php
header("Content-Type: image/svg+xml");
?>
```

We need to include the DOCTYPE declaration to conform to the XML specification and to validate our document:

```
<!DOCTYPE svg PUBLIC "-//W3C//DTD SVG 1.0//EN"
   "http://www.w3.org/TR/2001/REC-SVG-20010904/DTD/svg10.dtd">
```

The current SVG DTD can be found in the SVG W3C recommendation: http://www.w3.org/TR/SVG/.

SVG is XML and needs an XML declaration. So we'll use the bare minimum:

```
<?xml version="1.0"?>
```

The default namespace for SVG has been defined by the W3C as:

```
xmlns="http://www.w3.org/2000/svg"
```

The `xlink` namespace is required when linking internally or externally:

```
xmlns:xlink="http://www.w3.org/1999/xlink"
```

We can create a well-formed valid SVG document template by putting all of the above together.

There are two versions of the SVG document template. The first version is used when the SVG MIME type isn't sent automatically by the web server and PHP is parsing the file with short tags turned on:

```
<?php
header("Content-type: image/svg+xml");
?>
<?xml version="1.0"?>
<!DOCTYPE svg PUBLIC "-//W3C//DTD SVG 1.0//EN"
   "http://www.w3.org/TR/2001/REC-SVG-20010904/DTD/svg10.dtd">

<svg width="100%" height="100%"
     xmlns="http://www.w3.org/2000/svg"
     xmlns:xlink="http://www.w3.org/1999/xlink" >

  <-- SVG child elements... -->
</svg>
```

The second version is used when the web server is sending the SVG MIME type, and PHP is not parsing the file or the PHP short tags are turned `off`:

```
<?xml version="1.0"?>
<!DOCTYPE svg PUBLIC "-//W3C//DTD SVG 1.0//EN"
   "http://www.w3.org/TR/2001/REC-SVG-20010904/DTD/svg10.dtd">

<svg width="100%" height="100%"
   xmlns="http://www.w3.org/2000/svg"
   xmlns:xlink="http://www.w3.org/1999/xlink" >

  <-- SVG child elements... -->
</svg>
```

To turn PHP short tags off modify the `php.ini`. Under 'Language Options' change the `short_open_tag` directive to `Off`. This will force the use of the `<?php` open tag and therefore not parse the `<?xml` declaration which causes an error.

For all of the examples in this chapter we will be using the SVG document template above, with a width of 400 pixels and a height of 200 pixels (unless noted), like this:

```
<?xml version="1.0"?>
<!DOCTYPE svg PUBLIC "-//W3C//DTD SVG 1.0//EN"
   "http://www.w3.org/TR/2001/REC-SVG-20010904/DTD/svg10.dtd">

<svg width="400" height="200"
   xmlns="http://www.w3.org/2000/svg"
   xmlns:xlink="http://www.w3.org/1999/xlink" >

   <-- SVG examples here... -->
</svg>
```

Embedding SVG in HTML

There are three ways to embed SVG into an HTML page – using the `<embed>` element, the `<object>` element, or nesting both.

The `<embed>` element has never been a part of the W3C HTML specification, but it works on the majority of user agents:

```
<embed src="example.svg"
   type="image/svg+xml"
   pluginspace="http://www.adobe.com/svg/viewer/install/"
   width="400"
   height="200">
</embed>
```

The above HTML fragment inserts the `example.svg` file into the HTML page in the same way an image is inserted. The `src`, `width`, and `height` attributes are required. The `type` and `pluginspace` attributes help the user agent decide which plug-in to use and where it can be found if it isn't installed.

The `<object>` element is part of the W3C HTML specification and should be used if validation against the specification is required:

```
<object data="example.svg"
   type="image/svg+xml"
   pluginspace="http://www.adobe.com/svg/viewer/install/"
   width="400"
   height="200">
</object>
```

The basic attributes for `<object>` are the same as for `<embed>` with the notable exception of `data` replacing `src`.

However, not all user agents recognize the `<object>` tag, most notably Netscape Navigator. To ensure valid HTML that conforms to the specification, nest the two tags, as below:

```
<object data="example.svg"
  type="image/svg+xml"
  pluginspace="http://www.adobe.com/svg/viewer/install/"
  width="400"
  height="200">

  <embed src="example.svg"
    type="image/svg+xml"
    pluginspace="http://www.adobe.com/svg/viewer/install/"
    width="400"
    height="200">
  </embed>
</object>
```

The SVG specification also states that SVG should be able to be embedded using the `<img>` tag. However, currently no SVG user agents implement this part of the specification and therefore we cannot use the `<img>` tag to embed SVG.

Errors

Embedding PHP in SVG can be tricky. For one, when the user agent requests an SVG document that is embedded or standalone, it is expecting a document of type `image/svg+xml`. If a PHP error occurs, HTML text is sent instead of SVG. Sending the incorrect type of data causes some user agents to hang.

To avoid this problem we need to make sure that the right type of document is sent along with the PHP error. With some modifications to the `php.ini` file and the creation of a PHP error handler function we can solve the content type problem for both fatal and non-fatal errors.

To Display Fatal PHP Errors

To properly display fatal PHP errors we should update the following configuration directives in `php.ini`'s `Error handling` and `logging` sections and restart the web server:

```
error_reporting = E_ALL
display_errors = On
html_errors = Off
error_prepend_string =
                "<svg width = '100%' height = '100%'><text x='20' y='20'>"
error_append_string = "</text></svg>"
```

These settings configure PHP to show all errors, to not send the error string wrapped in HTML, and to wrap the error string in SVG. This solves the fatal PHP error content type problem because if SVG is expected, the user agent gets an SVG document, and if HTML is expected, the user agent ignores the SVG tags and displays the error text.

Unfortunately, we cannot use the PHP `ini_set()` function to set the configuration directives because PHP fatal errors are sent before the compilation of the code.

594

To Display Non-Fatal PHP Errors

If a non-fatal PHP error is encountered on a page, PHP outputs the error immediately and probably in the middle of the SVG document. This will cause the SVG to be malformed and not be displayed. Therefore, we need to erase the PHP buffer before sending the PHP SVG error string.

To erase the PHP buffer first we need to make sure PHP buffering is on.

In the Language Options section of php.ini set:

```
output_buffering = on
implicit_flush = off
```

This will ensure no PHP headers or output will be sent to the user agent before we get a chance to send the error message.

Next we create and set an error handler in PHP. The custom error handler is called instead of the standard PHP error handler. The custom error handler cleans the PHP buffer and outputs the error wrapped in SVG.

Define and set the custom error handler:

```php
<?php
function SvgErrorHandler($errno, $errstr, $errfile, $errline)
{
    // Clean the output buffer before outputting the error string.
    ob_end_clean();

    header("Content-type: image/svg+xml");
    print ("<?xml version=\"1.0\" standalone=\"no\"?>");
?>
<!DOCTYPE svg PUBLIC "-//W3C//DTD SVG 1.0//EN"
   "http://www.w3.org/TR/2001/REC-SVG-20010904/DTD/svg10.dtd">
<svg width="100%" height="100%">
   <g font-family="Verdana" font-size="12" fill="black" >
     <text x="20" y="20" >
       <?php print ($errstr); ?>
       <tspan x="20" y="40" >
         <?php print ($errfile); ?>
       </tspan>
       <tspan x="20" y="60" >
         <?php print ("Line: " . $errline); ?>
       </tspan>
     </text>
   </g>
</svg>

<?php
// Exit the script to fix the error.
exit();
}

// Set the error handler.
set_error_handler("SvgErrorHandler");
?>
```

We should include this function at the beginning of every SVG/PHP script to ensure the proper formatting of error strings. Now if an SVG/PHP file that is embedded in an HTML page throws a PHP error, the error string is displayed in the user agent.

> *There is another way to read what errors are taking place in a PHP script independent of the user agent – look in the PHP log file at the error. Turn logging on and set the PHP log file name and path in* `php.ini`.

In the `Error handling` and `logging` section of `php.ini` set:

```
log_errors = on
error_log = c:/temp/phperr.log; Works on Windows.
error_log = /tmp/phperr.log; Works on UNIX.
```

Container Elements

SVG container elements contain other elements. They are used to define or pass on attributes to their child elements.

<defs>

The `<defs>` element is a container element whose purpose is to define elements that are linked to by other tags. For example, the `<marker>` element is a child of the `<defs>` tag that then can be linked to by a `<line>` element:

```
<defs>
  <marker id="ArrowHead" refX="0" refY="4" markerUnits="userSpaceOnUse"
          markerWidth="10" markerHeight="8" orient="auto">
    <path d="M 0 0 L 10 4 L 0 8 z" />
  </marker>
</defs>

<line x1="0" y1="10" x2="300" y2="10" marker-end="url(#ArrowHead)"
      stroke-width="2" stroke="black" />
```

<g>

It is convenient to group elements that share common attributes. The container element `<g>` accomplishes this grouping. The attributes listed in `<g>` are inherited by its child elements:

```
<!-- Set child attributes -->
<g stroke="gray" style="stroke-width:5;">

  <!-- Draw a gray line with a width of 5 -->
  <line x1="30" y1="50" x2="350" y2="50" />

  <!-- Override stroke="gray" and draw a brown line with a 5 width -->
  <line x1="30" y1="100" x2="350" y2="100" style="stroke:brown;" />

</g>
```

To counter the effect of a <g> element attribute on a child element, set the offending attribute to another value or none.

<desc> and <title>

These two elements are not container elements but they assign descriptions and titles to container elements and graphic elements.

The <desc> element contains a description that can be used by different SVG parsers to discover and display what the SVG file is all about. This comes into play when the SVG script is rendered into something besides a visual media, like an aural presentation for the blind.

The <title> element is similar to <desc> and is used to supply a title to an element. In addition, the user agent can use the <title> to display a tool tip.

To make the SVG document accessible to the widest user base, the W3C specification suggests that there should be at least one <desc> and <title> tag near each <svg> tag in the document:

```
<desc>
   A very descriptive description about the SVG contained in the
   document detailing what is being rendered.
</desc>

<title>
   A descriptive title identifying the content of the SVG document.
</title>
```

Coordinate System

The SVG canvas is where the SVG content is drawn. The canvas is infinite in both the x and y directions. When the SVG document is created it specifies a viewport or a window onto this canvas. The content drawn within the viewport is viewable on the user agent.

Creating the Initial Viewport

All SVG documents contain an <svg> root element. The <svg> element defines the size and units of the initial viewport using the width and height properties:

```
<svg width="400" height="200">
```

The unit defaults for height and width are pixels but there are several others to choose from. The SVG unit identifiers match the unit identifiers in CSS:

Unit	Description
cm	Absolute centimetres.
em	Relative. Current font size.
ex	Relative. Current x-height of the font.

Table continued on following page

Unit	Description
in	Absolute inches.
mm	Absolute millimetres.
pc	Absolute picas. 1 pica is equal to 12 points.
pt	Absolute points. 1 point is 1/72nd of an inch.
px	Relative to the current viewing device.
percentages	Relative to the size of the viewport.

At the same time the viewport is created, a viewport coordinate system and a user coordinate system are created. Initially the viewport coordinate system and user coordinate system are equal with the origin in the upper-left corner of the viewport. In the initial coordinate system positive x coordinates are to the right of the origin and positive y coordinate are below the origin.

Here is the representation (initial_viewport.svg):

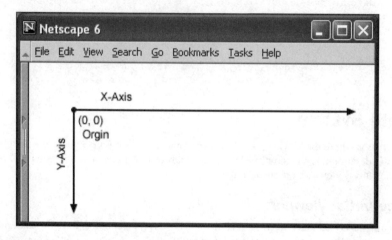

Creating a New User Coordinate System

It is often convenient to modify the user coordinate system. For example, to draw a group of concentric circles with their origins at (200, 100), we can move the user coordinate system origin to (200, 100) and then set the origin of the circles to (0, 0). To allow transformations of the user coordinate system we define an element's transform attribute.

transform

The transform attribute value is a transform-list. A transform-list is the different transformations separated by whitespace:

```
transform="scale(2) skewX(30) rotate(45)"
```

Currently there are six different transformations:

Transformation	Description
translate(x [y])	Moves the origin of the user coordinate system relative to the current coordinate system. If y is not specified it is assumed to be zero.
scale(x [y])	Scales the user coordinate system relative to the current coordinate system. If y is not specified it is assumed to be zero.
	If x or y are negative it has the effect of flipping the coordinate system in relation to that axis.
rotate(a [x y])	Rotates the user coordinate system around the current origin by angle a.
	If x and y are specified it rotates around point (x, y).
skewX(a)	Skews the x coordinates by angle a.
skewY(a)	Skews the y coordinates by angle a.
matrix(a b c d e f)	Changes the current coordinate system by multiplying the x and y coordinates by the matrix transformation: $$\begin{bmatrix} X \\ Y \\ 1 \end{bmatrix} x \begin{bmatrix} a & c & e \\ b & d & f \\ 0 & 0 & 1 \end{bmatrix}$$

All of the other transformations can be specified by the matrix() transformation. Graphic programs that create SVG often use the matrix() transformation to consolidate a list of other transformations.

Transformations are cumulative, so if we set rotate(45) on the parent element and rotate(45) on a child element, the total rotation for the child element would be 90°. But transformations are applied in the order in which they are specified. They are first applied to the parent and then to its children.

Therefore:

```
transform="rotate(45) skewX(45) rotate(45)"
```

is not the same as:

```
transform="rotate(90) skewX(45)"
```

The following example of translate() (translate.svg) draws two circles. It first translates the user coordinate system to the center of the viewport and then translates the second circle to be tangential to the bottom of the first:

```
<!-- Move to the middle of the viewport. -->
<g transform="translate(200 100)" style="stroke:black; stroke-width:2;">
  <circle cx="0" cy="0" r="50" style="fill:none;" />
```

```
    <!-- Draw a small circle tangential to the bottom of big circle. -->
    <circle cx="0" cy="20" r="20" style="fill:black;"
      transform="translate(0 50)"/>
</g>
```

Here is the output of the example:

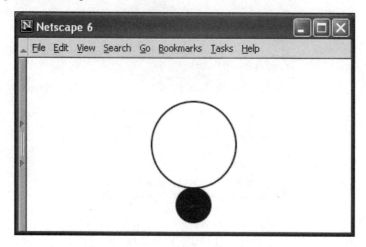

The scale() example (scale.svg) draws two similar ellipses at the center of the viewport but scales one by half:

```
<g transform="translate(200 100)" style="stroke:black; stroke-width:2;">
  <ellipse cx="0" cy="0" rx="150" ry="75" style="fill:none;" />

  <ellipse cx="0" cy="0" rx="150" ry="75" style="fill:black;"
        transform="scale(.5)"/>
</g>
```

Here is the output:

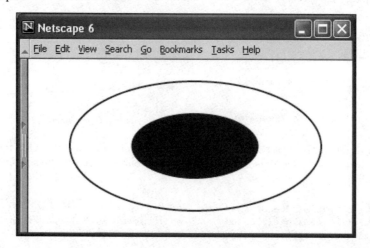

The `rotate()` transformation example (`rotate.svg`) rotates a rectangle 10 degrees around the center of the viewport:

```
<rect x="100" y="50" width="200" height="100"
  style="fill:none; stroke:black; stroke-width:2"
  transform="rotate(10 200 100)" />
```

Here is the output of the `rotate.svg` example file:

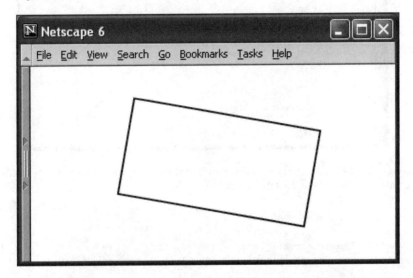

The `skewX()` and `skewY()` example skews two groups of elements. Note that the transform is applied to `<g>` container element instead of the individual `<text>` and `<rect>` elements. The first group uses `skewX()` and the second group uses `skewY()`:

```
<g transform="translate(50 30) skewX(45)" style="stroke:black;">
  <text x="0" y="0" style="font-family:Verdana;font-size:20" >
    skewX
  </text>
  <rect x="0" y="0" width="75" height="75" style="fill:none;
      stroke-width:2;"   />
</g>

<g transform="translate(250 30) skewY(45)" style="stroke:black;">
  <text x="0" y="0" style="font-family:Verdana;font-size:20" >
    skewY
  </text>
  <rect x="0" y="0" width="75" height="75" style="fill:none;
      stroke-width:2;" />
</g>
```

Here is the output:

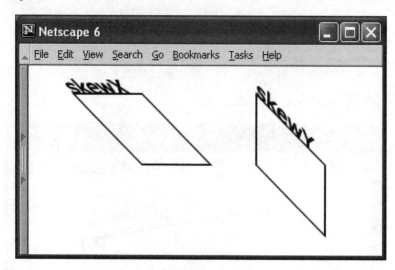

The following code (`matrix.svg`) uses a `matrix()` transformation to rotate an ellipse 45 degrees. The matrix for rotation is [cos(a) sin(a) – sin(a) cos(a) 0 0]:

```
<g transform="translate(200 100)" >
<ellipse cx="0" cy="0" rx="100" ry="75"
  style="fill:none; stroke:black; stroke-width:5"
  transform="matrix(.707 .707 -.707 .707 0 0)" />
</g>
```

Here is the result:

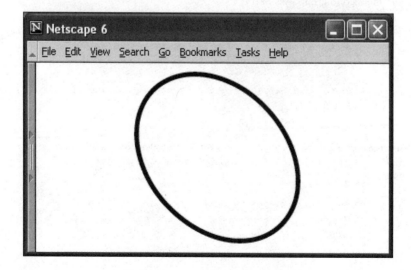

Style

Styles can be applied to SVG elements. The stylesheet can be external, internal, or defined inline in the element.

External Stylesheets

It is easy to create and link external stylesheets to SVG documents. First create a stylesheet (a CSS document) and link to it from the SVG document. Then the styles are applied once the elements are rendered.

Here is the `circle.css` stylesheet:

```
circle { stroke-width:5; fill:orange; stroke:rgb(0,128,0); }
```

Here is the `circle_style.svg` file:

```
<?xml version="1.0"?>
<?xml-stylesheet href="circle.css" type="text/css"?>
<!DOCTYPE svg PUBLIC "-//W3C//DTD SVG 1.0//EN"
  "http://www.w3.org/TR/2001/REC-SVG-20010904/DTD/svg10.dtd">

<svg width="400px" height="200px"
  xmlns="http://www.w3.org/2000/svg"
  xmlns:xlink="http://www.w3.org/1999/xlink">

  <circle cx="200" cy="100" r="50" />
</svg>
```

This draws a green bordered circle filled with orange:

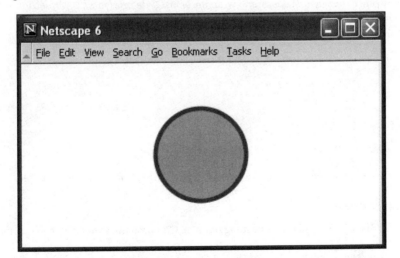

If the user agent supports CSS styling the `class` attribute can be used to apply different rules to the elements. For example, if we specify a `circle.red` rule in the stylesheet:

```
circle.red { fill:red; }
```

then set the circle class attribute to red:

```
<circle class="red" cx="200" cy="100" r="50" />
```

the result will be a red-filled circle:

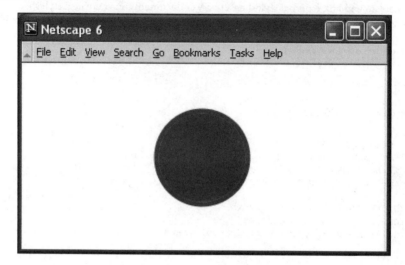

<style>

The `<style>` element is used to create embedded stylesheets in SVG content. The styles can then be referenced by other elements. Make sure to wrap the actual style rules in a CDATA section within the `<style>` element:

```
<defs>
  <style type="text/css">
    <![CDATA[
      circle { stroke-width:5; fill:orange; stroke:rgb(0,128,0); }
    ]]>
  </style>
</defs>

<circle cx="200" cy="100" r="50" />
```

This draws a green-bordered circle filled with orange like the external stylesheet example.

The style Attribute

The `style` attribute in SVG allows the setting of inline CSS properties within an SVG element:

```
<circle cx="200" cy="100" r="75"
        style=" stroke-width:5; fill:orange; stroke:rgb(0,128,0);" />
```

SVG supports many of the CSS styling properties in addition to defining many of its own.

These are the styling properties used in this chapter:

Styling Property	Description
fill	Sets the fill color of the element.
stroke	Sets the outline color of the element.
stroke-width	Sets the outline width of the element. Initially 0.
text-anchor	Sets the alignment of the string in the <text> element. Possible values are start, middle, and end.
font-family	Sets the font-family name for the element. Can be a prioritized list of font family names including generic font-family names like serif and sans-serif.
font-size	Sets the current size of the font.

A styling property color can be set by using a recognized color keyword or by using the rgb() function. Presently there are 147 recognized color keyword names like black, white, aliceblue, and yellowgreen. A complete list of recognized color keyword names and their RGB equivalents can be found in the W3C SVG recommendation located at http://www.w3.org/TR/SVG/types.html#ColorKeywords.

Also, the styling attributes can be listed individually as attributes of the element:

```
<circle cx="200" cy="100" r="75"
        stroke="black" stroke-width="2" fill="white" />
```

Creating Shapes

SVG has six basic shapes predefined. All of the basic shapes can be created using the <path> element, but have been defined for convenience. We will look at all six predefined shapes plus the <path> and the <marker> elements:

- ❑ <line>
- ❑ <rect>
- ❑ <circle>
- ❑ <ellipse>
- ❑ <polyline>
- ❑ <polygon>
- ❑ <path>
- ❑ <marker>

<line>

To draw a line we specify the line starting point (x1, y1) and ending point (x2, y2):

```
<g stroke="black">
  <line x1="125" y1="50" x2="275" y2="140" stroke-width="7" />
  <line x1="175" y1="50" x2="275" y2="110" stroke-width="5" />
  <line x1="225" y1="50" x2="275" y2="80" stroke-width="3" />
  <line x1="274" y1="50" x2="275" y2="51" stroke-width="1" />
</g>
```

Here is the result of the line.svg example file:

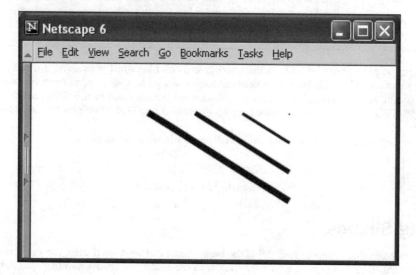

<rect>

The <rect> elements draws a rectangle with its upper-left corner at (x, y) and locates its lower-right corner width units to the right and height units down:

```
<g style="stroke:black; stroke-width:2;">
  <rect x="50" y="50" width="300" height="100" style="fill:none;" />
  <rect x="175" y="75" width="50" height="50" style="fill:black;" />
</g>
```

Here is the output of the rect.svg file:

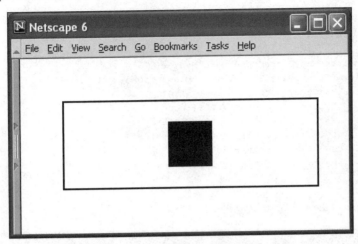

<circle>

The <circle> element sets its center at (cx, cy) and its radius to r. The circles in this example overlap and because they are filled the circle elements specified first are overwritten by the later circles:

```
<circle cx="200" cy="100" r="75"
    style="stroke:black; stroke-width:2; fill:white;" />

<!-- Translate the User Coordinate System to center of above circle -->
<g transform="translate(200 100)" style="stroke:black; stroke-width:2;">
  <circle cx="0" cy="-15" r="20" style="fill:gray;" />
  <circle cx="15" cy="15" r="20" style="fill:black;" />
  <circle cx="-15" cy="15" r="20" style="fill:white;" />
</g>
```

Here is the output of the circle.svg file:

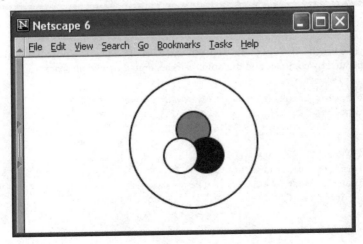

<ellipse>

For the <ellipse> element set (cx, cy) as its center, where rx is the radius in the x direction and ry is the radius in the y direction:

```
<!-- Translate the User Coordinate System -->
<g transform="translate(200 100)" style="stroke-width:2;">
  <ellipse cx="0" cy="0" rx="100" ry="50"
           style="stroke:black; fill:none;" />
  <ellipse cx="0" cy="-15" rx="30" ry="15"
           style="stroke:gray; fill:gray;" />
  <ellipse cx="0" cy="15" rx="30" ry="15"
           style="stroke:black; fill:black;" />
</g>
```

Here is the output of the ellipse.svg file:

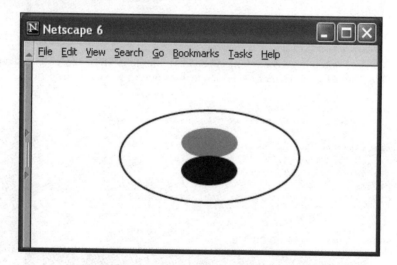

<polyline>

To draw a polyline use the <polyline> element, and a list of points. The point list is made up of x and y coordinates separated by commas, and the point pairs separated by a whitespace:

```
<polyline style="stroke:black; stroke-width:2; fill:none;"
          points="25,150 50,150 100,50 125,125 150,75
                  175,125 190,100 205,125 350,125" />

<!-- Draw a flag translated to the third point above -->
<g transform="translate(100 50)">
  <polyline style="stroke:black; stroke-width:2; fill:gray;"
            points="0,0 0,-30, 20,-30 20,-30 20,-15 0,-15" />
</g>
```

Here is the output of the `polyline.svg` file:

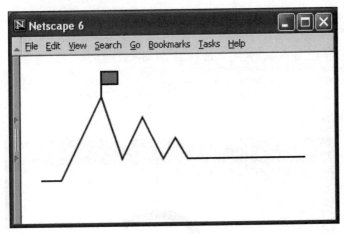

<polygon>

To draw a polygon we should specify a point list like in the `<polyline>` element:

```
<g transform="translate(75 100)" style="stroke:black; stroke-width:2;">
  <!-- The rocket ship body -->
  <polygon points="0,-25 200,-25 275,0 200,25 0,25"
           style="fill:white;"/>
  <!-- The fins -->
  <polygon points="0,-25 0,-50 50,-25" style="fill:black;" />
  <polygon points="0,25 0,50 50,25" style="fill:black;" />
  <!-- The flames -->
  <polygon transform="translate(-1 0)"
           points="0,-24 -30,-30 -20,-20 -40,-15 -20,-10 -50,0 -20,10
                   -40,15 -20,20 -30,30 0,24"
           style="fill:gray; stroke:none;" />
</g>
```

Here is the output of the `polygon.svg` file:

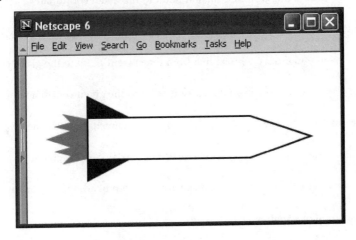

<path>

<path> is a complex and powerful element shape. We can create any vector-based shape or drawing using the <path> element:

```
<path style="fill:none; stroke:black; stroke-width:10;"
      d="M248.537 52.5552 C150.073 -6.52327 116.055 121.702 171.264
         154.828 C178.784 159.34 197.786 162.347 206.492 162.782 C226.626
         163.789 243.782 152.533 256.492 136.646" />
```

This path creates a simple C:

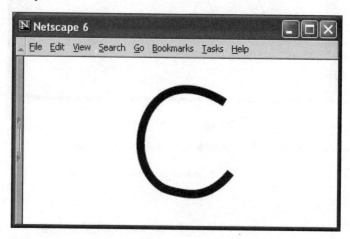

The path data uses several instructions to create the outline of a shape:

❑ **M**
  moveto – to move to a new point to start a path

❑ **Z**
  closepath – to close the current path by drawing a line from the current point to the path starting point

❑ **L**
  lineto – to draw a line from the current point to the given coordinate

❑ **H**
  horizontal lineto – to draw a horizontal line from the current point to the given coordinate

❑ **V**
  vertical lineto – to draw a vertical line from the current point to the given coordinate

❑ **C**
  curveto – to draw a curve from the current point to the given coordinate

❑ **S**
  smooth curveto – to draw a smooth curve from the current point to the given coordinate

❑ **Q**
  quadratic Bezier curveto – to specify a quadratic Bezier curve segment

❑ **T**
  smooth quadratic Bezier curveto – to specify a smooth quadratic Bezier curve segment

❑ **A**
  elliptical arc – to specify an elliptical arc

All of these instructions can be upper or lowercase. If the instruction is in lowercase, it means the instruction should be performed relative to the current point. If it is uppercase it means that the instruction should be performed absolutely in the user coordinate system.

Paths that create complex images will dominate the SVG file; the data will be thousands of lines long. Therefore it is not easy to code these SVG files manually. Fortunately, there are commercial graphics packages available to generate complex paths.

<marker>

The <marker> element creates shapes that can be linked to by other elements. It is useful for creating end-of-line markers like arrowheads:

```
<defs>
  <marker id="ArrowEnd" refX="0" refY="4" markerUnits="userSpaceOnUse"
          markerWidth="10" markerHeight="8" orient="auto">
    <path d="M 0 0 L 10 4 L 0 8 z" />
  </marker>
  <marker id="ArrowStart" refX="10" refY="5" markerUnits="userSpaceOnUse"
          markerWidth="10" markerHeight="10" orient="auto">
    <circle cx="6" cy="5" r="4" style="stroke:black; stroke-width:1" />
  </marker>
</defs>

<g transform="translate(200 100)" style="stroke:black; stroke-width:2;">
  <line x1="-100" y1="0" x2="100" y2="0"
        marker-start="url(#ArrowStart)" marker-end="url(#ArrowEnd)" />
  <line x1="0" y1="-50" x2="0" y2="50"
        style="marker-start:url(#ArrowStart);
        marker-end:url(#ArrowEnd);" />
</g>
```

Here is an example (marker.svg):

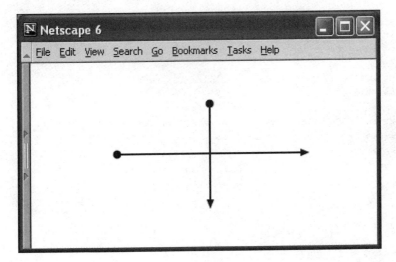

The marker properties used in this chapter are:

Marker Property	Description
id	Name of the marker. Used as link in other elements
refX	The x position of where the marker should attach itself on the linking element
refY	The y position of where the marker should attach itself on the linking element
markerUnits	stroke-width – sets the stroke to the current stroke-width
	userSpaceOnUse – renders the marker in the stroke-width specified in the marker property
markerWidth	The width of the marker
markerHeight	The height of the marker
orient	angle – the angle the marker rotates to after it attaches itself to the element
	auto – the markers' x-axis follows the current path of the element

Creating Basic Text

SVG has several elements to display and manipulate text. The two we are going to look at are:

- ❑ <text>
- ❑ <tspan>

<text>

To render text we use the <text> element and specify the text's position at (x, y):

```
<g style="font-family:Verdana; fill:black;">
  <text x="200" y="100" style="font-size:20; text-anchor:middle;">
    SVG and PHP
  </text>
  <text x="200" y="50" style="font-size:12; text-anchor:end;">
    Scalable
  </text>
  <text x="200" y="150" style="font-size:12; text-anchor:start;">
    Selectable
  </text>
</g>
```

Here is the output of the `text.svg` example file:

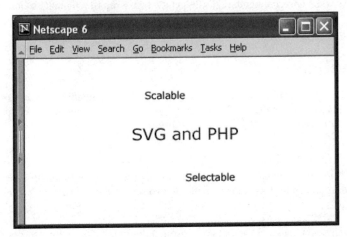

<tspan>

The `<tspan>` element changes the attributes of the text inside a `<text>` element:

```
<g style="font-family:Verdana; font-size:16; fill:black;" >
    <text x="70" y="50" >
        Text doesn't wrap unless
        <tspan x="70" y="80" >
         we use the tspan element.
        </tspan>
        <tspan x="70" y="140" >
         All lines are selectable too!
        </tspan>
    </text>
</g>
```

One of the major benefits of using the `<tspan>` element is the creation of multi-line text that is selectable.

Here is the output of the `tspan.svg` file:

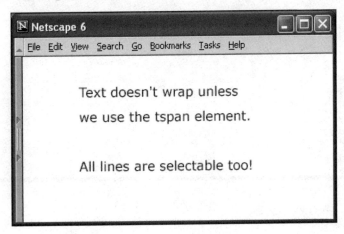

The next W3C SVG recommendation will include text-wrap functionality so look for it.

Basic Animation

Different element attributes can be animated using different SVG animation tags. In this chapter we shall describe the <animate> animation tag. For a description of the other animation elements in the SVG specification see http://www.w3.org/TR/SVG/animate.html.

<animate>

The <animate> element animates a single SVG element property over time. For example, we can make a circle grow in radius and change its color by defining two separate <animate> child elements – one for r and one for fill.

This SVG code snippet creates a circle that grows from a dot to full size in three seconds while changing from purple to orange:

```
<circle cx="200" cy="100" r="75"
        style="stroke:black; stroke-width:2; fill:purple;">
  <animate attributeName="r" attributeType="XML" from="0" to="75"
          dur="3s" fill="freeze" />
  <animate attributeName="fill" attributeType="CSS" from="purple"
          to="orange" dur="3s" fill="freeze" />
</circle>
```

Here is how it looks initially:

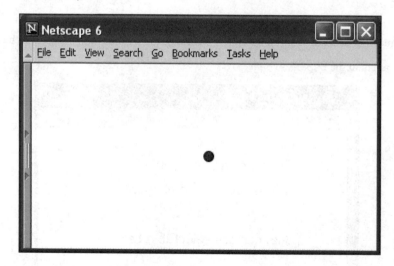

This is the way it looks when the animation is over:

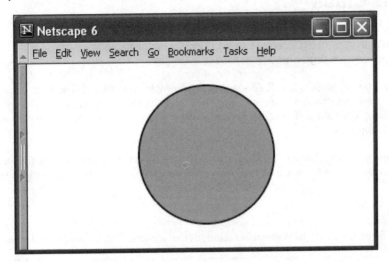

These are the `<animate>` attributes used in this chapter:

Animate Property	Description
`attributeName`	Name of the attribute to animate.
`attributeType`	Type of attribute named: ❑ CSS is an animatable CSS property. ❑ XML is an animatable property in the current XML namespace or a linked namespace. ❑ `auto` – decide depending on the `attributeName` in the target element. CSS is searched first and then XML.
`from`	The starting value of the animation.
`to`	The ending value of the animation.
`begin`	The time when the animation is started.
`dur`	How long the animation should last. A number followed by h, `min`, s, or ms.
`fill`	The action to take after the animation has completed: ❑ `freeze` – The effects of the animation are left ❑ `remove` – The effects of the animation are removed

PHP SVG Class

The SVG class, located at PHP Classes (http://www.phpclasses.org/), encapsulates all of the previous elements into individual PHP Classes. These SVG classes can be found at http://www.phpclasses.org/browse.html/package/457.html.

This SVG class is not just one class. Each element is its own derived class of type `SvgElement`. This makes adding a new class that communicates with the other classes as easy as extending `SvgElement`. This is because the basic idea behind `SvgElement` is to make it a container that holds references to other `SvgElement` objects.

After we are done creating all of the different instances that are needed for a complete document, a message is passed to the parent instance. The parent then recursively passes the `printElement()` message to all its children.

Methods

The `SvgElement` base class has three main methods that are inherited by the derived classes:

SvgElement Method	Description
`addChild()`	Make the passed object a child
`addParent()`	Make the passed object a parent
`printElement()`	Print the object's contents and send a `printElement()` message to all of its child objects

Animated Red Circle Example

This example uses the PHP SVG class to animate a circle and some text. The circle and text grow from a point to full size in three seconds. The circle also changes color from green to red during the same time period.

The `SVG_CLASS_BASE` constant is used within `svg.php` to include all of the different SVG element class files:

```php
<?php
define("SVG_CLASS_BASE", $_SERVER["DOCUMENT_ROOT"]."/ProPHPXML/classes/");
require_once(SVG_CLASS_BASE . "svg.php");
```

Next, we create an instance of type `SvgDocument`. All the other objects will have this instance as their 'parent':

```php
$svg =& new SvgDocument("400", "200");
```

Then we create an instance of type `SvgGroup`:

```php
$g =& new SvgGroup("stroke:black", "translate(200 100)");
```

All of the child objects of this instance will have a black stroke and be translated to the center of the viewport.

Now we make the instance $g a child of the $svg instance. There are two ways of accomplishing this. One is to send a message to $g requesting that it becomes the parent of $svg. The second is to send a message to $svg requesting that it includes $g as a child. In this example, we use the first method:

```
// Add a parent to the g instance.
$g->addParent($svg);
```

This is how we would send a message to $svg to request it to include $g as its child:

```
// The same results can be accomplished by making g a child of the SVG.
// $svg->addChild($g);
```

Now that we have the basics down, let us create an instance of type SvgCircle and make it animated. We do the same for an instance of SvgText and make both the $circle and $text children of the instance $g:

```
// Create and animate a circle.
$circle = new SvgCircle("0", "0", "100", "stroke-width:3", "");
$circle->addChild(new SvgAnimate("r", "XML", "0", "75", "", "3s", "freeze"));
$circle->addChild(new SvgAnimate("fill", "CSS", "green", "red", "", "3s",
                             "freeze"));

// Make the circle a child of g.
$g->addChild($circle);

// Create and animate some text.
$text = new SvgText("0", "0", "SVG and PHP",
                    "font-size:20;text-anchor:middle;", "");
$text->addChild(new SvgAnimate("font-size", "auto", "0", "20", "", "3s",
                             "freeze"));

// Make the text a child of g.
$g->addChild($text);
```

Once we have created all of the different objects necessary to create the intended SVG document, we pass the printElement() message to the $svg instance. This message is then passed down to all of the $svg object's children who pass the message to their children, and so on:

```
// Send a message to the SVG instance to start printing.
$svg->printElement();
?>
```

The result is a well-formed SVG file:

```
<?xml version="1.0" encoding="iso-8859-1"?>

<!DOCTYPE svg PUBLIC "-//W3C//DTD SVG 1.0//EN"
   "http://www.w3.org/TR/2001/REC-SVG-20010904/DTD/svg10.dtd">

<svg width="400" height="200" xmlns="http://www.w3.org/2000/svg"
```

```
                 xmlns:xlink="http://www.w3.org/1999/xlink" >
    <g style="stroke:black" transform="translate(200 100)" >
       <circle cx="0" cy="0" r="100" style="stroke-width:3" >
          <animate attributeName="r" attributeType="XML" from="0"
                   to="75" dur="3s" fill="freeze" />
          <animate attributeName="fill" attributeType="CSS" from="green"
                   to="red" dur="3s" fill="freeze" />
       </circle>
       <text x="0" y="0" style="font-size:20;text-anchor:middle;" >
          SVG and PHP
          <animate attributeName="font-size" attributeType="auto" from="0"
                   to="20" dur="3s" fill="freeze" />
       </text>
    </g>
  </svg>
```

And here is how it looks:

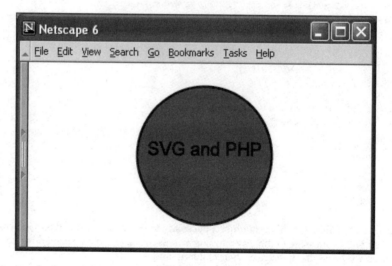

Because of the simple design of the SVG class, it is easy to extend. Objects that encapsulate other SVG elements can be added quickly. It is even possible to add classes that would compress an SVG object or convert an object to another graphics format like JPG. The possibilities are endless.

A Bar Chart Using SVG

To show off the SVG elements covered in this chapter let us develop an animated bar chart. The bar chart plots the occurrence of vowels on the http://www.example.com/ home page. It counts the vowels in the text and also in the tags of the page. This has no real-world application other than being fun and a mildly interesting statistical analysis. But we could easily use other data points from a web log or database to make the analysis more applicable. But for now we will be satisfied with counting the vowels on a page.

This is the bar chart after the animation has finished:

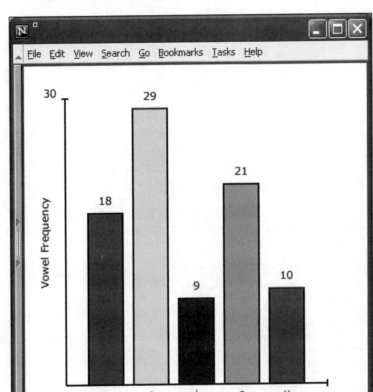

The animation consists of the bars growing for two seconds and as the bars reach their final height, the totals appear.

The Bar Chart Code

There are two versions of the code:

❑ The procedural version where PHP is embedded directly in the SVG elements

❑ The OO version using the PHP SVG class to create and print the SVG document

Both versions use the same load_data.php file to collect the data and define the graph attributes.

Defining the Graph Attributes and Collecting the Data

The file load_data.php defines and calculates the variables for use in both the procedural and object-oriented version of the bar chart code.

The following lines of code specify the file that is searched, the graph attributes, the viewport attributes, and the strings to search for.

```php
<?php
$file       = "http://www.example.com/";// The file to search
$offset_x   = 50;                       // Axis offset from edge of viewport
$offset_y   = 40;
$x_label    = $file;                    // Axis labels
$y_label    = "Vowel Frequency";
$bar_width  = 40;                       // Width of the bars
$svg_width  = 400;                      // SVG viewport height and width
$svg_height = 400;

$colors = array("red","yellow","blue","orange","green","violet"); // Bars
$srch_strings = array("a", "e", "i", "o", "u"); // Strings to search for
```

Next, we grab the file contents and loop, counting all of the $srch_strings occurrences in the file, and put the results into the $frequency[] associative array. We also update $scale making sure it is equal to the highest $frequency[]:

```php
$fcontents = join ("", file($file));       // Grab the contents of the $file
$num_data_points = sizeof($srch_strings);  // Get the number of data points.

$scale = 0;                                // Initial y-axis scale.

for ($i = 0; $i < $num_data_points; ++$i){ // Loop, counting the strings.
    $frequency[$srch_strings[$i]] =
        substr_count($fcontents, $srch_strings[$i]);

    if ($scale < $frequency[$srch_strings[$i]]) {   // Update scale.
        $scale = $frequency[$srch_strings[$i]];
    }
}
```

The above code sets the scale to the highest frequency. This is likely to be a number like 13 or 1724. To have the top of the scale equal a more appropriate number we need to round the scale off. So 13 becomes 20 and 1724 becomes 1800. This rounding gives the graph a more finished look:

```php
if ($scale < 100) {                    // Round scale up.
    $scale = ceil($scale/10) * 10;     // Up to tens.
} else {
    $scale = ceil($scale/100) * 100;   // Up to hundreds.
}
```

The bar chart automatically scales when $svg_width and $svg_height are changed. Therefore, we need to calculate the necessary graph presentation variables:

```php
$x_axis_start  = $offset_x;                // Axes attributes.
$x_axis_end    = $svg_width - $offset_x;
$x_axis_length = $x_axis_end - $x_axis_start;
```

Because the SVG coordinate system defines positive y-axis as down and the graph's positive y-axis is up we need to calculate the y-axis start from the bottom up:

```
$y_axis_start   = $svg_height - $offset_y;
$y_axis_end     = $offset_y;
$y_axis_length  = $y_axis_start - $y_axis_end;


// Calculate space between bars.
$bar_offset = ($x_axis_end - $x_axis_start - $bar_width)/$num_data_points;
```

Finally, we loop calculating the bar height, scaled to fit within the viewport, and store the results in an associative array, `$bar_height[]`:

```
// Calculate the height of bars.
for ($i = 0; $i < $num_data_points; ++$i){
    $bar_height[$srch_strings[$i]] =
        $frequency[$srch_strings[$i]] *
                    ($y_axis_start - $y_axis_end)/$scale;
}
?>
```

Generating SVG

Once we have collected the data and defined the graph variables we need to output the SVG. We create the `vowels.php` file that embeds PHP in SVG to create the bar chart.

The first part of `vowels.php` is dedicated to including the error handler, loading the data, and printing out the SVG Prolog:

```
<?php
// Include the custom error handler to view the PHP errors as SVG.
require_once("./svg_error_handler.php");

// Load the data and chart characteristics.
require_once("./load_data.php");

// Start sending SVG.
header("Content-Type: image/svg+xml");
print ("<?xml version=\"1.0\" ?>");
?>

<!DOCTYPE svg PUBLIC "-//W3C//DTD SVG 1.0//EN"
    "http://www.w3.org/TR/2001/REC-SVG-20010904/DTD/svg10.dtd">

<svg width="<?php print ($svg_width); ?>px"
    height="<?php print ($svg_height); ?>px"
    xmlns="http://www.w3.org/2000/svg"
    xmlns:xlink="http://www.w3.org/1999/xlink" >
```

Second, in keeping with the W3C recommendation, we output the `<desc>` and `<title>` elements. Also, we define a `<marker>` to use at the end of the axes:

```
<desc>
  A bar chart plotting the occurrences of vowels on example.com.
</desc>
<title>
  Vowels on example.com
</title>

<!-- Define an end of axis marker. -->
<defs>
  <marker id="AxisEnd" refX="0" refY="2" markerUnits="strokeWidth"
          markerWidth="1" markerHeight="4" orient="auto">
   <path d="M 0 0 L 0 4 L 1 4 L 1 0 Z" />
  </marker>
</defs>
```

Next, we start outputting the different SVG shapes that make up the graphs. The following is a two-pixel green border around the SVG viewport. The `<rect>` starts at $(1,1)$ and ends at ($svg_width - 2$, $svg_height - 2$). The offsets take into account the width of the stroke and the fact that half of the stroke is on the outside of the `<rect>` outline and half on the inside:

```
<!-- Draw border around viewport. -->
<rect x="1" y="1"
      width="<?php print ($svg_width - 2); ?>"
      height="<?php print ($svg_height - 2); ?>"
      style="fill:none; stroke:green; stroke-width:2;" />
```

The following lines of code draw the axes:

```
<!-- Draw axes with an end marker. -->
<g style="stroke:black; stroke-width:2;">
  <line x1="<?php print ($x_axis_start); ?>"
        y1="<?php print ($y_axis_start); ?>"
        x2="<?php print ($x_axis_end); ?>"
        y2="<?php print ($y_axis_start); ?>"
        marker-end="url(#AxisEnd)" />

  <line x1="<?php print ($x_axis_start); ?>"
        y1="<?php print ($y_axis_start); ?>"
        x2="<?php print ($x_axis_start); ?>"
        y2="<?php print ($y_axis_end); ?>"
        marker-end="url(#AxisEnd)" />
</g>
```

Here, the `marker-end` attribute links the `AxisEnd` `<marker>` defined above to the end of the lines. It could have been included in the `<g>` style attribute or the `<line>` style attribute. Because we are linking internally, make sure `xlns` is defined in the root SVG tag.

Now let's draw the bars. The bar rectangles are children of a `<g>` tag that transforms the user coordinate system by flipping the scale and translating the user coordinate system to the origin of the axis. The rectangles are then drawn up from the x-axis. However, the flipped scale distorts text so we only draw the bars. Also, `translate()` must precede `scale()` so the user coordinate system is moved into place first and then flipped.

It is possible that the `$colors[]` array will have fewer elements than the number of data points. If this is true the fill color of the bars will default to black. An enhancement to the code should reset the `colors[]` array when it reaches the last array element so that the bars stay color-coded.

An `<animate>` element is defined as a child of each bar `<rect>` element and these give the bars animation. The bars grow from zero to their final height in 2 seconds:

```
<!-- Draw Bars. Flip y scale(). -->
<g style="stroke:black; stroke-width:2;"
   transform="translate( <?php print ($x_axis_start); ?>
 <?php print ($y_axis_start); ?>  )
      scale(1 -1)" >

<?php
$x_point = $bar_offset/2;

for ($i = 0; $i < $num_data_points; ++$i){
    ?>
    <rect x="<?php print ($x_point); ?>" y="0"
        width="<?php print ($bar_width); ?>"
        height="<?php print ($bar_height[$srch_strings[$i]]); ?>"
        style="fill:<?php print ($colors[$i]); ?>;">
      <animate attributeType="XML" attributeName="height" from="0"
            to="<?php print ($bar_height[$srch_strings[$i]]); ?>"
            dur="2s" fill="freeze"/>
    </rect>
    <?php
    $x_point += $bar_offset;
}
?>
</g>
```

Now let's move on to the text part. All of the `<text>` elements are the children of the `<g>` tag that defines most of the `<text>` attributes and transforms the user coordinate system but does not flip the scale. Because we are not flipping the scale, the text is placed above the drawn y-axis by using a negative value and below by using a positive value:

```
<!-- Draw the text. Same translation as the bars but without scale(). -->
<g style="font-family:Verdana; font-size:12;
   fill:black; text-anchor:middle;"
   transform="translate( <?php print ($x_axis_start); ?>
 <?php print ($y_axis_start); ?> ) " >
```

Next we draw the text that labels the different bars. First we label the search strings at the base of the bar. Then we label the frequency above the bar.

Notice how the text above the bar is defined as `hidden`. This allows the `<animate>` tag to reveal the text two seconds after the document is loaded and place them as the bars reach their full height:

```
<!-- Label bars. -->
<?php
$x_point = $bar_offset/2 + $bar_width/2;

for ($i = 0; $i < $num_data_points; ++$i){
    ?>
    <text x="<?php print ($x_point); ?>" y="15" >
      <?php print ($srch_strings[$i]); ?>
    </text>
    <text x="<?php print ($x_point); ?>"
          y="-<?php print ($bar_height[$srch_strings[$i]] + 10); ?>"
          visibility="hidden">

      <?php print ($frequency[$srch_strings[$i]]); ?>

      <animate attributeType="CSS" attributeName="visibility"
               to="visible" begin="2s" fill="freeze" />
    </text>
    <?php
    $x_point += $bar_offset;
}                                                           // end for
?>
```

Finally, the axes are labeled. The label for the y-axis needs to be translated into place first and then rotated so the rotation is around the correct point:

```
<!-- Label x-axis -->
<text x="<?php print ($x_axis_length / 2); ?>" y="30" >
  <?php print ($x_label); ?>
</text>

<!-- Label y-axis end -->
<text x="-10"
      y="-<?php print ($y_axis_length - 3); ?>"
      text-anchor="end">
    <?php print ($scale); ?>
</text>

<!-- Label the y-axis. Move up y-axis then rotate()
     so text is vertical-->
<g transform="translate( -20
  -<?php print ($y_axis_length / 2); ?>)
  rotate(-90)">
  <text x="0" y="0">
    <?php print ($y_label); ?>
  </text>
</g>

</g>
</svg>
```

Generating SVG Using the SVG Base Class

If embedding PHP directly into SVG seems a little messy, we can use the PHP SVG class to create the SVG document.

Again, just like the procedural code, we should include all of the necessary files for error handling and data loading. In addition, we should include the SVG base class `svg.php`:

```php
<?php
// Include the custom error handler to view PHP errors as SVG.
require_once("./svg_error_handler.php");

// Load the data and chart characteristics.
require_once("./load_data.php");

// Include the SVG base classes. Define the path to the SVG class dir.
define("SVG_CLASS_BASE", $_SERVER["DOCUMENT_ROOT"]."/ProPHPXML/classes/");
require_once(SVG_CLASS_BASE . "svg.php");
```

The first instance we create is of type `SvgDocument`. All other instances will have this instance as their parent. The comment above the new statement is the class constructor definition. We will include it here for reference:

```php
// SvgDocument($width="100%", $height="100%", $style="")
$svg =& new SvgDocument($svg_width, $svg_height);
```

Next, let's create an instance of type `SvgDesc` and `SvgTitle` and make them the child of `$svg`:

```php
// SvgDesc($desc, $style="")
$svg->addChild(new SvgDesc("A bar chart plotting the occurrences
                            of vowels on example.com."));

// SvgTitle($title, $style="")
$svg->addChild(new SvgTitle("Vowels on Example.com"));
```

Here we create an end of axis `SvgMarker` instance. The instance must be the child of an `SvgDefs` instance and the parent of an `SvgPath` instance. So, we create the three corresponding SVG class instances and add them to their respective parent tags:

```php
// Create end of axis marker objects. SvgDefs($style="", $transform="")
$defs =& new SvgDefs();

// SvgMarker($id, $refX="", $refY="", $markerUnits="",
// $markerWidth="", $markerHeight="", $orient="")
$marker =& new SvgMarker("AxisEnd", "0", "2", "strokeWidth",
    "1", "4", "auto");

// SvgPath($d="", $style="", $transform="")
$marker->addChild(new SvgPath("M 0 0 L 0 4 L 1 4 L 1 0 Z"));

$defs->addChild($marker);
$svg->addChild($defs);
```

Next we create an `SvgRect` instance that will draw a rectangle around the viewport and add it to `$svg`:

```
// Create a rect object that draws a border around the viewport.
// SvgRect($x=0, $y=0, $width=0, $height=0,
// $style="", $transform="")
$svg->addChild(new SvgRect("1", "1", $svg_width - 2, $svg_height - 2,
                           "fill:none;stroke:green;stroke-width:2;"));
```

Now let us create an `SvgGroup` instance and make it the parent of the two `SvgLine` instances that make up the axes:

```
// Create the axes objects.
// SvgGroup($style="", $transform="")
$axisGroup = new SvgGroup("stroke:black;stroke-width:2;");

// SvgLine($x1=0, $y1=0, $x2=0,
// $y2=0, $style="", $transform="")
$axisGroup->addChild(new SvgLine($x_axis_start, $y_axis_start, $x_axis_end,
                                 $y_axis_start,
                                 "marker-end:url(#AxisEnd)"));

$axisGroup->addChild(new SvgLine($x_axis_start, $y_axis_start, $x_axis_start,
    $y_axis_end, "marker-end:url(#AxisEnd)"));

$svg->addChild($axisGroup);
```

The bar instances are added to the `SvgGroup` instance that translate the bars to the x-axis and flips them so they will print up from the y-axis:

```
// Create the bar objects.
$barGroup =& new SvgGroup("stroke:black; stroke-width:2;",
    "translate($x_axis_start $y_axis_start)
    scale(1 -1)");

$x_point = $bar_offset/2;

for ($i = 0; $i < $num_data_points; ++$i){

    $bar  =& new SvgRect($x_point, "0", $bar_width,
    $bar_height[$srch_strings[$i]], "fill:$colors[$i]");

    // SvgAnimate($attributeName, $attributeType="", $from="",
    // $to="", $begin="", $dur="", $fill="")
    $anim =& new SvgAnimate("height", "XML", "0",
    $bar_height[$srch_strings[$i]], "0", "2s", "freeze");

    $bar->addChild($anim);
    $barGroup->addChild($bar);

    $x_point += $bar_offset;

} // end for

$svg->addChild($barGroup);
```

Create another `SvgGroup` instance that will give all of the text similar attributes:

```
// Create the text objects.
$textGroup =& new SvgGroup("font-family:Verdana; font-size:12; fill:black;
text-anchor:middle;", "translate($x_axis_start $y_axis_start)");
```

Create the different `SvgText` instances that will print out the bar labels. Notice the creation of an `SvgAnimate` instance that will animate the bar totals making them appear when the bars reach their full height:

```
$x_point = $bar_offset/2 + $bar_width/2;
for ($i = 0; $i < $num_data_points; ++$i) {
    // x labels.
    // SvgText($x=0, $y=0, $text= "",
    // $style="", $transform="")
    $textGroup->addChild(new SvgText($x_point, "15", $srch_strings[$i]));

    // Frequencies printed above the bars; these are animated.
    $bar_label =& new SvgText($x_point, -$bar_height[$srch_strings[$i]]-10,
    $frequency[$srch_strings[$i]], "visibility:hidden;");

    $anim =& new SvgAnimate("visibility", "CSS", "", "visible", "2s", "",
                            "freeze");

    $bar_label->addChild($anim);
    $textGroup->addChild($bar_label);

    $x_point += $bar_offset;
}                                                               // end for
```

Here we are creating the axes label instances:

```
// Add the x-axis label.
$textGroup->addChild(new SvgText($x_axis_length / 2, "30", $x_label));

// Add the scale.
$textGroup->addChild(new SvgText("-10", -$y_axis_length - 3, $scale,
                                 "text-anchor:end"));

// Add the y-axis label. Create a group to rotate vertically first.
$y_trans = -$y_axis_length / 2;
$yLabelGroup = new SvgGroup("", "translate(-20 $y_trans) rotate(-90)");
$yLabelGroup->addChild(new SvgText("0", "0", $y_label));

// Add to the textGroup.
$textGroup->addChild($yLabelGroup);

$svg->addChild($textGroup);
```

The last step is to send a print message to the main `SvgDocument` instance. This message then sends messages to all of the instance's children telling them to print and so on down to the last child instance. Thus, it is all very neat and object-oriented:

```
$svg->printElement();
?>
```

Summary

In this chapter, we looked at the W3C's vector-based 2-dimensional graphics specification – SVG.

The three different user agents used to view SVG content were discussed, along with the difference between them. The correct structure of an SVG document was shown along with two templates that can be used when creating SVG. Error handling of PHP within an SVG document can be tricky, so several techniques for error handling were given. We looked at how to generate and render SVG. We then looked at how we can use PHP to add dynamic content to the SVG files. We also looked at two detailed examples:

❑ Embedding the PHP directly in the SVG file

❑ Using the PHP SVG class to generate an SVG document

Then several basic elements in the SVG specification were described and dissected along with the more advanced <path> and <animate>. Finally we concluded with two examples. One animated a circle and text. The other created and animated a bar chart.

PHP when combined with SVG provides limitless ways to present data in a graphical manner on the Internet. Some of the more promising possibilities include searchable maps and diagrams that we can even zoom. It is fairly easy to create interactive graphical displays using client and/or server processing, or to use PHP to pull information from a database to generate charts, graphs, diagrams, and other visual displays. The possibilities are endless using SVG.

For more information on SVG:

❑ The W3C SVG specification, a must read. Not too heavy – http://www.w3.org/TR/SVG/

❑ A tutorial on using ECMAScript, and SVG at http://www.devx.com/xml/articles/nm030402/nm030402-1.asp

❑ Samples of what the native SVG Mozilla build is capable of – http://www.croczilla.com/svg/

❑ A Perl extension of generating SVG – http://roasp.com/SVG.html

❑ This page contains a PHP class that translates svg files to png/jpeg images – http://php.chregu.tv/

❑ "SVG Elves is a collaborative work by developers and designers who enjoy tinkering with SVG and helping each other figure stuff out" – http://www.svgelves.com/

❑ Great site showing the many possibilities of creating maps using SVG – http://www.carto.net/

❑ Where to download the Adobe SVG Viewer plus many great examples of what can be done using SVG – http://www.adobe.com/svg/

❑ The SVG wiki, with examples, links, people, articles, documentation, and more – http://www.protocol7.com/svg-wiki/

❑ The SVG developer's mailing list at http://groups.yahoo.com/group/svg-developers/

Professional PHP4 XML Professional PHP4 XML Professional PHP4 XML

16

XML-RPC

In this chapter we are going to study one of the implementations of RPC that we can use to implement web services: XML-RPC. It is a very simple and elegant protocol, and has excellent ready-to-use PHP implementations. In this chapter we'll discuss the protocol in detail, and we'll see how we can use it from PHP to build web services. We will also implement small examples of XML-RPC clients and servers that we can use as skeletons to design our own services.

What Are RPCs?

RPC (Remote Procedure Call) was incorporated in UNIX as a powerful mechanism for distributed client-server applications. The first programs using RPC were written in C. It is based on extending the notion of conventional or local procedure calling, so that the called procedure doesn't need to exist in the same address space as the calling procedure. When the program wants to call a procedure running in another machine it calls a **stub** function, which is a function without the real code but with the ability to connect to the server and call the real procedure in the designated machine. Therefore the program does not realize it is calling a remote procedure.

To learn more about the roots of RPC computing visit
http://www.xmlrpc.com/stories/storyReader$555.

What Is XML-RPC?

There are several RPC models and implementations. One such implementation is XML-RPC. Let's start with a short history of XML-RPC.

The father of XML-RPC is Dave Winer. In 1998 Winer was working for Userland software in a product called Frontier. The product made extensive use of networking and since it had to run in several different platforms, they decided to base communications in XML and HTTP to form the communication protocol for Frontier. The protocol was simply called RPC. Later on people from Microsoft offered Dave Winer some help. Bob Atkinson and Mohsen Al-Ghosein introduced changes to the protocol and added composite data types. Soon XML-RPC was released. Dave and Microsoft continued working together and that's how SOAP (Simple Object Access Protocol) was created, but that's another story.

XML-RPC is a protocol that allows applications to make remote procedure calls. This protocol allows an application written in any language running on any operating system to use a procedure written in another language on any other operating system on some remote computer. A procedure call is sometimes referred to as a **function** call or a **subroutine** call. XML-RPC works by encoding the RPC requests into XML and sending them over a standard HTTP connection to a server or listener piece. The listener decodes the XML, executes the requested procedure, and then packages up the results in XML and sends them back over the wire to the client. The client decodes the XML, converts the results into standard language data types, and continues executing. As one would imagine this is quite a powerful mechanism.

There are a lot of client and server implementations of XML-RPC that allow us to write XML-RPC-based services or use them in a lot of different programming languages. See http://www.xmlrpc.com/directory/1568/implementations/ for a list of available implementations of XML-RPC.

What Are Web Services?

A web service is an interface that describes a collection of operations that are network accessible through standardized XML messaging. It is a procedure or method running on a server and is accessible using the Internet. Web services are important since they provide a universal API for applications no matter what language the application is written in and no matter where it runs. A web service allows us to execute functions from any platform to any other platform. This is the greatest degree of inter-operability and scope an application can achieve, and that's why web services are so useful.

SOAP and XML-RPC are two of the most popular protocols being used for most web services. For a more detailed reference on writing clients for SOAP web services refer to the section on SOAP in Chapter 14.

XML-RPC is a useful tool for developing web services that can be accessed by multiple computers. The most important thing to note here is it uses HTTP, and hence we don't have to worry about the operating system or programming language.

The XML-RPC Protocol

XML-RPC is a protocol based on XML and HTTP, where HTTP is used as a transport layer and XML is used for encoding. The protocol is based around a single HTTP POST containing a request payload and the corresponding response containing the result payload. The request payload contains a method name and a list of parameter values. Fundamental types supported are string, integer, floats, date/time, binary (via base64 encoding), and Boolean. Composite data types can be passed using the `<array>` and `<struct>` tags. To formalize the XML-RPC protocol we have to define three roles that a process may have in XML-RPC. A process can be a client, a server, or both.

The XML-RPC specifications are available at http://www.xmlrpc.com/spec/.

The Basic XML-RPC Protocol

The protocol to make a remote call can be explained in a number of steps:

❏   The calling application makes a procedure call on the XML-RPC client indicating the URI of the server, the procedure to be called on that server, and the parameters to be sent to that procedure

❏   The XML-RPC client takes the method and parameters and builds an XML container for them; the XML container is then sent over HTTP as a POST request

❏   The XML-RPC server that receives the POST requests parses the XML container and determines the method to be called and the parameters to this method

❏   The method is executed on the server returns a result

❏   The result is packaged as XML and the server returns the XML result container as the response of the POST request

❏   The client parses the XML response container and returns the result to the calling application

❏   The application processes the result

Before examining how the procedure call and its response are packaged as XML, there are several important points to consider about the protocol:

❏   **URIs are used to identify XML-RPC servers**
As an example we can have an XML-RPC server at http://www.foo.com/xml-rpc, or if we don't want the XML-RPC server to use the same port as our web server we can use http://www.foo.com:8088/xml-rpc (or any other port). Be aware that using the HTTP port is usually a good idea to evade firewalls and filters. If we can serve a web page we can serve a web service, and this is one of the advantages of XML-RPC.

❏   **An XML-RPC server can implement many methods**
We can serve any number of methods per-URI at the server, and can use URI directories to categorize methods if we want. We can also use a methodNames convention for categorization.

❑ **The protocol is synchronous**

This is an important consideration. In some applications we want the client to send some data to an XML-RPC server and continue its work immediately without waiting for the response; the server would then respond whenever the result is ready. We can't do this with a single XML-RPC call since the response of the server is returned as the response of the HTTP POST request that called the method. Furthermore the protocol specifies that the client must block until the server returns a response.

❑ **The protocol is stateless**

This is inherited from the HTTP protocol. Anyone who has created a dynamic web application is already familiar with this problem. We cannot preserve state between different XML-RPC calls. In a large majority of the cases this won't be a problem, however this could be a problem if, for example, we need to call a method and then call another method related to the first one, and make the server aware of that.

❑ **Authentication**

XML-RPC doesn't provide any kind of authentication mechanism. In many situations we need to provide some kind of authentication to prevent any unauthorized user from using our web services.

❑ **Encryption**

In some situations a web service may require some information that is confidential or sensitive. In these cases we may not want to disclose the information that will be transmitted over HTTP without any encryption.

We can implement encryption at the server side using SSL or at the application level. If we choose to use SSL, an XML-RPC implementation supporting SSL will be required. If we decide to encrypt at the application level, there are two ways we can implement this. The simplest solution is to agree a 'key' between the client and the server and use it to encrypt messages. However, this system cannot always be implemented and the security provided isn't comprehensive. The second approach is to implement login/logout methods and use the methods to establish a session key between the client and the server. We can encrypt messages using that key, and the key will change from session to session adding more security to our information transfer. There are methods such as the Diffie-Hellman method that allows the creation of a session key without sending the key over the network. A resource for this is available at http://www.ietf.org/rfc/rfc2631.txt. For data encryption a good choice would be an encryption algorithm like DES, RC4, or any other method that you are familiar with.

Extending the XML-RPC Protocol

In this section we will discuss extensions to the XML-RPC protocol. There are three main extensions to XML-RPC:

❑ Asynchronous

❑ State-preserving

❑ Authentication

An Asynchronous Protocol for XML-RPC

When we want to implement an asynchronous set of messages, we have to build them artificially on top of the synchronous protocol. This can be achieved only by having both processes become clients and servers. We can build this protocol as follows:

❑   The client makes an XML-RPC call to the server

❑   The server immediately returns an ID for the call without really processing it

❑   The client receives the ID and continues the operation

❑   (Time gap)

❑   The server processes the result and builds a result container

❑   The server makes a procedure call to the client with the ID of the client call and the result

❑   The client, as a server, receives the result of the call made in the first step

❑   The client processes the result

Let's sum up the protocol for XML-RPC:

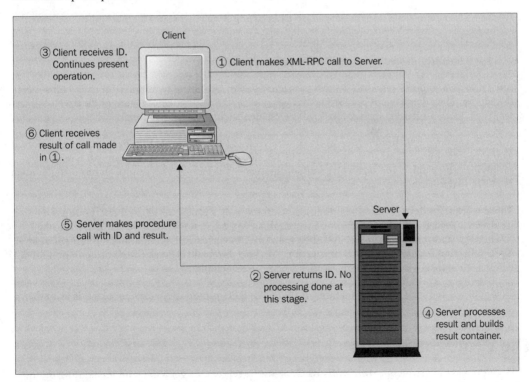

A State-Preserving Protocol for XML-RPC

Ordinarily we use cookies to preserve state. However in XML-RPC, to modify the protocol to preserve state, we will have to use the following protocol:

❑   The client makes an XML-RPC request passing an ID to the server

❑   The server processes the ID and returns a result

❑   (Time gap)

❑   The client makes a new XML-RPC call passing the same ID to the server

❑   The server is aware of which client is calling a method and proceeds accordingly

For this protocol we need a database or a similar mechanism to store sessions in the server.

A Protocol with Authentication for XML-RPC

One solution to implement authentication at the XML-RPC level is to define a login/logout procedure where a password hash is passed and a session is created. The session is then passed as a parameter in every other procedure call, as follows:

❑   The client issues a login procedure call passing a username and the hash of the password

❑   The server validates the login and if valid creates a session and returns it to the client

❑   The client passes the session to the server in each procedure call it makes

If we don't want to use sessions, we can pass a user/password set of parameters in each call we make to the server. The advantage of sessions is that we can use the session key to encrypt data we send to the server. A session-interchange protocol will be needed such as Diffie-Hellman.

A second approach to authenticate users is to rely on HTTP and use HTTP-based authentication. If the web server that hosts XML-RPC supports HTTP, then for authentication we can call a method supplying a user name and password, and let the server validate it. This approach has a slight advantage as HTTP-based authentication is enabled on most servers.

These workarounds are not very common since most web services won't need encryption. However, if we do face a situation where encryption is mandatory just remember that we can solve it using XML-RPC, and some extra work. Another solution is to use an SSL-compatible implementation of XML-RPC that lets us use an SSL connection for procedure calls. Check the documentation for XML-RPC to see if there's some kind of support for SSL connections.

Now that we know all the main features of the XML-RPC protocol, it's time to take a look at the protocol details.

The Protocol Details

If we do want to create our own XML-RPC clients or servers, or get a deep understanding on this protocol, then this section will be useful. The important points about XML-RPC that we will discuss in this section are:

❑   Data types

❑   Requests

❑   Responses

❑   DTD

❑   Schema

Data Types

There are different data types available in XML-RPC. Four of these are used far more than others. For single value data types `<string>` and `<int>`, which respectively denote string and integer data, are the most commonly used in XML-RPC programs. There are also two kinds of collection data types. Simple sequences of arbitrary data types are represented with the `<array>`, and records, structures, and associative arrays are represented by `<struct>`.

XML-RPC handles the following data types:

❑   Integers

❑   Floating point numbers

❑   Boolean

❑   Strings

❑   Date and time

❑   Binary data

❑   Arrays

❑   Structs

Integers

Integers represent 32-bit signed integers, and thus the allowed values are from -2,147,483,648 to 2,147,483,647. We can represent integers in XML-RPC as:

```
<value><int>42</int></value>
```

Or as:

```
<value><i4>42</i4></value>
```

Where `<i4>` is derived from the length of integers in 32-bit machines (4 bytes).

XML-RPC implementations recognize both representations as valid. We cannot put whitespace or other characters as an integer, only – or + as the first character, and then numeric digits.

Floating Point Numbers

XML-RPC uses IEEE754 double-precision numbers as floating point numbers. This implies that the allowed values range from $+/-10^{-323.3}$ to $+/-10^{308.3}$. We represent a floating point number in XML-RPC as:

```
<value><double>435.56</double></value>
```

In the `<double>` tag, XML-RPC only admits a + or – sign followed by digits, a decimal point, and further decimal digits. We cannot use a scientific notation with an exponential part.

> **Arbitrary precision numbers cannot be represented, so we have to observe the IEE754 specification for valid numbers.**

Some special numbers such as `-infinity`, `infinity`, `NaN`, and `indeterminate` cannot be represented in XML-RPC. If a method generates some of those numbers then we have to deal with them using **fault-codes**, which we will cover later in this chapter.

Boolean

A Boolean can be `TRUE` or `FALSE`, and in XML-RPC the Boolean `TRUE`/`FALSE` values are represented using 1 and 0 respectively. Boolean values are encoded as:

```
<value><boolean>1</boolean></value>
```

Strings

Strings are represented as any number of ASCII characters. There are two valid encodings for strings:

```
<value>Hello World</value>
<value><string>Hello World</string></value>
```

Both representations are equivalent for XML-RPC. A string can contain any valid XML ASCII characters, which means that characters not allowed in XML such as "&", "<", and ">" must be coded as XML entities, for example:

```
<value>Johnson &amp; Johnson</value>
```

There are several caveats about encoding strings in XML-RPC. The biggest issue is that the protocol states that only ASCII characters are valid which means than non-ASCII characters such as accents may not pass. However if the XML-RPC implementation is built over an XML 1.0-compliant parser then any XML valid character, using UTF-8, UTF-16, or ISO-8859-1, will be processed correctly. Test the XML-RPC implementation to get a good understanding of how strings are processed and which characters are valid inside a string.

Date and Time

XML-RPC defines a special data type for dates and times, and it uses the ISO8601 standard for them. The profile of the ISO standard used by the XML-RPC representation is defined as:

```
<value><dateTime.iso8601>CCYYMMDDTHH:MM:SS</dateTime.iso8601>
```

This format is useful for a lot of applications. Note that the minimum granularity allowed is the second, and that time zones are not represented in XML-RPC. Since clients don't know in which time zone the server is, the use of GMT timestamps is recommended when important.

We can find the ISO8601 standard at http://www.iso.ch/iso/en/prods-services/otherpubs/pdf/isonetmanual.pdf.

Here is an example:

```
<value><dateTime.iso8601>20020126T17:47:08</dateTime.iso8601>
```

This represents the 26th of January 2002 at 17:47:08 GMT.

Binary Data

Since strings are constrained to ASCII characters there's a special data type for arbitrary data such as images, binary files, and documents. XML-RPC uses the base64 data type as follows:

```
<base64>...binary-data....</base64>
```

The information inside the <base64> element must be base64 encoded. Of course the XML-RPC implementation handles the encoding and decoding of binary data so applications only deal with the pure binary information without any knowledge of how the data is transported over HTTP.

Base64 is defined in RFC2045 at http://www.ietf.org/rfc/rfc2045.txt. It's an encoding/decoding function that encodes arbitrary data as valid ASCII strings. In PHP, we have the base64_encode() and base64_decode() functions available to convert data to and from base64.

Here is an example:

```php
<?php
$data = "Hey this is a test";
print ("Result: ".base64_encode($data)."\n");
?>
```

Output of this will be:

Result: SGV5IHRoaXMgaXMgYSB0ZXN0

Arrays

Arrays are sequences of XML-RPC objects and are heterogeneous, which means that elements can be of different data types. Array members are not numbered as we may expect.

Arrays are represented in XML-RPC as follows:

```
<value>
  <array>
    <data>
      <value></value>
      <value></value>
      ...
      <value></value>
    </data>
  </array>
</value>
```

Data between `<value>` tags can be any valid XML-RPC data type. We can have arrays of arrays as multidimensional arrays, arrays of structures, and arrays with a mixture of integers, dates, binaries, and other items.

Here is an example. This array represents a fragment of the list of players of a football team:

```
<value>
  <array>
    <data>
       <value>QB: Brett Favre</value>
       <value>WR: Antonio Freeman</value>
       <value>WR: Bill Schoeder</value>
       ....
    </data>
  </array>
</value>
```

Structs

A struct allows the representation of associative arrays in XML-RPC. It is a list of members, where each member has a name and a value. The name must be an ASCII string while the value can be any XML-RPC data type including structs, arrays, and simple data types. A struct is encoded as:

```
<value>
  <struct>
    <member>
       <name></name>
       <value></value>
    </member>
    <member>
       <name></name>
       <value></value>
    </member>
  </struct>
</value>
```

The following structure represents information about a product:

```
<value>
  <struct>
    <member>
       <name>Product</name>
       <value>Blue Cheese</value>
    </member>
    <member>
       <name>Price</name>
       <value>5.50</value>
    </member>
  </struct>
</value>
```

The same structure can be represented in PHP as:

```php
<?php
$product = array("Product" => "Blue Cheese", "Price" => 5.50);
?>
```

Mixing arrays and structs we can find a better way to define our football team's list of players:

```
<value>
  <array>
    <data>
      <value>
        <struct>
          <member><name>position</name><value>QB</value></member>
          <member><name>name</name><value>Brett Favre</value></member>
        </struct>
      </value>
      <value>
        <struct>
          <member><name>position</name><value>WR</value></member>
          <member><name>name</name>
                <value>Antonio Freeman</value></member>
        </struct>
      </value>
      <value>
        <struct>
          <member><name>position</name><value>WR</value></member>
          <member><name>name</name><value>Bill Schroeder</value></member>
        </struct>
      </value>
        ....
    </data>
  </array>
</value>
```

The above XML-RPC data type can be represented in PHP as:

```php
<?php
$team = Array(
        Array("position" => "QB", "name" => "Brett Favre"),
        Array("position" => "WR", "name" => "Antonio Freeman"),
        Array("position" => "WR", "name" => "Bill Schoeder")
      );
?>
```

XML-RPC Requests

Now that we know how to represent data in XML-RPC we can take a look at how procedure calls and parameters are encoded in an XML container.

The XML-RPC request container has the following format:

```
<?xml version="1.0"?>
<methodCall>
  <methodName></methodName>
  <params>
    <param>
      <value></value>
    </param>
  </params>
</methodCall>
```

As we can see the request is enclosed in a `<methodCall>` element. The name of the method is defined in the `<methodName>` element and the parameters are encoded in the `<params>` element. The `<params>` element has an arbitrary number of `<param>` elements: one for each parameter the method may receive. Parameter values can be any of the XML-RPC data types that we have seen.

> **Even if the method requires no parameters, an empty `<params>` element must still be present.**

Method names may contain only alphanumeric characters (A-Z, a-z, 0-9) and the dot, colon, underscore, and slash characters. There's no definition about how method names should be defined between the client and the server.

Now that we can create an XML-RPC request object for a procedure call we only have to learn how to transmit this to the server.

Basic HTTP

HTTP is the protocol used by browsers and web servers to communicate. Browsers request pages using HTTP requests and servers send the requested page using HTTP responses. HTTP is a protocol built on top of another famous protocol: TPC/IP (Transmission Control Protocol/Internet Protocol). In TCP/IP, communication is established between two machines by indicating an IP address and a port. HTTP determines the IP address by resolving the URI using a DNS server. A DNS server converts URIs such as http://foo.com/ to an IP address, for example: 200.10.10.25. The standard port that HTTP uses is the port 80, so communication will be established to a web server in a machine with a public IP address listening on port 80.

In HTTP the client connects to the IP and port, and must issue an HTTP request. The protocol is defined using lines of text terminated by a carriage return. A very simple HTTP request is:

```
GET /index.html HTTP/1.1
```

This is telling the web server to return the page http://some.uri.com/index.html. If we know the IP address of a web server and a page, we can attempt to be a human browser using telnet:

```
telnet 10.15.20.30 80

GET /index.html HTTP/1.1
```

Press *Enter* twice after typing the request and the web server will return an HTTP response with some HTTP headers and the content of the page we requested. Congratulations! We hacked HTTP and we don't need a browser anymore.

HTTP requests consist of a request method (typically GET) followed by additional headers terminated in end-of-lines (\n), and then a second end-of-line terminating the HTTP request, for example:

```
GET /index.html HTTP/1.1  \n
Host: foo.mysite.com \n
\n
```

(\n means *Enter* and the ASCII character is 0x0A.) This uses an additional header indicating a virtual host to be used in the targeted machine. This is a new addition in HTTP 1.1.

Now that we know something about HTTP, we can issue POST requests by telnet and we can build our own web server or at least a standalone XML-RPC server that knows how to answer POST requests with the information that XML-RPC defines.

The HTTP Request

As we mentioned earlier in this chapter, XML-RPC uses HTTP as the transport protocol for XML-RPC requests. The request is an HTTP POST request where the body is in XML and the procedure is executed on the server. The value it returns is also formatted in XML. The following HTTP headers are mandatory: User-Agent, Host, Content-Type, and Content-Length. Since the Host header is mandatory, we must use an HTTP 1.1-compliant web server for XML-RPC implementations or create a stand alone XML-RPC server that can handle this format of POST requests.

Here is an example:

```
POST /services.php HTTP/1.1
User-Agent: SOME XML-RPC 0.1
Host: services.mysite.com
Content-Type: text/xml
Content-Length: 216
```

> While most XML-RPC servers are built on top of a web server, we may want to build a standalone XML-RPC server. In this case we have to handle the HTTP protocol that the XML-RPC uses by ourselves.

Additional Headers

The XML specification doesn't require more HTTP headers than the ones we've seen. However, some XML-RPC implementations may handle additional headers to improve the XML-RPC implementation. Authentication headers for example can be supported to provide basic HTTP authentication, so we can allow only authorized clients to access a web service. If we build commercial web services for profit, we must use some kind of authentication to control access to our services.

Another useful header may allow compressed data to be sent over HTTP. If we are implementing web services that will be handling or returning a lot of data (file conversion, for example) then this header can shorten the data that has to be sent, and in turn the time it takes to service the procedure call.

An Example of an XML-RPC Request

Here's an example of what will be transmitted by TCP/IP to the XML-RPC server for a procedure call. The call is made to a method that can add two integers and return the result:

```
POST /services.php HTTP/1.1
User-Agent: SOME XML-RPC 0.1
Host: services.mysite.com
Content-Type: text/xml
Content-Length: 187

<?xml version="1.0"?>
<methodCall>
  <methodName>math.addTwoNums</methodName>
    <params>
       <param><value><i4>5</i4></value></param>
       <param><value><i4>7</i4></value></param>
    </params>
</methodCall>
```

The `<methodCall>` element is used to enclose an XML-RPC request to a server. Inside the `<methodCall>` element we can find the `<methodName>` element where we put the name of the method to be executed on the server and the `<params>` element. The `<params>` element contains the parameters to be passed to the method. Each parameter is enclosed in a `<param>` element and inside the `<param>` element we put the parameter encoded as we explained in the XML-RPC data types section.

XML-RPC Responses

XML-RPC responses are encoded as XML, just like XML-RPC requests. There are two encodings for responses, one used for responses after the method was called and successfully executed and another used to report errors when a method fails. The first one is defined as follows:

```
<?xml version="1.0"?>
<methodResponse>
  <params>
     <param>
        <value></value>
     </param>
  </params>
</methodResponse>
```

As we can see this is very similar to a request, but there are restrictions. Only one `<param>` element can be used inside the `<params>` element. There is more to it, the `<params>` element cannot be empty. This typically produces two situations, one where we have methods that don't return anything and another for methods that return more than one value.

If we call a method that doesn't naturally return a value, for example, a logging method, we have to artificially define something to return, since we have to use a mandatory `<param>` element in the XML response. The alternatives are:

❑   Return a Boolean value.

❑   Return an arbitrary value that the client should ignore.

644

❑ Return the proposed 'nil' value as a NULL result. This is a recommendation by some XML-RPC implementers but it's not in the specification. The recommendation states that the NULL value may be represented in XML-RPC as `<value><nil/></value>`.

The other situation is where we have methods that return more than one value. If this is the case then, we have to obey the restriction of only one `<param>` element in the response, and since the `<param>` element can be any XML-RPC data type, we can return an array or a struct as a simple and elegant way of returning more than one value.

Handling Errors

If a procedure call produces an exception in some method, we can return a fault-report as the XML response of a procedure. The fault report is defined as follows:

```
<?xml version="1.0"?>
<methodResponse>
<fault>
  <value>
    <struct>
      <member>
        <name>faultCode</name>
        <value></value>
      </member>
      <member>
        <name>faultString</name>
        <value></value>
      </member>
    </struct>
  </value>
</fault>
</methodResponse>
```

We return a structure with two members, a faultCode and a faultString. The way in which faults are reported is not in the specification, but a number as a faultCode and a textual description for the problem as a faultString are common in XML-RPC implementations.

The HTTP Response

The HTTP headers sent by the server when responding to a method are similar to the headers used by the client in the request. In the following example, we can see a response generated as a result of our method to add two integers:

```
HTTP/1.1 200 OK
Date: Sun, 26 Jan 2002 18:38:35 GMT
Server: Apache/1.3.18 (Unix)
Connection: close
Content-Type: text/xml
Content-Length: 135

<?xml version="1.0"?>
<methodResponse>
  <params>
    <param>
```

```
        <value><i4>12</i4></value>
      </param>
    </params>
  </methodResponse>
```

The XML-RPC DTD

If we are implementing XLM-RPC, we may find this DTD useful to check if our requests and responses are valid according to the XML-RPC specifications. There's no official DTD for XML-RPC. Nevertheless, it's easy to write one. Indeed such a DTD may be a more easily understandable description of what is and isn't allowed than the prose specification:

```
<!DOCTYPE methodResponse [
<!ELEMENT i4 (#PCDATA)>
<!ELEMENT int (#PCDATA)>
<!ELEMENT boolean (#PCDATA)>
<!ELEMENT string (#PCDATA)>
<!ELEMENT double (#PCDATA)>
<!ELEMENT dateTime.iso8601 (#PCDATA)>
<!ELEMENT base64 (#PCDATA)>
<!ELEMENT data (value*)>
<!ELEMENT array (#PCDATA)>
<!ELEMENT name (#PCDATA)>
<!ELEMENT member (name,value)>
<!ELEMENT struct (member*)>
<!ELEMENT value
(i4|int|boolean|string|dateTime.iso8601|double|base64|struct|array)>
<!ELEMENT param (value)>
<!ELEMENT params (param*)>
<!ELEMENT methodName (#PCDATA)>
<!ELEMENT methodCall (methodName, params)>
<!ELEMENT fault (value)>
<!ELEMENT methodResponse (params|fault)>
]>
```

The DTD shown above states that a <methodCall> contains one <methodName> and one <params>, in that order. A <methodResponse> contains one <params> or one <fault> and a <value> element can contain an <i4>, <int>, <string>, <datetime>.<iso8601>, <double>, <base64>, <struct>, or <array>, and so forth. Note that the DTD can't check the correct values for data types and other constraints – we need a Schema for that. If we have a parser that can validate XML against a Schema then we should define an XML-RPC Schema and use it for finer validation of XML-RPC requests and responses.

The XML-RPC Schema

The DTD is instructive but it does not prescribe a norm or a standard. A Schema, on the other hand, validates the XML-RPC to ensure that they are strictly typed. This is a schema we can use to validate XML-RPC requests:

```
<?xml version="1.0" encoding="UTF-8"?>
<xs:schema xmlns:xs="http://www.w3.org/2001/XMLSchema"
elementFormDefault="qualified" attributeFormDefault="unqualified">
  <xs:element name="methodCall">
    <xs:annotation>
```

```
        <xs:documentation>Method Call for XML-RPC</xs:documentation>
    </xs:annotation>
<xs:complexType>
  <xs:sequence>
    <xs:element name="methodName" type="xs:string"/>
    <xs:element name="params">
      <xs:complexType>
        <xs:sequence>
          <xs:element name="param" maxOccurs="unbounded">
            <xs:complexType>
              <xs:sequence>
                <xs:element name="value">
                  <xs:complexType>
                    <xs:choice>
                      <xs:element name="i4" type="xs:int"/>
                      <xs:element name="int" type="xs:int"/>
                      <xs:element name="boolean" type="xs:boolean"/>
                      <xs:element name="string" type="xs:string"/>
                      <xs:element name="dateTime.iso8601"
                                  type="xs:string"/>
                      <xs:element name="double" type="xs:double"/>
                      <xs:element name="base64" type="xs:base64Binary"/>
                      <xs:element name="struct">
                        <xs:complexType>
                          <xs:sequence>
                            <xs:element name="member"
                                        maxOccurs="unbounded">
                          <xs:complexType>

                              <xs:sequence>
                                <xs:element name="name"

                                            type="xs:string"/>
                                <xs:element ref="value"/>
                              </xs:sequence>
                            </xs:complexType>
                          </xs:element>
                        </xs:sequence>
                      </xs:complexType>
                    </xs:element>
                    <xs:element name="array">
                      <xs:complexType>
                        <xs:sequence>
                          <xs:element name="data">
                            <xs:complexType>
                              <xs:sequence>
                                <xs:element ref="value"
                                            maxOccurs="unbounded"/>
                              </xs:sequence>
                            </xs:complexType>
                          </xs:element>
                        </xs:sequence>
                      </xs:complexType>
                    </xs:element>
```

647

```
                    </xs:choice>
                </xs:complexType>
            </xs:element>
        </xs:sequence>
    </xs:complexType>
    </xs:element>
    </xs:sequence>
    </xs:complexType>
    </xs:element>
    </xs:sequence>
    </xs:complexType>
</xs:element>
<xs:element name="value"/>
</xs:schema>
```

This is a valid Schema for XML-RPC responses:

```
<?xml version="1.0" encoding="UTF-8"?>
<xs:schema xmlns:xs="http://www.w3.org/2001/XMLSchema"
elementFormDefault="qualified" attributeFormDefault="unqualified">
  <xs:element name="methodResponse">
    <xs:annotation>
      <xs:documentation>Method Responsel for XML-RPC</xs:documentation>
    </xs:annotation>
    <xs:complexType>
      <xs:choice>
        <xs:element name="params">
          <xs:complexType>
            <xs:sequence>
              <xs:element name="param" maxOccurs="unbounded">
                <xs:complexType>
                  <xs:sequence>
                    <xs:element name="value">
                      <xs:complexType>
                        <xs:choice>
                          <xs:element name="i4" type="xs:int"/>
                          <xs:element name="int" type="xs:int"/>
                          <xs:element name="boolean" type="xs:boolean"/>
                          <xs:element name="string" type="xs:string"/>
                          <xs:element name="dateTime.iso8601"
                                      type="xs:string"/>
                          <xs:element name="double" type="xs:double"/>
                          <xs:element name="base64" type="xs:base64Binary"/>
                          <xs:element name="struct">
                            <xs:complexType>
                              <xs:sequence>
                                <xs:element name="member"
                                            maxOccurs="unbounded">
                                  <xs:complexType>
                                    <xs:sequence>
                                      <xs:element name="name"
                                                  type="xs:string"/>
                                      <xs:element ref="value"/>
```

```
                            </xs:sequence>
                          </xs:complexType>
                        </xs:element>
                      </xs:sequence>
                    </xs:complexType>
                  </xs:element>
                  <xs:element name="array">
                    <xs:complexType>
                      <xs:sequence>
                        <xs:element name="data">
                          <xs:complexType>
                            <xs:sequence>
                              <xs:element ref="value"
                                          maxOccurs="unbounded"/>
                            </xs:sequence>
                          </xs:complexType>
                        </xs:element>
                      </xs:sequence>
                    </xs:complexType>
                  </xs:element>
                </xs:choice>
              </xs:complexType>
            </xs:element>
          </xs:sequence>
        </xs:complexType>
      </xs:element>
    </xs:sequence>
  </xs:complexType>
</xs:element>
<xs:element name="fault">
  <xs:complexType>
    <xs:sequence>
      <xs:element ref="value"/>
    </xs:sequence>
  </xs:complexType>
</xs:element>
          </xs:choice>
        </xs:complexType>
      </xs:element>
      <xs:element name="value"/>
    </xs:schema>
```

XML-RPC in PHP

So far in this chapter we have discussed the details of XML-RPC. In this section we will see how to implement web services using PHP.

What we need to implement XML-RPC clients and services, is a PHP implementation of XML-RPC. In this chapter we'll be using the XML-RPC library from http://www.usefulinc.com/. There is a new experimental XML-RPC extension in PHP 4.1 that will provide native XML-RPC functionality to PHP, but since the extension is experimental, and lacks enough documentation and examples, it's more convenient at the time this book was written to use a library. As we'll see, the use of this library only requires downloading two .inc scripts and including them in a directory accessible from our PHP script, so it's really easy.

Using the XML-RPC Library from Usefulinc

The library by Usefulinc can be downloaded from
http://sourceforge.net/project/showfiles.php?group_id=34455.

We'll need two `.inc` scripts: `xmlrpc.inc`, which provides the client functionality, and `xmlrpcs.inc`, which provides the server functionality. We then will have to put these files in a directory accessible from our PHP scripts in a way that we can `include()` these scripts from our PHP code. After this basic installation procedure, we are ready to use XML-RPC.

> If we install and compile PHP 4.1.x with `--with-xml-rpc`, we may find a name collision between the functions in the native XML-RPC implementation and the Usefulinc class. If you use Usefulinc's library then compile PHP without `--with-xml-rpc`. In some PHP installations, we may get a warning about an undefined index in `xmlrpc.inc`. We need to fix it to make XML-RPC work, but the fix is simple and described below.

A Fix

In some PHP installations, we may get a warning message such as undefined index ac at line 333 of xmlrpc.inc. This warning may break the whole XML-RPC service since it will prevent HTTP headers from being correctly sent. We can fix it as follows:

Find the following piece of code at line 333 of `xmlrpc.inc`:

```
$_xh[$parser]['ac'].=str_replace('$', '\$',
        str_replace('"', '\"', str_replace(chr(92),
            $xmlrpc_backslash, $data)));
}
```

and replace it with:

```
if(!isset($_xh[$parser]['ac'])) {$_xh[$parser]['ac']='';}
    $_xh[$parser]['ac'].=str_replace('$', '\$',
            str_replace('"', '\"', str_replace(chr(92),
                    $xmlrpc_backslash, $data)));
    }
```

Writing Clients

To write a client we need to:

❑ Encode PHP data types as XML-RPC data

❑ Connect to an XML-RPC server

❑ Call a method and pass parameters previously encoded as XML-RPC data types

As one would expect, the `xmlrpc.inc` class provides this functionality and we are going to study it very soon, but first things first. A lot of experienced programmers are used to coding by example. If you are one of them, and only want to see a working client to modify it and build your own, here it is.

An XML-RPC Client

This is a very simple XML-RPC client, it is used to show an HTML form asking for a number, and if the number is entered it packs the number as an XML-RPC integer and calls a method `multiply()` on a server. The `multiply()` method on the server multiplies the number entered by two. The server shows the XML response or an error message. With this sample client, and a sample server, we have all that we need to set up a web service. All we need to know now is how to manage other data types. The server for this program (`servfoo.php`) is given later in the chapter. The server program will have to be accessible by the client program. Save the program below as `client.php`:

```php
<html>
  <head>
    <title>xmlrpc</title>
  </head>
  <body>
    <h2>XML-RPC test</h2>

<?php
include("../classes/xmlrpc.inc");

if (!empty($_REQUEST["number"])) {
// first we create an xmlrpc message to call the method "multiply"
// passing $number as an xmlrpc int data type
    $f = new xmlrpcmsg('multiply',
                    array(new xmlrpcval($_POST["number"], "int")));

    // Now we create an xmlrpc_client connecting to the xmlrpc server
    $c = new xmlrpc_client("/ProPHPXML/Chapter16/servfoo.php",
                    "localhost", 80);
    $c->setDebug(0);

    // We send the xmlrpc message
    $r = $c->send($f);
    // And get the response
    $v = $r->value();

    // Check for Errors
    if (!$r->faultCode()) {
        print ("Number ". $number . " is " . $v->scalarval() . "<br />");
        print ("<hr>I got this value back<br /><pre>" .
                htmlentities($r->serialize()). "</pre><hr>\n");
    } else {
        print ("Fault: ");
        print ("Code: " . $r->faultCode() .
                " Reason '" .$r->faultString()."'<br />");
    }
} else {
    $number = 0;
}
print ("<form method=\"post\">
            <input name=\"number\" value=\"{$number}\">
            <input type=\"submit\" value=\"go\" name=\"submit\">
        </form><p>
        enter a number");
?>
  </body>
</html>
```

Client Functions

When writing a client using this library, we need to create a client object. The client object receives in its constructor the path, hostname, and port of the server:

```
$client = new xmlrpc_client($serverpath, $hostname, $port);
```

Here is an example:

```
$client = new xmlrpc_client("/ProPHPXML/Chapter16/fooserv.php",
                            "localhost", 80);
```

Before using the client to call a method on the server, we can set some parameters for the client:

```
$client->setDebug(0);  // sets debug mode off
$client->setDebug(1); // sets debug mode on
```

If debug mode is On we get a verbose description of what happened when the error occurred. This is a useful setting when developing the client and server scripts:

```
$client->setCredentials($username, $password);
```

This sets the username and password to be used if the server is using HTTP authentication for methods. Once we create the client object, we need to create the message to send to the server:

```
$msg = new xmlrpcmsg($methodname, $parameters);
```

$methodname is a string with the name of the method to be called, $parameters is an array of XML-RPC objects, one for each parameter.

Here is an example:

```
$n1 = xmlrpc_encode(15);
$n2 = xmlrpc_encode(23);
$client = new xmlrpc_client("/ProPHPXML/Chapter16/fooserv.php",
                            "localhost",80);
$msg = new xmlrpcmsg("add", array($n1,$n2));
```

If we want to see the XML container created for the message, we can use $msg->serialize() to get a serialization of the XML we'll send to the server.

After the message is ready, we send it to the server in either of the two ways shown below:

```
$result = $client->send($msg);
```

or by specifying a timeout in seconds:

```
$result = $client->send($msg,40);
```

We get a $result variable with the result. If $result is FALSE then a low-level error occurs. For example, the server is down, the timeout expired, or there's no network connection to the server.

If $result is true then the client and the server interchanged messages, and we can check for logic errors. If $result->value() is TRUE then the method returns a valid result. If $result->value() is FALSE then the method produces an exception.

We can decode the fault message for an exception using:

```
if (!$value->result) {
    print ("Error: " $result->faultCode()."\n");
    print ("Text: ". $result->faultString()."\n");
}
```

The XML-RPC library from Usefulinc defines the following errors for some common XML-RPC-related problems the server may find:

Error Code	Error Text	Description
1	Unknown method	The client tried to execute a method that the server can't find or recognize. A common error is to misspell the method name.
2	Invalid return payload: enabling debugging to examine incoming payload	The server received an invalid XML-RPC request. This error occurs frequently if the xmlrpc.inc class produces a warning message or we have an error in our client.
3	Incorrect parameters passed to method	We sent an incorrect number or type of parameter to a method in the server.
4	Can't introspect method unknown	We tried to find a method in the server that doesn't exist (see the *Introspection* section later in this chapter).
5	Didn't receive 200 OK from server	There was an HTTP error. Perhaps we need to pass credentials or our credentials are invalid. If the server is trying to authenticate, set debug mode to On to get a further description of the error.

Writing Servers

When writing servers we need to:

❑ Create the methods that the client will call

❑ Initialize a server object binding the methods we created with the method names that the server recognizes

Again, the Usefulinc library provides us with much of this functionality.

An XML-RPC Server

The server has to be placed in a directory where our client program can access it. The server program is also written in PHP and this makes it easier as we just have to manage it like a standard PHP script. Make sure that the server program has access to both the xmlrpc.inc and xmlrpcs.inc scripts. Name the file below as servfoo.php:

```php
<?php
include("../classes/xmlrpc.inc");
include("../classes/xmlrpcs.inc");

function foo($params)
{
    // $params is an Array of xmlrpcval objects
    $vala = $params->params[0];
    $sval = $vala->scalarval();
    $ret = $sval * 2;
    return new xmlrpcresp(new xmlrpcval($ret, "int"));
}

$s = new xmlrpc_server(array("multiply" => array("function" => "foo")));
?>
```

Shown below is the output when the client.php program written earlier is executed. The number 23 was entered. The server received this in the XML-RPC format, multiplied it by two, and sent the response back. The XML-RPC response is also echoed to the screen:

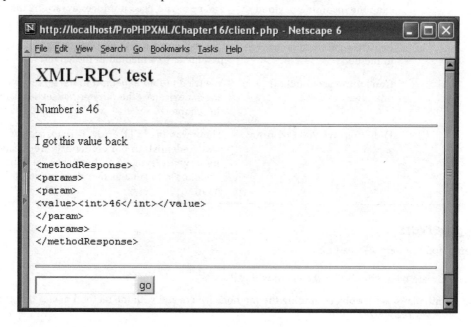

Server Functions

A method has the following prototype:

```
function any_name($params) {}
```

We can access `params` using `$params->getParam(0)` and `$params->getParam(1)`. Each `param` is an `xmlrpc` object, and we have to decode it to PHP `vars` before processing them. Once we have the parameters as PHP data, and we process them, we have to create a response object. We have two constructors for a response:

```
$result = new xmlrpcresp(0, $errno, $errmsg);
```

or:

```
$result = new xmlrpcresp(new xmlrpcval());
```

In the first constructor, we are returning a fault code, and we can indicate the error number and error message, in the second constructor we create an XML-RPC object for the response and return it.

Binding

Once we have all the methods created, we need to create a binding between those methods and the methods the server will recognize. A basic way to do the binding is:

```
$s = new xmlrpc_server(array("methodname" =>
                       array("function" => "php_function_name")));
```

The Library Details

Now that we can write a skeleton XML-RPC client and server, we are going to study how to encode/decode PHP data types from and to XML-RPC. We may also need some details for a full XML-RPC implementation of web services using PHP.

Encoding Data from PHP To XML-RPC

We use the `xmlrpcval()` constructors to build XML-RPC data types from PHP data. The constructors are used as described below:

- Encoding strings:
  `$xmlrpc_string = xmlrpcval("Hello world", "string")`

- Encoding integers:
  `$xmlrpc_int = xmlrpcval(25, "int")`

- Encoding floating-point numbers:
  `$xmlrpc_float = xmlrpcval(3.1415, "double")`

- Encoding Booleans:
  `$xmlrpc_boolean = xmlrpcval(1, "boolean")`

❑ Encoding dates:
```
$xmlrpc_data = ("2002-01-28T13:17:57", "dateTime.iso8601")
```

❑ Encoding binary dates:
```
$xmlrpc_binary = xmlrpcval($data, "base64")
```

❑ Encoding arrays:
```
$xmlrpc_array = xmlrpcval(array(new xmlrpcval("one", "string"), new
xmlrpcval("two", "string")), "array");
```

❑ Encoding structs:
```
$xmlrpc_struct = xmlrpcval(array("name" => new xmlrpcval("John",
"string"), "age" => new xmlrpcval(27, "int")), "struct")
```

In the code you can see how we can create XML-RPC data types from PHP data. Of course we can compose the functions to create arrays of arrays of structs and so on.

Decoding XML-RPC Data To PHP

When we get an XML-RPC object, we can check the XML-RPC data type associated with it. We use the kindOf property of the object:

```
// let $x be an XML-RPC object
if ($x->kindOf=="scalar") {
    print ("X is an scalar\n");
} elseif ($x->kindOf == "array" ) {
    print ("X is an array\n");
} elseif($x->kindOf == "struct") {
    print ("X is a struct");
} else {
    print ("Something weird is happening here\n");
}
```

Scalars

As we know an XML-RPC scalar can be:

❑ Boolean

❑ Integer

❑ Double

❑ String

❑ date/time

❑ base64-encoded binary

We can determine the type of an XML-RPC scalar using $x->scalartype() and we can get the value with $x->scalarval().

Arrays

XML-RPC arrays are managed using two methods: $x->arraysize(), which determines the size of the array, while $x->arraymem(i) gets the i'th value of the array.

Here is an example:

```
if ($x->kindOf=="array") {
    //check
    for ($i = 0; $i<$x->arraysize; $i++) {
        print ("Array[$i] = ".$x->arraymem($i)."\n");
    }
}
```

Structs

Structs are handled with the `structmem()` function. We use `$x->structmem("key")` to get the value of the given key. The value is an XML-RPC object so we need to process it accordingly.

We can also use the `structeach()` method to iterate a struct:

```
while (($key, $val) = $x->structeach()){
    ...
    // $key is a php string with the struct key
    // $val is an XML-RPC object with the value
}
```

Shortcuts for Encoding and Decoding Data

There are some shortcuts that we can use to reduce the amount of code we have to write to handle encoding and decoding of data. We can use the `xmlrpc_encode()` and `xmlrpc_decode()` functions as follows:

```
$xmprpc_in = xmlrpc_encode(23);
$xmlrpc_string = xmlrpc_encode("Hello world");
$xmlrpc_double = xmlrpc_encode(3.1415);
```

We can't use `xmlrpc_encode()` on date or binary since PHP doesn't have native data types for them.

To encode structs:

```
$xmlrpc_struct = xmlrpc_encode(array("name"=>"John", "age"=>27));
```

To decode use `xmlrpc_decode()`:

```
$phpvar = xmlrpc_decode($xmlrpc_object);
```

And we get a PHP integer/string/double or array depending on the data type of the `xmlrpc_object`.

Service Descriptions

A better way to define the server that allows a mechanism called **introspection** is to use a **Dispatch Map**. To create a binding using a Dispatch Map, we need to create a **signature** and documentation for each method. The signature indicates the parameters the method receives and its types. The signature is an array of n+1 values, n being the number of parameters the method receives. Note the index n+1. This is because the first element of the signature array is the data type that the method returns.

Here is an example:

```
$method_sig = array(array($xmlrpcInt, $xmlrpcInt, $xmlrpcInt));
$method_doc = 'This method adds two numbers';

$map = array("math.add" => array("function" => "add",
                                 "signature" => $method_sig,
                                 "docstring" => $method_doc),
             ....
       );

new xmlrpc_server(dispatchmap);
```

Introspection

Introspection is a mechanism to get a list and description of services an XML-RPC server provides. The recommendation for implementations supporting introspection is to provide the following services:

❑ `system.listMethods()`
This method must return an array of strings with the names of the methods the server supports

❑ `system.methodSignature(methodName)`
This method receives a string with a method name and returns an array of signatures for this method (a method can be overloaded)

❑ `system.methodHelp(methodName)`
This method returns a string with the documentation for the method passed as argument

> If we use the Usefulinc library we don't need to code the `system.listMethods()`, `system.methodSignature()`, and `system.methodHelp()` methods. We just need to provide the information and initialize the server, and the library itself will implement the methods.

Introspection is a good way to query methods and to get documentation and description of methods from an XML-RPC server.

An Example

In this basic example we create a library of services to manipulate integer numbers. We define a method for adding numbers and a method for subtracting numbers and use a Dispatch Map to describe the services.

This is the server. The signature is an array inside an array because we can specify alternative method signatures as arrays alongside each other. Simply omitting an argument from subsequent arrays labels it as optional:

```
<?php
include("../classes/xmlrpc.inc");
include("../classes/xmlrpcs.inc");

$add_sig = array(array($xmlrpcInt, $xmlrpcInt, $xmlrpcInt));
```

```
$add_doc = 'This method adds two numbers';

$sub_sig = array(array($xmlrpcInt, $xmlrpcInt, $xmlrpcInt));
$sub_doc = 'This method substracts two numbers';

$map = array("math.add" => array("function" => "PhpAdd",
                                 "signature" => $add_sig,
                                 "docstring" => $add_doc),
             "math.sub" => array("function" => "PhpSub",
                                 "signature" => $sub_sig,
                                 "docstring" => $sub_doc));

function PhpAdd($params)
{
    // $params is an Array of xmlrpcval objects
    $vala = $params->getParam(0);
    $svala = $vala->scalarval();
    $valb = $params->getParam(1);
    $svalb = $valb->scalarval();
    $ret = $svala+$svalb;
    return new xmlrpcresp(new xmlrpcval($ret, "int"));
}

function PhpSub($params)
{
    // $params is an Array of xmlrpcval objects
    $vala = $params->getParam(0);
    $svala = $vala->scalarval();
    $valb = $params->getParam(1);
    $svalb = $valb->scalarval();
    $ret = $svala-$svalb;
    return new xmlrpcresp(new xmlrpcval($ret, "int"));
}

$s = new xmlrpc_server($map);
?>
```

In the client we use introspection to find server methods, and then use a simple dynamic form asking for two numbers and a method name, and then we call the method and show the result. Alternatively, we can input a method name and get Help on it or see its signature.

This is the client:

```
<html>
  <head>
    <title>xmlrpc</title>
  </head>
  <body>
    <h2>XML-RPC test2</h2>

<?php
include("../classes/xmlrpc.inc");
```

```
$serverPath = "/ProPHPXML/Chapter16/XML-RPCserver.php";
$serverHost = "localhost";
$serverPort = 80;

// We use introspection to get a list of server methods and put methods in
// an array
$f = new xmlrpcmsg('system.listMethods');
$c = new xmlrpc_client($serverPath, $serverHost, $serverPort);
$c->setDebug(0);
$methods = Array();
$r = $c->send($f);
$v = $r->value();
if (!$r->faultCode()) {
    $list = xmlrpc_decode($v);
    foreach ($list as $elem) {
        $methods[] = $elem;
    }
} else {
    print ("Fault: ");
    print ("Code: " . $r->faultCode() .
            " Reason '" .$r->faultString()."'<br />");
}

// Here we call the submitted method on the xmlrpcserver
if (!empty($_REQUEST["method"])) {
```

If we chose to see the results of calling `system.listMethods` we carry out the same process above, and output the results and the XML-RPC response to the screen:

```
    // check if we want to list the methods
    if ($_REQUEST["method"] == "system.listMethods") {
        $f = new xmlrpcmsg("system.listMethods");
        $c = new xmlrpc_client($serverPath, $serverHost, $serverPort);
        $c->setDebug(0);
        $r = $c->send($f);
        $v = $r->value();
        $methods =Array();
        $list = xmlrpc_decode($v);
        foreach ($list as $elem) {
            $methods[] = $elem;
        }
        print ("Result is ");
        foreach ($methods as $m) {
            print ("\n<br />" . $m);
        }
        print ("<hr>I got this value back<br /><pre>" .
                htmlentities($r->serialize()). "</pre><hr>\n");
```

If we asked for the `system.methodHelp` introspection method, then call this method on the server with the name of the method we require help with. Once we receive a response, we extract the Help text and display the XML-RPC response to the screen:

```
    // check if we want to get some help
    } elseif ($_REQUEST["method"] == "system.methodHelp") {
        $f = new xmlrpcmsg("system.methodHelp",
                    array(new xmlrpcval($_POST["arg1"], "string")));
        $c = new xmlrpc_client($serverPath, $serverHost, $serverPort);
        $c->setDebug(0);
        $r = $c->send($f);
        $v = $r->value();
        print ("Result  is " . $v->scalarval() . "<br />");
        print ("<hr>I got this value back<br /><pre>" .
            htmlentities($r->serialize()). "</pre><hr>\n");
```

The `system.methodSignature` introspection method requires more work. As some methods can have optional arguments, we need to handle these properly:

```
    // check if we want to see the method signature
    } elseif ($_REQUEST["method"] == "system.methodSignature") {
        $f = new xmlrpcmsg("system.methodSignature",
                    array(new xmlrpcval($_POST["arg1"], "string")));
        $c = new xmlrpc_client($serverPath, $serverHost, $serverPort);
        $c->setDebug(0);
        $r = $c->send($f);
        $v = $r->value();
        $parameters =Array();
        $paramlist = xmlrpc_decode($v);
```

Up until now there's nothing new to see. Next we have to remember the total number of possible arguments just in case some of them are optional. Note that the first parameter is the return type and so should be factored out:

```
    // remember the total possible number of arguments
    $total_possible = count($paramlist[0]) - 1;
```

We'll now check each parameter in the list of parameters. If it is an array, then it contains one of the possible method signatures. We'll need to remember how many parameters are required in this version as it may be less than the possible maximum:

```
    // check each array in the parameter list
    foreach ($paramlist as $arr) {
        // if this is an array, then it must contain a possible method
        // signature
        if (gettype($arr) == "array") {
            // remember how many arguments this one takes
            $temp_num_params = count($arr) - 1;
        }
    }
```

Now that we know the minimum number of arguments this method can take, we can calculate how many optional arguments there are:

```
        // the number of optional arguments is equal to the number
        // of possible ones minus the minimum number required
        $num_optional = $total_possible - $temp_num_params;
```

Now we populate an array with all the possible arguments ready for output:

```
        foreach ($paramlist[0] as $elem) {
            $parameters[] = $elem;
        }
```

We first print the return type:

```
        print ("Result  is ");
        print ("<b>".$parameters[0] . " " . $_POST["arg1"] . " (");
```

Then we print the non-optional arguments:

```
        // here we only print non-optional arguments
        for ($i = 1; $i < count($parameters) - $num_optional; ++$i) {
            print (" " . $parameters[$i]);
        }
```

Finally we print any remaining optional arguments in square brackets then show the entire XML-RPC response:

```
        // print the optional arguments
        for (; $i < count($parameters); ++$i) {
            print (" [" . $parameters[$i] . "]");
        }

        print (" )</b>");

        print ("<hr>I got this value back<br /><pre>" .
            htmlentities($r->serialize()). "</pre><hr>\n");
    }
```

The default case is when we have called one of the `math.*` methods:

```
    else {
    $f = new xmlrpcmsg($_REQUEST["method"],
                    array(new xmlrpcval($_POST["arg1"], "int"),
                        new xmlrpcval($_POST["arg2"], "int")));
    $c = new xmlrpc_client($serverPath, $serverHost, $serverPort);
    $c->setDebug(0);
    $r = $c->send($f);
    $v = $r->value();
    if (!$r->faultCode()) {
        print ("Result  is " . $v->scalarval() . "<br />");
        print ("<hr>I got this value back<br /><pre>" .
            htmlentities($r->serialize()). "</pre><hr>\n");
    } else {
        print ("Fault: ");
        print ("Code: " . $r->faultCode() .
          " Reason '" .$r->faultString()."'<br />");
    }
```

```
    }
} else {
    $arg1 = 0; $arg2 = 0;
}
?>

    <form method="post">
      <input name="arg1" value="<?php print ($arg1); ?>">
      <select name="method">
        <?php
        foreach ($methods as $m) {
            print ("<option value=\"$m\">$m</option>");
        }
        ?>
      </select>
      <input name="arg2" value="<?php print ($arg2); ?>">
      <input type="submit" value="go" name="submit">
    </form>
  </body>
</html>
```

This is the response of the client web page:

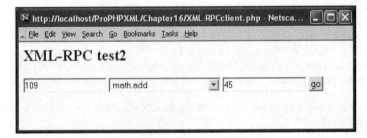

When this is passed to the server it invokes the `math.add` method. The output is shown below:

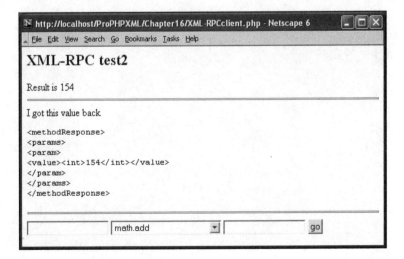

Resources

❑   The XML-RPC home page: http://www.xmlrpc.com/

❑   To download Usefulinc library:

http://sourceforge.net/project/showfiles.php?group_id=34455

Summary

XML-RPC is a very simple protocol, but has enough power to let us implement web services with service descriptions and introspection mechanisms. The services we create using XML-RPC can be accessed by a very wide range of languages, so there can be as many interfaces as needed for a particular service. The combination of XML and HTTP makes XML-RPC simple and very easy to use from PHP.

In this chapter we examined the XML-RPC protocol in detail, in fact we covered the whole protocol, studying how data types are represented as XML and how the XML packet is sent using HTTP. Then we showed how to use the Usefulinc library to write XML-RPC clients and servers. With this information you are ready to write clients and servers.

If we are providing XML-RPC services, we have to know that our services can be accessed from: AppleScript, ASP, C, C++, ColdFusion, COM, Delphi, Dylan, Flash, Guile, Java, JavaScript, K, Lingo, Lisp, .NET, Objective C, Perl , Python, RealBasic, Rebol, Ruby, Scheme, Squeak, TCL, and of course PHP.

In the next chapter we will see a full case study on how XML-RPC can be used to implement a working distributed application.

17

Case Study: A Calendar Server Using XML-RPC

In this chapter, we'll develop a client-server calendar using XML-RPC. First, we'll construct the server using PHP and an XML-RPC library. Next, we'll build a web client using PHP and HTML, and a command-line client using Perl. XML-RPC is a protocol to implement remote procedure calls using XML and HTTP. It is one of the protocols used to deploy web services, the other one being SOAP. We covered XML-RPC in Chapter 16.

By the end of the chapter we will know:

- ❑ How to use an XML-RPC library from PHP
- ❑ How to create XML-RPC servers using PHP
- ❑ How to create XML-RPC clients using PHP and HTML
- ❑ How to build a client-server application using PHP and XML-RPC
- ❑ How we can iteratively build a server adding functionality as and when it is needed

The Calendar Application

The calendar application we'll be designing will allow multiple users to log in/log out and schedule their appointments and events. It should allow users to check their agenda and scroll through the calendar. A MySQL database will contain the username and passwords for the users. Let's study the initial requirements for our calendar application:

❑ It will be a client-server application, where multiple clients may access the server simultaneously.

❑ It should have a simple and easy-to-use user interface.

❑ It must be very easy to access. A user must be able to access it from any application.

❑ It must be extensible, that is, it should be easy to add more functionality as and when it is needed.

Methodology

To build the calendar application, we will use an iterative approach towards the software development process. This means that the server application will be built to meet our basic requirements, and once the server is working, clients will start using the server methods to access the calendar. If any errors are found, the server application will be modified to make it stable. If required, new functionality can be added in response to user comments, and a new release can be generated.

This methodology allows us to swiftly deploy a working calendar server, which allows programmers to integrate the calendar, or to build ad-hoc client applications as early as possible. When new functionality is added, the existing clients need not be modified. They can run as they did before but the new methods will be made available to them.

To successfully apply such an iterative software development approach, we need to design our server application very carefully and make it as extensible as we can. The following diagram illustrates the process that we'll be using for building the calendar server application:

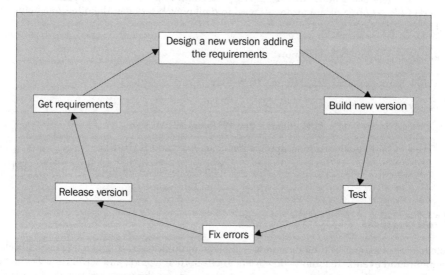

Technologies To Be Used

Now that we have an idea about what our calendar application is expected to do, it's time to decide on the technologies we will be using for its development.

Communication Protocol

It is a good idea to define how we'll handle communication between the client and the server since our application is a client-server application. Many times the communication technology will be a key determinant when choosing a programming language for the server. Our options are:

❑ Use TCP/IP and define a format for messages

❑ Use HTTP and use GET/POST requests

❑ Use XML-RPC

A messaging format over TCP/IP is a very common option that can be applied to all kinds of applications. However, it will require us to define a messaging format and define messages for each function the server will provide. We may need to develop a proprietary format if we can't find a standard that suits our needs.

HTTP is one of the most widely used protocols for client-server applications. A calendar client will have to issue HTTP GET or POST requests to execute methods and have to parse an HTTP response on the way back. It is true that HTTP can be used from almost any programming language but it doesn't seem to be the right choice since responses are documents and we want responses to easily return data that can be used from a programming language.

Finally we consider implementing the messages using XML-RPC. There are however some restrictions that apply to client-server applications based on XML-RPC:

❑ Messages must be synchronous

❑ Messages are stateless

❑ Authentication must be handled at the application level

None of the restrictions present a disadvantage to our calendar: calling a calendar function is always synchronous, we don't need to preserve state between calls to the server, and we may handle authentication at the application level without problems.

Since we won't have a problem using XML-RPC we'll pick XML-RPC for our client-server interface. XML-RPC provides us with the following advantages:

❑ Messaging between clients and servers is handled by XML-RPC transparently for the application. What this means is that clients just call functions without knowing how the parameters or the method are encoded.

❑ There are XML-RPC libraries for many programming languages such as PHP, Perl, and Python. This provides us with a greater degree of interoperability.

By using XML-RPC we can allow a PHP application, a web site, or any other application to act as a client for our calendar server. This is a great advantage for users who need to align or modify their calendars from many different applications.

Note that not all kinds of client-server applications can easily use XML-RPC. For example, a gaming server needs to provide a way for its clients to wait for a particular event – another player's move, for example, which occurs in the server. We could emulate this behavior in many ways using XML-RPC but the result will not achieve the desired efficiency. A generic messaging approach using TCP/IP, and blocking on socket reads is clearly better for such applications. In some occasions, a combination of a TCP/IP server using sockets and XML-RPC can also be a good solution.

For our calendar application we'll be using Usefulinc's XML-RPC library 1.01 that we studied in Chapter 16. It is available for download from http://sourceforge.net/project/showfiles.php?group_id=34455.

Web Server Application

Since XML-RPC is a protocol based on HTTP, it would be a good idea to build the XML-RPC server using a widely known, stable, and efficient web server such as Apache. We'll use Apache 1.3.24 that can be downloaded from http://www.apache.org/dist/httpd/binaries/.

Server-Side Programming Language

The messaging protocol and the web server have been defined. We now have to determine the language for building the server application. Since we'll be using XML-RPC, we have many options like PHP, Perl, Python, Java, C, or C++ to choose from.

PHP is a language that runs extremely well as an Apache module and there are some very good and simple XML-RPC libraries for PHP. Hence, we'll use PHP as the programming language for our calendar server application.

Storage

Information about users and their calendars need to be stored in the server. There are several options for the storage of information in the server:

- A relational database
- Plain files
- XML

The storage requirements for our calendar application are the following:

- Data won't be sent, imported, or exported from the server to other systems
- The size of the information to be stored is not a big issue
- Data must be retrieved as quickly as possible
- Information will be updated as often as it is queried

We can discard a data model based on plain files as plain files are normally used when a database or an XML-based model falls short because we have a huge amount of information that must be handled with very specific compression or indexing methods.

XML or a relational database can be used to store calendar information since we are dealing with a very dynamic data set (events are added and removed frequently). Since we won't be sending or exchanging data entities between systems, a relational database seems to be the better option.

We now need to pick a RDBMS. Some choices are:

- MySQL
- PostgresSQL
- A commercial DBMS

Since both MySQL and PostgresSQL provide all the functionality we need for the calendar we can start by discarding commercial DBMSs. The choice between MySQL and PostgresSQL depends on personal preference, but for this case study we'll use MySQL.

To sum it up, we'll build our server using PHP and implement the interface between clients and servers using XML-RPC. Clients can be built using any language where an XML-RPC implementation is available. We'll use a database in the server to store calendars and we'll use MySQL as our RDBMS.

Now that all the technologies have been defined we have a clear picture of our calendar application:

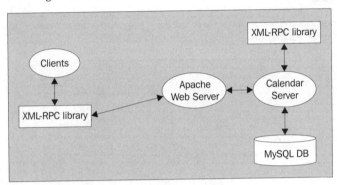

The Server Application (Iteration 1)

We'll now start building our calendar server. As a start we'll choose simple requirements so we can build a server as soon as possible.

The following are the basic initial requirements for our calendar server:

- ❑ Users will be identified by a login name and a password
- ❑ Users can add events to the calendar indicating day, month, year, start hour, duration, and title
- ❑ The calendar will be split at 1 hour intervals
- ❑ Users can ask for their agenda for a given day by indicating day, month, and year
- ❑ Users may define the start and the end hour for a working day

From these initial requirements we can identify the following entities for our server application:

- ❑ **Users**
  Users are people using the calendar. They will be identified by a username and a password.

- ❑ **Events**
  An event is an activity in a user calendar. Events start at some time and have a fixed duration.

- ❑ **Preferences**
  The calendar will have some parameters to make it configurable. When a user sets one of these parameters he will be setting a 'preference'.

- ❑ **Agenda**
  The agenda is the list of events for a user in a period of time.

A user can have zero or more events, and can also define preferences such as the start and the end hour for a working day. We have to make the server application extensible to allow the use of several user preferences in the future. Preferences will be stored in the server so that multiple clients can set them. However, if there are client-level preferences, color for example, they must be maintained by the client. Since the agenda can be constructed by analyzing all the events a given user has for a particular day, we don't need to store this information on the server.

The Database

Our calendar server database will have three tables - users, preferences, and events. Let's draw an Entity Relationship Diagram (ERD) for our basic data model:

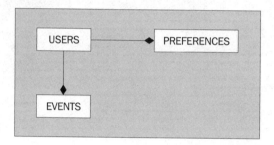

The implementation for the tables that we need is as follows.

Table – Events

In the tables shown below 'PK' stands for primary key, and 'FK' refers to foreign key.

Column Name	Type	Description
eventId	varchar(32)	Event ID (PK)
userId	int(8)	User ID (PK), an event belongs to one and only one user
start	int(14)	Event start as UNIX timestamp
end	int(14)	Event end as UNIX timestamp
title	varchar(200)	Event's title
type	varchar(40)	Event's type

The eventId will be a varchar(32) as a security measure. If users can't predict the ID of events, it is rather unlikely that a malicious user can, for example, delete an event of some other user.

Table – Users

Column Name	Type	Description
userId	int(8)	User ID (PK)
userLogin	varchar(20)	Login name for the user
userName	varchar(80)	Full name
password	varchar(40)	Password

Table – Preferences

Column Name	Type	Description
userId	int(8)	User ID (PK)(FK)
preferenceName	varchar(30)	Name of the preference (PK)
preferenceValue	varchar(250)	Preference value

Creating the Database

First, to create the database for our application, we'll use `mysqladmin`. Type the following lines in the `mysql>` prompt. Let's set the `root` password:

```
mysqladmin --user=root password phpxml
```

Now, MySQL will ask for the `root` password for creating the database and importing the tables:

```
mysql --user=root -p
```

As a `root` user, let's create our calendar database:

```
mysql> CREATE DATABASE calendar;
```

We will write a MySQL script, `calendar.sql`, to create these tables in our `calendar` database.

Save the file given below as `calendar.sql`. Windows users should save this in `c:\mysql\bin` and Linux users should save it in `/usr/local/mysql/bin`:

```
##### Calendar.sql

# Table structure for table 'events'

CREATE TABLE events (
  eventId varchar(32) NOT NULL default '',
  userId int(8) default NULL,
  start int(14) default NULL,
```

673

```
    end int(14) default NULL,
    title varchar(200) default NULL,
    type varchar(40) default NULL,
    PRIMARY KEY (eventId)
) TYPE=MyISAM;

# Table structure for table 'preferences'

CREATE TABLE preferences (
    userId int(8) NOT NULL default '0',
    preferenceName varchar(30) NOT NULL default '',
    preferenceValue varchar(250) default NULL,
    PRIMARY KEY (userId,preferenceName)
) TYPE=MyISAM;

# Table structure for table 'users'

CREATE TABLE users (
    userLogin varchar(20) default NULL,
    userName varchar(80) default NULL,
    password varchar(40) default NULL,
    userId int(8) NOT NULL auto_increment,
    PRIMARY KEY (userId)
) TYPE=MyISAM;

# Dumping data for table 'users'

INSERT INTO users VALUES ('test','The tester','test',1);
CREATE index events_search ON events (userId,start,end);
CREATE index user_search ON users(userLogin,password);

GRANT SELECT,INSERT,UPDATE,DELETE ON calendar.* TO calendar@localhost IDENTIFIED
BY 'wrox';
```

The script can also be executed from the command prompt in Windows by typing:

```
C:\mysql\bin>mysqladmin create calendar
C:\mysql\bin>mysql calendar < calendar.sql
```

Note that we added a line to insert a `test` user into the database.

Adding Indices

The tables are created, and by now we know our server methods, so let's analyze the queries that the server uses. If we find a query that is used in many functions, we may want to add an index to speed up the query execution time.

We may also want to read the code for our calendar server, with special considerations to the $query variables that are later used in `mysql_query()` instructions to execute queries to the database. To do this we must keep in mind two important queries on the database server.

The first one is the query used to find the user ID of the calendar user, by using the login name and password. This query is important because it is used in almost all the functions of the calendar server. If there are a lot of users in the `users` table, we want the query to be executed as fast as possible. Since the query searches for `userId`, given `userLogin` and `password`, an index to the `users` table with `userLogin` and `password` as the index columns needs to be created.

This is the MySQL instruction that can be used to create the index on the `users` table:

```
CREATE INDEX user_search ON users(userLogin,password);
```

Each time the query is run, the MySQL server can use the index to speed up the query. When the index is used the MySQL server won't have to scan all the rows in the table to find the proper user, it can use the index and perform a logarithmic time search using a binary tree or some other indexing technique.

The second important query is found on the `_findEvent()` and `_findOverlappingEvent()`. These methods are intensively used in the `GetAgenda()` method to analyze the events that are occupying certain time slots or the free time slots, if no events are found touching them. The query looks for information from the `events` table, given the `userId`, `start`, and `end` variables. As with the previous query, we create an index of those values:

```
CREATE INDEX events_search ON events(userId,start,end);
```

User Management

User management can seem easy, but there are many design decisions we have to make in this area. We know that some kind of authentication mechanism must be implemented in the server, to prevent a user from setting or removing events that belong to other users. All the users will be identified by a username and a password. For every event, the server should have the details of the user who sets that event.

There are several ways to authenticate users. An important issue is whether to use sessions or not. If we don't use sessions then for each method that needs to identify a user, clients must provide a login name and password.

If we use sessions, the server will have to implement login/logout procedures, and a session would be created when a client issues a successful login. This technique will involve the following steps:

❏ Clients identify themselves and send a login request indicating the client ID, the login name, and the password

❏ The server validates login name and password, and if they are valid, a session is created and returned to the client

❏ For each method the client calls, it uses a unique session ID that is used by the server to determine the `userId` for that user

As sessions need to be stored in the server, a session cleanup mechanism must be used to remove inactive sessions from the server.

Using sessions:

❏ **Makes the server more secure**
When using sessions, the login name and password are sent only once. The session ID is used to determine these details for each method called in that session. Sending the password frequently over the network makes it prone to being intercepted. Hence, the fewer times we send the password, the safer it is for our application. Though sessions can also be intercepted, the eavesdropper can't take advantage of a stolen session for long, because of its short lifetime.

❑ **Makes interaction between the clients and the server more complex**
Clients should be aware of the login/logout procedure when using sessions. We process or generate a client ID and store the session ID to use it when a server method is called. It's easier for a client to ask the user for a login name and password, and then just send them in every time a method is called, leaving all the authentication details and user management to the server.

❑ **Allows the server to track client activity**
If we don't use a session mechanism, we can't determine the activities of each client application at a given instance. If we want to know what a client did, or a history of method calls of any client, we need to track clients by using sessions. Web sites are popular examples of the need for sessions. In the case of web sites a log of pages visited by the user is an important piece of information.

For our calendar application, though security is important it is not crucial. Another consideration is simplicity of the interface between the client and the server. Therefore, we are not going to use sessions for our calendar server application. Each method that needs to identify the user for invoking a function will receive the login name and password as arguments. An additional security cover can be added by using SSL. This would enable the communication between a client and a server to be encrypted.

A spin-off of this arrangement is that the server API will be cleaner since each server method can be called independently of others. A client application can be written easily as a developer just has to call one method without worrying about the login/logout protocols.

We have the database ready, so let's deploy the server and implement each method to get our calendar server working.

Initializing the Server

Before we write any functions we have to include the XML-RPC library, define the methods, and bind the XML-RPC method names to the names of PHP functions that will be used to implement the methods. Save the file shown below as `server.php`:

```php
<?php
include_once("xmlrpc/xmlrpc.inc");
include_once("xmlrpc/xmlrpcs.inc");

define("DEFAULT_START_HOUR", 8);
define("DEFAULT_END_HOUR", 17);

// Definition of the methods provided by the server
$map = array (
    "ValidateUser"=>array("function"=>"ValidateUser"),
    "GetPreference"=>array("function"=>"GetPreference"),
    "SetPreference"=>array("function"=>"SetPreference"),
    "AddEvent"=>array("function"=>"AddEvent"),
    "RemoveEvent"=>array("function"=>"RemoveEvent"),
    "GetAgenda"=>array("function"=>"GetAgenda"),
    "GetUnixTimeStamp"=>array("function"=>"GetUnixTimeStamp"),
    );
```

```
mysql_connect("localhost", "calendar", "wrox");
mysql_select_db("calendar");

// Intercepting and reporting database errors to a log
$s = new xmlrpc_server($map);
```

In the server initialization, we define an associative array with all the XML-RPC method names as keys, and another associative array as their value. In this associative array, we define the function key indicating the name of the PHP function that will be used to implement the method. For clarity, we are using the same name for the XML-RPC method and the corresponding PHP function.

The next step is to connect to our calendar database so that we can use it from all our functions in the server. We also select this database as our current database, and finally, we instantiate the XML-RPC server. Once the XML-RPC server is created, the script will be ready to process HTTP POST requests as XML-RPC requests by calling the appropriate function and executing it.

Server Functions

Now, we'll describe the public and private PHP functions for the calendar server. The public functions will be called from XML-RPC and executed as a result of the client's request. However, the internal functions can't be called by the clients using XML-RPC. They will be used from the public functions (or other internal functions if needed). The functions given below need to be saved in the server.php file.

Validating Users

Let's start with some basic functions. We need an internal function to get the user ID, given a login name and password, and a function to let the clients validate the login name and password.

_getUserId(userLogin, password)

Input	Output	Description
userLogin – Login name for the user password – User password	userId, if the login name, and password match. FALSE, if they don't.	Finds the user in the users table and returns its user ID, if the login name and password match. Returns FALSE, if the login name and password don't match or the user doesn't exist.

This internal function will receive a user login and a password. It will return the user ID from the users table if the user login and password match and FALSE if they don't. In our application many other functions will use this function for user authentication:

```
function _getUserId($user, $pass)
{
    $query = "SELECT userId FROM users WHERE userLogin='$user'
            AND password='$pass'";
    $result = mysql_query($query);
```

```
        if (mysql_num_rows($result)) {
            $res = mysql_fetch_assoc($result);
            $id = $res["userId"];
            return $id;
        } else {
            return false;
        }
    }
```

ValidateUser(userLogin, password)

Input	Output	Description
userLogin – Login name for the user password – User password	TRUE if the login name and password match or an exception if an error occurs	Checks if the user with the given login name and password exists in the users table

This function will receive userLogin and password and validate them against the users table in the database. If the userLogin and password match a record in the database then TRUE will be returned. If a match does not take place, an exception will be returned indicating that the userLogin or password is wrong:

```
function ValidateUser($params)
{
    $userp = $params->getParam(0);
    $user = $userp->scalarval();
    $passp = $params->getParam(1);
    $pass = $passp->scalarval();

    if (_getUserId($user, $pass)) {
        return new xmlrpcresp(new xmlrpcval(1, "boolean"));
    } else {
        return new xmlrpcresp(0, 101,
                        "userLogin error: Invalid username or password");
    }
}
```

The XML-RPC library passes the XML-RPC object params to this function. The parameters required by the function are then extracted. First, we get the parameter and then convert it to its scalar value by calling the scalarval() method of the object. The function is straightforward, and uses the _getUserId() internal function. The function returns TRUE to the client or an error expression if the _getUserId() function returns FALSE.

> **Security Tip: when validating a username and password, if something is wrong, don't explain too much, just return "invalid username and password". This way attackers can't know if they have randomly chosen a valid username for our system.**

Note that our calendar application won't permit addition or removal of users from the calendar server. To create a user we simply make an entry into the database. The way in which users will be created, modified, or removed is left to the reader. Perhaps we may want to use the users from our site, or we may want to create a web application for the user registration. It is worthwhile noting that even phpMyAdmin can be used for such a task. Regardless of which method we use, the objective is to allow the client to create, delete, or modify users. If we still want to let the client manipulate users, we can add a public function.

Adding and Removing Events

To allow the clients to connect to our calendar server, we provide functions to add or remove events for a particular user.

_getEvent(eventId)

Input	Output	Description
eventId – event ID of an event	If the event doesn't exist, FALSE, or an associative array with eventId, userId, start, end, type, title as keys.	Retrieves the event from the database. If no event is found, returns FALSE.

The _getEvent() function is an internal function used to retrieve information about an event, given an eventId. The function returns an associative array containing the information for that event:

```
function _getEvent($eventId)
{
    $query = "SELECT userId,start,end,title,type FROM events WHERE
              eventId='$eventId'";
    $result = mysql_query($query);
    if (!mysql_num_rows($result)) {
        return false;
    } else {
        $res = mysql_fetch_array($result);
        $ret = Array();
        $ret["eventId"] = $eventId;
        $ret["userId"] = $res["userId"];
        $ret["start"] = $res["start"];
        $ret["end"] = $res["end"];
        $ret["title"] = $res["title"];
        $ret["type"] = $res["type"];
        return $ret;
    }
}
```

_findEvent(userId, e_start, e_end)

Input	Output	Description
userId – User ID of the user e_start – UNIX timestamp with the beginning of the time window e_end – UNIX timestamp with the ending of the time window	If no event matches then false. If one or more events are found matching then an array of associative array of events is returned.	Retrieves all matching events from the database, and builds an array where each member describes an event.

_findEvent() is an internal function used to check for events that are completely enclosed within a given time slot for the user with the userId passed as the first argument. We will use a SQL query to find the events. The _findEvent() function returns an array with one element for each event that matches the given time slot. Each event will be represented in the array as an associative array containing the information for the event:

```
function _findEvent($userId, $e_start, $e_end)
{
    $query = "SELECT eventId,userId,start,end,title,type FROM events WHERE
              userId='$userId' AND start<='$e_start' AND end>='$e_end'";
    $result = mysql_query($query);
    if (!mysql_num_rows($result)) {
        return false;
    } else {
        $allret = Array();
        while ($res = mysql_fetch_array($result)) {
            $ret = Array();
            $ret["eventId"] = $res["eventId"];
            $ret["userId"] = $res["userId"];
            $ret["start"] = $res["start"];
            $ret["end"] = $res["end"];
            $ret["title"] = $res["title"];
            $ret["type"] = $res["type"];
            $allret[] = $ret;
        }
        return $allret;
    }
}
```

_findOverlappingEvent(userId, e_start, e_end)

Input	Output	Description
userId – User ID of the user e_start – UNIX timestamp with the beginning of the time slot e_end – UNIX timestamp with the ending of the time slot	FALSE, if no event matches. An array containing associative arrays of events, if one or more events are found matching the time slot.	Retrieves all the matching events from the database, and builds an array where each member describes an event.

This function is similar to _findEvent(), but it returns all the events that overlap with the given time slot even if they are not completely enclosed in it. Events overlapping the start and end arguments could be of two types:

❑ Events that start after the time slot begins, but before it ends, no matter when the events end

❑ Events that start before the time slot begins, and end after the time window begins

For example, if we check for events for the time window 13 to 17, an event starting at 12 and ending at 14 is an overlapping event.

By definition, this function returns all the events returned by _findEvent(), and may return more events. It can't return fewer events than _findEvent(), because events enclosed between the time window are defined as overlapping events:

```
function _findOverlappingEvent($userId, $e_start, $e_end)
{
    $query = "SELECT eventId,userId,start,end,title,type FROM events
      WHERE userId='$userId' AND ( (start='$e_start')
      OR (start<='$e_start' AND end>'$e_start') OR (start>'$e_start'
      AND end<='$e_end') OR (start<'$e_end' AND end>='$e_end'))";
    $result = mysql_query($query);
    if (!mysql_num_rows($result)) {
        return false;
    } else {
        $allret = Array();
        while ($res = mysql_fetch_array($result)) {
            $ret = Array();
            $ret["eventId"] = $res["eventId"];
            $ret["userId"] = $res["userId"];
            $ret["start"] = $res["start"];
            $ret["end"] = $res["end"];
            $ret["title"] = $res["title"];
            $ret["type"] = $res["type"];
            $allret[] = $ret;
        }
        return $allret;
    }
}
```

AddEvent(userLogin, password, start, end, type, title)

Input	Output	Description
userLogin – Login name for the user password – User password start – Event start time in UNIX timestamp end – Event end time in UNIX timestamp type – Type of the event title – Title of the event	EventId, if the event was set, or an exception, if an error occurs.	Validates the user, gets the user Id by calling _getUserId(). Checks that no other event overlaps with this event (calls _findOverlappingEvent( )), and then inserts the event in the events table.

The `AddEvent()` method adds an event for a given user into the calendar. The start and end time for the event are passed as UNIX timestamps to allow clients to add the events starting at any time. The `type` allows the clients to classify events. For example, we may have public and private events, and we can allow the users to share their calendars by showing their public events to the other users:

```
function AddEvent($params)
{
    global $xmlrpcerruser;
    // import user errcode value
    $userp = $params->getParam(0);
    $user = $userp->scalarval();
    $passp = $params->getParam(1);
    $pass = $passp->scalarval();
    $startp = $params->getParam(2);
    $start = $startp->scalarval();
    $endp = $params->getParam(3);
    $end = $endp->scalarval();
    $titlep = $params->getParam(4);
    $title = $titlep->scalarval();
    $typep = $params->getParam(5);
    $type = $typep->scalarval();

    if (empty($title)) {
        return new xmlrpcresp(0, 106, "AddEvent error:
                            Cannot add event without a title");
    }

    $userId = _getUserId($user, $pass);

    if (!$userId) {
        return new xmlrpcresp(0, 107, "AddEvent error:
                            Invalid username or password");
    }

    _lockEvents();

    // Check for pre-existent overlapping event
    if (_findOverlappingEvent($userId, $start, $end)) {
        _unlock();
        return new xmlrpcresp(0, 108, "AddEvent error:
            Cannot add event, it overlaps with another event");
    }

    $evId = md5(uniqid(rand()));
    $query = "INSERT INTO events(eventId,userId,start,end,title,type)
            VALUES('$evId','$userId',$start,$end,'$title','$type')";
    mysql_query($query);
    _unlock();
    return new xmlrpcresp(new xmlrpcval(1, "boolean"));
}
```

This function validates that the title is not blank using the PHP `empty()` function, and retrieves the user ID after validating the user. Next, the function calls `_findOverlappingEvent()` to check if there is an event that overlaps with the event we are trying to set. If that is the case, an exception is returned, otherwise it creates an event ID for the event and adds it to the `events` table in the database. Note that we created the event ID using `md5(uniqid(rand()))`, which creates a random ID of 32 bytes. Random event IDs are a good way to prevent users from querying, trying to delete, or do strange things with events. Note that the events table is locked during the operation to prevent another process from occupying a time slot that was free when our process was checking.

RemoveEvent(userLogin, password, event)

Input	Output	Description
userLogin – Login name for the user password – User password event – Event ID of the event to be removed	TRUE, if the event was removed, or an exception, if an error occurs	Validates the user and gets the user ID (calls `_getUserId()`). Checks that the event exists and belongs to the user. Removes the event from the `events` table.

The `RemoveEvent()` method deletes an event from the calendar. The client must know the `eventId` which is a 32-character string generated by the server:

```
function RemoveEvent($params)
{
    global $xmlrpcerruser;
    // import user errcode value
    $userp = $params->getParam(0);
    $user = $userp->scalarval();
    $passp = $params->getParam(1);
    $pass = $passp->scalarval();
    $eventp = $params->getParam(2);
    $event = $eventp->scalarval();

    $userId = _getUserId($user, $pass);

    if (!$userId) {
    return new xmlrpcresp(0, 109, "RemoveEvent error: Invalid username or
                        password");
    }

    // Check that the event exists
    if (!_getEvent($event)) {
        return new xmlrpcresp(0, 110, "RemoveEvent error:
                            Unexistant event or wrong eventId");
    }
    // Only delete the event if it belongs to the user passed as argument
    $query = "DELETE FROM events WHERE eventId='$event' AND
            userId='$userId'";
    mysql_query($query);
    return new xmlrpcresp(new xmlrpcval(1, "boolean"));
}
```

This function removes an event from the database. We validate the user and check if the event exists. Then we delete the event from the events table. We also validate that the event belongs to the same user who requested the event to be removed.

Setting and Getting Preferences

Clients can allow the users to configure the calendar by using preferences. Let's see the functions that allow the calendar clients to access and query the preferences for a user.

_getPreference(preference, userId)

Input	Output	Description
userId – User ID preference – Preference name	The preference value or FALSE, if preference doesn't exist	Gets the preference value from the preferences table

This internal function _getPreference() retrieves the preference value (or FALSE if it doesn't exist), given the userId and preference:

```
function _getPreference($pref, $userId)
{
    $query = "SELECT preferenceValue FROM preferences WHERE userId='$userId'
            AND preferenceName='$pref'";
    $result = mysql_query($query);
    if (!mysql_num_rows($result)) {
        return false;
    }
    $res = mysql_fetch_array($result);
    $value = $res["preferenceValue"];
    return $value;
}
```

GetPreference(userLogin, password, preference)

Input	Output	Description
userLogin – Login name for the user password – User password preference – Name of the preference to retrieve	The preference value or an exception if the preference doesn't exist.	Validates the user and gets userId (calls _getUserId()). Retrieves the preference from the preferences table

The GetPreference() method returns the value of a preference for a given user:

```
function GetPreference($params)
{
    $userp = $params->getParam(0);
    $user = $userp->scalarval();
    $passp = $params->getParam(1);
    $pass = $passp->scalarval();
    $prefp = $params->getParam(2);
    $pref = $prefp->scalarval();

    $userId = _getUserId($user, $pass);

    if (!$userId) {
        return new xmlrpcresp(0, 103, "GetPreference error: Invalid username
                            or password, cannot get preference");
    }

    if ($value = _getPreference($pref, $userId)) {
        return new xmlrpcresp(new xmlrpcval($value, "string"));
    } else {
        return new xmlrpcresp(0, 104, "GetPreference error: Cannot get
                            preference value for $pref does it exist?");
    }
}
```

This function calls _getPreference() to retrieve the value for the preference once the userId was obtained. Note that the function _getUserId() retrieves the userId by using the login name and password. If the _getUserId() function returns FALSE, an exception is returned immediately. This validation pattern will be repeated in most of the server methods.

SetPreference(userLogin, password, preference, value)

Input	Output	Description
userLogin – Login name for the user password – User password preference – Name of the preference value – Preference value	TRUE, if the preference was successfully updated or created or an error if something goes wrong.	Validates the user, and gets the userId (calls _getUerId()). Updates or inserts the preference in the preferences table.

This function allows the client to set the value of a preference for a user. If the preference doesn't exist it will be created, and if it exists, it will be updated with the new value:

```
function SetPreference($params)
{
    $userp = $params->getParam(0);
    $user = $userp->scalarval();
    $passp = $params->getParam(1);
    $pass = $passp->scalarval();
    $prefp = $params->getParam(2);
    $pref = $prefp->scalarval();
    $prefvalp = $params->getParam(3);
    $prefval = $prefvalp->scalarval();

    $userId = _getUserId($user, $pass);

    if (!$userId) {
        return new xmlrpcresp(0, 105, "SetPreference error: Invalid username
                              or password");
    }

    $query = "REPLACE INTO
              preferences(preferenceName,preferenceValue,userId)
              VALUES('$pref','$prefval','$userId')";
    $result = mysql_query($query);
    return new xmlrpcresp(new xmlrpcval(1, "boolean"));
}
```

This function uses the MySQL REPLACE syntax to automatically update a preference, if it did previously exist, or to insert a new record if the preference is new.

Getting the Agenda

The GetAgenda() method is one of the most important methods in our server. This method will return a description of the agenda for the user for a particular day. This method will slice the day into intervals of 1 hour (of course, it can be changed later to use intervals defined by the user). It will return a description for each interval indicating the event ID and event title. If the time slot is free, it will return nothing. Since the format for the agenda can be complex, we will return it in XML format. The XML vocabulary that we'll be returning from the GetAgenda() method will have the following format:

```
<agenda>
  <day></day>
  <month></month>
  <year></year>
  <slot>
    <hourstart></hourstart>
    <minstart></minstart>
    <hourend></hourend>
    <minend></minend>
    <title></title>
    <type></type>
    <eventId></eventId>
  </slot>
</agenda>
```

If the title is empty (and `<eventId>` is also empty), the interval is free. The clients are free to convert the XML returned by the `GetAgenda()` method into any other format they want: text, an internal structure, HTML, or other presentations.

We'll return the agenda as an XML string instead of another format. Doing this has the following advantages:

❑   It allows us to modify the XML format by adding new elements for an event without modifying existing clients

❑   PHP supports associative arrays and can easily manipulate an array of associative arrays

❑   There are easy-to-use tools to manipulate XML in all the programming languages

❑   We can transform the result to multiple presentation formats using XSLT

Now, let's create the `GetAgenda()` method.

GetAgenda(userLogin, password, day, month, year)

Input	Output	Description
`userLogin` – Login name for the user `password` – User password `day` – Day (1-31) `month` – Month (1-12) `year` – Year (in YYYY format)	An XML string with the agenda for the given day, in the format shown above.	Validates the user, and gets `userId` (calls `_getUserID()`). Iterates through all the intervals for the given day and checks if there's an event touching that interval. It calls `_findEvent()` and generates the XML result, filling the event ID, title, start and end hour, or leaving it blank if no event is found for the interval.

We set the interval to one hour (3600 seconds). In the next implementation of the server, we could allow the user to define a preference for the interval. For example, a little modification to this function allows the users to see their calendars at half-hourly intervals. It is important to note that this in no way affects the other clients:

```
function GetAgenda($params)
{
    $userp = $params->getParam(0);
    $user = $userp->scalarval();
    $passp = $params->getParam(1);
    $pass = $passp->scalarval();
    $dayp = $params->getParam(2);
    $day = $dayp->scalarval();
    $monthp = $params->getParam(3);
    $month = $monthp->scalarval();
    $yearp = $params->getParam(4);
    $year = $yearp->scalarval();

    $interval = 3600;
```

In this method we validate the user and get the userId. Next, we check if there's a preference in the preferences table for the start and end hour of the day. If no preference is found, we default the start and the end hour to 8 and 17 respectively:

```
$userId = _getUserId($user, $pass);

if (!$userId) {
    return new xmlrpcresp(0, 111, "GetAgenda error:
                            Invalid username or password");
}

// If the user has no preference for the start and
// end hour of a day we set defaults
if (!$startHour = _getPreference("startHour", $userId)) {
    $startHour = DEFAULT_START_HOUR;
}
if (!$endHour = _getPreference("endHour", $userId)) {
    $endHour = DEFAULT_END_HOUR;
}
$last_title = '';
$unixtime = mktime($startHour, 0, 0, $month, $day, $year);
$lasttime = mktime($endHour, 0, 0, $month, $day, $year);
$values = Array();
$value = false;
while ($unixtime<$lasttime) {
    $atitle = _findEvent($userId, $unixtime, $unixtime+3600);
    if (!$atitle) {
        $title = '';
        $evid = '';
        $type = '';
    } else {
        $title = $atitle[0]["title"];
        $evid = $atitle[0]["eventId"];
        $type = $atitle[0]["type"];
    }
    if (($title<>$last_title) || (empty($title))) {
        if ($value) {
            $values[] = $value;
        }
        $value["hourstart"] = date("H", $unixtime);
        $value["hourend"] = date("H", $unixtime+$interval);
        $value["minstart"] = date("i", $unixtime);
        $value["minend"] = date("i", $unixtime+$interval);
        $value["title"] = $title;
        $value["eventId"] = $evid;
        $value["type"] = $type;
        $last_title = $title;
    } else {
        $value["hourend"] = date("H", $unixtime+$interval);
        $value["minend"] = date("i", $unixtime+$interval);
    }
    $unixtime+=$interval;
}
$value["end"] = date("H", $unixtime);
```

```
        $value["title"] = $last_title;
        $values[] = $value;
        $xml = "<agenda><day>$day</day><month>$month</month><year>$year</year>";
        foreach ($values as $value) {
            $xml.="<slot><eventId>".$value["eventId"]."</eventId>
                    <hourstart>".$value["hourstart"]."</hourstart>
                    <hourend>".$value["hourend"]."</hourend>
                    <minstart>".$value["minstart"]."</minstart>
                    <minend>".$value["minend"].
                    "</minend><title>".$value["title"]."</title></slot>";
        }
        $xml.='</agenda>';
        return new xmlrpcresp(new xmlrpcval($xml, "string"));
}
```

Finally, we iterate all the intervals for the given day by searching for events that touch each interval (by calling _findEvent()). If an event was found we fill a record, which is added to an array each time the title changes. If we have an event lasting for more than one interval, we return just one interval. After building an array with the proper information for each interval, we iterate the array and build the XML string that will be returned to the client.

Other Functions

GetUnixTimeStamp()

Input	Output	Description
hour, minute, sec, month, day, and year	UNIX timestamp for the given time	This is a conversion function provided for clients that can't easily construct a UNIX timestamp

```
function GetUnixTimeStamp($params)
{
    $dayp = $params->getParam(0);
    $day = $dayp->scalarval();
    $monthp = $params->getParam(1);
    $month = $monthp->scalarval();
    $yearp = $params->getParam(2);
    $year = $yearp->scalarval();
    $hourp = $params->getParam(3);
    $hour = $hourp->scalarval();
    $minp = $params->getParam(4);
    $min = $minp->scalarval();
    $secp = $params->getParam(5);
    $sec = $secp->scalarval();

    $unixtime = mktime($hour, $min, $sec, $month, $day, $year);
    return new xmlrpcresp(new xmlrpcval($unixtime, "int"));
}
```

This is a function provided for clients that can't handle UNIX timestamps, since the `AddEvent()` function uses UNIX timestamps. Clients that can't convert from or to UNIX timestamps can call this conversion method.

_lockEvents()

Input	Output	Description
Nothing	Nothing	Locks the events table to prevent other threads/processes from using the table

```
function _lockEvents()
{
    $query = "LOCK TABLES events WRITE";
    mysql_query($query);
}
```

_unlock()

Input	Output	Description
Nothing	Nothing	Unlocks the events table.

```
function _unlock()
{
    $query = "UNLOCK TABLES";
    mysql_query($query);
}
```

Server Exceptions

An examination of the code will reveal that public methods return some XML-RPC fault codes, if an error occurs. This is a list of all the possible errors that may occur. The clients however, are free to handle errors as they want:

Error Number	Description
101	`userLogin` error: invalid username or password.
102	`userLogout` error: invalid username or password. Cannot log out.
103	`GetPreference` error: invalid username or password. Cannot get preference.
104	`GetPreference` error: cannot get preference value for `$pref`. Does it exist?
105	`SetPreference` error: invalid username or password.
106	`AddEvent` error: cannot add event without a title.
107	`AddEvent` error: invalid username or password.

Error Number	Description
108	AddEvent error: cannot add event, it overlaps with another event.
109	RemoveEvent error: invalid username or password.
110	RemoveEvent error: non-existent event or wrong eventId.
111	GetAgenda error: invalid username or password.
112	GetSlots error: invalid username or password.

Installing the Server

To use this application, we'll need PHP installed with MySQL and XSLT support. PHP4.2 has a built-in support for MySQL. To provide XSLT support we need to install the Sablotron engine. For a reference on how to enable the XSLT extension with PHP refer to Chapter 8.

We'll need to uncompress the calendar.zip (available for download at http://www.wrox.com/) to a directory under the document root. For now, let's not look at all the files that are downloaded, we'll see these files as we go along with the chapter.

If everything worked fine and everything is installed, point the browser to main.php, and log in as test with the password test. The calendar screen should be displayed in the browser window.

The Client Application

Our calendar client will be a web-based application that will implement all the functionality the calendar server provides. The client will implement all the server methods. As already discussed in Chapter 16, we'll use Usefulinc's XML-RPC library to call the server methods from this web client.

The web client application should be able to display the user's agenda for any particular day, month, or year. The application should allow the user to add and remove events from the calendar. It also permits the user to set the start hour and end hour of the calendar as per his preferences.

We'll use a basic login/logout method for our web application. When the user logs in, the client calls the ValidateUser() method on the server. If the user is valid, our client sets the userlogin and password as session variables that are unregistered at the time of logout. During a session when these methods are called, these session variables will be sent.

The following is the functionality our client application should provide:

❑ Login/logout
❑ Viewing the agenda
❑ Navigating the calendar
❑ Adding events
❑ Removing events
❑ Setting preferences

Interface Design

The idea is to provide a simple, elegant, and functional interface. The layout of our web client application will look like:

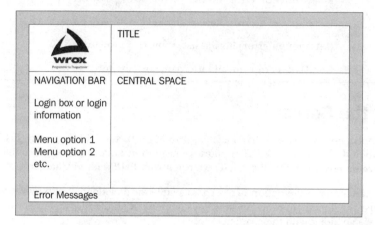

As seen above, we'll have a navigation bar on the left. This bar will have a login box, or the login information (if the user is already logged in), and a menu with all the possible sections of the calendar. The central space will display the body of the active section. In this client application, we could find the following sections:

❑   **Agenda**
In this section the user will see the agenda for any day that the section may receive or the current day if no day is passed. Hence, this is going to be our default section. We'll also provide a way to navigate the calendar.

❑   **Schedule**
This section will display a form where the user can enter information for an event, and then the form will be processed to add that event to the calendar by calling the appropriate server methods.

❑   **Preferences**
This section will display a form with the actual values of the start and end hours for an agenda. The user will be able to change the preferences by manipulating the form values. When the form is submitted, the user preferences will be updated by calling the SetPreference() method on the server.

For design details such as colors, fonts, and font size we'll use a main.css file provided along with the calendar.zip. It will be easy to change the whole look of our web-based client just by modifying this .css file.

Application Design

Let's use a simple and extensible approach to design our web-based client in PHP. We are going to display the main layout of the application from a script called main.php and then implement the body of each section in a separate .php file called section_XX.php. We'll pass a GET variable to our main.php script indicating which section the application has to display in the central space.

For example, `main.php?section=schedule` will display the layout, and include `section_schedule.php` in the central space. As we saw earlier, agenda is going to be our default section, that is, if we don't pass the `GET` variable, agenda will be the active section in the central space of our layout.

Using this approach, we can add a new section simply by adding it to the menu, and creating a separate PHP script, without making any major changes to `main.php`.

If a section uses a form, the action of the form will be `main.php`, and the form will be submitted as a `POST` request. Hence we'll place all the code needed to process each form in `main.php`, and since all the forms will be managed from `main.php`, we'll include the XML-RPC library in that script.

The forms that our `main.php` will process are:

❑ **Login**
  The login form will be displayed from `main.php` in the navigation bar, when the user is not logged in (the variable `userId` is not registered in the session).

❑ **Logout**
  The logout form is a link that will be used to log out from the application. When we process a logout form, the `userId` variable is reset.

❑ **Schedule**
  The schedule form displays the information needed to add an event to the calendar. Processing a logout form will imply calling the `AddEvent()` method on the calendar server.

❑ **SetPreference**
  The set preference form will display the user preferences with the values that are set in the server or the default values (clients might decide their own default preferences, if no preference is stored in the server). When we process this form, we call the `SetPreference()` method on the server to change each preference that the user has changed in the form.

The name of the submit button will be used to identify which form is to be processed. For example, if we have a form with a submit button called `foo`, we can do an `if(isset($foo))` check to see if we have to process the `foo` form. This mechanism will be used to process all the forms from our `main.php` script.

Developing the Client Application

Now it's time to start our client implementation. We'll start with the `main.php` script, and then we'll move on to each section.

main.php

In `main.php`, we have the following tasks:

❑ Retrieve user preferences for the start and end hour of a day (or default them) and register the values in the session

❑ Process forms which are submitted to the `main.php` script.

❑ Create the layout for the client and display the login box or login information, and the navigation bar

❑ Determine the section to show on the central part of the layout or default it to agenda

❑ Include the script for every section in the central space of the layout

Initialization

First, the general initialization of the client:

```php
<?php

$server_port = 80;
$server_uri = "localhost";
$server_path = "/ProPHPXML/Chapter17/server.php";

include_once("xmlrpc/xmlrpc.inc");

define("DEFAULT_START_HOUR", 8);
define("DEFAULT_END_HOUR", 17);

$PHP_SELF = $_SERVER["PHP_SELF"];

session_start();

if (isset($_SESSION["user"])) {
    $user = $_SESSION["user"];
}
if (isset($_SESSION["pass"])) {
    $pass = $_SESSION["pass"];
}
if (isset($_SESSION["startHour"])) {
    $startHour = $_SESSION["startHour"];
}
if (isset($_SESSION["endHour"])) {
    $endHour = $_SESSION["endHour"];
}
if (isset($_REQUEST["day"])) {
    $day = $_REQUEST["day"];
}
if (isset($_REQUEST["mon"])) {
    $mon = $_REQUEST["mon"];
}
if (isset($_REQUEST["year"])) {
    $year = $_REQUEST["year"];
}

$errorMsg = '';
$client = new xmlrpc_client("$server_path", "$server_uri", $server_port);
$client->setDebug(0);
```

We have included the XML-RPC library that will be used in the client. Next, we define the default start and end hour for the client if no preference is stored in the server. We also start the session, initialize the error message to an empty string, and create the XML-RPC client pointing it to the calendar server. We need to replace the values in our XML-RPC client instantiation with the proper values for our XML-RPC calendar server. The session will be used to keep the user login and password that the user entered because the client needs to send them to the server in each method called. We also get the $section variable from the GET section variable if it is passed, or we default to the agenda section.

Removing Events

To remove an event in the client, we must call main.php by passing the removeEvent variable with the eventId. For example, to remove the event with event ID as 1234, we'll use the link:

```
<a href="main.php?removeEvent=1234"> remove an event</a>
```

Hence, if the $removeEvent variable is set, we proceed to remove the event:

```
// Process a request to remove an event
if (isset($_REQUEST["removeEvent"])) {
    $removeEvent = $_REQUEST["removeEvent"];
}
if (isset($removeEvent)) {
    $removeMsg = new xmlrpcmsg('RemoveEvent',
    array(new xmlrpcval($user, "string"),
    new xmlrpcval($pass, "string"),
    new xmlrpcval($removeEvent, "string")));
    $result = $client->send($removeMsg);
    if (!$result) {
        $errorMsg = 'Cannot log in to server maybe the server is down';
    } else {
        if (!$result->faultCode()) {
        // We have a response
        } else {
            $errorMsg = $result->faultstring();
        }
    }
}
```

Note that we create an XML-RPC message for the RemoveEvent() method on the server. We then pass the userId, pass, and removeEvent variables. userId, and pass are session variables that we stored when the user logged into the client.

Setting Preferences

We'll name the submit button in the preferences form as setpref. When setpref is defined we know that we are in main.php, after the user submitted the preferences form. We process the set preferences form by sending the calendar server a SetPreference message for the start hour and another message for the end hour. An addition to this program would be to check if the values of the start and end time have been changed. We could then prevent the client from sending unnecessary messages to the server. Here's the code to process a change in the user preferences:

```
// Process a request to set preferences
if (isset($_REQUEST["setpref"])) {
    $setpref = $_REQUEST["setpref"];
}

if (isset($setpref)) {
    // Set Start Hour Preference
    $sstartHour = $_REQUEST["sstartHour"];
    $sendHour = $_REQUEST["sendHour"];
```

```
    if ($sstartHour <> $startHour) {
        $prefMsg = new xmlrpcmsg('SetPreference',
        array(new xmlrpcval($user, "string"),
        new xmlrpcval($pass, "string"),
        new xmlrpcval("startHour", "string"),
        new xmlrpcval($sstartHour, "string")));
        $result = $client->send($prefMsg);
        if (!$result) {
            $errorMsg =
                'Cannot send message to server.maybe the server is down';
        } else {
            if (!$result->faultCode()) {
                $errorMsg = '';
                // We have a response
                $startHour = $sstartHour;
                session_register("startHour");
                $_SESSION["startHour"] = $startHour;
            } else {
                $errorMsg = $result->faultstring();
            }
        }
    }

    if ($sendHour <> $endHour) {
        // Set endHour Preference
        $prefMsg = new xmlrpcmsg('SetPreference',
        array(new xmlrpcval($user, "string"),
        new xmlrpcval($pass, "string"),
        new xmlrpcval("endHour", "string"),
        new xmlrpcval($sendHour, "string")));
        $result = $client->send($prefMsg);
        if (!$result) {
            $errorMsg =
                'Cannot send message to server maybe the server is down';
        } else {
            if (!$result->faultCode()) {
                $errorMsg = '';
                // We have a response
                $endHour = $sendHour;
                session_register("endHour");
                $_SESSION["endHour"] = $endHour;
            } else {
                $errorMsg = $result->faultstring();
            }
        }
    }
    $startHour = $sstartHour;
    $endHour = $sendHour;
}
```

Adding an Event

While adding an event we are processing the schedule form. We can determine whether the schedule form was submitted from the status of the $schedule variable:

```
// Process a request to schedule an event
if (isset($_REQUEST["schedule"])) {
    $schedule = $_REQUEST["schedule"];
}

if (isset($schedule)) {
    $sday = $_REQUEST["sday"];
    $shour = $_REQUEST["shour"];
    $smon = $_REQUEST["smon"];
    $syear = $_REQUEST["syear"];
    $stitle = $_REQUEST["stitle"];
    $sduration = $_REQUEST["sduration"];

    // sday, smon, syear, stitle, sduration
    $unixStart = mktime($shour, 0, 0, $smon, $sday, $syear);
    $unixEnd = $unixStart+($sduration*3600);
    $stype = "private";
    $schMsg = new xmlrpcmsg('AddEvent',
    array(new xmlrpcval($user, "string"),
    new xmlrpcval($pass, "string"),
    new xmlrpcval($unixStart, "int"),
    new xmlrpcval($unixEnd, "int"),
    new xmlrpcval($stitle, "string"),
    new xmlrpcval($stype, "string")));
    $result = $client->send($schMsg);
    if (!$result) {
        $errorMsg = 'Cannot log in to server maybe the server is down';
    } else {
        if (!$result->faultCode()) {
            $errorMsg = '';
            // We have a response
        } else {
            $errorMsg = $result->faultstring();
        }
    }
}
```

Note that we convert the day, month, year, and hour of the event to a UNIX timestamp, and create the end time for the event by adding the duration multiplied by 3600. Next, we simply build the XML-RPC message and call the calendar server.

Processing a Login

The `$user` variable is set when we are processing a login. We validate the user by calling the `ValidateUser()` method on the calendar server, and then we set the `userId` with the help of `user` and `pass` variables:

```
// Process a login
if (isset($_REQUEST["user"])) {
    $user = $_REQUEST["user"];
}

if (isset($_REQUEST["pass"])) {
```

697

```
        $pass = $_REQUEST["pass"];
    }

if (isset($user)) {
    if (!session_is_registered("user")) {
        // Call the userLogin method from the games server
        $loginMsg = new xmlrpcmsg('ValidateUser',
        array(new xmlrpcval($user, "string"),
        new xmlrpcval($pass, "string")));
        $result = $client->send($loginMsg);
        if (!$result) {
            $errorMsg = 'Cannot log in to server maybe the server is down';
        } else {
            if (!$result->faultCode()) {
                // We obtain the user ID from the server
                session_register("user");
              session_register("pass");
            } else {
                $errorMsg = $result->faultstring();
            }
        }
    }
}
```

Processing a Logout

Logging out of the client is a simple process. If the $logout variable is set, we reset the userId from the session that logs out the user:

```
// Process a logout request
if (isset($_REQUEST["logout"])) {
    $logout = $_REQUEST["logout"];
}
if (isset($logout)) {
    session_unregister("user");
    session_unregister("pass");
    session_unregister("startHour");
    session_unregister("endHour");
    unset($user);
}
```

Getting Preferences

In this section if the user is logged in, we retrieve the startHour and endHour preferences for the user:

```
// Only get preferences if user is registered in the session
if (session_is_registered("user")) {
    if (!session_is_registered("startHour")) {
        // Try to get hourStart from preferences
        $getMsg = new xmlrpcmsg('GetPreference',
        array(new xmlrpcval($user, "string"),
        new xmlrpcval($pass, "string"),
```

```php
            new xmlrpcval("startHour", "string")));
        $result = $client->send($getMsg);
        if (!$result) {
            $errorMsg = 'Cannot log in to server maybe the server is down';
        } else {
            if (!$result->faultCode()) {
                // We have a response
                $startHour = xmlrpc_decode($result->value());
                session_register("startHour");
            } else {
                $startHour = DEFAULT_START_HOUR;
                session_register("startHour");
            }
        }
    }

    if (!session_is_registered("endHour")) {
        // Try to get hourStart from preferences
        $getMsg = new xmlrpcmsg('GetPreference',
        array(new xmlrpcval($user, "string"),
        new xmlrpcval($pass, "string"),
        new xmlrpcval("endHour", "string")));
        $result = $client->send($getMsg);
        if (!$result) {
            $errorMsg = 'Cannot log in to server maybe the server is down';
        } else {
            if (!$result->faultCode()) {
                // We have a response
                $endHour = xmlrpc_decode($result->value());
                session_register("endHour");
            } else {
                $endHour = DEFAULT_END_HOUR;
                session_register("endHour");
            }
        }
    }
}


// Sets the default section
if (isset($_REQUEST["section"])) {
    $section = $_REQUEST["section"];
} else {
    $section = "agenda";
}
?>
```

The Layout

Finally, we produce the HTML needed to render the application layout, the login box or login information, the navigation bar, and the main section:

```html
<html>
  <head>
    <title>My Calendar</title>
    <link rel="stylesheet" href="css/main.css" type="text/css">
  </head>

  <body>
    <table border="1" width="100%" bgcolor="#666666">
      <tr width="100%">
        <td align="center"><a href="<?php print ($PHP_SELF)?>">
          <img border="0" src="wrox.gif" width="90" height="90"/></a>
        </td>
        <td><h2>The calendar</h2></td>
      </tr>

      <tr>
        <td width="20%" class="text" valign="top">

          <table height="20%" width="100%" bgcolor="#777777"><tr>
            <td class="text" valign="center">
              <?php if(session_is_registered("user")) {?>
                You are logged in as: <?php print ($user)?><br />
              <a class="menu" href="
              <?php print ($PHP_SELF) ?>?logout=yes">logout</a>
              <?php } else { ?>
              You are not logged in.<br />
              Please login:<br />
              <form action="<?php print ($PHP_SELF) ?>" method="post">
                <table>
                  <tr><td class="text">user:</td><td>
                    <input type="text" name="user" />
                  </td></tr>
                  <tr><td class="text">pass:</td><td>
                    <input type="pass" name="pass" />
                  </td></tr>
                  <tr><td> </td>
                    <td><input type="submit" value="login" /></td>
                  </tr>
                </table>
              </form>
              <?php } ?>
          </td></tr>
        </table>
        <table bgcolor="#666666" width="100%" height="80%">
          <tr><td valign="top">
            <table width="100%">
              <tr><td valign="top">
                <a class="menu" href="
                  <?php print ($PHP_SELF) ?>?section=agenda">Agenda</a>
```

```
        </td></tr>
        <tr><td valign="top">
          <a class="menu" href="
            <?php print ($PHP_SELF) ?>?section=schedule">Schedule
          </a>
        </td></tr>
        <tr><td valign="top">
          <a class="menu" href="
            <?php print ($PHP_SELF) ?>?section=preferences">
            Preferences
          </a>
        </td></tr>
        <tr><td valign="top">
          <a class="menu" href="
            <?php print ($PHP_SELF) ?>?section=getslots">Allocate
          </a>
        </td></tr>
      </table>
    </td></tr>
  </table>
</td>
<td width="80%">
  <table width="100%">
    <tr><td>
      <?php
      $include_name="./section_".$section.".php";
      include("$include_name");
      ?>
    </td></tr>
  </table>
</td>
</tr>

<tr>
  <td colspan="2" class="text">Errors: <?php if($errorMsg)
          {print($errorMsg);}?>
  </td>
</tr>
  </table>
</body>
</html>
```

> We didn't use `include($section)` directly. If we had done it that way, there would have been a serious security problem if the user passed `$section="/etc/passwd"`, but things could have been even worse. If the option in `php.ini` had been enabled, the user could have executed arbitrary PHP code even using scripts from other sites. This could happen if `$section` has been set as
> `"http://badsite.com/some.php"`, using a path like `"./section_$section"`. We force our script to include a file from our server and with a specific name.

Once our calendar application is ready, the default screen will look like this:

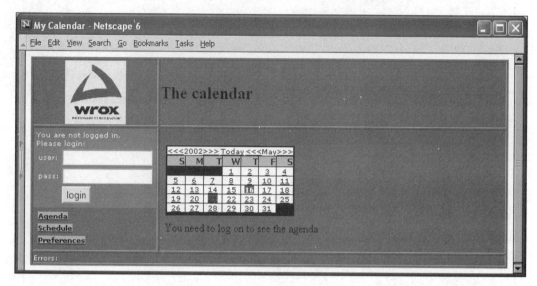

When a valid login name and password is entered (test and test for example), we can see a very similar screen with the login information replacing the login form:

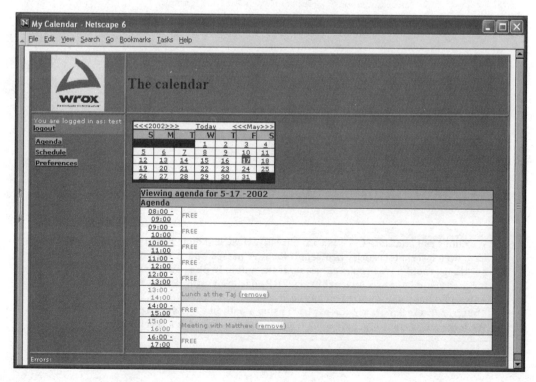

section_agenda.php

This script does two things – first, it shows a navigable calendar and second, it shows the agenda for the day selected. The calendar works based on a day passed by GET variables to the script, and if no variables are passed it defaults to the current day. The calendar allows the user to navigate to a given day, month, or year. Once we are positioned at a day on the calendar, the agenda for that selected day is shown below the calendar.

We are not going to see how we constructed the calendar, it's a simple PHP program with some date management. We will use the class_calendar.php class that provides some of the functionality we need to build the calendar. It can be downloaded from the code download section at http://www.wrox.com/.

On the calendar, the days are linked to main.php passing $day, $mon, and $year as GET variables. It is useful to remember that if no $day is set, we default the $day, $mon, and $year to the current date. To display the agenda, we call the GetAgenda() method on the calendar server, and then transform the XML to HTML using an XSLT stylesheet. Here's the XSLT stylesheet, agenda2html.xsl:

```
<?xml version="1.0" encoding="iso-8859-1"?>
<xsl:stylesheet xmlns:xsl="http://www.w3.org/1999/XSL/Transform"
                        version="1.0">
  <xsl:output method="html" encoding="iso-8859-1" />


  <xsl:template match="/">
    <table width="95%" border="0" cellspacing="0" cellpadding="0"
                    align="center">
      <tr>
        <td class="ft">
          <table width="100%" border="0" cellspacing="1" cellpadding="0"
                            bordercolor="#FF0000" align="center">
            <tr>
              <td class="date" colspan="3">Viewing agenda for
              <xsl:value-of select="/agenda/month" />
              -
              <xsl:value-of select="/agenda/day" />


              -
              <xsl:value-of select="/agenda/year" />
              </td>
            </tr>

            <tr>
              <td class="date" colspan="3">Agenda</td>
            </tr>

            <xsl:apply-templates select="/agenda/slot" />
          </table>
        </td>
      </tr>
    </table>
```

```
    </xsl:template>

<xsl:template match="/agenda/slot">
  <xsl:choose>
    <xsl:when test="normalize-space(./title)=''">
      <tr class="fc">
        <xsl:variable name="h" select="(normalize-space(./hourend)-
                      normalize-space(./hourstart))*20" />

        <td class="fc" align="center" width="10%">
          <xsl:attribute name="height">
            <xsl:value-of select="$h" />
          </xsl:attribute>

          <a class="day">
          <xsl:attribute name="href">main.php?section=schedule&amp;day=
          <xsl:value-of select="/agenda/day" />

          &amp;mon=
          <xsl:value-of select="/agenda/month" />

          &amp;year=
          <xsl:value-of select="/agenda/year" />

          &amp;hour=
          <xsl:value-of select="hourstart" />
          </xsl:attribute>

          <xsl:value-of select="hourstart" />
          :
          <xsl:value-of select="minstart" />
          -
          <xsl:value-of select="hourend" />
          :
          <xsl:value-of select="minend" />
          </a>
        </td>

        <td class="fc" align="left" width="75%">FREE</td>
      </tr>
      </xsl:when>

      <xsl:otherwise>
        <tr>
          <xsl:variable name="h" select="(normalize-space(./hourend)-
                        normalize-space(./hourstart))*20" />

          <td class="fc" align="center" width="10%">
          <xsl:attribute name="height">
```

```
                    <xsl:value-of select="$h" />
                    </xsl:attribute>

                    <xsl:value-of select="hourstart" />
                    :
                    <xsl:value-of select="minstart" />
                    -
                    <xsl:value-of select="hourend" />
                    :
                    <xsl:value-of select="minend" />
                    </td>

                    <td class="ac" align="left" width="75%">
                    <xsl:value-of select="title" />

                    (
                    <a class="fc">
                    <xsl:attribute
                    name="href">main.php?section=agenda&amp;removeEvent=
                    <xsl:value-of select="eventId" />

                    &amp;day=
                    <xsl:value-of select="/agenda/day" />

                    &amp;mon=
                    <xsl:value-of select="/agenda/month" />

                    &amp;year=
                    <xsl:value-of select="/agenda/year" />
                    </xsl:attribute>

                    remove</a>

                )</td>
            </tr>
        </xsl:otherwise>
      </xsl:choose>
    </xsl:template>
</xsl:stylesheet>
```

In this stylesheet, we can see how to build links to the schedule section of the main.php to schedule an event for a free time slot, or a link passing removeEvent to main.php to delete an existing event. We also use some HTML to show longer events in bigger cells and shorter events in shorter cells. This is done by creating an XSLT variable for the table height and using the <xsl:attribute> syntax to create the height attribute for the cell where the event is displayed. Note that we used <xsl:when> to generate a branch in the stylesheet and to create different formats for the free and occupied time slots.

This is a good example of how XSLT can easily be used to produce a presentation format from an XML stream. In our web client, we used XSLT to generate HTML, but if we were building a WAP interface for the calendar, we would have used an XSLT to generate WML, all without requiring a single change on the calendar server.

This is the code for `section_agenda.php`. This program calls the `GetAgenda()` method, transforms it and shows the result:

```php
<?php
if (session_is_registered("user")) {
    $agendaMsg = new xmlrpcmsg('GetAgenda',
    array(new xmlrpcval($user, "string"),
    new xmlrpcval($pass, "string"),
    new xmlrpcval($day, "int"),
    new xmlrpcval($mon, "int"),
    new xmlrpcval($year, "int")) );
    $result = $client->send($agendaMsg);
    if (!$result) {
        $errorMsg =
                    'Cannot send message to server maybe the server is down';
    } else {
        if (!$result->faultCode()) {
            $agenda = xmlrpc_decode($result->value());
        } else {
            $errorMsg = $result->faultstring();
        }
    }
    if (isset($agenda)) {
        include_once("classes/class_xslt.php");
        $xslt = new xslt();
        $xslt->setXmlString($agenda);
        $xslt->setXsl("agenda2html.xsl");
        if ($xslt->transform()) {
            $ret = $xslt->getOutput();
            print ($ret);
        } else {
            print ("Error:".$xslt->getError());
        }
    }
} else {
    print("You need to log on to see the agenda<br />");
}
?>
```

We used `class_xslt.php` which is a XSLT class to abstract the XSLT processor from the calendar application. This allows us to change the XSLT processor without changing the application code. Here is the `class_xslt.php`:

```php
<?php
class xslt {

    var $xsl, $xml, $output, $error ;

    // Constructor //
    function xslt()
    {
        $this->processor = xslt_create();
    }
```

```
    // Destructor
    function destroy()
    {
        xslt_free($this->processor);
    }

    // output methods
    function setOutput($string)
    {
        $this->output = $string;
    }
    function getOutput()
    {
        return $this->output;
    }

    // set methods
    function setXmlString($xml)
    {
        $this->xml = $xml;
        return true;
    }

    function setXslString($xsl)
    {
        $this->xsl = $xsl;
        return true;
    }

    function setXml($uri)
    {
        if ($doc = new docReader($uri)) {
            $this->xml = $doc->getString();
            return true;
        } else {
            $this->setError("Could not open $xml");
            return false;
        }
    }

    function setXsl($uri)
    {
        if ($doc = new docReader($uri)) {
            $this->xsl = $doc->getString();
            return true;
        } else {
            $this->setError("Could not open $uri");
            return false;
        }
    }

    // transform method
    function transform()
```

```
    {
        $arguments = array (
                        '/_xml' => $this->xml,
                        '/_xsl' => $this->xsl
                      );
        $ret = xslt_process($this->processor, 'arg:/_xml', 'arg:/_xsl',
                        NULL, $arguments);
        if (!$ret) {
            $this->setError(xslt_error($this->processor));
            return false;
        } else {
            $this->setOutput($ret);
            return true;
        }
    }

    // Error Handling
    function setError($string)
    {
        $this->error = $string;
    }
    function getError()
    {
        return $this->error;
    }
}

// docReader -- read a file or URL as a string
// test
/*
$docUri = new docReader('http://www.someurl.com/doc.html');
print ($docUri->getString());
*/
class docReader
{
    var $string;
    // public string representation of file
    var $type;
    // private URI type: 'file','url'
    var $bignum = 1000000;
    var $uri;
    // public constructor
    function docReader($uri)
    {
        // returns integer        $this->setUri($uri);
        $this->uri = $uri;
        $this->setType();
        $fp = fopen($this->getUri(), "r");
        if ($fp) { // get length
            if ($this->getType() == 'file') {
                $length = filesize($this->getUri());
            } else {
                $length = $this->bignum;
            }
```

```
                $this->setString(fread($fp, $length));
                return 1;
            } else {
                return 0;
            }
        }

        // determine if a URI is a file name or URL
        function isFile($uri)
        { // returns boolean
            if (strstr($uri, 'http://') == $uri) {
                return false;
            } else {
                return true;
            }
        }
        // set and get methods
        function setUri($string)
        {
            $this->uri = $string;
        }
        function getUri()
        {
            return $this->uri;
        }
        function setString($string)
        {
            $this->string = $string;
        }
        function getString()
        {
            return $this->string;
        }
        function setType()
        {
            if ($this->isFile($this->uri)) {
                $this->type = 'file';
            } else {
                $this->type = 'url';
            }
        }
        function getType()
        {
            return $this->type;
        }
    }
?>
```

In our application, if we click on the Agenda link on the navigation bar, we can see the agenda for 'today', and the navigable calendar. We can navigate the calendar by clicking on any day, or advancing and rewinding the month or year. We can click the Today link to return to the current date.

section_schedule.php

The `section_schedule.php` is a simple script where a form is displayed allowing the user to enter the information needed to add an event to the calendar.

The only detail to notice is that we can pass the day, month, year, start hour, and duration to `section_schedule.php`. These details will be the values shown in the form. This is used, for example from the agenda, when we click on a free time slot. In this case, we are automatically directed to the schedule form, and the day, month, year, and start hour for the event are already filled with the values for the interval that was selected. For example, if we want to call the form to set an event for February 2, 2002 at 9:00, the browser will point to:

http://localhost/ProPHPXML/Chapter17/main.php?section=schedule&day=2&mon=2&year=2002&hour=9

In this script we will check if $day is set. If $day is not set, we default $day, $mon, $year, and $hour to the current day, month, year, and hour. We also default the event duration to 1 hour when $duration is not set:

```php
<?php
if (isset($_REQUEST["day"])) {
    $day = $_REQUEST["day"];
}
if (isset($_REQUEST["mon"])) {
    $mon = $_REQUEST["mon"];
}
if (isset($_REQUEST["year"])) {
    $year = $_REQUEST["year"];
}
if (isset($_REQUEST["hour"])) {
    $hour = $_REQUEST["hour"];
}
if (isset($_REQUEST["duration"])) {
    $duration = $_REQUEST["duration"];
}


if (session_is_registered("user")) {
    include_once("classes/class_calendar.php");
    if (!isset($day)) {
        $day = date("d");
        $mon = date("m");
        $year = date("Y");
        $hour = date("H");
    }
    if (!isset($duration)) {
        $duration = 1;
    }
    $c = new Calendar("en");
?>

<form action="main.php?section=agenda" method="post">
  <table width="100%">
    <tr><td colspan="2" valign="top" height="45" class="textbl">
```

```
                    Schedule an event</td></tr>
   <tr><td width="20%" class="text">Setting Event for:
   </td><td class="text">
   <?php $c->buildDayBox("sday",$day,$mon,$year);?> of
   <?php $c->buildMonthBox("smon", $mon)?>
   <?php $c->buildYearBox("syear", $year)?></td></tr>
   <tr><td class="text">At:</td><td class="text">
   <?php $c-> buildHourBox("shour", $hour)?>:00</td></tr>
   <input type="hidden" name="day" value="<?php print ($day)?>"/>
   <input type="hidden" name="mon" value="<?php print ($mon)?>"/>
   <input type="hidden" name="year" value="<?php print ($year)?>"/>
   <tr><td class="text">Title:</td><td class="text">
   <input type="text" name="stitle"></td></tr>
   <tr><td class="text">Duration:</td><td class="text">
   <?php $c->buildIntBox("sduration", 1, 10, 1, $duration)?>
   hours</td></tr>
   <tr><td class="text"> </td><td class="text">
   <input type="submit" name="schedule" value="schedule" /></td></tr>
   </table>
</form>

<?php
} else {
    print ("You are not logged in<br />");
}
?>
```

Here, the class_calendar script is included to use some of its methods that generate HTML, and select boxes for days, months, years, and hours. The methods are useful, since they know how many dates there are in a month, and so on.

If there aren't any events for a particular time slot, and we want to add a new event, we can click on the **Schedule** link on the navigation bar. We can also click one of the intervals of the agenda to go to the schedule form with the starting hour preset. Here is the schedule form:

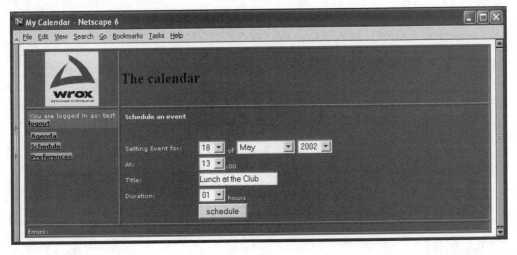

section_preferences.php

The section_preferences.php script displays the form for the preferences section. It is very similar to the schedule section. It's worth remembering that the main.php script stores the start and end hour as session variables. This script simply displays the start hour and end hour preferences, which can be changed by the user:

```php
<?php
if (session_is_registered("user")) {
    include_once("classes/class_calendar.php");
    $c = new Calendar("en");
?>

<form action="main.php?section=agenda" method="post">
  <table width="100%">
  <tr><td colspan="2" valign="top" height="45" class="textbl">
                   Set Preferences:</td></tr>
  <tr><td width="20%" class="text">StartHour</td><td class="text">
  <?php $c->buildHourBox("sstartHour", $startHour)?>
  </td></tr>
  <tr><td class="text">EndHour:</td><td class="text">
  <?php $c->buildHourBox("sendHour", $endHour)?>
  </td></tr>
  <tr><td class="text"> </td><td class="text">
  <input type="submit"
  name="setpref" value="set" /></td></tr>
  </table>
</form>

<?php
} else {
    print ("You are not logged in<br />");
}
?>
```

In this form, we again used the class_calendar class to construct some HTML, and select boxes.

Let's have a look at the preferences screen:

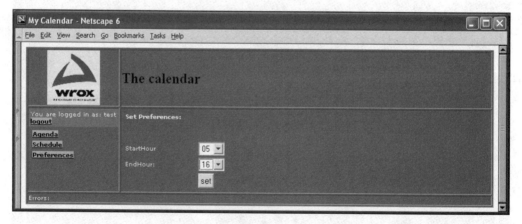

As can be seen, we can change the start and end hour for a day. Here, we set the start hour to be 5 and the end hour to 16.

Installing the Client

Installation of the client is fairly simple. If the `calendar.zip` file was decompressed with all the sourcecode for the calendar, then just point the browser to the URI where the scripts can be reached and click on `main.php`. No parameter needs to be passed to `main.php` since everything will be defaulted. After logging in the agenda for the current day, the navigable calendar will be displayed and it's ready to use.

The Command-Line Client

To demonstrate the language-independence of XML-RPC we'll build a command-line client that will display the user agenda for the current date using Perl. The purpose of this tool is to let the user know his calendar by using a simple command at the command-line. Although we have used Perl here, the command-line client could have been developed in any other language (and of course PHP).

We'll be getting the day, month, and year from the system time, and call the `GetAgenda()` method on the calendar server. We then transform the XML agenda to a text representation using XSLT. The XSLT file `agenda2txt.xsl`, which we are going to use, is as follows:

```
<?xml version="1.0" encoding="iso-8859-1"?>
<xsl:stylesheet xmlns:xsl="http://www.w3.org/1999/XSL/Transform"
                           version="1.0">
  <xsl:output method="text" encoding="iso-8859-1" />

  <xsl:template match="/">Agenda
  <xsl:apply-templates select="/agenda/slot"/>
  </xsl:template>

  <xsl:template match="/agenda/slot">
    <xsl:choose>
      <xsl:when test="normalize-space(./title)=''">
        <xsl:value-of select="hourstart"/>
        :
        <xsl:value-of select="minstart" />
        -
        <xsl:value-of select="hourend" />
        :
        <xsl:value-of select="minend" />
        FREE</xsl:when>
        <xsl:otherwise>
        <xsl:value-of select="hourstart" />
        :
        <xsl:value-of select="minstart" />
        -
        <xsl:value-of select="hourend" />
        :
        <xsl:value-of select="minstart" />
        [<xsl:value-of select="title" />]
        </xsl:otherwise>
    </xsl:choose>
  </xsl:template>
</xsl:stylesheet>
```

The code shown below is the Perl script, `perl_client.pl`, for our command-line client:

```perl
#!/usr/bin/perl

use Frontier::Client;
use XML::Xalan;
use POSIX qw(strftime);


my $tr = new XML::Xalan::Transformer;


$server = Frontier::Client->new( 'url' => 'WWW.YOURSITE.COM/calendar/server.php'
);
$day = strftime "%d", localtime;
$mon = strftime "%m", localtime;
$year = strftime "%Y", localtime;
$user = $server->string('test');
$pass = $server->string('test');

if($ARGV[0] eq "") {
  $option="display"
} else {
  $option = $ARGV[0];
}

if ($option=="display") {
  print("Agenda for: $day of $mon $year\n");
  @params = ($user, $pass, $day, $mon, $year);
  $ret = $server->call("GetAgenda", @params);
  my $parsed = $tr->parse_string($ret);
  my $res = $tr->transform_to_data($parsed, "agenda2txt.xsl");
  print("$res\n");
}
```

Note that the username and password were written in the Perl file. This could of course have been read from a configuration file or taken from the command line.

Using the Command-Line Client

Once everything is properly installed, we can test the Perl client. Make sure the XSLT stylesheet, `agenda2txt.xsl`, is in the same directory as the client.

To run the command-line client we will need a Perl installation with XSLT support. The command `perl perl_client.pl` will display the calendar:

```
root@wroxtest:/tmp/perl_client                                    _ □ ×

File   Edit   Settings   Help

[root@wroxtest perl_client]# perl perl_client.pl
Agenda for: 21 of 05 2002

     Agenda
     08:00 - 09:00 FREE
     09:00 - 10:00 FREE
     10:00 - 11:00 FREE
     11:00 - 12:00 FREE
     12:00 - 13:00 [Meeting with Girish]
     13:00 - 14:00 [Lunch]
     14:00 - 15:00 FREE
     15:00 - 17:00 [Salary Review]

[root@wroxtest perl_client]# []
```

As can be seen above, we can easily get the agenda for the current date with this command-line client. Perl also allows us to add commands to perform tasks like adding and removing events to the same calendar server.

We now have a working calendar server using XML-RPC, and a web client implementing the full package of services that the server provides. More functionality could be added to the calendar server and the clients can be implemented immediately. Programmers can also start integrating the calendar to their existing applications.

New Requirements (Iteration 2)

We have chosen an iterative approach to developing our client-server application. After building the server, the web client, and the Perl command-line client, it's time to consider adding more functionality to the application.

We can enter events, remove them, and see the agenda with our existing calendar. However, since the calendar doesn't allow scheduling an event for a time slot that is already occupied by another event, users with a very dense agenda will have trouble finding empty slots for new events.

Without an additional visual interface, users can still flip through their agenda, and find a slot for an event. However, a good calendar should have a feature that will allow them to automatically find empty slots for an event.

We need a way to find empty slots for an event. To accomplish this we will construct a new method, GetSlots(), in the calendar server. This method should return an XML string of the following format that describes all the possible time intervals for the event:

```
<slots>
  <duration></duration>
  <slot>
    <day></day>
    <month></month>
    <year></year>
    <hourstart></hourstart>
    <minstart></minstart>
    <hourend></hourend>
    <minend></minend>
  </slot>
    ...
</slots>
```

The client can do whatever it needs to do with the returned information – for example, display a list of options to the user, or suggest an interval closer to the current date.

GetSlots()

Input	Output	Description
userLogin – Login name for the user	An XML string with the list of slots that match the search criteria.	Generates all the possible slots, and checks if there's an event touching each slot. If not then adds that slot to the result.
password – User password		
fromDay – Day for the date to start searching		
fromMonth – Month for the date to start searching		
fromYear – Year for the date to start searching		
toDay – Day for the date to stop searching		
toMonth – Month for the date to stop searching		
toYear – Year for the date to stop searching		
fromHour – Search for time slots from this hour		
toHour – Search for time slots up to this hour		
duration – Duration of the event (search for slots of at least this length)		

This method will search the given user's calendar for a given range of days, and check each day for time slots where an event of certain length could be allocated.

Modifying the Server

At the server, we only have to add the method and include it in the server initialization. This is easily done by adding a line in the //Definition of Methods provided by the server section. The line provides the mapping for the GetSlots() function:

```
"GetSlots"=>array("function"=>"GetSlots")
```

The GetSlots() method will be as follows:

```
function GetSlots($params)
{
    $userp = $params->getParam(0);
    $user = $userp->scalarval();
    $passp = $params->getParam(1);
    $pass = $passp->scalarval();
    $fromdayp = $params->getParam(2);
    $fromday = $fromdayp->scalarval();
    $frommonthp = $params->getParam(3);
    $frommonth = $frommonthp->scalarval();
    $fromyearp = $params->getParam(4);
    $fromyear = $fromyearp->scalarval();
    $todayp = $params->getParam(5);
    $today = $todayp->scalarval();
    $tomonthp = $params->getParam(6);
    $tomonth = $tomonthp->scalarval();
    $toyearp = $params->getParam(7);
    $toyear = $toyearp->scalarval();
    $fromhourp = $params->getParam(8);
    $fromhour = $fromhourp->scalarval();
    $tohourp = $params->getParam(9);
    $tohour = $tohourp->scalarval();
    $durationp = $params->getParam(10);
    $duration = $durationp->scalarval();

    $interval = 3600;

    $userId = _getUserId($user, $pass);

    if (!$userId) {
        return new xmlrpcresp(0, 112, "GetSlots error: Invalid username or
                        password");
    }

    $timebegin = mktime($fromhour, 0, 0, $frommonth, $fromday, $fromyear);
    $timeend = mktime($tohour, 0, 0, $tomonth, $today, $toyear);
```

```
$time = $timebegin;
$values = Array();
while ($time<$timeend) {
    if ((date("H", $time)>=$fromhour) &&
        (date("H", $time)+$duration<$tohour)) {
        $slotfin = $time+($interval * $duration);
        $atitle = _findOverlappingEvent($userId, $time, $slotfin);
        if (!$atitle) {
            $value["day"] = date("d", $time);
            $value["month"] = date("m", $time);
            $value["year"] = date("Y", $time);
            $value["hourstart"] = date("H", $time);
            $value["hourend"] = date("H", $slotfin);
            $value["minstart"] = date("i", $time);
            $value["minend"] = date("i", $slotfin);
            $values[] = $value;
        }
    }
    $time+=$interval;
}
$xml = '<slots><duration>'.$duration.'</duration>';
foreach ($values as $value) {
    $xml.='<slot>';
    $xml.='<day>'.$value["day"].'</day>';
    $xml.='<month>'.$value["month"].'</month>';
    $xml.='<year>'.$value["year"].'</year>';
    $xml.='<hourstart>'.$value["hourstart"].'</hourstart>';
    $xml.='<minstart>'.$value["minstart"].'</minstart>';
    $xml.='<hourend>'.$value["hourend"].'</hourend>';
    $xml.='<minend>'.$value["minend"].'</minend>';
    $xml.='</slot>';
}
$xml.='</slots>';
return new xmlrpcresp(new xmlrpcval($xml, "string"));
}
```

In this method, we check for slots at 1 hour (3600 seconds) intervals. If later implementations of the calendar allow the user to set the calendar granularity, we only need to change this method to retrieve the `$interval` variable from the user preferences or default it to 3600 if no preference is found. In fact, we could have coded the method to do this and left it to the clients to allow the user to set the preference.

The method is similar to `GetAgenda()`, but only free intervals are returned as valid time slots for the event.

> The compressed file with all the code for this case study, both the server, and the client have this new functionality already added.

Modifying the Web Client

Once this new method is added to the server, we'll need to modify our web client so that the user can allocate a time interval for an event.

First, let's add a new option called **Allocate** to the navigation bar on the left of our layout, and link it to a new PHP script `section_getslots.php` (shown below). This can be easily done by adding the following line to the layout section of `main.php`:

```
<tr><td valign="top">
       <a class="menu"
          href="<? print ($PHP_SELF)?>?section=getslots">Allocate</a>
     </td></tr>
```

The **Allocate** link will take us to the `section_getslots.php` script given below:

```php
<?php
if (session_is_registered("user")) {
    if (isset($_REQUEST["day"])) {
        $day = $_REQUEST["day"];
    }
    if (isset($_REQUEST["mon"])) {
        $mon = $_REQUEST["mon"];
    }
    if (isset($_REQUEST["year"])) {
        $year = $_REQUEST["year"];
    }
    if (isset($_REQUEST["hour"])) {
        $hour = $_REQUEST["hour"];
    }
    include_once("class_calendar.php");
    if (!isset($day)) {
        $day = date("d");
        $mon = date("m");
        $year = date("Y");
        $hour = date("H");
    }
    $c = new Calendar("en");
?>

<form action="main.php?section=agenda" method="post">
  <table width="100%">
  <tr><td colspan="2" valign="top" height="45" class="textbl">
      Allocate time for an event</td></tr>
  <!-- DATA:
    From Day
    From Month
    From Year
    To Day
```

```
      To Month
      To year
      From Hour
      To Hour
      Duration
  -->

  <tr><td width="20%" class="text">Search from:</td><td class="text">
  <?php $c->buildDayBox("sdayfrom", $day, $mon, $year)?> of
  <?php $c->buildMonthBox("smonfrom", $mon)?>
  <?php $c->buildYearBox("syearfrom", $year)?>
  </td></tr>
  <tr><td width="20%" class="text">Search to:</td><td class="text">
  <?php $c->buildDayBox("sdayto", $day, $mon, $year)?> of
  <?php $c->buildMonthBox("smonto", $mon)?>
  <?php $c->buildYearBox("syearto", $year)?>
  </td></tr>

  <tr><td class="text">Search from hour:</td><td class="text">
  <?php $c-> buildHourBox("shourfrom", $startHour)?>:00</td></tr>
  <tr><td class="text">Search to hour:</td><td class="text">
  <?php $c-> buildHourBox("shourto", $endHour)?>:00</td></tr>
  <input type="hidden" name="day" value="<?php print ($day)?>"/>
  <input type="hidden" name="mon" value="<?php print ($mon)?>"/>
  <input type="hidden" name="year" value="<?php print ($year)?>"/>
  <tr><td class="text">Duration:</td><td class="text">
  <?php $c->buildIntBox("sduration", 1, 10, 1, 1)?> hours</td></tr>
  <tr><td class="text"> </td><td class="text">
  <input type="submit" name="search" value="search" /></td></tr>
  </table>
</form>

<?php
} else {
    print ("You are not logged in<br />");
}
?>
```

This script displays a form letting the user query for available time slots during a given period. It lets the user enter the day, month, and year for both the start and end days for that period. The submit button has been named search. We can check for $search that will be set at main.php to determine if we are processing the 'get slots' form.

The following screenshot shows the calendar web client with the new form, and the new Allocate option in the navigation bar menu:

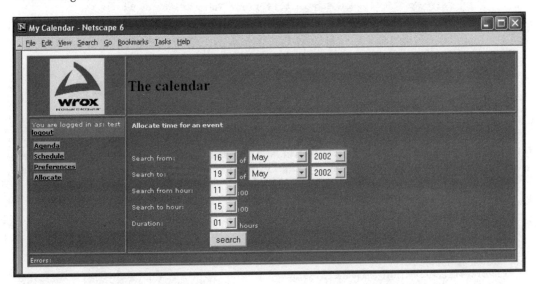

This is the addition to be made to `main.php`, which will process the search:

```
// Process a request to allocate events
if(isset($_REQUEST["search"])) {
  $search=$_REQUEST["search"];
}
if (isset($search)) {
    $sdayfrom = $_REQUEST["sdayfrom"];
    $smonfrom = $_REQUEST["smonfrom"];
    $sdayto = $_REQUEST["sdayto"];
    $smonto = $_REQUEST["smonto"];
    $syearfrom = $_REQUEST["syearfrom"];
    $syearto = $_REQUEST["syearto"];
    $shourfrom = $_REQUEST["shourfrom"];
    $shourto = $_REQUEST["shourto"];
    $sduration = $_REQUEST["sduration"];
    //sdayfrom smonfrom syearfrom sdayto smonto syearto shourfrom shourto
    //sduration
    $searchMsg = new xmlrpcmsg('GetSlots',
    array(new xmlrpcval($user, "string"),
          new xmlrpcval($pass, "string"),
          new xmlrpcval($sdayfrom, "string"),
          new xmlrpcval($smonfrom, "string"),
          new xmlrpcval($syearfrom, "string"),
          new xmlrpcval($sdayto, "string"),
          new xmlrpcval($smonto, "string"),
          new xmlrpcval($syearto, "string"),
          new xmlrpcval($shourfrom, "string"),
          new xmlrpcval($shourto, "string"),
          new xmlrpcval($sduration, "string")));
```

```
                $result = $client->send($searchMsg);
    if (!$result) {
        $errorMsg = 'Cannot log in to server. The server may be down';
    } else {
        if (!$result->faultCode()) {
            // We have a response
            $xmlsearch = xmlrpc_decode($result->value());
            $section = 'search';
        } else {
            $errorMsg = $result->faultstring();
        }
    }
}
```

We call the GetSlots() method on the server, and store the resulting XML in $xmlsearch. Then, we change the value of $section to search. This includes the section_search.php script that will display the result of the search in the central space of our web application.

This is the section_search.php script, from where the results of the search will be displayed:

```
<?php
include_once("class_xslt.php");
$xslt = new xslt();
$xslt->setXmlString($xmlsearch);
$xslt->setXsl("slots2html.xsl");
if ($xslt->transform()) {
    $ret = $xslt->getOutput();
    print ($ret);
} else {
    print ("Error:".$xslt->getError());
}
?>
```

We called the XSLT class to transform the resulting XML to HTML using the following XSLT, slots2html.xsl:

```
<?xml version="1.0" encoding="iso-8859-1"?>
<xsl:stylesheet xmlns:xsl="http://www.w3.org/1999/XSL/Transform"
                         version="1.0">
  <xsl:output method="html" encoding="iso-8859-1" />

  <xsl:template match="/">
    <table width="95%" border="0" cellspacing="0" cellpadding="0"
                     align="center">
      <tr>
        <td class="ft">
          <table width="100%" border="0" cellspacing="1" cellpadding="0"
                             bordercolor="#FF0000" align="center">
            <tr>
              <td class="date" colspan="3">Slots</td>
            </tr>

            <xsl:apply-templates select="/slots/slot" />
          </table>
        </td>
      </tr>
```

```
      </table>
  </xsl:template>

  <xsl:template match="/slots/slot">
    <tr class="fc">
      <td class="fc" width="20%">
      <xsl:value-of select="./month" />
      /
      <xsl:value-of select="./day" />
      /
      <xsl:value-of select="./year" />
      </td>
      <td class="fc" width="20%">
      <xsl:value-of select="./hourstart" />
      :
      <xsl:value-of select="./minstart" />
      -
      <xsl:value-of select="./hourend" />
      :
      <xsl:value-of select="./minend" />
      </td>

      <td class="fc">
        <a>
        <xsl:attribute name="href">main.php?section=schedule&amp;day=
        <xsl:value-of select="./day" />

        &amp;mon=
        <xsl:value-of select="./month" />

            &amp;year=
        <xsl:value-of select="./year" />

        &amp;hour=
        <xsl:value-of select="./hourstart" />

        &amp;duration=
        <xsl:value-of select="/slots/duration" />
        </xsl:attribute>

        Alocate</a>
      </td>
    </tr>
  </xsl:template>
</xsl:stylesheet>
```

In this simple XSLT file, for each slot we display the date, the hour where the slot begins, the hour where the slot ends, and a link to http://localhost/ProPHPXML/Chapter17/main.php?section=schedule passing the parameters to schedule an event for that interval. We pass the day, month, year, hour, and duration to the schedule form, so the form will be pre-filled with that information. The user then just enters the title of the event and the event can be allocated to the interval selected by the user. The following screenshot displays the time slots after the XSLT converts the XML to HTML:

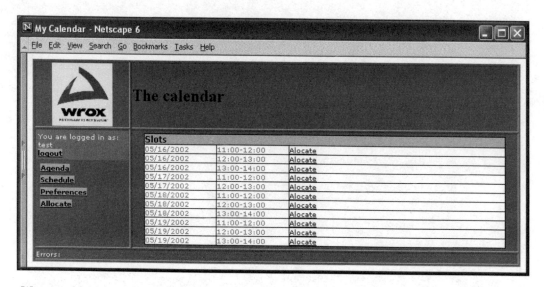

We can add this cool feature to other clients or integrate the feature into existing applications.

Our experience with the GetSlots() method demonstrates how additional features can be iteratively added to the calendar server and client, while maintaining compatibility with previous versions.

Future Requirements

With the iterative approach, we have added new functionality to our calendar server and the client. Our application is quite user-friendly for simple calendars that have to be accessed from different applications.

Once the clients incorporate our calendar, and users start using it, we'll probably receive a huge amount of requests for new functionality. We can easily fulfill such requirements, and go through a new iteration generating a new calendar server release.

Listed below are a few ideas we could incorporate into our application. A brief description about how this can be achieved follows. If these suggestions were to be implemented, we'll end up with an excellent calendar server.

Editing Events

Our web client didn't allow the user to modify an existing event. An **Edit** link can easily be added to the navigation bar. An EditEvent() method can be added to the server which would remove an existing event and add a new event with the modified data. The EditEvent() would be supplied the username, password, event ID, and event information (including unchanged information) as parameters. Then we can just update the event in the database and the event would have been edited. More granular methods such as EventChangeTitle() and EventChangeDuration() could also be added. These methods would call EditEvent() to make the necessary modifications.

Repeating Events

Sometimes users want to schedule an event that occurs on a regular basis. For example, a visit to the masseuse on Mondays at 17:00 will be repeated four (or more) times a month. This is a feature that should be implemented at the client level. We can add a form in the schedule section to let the user indicate if the event is a repeating event, and let them provide information like when, and for how long, does it repeat. When we process the form, we should call AddEvent() several times to add all the events to the calendar. If some of the AddEvent() calls fail, the user will be sent a message, and we can remove the event ID that was added until the error occurred.

Searching for Events

We can also include a powerful search feature. This would allow users to search for an event using several filters. For example, events on Mondays between 9 and 14 that have 'interview' in their title. To add this functionality, we must add a SearchEvent() method in the server which can return XML with the information for all the events that matched the search criteria. The clients can display or use the events as they want, just by parsing the XML file. This method would take the following parameters:

- userLogin
  Login name for the user

- password
  The user password

- daysOfWeek
  A string with 7 letters, indicating the days of the week valid in search results (for example, "nyyyyyn" = Monday to Friday only)

- fromDay
  UNIX timestamp of the day to start the search

- toDay
  UNIX timestamp of the day to end the search

- fromHour
  Search for the events that start at or after this hour

- toHour
  Search for the events that end before this hour

- minDuration
  Minimum duration of events to be retrieved (in seconds)

- maxDuration
  Maximum duration of events to be retrieved (in seconds)

- titleContains
  Words separated by whitespace, which the title of any event must contain

Attachments

Another useful feature is to let the users attach files to the events. The clients can allow a user to attach, remove, or retrieve a file to an event. This feature can be implemented by adding support for attachments in the server. For this feature, we'll need a table where attachments can be stored.

Table – Attachments

Column Name	Definition
attachmentId	integer(8) NOT NULL auto_increment
eventId	varchar(32) NOT NULL
filename	varchar(40)
filetype	varchar(120)
filesize	integer(10)
data	longblob

The primary key for this table would be attachmentId, and the methods to manipulate attachments would be as follows:

```
addAttachment(username,password,eventId,filename,filetype,filesize,filedata)
removeAttachment(username,password,eventId,attachmentId)
findAttachments(username,password,eventId)
removeAllAttachments(username,password,eventId)
```

We can also modify the XML returned by GetAgenda() to list the attachments for an event:

```xml
<attachments>
  <attachment>
    <id></id>
    <filename></filename>
  <filesize></filesize>
  </attachment>
</attachments>
```

Note that the clients already calling GetAgenda() won't need to be modified, since the XML structure that they are using is still working. However, more data has been added to the XML response. Clients unaware of attachments should simply ignore the attached information and proceed as they did before.

Sharing the Calendar

Some applications allow users to share their calendar, so that the agenda for a given day can be checked by other users. To implement this in our calendar server, we need to use the type attribute of the events table. We should define that the events can either be public or private. The public events can be shown to other users if the calendar is shared, while private events are only visible to the user that owns the calendar.

We also define the sharing preference that can be y or n, indicating if the calendar is being shared. The default will be n.

Finally we provide a method so that users can retrieve the agenda of some other user:

```
GetPublicAgenda(username, day, month, year)
```

This method will return an XML format similar to `GetAgenda()` but `eventIds` won't be set, since the users can't modify events that don't belong to them. Implementing this function in the server should be easy. We have to be careful and check that the user exists, the calendar is shared, and only public events are considered for the public agenda.

Reminders

When we set an event, we may want to be reminded some minutes, hours, or days before the event (wedding anniversary) occurs. We implement reminders by adding a `reminders` table in the server. We then program a daemon that checks the `reminders` table every 1 minute, for example. The method will check if there are some reminders that have to be sent.

Task List

You can add a task list manager to the calendar that allows the calendar clients to display a task list for users. Tasks are events without a defined time window. They are always active until the user decides that the task is completed. Managing tasks is fairly simple, since we can store tasks in a `tasks` table:

Table – tasks

Column Name	Definition
tasked	integer(8) NOT NUL auto_increment
userId	integer(8) NOT NULL
taskTitle	varchar(80)
taskDescription	text (64Kb maximum)

The primary key for this table would be `taskId`. We'll have to implement the following methods to manage tasks:

```
AddTask(username, password, taskTitle, taskDescription)
FindAllTasks(username, password)
RemoveTask(username, password, taskId)
```

The `FindAllTasks()` method can return an XML string with the information for all the tasks the user has.

Describing Events

A useful addition would be displaying a description of the events in our calendar server. We are storing the event title in the events base, but some users may want to add a description to the events. We can't modify the `events` table or the `AddEvent()` method, since this will impact existing clients, and they may stop working. We have to add this feature without changing the way clients work. Let's build a satellite table.

Table – eventDescriptions

Column Name	Definition
eventide	char(32) NOT NULL
description	text

The primary key for this `eventDescriptions` table would be `eventId`. The methods we will use are as follows:

```
AddDescription(username, password, eventId, description)
GetDescription(username, password, eventId)
```

After removing the event, the `RemoveEvent()` method should be modified to remove the event description if it exists.

The description can also be added to the XML format returned by `GetAgenda()` without disturbing the behavior of existing clients.

More Features

A lot of other features can be added some of which may require modifications to the server. Our application allows our imagination to build a calendar as comprehensive as we want. Irrespective of what we add to the calendar, our design allows very primitive clients, such as the ones we presented earlier in this chapter, to keep working as if nothing had changed.

Summary

In this chapter, we designed and built a calendar server using XML-RPC, and showed how to build a web client and a command-line client for XML-RPC. We also stressed the concept of an extensible server where new features can be added without modifying existing clients.

The calendar that we constructed can add events, remove them, display the user agenda, set user preferences common to all the clients, and search for time slots for an event. We also discussed some ideas that can be implemented in our calendar application. Now, we can build our own calendar with all the features we want, and integrate it to some other applications we have developed using XML-RPC.

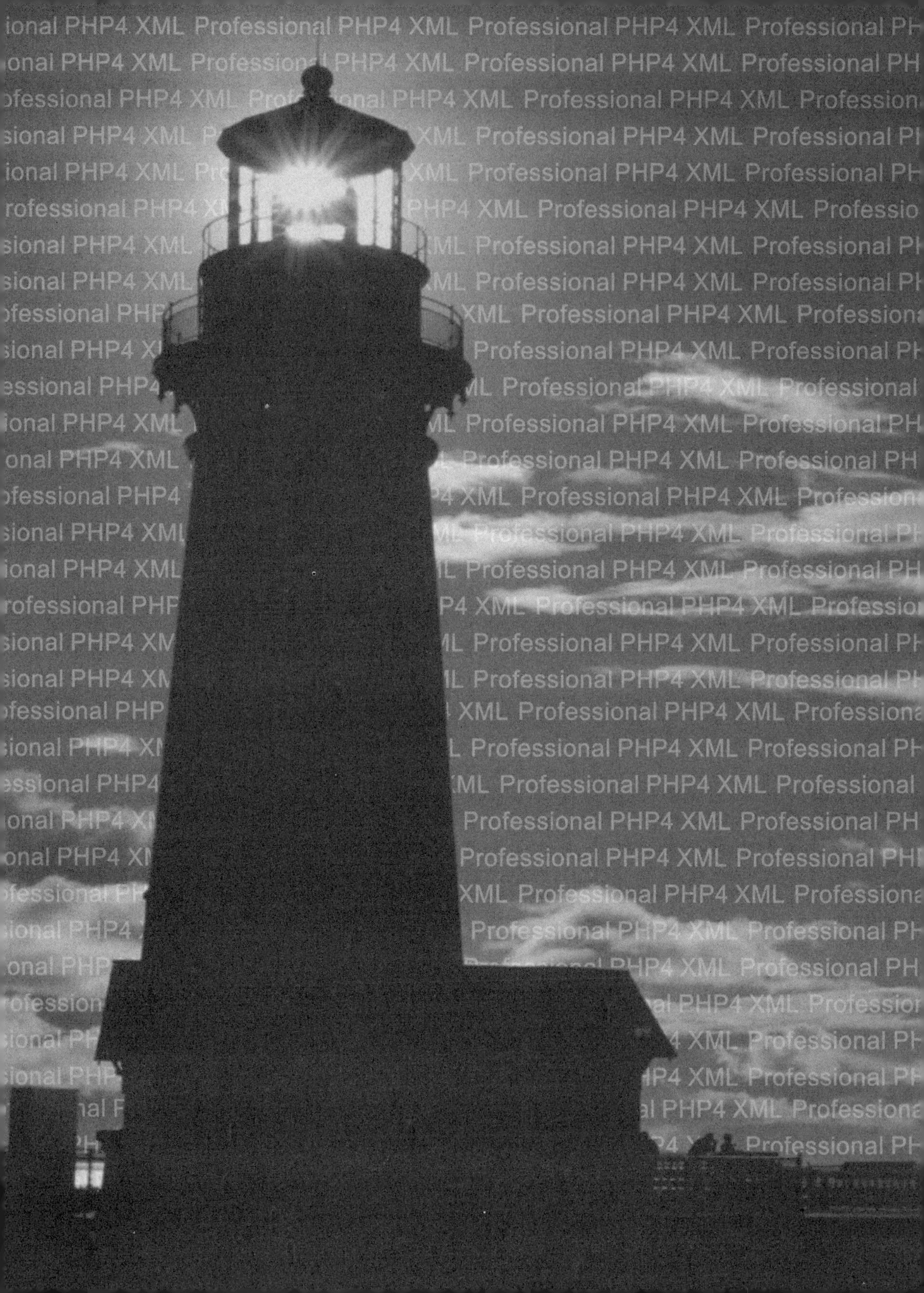
Professional PHP4 XML

PHP4 XML Language Reference

PHP has built-in XML support via inclusion of the popular Expat XML parser developed by James Clark (http://www.jclark.com/xml/).

Some characteristics of Expat:

❑   It is an event-based parser

❑   It checks for well-formedness of the XML document

❑   It does not check the validity of the XML document

❑   It provides UNICODE support

❑   Its default source encoding is ISO-8859-1

❑   It supports source encoding and target encoding

We must ensure that our build of PHP is configured to use the parser. On Windows, make sure that the `expat.dll` file is present in `C:\Windows\System` for Widows9x/ME and `C:\WINNT\System32` for WindowsNT/2000 systems. On UNIX, run configure with `--with-xml`.

Common Steps When Employing XML Parser

Instantiate XML Parser

To instantiate a parser simply call the `xml_parser_create()` function:

```
$parser = xml_parser_create();
```

There is an optional `char` encoding parameter with the following options:

❑   ISO-8859-1 (the default)

❑   UTF-8

❑   US-ASCII

Register Callback Functions (Handler Functions)

In an event-based parser, such as Expat, the XML **streams** through a logical filter instead of building a memory resident tree representation of the data. With callback functions we can register a handler to activate and process XML flows through this filter.

Review the following XML snippet:

```
<test>
  <tag>How now brown cow</tag>
  <tag name="jane">See jane run with spot</tag>
</test>
```

We could use the various handler functions to activate when the parser finds a `<test>` element or a name attribute.

The parser instance must be passed as the first argument for all of the handler functions:

```
xml_set_element_handler($parser, "start_element", "stop_element");
```

The above instruction fires the user-defined function `start_element()` whenever the parser encounters the beginning element. Whenever a closing element tag is parsed, the user-defined function `stop_element()` is activated.

Handler functions can be named anything, but it's good practice to follow a certain prototype, the form of which is given in the handler function table later in the chapter.

Parse Data

To process data through the parser we use the `xml_parse()` function:

```
// set a file to process
$file = "test.xml";

//test file existence
if(!file_exists($file)) {
    die("can't find file \"$file\".");
}

// set pointer to file
if(!($fp = fopen($file, "r"))) {
    die("Can't open file \"$file\".");
}

//read data from file in 1024 byte chunks and place in variable
while($data = fread($fp, 1024)) {
    //parse data in 1024 byte chunks, checking for end of file condition
    if(!xml_parse($parser, $data, feof($fp))) {
        return FALSE;
    }
}

// close the file resource
fclose($fp);
```

`xml_parse()` takes in chunks of data. This is useful when processing large XML files; it also is the perfect method for handling streaming XML data.

Destroy and Free XML Parser

When done with a parser it is good practice to free up the resources by using the `xml_parser_free()` function:

```
xml_parser_free($parser);
```

This returns TRUE if successful and FALSE if no parser exists.

The PHP XML API

The following sections describe the common format for function definitions by supplying functional prototype, parameters, return values, and a description.

Parser

xml_parser_create(string encoding)

> Instantiates an XML parser. Returns a handle to parser if successful. Returns FALSE if a parser cannot be created.
>
> **Parameters:**   string encoding – UTF-8, US-ASCII, ISO-8859-1
>
> **Returns:**   This function creates an XML parser and returns a handle for use by other XML functions. Returns FALSE on failure.

xml_parser_free(resource parser)

> Releases the handle and frees up parser and associated resources. Returns TRUE if the operation was successful, FALSE if no parser exists.
>
> **Parameters:**   resource parser – A reference to the XML parser to free
>
> **Returns:**   This function returns FALSE if parser does not refer to a valid parser, or else it frees the parser and returns TRUE.

xml_set_object(resource parser, object &object)

> Use this function to encapsulate all parsing functions, including all the handler functions, within an object.
>
> **Parameters:**   resource parser – Handle to parser
>
>   object &object – Pointer to an instantiated object
>
> **Returns:**   void

Example:

```
class xml
{
    var $parser;

    function xml()
    {
        $this->parser = xml_parser_create();
        xml_set_object($this->parser, &$this);
    }

    function parsethis()
    {
        xml_parse($this->parser, $data);
    }
}

$parser = new xml();
$parser->parsethis("<test name=\"jim\">watch spot run</test>");
```

xml_parse(resource parser, string data [, bool is_final])

This function starts processing data in chunks, through the parser. All registered handlers will activate as many times as required, and as long as data continues to be handed to the parser. The parser will continue to use these handlers until the is_final parameter is set to TRUE which instructs the parser that the current data is the last data. This indirection gives a chance to register different handlers within a single parsing process.

Parameters:	resource parser – A reference to the XML parser to use.
	string data – Chunk of data to parse. A document may be parsed piece-wise by calling xml_parse() several times with new data, as long as the is_final parameter is set and TRUE when the last block of data is parsed.
	bool is_final (optional) – If set and TRUE, data is the last piece of data sent in this parse.
Returns:	TRUE is returned if the parse was successful, FALSE if it was not successful or if parser does not refer to a valid parser.

Example:

```
$fp = fopen("somefile.xml", "r")
//read data from file in 4096 byte chunks and place in variable
while($data = fread($fp, 4096)) {
    //parse data in 4096, checking for end of file condition
    if(!xml_parse($parser, $data, feof($fp))) {
        return FALSE;
    }
}
```

xml_parse_into_struct(resource parser, string data, array &values, array &index)

This function parses XML data into 2 arrays. The first array holds pointers to the 2nd array, which holds the values. This is useful when we want to use XML data within PHP, without using DOM or XML functions.

Parameters:	resource parser – Handle to parser
	string data – Variable containing current chunk of XML data to be processed
	array &values – Array holding values
	array &index – Array holding pointers to values
Returns:	int

xml_parser_get_option(resource parser, int option)

Gets the current setting value of an option.

Parameters:	resource parser – Handle to parser.
	int option – XML_OPTION_CASE_FOLDING* | XML_OPTION_TARGET_ENCODING
Returns:	This function returns FALSE if parser does not refer to a valid parser, or if the option could not be set. Else the option's value is returned.

*Case folding: forces element names to be parsed into uppercase.

Example:

```
$parser = xml_parser_create("UTF-8");
xml_parser_get_option($parser, XML_OPTION_CASE_FOLDING);
```

xml_parser_set_option(resource parser, int option, mixed value)

Sets an option on a selected parser.

XML_OPTION_CASE_FOLDING is enabled by default.

XML_OPTION_TARGET_ENCODING sets the target encoding for the parser (UTF-8, US-ASCII, ISO-8859-1).

Parameters:	resource parser – Handle to parser.
	int option – XML_OPTION_CASE_FOLDING | XML_OPTION_TARGET_ENCODING
	mixed value – Value of the chosen option (option integer | string).
Returns:	This function returns FALSE if parser does not refer to a valid parser, or if the option could not be set. Else the option is set and TRUE is returned.

Example:

```
$parser= xml_parser_create("UTF-8");
xml_parser_set_option($parser,XML_OPTION_CASE_FOLDING,true);
```

Handler Functions

Default

xml_set_default_handler(resource parser, string defaultHandler)

Sets the default handler function for the XML parser parser. handler is a string containing the name of a function that must exist when xml_parse() is called.

Parameters:	resource parser – Handle to parser.
	string defaultHandler – Function name which handles default string.
Returns:	TRUE is returned if the handler is set up, FALSE if parser is not a parser.

Example:

```
function generic()
{
    print ("do nothing to this XML node");
}

xml_set_default_handler($parser, 'generic');
```

Element

xml_set_element_handler(resource parser, string startElementHandler, string endElementHandler)

Defines handler functions for elements. The starting and ending tag/elements have separate callback functions.

Parameters:	resource parser – Handle to parser.
	startElementHandler and endElementHandler are strings containing the names of functions that must exist when xml_parse() is called for parsing.
	The function named by startElementHandler must accept three parameters: resource parser, string name, array attribs.
	The function named by endElementHandler must accept two parameters: resource parser, string name.
Returns:	TRUE is returned if the handlers are set up, FALSE if parser is not a parser.

startElementHandler(resource parser, string name, array attribs)

Function prototype for start element handler.

Parameters: `resource parser` – A reference to the XML parser calling the handler.

`string name` – Contains the name of the element for which this handler is called. If case folding is in effect for this parser, the element name will be in uppercase letters.

`array attribs` – Contains an associative array with the element's attributes (if any). The keys of this array are the attribute names and the values are the attribute values. Attribute names are case-folded on the same criteria as element names. Attribute values are not case-folded.

The original order of the attributes can be retrieved by walking through `attribs` the normal way, using `each()`. The first key in the array was the first attribute, and so on.

endElementHandler(resource parser, string name)

Function prototype for start element handler.

Parameters: `resource parser` – A reference to the XML parser calling the handler.

`string name` – Contains the name of the element for which this handler is called. If case folding is in effect for this parser, the element name will be in uppercase letters.

If a handler function is set to an empty string, or `FALSE`, the handler in question is disabled.

Character Data

xml_set_character_data_handler(resource parser, string characterDataHandler)

Sets the handler function for processing character data. Character data is Unicode data between elements.

Parameters: `resource parser` – Handle to parser.

`string characterDataHandler` – Function name which handles character data.

Returns: `TRUE` is returned if the handler is set up, `FALSE` if `parser` is not a parser.

characterDataHandler(resource parser, string data)

Function prototype for character data handling.

Parameters: `resource parser` – Handle to parser.

`string data` – Current XML character node.

Processing Instructions

xml_set_processing_instruction_handler(resource parser, string processingInstructionHandler)

Sets the handler function for processing processing instructions.	
Parameters:	resource parser – Handle to parser
	string processingInstructionHandler – Function name which handles the processing instructions
Returns:	TRUE is returned if the handler is set up, FALSE if parser is not a parser

processingInstructionHandler(resource parser, string target, string data)

Function prototype for processing instruction handler.	
Parameters:	resource parser – Handle to parser
	string target – PI target
	string data – Data in the body of PI

External Entities

xml_set_external_entity_ref_handler(resource parser, string externalEntityRefHandler)

Sets the external entity reference handler function for the XML parser.	
Parameters:	resource parser – Handle to parser
	string externalEntityRefHandler –Function name which handles external entity references
Returns:	TRUE is returned if the handler is set up, FALSE if parser is not a parser

externalEntityRefHandler(resource parser, string open_entity_names, string base, string systemID, string publicID)

Function prototype for external entity reference handler.

Parameters: resource parser – The first parameter, parser, is a reference to the XML parser calling the handler.

string open_entity_names – A space-separated list of the names of the entities that are open for the parsing of this entity (including the name of the referenced entity).

string base – This is the base for resolving the system identifier (system_id) of the external entity. Currently this parameter will always be set to an empty string.

string systemID – The system identifier as specified in the entity declaration.

string publicID – The public identifier as specified in the entity declaration, or an empty string if none was specified. The whitespace in the public identifier will have been normalized as required by the XML specifications.

Unparsed External Entities

xml_set_unparsed_entity_decl_handler(resource parser, string unparsedEntityDeclHandler)

Sets the unparsed entity declaration handler function for the XML parser.

Parameters: resource parser – Handle to parser

string unparsedEntityDeclHandler – Name which handles unparsed entity declaration

Returns: TRUE is returned if the handler is set up, FALSE if parser is not a parser

unparsedEntityDeclHandler(resource parser, string entityName, string base, string systemID, string publicID, string notationName)

Function prototype for handling unparsed entity declarations.

Parameters: resource parser – A reference to the XML parser calling the handler.

string entityName – The name of the entity that is about to be defined.

string base – This is the base for resolving the system identifier (systemId) of the external entity. Currently this parameter will always be set to an empty string.

string systemID – System identifier for the external entity.

string publicID – Public identifier for the external entity.

string notationName – Name of the notation of this entity.

Notation Declarations

xml_set_notation_decl_handler(resource parser, string notationDeclarationHandler)

Sets the notation declaration handler function for the XML parser.	
Parameters:	resource parser – Handle to parser
	string notationDeclarationHandler – Name which handles notation declaration
Returns:	TRUE is returned if the handler is set up, FALSE if parser is not a parser

A notation declaration is part of the document's DTD and has the following format:

```
<!NOTATION name {system_id | public_id}>
```

Note: Instead of a function name, an array containing an object reference and a method name can also be supplied.

notationDeclarationHandler(resource parser, string notationName, string base, string systemID, string publicID)

Function prototype for handling notation declaration.	
Parameters:	resource parser – A reference to the XML parser calling the handler.
	string notationName – This is the notation's name, as per the notation format described above.
	string base – This is the base for resolving the system identifier (system_id) of the notation declaration. Currently this parameter will always be set to an empty string.
	string systemID – System identifier of the external notation declaration.
	string publicID – Public identifier of the external notation declaration.

Utility Functions

Current

xml_get_current_line_number(resource parser)

Returns the current line number.	
Parameters:	resource parser – Handle to parser
Returns:	This function returns FALSE if parser does not refer to a valid parser, or else it returns which line the parser is currently at in its data buffer

xml_get_current_column_number(resource parser)

Returns the current column number.	
Parameters:	resource parser – Handle to parser
Returns:	This function returns FALSE if parser does not refer to a valid parser, or else it returns which column on the current line (as given by xml_get_current_line_number()) the parser is currently on

xml_get_current_byte_index(resource parser)

Returns current byte index.	
Parameters:	resource parser – Handle to parser
Returns:	This function returns FALSE if parser does not refer to a valid parser, or else it returns which byte index the parser is currently at in its data buffer (starting at 0)

UTF-8

utf8_encode(string data)

This function encodes the string data to UTF-8, and returns the encoded version.	
Parameters:	string data – Data to be converted
Returns:	string

Example:

```
$iso88591toutf8 = utf8_encode($data);
```

utf8_decode(string data)

This function encodes the string data to UTF-8, and returns the encoded version.	
Parameters:	string data – Data to be converted
Returns:	string

Example:

```
$utf8toiso88591 = utf8_encode($data);
```

Namespace

Currently the namespace functions are not documented. Refer to http://www.php.net/manual/en/ref.xml.php for updates.

Error

xml_get_error_code(resource parser)

Accesses current error code for selected parser.	
Parameters:	resource parser – A reference to the XML parser to get error code from
Returns:	This function returns FALSE if parser does not refer to a valid parser, or else it returns one of the error codes

xml_error_string (int code)

Return text description of a particular error code.	
Parameters:	int code – Error code
Returns:	Returns a string with a textual description of the error code, or FALSE if no description was found

Example:

```
$error_message = xml_error_string($errorcode);
print ("error: $error_message");
```

XML Parsing Error Codes

The following constants are defined for XML error codes (as returned by xml_parse()):

Error Code	Description
XML_ERROR_NONE	No Error
XML_ERROR_NO_MEMORY	XML parser has run out of memory
XML_ERROR_SYNTAX	General error in syntax
XML_ERROR_NO_ELEMENTS	No elements are found
XML_ERROR_INVALID_TOKEN	Invalid XML token, not well-formed
XML_ERROR_UNCLOSED_TOKEN	Unclosed XML token
XML_ERROR_PARTIAL_CHAR	Unclosed token

Table continued on following page

Error Code	Description
XML_ERROR_TAG_MISMATCH	Mismatched element tags
XML_ERROR_DUPLICATE_ATTRIBUTE	Element has the same attribute at least twice, not valid XML
XML_ERROR_JUNK_AFTER_DOC_ELEMENT	Text after root element, which is not valid XML
XML_ERROR_PARAM_ENTITY_REF	Illegal parameter entity reference
XML_ERROR_UNDEFINED_ENTITY	PHP XML parser does not recognize entity
XML_ERROR_RECURSIVE_ENTITY_REF	Entity refers to itself
XML_ERROR_ASYNC_ENTITY	Asynchronous entity
XML_ERROR_BAD_CHAR_REF	Reference to invalid character numbers
XML_ERROR_BINARY_ENTITY_REF	Reference to binary entity
XML_ERROR_ATTRIBUTE_EXTERNAL_ENTITY_REF	Reference to external entity in attribute
XML_ERROR_MISPLACED_XML_PI	XML processing instruction not at the beginning of external entity
XML_ERROR_UNKNOWN_ENCODING	PHP XML parser does not understand character encoding
XML_ERROR_INCORRECT_ENCODING	Incorrect char encoding as specified in XML declaration
XML_ERROR_UNCLOSED_CDATA_SECTION	<![CDATA[ ]]> not closed off properly
XML_ERROR_EXTERNAL_ENTITY_HANDLING	Error in processing external entity reference

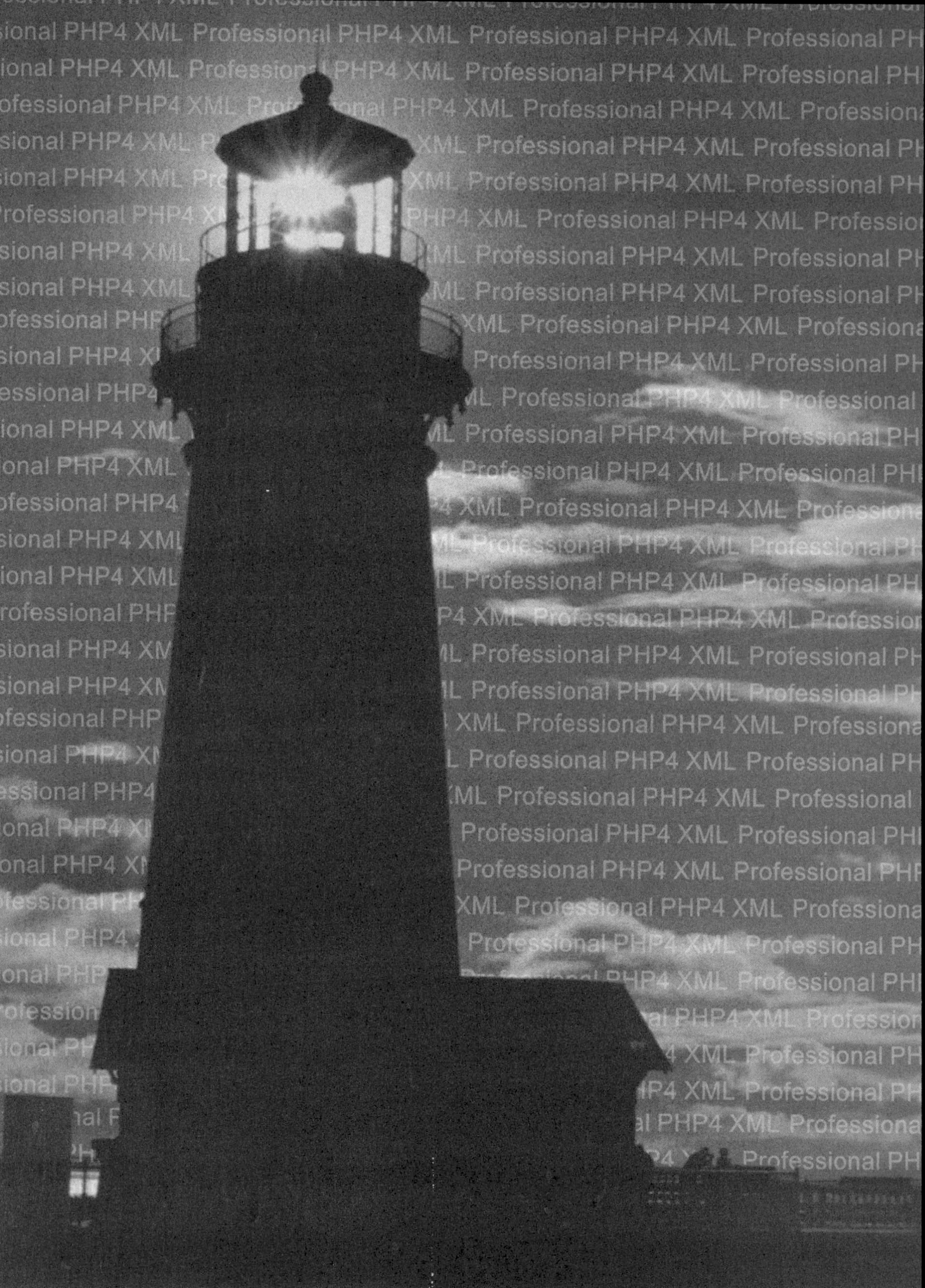
Professional PHP4 XML

B

Installing PHP4 and Apache

There are various methods to install PHP on either UNIX-like or Windows operating systems: Install Wizards, RPMs, and ports are available for most platforms. This makes sourcecode compilation one of the options. In this appendix we'll give you an overview of the installation instructions for the more common options. But first let's see some high-level decisions that need to be made before we install PHP.

Which Operating System?

The decision of which operating system you have to use is usually pre-determined. However, we might add that PHP runs better on a UNIX-like OS. While the core of PHP itself runs flawlessly under Windows, some of the more esoteric and interesting third-party software packages are unavailable for Windows, or can safely be run only via a CGI (Common Gateway Interface) rather than as a module.

Installation may be slightly harder under UNIX-like OSs, but the feature set and reliability will usually be worth it for most users. More about CGI versus module installation in the next section, but for now, be aware that a critical performance difference is noticeable only under extremely heavy loads. So unless your site is getting or truly expecting millions of hits a day, your OS decision should be based on factors other than PHP, which will happily plod away on almost any OS.

Module or CGI?

Next, you need to decide whether to install PHP as a module or as a CGI. As a module, PHP becomes a part of the web server. When the web server is started, PHP is always there with the web server, ready and waiting. When run as a CGI, PHP is run as a separate program every time a request for a web page is made. That is, a user asks for a URL, the web server runs PHP to get the content, and then PHP quits.

Running PHP as a module is usually far more efficient than running it as CGI, since the PHP program doesn't need to start and quit for every request. Also, tighter integration between the web server and modules allows features that are not possible when running PHP as a CGI. However, there are some specific cases where running as a CGI provides flexibility that is not available as a module. Specifically, PHP running as a CGI can be configured to run as a different user with more (or less) privileges than PHP running as a module of the web server.

Note that running PHP as a module does not stop you from having it available as a CGI, which is also useful for non-web activities such as scheduled events. For example, you may use PHP as a module on your web site, while using the CGI as a standalone interpreter to do routine maintenance of database tables or schedule e-mails.

In some cases, the decision is taken out of your hands, since PHP cannot run as a module for every web server. PHP can run as a CGI on every web server that supports CGI (virtually all web servers support CGI). Module support for UNIX-based servers are offered by Apache, thttpd, fhttpd, Zeus, Roxen, and pi3Web and module support for Windows-based web servers is offered by Microsoft IIS 4.0, 5.0*, AOLServer, WebSphere, Netscape web server, iPlanet (a Sun & NetScape joint venture), any ISAPI Compliant server, and Apache.

Which Web Server?

Your final major choice is the web server to go with PHP. This also may be pre-ordained by external factors such as management, or what is already available and in use. If not, Apache is probably the best bet for most users. It's on a par with or superior to the other choices. From a technical standpoint, it runs well under both Windows and UNIX-like operating systems, and the freely available Help resources are far more numerous than the other options.

You need to make these high-level decisions that affect how you should install PHP, before you embark on the installation process. We will discuss first the installation procedure for UNIX. Note that most UNIX distributions will most likely have a pre-packaged version of PHP configured as a module or as a CGI binary. Usually the packaged versions are easier to manage and upgrade, so check the existing PHP packages before compiling.

We then discuss installing PHP on Windows. It is much simpler because there is no compilation. However, that also takes away some flexibility. If necessary, we can compile PHP on Windows ourselves. Because of the complexity of doing so, it will not be covered here.

Once you have made your OS, module/CGI, and web server choices, you need to decide how to install PHP itself. Under Windows, an Install Wizard is probably the fastest and easiest way to do it. We'll provide step-by-step instructions along with suggestions for where to look if things go wrong, but Install Wizards make installations fairly easy.

For UNIX-like installations, you're probably better off with a sourcecode compilation for Apache and PHP. While the RPMs are wonderful for most software packages, when it comes to PHP, RPMs can be a little problematic. RPMs are created with one specific set of installation options tied to the various versions of the other third-party software installed. If you have a different version of MySQL, for example, the RPM is unlikely to work. Since there are 107 different installation switches, the odds of any given RPM being exactly what you want are slim.

You can probably work with an RPM and cope with the missing or extra features, and even be very careful about version numbers to be sure everything matches up. You can even edit the RPM sourcecode itself to alter it, but that's at least as hard as compiling PHP from source and getting precisely what you want. In the final analysis, compiling the source is usually the fastest and easiest way to get up-and-running.

Windows Installation

Installing PHP on Windows is easier than on UNIX because compilation is not required. However, because of this, it is not as flexible. PHP can be compiled on Windows but it requires Microsoft Visual C++. There is very little information available on compiling PHP on Windows systems; it is easiest to use the compiled version available from the PHP web site.

Note that there is an installer package called PHPTriad, available from http://www.phpgeek.com/, which bundles PHP with Apache, MySQL, Perl, and phpmyAdmin. PHPTriad is probably the easiest way to create a PHP development environment on a Windows machine.

We will first detail the installation of Apache and then move onto discussing the PHP installation for Windows.

Installing Apache

Download the Apache Install Wizard from:

http://www.apache.org/dist/httpd/

Double-click on the installer file and click Next on the standard introductory screen, and you should reach a screen like this:

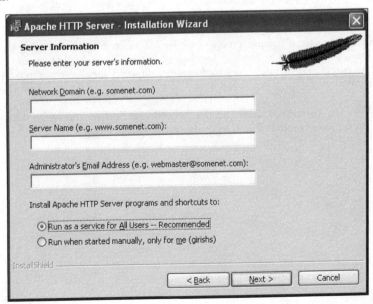

If you are configuring a live web server, you will want to use your real domain name and server name for Network Domain and Server Name. If this is to be a development web server you should use `localhost` or `127.0.0.1` as the Network Domain and Server Name. In either case, you should use a real e-mail address that you check, or one that is forwarded for the Administrator's Email Address.

> For a live web server, just configuring Apache to correctly serve web pages for that domain name is not sufficient to "go live". There must be a DNS server that has records associating your domain name with your IP address.

Near the bottom of this screen, you will be asked to install Apache as a service or as an application. Windows 9x doesn't support the service option, so you might as well choose application under Win 9x/ME. Windows NT/2000 users should choose service unless you have a very specific reason not to do so. A service always runs behind the scenes no matter who is logged in or even if nobody is logged in, but an application can only be run by a user logged in to the system. When a user logs out, any application they are running is exited.

After installing under Windows 9x/ME, you can put a shortcut to the Apache application in the startup directory for all users, which will mean that any user logged in will have Apache running. Adding this shortcut will automatically start Apache for Win9x/ME users, and be almost as good as installing as a service.

On the next screen, you are asked whether to do a complete install or a custom install. The complete installation is probably best for most users, but if your hard drive is getting full and you're online most of the time anyway, you may opt for the custom install and uncheck the Documentation and Sourcecode selections. The documentation and source are all online at http://apache.org/. If you choose the custom installation, you should probably keep the default install directory of `C:\Program Files\Apache Group` unless you have a really good reason not to do so. You'll definitely need to be able to find the directory you choose, so be sure you know where you installed Apache.

After the installation finishes, if you did not select service (either because you are using Win9x/ME or for some other reason) you will need to start the Apache web server. There should be menu items in your Start menu. You may want to drag that shortcut into the startup directory for all users or into your shortcuts in the desktop toolbar.

Once you have started Apache you should be able to open your browser and surf to http://localhost/ and see this web page on your newly installed web server from the Apache group:

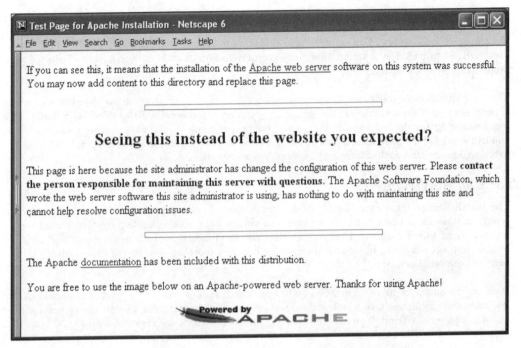

Note that this message is directed to users surfing to your web site, and you are the person responsible for maintaining this server. You could send yourself an e-mail to say that you haven't finished building your web site, but it would be much more useful to actually build it, wouldn't it?

You can try adding a couple of HTML files to your document root directory. In the default setup, this is usually `C:\Program Files\Apache Group\Apache\htdocs`. You should see an `index.html` document, which contains the HTML for the above displayed page.

Once you get the hang of adding files to your web server, you can change your document root to any directory you like by editing `httpd.conf`, which is by default in `C:\Program Files\Apache Group\Apache\conf\httpd.conf`:

```
DocumentRoot "C:/Apache/htdocs"
```

Make a backup copy before you edit, however, since a simple typo in `httpd.conf` can make your web server display **500 Internal Server Error** in your browser. Also, you need to restart Apache for changes to take effect. Make sure and check that the settings you changed actually work after every edit of `httpd.conf`.

If you chose to install Apache in a different location, you'll find the `httpd.conf` file and `htdocs` directory in that location specified. Note that when you change `DocumentRoot` in `httpd.conf`, you must also change the `<Directory...>` setting below that to match.

You can only have one main `DocumentRoot` in `httpd.conf`. While it is possible to add `<VirtualHost...>` settings and have a different `DocumentRoot` setting for each `VirtualHost`, that's a little beyond the scope of this book.

You may find it easier to organize your projects or clients or similar entities into sub directories within your `DocumentRoot` directory. This provides an easy way to maintain multiple web sites without editing `httpd.conf` for each one. You can even alter `Options` to include `Indexes` and get rid of the default `index.html` provided by Apache. Then, when you surf to http://localhost/ you'll have a listing of your projects served up by Apache.

There are innumerable other incredibly useful settings in `httpd.conf` that you may want to research and experiment with. Take a quick read-through of `httpd.conf`, and see which directives seem useful to your requirement. Ignore the rest for now, but a few simple experiments to configure your web server, the way you like it, might be a good idea. Be sure to keep a valid working backup copy of `httpd.conf`, and be sure to restart Apache after each change and thoroughly test your changes.

What Can Go Wrong?

The Install Wizard takes care of most of the installation. As stated before, it's very easy to make a typing mistake in `httpd.conf`. So be sure you always have a valid backup copy of a working `httpd.conf` to fall back on. That way, even if you can't figure out how to get exactly what you want out of your web server right now, you can at least have a working web server to use while you research the settings more.

Read the document for more information on `httpd.conf`. It does take a little practice to get used to the documentation format, so take a look at the directives you already understand before diving into the ones you don't quite understand. If you are interested in finding out more, see *Professional Apache* 2.0 from *Wrox Press (ISBN 1-861007-22-1)*.

For each URL request to your web site, Apache logs the request and the status of the fulfilment. These logs are kept in Apache's `logs` directory, which by default is in `C:\Program Files\Apache Group\Apache\logs`. This directory contains an `error_log` and an `access_log` file. Looking at the last line of `error_log` when something is going wrong is often extremely useful. You can try and rectify whatever is wrong by reading the message.

If there is nothing relevant in the `error_log` or `access_log` file, and if you are running Apache as a service or automatically on startup, try stopping Apache and running it by double-clicking on the `Apache.exe` file directly. Ideally, you'll get an MS DOS console window with some useful messages as Apache starts up that might provide some clues.

If `localhost` returns a **Server not found** or similar message, or if your browser ends up trying to find http://localhost.com/ and similar URLs, try http://127.0.0.1/ instead. If `127.0.0.1` works but `localhost` does not, you need to copy the sample `hosts.sam` file in your Windows system directory and rename it as `hosts` (no extension). That file should contain:

```
127.0.0.1    localhost
```

This is required to make Windows aware that the domain name `localhost` is really just `127.0.0.1`. In any networked computer, `127.0.0.1` is always an IP address that refers to the local machine. But the computer only knows what `localhost` means if it's in a `hosts` file.

Installing PHP

The PHP Install Wizard supports the following web servers:

- ❏ Microsoft PWS on Windows 9x or ME
- ❏ Microsoft PWS on Windows NT workstation
- ❏ Microsoft IIS 3 and lower
- ❏ Microsoft IIS 4 and higher
- ❏ Apache for Windows
- ❏ Xitami for Windows

First, download the PHP Windows distribution from http://php.net/downloads.php.

Next, stop your Apache web server and any database servers, if they are already running. Double-click on the setup program to begin. After a standard introductory screen and a license agreement, you will be asked to choose Standard or Advanced. While Standard is recommended, and is the path we'll be taking, experienced users may want to explore Advanced. You can always click Back or even Cancel and start all over again.

Following the Standard path, you will next be presented with a dialog to choose where to install PHP. The default location of c:\php is best unless you have a very good reason to choose otherwise.

Next, you'll be asked to configure PHP to be able to send e-mail using the built-in mail function. This dialog requests a valid SMTP server and a default From: address. If you know your SMTP server for outgoing e-mail, and if you know that it only checks your From: address to authorize you to send e-mail, you can use those values. If you are unsure what your SMTP server is, or if it requires a username/password as well as a valid From: address to authenticate, you can simply use localhost as the SMTP server, and your usual e-mail address as the From:.

Since most Windows versions do not provide an SMTP server, localhost won't actually work unless you have installed an SMTP server on your computer. Fortunately, we'll be able to reconfigure this easily later on, and there are freely available tools to provide the functionality you may require.

If you are thoroughly confused by the preceding two paragraphs, simply use localhost for the SMTP server, and your regular e-mail ID for the Email setting. You can always fix it later.

Finally, you'll be asked which web server to configure to run PHP. This book assumes you've chosen Apache.

> If you have chosen a web server other than those listed in the Wizard dialog, and if you have a tough time installing PHP, here's a tip: that web server probably comes with instructions for installing Perl. The php.exe program can be installed in exactly the same way as Perl by substituting the appropriate paths and using "php" instead of "perl".

Finally, you have finished making all your decisions, and you are ready to install. Click on that last Next button, and the installer will begin.

The Install Wizard does not currently automatically configure Apache's httpd.conf file, so you'll probably see a dialog about this. Don't worry, we'll go through the configuration of Apache to use PHP next.

After the installation is finished, you'll be presented with a dialog declaring successful installation and an **OK** button. Click **OK**, and we'll move on to configuring Apache.

Configuring Apache To Use PHP

We'll be configuring Apache to use PHP as a CGI under Windows, due to the instability of third-party software under Windows threading. Even if you plan on going the ISAPI module route, you probably should follow these instructions and do the CGI configuration first and make sure everything works. It's much easier to switch to ISAPI module usage after everything else is working. You'll need to do a lot of stress testing under ISAPI to be sure your web server is stable.

First, make sure Apache is not running. In the PHP directory, default `c:\php`, you should find a file named `php4ts.dll`. Windows 9x/ME users should copy it to `C:\Windows\System` while Windows NT/2000 users should copy it to `C:\WinNT\System32`.

Find the `httpd.conf` file, which by default is in `C:\Program Files\Apache Group\Apache\conf`. Make a backup copy of this file before you edit it.

Open this file with a text editor. Use the **Find** menu item to search for a `ScriptAlias` section. It's usually in between `<IfModule mod_alias.c>` and `</IfModule>`. There may be several `ScriptAlias` sections, and the `IfModule` lines may be separated by a considerable amount of text. In the `ScriptAlias` section, add the following line:

```
ScriptAlias /php/ "c:/php/"
```

This tells Apache where to find the various PHP files, and creates an **alias** to use later on in `httpd.conf` to reference that directory. If you installed PHP in a non-default location, you'll need to change the path above. Don't use Windows \ in `httpd.conf`, use / instead.

If there doesn't seem to be any existing `ScriptAlias` section, add the line above directly after the `<Directory...>` line, which corresponds to your `DocumentRoot`. More explanation was provided about these in the Apache installation instructions.

Second, locate the `AddType` section of `httpd.conf`. There should already be a couple of PHP4.x lines. You can uncomment (remove the # character at the beginning) or you can type in a line below those comments:

```
AddType application/x-httpd-php .php
```

This tells Apache the files that end in `.php` should be treated as MIME-type `application/x-httpd-php`. Just as GIF files are of MIME-type `image/gif` and JPEG files are `image/jpg`. If there doesn't seem to be an `AddType` section, put this line inside the `<Directory...>` section as described above.

Finally, locate the `Action` section of `httpd.conf`. This typically has a couple of example `Format:` lines.

Add the following line in the `Action` section:

```
Action application/x-httpd-php "/php/php.exe"
```

This tells Apache that a file whose MIME-type is `application/x-httpd-php`, which we defined with the `AddType` above, should be acted upon by the file named php.exe which is located in the directory defined by the `ScriptAlias "/php/"` that we typed above.

Once again, if there doesn't seem to be an `Action` section in your `httpd.conf`, simply add this inside the `Directory` section as above. Review the lines you have added for typing errors. While they are spread throughout the `httpd.conf` file to keep them organized by their command, these three lines act together to tell Apache how to cope with PHP files.

You may want to alter that second line so that files ending in `.php3` (older scripts you may find) or even `.htm` and `.html` files are passed through PHP. Forcing all HTML files through PHP will not slow down the response time appreciably. Also, including older extensions will allow you to add PHP features in all sorts of places in existing HTML files, without having to re-link to your web site. It also allows the use of `.htm` or `.html` which users are used to, instead of `.php`.

Your `AddType` line may end up looking like this:

```
AddType application/x-httpd-php .php .htm .html .php3
```

The order of the file endings is irrelevant, and you can add as many as you like that make sense. For example, it usually doesn't make a lot of sense to pass `.mp3` files through PHP. In fact, that will probably break your MP3 URLs, since PHP will add some default headers.

Once you've made and reviewed all your changes, save the `httpd.conf` file, and restart Apache.

What Can Go Wrong?

If Apache doesn't start at this point, review the three lines you added for typing errors. Also make sure:

- ❏ That you have the correct directory for your PHP installation in the `ScriptAlias` line.

- ❏ That you used / instead of \ in that path.

- ❏ The MIME-type `application/x-httpd-php` is the same on both the `AddType` and the `Action` lines. Copy and paste the two, so you are sure they are the same.

- ❏ That php.exe actually is in the right directory.

- ❏ You copied `php4ts.dll` into your Windows system directory.

If you've double-checked all the above, and stopped/restarted Apache and it still doesn't work, review the *What Can Go Wrong?* section under *Installing Apache*. In particular, check the error logs and the MS DOS console window for errors.

If all else fails, try copying `php4ts.dll` into the same directory as the php.exe file. By all rights, Windows is supposed to be able to find it in the system directory and load it, but if not, PHP can probably find it if it's sitting in the same directory as the php.exe file.

Testing the PHP Installation

In your httpd.conf file, there is a setting called DocumentRoot. There is also a <Directory ...> setting with the same path as the DocumentRoot setting. If you haven't changed them, and if you installed with the default settings, they are probably set to C:\Program Files\Apache Group\Apache\htdocs.

The DocumentRoot is where the homepage for your web server lives. There is already a file named index.html there, which serves any request made to your site.

Create a folder called prophpxml and place a text file called phpinfo.php in it. Add the following single line of text to the file:

```php
<?php
phpinfo();
?>
```

Save that file in your DocumentRoot. Use your web browser to surf to http://localhost/prophpxml/phpinfo.php.

If you have correctly installed PHP, you should see the following page that details your PHP installation's properties:

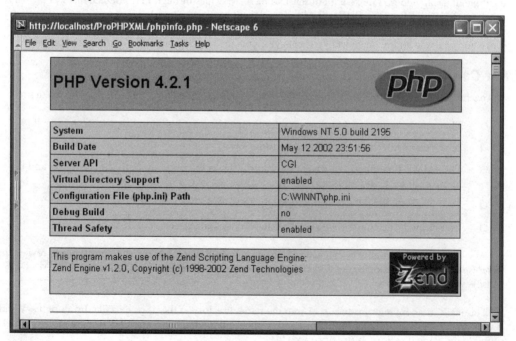

What Can Go Wrong?

If you see 404 Document not found or a similar error, you probably did not save phpinfo.php in the correct directory, or you spelled the file name wrong, or you typed the URL incorrectly. If you see 500 Internal Server Error you probably have a typing error in httpd.conf.

If you changed DocumentRoot, be sure that the corresponding <Directory...> setting has been changed to exactly the same directory. If those don't match up, Apache will not work. Check the Apache error logs as discussed in *What Can Go Wrong?* in the *Installing Apache* section previously.

If you see nothing, try using the View Source menu item in your browser. If that shows <?php phpinfo();?> then Apache is serving up the web page, but it is not correctly configured to hand it off to PHP first. So one of the three ScriptAlias/AddType/Action lines you added to httpd.conf must be wrong. Or you forgot to stop and restart Apache. Apache only reads httpd.conf once, when it starts. You must restart Apache for changes to httpd.conf to take effect.

If you see nothing and the View Source menu item isn't available, check the Apache error logs and review the httpd.conf settings. Something is probably configured badly enough to crash Apache.

If all else fails, try commenting out the three lines you've added to httpd.conf by inserting a # sign in front of them, and restart Apache. If Apache then works, but PHP doesn't, at least you know it's something in those three lines that is wrong or your installation of PHP itself.

If you cannot find anything wrong with what you typed in httpd.conf, test that PHP itself is working properly independent of the browser. Open up an MS DOS console window and change directory to the C:\php or wherever your PHP is installed. Then type:

```
php C:\Program Files\Apache Group\Apache\htdocs\phpinfo.php
```

You may need to substitute a different path if your phpinfo.php file is in a different directory.

php.exe is invoked, as you are actually handing it your phpinfo.php file to work with. PHP should execute the code in that file and return HTML. If PHP displays the HTML, then you know php.exe is working properly, and that there is something wrong in the way Apache is invoking PHP. Review your httpd.conf settings once again.

If php.exe works by itself, and Apache works without the three lines to invoke PHP, but they don't work together, your mistake has to be in those three lines.

Post-Installation

When you install PHP, a file named php.ini gets installed with it. Your phpinfo.php page should also describe where PHP is looking for your php.ini file. Make a backup copy of this php.ini file and make sure that phpinfo.php is looking in the place where your php.ini file exists.

If there simply is no php.ini file anywhere, look for a php.ini-dist file and copy that over to php.ini in the appropriate directory listed in phpinfo.php.

Open php.ini file with a text editor, and skim through it to see all the settings. You may want to experiment a little with some of them, and you may want to do some research online at http://php.net/ to see what a particular setting does.

First, if you are not an experienced programmer, it is recommended to increase error_reporting one notch to E_ALL. Find the Error handling and logging section, and change the line that reads:

```
error_reporting = E_ALL & ~E_NOTICE ;show all errors, except for notices
```

to the following:

```
error_reporting = E_ALL ; show all errors
```

The point of this `error_reporting` setting is: imagine you have typed some PHP code, and imagine you spelled a variable name incorrectly like this:

```
$name = "Rich";
print ($nam);
```

Notice how $nam is missing an 'e' at the end in the second line. With the default settings, PHP does not complain when you do this. By changing the `error_reporting` to E_ALL, you have instructed PHP to help you more. PHP will notice problems like this, and complain about variables you use that don't have anything in them, as well as some other minor errors you are likely to make as a beginner.

There is no significant performance decrease for this change. You are likely to catch typos and logical errors much earlier with `error_reporting` cranked up to E_ALL.

Next, search through `php.ini` for the `Paths and Directories` section. Change the `extension_dir` to:

```
extension_dir = "C:/php/extensions"
```

Search through `php.ini` for the `Dynamic Extensions` section. Each line that looks like:

```
;extension=php_XXX.dll
```

is a third-party software package that you may find useful to integrate with PHP and utilize in your web pages.

PHP usually comes with the extension software (`php_XXX.dll`) for the following:

- ❏ MySQL
- ❏ PostgreSQL
- ❏ Interbase
- ❏ ODBC
- ❏ FTP
- ❏ Calendar
- ❏ BCMath
- ❏ COM
- ❏ PCRE
- ❏ Sessions
- ❏ WDDX
- ❏ XML

You still need to download, install, and test the actual third-party software in most cases. The php_XXX.dll files just tell PHP how to communicate with third-party software. When PHP is required to interface with the new technologies, they only need to write the software to build this bridge.

PHP's side of the bridge, and how to hook that bridge in to PHP, is very well-defined and clear-cut. The bridge itself is usually easy. The only question remaining is how easy the other software makes it to hook in a bridge to their software. Some make it easy. Some make it virtually impossible. At least PHP's side of the bridge, and the bridge itself, are usually straightforward, and that's two thirds of the battle.

To enable an extension, you will need to do four things:

❑   Install, configure, and test the third-party software.

❑   Make sure your extension_dir is set correctly.

❑   Make sure you have the DLL file named in php.ini in that extension_dir.

❑   Uncomment the line by removing the semicolon at the beginning.

❑   ISAPI users need to stop/restart Apache, since PHP under ISAPI only reads php.ini when Apache starts up. Under CGI, PHP reads php.ini for every web page hit.

After that, you simply write some PHP code to test your extension.

Upgrading To ISAPI

If you absolutely must use ISAPI to get the performance you need, here are some tips:

❑   Back up your working CGI-style httpd.conf file, as well as your php.ini file.

❑   Follow the instructions that came with PHP for installing ISAPI. Make sure to comment out the Action line in httpd.conf that you added for the CGI installation.

❑   Comment all extensions you may have enabled in php.ini by adding a semicolon to the beginning of the lines.

❑   Stop and restart Apache, and stress test the core PHP functions you will be using. Core functions are functions that are not in the extensions you just commented. Make sure you test every function you are currently using or plan to use under heavy load. The issues with ISAPI appear only under multi-thread conditions involving heavy load. A simple viewing of phpinfo() in a single browser is not a valid test: you need to have multiple browsers hitting the same functions at the same time to have a valid test.

❑   Stop Apache and edit php.ini. Uncomment one, but only one, of the extensions you use. Restart Apache, and now stress test every function you use or plan to use in that extension. Once again, it is important to test the functions under heavy load, as noted above.

❑   Repeat the fifth step for each and every extension you use, with regression testing of all the extensions and core functionality every time. You may find functions, or even whole extensions, that simply haven't been made thread-safe for use with ISAPI.

Installing on UNIX-Like Systems

You should have made the decision to install PHP as a module as opposed to a CGI. If installing from sourcecode is a nightmare for you, and you really want to use an Install Wizard, there are some viable UNIX-based options. One of them is available from NuSphere at http://www.nusphere.com/. It installs PHP/Apache/MySQL/Perl quite easily.

You have still more flexibility if you compile from source. We'll be demonstrating this here. First, we'll install, configure, and test Apache to be sure we have a working web server. Then, we'll install, configure, and test PHP and integrate it with Apache.

While we won't be configuring Apache to use PHP as a CGI, we will still be compiling PHP as a standalone binary (CGI) because it's extremely useful for quickly running PHP scripts from a command line without firing up a web browser, and for cron jobs – executing PHP scripts for routine, periodic, scheduled events.

Installing Apache

First, download the latest stable version from http://apache.org/ and store it in your /usr/local/src directory. You probably still want to stick with version 1.3.x unless you are certain PHP is compatible. There is some lag between Apache 2.0 and PHP compatibility.

Next, untar or ungzip it:

```
tar -xzf apache_1.x.xx.xx.tar.gz
```

Change into the sourcecode directory and configure:

```
cd apache_1.x.xx.xx
./configure --prefix=/usr/local/apache/ \
 --enable-shared=max \
 --enable-module=most
```

If everything goes well, you should then do:

```
make
make install
```

To start Apache up:

```
/usr/local/apache/bin/apachectl start
```

You should now be able to use a browser on your computer to surf to your web site:

```
lynx http://localhost/
```

If you are running X Windows, you can use a browser that's more graphics-oriented than lynx such as Konquerer or Netscape.

If `localhost` doesn't work, try `127.0.0.1` instead. `127.0.0.1` is always your local computer. If `127.0.0.1` works, and `localhost` doesn't, edit `/etc/hosts` and add a line that reads:

```
127.0.0.1 localhost
```

You can also verify whether Apache is running by doing:

```
ps auxwww | grep httpd
```

You should see five different processes running, all named `httpd`. That's perfectly normal. When Apache starts up, it actually runs multiple copies of itself. Thus, with the five processes, you now have Apache running. Now Apache is ready and waiting for five people to visit your web site, and Apache will be able to very quickly service their requests. Apache also automatically adjusts how many servers are ready and waiting to conform to other settings in `httpd.conf` (see below). You probably don't need to change the number of servers unless you are an ISP and know what you are doing.

When you need to stop Apache, or stop/restart Apache, you can use one of these commands:

```
/usr/local/apache/bin/apachectl stop
/usr/local/apache/bin/apachectl restart
```

Apache Post-Installation

Much of Apache's behavior is controlled by the `httpd.conf` file, which should be in `/usr/local/apache/conf` directory.

Make a backup copy of this file, and use your favorite editor to review the settings. If you don't like the default `DocumentRoot` where all your web pages will go, which is `/usr/local/apache/htdocs`, you can alter the setting in `<Directory ...>`. You'll also be editing this `httpd.conf` later to integrate PHP with Apache.

You can skim through the file to see what other options Apache has available for you. It's handy to have some kind of idea what's in there if you run into trouble later or want to implement a new feature on your web server that requires altering Apache configuration.

If you have Apache working properly, you probably want Apache to be always running and automatically start on boot. You can add a script in `/etc/rc.d/init.d` and name it `apache` with the following line in it:

```
/usr/local/apache/bin/apachectl start
chmod 755 /etc/rc.d/init.d/apache
```

You'll need to change the path if you have deviated from the above instructions. Then, in `/etc/rc.d/rc3.d` you can do:

```
ln -s ../init.d/apache S99apache
```

The first two commands create an executable shell script that is available for any of the 6 different boot levels. Usually your computer boots into level 3, but in case of an emergency, you can boot into level 1 where fewer applications are started. The last command creates a soft link in the `rc3.d` directory. Commands in that directory that begin with 'S' are executed at boot time in alphabetical order. Since you want Apache to start rather late in the process, we started it with S99 rather than a lower number.

If you are not running Linux, or even if you are running a different distribution of Linux, the directory structure for the `rc.d`, `init.d`, and `rcX.d` directories (where X is 1 through 6) might be different, but most Linux distributions have a similar setup.

What Can Go Wrong?

If `configure` or `make` fails, search the Apache web site for your operating system. There may be some information to help you install Apache.

If `configure`, `make`, and `make install` seemed to go OK, but Apache doesn't start, check the `error_log` file which is in `/usr/local/apache/logs/error_log` by default.

If Apache works fine when you start it by hand but not during reboot, do this right after a reboot:

```
tail /var/log/messages
```

The `tail` command shows you the last 10 lines from the file supplied. `/var/log/messages` is a log of operating system messages. It should have some messages about Apache's attempt to start up. If you see absolutely nothing about Apache, you may need to view more lines using:

```
tail -n 20 /var/log/messages
```

This will show the last 20 lines rather than the default 10. You can also add | `grep apache` to the end of the command to search for `apache` in the output.

If nothing at all appears, check the file name and link in `/etc/rc.d` that you created.

Installing PHP

You're finally ready to actually configure, compile, and install PHP now. First download the latest stable source release from http://php.net/ into your `/usr/local/src` directory. Untar/ungzip the files:

```
tar -xzf php-4.x.x.tar.gz
```

Change into the PHP directory:

```
cd php-4.x.x
```

You could jump right in and do `./configure`. However, if you added any other third-party software other than Apache to your computer, and want to integrate PHP with it, you may find yourself reconfiguring the other third-party software. In the meantime, the `configure` command that you used to install PHP will have scrolled off the screen. Rather than try to dig back through your history list to find it, we're going to create a shell script to configure PHP. Create a file named `config.sh` and put the following lines in it:

```
./configure \
--with-apxs=/usr/local/apache/bin/apxs
```

If you have any other PHP extensions you want to add, put them in on separate lines with \ at the end. Make sure the last line does not end with a \.

Note that `--with-apxs` is used instead of `--with-apache`. This allows you to install PHP as a dynamic shared object (DSO) instead of a static module. This means you'll be able to upgrade PHP, without having to recompile Apache just because you want to upgrade PHP. If you use `--with-apache`, you'll need to re-compile Apache when it's time to upgrade PHP. If you are using a web server other than Apache, you'll need to substitute something appropriate for `--with-apxs`.

Save the file and do:

```
chmod 755 config.sh
```

You can now do:

```
./config.sh
```

This attempts to configure PHP.

If you are following these instructions without deviations, everything should work just fine. If you deviated a little to add more features, the script will let you easily configure with and without them by editing the `config.sh` file and deleting or adding lines.

Pay attention as `configure` prints out various status messages: some of the configure flags (for any third-party software) might fail, but the configure itself will continue successfully.

At the end, you should see a message in an ASCII art box:

```
+--------------------------------------------------------------------+
| License:|
| This software is subject to the PHP License, available in this|
| distribution in the file LICENSE> By continuing this installation|
| process, you are bound by the terms of this license agreement.|
| If you do not agree with the terms of this license, you must abort|
| the installation process at this point.|
+--------------------------------------------------------------------+
```

What Can Go Wrong?

Sometimes you might see error messages such as these:

```
*** WARNING ***
Your /usr/local/apache/bin/apxs script is most likely broken.
```

```
*** WARNING ***
You will be compiling the CGI version of PHP without any redirection checking...
```

If you see any of these, then don't go ahead with `make` and `make install`, as they will not work.

The first one actually gives you a link to the PHP FAQ. It's unlikely that you'll see this one, unless you managed to install an old version of Apache, or used the path to the old version of the `apxs` script instead of the one you installed above.

The second one about compiling the CGI version of PHP without redirection checking means that you misspelled (or forgot) the `--with-apxs` line in your `config.sh` file above, or that you provided an invalid path to the `apxs` script.

If you are trying to use other PHP extensions and are having trouble with `configure`, review the `config.log` file for any error messages that seem related to the problem. Also double-check your spelling in `config.sh` as well as any directories. You can do:

```
configure --help | less
```

Use the space bar and arrow keys to get a very brief overview of the options to `configure`. It's very easy to misspell one of the directives or a path or forget to use a path. Also note that some directives require other directives to be useful. `--with-gd`, for example, is rather pointless without at least one of `--with-jpeg-dir`, `--with-png-dir`, or `--with-tiff-dir` since GD itself relies on the underlying graphics technologies to do its job.

If you attempt to do `config.sh` again, do `rm config.cache` and `make clean` first:

```
rm config.cache
make clean
./config.sh
```

If you don't do this, `configure` is likely to remember the old, broken settings and simply repeat the same mistake as before, ignoring the new directives you have provided.

Similarly, if you don't do `make clean`, the compiler might not realize that you've altered the `configure` settings, and think that the files it has already compiled can be safely skipped. This actually is usually correct, since the files that were successfully compiled are usually fine, but since there are rare occurrences where it matters, it's safer to do `make clean` anyway. It will take longer to compile, but you'll know you're getting what you asked for this time with the new `configure` options:

```
make distclean
```

This should completely reset everything to exactly the way it was after you untared/ungzipped PHP; the way it was before you did `configure`, `make`, or `make install`.

Compiling PHP

After you've successfully done `config.sh`, you can do:

```
make
```

If that works without error, do:

```
make install
```

If `configure` seemed to work, but `make` failed, then you need to review `config.sh` and try again. The output from `make` seems rather obscure, but you can usually tell which extension was being compiled at the time that it failed. You can do `make` again and it will probably quickly repeat the error message. It doesn't need to recompile all the files it compiled already, and will rush through them and get right to the one that didn't work. But be sure to do `make clean` (see above) when you're ready to try again with different settings.

What Can Go Wrong?

If things are going wrong at this point, and are not already covered in this book, then copy the error message, and go to http://php.net/support.php. Then click on the link to the PHP-General mailing list archive and paste in your error message to the search engine. Also read the FAQ at http://php.net/FAQ.php.

Post-Installation

In your PHP source directory is a file named `php.ini-dist`. You may need to copy this file to `php.ini` in the appropriate place, which by default is `/usr/local/lib/php.ini`.

If there is already a `php.ini` file there from a previous installation, make a backup copy of the old `php.ini`, and copy the `php.ini-dist` file from your PHP source directory to that location:

```
cp /usr/local/src/php-4.xx.xx/php.ini-dist \
/usr/local/lib/php.ini
```

Open up this `php.ini` file and skim through it to see all the settings. You may want to experiment a little with some of them, and you may want to do some research online at http://php.net/.

Increase the `error_reporting` level one notch to `E_ALL`. Find the `Error handling and logging` section, and change the lines accordingly as described in the *Post-Installation* section under *Installing on Windows* above.

Integrating PHP with Apache

`make install` should have copied a file named `libphp4.so` into the directory `/usr/local/apache/libexec`. To get Apache to use that module and enable PHP, you'll need to edit `httpd.conf`:

```
pico /usr/local/apache/conf/httpd.conf
```

Search for the `Dynamic Shared Object (DSO) Support` section. If you can't find that, then search from the top for `LoadModule`.

Near the end of the `LoadModule` section, there should be one that looks something like this:

```
LoadModule php4_module libexec/libphp4.so
```

If it isn't there, add it. If there are other `LoadModule` lines there, make your line look as much like them as possible. If they have `libexec` for the modules that are in `/usr/local/apache/libexec`, you should also have one. If they don't, you shouldn't either.

This line is what actually loads in the `libphp4.so` that you just compiled and installed. Search for the directive `AddType` and then find the part that looks like this:

```
# And for PHP 4.x use:
#
# AddType application/x-httpd-php .php
# AddType application/x-httpd-php-source .phps
```

Uncomment the first `AddType` line by removing the "#" at the beginning. If you want to make it easy for you to give users your PHP scripts, also uncomment the second `AddType` line. The purpose of these lines is to tell Apache that files that end in `.php` are of the MIME-type `application/x-httpd-php`. The `libphp4.so` loaded from the `LoadModule` line will have told Apache that PHP knows how to handle files whose MIME-type is `application/x-httpd-php`. Similarly, the MIME-type `application/x-httpd-php-source` can be set up so PHP can display color-coded syntax-aware PHP sourcecode for files that end in `.phps`.

> Just using `AddType` with `.phps` does not expose your PHP sourcecode. You'll need to create `.phps` files that are copies of your `.php` files to expose your PHP source. A good way to do this is not to copy the files, but to make symbolic links to the actual sourcecode files that you want to expose to the public. Sample code to do this on a widespread basis is available at **http://php.net/**. There is a link at the bottom of every single page on the PHP web site, which gives you access to the PHP sourcecode that drives the PHP site. If you want to see how the experts code PHP, try clicking on that link on the more interesting pages.

While you're at it, you may wish to add more extensions to the first `AddType` line. For example, if you have, or download, old `.php3` scripts and add them to your web site, it would be nice if the old `.php3` scripts were sent through PHP. You may also want to have **all** your `.htm` and `.html` files sent through PHP. Forcing all HTML files through PHP will only slow down their response time by about 5%, and will allow you to add PHP features in all sorts of places in existing HTML files without having to re-link your web site.

It also does not allow users to know you are using PHP, and to not have to remember to use `.php` at the end of URLs. Instead, they still use `.htm` or `.html`, which they are used to.

Thus, your `AddType` line may end up looking like:

```
AddType application/x-httpd-php .php .htm .html .php3
```

The order of the file endings is irrelevant, and you can add as many as you like that make sense. For example, it usually doesn't make a lot of sense to pass `.mp3` files through PHP. In fact, that will probably break your MP3 URLs, since PHP will add some default headers. However, you might actually find some **extremely** old PHP sourcecode that still works but has `.phtml` as the file extension. So, you might even want to add `.phtml` at the end of that `AddType` line.

Once you've made and reviewed all your changes, save the `httpd.conf` file, and restart Apache. Then, create a text file in `DocumentRoot/prophpxml` named `phpinfo.php` with this single line in it:

```
<?php
phpinfo();
?>
```

No HTML tags are needed: the `phpinfo()` function will return a large page giving you a complete status report on your PHP installation. If you go to **http://localhost/prophpxml/phpinfo.php**, you should see something like this:

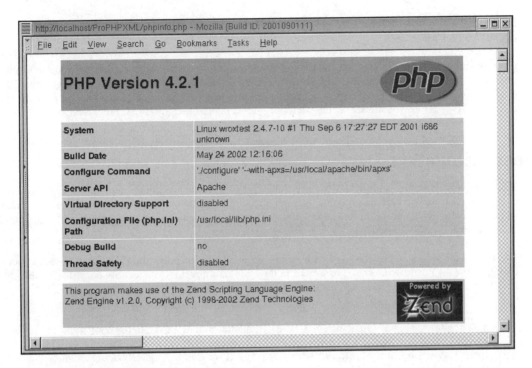

What Can Go Wrong?

Here is the real crux of the installation. Hopefully, you've followed the instructions exactly, and not added anything or deviated from them, and everything worked.

However, if that's not the case, you may be getting an error message on the console from Apache as it tries to start up. If that involves some extension you added to PHP, go back and delete it from `config.sh`, and do `rm config.cache`, make `clean`, `./config.sh`, and repeat the `make` and `make install` steps.

If there is no message on the console, there may be one in `/usr/local/apache/logs/error_log`. Apache writes all useful messages there, so take a look at the end of that file:

```
tail /usr/local/apache/logs/error_log
```

If you deviated from the configuration of Apache, this `error_log` may be somewhere else on your hard drive.

Stop and restart Apache. Apache only reads `httpd.conf` when it starts up, so changes don't take effect unless you stop and restart it. Just to be sure, stop Apache, do `ps auxwww | grep httpd` to be sure it's really gone, and then start it again. Then try to surf to your `phpinfo()` page again.

If you see a 404 Document not found error, or something similar, you probably spelled the file name or URL for `phpinfo.php` incorrectly, or placed the file somewhere other than the `DocumentRoot`. Check the `DocumentRoot` setting in `httpd.conf`.

If you get a 500 Internal Server Error you probably have a typo in `httpd.conf`. Check the Apache `error_log` for a message.

If you see nothing in the browser, use the View Source menu to see what might be there. If you see `<?php phpinfo();?>` in the browser, then Apache is not correctly configured in `httpd.conf` to know that PHP handles documents of MIME-type `applications/x-httpd-php` and that files that end in `.php` are of that MIME-type. Thus, you are seeing the file as if it were a regular text (or HTML) file. Review the `httpd.conf` settings that involve PHP.

Post-Installation

While you are compiling, you might as well compile PHP as a standalone binary (also known as CGI). Even though we are installing PHP as a module, and not a CGI, the standalone binary is incredibly useful. With it, you can execute PHP scripts from the command-line, and thus you can use `cron` to schedule PHP scripts to be executed at specific times/dates.

There are some security issues involved with using PHP as a CGI. Including the PHP binary we are about to create, **inside** the `DocumentRoot` directory or in the `cgi-bin` directory is a security hazard. You already have PHP as a module, and have no need for PHP as a CGI.

> **You might want to have PHP installed, both as a module and as a CGI, in the same web server. In that case, read the security chapter of the online PHP manual carefully (http://www.php.net/manual/en/security.php). If you don't completely understand that, do not put a PHP CGI binary in your web directory. It would cause a fairly big security hole.**

To compile PHP as a standalone binary, change into the PHP source directory, and copy the `config.sh` script to `config.cgi.sh`:

```
cd /usr/local/src/php-4.x.xx.xx
cp config.sh config.cgi.sh
```

Edit the new `config.cgi.sh` file and delete the line that has `--with-apxs=` in it.

We won't be putting the resulting binary in the `DocumentRoot`. For security reasons, you should add the following two lines in case you do that when you've been told not to:

```
--enable-discard-path \
--enable-force-cgi-redirect \
```

Be sure that all the lines **except** the last line have \ at the end.

> **Never copy the php binary into the web tree or cgi-bin directories.**

Save and quit, and then do:

```
./config.cgi.sh
make
```

This should create a file named `php` in the source directory.

You can then safely copy that file to the `/usr/bin/` directory or `/usr/sbin/` or `/usr/local/bin/` or wherever you feel is most appropriate. If you want to be consistent with your operating system, use `whereis perl` to find out where the `perl` binary is, and put the `php` binary in the same directory.

If you have no idea what `perl` is, and are getting really confused by the appropriateness of directories, just use `/usr/bin/`.

Now you can do something like this:

```
php /usr/local/apache/htdocs/phpinfo.php
```

You've just executed the PHP script `phpinfo.php` from the command-line with no web server involved. This is exceedingly handy for all sorts of things. If you can't think of any right now, they will occur to you once you start creating the scripts.

You can also create PHP scripts that are executables, just like Perl. Try this: change to your home directory (just use `cd` with no path) and create a file named `hello` (no extension needed) with the following in it:

```
#!/usr/bin/php -q
<?php
print ("Hello World\n");
?>
```

Save and quit your editor, and then do:

```
chmod 755 hello
./hello
```

By making this file executable (`chmod 755 hello`) you have created a standalone command, just like `cd` and `ls` and all the other UNIX commands we've been using, but your command starts off with `#!/usr/bin/php -q` which tells it to use your PHP binary to execute the instructions.

The `-q` part stands for quiet, which tells PHP not to output some default headers for the Web that it usually sends out. You can try it without the `-q` to see the difference if you like. `print()` prints the text inside the quotes to the console. The `\n` bit adds a new line at the end. Without it, your shell prompt ends up on the same line as the Hello World output.

Further Resources

Wrox.com

If the tutorials do not produce the expected results repeatedly, there are a number of other sources to consult for more information and assistance. For all three software packages, an online discussion forum is available on the Wrox web site at: http://p2p.wrox.com/ or http://www.lamplists.com/.

PHP.net

These pages on the PHP web site might prove useful:

❑   http://php.net/FAQ.php. The PHP FAQ.

❑   http://php.net/funcref/. Follow each link in the body and read the overview.

❑   http://www.php.net/langref/. Read this whole section both before and after this book.

You also should be aware of the PHP mailing lists at http://php.net/support.php. These lists are archived, and most are a gateway to a newsgroup.

Most are also available in a digest mode with one big message, much less frequently, which contains all the messages since the last digest. PHP-General digest is twice daily, but is still a very large e-mail.

The PHP mailing lists are very pleasant (generally) and extremely tolerant of newbie questions, but do follow these rules:

❑   Read the manual

❑   Re-read the FAQs before you send your question

❑   Search the archives before you send your question

❑   Use the right list

❑   Do not cross-post

❑   Use an intelligent subject

Be sure you read the descriptions of the various mailing lists before you choose to send an e-mail to one of them. Install questions should go to PHP-Install, not PHP-General. Similarly, database-related questions should go to one of the various database-related mailing lists. PHP-QA is not "Question and Answer", but is an internal list for "Quality Assurance" by the PHP quality assurance team.

If you are looking for some help in how to code a particular feature, then search the code archives.

There are literally thousands, maybe even millions, of sample snippets of PHP scripts on innumerable PHP-related web site, that you can read, copy, and modify to help you learn and to help you develop your web site. In some cases, entire applications and libraries are available that you can use to build a good web site with some nice features, without you having to write a single line of PHP code. Some good code samples are generally on the sites linked from: http://php.net/links.php.

If you ever find yourself in the situation of not understanding the documentation, but you eventually figure out how something works, you are **strongly** encouraged to contribute a note to this system. Intellectual contributions of thousands of users are what make open-source projects such as PHP flourish.

The PHP documentation team routinely goes through these notes and incorporates them into the official documentation, throws out the bad posts, and, in some cases, leaves the best notes as-is for posterity. So your contribution could easily end up as a part of the official documentation.

Zend.com

❑   http://zend.com/. Commercial products for enterprise-class PHP users.

php4win.de

❑   http://www.php4win.de/. A great place to get help with Windows-based PHP.

❑   http://forum.dynapolis.com/. A Macintosh-specific Apache/MySQL/PHP mailing list and web forum.

Printed Resources Available from Wrox

❑   Beginning PHP4 *(ISBN 1-861003-73-0)*

❑   Professional PHP4 *(ISBN 1-861006-91-8)*

❑   Professional Apache 2.0 *(ISBN 1-86100-7-22-1)*

Apache

❑   http://httpd.apache.org/docs/. The complete Apache documentation.

❑   http://httpd.apache.org/docs/misc/FAQ.html. A very comprehensive FAQ on everything Apache.

Summary

You have now successfully installed and tested PHP and Apache on your computer. You have a working Apache web server, with PHP enabled. You also have a command-line php binary available to execute PHP scripts independent of the web server.

SAX 2.0: The Simple API for XML

This appendix contains the specification of the SAX interface, version 2.0, some of which is explained in Chapter 5. It is taken largely verbatim from the definitive specification to be found at http://www.saxproject.org/.

The classes and interfaces are described in alphabetical order. Within each class, the methods are also listed alphabetically.

The SAX specification is in the public domain – see the web site quoted above for a statement of policy on copyright. Essentially the policy is: do what you like with it, copy it as you wish, but no one accepts any liability for errors or omissions.

The SAX distribution also includes two other helper classes:

❑ LocatorImpl is an implementation of the Locator interface

❑ ParserFactory is a class that enables you to load a parser identified by a parameter at run-time

The documentation of these helper classes is not included here. For this, and for SAX sample applications, see the SAX distribution available at http://www.saxproject.org/apidoc/org/xml/sax/helpers/package-summary.html.

SAX2 contains complete namespace support, which is available by default from any XMLReader object. An XML reader can also optionally supply raw XML 1.0 names.

An XML reader is fully configurable: it is possible to attempt to query or change the current value of any feature or property. Features and properties are identified by fully-qualified URIs, and parties are free to invent their own names for new extensions.

The ContentHandler and Attributes interfaces are similar to the deprecated DocumentHandler and AttributeList interfaces, but they add support for namespace-related information. ContentHandler also adds a callback for skipped entities, and Attributes adds the ability to look up an attribute's index by name.

The following interfaces have been deprecated:

- ❑ org.xml.sax.Parser
- ❑ org.xml.sax.DocumentHandler
- ❑ org.xml.sax.AttributeList
- ❑ org.xml.sax.HandlerBase

The following interfaces and classes have been added to SAX2.0:

- ❑ org.xml.sax.XMLReader (replaces Parser)
- ❑ org.xml.sax.XMLFilter (extends XMLReader)
- ❑ org.xml.sax.ContentHandler (replaces DocumentHandler)
- ❑ org.xml.sax.Attributes (replaces AttributeList)
- ❑ org.xml.sax.SAXNotSupportedException (extends SAXException)
- ❑ org.xml.sax.SAXNotRecognizedException (extends SAXException)

Class and Interface Hierarchies

The following diagrams show the class and interface hierarchies of SAX 2.0. We covered some of these classes in Chapter 5, although many were left out as they are outside the scope of what we needed to know. However, this appendix covers them all, and further details can be found at the SAX web site.

Class Hierarchy

```
- class java.lang.Object
    - class org.xml.sax.helpers.AttributeListImpl
            (implements org.xml.sax.AttributeList)
    - class org.xml.sax.helpers.AttributesImpl
            (implements org.xml.sax.Attributes)
        - class org.xml.sax.ext.Attributes2Impl
                (implements org.xml.sax.ext.Attributes2)
    - class org.xml.sax.helpers.DefaultHandler
            (implements org.xml.sax.ContentHandler, org.xml.sax.DTDHandler,
            org.xml.sax.EntityResolver, org.xml.sax.ErrorHandler)
        - class org.xml.sax.ext.DefaultHandler2
                (implements org.xml.sax.ext.DeclHandler,
                org.xml.sax.ext.EntityResolver2,
                org.xml.sax.ext.LexicalHandler)
    - class org.xml.sax.HandlerBase
            (implements org.xml.sax.DocumentHandler,
            org.xml.sax.DTDHandler, org.xml.sax.EntityResolver,
            org.xml.sax.ErrorHandler)
    - class org.xml.sax.InputSource
    - class org.xml.sax.helpers.LocatorImpl
            (implements org.xml.sax.Locator)
        - class org.xml.sax.ext.Locator2Impl
                (implements org.xml.sax.ext.Locator2)
    - class org.xml.sax.helpers.NamespaceSupport
    - class org.xml.sax.helpers.ParserAdapter
            (implements org.xml.sax.DocumentHandler, org.xml.sax.XMLReader)
    - class org.xml.sax.helpers.ParserFactory
    - class java.lang.Throwable
            (implements java.io.Serializable)
        - class java.lang.Exception
            - class org.xml.sax.SAXException
                - class org.xml.sax.SAXNotRecognizedException
                - class org.xml.sax.SAXNotSupportedException
                - class org.xml.sax.SAXParseException
    - class org.xml.sax.helpers.XMLFilterImpl
            (implements org.xml.sax.ContentHandler,
            org.xml.sax.DTDHandler, org.xml.sax.EntityResolver,
            org.xml.sax.ErrorHandler, org.xml.sax.XMLFilter)
    - class org.xml.sax.helpers.XMLReaderAdapter
            (implements org.xml.sax.ContentHandler, org.xml.sax.Parser)
    - class org.xml.sax.helpers.XMLReaderFactory
```

Interface Hierarchy

> interface org.xml.sax.**AttributeList**
> interface org.xml.sax.**Attributes**
> interface org.xml.sax.ext.**Attributes2**
> interface org.xml.sax.**ContentHandler**
> interface org.xml.sax.ext.**DeclHandler**
> interface org.xml.sax.**DocumentHandler**
> interface org.xml.sax.**DTDHandler**
> interface org.xml.sax.**EntityResolver**
> interface org.xml.sax.ext.**EntityResolver2**
> interface org.xml.sax.**ErrorHandler**
> interface org.xml.sax.ext.**LexicalHandler**
> interface org.xml.sax.**Locator**
> interface org.xml.sax.ext.**Locator2**
> interface org.xml.sax.**Parser**
> interface org.xml.sax.**XMLReader**
> interface org.xml.sax.**XMLFilter**

Interface org.xml.sax.Attributes (SAX 2.0 – Replaces AttributeList)

Interface for a list of XML attributes – this interface allows access to a list of attributes in three different ways:

❑   By attribute index

❑   By namespace-qualified name

❑   By qualified (prefixed) name

The list will not contain attributes that were declared #IMPLIED but not specified in the start tag. It will also not contain attributes used as namespace declarations (xmlns*) unless the http://xml.org/sax/features/namespace-prefixes feature is set to True (it is False by default).

If the http://xml.org/sax/features/namespaces/ feature is False, access by namespace-qualified names may not be available.

This interface replaces the now-deprecated SAX 1.0 AttributeList interface, which does not contain namespace support. In addition to namespace support, it adds the getIndex() methods (below).

The order of attributes in the list is unspecified, and will vary from implementation to implementation:

Method	Description
public int getIndex(String qName)	Looks up the index of an attribute by XML 1.0-qualified name.
	Parameters:
	qName – the qualified (prefixed) name.

Method	Description
	Returns: The index of the attribute, or -1 if it does not appear in the list.
`public int getIndex(String uri, String localName)`	Looks up the index of an attribute by namespace name.
	Parameters:
	`uri` – the namespace URI, or the empty string if the name has no namespace URI.
	`localName` – the attribute's local name.
	Returns: The index of the attribute, or -1 if it does not appear in the list.
`public int getLength()`	Returns the number of attributes in the list. Once you know the number of attributes, you can iterate through the list.
	Returns: The number of attributes in the list.
`public String getLocalName(int index)`	Looks up an attribute's local name by index.
	Parameters:
	`index` – the attribute index (zero-based).
	Returns: The local name, or the empty string if namespace processing is not being performed, or NULL if the index is out of range.
`public String getQName(int index)`	Look up an attribute's XML 1.0 qualified name by index.
	Parameters:
	`index` – the attribute index (zero-based).
	Returns: The XML 1.0-qualified name, or the empty string if none is available, or NULL if the index is out of range.
`public String getType(int index)`	Looks up an attribute's type by index.
	The attribute type is one of the strings 'CDATA', 'ID', 'IDREF', 'IDREFS', 'NMTOKEN', 'NMTOKENS', 'ENTITY', 'ENTITIES', or 'NOTATION' (always in uppercase).
	If the parser has not read a declaration for the attribute, or if the parser does not report attribute types, then it must return the value 'CDATA' as stated in the XML 1.0 Recommendation (clause 3.3.3, 'Attribute-Value Normalization').
	For an enumerated attribute that is not a notation, the parser will report the type as 'NMTOKEN'.

Table continued on following page

Method	Description
	Parameters: `index` – the attribute index (zero-based). **Returns:** The attribute's type as a string, or NULL if the index is out of range.
`public String getType(String qName)`	Looks up an attribute's type by XML 1.0-qualified name. See `getType(int)` for a description of the possible types. **Parameters:** `qName` – the XML 1.0-qualified name. **Returns:** The attribute type as a string, or NULL if the attribute is not in the list or if qualified names are not available.
`public String getType(String uri, String localName)`	Looks up an attribute's type by namespace name. See `getType(int)` for a description of the possible types. **Parameters:** `uri` – the namespace URI, or the empty string if the name has no namespace URI. `localName` – the local name of the attribute. **Returns:** The attribute type as a string, or NULL if the attribute is not in the list or if namespace processing is not being performed.
`public String getURI(int index)`	Looks up an attribute's namespace URI by index. **Parameters:** `index` – the attribute index (zero-based). **Returns:** The namespace URI, or the empty string if none is available, or NULL if the index is out of range.
`public String getValue(int index)`	Looks up an attribute's value by index. If the attribute value is a list of tokens (IDREFS, ENTITIES, or NMTOKENS), the tokens will be concatenated into a single string with each token separated by a single space. **Parameters:** `index` – the attribute index (zero-based). **Returns:** The attribute's value as a string, or NULL if the index is out of range.
`public String getValue(String qName)`	Looks up an attribute's value by XML 1.0-qualified name. See `getValue(int)` for a description of the possible values.

Method	Description
	Parameters:
	qName – the XML 1.0-qualified name.
	Returns: The attribute value as a string, or NULL if the attribute is not in the list or if qualified names are not available.
`public String getValue(String uri, String localName)`	Looks up an attribute's value by namespace name.
	See `getValue(int)` for a description of the possible values.
	Parameters:
	uri – the namespace URI, or the empty string if the name has no namespace URI.
	localName – the local name of the attribute.
	Returns: The attribute value as a string, or NULL if the attribute is not in the list.

Interface org.xml.sax.ext.Attributes2

The `Attributes2` interface and its `Attributes2Impl` implementation class expose those attributes that were specified in the source text, rather than defaulted through the DTD. This is important when implementing DOM as a clean layer over SAX.

This is a SAX2 extension to augment the per-attribute information provided through `Attributes`. If an implementation supports this extension, the attributes provided in `ContentHandler.startElement()` will implement this interface, and the http://xml.org/sax/features/use-attributes2/ feature flag will have the value TRUE.

This is a new extension that extends the class `Attributes`:

Method	Description
`public boolean isSpecified(int index)`	Returns TRUE unless the attribute value was provided by DTD defaulting.
	Parameters:
	index – the attribute index (zero-based).
	Returns: TRUE if the value was found in the XML text, FALSE if the value was provided by DTD defaulting.
	Throws: ArrayIndexOutOfBoundsException – when the supplied index does not identify an attribute.
`public boolean isSpecified( String qName)`	Returns TRUE unless the attribute value was provided by DTD defaulting.

Table continued on following page

Method	Description
	Parameters:
	qName – The XML 1.0-qualified name.
	Returns: TRUE if the value was found in the XML text, FALSE if the value was provided by DTD defaulting.
	Throws: IllegalArgumentException – when the supplied name does not identify an attribute.
public boolean isSpecified(String uri, String localName)	Returns TRUE unless the attribute value was provided by DTD defaulting.
	Parameters:
	uri – The namespace URI, or the empty string if the name has no namespace URI.
	localName – The attribute's local name.
	Returns: TRUE if the value was found in the XML text, FALSE if the value was provided by DTD defaulting.
	Throws: IllegalArgumentException – when the supplied names do not identify an attribute.

Interface org.xml.sax.AttributeList – Deprecated

An AttributeList is a collection of attributes appearing on a particular start tag. The parser supplies the DocumentHandler with an AttributeList as part of the information available on the startElement event. The AttributeList is essentially a set of name-value pairs for the supplied attributes; if the parser has analyzed the DTD it may also provide information about the type of each attribute.

The AttributeListImpl helper class provides a convenience implementation for use by parser or application writers:

Method	Description
public int getLength()	Returns the number of attributes in this list.
	The SAX parser may provide attributes in any arbitrary order, regardless of the order in which they were declared or specified. The number of attributes may be zero.
	Returns: The number of attributes in the list.

Method	Description
public String getName(int index)	Return the name of an attribute in this list (by position). The names must be unique: the SAX parser shall not include the same attribute twice. Attributes without values (those declared #IMPLIED without a value specified in the start tag) will be omitted from the list. If the attribute name has a namespace prefix, the prefix will still be attached. **Parameters:** index – the index of the attribute in the list (starting at 0). **Returns:** The name of the indexed attribute, or NULL if the index is out of range.
public String getType(int index)	Returns the type of an attribute in the list (by position). The attribute type is one of the strings "CDATA", "ID", "IDREF", "IDREFS", "NMTOKEN", "NMTOKENS", "ENTITY", "ENTITIES", or "NOTATION" (always in uppercase). If the parser has not read a declaration for the attribute, or if the parser does not report attribute types, then it must return the value "CDATA" as stated in the XML 1.0 Recommendation (clause 3.3.3, "Attribute-Value Normalization"). For an enumerated attribute that is not a notation, the parser will report the type as "NMTOKEN". **Parameters:** index – the index of the attribute in the list (starting at 0). **Returns:** The attribute type as a string, or NULL if the index is out of range.
public String getType(String name)	Returns the type of an attribute in the list (by name). The return value is the same as the return value for getType(int). If the attribute name has a namespace prefix in the document, the application must include the prefix here. **Parameters:** name – the name of the attribute. **Returns:** The attribute type as a string, or NULL if no such attribute exists.

Table continued on following page

781

Method	Description
`public String getValue(int index)`	Returns the value of an attribute in the list (by position).
	If the attribute value is a list of tokens (`IDREFS`, `ENTITIES`, or `NMTOKENS`), the tokens will be concatenated into a single string separated by whitespace.
	Parameters:
	`index` – the index of the attribute in the list (starting at 0).
	Returns: The attribute value as a string, or `NULL` if the index is out of range.
`public String getValue(String name)`	Returns the value of an attribute in the list (by name).
	The return value is the same as the return value for `getValue(int)`.
	If the attribute name has a namespace prefix in the document, the application must include the prefix here.
	Parameters:
	`name` – the name of the attribute.
	Returns: The attribute value as a string, or `NULL` if no such attribute exists.

Interface org.xml.sax.ContentHandler (SAX 2.0 – Replaces DocumentHandler)

Every SAX application is likely to include a class that implements this interface, either directly or by subclassing the supplied class `HandlerBase`.

This is the main interface that most SAX applications implement. If the application needs to be informed of basic parsing events, it implements this interface and registers an instance with the SAX parser using the `setContentHandler()` method. The parser uses the instance to report basic document-related events like the start and end of elements and character data.

The order of events in this interface is very important, and mirrors the order of information in the document itself. For example, all of an element's content (character data, processing instructions, and/or subelements) will appear, in order, between the `startElement` event and the corresponding `endElement` event.

This interface is similar to the now-deprecated SAX 1.0 `DocumentHandler` interface, but it adds support for namespaces and for reporting skipped entities (in non-validating XML processors).

Implementers should note that there is also a Java class `ContentHandler` in the `java.net` package; that means that it's probably a bad idea to do the following (more like a feature than a bug anyway, as `import ... *` is a sign of bad programming):

```
import java.net.*;
import org.xml.sax.*;
```

Method	Description
public void characters (char[] ch, int start, int length)	Receives notification of character data.
	The parser will call this method to report each chunk of character data. SAX parsers may return all contiguous character data in a single chunk, or they may split it into several chunks; however, all of the characters in any single event must come from the same external entity so that the locator provides useful information.
	The application must not attempt to read from the array outside the specified range.
	Note that some parsers will report whitespace in element content using the ignorableWhitespace method rather than this one (validating parsers must do so).
	Parameters:
	ch – the characters from the XML document.
	start – the start position in the array.
	length – the number of characters to read from the array.
	Throws: SAXException – any SAX exception, possibly wrapping another exception.
public void endDocument ()	Receives notification of the end of a document.
	The SAX parser will invoke this method only once, and it will be the last method invoked during the parse. The parser shall not invoke this method until it has either abandoned parsing (because of an unrecoverable error) or reached the end of input.
	Throws: SAXException – any SAX exception, possibly wrapping another exception.
public void endElement(String namespaceURI, String localName, String qName)	Receives notification of the end of an element.
	The SAX parser will invoke this method at the end of every element in the XML document; there will be a corresponding startElement event for every endElement event (even when the element is empty).
	For information on the names, see startElement.

Table continued on following page

Method	Description
	Parameters:
	`uri` – the namespace URI, or the empty string if the element has no namespace URI or if namespace processing is not being performed.
	`localName` – the local name (without prefix), or the empty string if namespace processing is not being performed.
	`qName` – the qualified XML 1.0 name (with prefix), or the empty string if qualified names are not available.
	Throws: `SAXException` – any SAX exception, possibly wrapping another exception.
`public void endPrefixMapping (String prefix)`	Ends the scope of a prefix-URI mapping.
	See `startPrefixMapping` for details. This event will always occur after the corresponding `endElement` event, but the order of `endPrefixMapping` events is not otherwise guaranteed.
	Parameters:
	`prefix` – the prefix that was being mapped.
	Throws: `SAXException` – the client may throw an exception during processing.
`public void ignorableWhitespace( char[] ch, int start, int length)`	Receives notification of ignorable whitespace in element content.
	Validating parsers must use this method to report each chunk of whitespace in element content (see the W3C XML 1.0 Recommendation, section 2.10): non-validating parsers may also use this method if they are capable of parsing and using content models.
	SAX parsers may return all contiguous whitespace in a single chunk, or they may split it into several chunks; however, all of the characters in any single event must come from the same external entity, so that the locator provides useful information.
	The application must not attempt to read from the array outside the specified range.
	Parameters:
	`ch` – the characters from the XML document.
	`start` – the start position in the array.
	`length` – the number of characters to read from the array.
	Throws: `SAXException` – any SAX exception, possibly wrapping another exception.

Method	Description
public void processing Instruction(String target, String data)	Receives notification of a processing instruction.
	The parser will invoke this method once for each processing instruction found: note that processing instructions may occur before or after the main document element.
	A SAX parser must never report an XML declaration (XML 1.0, section 2.8) or a text declaration (XML 1.0, section 4.3.1) using this method.
	Parameters:
	target – the processing instruction target.
	data – the processing instruction data, or NULL if none was supplied. The data does not include any whitespace separating it from the target.
	Throws: SAXException – any SAX exception, possibly wrapping another exception.
public void setDocumentLocator(L ocator locator)	Receives an object for locating the origin of SAX document events.
	SAX parsers are strongly encouraged (though not absolutely required) to supply a locator: if they do so, they must supply the locator to the application by invoking this method before invoking any of the other methods in the ContentHandler interface.
	The locator allows the application to determine the end position of any document-related event, even if the parser is not reporting an error. Typically, the application will use this information for reporting its own errors (such as character content that does not match an application's business rules). The information returned by the locator is probably not sufficient for use with a search engine.
	Note that the locator will return correct information only during the invocation of the events in this interface. The application should not attempt to use it at any other time.
	Parameters:
	locator – an object that can return the location of any SAX document event.
public void skippedEntity(String name)	Receives notification of a skipped entity.
	The parser will invoke this method once for each entity skipped. Non-validating processors may skip entities if they have not seen the declarations (because, for example, the entity was declared in an external DTD subset). All processors may skip external entities, depending on the values of the http://xml.org/sax/features/external-general-entities/ and the http://xml.org/sax/features/external-parameter-entities/ properties.

Table continued on following page

Method	Description
	Parameters:
	name – the name of the skipped entity. If it is a parameter entity, the name will begin with '%', and if it is the external DTD subset, it will be the string "[dtd]".
	Throws: SAXException – any SAX exception, possibly wrapping another exception.
`public void startDocument()`	Receives notification of the beginning of a document.
	The SAX parser will invoke this method only once, before any other methods in this interface or in DTDHandler (except for setDocumentLocator).
	Throws: SAXException – any SAX exception, possibly wrapping another exception.
`public void startElement(String namespaceURI, String localName, String qName, Attributes atts)`	Receives notification of the beginning of an element.
	The parser will invoke this method at the beginning of every element in the XML document; there will be a corresponding endElement event for every startElement event (even when the element is empty). All of the element's content will be reported, in order, before the corresponding endElement event.
	This event allows up to three name components for each element:
	❑ The namespace URI
	❑ The local name
	❑ The qualified (prefixed) name
	Any or all of these may be provided, depending on the values of the http://xml.org/sax/features/namespaces/ and the http://xml.org/sax/features/namespace-prefixes/ properties:
	The namespace URI and local name are required when the namespaces property is TRUE (the default), and are optional when the namespaces property is FALSE (if one is specified, both must be).
	The qualified name is required when the namespace-prefixes property is TRUE, and is optional when the namespace-prefixes property is FALSE (the default).
	Note that the attribute list provided will contain only attributes with explicit values (specified or defaulted): #IMPLIED attributes will be omitted. The attribute list will contain attributes used for namespace declarations (xmlns* attributes) only if the http://xml.org/sax/features/namespace-prefixes property is TRUE (it is FALSE by default, and support for a TRUE value is optional).

Method	Description
	Parameters:
	`uri` – the namespace URI, or the empty string if the element has no namespace URI or if namespace processing is not being performed.
	`localName` – the local name (without prefix), or the empty string if namespace processing is not being performed.
	`qName` – the qualified name (with prefix), or the empty string if qualified names are not available.
	`atts` – the attributes attached to the element. If there are no attributes, it shall be an empty `Attributes` object.
	Throws: SAXException – any SAX exception, possibly wrapping another exception.
`public void startPrefixMapping(String prefix, String uri)`	Begins the scope of a prefix-URI namespace mapping.
	The information from this event is not necessary for normal namespace processing: the SAX XML reader will automatically replace prefixes for element and attribute names when the http://xml.org/sax/features/namespaces/ feature is TRUE (the default).
	There are cases, however, when applications need to use prefixes in character data or in attribute values, where they cannot safely be expanded automatically; the `start/endPrefixMapping` event supplies the information to the application to expand prefixes in those contexts itself, if necessary.
	Note that `start/endPrefixMapping` events are not guaranteed to be properly nested relative to each-other: all `startPrefixMapping` events will occur before the corresponding `startElement` event, and all `endPrefixMapping` events will occur after the corresponding `endElement` event, but their order is not otherwise guaranteed.
	There should never be `start/endPrefixMapping` events for the "xml" prefix, since it is pre-declared and immutable.
	Parameters:
	`prefix` – the namespace prefix being declared.
	`uri` – the namespace URI the prefix is mapped to.
	Throws: SAXException – the client may throw an exception during processing.

Table continued on following page

Interface org.xml.sax.ext.DeclHandler

This interface is a SAX2 extension handler for DTD declaration events. This is an optional extension handler to provide more complete information about DTD declarations in an XML document. XML readers are not required to recognize this handler, and it is not part of core-only SAX2 distributions.

Note that data-related DTD declarations (unparsed entities and notations) are already reported through the DTDHandler interface. Implementers must note that if they are using the declaration handler together with a lexical handler, all of the events will occur between the startDTD and the endDTD events.

To set the DeclHandler for an XML reader, use the setProperty method with the property name http://xml.org/sax/properties/declaration-handler/ and an object implementing this interface (or NULL) as the value. If the reader does not report declaration events, it will throw a SAXNotRecognizedException when we attempt to register the handler:

Method	Description
public void attributeDecl(String eName, String aName, String type, String Mode, String value)	Reports an attribute type declaration. Only the effective (first) declaration for an attribute will be reported. The type will be one of the strings "CDATA", "ID", "IDREF", "IDREFS", "NMTOKEN", "NMTOKENS", "ENTITY", "ENTITIES", a parenthesized token group with the separator "|" and all whitespace removed, or the word "NOTATION" followed by a space followed by a parenthesized token group with all whitespace removed. The value will be the value as reported to applications, appropriately normalized and with entity and character references expanded. **Parameters:** eName – The name of the associated element. aName – The name of the attribute. type – A string representing the attribute type. mode – A string representing the attribute defaulting mode ("#IMPLIED", "#REQUIRED", or "#FIXED") or NULL if none of these applies. value – A string representing the attribute's default value, or NULL if there is none. **Throws:** SAXException – The application may raise an exception.

Method	Description
`public void elementDecl( String name, String model)`	Reports an element type declaration. The content model will consist of the string "EMPTY", the string "ANY", or a parenthesized group, optionally followed by an occurrence indicator. The model will be normalized so that all parameter entities are fully resolved and all whitespace is removed, and will include the enclosing parentheses. Other normalization (such as removing redundant parentheses or simplifying occurrence indicators) is at the discretion of the parser. **Parameters:** `name` – The element type name. `model` – The content model as a normalized string. **Throws:** `SAXException` – The application may raise an exception.
`public void externalEntityDecl(String name, String publicId, String systemId)`	Reports a parsed external entity declaration. Only the effective (first) declaration for each entity will be reported. **Parameters:** `name` – The name of the entity. If it is a parameter entity, the name will begin with '%'. `publicId` – The declared public identifier of the entity, or `NULL` if none was declared. `systemId` – The declared system identifier of the entity. **Throws:** `SAXException` – The application may raise an exception.
`public void internalEntityDecl(String name, String value)`	Reports an internal entity declaration. Only the effective (first) declaration for each entity will be reported. All parameter entities in the value will be expanded, but general entities will not. **Parameters:** `name` – The name of the entity. If it is a parameter entity, the name will begin with '%'. `value` – The replacement text of the entity. **Throws:** `SAXException` – The application may raise an exception.

Interface org.xml.sax.DocumentHandler – Deprecated

Every SAX application is likely to include a class that implements this interface, either directly or by subclassing the supplied class `HandlerBase`.

This is the main interface that most SAX applications implement: if the application needs to be informed of basic parsing events, it implements this interface and registers an instance with the SAX parser using the `setDocumentHandler()` method. The parser uses the instance to report basic document-related events like the start and end of elements and character data.

The order of events in this interface is very important, and mirrors the order of information in the document itself. For example, all of an element's content (character data, processing instructions, and/or sub-elements) will appear, in order, between the `startElement` event and the corresponding `endElement` event.

Application writers who do not want to implement the entire interface can derive a class from `HandlerBase`, which implements the default functionality; parser writers can instantiate `HandlerBase` to obtain a default handler. The application can find the location of any document event using the locator interface supplied by the parser through the `setDocumentLocator()` method:

Method	Description
`public void characters(char ch[], int start, int length)`	Receives notification of character data.
	The parser will call this method to report each chunk of character data. SAX parsers may return all contiguous character data in a single chunk, or they may split it into several chunks; however, all of the characters in any single event must come from the same external entity, so that the locator provides useful information.
	The application must not attempt to read from the array outside the specified range *and must not attempt to write to the array.*
	Note that some parsers will report whitespace using the `ignorableWhitespace()` method rather than this one (validating parsers *must* do so).
	Parameters:
	`ch` – the characters from the XML document.
	`start` – the start position in the array.
	`length` – the number of characters to read from the array.
	Throws: `SAXException` – any SAX exception, possibly wrapping another exception.
`public void endDocument()`	Receives notification of the end of a document.
	The SAX parser will invoke this method only once *for each document,* and it will be the last method invoked during the parse. The parser shall not invoke this method until it has either abandoned parsing (because of an unrecoverable error) or reached the end of input.
	Throws: `SAXException` – any SAX exception, possibly wrapping another exception.

Method	Description
`public void` `endElement(String name)`	Receives notification of the end of an element. The SAX parser will invoke this method at the end of every element in the XML document; there will be a corresponding `startElement()` event for every `endElement()` event (even when the element is empty). If the element name has a namespace prefix, the prefix will still be attached to the name. **Parameters:** `name` – the element type name. **Throws:** `SAXException` – any SAX exception, possibly wrapping another exception.

`public void`
`ignorableWhitespace(`
`char ch[], int start, int`
`length)`
	Receives notification of ignorable whitespace in element content.
	
	Validating parsers must use this method to report each chunk of ignorable whitespace (see the W3C XML 1.0 Recommendation, section 2.10): non-validating parsers may also use this method if they are capable of parsing and using content models.
	
	SAX parsers may return all contiguous whitespace in a single chunk, or they may split it into several chunks; however, all of the characters in any single event must come from the same external entity, so that the locator provides useful information.
	
	The application must not attempt to read from the array outside the specified range.
	
	Parameters:
	
	`ch` – the characters from the XML document.
	
	`start` – the start position in the array.
	
	`length` – the number of characters to read from the array.
	
	Throws: `SAXException` – any SAX exception, possibly wrapping another exception.

`public void`
`processingInstruction(`
`String target, String`
`data)`
	Receives notification of a processing instruction.
	
	The parser will invoke this method once for each processing instruction found: note that processing instructions may occur before or after the main document element.
	
	A SAX parser should never report an XML declaration (XML 1.0, section 2.8) or a text declaration (XML 1.0, section 4.3.1) using this method.

Table continued on following page

Method	Description
	Parameters:
	`target` – the processing instruction target.
	`data` – the processing instruction data, or NULL if none was supplied.
	Throws: SAXException – any SAX exception, possibly wrapping another exception.
`public void setDocumentLocator( Locator locator)`	Receives an object for locating the origin of SAX document events.
	A SAX parser is strongly encouraged (though not absolutely required) to supply a locator: if it does so, it must supply the locator to the application by invoking this method before invoking any of the other methods in the `DocumentHandler` interface.
	The locator allows the application to determine the end position of any document-related event, even if the parser is not reporting an error. Typically, the application will use this information for reporting its own errors (such as character content that does not match an application's business rules). The information returned by the locator is probably not sufficient for use with a search engine.
	Note that the locator will return correct information only during the invocation of the events in this interface. The application should not attempt to use it at any other time.
	Parameters:
	`locator` – an object that can return the location of any SAX document event.
`public void startDocument()`	Receives notification of the beginning of a document.
	The SAX parser will invoke this method only once *for each document*, before any other methods in this interface or in `DTDHandler` (except for `setDocumentLocator`).
	Throws: SAXException – any SAX exception, possibly wrapping another exception.

Method	Description

`public void startElement(`
`String name,`
`AttributeList atts)`
	Receives notification of the beginning of an element.
	
	The parser will invoke this method at the beginning of every element in the XML document; there will be a corresponding `endElement()` event for every `startElement()` event (even when the element is empty). All of the element's content will be reported, in order, before the corresponding `endElement()` event.
	
	If the element name has a namespace prefix, the prefix will still be attached. Note that the attribute list provided will contain only attributes with explicit values (specified or defaulted): `#IMPLIED` attributes will be omitted.
	
	Parameters:
	
	`name` – the element type name.
	
	`atts` – the attributes attached to the element, if any.
	
	Throws: `SAXException` – any SAX exception, possibly wrapping another exception.

Interface org.xml.sax.DTDHandler

This interface should be implemented by the application if it wants to receive notification of events related to the DTD. SAX does not provide full details of the DTD, but this interface is available because without it, it would be impossible to access notations and unparsed entities referenced in the body of the document.

Notations and unparsed entities are rather specialized facilities in XML, so most SAX applications will not need to use this interface.

If a SAX application needs information about notations and unparsed entities, then the application implements this interface and registers an instance with the SAX parser using the parser's `setDTDHandler()` method. The parser uses the instance to report notation and unparsed entity declarations to the application.

The SAX parser may report these events in any order, regardless of the order in which the notations and unparsed entities were declared; however, all DTD events must be reported after the document handler's `startDocument` event, and before the first `startElement` event.

It is up to the application to store the information for future use (perhaps in a hash table or object tree). If the application encounters attributes of type "NOTATION", "ENTITY", or "ENTITIES", it can use the information that it obtained through this interface to find the entity and/or notation corresponding with the attribute value.

The `HandlerBase` class provides a default implementation of this interface, which simply ignores the events:

Method	Description
`public void notationDecl(String name, String publicId, String systemId)`	Receives notification of a notation declaration event. It is up to the application to record the notation for later reference, if necessary. If a system identifier is present, and it is a URL, the SAX parser must resolve it fully before passing it to the application. **Parameters:** `name` – the notation name. `publicId` – the notation's public identifier, or NULL if none was given. `systemId` – the notation's system identifier, or NULL if none was given. **Throws:** SAXException – any SAX exception, possibly wrapping another exception.
`public void unparsedEntityDecl(String name, String publicId, String systemId, String notationName)`	Receives notification of an unparsed entity declaration event. Note that the notation name corresponds to a notation reported by the `notationDecl()` event. It is up to the application to record the entity for later reference, if necessary. If the system identifier is a URL, the parser must resolve it fully before passing it to the application. **Parameters:** `name` – the unparsed entity's name. `publicId` – the entity's public identifier, or NULL if none was given. `systemId` – the entity's system identifier (it must always have one). `notationName` – the name of the associated notation. **Throws:** SAXException – any SAX exception, possibly wrapping another exception.

Interface org.xml.sax.EntityResolver

When the XML document contains references to external entities, the URL will normally be analyzed automatically by the parser: the relevant file will be located and parsed where appropriate. This interface allows an application to override this behavior. This might be needed, for example, if you want to retrieve a different version of the entity from a local server, or if the entities are cached in memory or stored in a database, or if the entity is really a reference to variable information such as the current date.

When the parser needs to obtain an entity, it calls this interface, which can respond by supplying any `InputSource` object.

If a SAX application needs to implement customized handling for external entities, it must implement this interface and register an instance with the SAX parser using the parser's `setEntityResolver()` method.

The parser will then allow the application to intercept any external entities (including the external DTD subset and external parameter entities, if any) before including them.

Many SAX applications will not need to implement this interface, but it will be especially useful for applications that build XML documents from databases or other specialized input sources, or for applications that use URI types other than URLs.

The application can also use this interface to redirect system identifiers to local URIs or to look up replacements in a catalog (possibly by using the public identifier).

The `HandlerBase` class implements the default behavior for this interface, which is simply always to return `NULL` (to request that the parser use the default system identifier):

Method	Description
`public InputSource resolveEntity(String publicId, String systemId)`	Allows the application to resolve external entities.
	The parser will call this method before opening any external entity except the top-level document entity (including the external DTD subset, external entities referenced within the DTD, and external entities referenced within the document element): the application may request that the parser resolve the entity itself, that it use an alternative URI, or that it use an entirely different input source.
	Application writers can use this method to redirect external system identifiers to secure and/or local URIs, to look up public identifiers in a catalogue, or to read an entity from a database or other input source (including, for example, a dialog box).
	If the system identifier is a URL, the SAX parser must resolve it fully before reporting it to the application.

Table continued on following page

Method	Description
	Parameters:
	`publicId` – the public identifier of the external entity being referenced, or `NULL` if none was supplied.
	`systemId` – the system identifier of the external entity being referenced.
	Returns:
	An `InputSource` object describing the new input source, or `NULL` to request that the parser open a regular URI connection to the system identifier.
	Throws:
	`SAXException` – any SAX exception, possibly wrapping another exception.
	`IOException` – a Java-specific IO exception, possibly the result of creating a new `InputStream` or `Reader` for the `InputSource`.

Interface org.xml.sax.ext.EntityResolver2

This class extends the interface `EntityResolver`. It provides an extended interface for mapping external entity references to input sources, or providing a missing external subset. The `XMLReader.setEntityResolver()` method is used to provide implementations of this interface to parsers. When a parser uses the methods in this interface, the `EntityResolver2.resolveEntity()` method (in this interface) is used instead of the older (SAX 1.0) `EntityResolver.resolveEntity()` method.

If a SAX application requires the customized handling that this interface defines for external entities, it must ensure that it uses an `XMLReader` with the http://xml.org/sax/features/use-entity-resolver2/ feature flag set to `TRUE` (which is its default value when the feature is recognized). If that flag is unrecognized, or its value is `FALSE`, or the resolver does not implement this interface, then only the `EntityResolver` method will be used.

That supports three categories of application that modify entity resolution. Old style applications won't know about this interface; they will provide an `EntityResolver`. Transitional Mode provides an `EntityResolver2` and automatically gets the benefit of its methods in any systems (parsers or other tools) supporting it, due to polymorphism. Both Old Style and Transitional Mode applications will work with any SAX2 parser. New-style applications will fail to run except on SAX2 parsers that support this particular feature. They will insist that feature flag have a value of `TRUE`, and the `EntityResolver2` implementation they provide might throw an exception if the original SAX 1.0 style entity resolution method is invoked:

Method	Description
`public InputSource getExternalSubset (String name, String baseURI)`	Allows applications to provide an external subset for documents that don't explicitly define one. Documents with `DOCTYPE` declarations that omit an external subset can thus augment the declarations available for validation, entity processing, and attribute processing (normalization, defaulting, and reporting types including ID). This augmentation is reported through the `startDTD()` method as if the document text had originally included the external subset; this callback is made before any internal subset data or errors are reported.

	This method can also be used with documents that have no `DOCTYPE` declaration. When the root element is encountered, but no `DOCTYPE` declaration has been seen, this method is invoked. If it returns a value for the external subset, that root element is declared to be the root element, giving the effect of splicing a `DOCTYPE` declaration at the end of the Prolog of a document that could not otherwise be valid. The sequence of parser callbacks in that case logically resembles this:
	
	... comments and PIs from the Prolog (as usual)
	
	`startDTD ("rootName", source.getPublicId (), source.getSystemId ());`
	
	`startEntity(" [dtd] ");`
	
	... declarations, comments, and PIs from the external subset
	
	`endEntity (" [dtd] ");`
	
	`endDTD();`
	
	... then the rest of the document (as usual)
	
	`startElement (..., "rootName", ...);`
	
	Note that the `InputSource` gets no further resolution. Implementations of this method may wish to invoke `resolveEntity()` to gain benefits such as use of local caches of DTD entities. Also, this method will never be used by a (non-validating) processor that is not including external parameter entities.

	Uses for this method include facilitating data validation when interoperating with XML processors that would always require undesirable network accesses for external entities, or which for other reasons adopt a "no DTDs" policy. Non-validation motives include forcing documents to include DTDs so that attributes are handled consistently. For example, an XPath processor needs to know which attributes have type `"ID"` before it can process a widely used type of reference.
	Warning: Returning an external subset modifies the input document. By providing definitions for general entities, it can make a malformed document appear to be well formed.

Table continued on following page

Method	Description
	Parameters:
	name – Identifies the document root element. This name comes from a DOCTYPE declaration (where available) or from the actual root element.
	baseURI – The document's base URI, serving as an additional hint for selecting the external subset. This is always an absolute URI, unless it is null because the XMLReader was given an InputSource without one.
	Returns: An InputSource object describing the new external subset to be used by the parser, or null to indicate that no external subset is provided.
	Throws:
	SAXException – Any SAX exception, possibly wrapping another exception.
	IOException – Probably indicating a failure to create a new InputStream or Reader, or an illegal URL.
public InputSource resolveEntity(String name, String publicId, String baseURL, String systemId)	Allows applications to map references to external entities into input sources, or tell the parser it should use conventional URI resolution. This method is only called for external entities which have been properly declared. This method provides more flexibility than the EntityResolver interface, supporting implementations of more complex catalogue schemes such as the one defined by the OASIS XML Catalogs specification.
	Parsers configured to use this resolver method will call it to determine the input source to use for any external entity being included because of a reference in the XML text. That excludes the document entity, and any external entity returned by getExternalSubset(). When a (non-validating) processor is configured not to include a class of entities (parameter or general) through use of feature flags, this method is not invoked for such entities.
	Note that the entity naming scheme used here is the same one used in the LexicalHandler, or in the ContentHandler.skippedEntity() method.

Method	Description
	Parameters: name – Identifies the external entity being resolved. Either " [dtd] " for the external subset, or a name starting with "%" to indicate a parameter entity, or else the name of a general entity. This is never null when invoked by a SAX2 parser. publicId – The public identifier of the external entity being referenced (normalized as required by the XML specification), or NULL if none was supplied. baseURI – The URI with respect to which relative system IDs are interpreted. This is always an absolute URI, unless it is NULL (likely because the XMLReader was given an InputSource without one). This URI is defined by the XML specification to be the one associated with the "<" starting the relevant declaration. systemId – The system identifier of the external entity being referenced; either a relative or absolute URI. This is never NULL when invoked by a SAX2 parser; only declared entities, and any external subset, are resolved by such parsers. **Returns:** An InputSource object describing the new input source to be used by the parser. Returning NULL directs the parser to resolve the system ID against the base URI and open a connection to the resulting URI. **Throws:** SAXException – Any SAX exception, possibly wrapping another exception. IOException – Probably indicating a failure to create a new InputStream or Reader, or an illegal URL.

Interface org.xml.sax.ErrorHandler

You may implement this interface in your application if you want to take special action to handle errors. There is a default implementation provided within the HandlerBase class.

If a SAX application needs to implement customized error handling, it must implement this interface and then register an instance with the SAX parser using the parser's setErrorHandler() method. The parser will then report all errors and warnings through this interface.

The parser shall use this interface instead of throwing an exception: it is up to the application whether to throw an exception for different types of errors and warnings. Note, however, that there is no requirement that the parser continue to provide useful information after a call to fatalError (in other words, a SAX driver class could catch an exception and report a fatalError).

The `HandlerBase` class provides a default implementation of this interface, ignoring warnings and recoverable errors and throwing a `SAXParseException` for fatal errors. An application may extend that class rather than implementing the complete interface itself:

Method	Description
`public void error(SAXParseException exception)`	Receives notification of a recoverable error.
	This corresponds to the definition of "error" in section 1.2 of the W3C XML 1.0 Recommendation. For example, a validating parser would use this callback to report the violation of a validity constraint. The default behavior is to take no action.
	The SAX parser must continue to provide normal parsing events after invoking this method: it should still be possible for the application to process the document through to the end. If the application cannot do so, then the parser should report a fatal error even if the XML 1.0 Recommendation does not require it to do so.
	Parameters:
	`exception` – the error information encapsulated in a SAX parse exception.
	Throws:
	`SAXException` – any SAX exception, possibly wrapping another exception.
`public void fatalError(SAXParseException exception)`	Receives notification of a non-recoverable error.
	This corresponds to the definition of "fatal error" in section 1.2 of the W3C XML 1.0 Recommendation. For example, a parser would use this callback to report the violation of a well-formedness constraint.
	The application must assume that the document is unusable after the parser has invoked this method, and should continue (if at all) only for the sake of collecting additional error messages: in fact, SAX parsers are free to stop reporting any other events once this method has been invoked.
	Parameters:
	`exception` – the error information encapsulated in a SAX parse exception.
	Throws:
	`SAXException` – any SAX exception, possibly wrapping another exception.

Method	Description
`public void warning(` `SAXException exception)`	Receives notification of a warning.
	SAX parsers will use this method to report conditions that are not errors or fatal errors as defined by the XML 1.0 Recommendation. The default behavior is to take no action.
	The SAX parser must continue to provide normal parsing events after invoking this method: it should still be possible for the application to process the document through to the end.
	Parameters:
	`exception` – the warning information encapsulated in a SAX parse exception.
	Throws:
	`SAXException` – any SAX exception, possibly wrapping another exception.

Interface org.xml.sax.ext.LexicalHandler

This is a SAX2.0 extension for handling Lexical events. This is an optional extension handler for SAX2 to provide lexical information about an XML document, such as comments and CDATA section boundaries. XML readers are not required to recognize this handler, and it is not part of core-only SAX2.0 distributions.

The events in the lexical handler apply to the entire document, not just to the document element, and all lexical handler events must appear between the content handler's `startDocument` and `endDocument` events.

To set the `LexicalHandler` for an XML reader, use the `setProperty` method with the property name http://xml.org/sax/properties/lexical-handler/ and an object implementing this interface (or `NULL`) as the value. If the reader does not report lexical events, it will throw a `SAXNotRecognizedException` when we attempt to register the handler:

Method	Description
`public void endCDATA()`	Reports the end of a CDATA section.
	Throws:
	`SAXException` – The application may raise an exception.

Table continued on following page

Method	Description
`public void endDTD()`	Reports the end of DTD declarations. This method is intended to report the end of the `DOCTYPE` declaration; if the document has no `DOCTYPE` declaration, this method will not be invoked. **Throws:** `SAXException` – The application may raise an exception.
`public void endEntity(String name)`	Reports the end of an entity. **Parameters:** `name` – The name of the entity that is ending. **Throws:** `SAXException` – The application may raise an exception.
`public void startCDATA()`	Reports the start of a CDATA section. The contents of the CDATA section will be reported through the regular `characters` event; this event is intended only to report the boundary. **Throws:** `SAXException` – The application may raise an exception.
`public void startDTD(String name, String publicId, String systemId)`	Report the start of DTD declarations, if any. This method is intended to report the beginning of the `DOCTYPE` declaration; if the document has no `DOCTYPE` declaration, this method will not be invoked. All declarations reported through `DTDHandler` or `DeclHandler` events must appear between the `startDTD` and `endDTD` events. Declarations are assumed to belong to the internal DTD subset unless they appear between `startEntity` and `endEntity` events. Comments and processing instructions from the DTD should also be reported between the `startDTD` and `endDTD` events, in their original order of (logical) occurrence; they are not required to appear in their correct locations relative to `DTDHandler` or `DeclHandler` events, however. Note that the `start/endDTD` events will appear within the `start/endDocument` events from `ContentHandler` and before the first `startElement` event.

Method	Description
	Parameters: name – The document type name. publicId – The declared public identifier for the external DTD subset, or NULL if none was declared. systemId – The declared system identifier for the external DTD subset, or NULL if none was declared. Note that this is not resolved against the document base URI. **Throws:** SAXException – The application may raise an exception.
public void startEntity(String name)	Reports the beginning of some internal and external XML entities. The reporting of parameter entities (including the external DTD subset) is optional, and SAX2.0 drivers that report LexicalHandler events may not implement it; you can use the http://xml.org/sax/features/lexical-handler/parameter-entities/ feature to query or control the reporting of parameter entities. General entities are reported with their regular names, parameter entities have '%' prepended to their names, and the external DTD subset has the pseudo-entity name "[dtd]". When a SAX2.0 driver is providing these events, all other events must be properly nested within start/end entity events. There is no additional requirement that events from DeclHandler or DTDHandler be properly ordered. Note that skipped entities will be reported through the skipped entity event, which is part of the ContentHandler interface. Because of the streaming event model that SAX uses, some entity boundaries cannot be reported under any circumstances: ❑ General entities within attribute values ❑ Parameter entities within declarations These will be silently expanded, with no indication of where the original entity boundaries were. Note also that the boundaries of character references (which are not really entities anyway) are not reported. All start/endEntity events must be properly nested.

Table continued on following page

Method	Description
	Parameters:
	name – The name of the entity. If it is a parameter entity, the name will begin with '%', and if it is the external DTD subset, it will be "[dtd]".
	Throws:
	SAXException – The application may raise an exception.

Class org.xml.sax.HandlerBase – Deprecated

This class is supplied with SAX itself: it provides default implementations of most of the methods that would otherwise need to be implemented by the application. If you write classes in your application as subclasses of HandlerBase, you need only code those methods where you want something other than the default behavior.

This class implements the default behavior for four SAX interfaces: EntityResolver, DTDHandler, DocumentHandler, and ErrorHandler.

Application writers can extend this class when they need to implement only part of an interface; parser writers can instantiate this class to provide default handlers when the application has not supplied its own.

Note that the use of this class is optional.

In the description below, only the behavior of each method is described. For the parameters and return values, see the corresponding interface definition:

Method	Description
`public void characters(char ch[], int start, int length) throws SAXException`	By default, do nothing. Application writers may override this method to take specific actions for each chunk of character data (such as adding the data to a node or buffer, or printing it to a file).
`public void comment(char[] ch, int start, int length)`	Reports an XML comment anywhere in the document. This callback will be used for comments inside or outside the document element, including comments in the external DTD subset (if read). Comments in the DTD must be properly nested inside start/endDTD and start/endEntity events (if used).

Method	Description
	Parameters:
	`ch` – An array holding the characters in the comment.
	`start` – The starting position in the array.
	`length` – The number of characters to use from the array.
	Throws:
	`SAXException` – The application may raise an exception.
`public void endDocument()` `throws SAXException`	Receives notification of the end of the document. By default, do nothing. Application writers may override this method in a subclass to take specific actions at the beginning of a document (such as finalizing a tree or closing an output file).
`public void endElement(String` `name) throws SAXException`	By default, do nothing. Application writers may override this method in a subclass to take specific actions at the end of each element (such as finalizing a tree node or writing output to a file).

`public void`
`error(SAXParseException e)`
`throws SAXException`
	The default implementation does nothing. Application writers may override this method in a subclass to take specific actions for each error, such as inserting the message in a log file or printing it to the console.

`public void fatalError(`
`SAXParseException e) throws`
`SAXException`
	The default implementation throws a `SAXParseException`. Application writers may override this method in a subclass if they need to take specific actions for each fatal error (such as collecting all of the errors into a single report): in any case, the application must stop all regular processing when this method is invoked, since the document is no longer reliable, and the parser may no longer report parsing events.

`public void`
`ignorableWhitespace(char`
`ch[], int start, int length)`
`throws SAXException`
	By default, do nothing. Application writers may override this method to take specific actions for each chunk of ignorable whitespace (such as adding data to a node or buffer, or printing it to a file).

`public void`
`notationDecl(String name,`
`String publicId, String`
`systemId)`
	By default, do nothing. Application writers may override this method in a subclass if they wish to keep track of the notations declared in a document.

`public void`
`processingInstruction(String`
`target, String data) throws`
`SAXException`
	By default, do nothing. Application writers may override this method in a subclass to take specific actions for each processing instruction, such as setting status variables or invoking other methods.

Table continued on following page

805

Method	Description
`public InputSource resolveEntity(String publicId, String systemId) throws SAXException`	Always return NULL, so that the parser will use the system identifier provided in the XML document. This method implements the SAX default behavior: application writers can override it in a subclass to do special translations such as catalog lookups or URI redirection.
`public void setDocumentLocator(Locator locator)`	By default, do nothing. Application writers may override this method in a subclass if they wish to store the locator for use with other document events.
`public void startDocument() throws SAXException`	By default, do nothing. Application writers may override this method in a subclass to take specific actions at the beginning of a document (such as allocating the root node of a tree or creating an output file).
`public void startElement(String name, AttributeList attributes) throws SAXException`	By default, do nothing. Application writers may override this method in a subclass to take specific actions at the start of each element (such as allocating a new tree node or writing output to a file).
`public void unparsedEntityDecl(String name, String publicId, String systemId, String notationName)`	By default, do nothing. Application writers may override this method in a subclass to keep track of the unparsed entities declared in a document.
`public void warning(SAXParseException e) throws SAXException`	The default implementation does nothing. Application writers may override this method in a subclass to take specific actions for each warning, such as inserting the message in a log file or printing it to the console.

Class org.xml.sax.InputSource

An `InputSource` object represents a container for the XML document or any of the external entities it references (technically, the main document is itself an entity). The `InputSource` class is supplied with SAX: generally the application instantiates an `InputSource` and updates it to say where the input is coming from, and the parser interrogates it to find out where to read the input from.

The `InputSource` object provides three ways of supplying input to the parser: a system identifier (or URL), a `Reader` (which delivers a stream of Unicode characters), or an `InputStream` (which delivers a stream of uninterpreted bytes).

This class allows a SAX application to encapsulate information about an input source in a single object, which may include a public identifier, a system identifier, a byte stream (possibly with a specified encoding), and/or a character stream.

There are two places that the application will deliver this input source to the parser: as the argument to the `Parser.parse()` method, or as the return value of the `EntityResolver.resolveEntity()` method.

The SAX parser will use the InputSource object to determine how to read XML input. If there is a character stream available, the parser will read that stream directly; if not, the parser will use a byte stream, if available; if neither a character stream nor a byte stream is available, the parser will attempt to open a URI connection to the resource identified by the system identifier.

An InputSource object belongs to the application: the SAX parser shall never modify it in any way (it may modify a copy if necessary).

If you supply input in the form of a Reader or InputStream, it may be useful to supply a system identifier as well. If you do this, the URI will not be used to obtain the actual XML input, but it will be used in diagnostics, and more importantly to resolve any relative URIs within the document, for example entity references.

Method	Description
public InputSource()	Zero-argument default constructor.
public InputSource(String systemId)	Creates a new input source with a system identifier.
	Applications may use setPublicId to include a public identifier as well, or setEncoding to specify the character encoding, if known.
	If the system identifier is a URL, it must be fully resolved.
	Parameters:
	systemId – the system identifier (URI).
public InputSource(InputStream byteStream)	Creates a new input source with a byte stream.
	Application writers may use setSystemId to provide a base for resolving relative URIs, setPublicId() to include a public identifier, and/or setEncoding() to specify the object's character encoding.
	Parameters:
	byteStream – the raw byte stream containing the document.
public InputSource(Reader characterStream)	Creates a new input source with a character stream.
	Application writers may use setSystemId() to provide a base for resolving relative URIs, and setPublicId() to include a public identifier.
	The character stream shall not include a byte order mark.
public InputStream getByteStream()	Gets the byte stream for this input source.
	The getEncoding() method will return the character encoding for this byte stream, or NULL if unknown.

Table continued on following page

Method	Description
	Returns: The byte stream, or NULL if none was supplied.
`public Reader getCharacterStream()`	Gets the character stream for this input source.
	Returns: The character stream, or NULL if none was supplied.
`public String getEncoding()`	Gets the character encoding for a byte stream or URI.
	Returns: The encoding, or NULL if none was supplied.
`public String getPublicId()`	Gets the public identifier for this input source.
	Returns: The public identifier, or NULL if none was supplied.
`public String getSystemId()`	Gets the system identifier for this input source.
	The `getEncoding()` method will return the character encoding of the object pointed to, or NULL if unknown.
	If the system ID is a URL, it will be fully resolved.
	Returns: The system identifier.
`public void setByteStream(InputStream byteStream)`	Sets the byte stream for this input source.
	The SAX parser will ignore this if there is also a character stream specified, but it will use a byte stream in preference to opening a URI connection itself.
	If the application knows the character encoding of the byte stream, it should set it with the `setEncoding()` method.
	Parameters:
	`byteStream` – a byte stream containing an XML document or other entity.
`public void setCharacterStream(Reader characterStream)`	Sets the character stream for this input source.
	If there is a character stream specified, the SAX parser will ignore any byte stream and will not attempt to open a URI connection to the system identifier.
	Parameters:
	`characterStream` – the character stream containing the XML document or other entity.

Method	Description
`public void setEncoding(String encoding)`	Sets the character encoding, if known.
	The encoding must be a string acceptable for an XML encoding declaration (see section 4.3.3 of the XML 1.0 Recommendation).
	This method has no effect when the application provides a character stream.
	Parameters:
	`encoding` – a string describing the character encoding.
`public void setPublicId(String publicId)`	Sets the public identifier for this input source.
	The public identifier is always optional: if the application writer includes one, it will be provided as part of the location information.
	Parameters:
	`publicId` – the public identifier as a string.
`public void setSystemId(String systemId)`	Sets the system identifier for this input source.
	The system identifier is optional if there is a byte stream or a character stream, but it is still useful to provide one, since the application can use it to resolve relative URIs and can include it in error messages and warnings (the parser will attempt to open a connection to the URI only if there is no byte stream or character stream specified).
	If the application knows the character encoding of the object pointed to by the system identifier, it can register the encoding using the `setEncoding()` method.
	If the system ID is a URL, it must be fully resolved.
	Parameters:
	`systemId` – the system identifier as a string.

Interface org.xml.sax.Locator

This interface provides methods that the application can use to determine the current position in the source XML document.

If a SAX parser provides location information to the SAX application, it does so by implementing this interface and then passing an instance to the application using the document handler's `setDocumentLocator()` method. The application can use the object to obtain the location of any other document handler event in the XML source document.

Note that the results returned by the object will be valid only during the scope of each document handler method: the application will receive unpredictable results if it attempts to use the locator at any other time.

SAX parsers are not required to supply a locator, but they are very strongly encouraged to do so. If the parser supplies a locator, it must do so before reporting any other document events. If no locator has been set by the time the application receives the `startDocument` event, the application should assume that a locator is not available:

Method	Description
`public int getColumnNumber()`	Returns the column number where the current document event ends. Note that this is the column number of the first character after the text associated with the document event. The first column in a line is position 1. **Returns:** The column number, or `-1` if none is available.
`public int getLineNumber()`	Returns the line number where the current document event ends. Note that this is the line position of the first character after the text associated with the document event. In practice some parsers report the line number and column number where the event starts. **Returns:** The line number, or `-1` if none is available.
`public String getPublicId()`	Returns the public identifier for the current document event. **Returns:** A string containing the public identifier, or `NULL` if none is available.
`public String getSystemId()`	Returns the system identifier for the current document event. If the system identifier is a URL, the parser must resolve it fully before passing it to the application. **Returns:** A string containing the system identifier, or `NULL` if none is available.

Interface org.xml.sax.ext.Locator2

This is a SAX2.0 extension to augment the entity information provided through a `Locator`. If an implementation supports this extension, the `Locator` provided in `ContentHandler.setDocumentLocator()` will implement this interface, and the http://xml.org/sax/features/use-locator2/ feature flag will have the value `TRUE`.

`XMLReader` implementations are not required to support this information, and it is not part of core-only SAX2.0 distributions:

Method	Description
`public String getEncoding()`	Returns the name of the character encoding for the entity.
	If the encoding was declared externally (for example, in a MIME `Content-Type` header), that will be the name returned. Else if there was an `<?xml ...encoding='...'?>` declaration at the start of the document, that encoding name will be returned. Otherwise the encoding will be inferred (normally to be UTF-8, or some UTF-16 variant), and that inferred name will be returned.
	When an `InputSource` is used to provide an entity's character stream, this method returns the encoding provided in that input stream.
	Note that some recent W3C specifications require that text in some encodings be normalized, using Unicode Normalization Form C, before processing. Such normalization must be performed by applications, and would normally be triggered based on the value returned by this method.
	Encoding names may be those used by the underlying JVM, and comparisons should be case-insensitive.
	Returns: Name of the character encoding being used to interpret the entity's text, or `NULL` if this was not provided for a character stream passed through an `InputSource`.
`public String getXMLVersion()`	Returns the version of XML used for the entity. This will normally be the identifier from the current entity's `<?xml version='...' ...?>` declaration, or be defaulted by the parser.
	At this writing, only one version ("1.0") is defined, but it seems likely that a new version will be defined which has slightly different rules about which characters are legal in XML names.
	Returns: Identifier for the XML version being used to interpret the entity's text.

Interface org.xml.sax.XMLReader (SAX 2.0 – Replaces Parser)

Every SAX 2.0 parser must implement this interface for reading documents using callbacks. An application parses an XML document by creating an instance of a parser (that is, a class that implements this interface) and calling one of its `parse()` methods.

Interface for reading an XML document using callbacks. `XMLReader` is the interface that an XML parser's SAX2 driver must implement. This interface allows an application to set and query features and properties in the parser, to register event handlers for document processing, and to initiate a document parse.

All SAX interfaces are assumed to be synchronous: the parse methods must not return until parsing is complete, and readers must wait for an event-handler callback to return before reporting the next event. This interface replaces the (now deprecated) SAX 1.0 parser interface. The XMLReader interface contains two important enhancements over the old Parser interface:

❑ It adds a standard way to query and set features and properties

❑ It adds namespace support, which is required for many higher-level XML standards

There are adapters available to convert a SAX1.0 Parser to a SAX2.0 XMLReader and vice-versa:

Method	Description
public ContentHandler getContent Handler()	Returns the current content handler. **Returns:** The current content handler, or NULL if none has been registered.
public DTDHandler getDTDHandler()	Returns the current DTD handler. **Returns:** The current DTD handler, or NULL if none has been registered.
public getEntity Resolver()	Returns the current entity resolver. **Returns:** The current entity resolver, or NULL if none has been registered.
public ErrorHandler getErrorHandler()	Returns the current error handler. **Returns:** The current error handler, or NULL if none has been registered.
public boolean getFeature(String name)	Looks up the value of a feature The feature name is any fully-qualified URI. It is possible for an XMLReader to recognize a feature name but to be unable to return its value; this is especially true in the case of an adapter for a SAX1.0 Parser, which has no way of knowing whether the underlying parser is performing validation or expanding external entities. For more on getFeature() usage, see the explanation below this table. **Parameters:** name – the feature name, which is a fully-qualified URI **Returns:** The current state of the feature (TRUE or FALSE) **Throws:** SAXNotRecognizedException SAXNotSupportedException

Method	Description
public Object getProperty(String name)	Looks up the value of a property.
	The property name is any fully-qualified URI. It is possible for an XMLReader to recognize a property name but to be unable to return its state; this is especially true in the case of an adapter for a SAX1.0 Parser.
	Parameters:
	name – the feature name, which is a fully-qualified URI
	Returns: The current value of the property
	Throws:
	SAXNotRecognizedException
	SAXNotSupportedException
public void parse(InputSource input)	Parses an XML document.
	The application can use this method to instruct the XML reader to begin parsing an XML document from any valid input source (a character stream, a byte stream, or a URI).
	Applications may not invoke this method while a parse is in progress (they should create a new XMLReader instead for each nested XML document). Once a parse is complete, an application may reuse the same XMLReader object, possibly with a different input source.
	During the parse, the XMLReader will provide information about the XML document through the registered event handlers.
	This method is synchronous: it will not return until parsing has ended. If a client application wants to terminate parsing early, it should throw an exception.
	Parameters:
	source – the input source for the top level of the XML document.
	Throws:
	SAXExeception – any SAX exception, possibly wrapping another exception.
	java.io.IOException – an IO exception from the parser, possibly from a byte stream or character stream supplied by the application.
public void parse(String systemId)	Parse an XML document from a system identifier (URI).
	If the system identifier is a URL, it must be fully resolved by the application before it is passed to the parser.
	Parameters:
	systemId – the system identifier (URI).

Table continued on following page

Method	Description
	Throws:
	`SAXExeception` – any SAX exception, possibly wrapping another exception.
	`java.io.IOException` – an IO exception from the parser, possibly from a byte stream or character stream supplied by the application.
`public void setContentHandler (ContentHandler handler)`	Allows an application to register a content event handler.
	If the application does not register a content handler, all content events reported by the SAX parser will be silently ignored. Applications may register a new or different handler in the middle of a parse, and the SAX parser must begin using the new handler immediately.
	Parameters:
	`handler` – the content handler.
	Throws:
	`java.lang.NullPointerException` – if the handler argument is NULL
`public void setDTDHandler( DTDHandler handler)`	Allows an application to register a DTD event handler.
	If the application does not register a DTD handler, all DTD events reported by the SAX parser will be silently ignored.
	Applications may register a new or different handler in the middle of a parse, and the SAX parser must begin using the new handler immediately.
	Parameters:
	`handler` – the DTD handler.
	Throws:
	`java.lang.NullPointerException` – if the handler argument is NULL
`public void setEntity Resolver( EntityResolver resolver)`	Allows an application to register an entity resolver.
	If the application does not register an entity resolver, the `XMLReader` will perform its own default resolution.
	Applications may register a new or different resolver in the middle of a parse, and the SAX parser must begin using the new resolver immediately.
	Parameters:
	`resolver` – the entity resolver.

Method	Description
	Throws: `java.lang.NullPointerException` – if the resolver argument is NULL
`public void setErrorHandler( ErrorHandler handler)`	Allows an application to register an error event handler. If the application does not register an error handler, all error events reported by the SAX parser will be silently ignored; however, normal processing may not continue. It is highly recommended that all SAX applications implement an error handler to avoid unexpected bugs. Applications may register a new or different handler in the middle of a parse, and the SAX parser must begin using the new handler immediately. **Parameters:** `handler` – the error handler. **Throws:** `java.lang.NullPointerException` – if the handler argument is NULL.

`public void setFeature(String name, boolean value)`	Sets the state of a feature.
	
	The feature name is any fully-qualified URI. It is possible for an `XMLReader` to recognize a feature name but to be unable to set its value; this is especially true in the case of an adapter for a SAX1.0 `Parser`, which has no way of affecting whether the underlying parser is validating, for example.
	
	Parameters:
	
	`name` – the feature name, which is a fully-qualified URI
	
	`state` – the requested state of the feature (TRUE or FALSE)
	
	Throws:
	
	`SAXNotRecognizedException`
	
	`SAXNotSupportedException`

`public void setProperty( String name, Object value)`	Sets the value of a property. The property name is any fully-qualified URI. It is possible for an `XMLReader` to recognize a property name but to be unable to set its value; this is especially true in the case of an adapter for a SAX1.0 `Parser`. **Parameters:** `name` – the feature name, which is a fully-qualified URI `state` – the requested value for the property

Table continued on following page

Method	Description
	Throws:
	SAXNotRecognizedException
	SAXNotSupportedException

All XMLReader objects are required to recognize the http://xml.org/sax/features/namespaces/ and the http://xml.org/sax/features/namespace-prefixes/ feature names.
Some feature values may be available only in specific contexts, such as before, during, or after a parse.

Implementers are free (and encouraged) to invent their own features, using names built on their own URIs.

Interface org.xml.sax.Parser – Deprecated

Every SAX 1.0 parser must implement this interface. An application parses an XML document by creating an instance of a parser (that is, a class that implements this interface) and calling one of its parse() methods.

All SAX parsers must implement this basic interface: it allows applications to register handlers for different types of events and to initiate a parse from a URI, or a character stream.

All SAX parsers must also implement a zero-argument constructor (though other constructors are also allowed).

SAX parsers are reusable but not re-entrant: the application may reuse a parser object (possibly with a different input source) once the first parse has completed successfully, but it may not invoke the parse() methods recursively within a parse:

Method	Description
`public void parse(InputSource source)`	Parses an XML document.
	The application can use this method to instruct the SAX parser to begin parsing an XML document from any valid input source (a character stream, a byte stream, or a URI).
	Applications may not invoke this method while a parse is in progress (they should create a new parser instead for each additional XML document). Once a parse is complete, an application may reuse the same parser object, possibly with a different input source.
	Parameters:
	source – the input source for the top-level of the XML document.

Method	Description
	Throws:
	`SAXException` – any SAX exception, possibly wrapping another exception.
	`IOException` – an IO exception from the parser, possibly from a byte stream or character stream supplied by the application.
`public void parse(String systemId)`	Parses an XML document from a system identifier (URI).
	This method is a shortcut for the common case of reading a document from a system identifier. It is the exact equivalent of the following:
	`parse(new InputSource(systemId));`
	If the system identifier is a URL, it must be fully resolved by the application before it is passed to the parser.
	Parameters:
	`systemId` – the system identifier (URI).
	Throws:
	`SAXException` – any SAX exception, possibly wrapping another exception.
	`IOException` – an IO exception from the parser, possibly from a byte stream or character stream supplied by the application.
`public void setDocumentHandler( DocumentHandler handler)`	Allows an application to register a document event handler.
	If the application does not register a document handler, all document events reported by the SAX parser will be silently ignored (this is the default behavior implemented by `HandlerBase`).
	Applications may register a new or different handler in the middle of a parse, and the SAX parser must begin using the new handler immediately.
	Parameters:
	`handler` – the document handler.

Table continued on following page

817

Method	Description
`public void setDTDHandler(DTDHandler handler)`	Allows an application to register a DTD event handler. If the application does not register a DTD handler, all DTD events reported by the SAX parser will be silently ignored (this is the default behavior implemented by `HandlerBase`). Applications may register a new or different handler in the middle of a parse, and the SAX parser must begin using the new handler immediately. **Parameters:** `handler` – the DTD handler.
`public void setEntityResolver( EntityResolver resolver)`	Allows an application to register a custom entity resolver. If the application does not register an entity resolver, the SAX parser will resolve system identifiers and open connections to entities itself (this is the default behavior implemented in `HandlerBase`). Applications may register a new or different entity resolver in the middle of a parse, and the SAX parser must begin using the new resolver immediately. **Parameters:** `resolver` – the object for resolving entities.
`public void setErrorHandler( ErrorHandler handler)`	Allows an application to register an error event handler. If the application does not register an error event handler, all error events reported by the SAX parser will be silently ignored, except for `fatalError`, which will throw a `SAXException` (this is the default behavior implemented by `HandlerBase`). Applications may register a new or different handler in the middle of a parse, and the SAX parser must begin using the new handler immediately. **Parameters:** `handler` – the error handler.
`public void setLocale(Locale locale)`	Allows an application to request a locale for errors and warnings. SAX parsers are not required to provide localization for errors and warnings; if they cannot support the requested locale, however, they must throw a SAX exception. Applications may not request a locale change in the middle of a parse.

Method	Description
	Parameters:
	`locale` – a Java `Locale` object.
	Throws:
	`SAXException` – throws an exception (using the previous or default locale) if the requested locale is not supported.

Class org.xml.sax.SAXException

This class is used to represent an error detected during processing either by the parser or by the application.

This class can contain basic error or warning information from either the XML parser or the application: a parser writer or application writer can subclass it to provide additional functionality. SAX handlers may throw this exception or any exception subclassed from it.

If the application needs to pass through other types of exceptions, it must wrap those exceptions in a `SAXException` or an exception derived from a `SAXException`.

If the parser or application needs to include information about a specific location in an XML document, it should use the `SAXParseException` subclass:

Method	Description
`public Exception getException()`	Returns the embedded exception, if any.
	Returns: The embedded exception, or `NULL` if there is none.
`public String getMessage()`	Return a detailed message for this exception.
	If there is an embedded exception, and if the `SAXException` has no detailed message of its own, this method will return the detailed message from the embedded exception.
	Returns: The error or warning message.
`public String toString()`	Converts this exception to a string.
	Returns: A string version of this exception.

Class org.xml.sax.SAXParseException

Extends `SAXException`. This exception class represents an error or warning condition detected by the parser or by the application. In addition to the basic capability of `SAXException`, a `SAXParseException` allows information to be retained about the location in the source document where the error occurred. For an application-detected error, this information might be obtained from the `Locator` object.

This exception will include information for locating the error in the original XML document. Note that although the application will receive a SAXParseException as the argument to the handlers in the ErrorHandler interface, the application is not actually required to throw the exception; instead, it can simply read the information in it and take a different action.

Since this exception is a subclass of SAXException, it inherits the ability to wrap another exception:

Method	Description
public SAXParseException(String message, Locator locator)	Creates a new SAXParseException from a message and a locator. This constructor is especially useful when an application is creating its own exception from within a DocumentHandler callback. **Parameters:** message – the error or warning message. locator – the locator object for the error or warning.
public SAXParseException(String message, Locator locator, Exception e)	Wraps an existing exception in a SAXParseException. This constructor is especially useful when an application is creating its own exception from within a DocumentHandler callback, and needs to wrap an existing exception that is not a subclass of SAXException. **Parameters:** message – the error or warning message, or NULL to use the message from the embedded exception. locator – the locator object for the error or warning. e – Any exception
public SAXParseException(String message, String publicId, String systemId, int lineNumber, int columnNumber)	Creates a new SAXParseException. This constructor is most useful for parser writers. If the system identifier is a URL, the parser must resolve it fully before creating the exception.

Method	Description
	Parameters: message – the error or warning message. publicId – the public identifier of the entity that generated the error or warning. systemId – the system identifier of the entity that generated the error or warning. lineNumber – the line number of the end of the text that caused the error or warning. columnNumber – the column number of the end of the text that caused the error or warning.
public SAXParseException(String message, String publicId, String systemId, int lineNumber, int columnNumber, Exception e)	Creates a new SAXParseException with an embedded exception. This constructor is most useful for parser writers who need to wrap an exception that is not a subclass of SAXException. If the system identifier is a URL, the parser must resolve it fully before creating the exception. **Parameters:** message – the error or warning message, or NULL to use the message from the embedded exception. publicId – the public identifier of the entity that generated the error or warning. systemId – the system identifier of the entity that generated the error or warning. lineNumber – the line number of the end of the text that caused the error or warning. columnNumber – the column number of the end of the text that caused the error or warning. e – another exception to embed in this one.
public int getColumnNumber()	The column number of the end of the text where the exception occurred. The first column in a line is position 1. **Returns:** An integer representing the column number, or -1 if none is available.
public int getLineNumber()	The line number of the end of the text where the exception occurred. **Returns:** An integer representing the line number, or -1 if none is available.

Table continued on following page

Method	Description
public String getPublicId()	Gets the public identifier of the entity where the exception occurred. **Returns:** A string containing the public identifier, or NULL if none is available.
public String getSystemId()	Gets the system identifier of the entity where the exception occurred. Note that the term "entity" includes the top-level XML document. If the system identifier is a URL, it will be resolved fully. **Returns:** A string containing the system identifier, or NULL if none is available.

Class org.xml.sax.SAXNotRecognizedException (SAX 2.0)

Exception class for an unrecognized identifier – an XML reader will throw this exception when it finds an unrecognized feature or property identifier; SAX applications and extensions may use this class for other, similar purposes:

Method	Description
public SAXNotRecognizedException (String message)	Constructs a new exception with the given message. **Parameters:** message – the text message of the exception.

This class has also inherited a lot of methods from other classes. These are summarized below:

Methods inherited from class org.xml.sax.SAXException:

- ❑ getException()
- ❑ getMessage()
- ❑ toString()

Methods inherited from class java.lang.Throwable:

- ❑ fillInStackTrace()
- ❑ getLocalizedMessage()
- ❑ printStackTrace()

Methods inherited from class `java.lang.Object`:

- ❑ `equals()`
- ❑ `getClass()`
- ❑ `hashCode()`
- ❑ `notify()`
- ❑ `notifyAll()`
- ❑ `wait()`

Class org.xml.sax.SAXNotSupportedException (SAX 2.0)

Exception class for an unsupported operation – an `XMLReader` will throw this exception when it recognizes a feature or property identifier, but cannot perform the requested operation (setting a state or value). Other SAX2.0 applications and extensions may use this class for similar purposes:

Method	Description
`public SAXNotSupported Exception(String message)`	Constructs a new exception with the given message.
	Parameters:
	`message` – the text message of the exception.

This class has also inherited a lot of methods from other classes. These are summarized below:

Methods inherited from class `org.xml.sax.SAXException`:

- ❑ `getException()`
- ❑ `getMessage()`
- ❑ `toString()`

Methods inherited from class `java.lang.Throwable`:

- ❑ `fillInStackTrace()`
- ❑ `getLocalizedMessage()`
- ❑ `printStackTrace()`

Methods inherited from class `java.lang.Object`:

- ❑ `equals()`
- ❑ `getClass()`
- ❑ `hashCode()`

❑ notify()

❑ notifyAll()

❑ wait()

Interface org.xml.sax.XMLFilter (SAX 2.0)

This interface is like the reader, except it is used to read documents from a source other than a document or database. It can also modify events on the way to an application (extends XMLReader).

Interface for an XML filter – an XML filter is like an XML reader, except that it obtains its events from another XML reader rather than a primary source like an XML document or database. Filters can modify a stream of events as they pass on to the final application.

The XMLFilterImpl helper class provides a convenient base for creating SAX2.0 filters, by passing on all EntityResolver, DTDHandler, ContentHandler, and ErrorHandler events automatically:

Method	Description
public XMLReader getParent()	Gets the parent reader.
	This method allows the application to query the parent reader (which may be another filter). It is generally a bad idea to perform any operations on the parent reader directly: they should all pass through this filter.
	Returns: The parent filter, or NULL if none has been set.
public void setParent(XMLReader parent)	Sets the parent reader.
	This method allows the application to link the filter to a parent reader (which may be another filter). The argument may not be NULL.
	Parameters:
	parent – the parent reader.

The XML DOM (Document Object Model)

This appendix lists all of the interfaces in the DOM Level 2 Core, both the **Fundamental Interfaces** and the **Extended Interfaces**, including all of their properties and methods. Examples of how to use some of these interfaces were given in Chapter 6.

Further information on these interfaces can be found at:
http://www.w3.org/TR/1999/CR-DOM-Level-2-19991210/core.html#ID-1590626200

To activate PHP's DOM support we need to ensure that the php_domxml.dll file is found in the extensions folder of our PHP installation. The php_domxml.dll extension will not be extracted to the extensions folder by default. It can be found in the experimental directory of the PHP installation. You must move php_domxml.dll to the extensions folder before you can use the DOM API.

Fundamental Interfaces

The DOM Fundamental Interfaces are interfaces that all DOM implementations must provide, even if they aren't designed to work with XML documents. The list of interfaces covered in this section is:

- ❑ DOMException
- ❑ Node
- ❑ Document

- ❑ DOMImplementation
- ❑ DocumentFragment
- ❑ NodeList
- ❑ Element
- ❑ NamedNodeMap
- ❑ Attr
- ❑ CharacterData
- ❑ Text
- ❑ Comment

DOMException

An object implementing the DOMException interface is raised whenever an error occurs in the DOM:

Property	Description
code	An integer, representing which **exception code** this DOMException is reporting

The code property can take the following values:

Exception Code	Integer Value	Description
INDEX_SIZE_ERR	1	The index or size is negative, or greater than the allowed value.
DOMSTRING_SIZE_ERR	2	The specified range of text does not fit into a DOMString.
HIERARCHY_REQUEST_ERR	3	The node is inserted somewhere it doesn't belong.
WRONG_DOCUMENT_ERR	4	The node is used in a different document than the one that created it, and that document doesn't support it.
INVALID_CHARACTER_ERR	5	A character has been passed which is not valid in XML.
NO_DATA_ALLOWED_ERR	6	Data has been specified for a node that does not support data.
NO_MODIFICATION_ ALLOWED_ERR	7	An attempt has been made to modify an object that doesn't allow modifications.
NOT_FOUND_ERR	8	An attempt was made to reference a node that does not exist.

Exception Code	Integer Value	Description
NOT_SUPPORTED_ERR	9	The implementation does not support the type of object requested.
INUSE_ATTRIBUTE_ERR	10	An attempt was made to add a duplicate attribute or an attempt is made to add an attribute that is already in use elsewhere.
INVALID_STATE_ERR	11	An attempt was made to use an object that is not, or is no longer, useable.
SYNTAX_ERR	12	An invalid or illegal string was passed.
INVALID_MODIFICATION_ERR	13	An attempt was made to modify the type of the underlying object.
NAMESPACE_ERR	14	An attempt was made to create or change an object in a way that is incompatible with namespaces.
INVALID_ACCESS_ERR	15	A parameter was passed or an operation attempted which is not supported by the underlying object.

Node

The Node interface is the primary data type for the entire Document Object Model. It represents a single node in the document tree. While all objects implementing the Node interface expose methods for dealing with children, not all objects implementing the Node interface may have children. For example, Text nodes may not have children, and adding children to such nodes results in a DOMException being raised.

The attributes nodeName, nodeValue, and attributes are included as a mechanism to get at node information without casting down to the specific derived interface. In cases where there is no obvious mapping of these attributes for a specific nodeType (that is, nodeValue for an Element or attributes for a Comment), this returns NULL. Note that the specialized interfaces may contain additional and more convenient mechanisms to get and set the relevant information.

The Node interface is the base interface upon which most of the DOM objects are built. It contains methods and attributes that can be used for all types of nodes. The interface also includes some helper methods and attributes which only apply to particular types of nodes:

Property	Description
attributes	A NamedNodeMap containing the attributes of this node. If the node is not an element, this returns NULL.
childNodes	A NodeList containing all of this node's children. If there are no children, an empty NodeList will be returned, not NULL.

Table continued on following page

Property	Description
firstChild	The first child of this node. If there are no children, this returns NULL.
lastChild	The last child of this node. If there are no children, this returns NULL.
localName	Returns the local part of this node's qualified name.
namespaceURI	The namespace URI of this node. Returns NULL if a namespace is not specified.
nextSibling	The node immediately following this node. If there is no following node, this returns NULL.
nodeName	The name of the node. Will return different values, depending on the nodeType, as listed in the next table.
nodeType	The type of node. Will be one of the values from the next table.
nodeValue	The value of the node. Will return different values, depending on the nodeType, as listed in the next table.
ownerDocument	The Document object associated with this node. This is also the Document object used to create new nodes. When this node is a Document or a DocumentType that is not used with any Document yet, this is NULL. The document to which this node belongs.
parentNode	The node that is this node's parent. If a node has just been created and not yet added to the tree, or if it has been removed from the tree, this returns NULL.
prefix	The namespace prefix of this node. Returns NULL if a namespace is not specified.
previousSibling	The node immediately preceding this node. If there is no preceding node, this returns NULL.

The value of the nodeName and nodeValue properties depend on the value of the nodeType property, which can return one of the following constants:

nodeType Property Constant	nodeName	nodeValue
ATTRIBUTE_NODE	Name of attribute	Value of attribute
CDATA_SECTION_NODE	#cdata-section	Content of the CDATA section
COMMENT_NODE	#comment	Content of the comment
DOCUMENT_FRAGMENT_NODE	#document-fragment	NULL
DOCUMENT_NODE	#document	NULL

nodeType Property Constant	nodeName	nodeValue
DOCUMENT_TYPE_NODE	Document type name	NULL
ELEMENT_NODE	Tag name	NULL
ENTITY_NODE	Entity name	NULL
ENTITY_REFERENCE_NODE	Name of entity referenced	NULL
NOTATION_NODE	Notation name	NULL
PROCESSING_INSTRUCTION_NODE	Target	Entire content excluding the target
TEXT_NODE	#text	Context of the text node

Method	Description
appendChild(newChild)	Adds newChild to the end of the list, and returns it. If the newChild is already in the tree, it is first removed.
cloneNode(deep)	Returns a duplicate of this node. If the Boolean deep parameter is TRUE, this will recursively clone the subtree under the node, otherwise it will only clone the node itself.
hasChildNodes()	Returns a Boolean; TRUE if the node has any children, FALSE otherwise.
insertBefore(newChild, refChild)	Inserts the newChild node before the existing refChild. If refChild is NULL, inserts the node at the end of the list. Returns the inserted node.
normalize()	If there are multiple adjacent Text child nodes (from a previous call to Text.splitText()) this method will combine them again. It doesn't return a value.
removeChild(oldChild)	Removes oldChild from the list, and returns it.
replaceChild(newChild, oldChild)	Replaces oldChild with newChild. Returns oldChild.
supports(feature, version)	Indicates whether this implementation of the DOM supports the feature passed. Returns a Boolean, TRUE if it supports the feature, FALSE otherwise.

Document

An object implementing the Document interface represents the entire XML document. This object is also used to create other nodes at run-time.

The Document interface extends the Node interface:

Property	Description
doctype	Returns a DocumentType object, indicating the document type associated with this document. If the document has no document type specified, returns NULL.
documentElement	This is a convenience attribute that allows direct access to the child node that is the root element of the document. For HTML documents, this is the element with the tagName <html>.
implementation	The DOMImplementation object used for this document.

Method	Description
createAttribute(name)	Creates an attribute, with the specified name.
createAttributeNS(namespaceURI, qualifiedName)	Creates an attribute, with the specified namespace and QName.
createCDATASection(data)	Creates a CDATASection node, containing the text in data.
createComment(data)	Creates a Comment node, containing the text in data.
createDocumentFragment()	Creates an empty DocumentFragment object.
createElement(tagName)	Creates an element, with the tagName specified.
createElementNS(namespaceURI, qualifiedName)	Creates an element, with the specified namespace and QName.
createEntityReference(name)	Creates an entity reference, with the specified name.
createProcessingInstruction(target, data)	Creates a ProcessingInstruction node, with the specified target and data.
createTextNode(data)	Creates a Text node, containing the text in data.
getElementByID(elementID)	Returns the element with the ID specified in elementID. If there is no such element, returns NULL.
getElementsByTagName(tagname)	Returns a NodeList of all elements in the document with this tagname. The elements are returned in document order.
getElementsByTagNameNS(namespaceURI, localName)	Returns a NodeList of all the elements in the document that have the specified local name, and are in the namespace specified by namespaceURI.

Method	Description
importNode(importedNode, deep)	Imports a node importedNode from another document into this one. The original node is not removed from the old document, it is just cloned. (The Boolean deep parameter specifies if it is a deep or shallow clone: deep – subtree under node is also cloned, shallow – only node itself is cloned.) Returns the new node.

Note: all of the createXxx() *methods return the node created.*

DOMImplementation

The DOMImplementation interface provides methods which are not specific to any particular document, but to any document from this DOM implementation. You can get a DOMImplementation object from the implementation property of the Document interface:

Method	Description
createDocument(namespaceURI, qualifiedName, doctype)	Creates a Document object, with the document element specified by qualifiedName. The doctype property must refer to an object of type DocumentType.
createDocumentType (qualifiedName, publicID, systemID, internalSubset)	Creates a DocumentType object, with the specified attributes.
hasFeature(feature, version)	Returns a Boolean, indicating whether this DOM implementation supports the feature requested. version is the version number of the feature to test.

DocumentFragment

A document fragment is a temporary holding place for a group of nodes, usually with the intent of inserting them back into the document at a later point.

The DocumentFragment interface extends the Node interface, without adding any additional properties or methods. DocumentFragment is a lightweight or minimal Document object. It is very common to want to be able to extract a portion of a document's tree or to create a new fragment of a document. Imagine implementing a user command like cut or rearranging a document by moving fragments around. It is desirable to have an object that can hold such fragments and it is quite natural to use a Node for this purpose.

While it is true that a Document object could fulfill this role, a Document object can potentially be a heavyweight object, depending on the underlying implementation. What is really needed for this is a very lightweight object. DocumentFragment is such an object. Furthermore, various operations such as inserting nodes as children of another node may take DocumentFragment objects as arguments. This results in all the child nodes of the DocumentFragment being moved to the child list of this node.

The children of a DocumentFragment node are zero or more nodes representing the tops of any subtrees defining the structure of the document. DocumentFragment nodes do not need to be well-formed XML documents (although they do need to follow the rules imposed upon well-formed XML parsed entities, which can have multiple top nodes). For example, a DocumentFragment might have only one child and that child node could be a Text node. Such a structure model represents neither an HTML document nor a well-formed XML document.

When a DocumentFragment is inserted into a Document (or indeed any other node that may take children) the children of the DocumentFragment and not the DocumentFragment itself are inserted into the Node. This makes the DocumentFragment very useful when the user wishes to create nodes that are siblings. The DocumentFragment acts as the parent of these nodes so that the user can use the standard methods from the Node interface, such as insertBefore() and appendChild().

NodeList

The NodeList interface provides the abstraction of an ordered collection of nodes, without defining or constraining how this collection is implemented. The items in the NodeList are accessible via an integral index, starting from 0:

Property	Description
length	The number of nodes contained in this list. The range of valid child node indices is 0 to length-1 inclusive.

Method	Description
item(index)	Returns the Node in the list at the indicated index. If index is same or greater than length, returns NULL.

Element

Provides properties and methods for working with an element.

The Element interface extends the Node interface:

Property	Description
tagName	The name of the element

Method	Description
getAttribute(name)	Returns the value of the attribute with the specified name, or an empty string if that attribute does not have a specified or default value.
getAttributeNode(name)	Returns an Attr node, containing the named attribute. Returns NULL if there is no such attribute.

Method	Description
`getAttributeNS(namespaceURI, localName)`	Returns the value of the specified attribute, or an empty string if that attribute does not have a specified or default value.
`getElementsByTagName(name)`	Returns a `NodeList` of all descendants with the given node name.
`getElementsByTagNameNS namespaceURI, localName)`	Returns a `NodeList` of all of the elements matching these criteria.
`removeAttribute(name)`	Removes the specified attribute. If the attribute has a default value, it is immediately replaced with an identical attribute, containing this default value.
`removeAttributeNode(oldAttr)`	Removes the specified `Attr` node, and returns it. If the attribute has a default value, it is immediately replaced with an identical attribute, containing this default value.
`removeAttributeNS(namespaceURI, localName)`	Removes the specified attribute. If the attribute has a default value, it is immediately replaced with an identical attribute, containing this default value.
`setAttribute(name, value)`	Sets the value of the specified attribute to this new value. If no such attribute exists, a new one with this name is created.
`setAttributeNode(newAttr)`	Adds a new attribute node. If an attribute with the same name already exists, it is replaced. If an `Attr` has been replaced, it is returned, otherwise `NULL` is returned.
`setAttributeNS(namespaceURI, qualifiedName, value)`	Sets the value of the specified attribute to this new value. If no such attribute exists, a new one with this namespace URI and QName is created.
`setAttributeNodeNS(newAttr)`	Adds a new `Attr` node to the list. If an attribute with the same namespace URI and local name exists, it is replaced. If an `Attr` object is replaced, it is returned, otherwise `NULL` is returned.

NamedNodeMap

A named node map represents an unordered collection of nodes, retrieved by name:

Property	Description
`length`	The number of nodes in the map

Method	Description
getNamedItem(name)	Returns a Node, where the nodeName is the same as the name specified, or NULL if no such node exists.
getNamedItemNS (namespaceURI, localName)	Returns a Node, matching the namespace URI and local name, or NULL if no such node exists.
item(index)	Returns the Node at the specified index. If index is the same as or greater than length, returns NULL.
removeNamedItem(name)	Removes the Node specified by name, and returns it.
removeNamedItemNS (namespaceURI, localName)	Removes the specified node, and returns it.
setNamedItem(arg)	The arg parameter is a Node object, which is added to the list. The nodeName property is used for the name of the node in this map. If a node with the same name already exists, it is replaced. If a Node is replaced it is returned, otherwise NULL is returned.
setNamedItemNS(arg)	The arg parameter is a Node object, which is added to the list. If a node with the same namespace URI and local name already exists, it is replaced. If a Node is replaced it is returned, otherwise, NULL is returned.

Attr

Provides properties for dealing with an attribute.

The Attr interface extends the Node interface:

Property	Description
name	The name of the attribute
ownerElement	An Element object representing the element to which this attribute belongs
specified	A Boolean, indicating whether this attribute was specified (TRUE), or just defaulted (FALSE)
value	The value of the attribute

CharacterData

Provides properties and methods for working with character data.

The CharacterData interface extends the Node interface:

Property	Description
data	The text in this `CharacterData` node
length	The number of characters in the node

Note that none of the methods explained below return any value.

Method	Description
appendData(arg)	Appends the string in `arg` to the end of the string.
deleteData(offset, count)	Deletes a portion of the string, starting at the `offset`. Will delete the number of characters specified in `count`, or until the end of the string, whichever is less.
insertData(offset, arg)	Inserts the string in `arg` into the middle of the string, starting at the position indicated by `offset`.
replaceData(offset, count, arg)	Replaces a portion of the string, starting at the `offset`. Will replace the number of characters specified in `count`, or until the end of the string, whichever is less. The `arg` parameter is the new string to be inserted.
substringData(offset, count)	Returns a portion of the string, starting at the `offset`. Will return the number of characters specified in `count`, or until the end of the string, whichever is less.

Text

Provides an additional method for working with text nodes.

The Text interface extends the `CharacterData` interface:

Method	Description
splitText(offset)	Separates this single `Text` node into two adjacent `Text` nodes. All of the text up to the `offset` point goes into the first `Text` node, and all of the text starting at the `offset` point to the end goes into the second `Text` node. It returns the new `Text` node.

Comment

Encapsulates an XML comment.

The Comment interface extends the `CharacterData` interface, without adding any additional properties or methods.

Extended Interfaces

The DOM Extended Interfaces need only be provided by DOM implementations that will be working with XML documents. The extended interfaces covered in this section are:

❑ CDATASection

❑ ProcessingInstruction

❑ DocumentType

❑ Notation

❑ Entity

❑ EntityReference

CDATASection

Encapsulates an XML CDATA section.

The CDATASection interface extends the Text interface, without adding any additional properties or methods.

ProcessingInstruction

Provides properties for working with an XML processing instruction (PI). It is used in XML as a way to keep processor-specific information in the text of the document.

The ProcessingInstruction interface extends the Node interface:

Property	Description
data	The content of the PI
target	The PI target, in other words the name of the application to which the PI should be passed

DocumentType

Provides properties for working with an XML document type. Can be retrieved from the doctype property of the Document interface. (If a document doesn't have a document type, doctype will return NULL.)

DocumentType extends the Node interface:

Property	Description
entities	A NamedNodeMap containing all entities declared in the DTD (both internal and external). Parameter entities are not contained, and duplicates are discarded, according to the rules followed by validating XML parsers.

Property	Description
internalSubset	The internal subset, as a string.
name	The name of the DTD (Document Type Definition)
notations	A NamedNodeMap containing the notations contained in the DTD. Duplicates are discarded.
publicID	The public identifier of the external subset.
systemID	The system identifier of the external subset.

Notation

Provides properties for working with an XML notation. Notations are read-only in the DOM.

The Notation interface extends the Node interface:

Property	Description
publicID	The public identifier of this notation. If the public identifier was not specified, returns NULL
systemID	The system identifier of this notation. If the system identifier was not specified, returns NULL

Entity

Provides properties for working with parsed and unparsed entities. Entity nodes are read-only.

The Entity interface extends the Node interface:

Property	Description
notationName	For unparsed entities, the name of the notation for the entity. NULL for parsed entities.
publicID	The public identifier associated with the entity, or NULL if none is specified.
systemID	The system identifier associated with the entity, or NULL if none is specified.

EntityReference

Encapsulates an XML entity reference.

The EntityReference extends the Node interface, without adding any properties or methods.

XSLT Reference

This reference appendix describes the elements and functions that are part of XSLT. For the XPath functions that can also be used with XSLT, see Appendix B.

The XSLT 1.0 specification became a W3C Recommendation on 16 November 1999. Version 1.1 was a Working Draft at the time of writing, as were the requirements for version 2.0. As in Appendix B, we will describe not only the functionality as described in the specifications, but also in which releases of the MSXML library the feature is implemented, since some older partial implementations of this library can still be found in many environments.

This is not done for the many other implementations, such as Xalan and Saxon. Distributions of XSLT processors will normally come with a description of the conformance to the XSLT 1.0 specification.

Both the attributes on XSLT elements and the parameters of XSLT functions can be of several types. At the end of this appendix, you will find a list of the types used in the elements and functions of XSLT.

You can find an online version of this reference at: http://www.vbxml.com/xsl/XSLTRef.asp.

Elements

The XSLT stylesheet is itself an XML document, using a number of special elements in its own namespace. This namespace is http://www.w3.org/1999/XSL/Transform, but in this appendix (and the rest of this book) we simply use the prefix xsl.

Given overleaf is a short description of the elements and their use. (A more detailed explanation follows. For each element we have given a description of its use, described the attributes that can or must be used on the element, and indicated where in the stylesheet the element can occur (as a child of which other elements):

Element	Description
`<xsl:apply-imports>`	Applies a template from an imported stylesheet
`<xsl:apply-templates>`	Applies a template to the current element
`<xsl:attribute>`	Adds an attribute to the nearest containing element
`<xsl:attribute-set>`	Defines a named set of attributes
`<xsl:call-template>`	Provides a way to call a named template
`<xsl:choose>`	Provides a way to choose between a number of alternatives based on conditions
`<xsl:comment>`	Creates an XML comment
`<xsl:copy>`	Copies the current node without child nodes and attributes to the output
`<xsl:copy-of>`	Copies the current node with child nodes and attributes to the output
`<xsl:decimal-format>`	Defines the character/string to be used when converting numbers into strings, with the format-number function
`<xsl:document>`	Switches the target of the result tree to another document
`<xsl:element>`	Adds a new element node to the output
`<xsl:fallback>`	Provides a way to define an alternative for not-implemented instructions
`<xsl:for-each>`	Provides a way to create a loop in the output stream
`<xsl:if>`	Provides a way to write a conditional statement
`<xsl:import>`	Imports a stylesheet
`<xsl:include>`	Includes a stylesheet
`<xsl:key>`	Provides a way to define a key
`<xsl:message>`	Writes a message to the output
`<xsl:namespace-alias>`	Provides a way to map a namespace to another namespace
`<xsl:number>`	Writes a formatted number to the output
`<xsl:otherwise>`	Indicates what should happen when none of the `<xsl:when>` elements inside an `<xsl:choose>` element is satisfied
`<xsl:output>`	Provides a way to control the transformed output
`<xsl:param>`	Provides a way to define parameters
`<xsl:preserve-space>`	Provides a way to define the handling of whitespace

Element	Description
`<xsl:processing-instruction>`	Writes a processing instruction to the output
`<xsl:sort>`	Provides a way to define sorting
`<xsl:strip-space>`	Provides a way to define the handling of whitespace
`<xsl:stylesheet>`	Defines the root element of the stylesheet
`<xsl:template>`	Defines a template for output
`<xsl:text>`	Writes text to the output
`<xsl:transform>`	Defines the root element of the stylesheet
`<xsl:value-of>`	Creates a text node and inserts a value into the result tree
`<xsl:variable>`	Provides a way to declare a variable
`<xsl:when>`	Defines a condition to be tested and performs an action if the condition is true. This element is always a child element of `<xsl:choose>`
`<xsl:with-param>`	Provides a way to pass parameters to templates

`<xsl:apply-imports>`

For calling a template from an imported stylesheet that was overruled in the importing stylesheet. This is normally used if you want to add functionality to a standard template that you imported using `<xsl:import>`.

Implemented:	W3C 1.0 specification (recommendation) W3C 1.1 specification (working draft) MSXML 3.0 MSXML 4.0
Can contain:	No other elements
Can be contained by:	`<xsl:attribute>`, `<xsl:comment>`, `<xsl:copy>`, `<xsl:document>`, `<xsl:element>`, `<xsl:fallback>`, `<xsl:for-each>`, `<xsl:if>`, `<xsl:message>`, `<xsl:otherwise>`, `<xsl:param>`, `<xsl:processing-instruction>`, `<xsl:template>`, `<xsl:variable>`, `<xsl:when>`

\<xsl:apply-templates\>

Used to pass the context on to another template. The `select` attribute specifies which nodes should be transformed now; the processor decides which templates will be used.

Attributes:

`select` (optional)	Expression describing which nodes in the source document should be transformed next. Defaults to `child::*`.

<table>
<tr><td></td><td>Type:</td><td><code>node-set-expression</code></td></tr>
<tr><td></td><td>Attribute Value Template:</td><td>no</td></tr>
</table>

`mode` (optional)	By adding a `mode` attribute, the processor will transform the indicated source document nodes using only templates with this same `mode` attribute. This allows us to process the same source node in different ways.

<table>
<tr><td></td><td>Type:</td><td><code>qname</code></td></tr>
<tr><td></td><td>Attribute Value Template:</td><td>no</td></tr>
</table>

Implemented:	W3C 1.0 specification (recommendation) W3C 1.1 specification (working draft) MSXML 2.0 (IE5) MSXML 2.6 (January 2000 preview) MSXML 3.0 MSXML 4.0
Can contain:	`<xsl:sort>`, `<xsl:with-param>`
Can be contained by:	`<xsl:attribute>`, `<xsl:comment>`, `<xsl:copy>`, `<xsl:document>`, `<xsl:element>`, `<xsl:fallback>`, `<xsl:for-each>`, `<xsl:if>`, `<xsl:message>`, `<xsl:otherwise>`, `<xsl:param>`, `<xsl:processing-instruction>`, `<xsl:template>`, `<xsl:variable>`, `<xsl:when>`

\<xsl:attribute\>

Generates an attribute in the destination document. It should be used in the context of an element (either a literal, \<xsl:element\>, or some other element that generates an element in the output). It must occur before any text or element content is generated.

Attributes:

name (required)	The name of the attribute.	
	Type:	qname
	Attribute Value Template:	yes
namespace (optional)	The namespace (the default uses the namespace of the element the attribute is placed on).	
	Type:	uri-reference
	Attribute Value Template:	yes

Implemented:
W3C 1.0 specification (recommendation)
W3C 1.1 specification (working draft)
MSXML 2.0 (IE5)
MSXML 2.6 (January 2000 preview)
MSXML 3.0
MSXML 4.0

Can contain:
\<xsl:apply-imports\>, \<xsl:apply-templates\>, \<xsl:call-template\>, \<xsl:choose\>, \<xsl:copy\>, \<xsl:copy-of\>, \<xsl:fallback\>, \<xsl:for-each\>, \<xsl:if\>, \<xsl:message\>, \<xsl:number\>, \<xsl:text\>, \<xsl:value-of\>, \<xsl:variable\>

Can be contained by:
\<xsl:attribute-set\>, \<xsl:copy\>, \<xsl:document\>, \<xsl:element\>, \<xsl:fallback\>, \<xsl:for-each\>, \<xsl:if\>, \<xsl:message\>, \<xsl:otherwise\>, \<xsl:param\>, \<xsl:template\>, \<xsl:variable, xsl:when\>

<xsl:attribute-set>

Used to define a set of attributes that can then be added to an element as a group by specifying the `<xsl:attribute-set>` element's name attribute value in the `use-attribute-sets` attribute on the `<xsl:element>` element.

Attributes:

`name` (required)	Name that can be used to refer to this set of attributes.
	Type: qname
	Attribute Value Template: no
`use-attribute-sets` (optional)	For including an existing attribute set in this attribute set.
	Type: qnames
	Attribute Value Template: no
Implemented:	W3C 1.0 specification (recommendation) W3C 1.1 specification (working draft) MSXML 3.0 MSXML 4.0
Can contain:	`<xsl:attribute>`
Can be contained by:	`<xsl:stylesheet>`, `<xsl:transform>`

<xsl:call-template>

Used to call a template by name. Causes no context switch (change of context node) as `<xsl:apply-templates>` and `<xsl:for-each>` do. The template you call by name will still be processing the same context node as your current template. This element can be used to reuse the same functionality in several templates.

Attributes:

`name` (required)	Name of the template you want to call.
	Type: qname
	Attribute Value Template: no
Implemented:	W3C 1.0 specification (recommendation) W3C 1.1 specification (working draft) MSXML 3.0 MSXML 4.0
Can contain:	`<xsl:with-param>`
Can be contained by:	`<xsl:attribute>`, `<xsl:comment>`, `<xsl:copy>`, `<xsl:document>`, `<xsl:element>`, `<xsl:fallback>`, `<xsl:for-each>`, `<xsl:if>`, `<xsl:message>`, `<xsl:otherwise>`, `<xsl:param>`, `<xsl:processing-instruction>`, `<xsl:template>`, `<xsl:variable>`, `<xsl:when>`

<xsl:choose>

For implementing the choose/when/otherwise construct. Compare to Case/Select in Visual Basic or switch in C and Java.

Implemented:	W3C 1.0 specification (recommendation)
	W3C 1.1 specification (working draft)
	MSXML 2.0 (IE5)
	MSXML 2.6 (January 2000 preview)
	MSXML 3.0
	MSXML 4.0
Can contain:	`<xsl:otherwise>`, `<xsl:when>`
Can be contained by:	`<xsl:attribute>`, `<xsl:comment>`, `<xsl:copy>`, `<xsl:document>`, `<xsl:element>`, `<xsl:fallback>`, `<xsl:for-each>`, `<xsl:if>`, `<xsl:message>`, `<xsl:otherwise>`, `<xsl:param>`, `<xsl:processing-instruction>`, `<xsl:template>`, `<xsl:variable>`, `<xsl:when>`

<xsl:comment>

For generating a comment node in the destination document.

Implemented:	W3C 1.0 specification (recommendation)
	W3C 1.1 specification (working draft)
	MSXML 2.0 (IE5)
	MSXML 2.6 (January 2000 preview)
	MSXML 3.0
	MSXML 4.0
Can contain:	`<xsl:apply-imports>`, `<xsl:apply-templates>`, `<xsl:call-template>`, `<xsl:choose>`, `<xsl:copy>`, `<xsl:copy-of>`, `<xsl:fallback>`, `<xsl:for-each>`, `<xsl:if>`, `<xsl:message>`, `<xsl:number>`, `<xsl:text>`, `<xsl:value-of>`, `<xsl:variable>`
Can be contained by:	`<xsl:copy>`, `<xsl:document>`, `<xsl:element>`, `<xsl:fallback>`, `<xsl:for-each>`, `<xsl:if>`, `<xsl:message>`, `<xsl:otherwise>`, `<xsl:param>`, `<xsl:template>`, `<xsl:variable>`, `<xsl:when>`

<xsl:copy>

Generates a copy of the context node in the destination document. Does not copy any children or attributes.

Attributes:

use-attribute-sets (optional)	For adding a set of attributes to the copied node.

Type:	qnames
Attribute Value Template:	no

Implemented:	W3C 1.0 specification (recommendation) W3C 1.1 specification (working draft) MSXML 2.0 (IE5) MSXML 2.6 (January 2000 preview) MSXML 3.0 MSXML 4.0
Can contain:	<xsl:apply-imports>, <xsl:apply-templates>, <xsl:attribute>, <xsl:call-template>, <xsl:choose>, <xsl:comment>, <xsl:copy>, <xsl:copy-of>, <xsl:document>, <xsl:element>, <xsl:fallback>, <xsl:for-each>, <xsl:if>, <xsl:message>, <xsl:number>, <xsl:processing-instruction>, <xsl:text>, <xsl:value-of>, <xsl:variable>
Can be contained by:	<xsl:attribute>, <xsl:comment>, <xsl:copy>, <xsl:document>, <xsl:element>, <xsl:fallback>, <xsl:for-each>, <xsl:if>, <xsl:message>, <xsl:otherwise>, <xsl:param>, <xsl:processing-instruction>, <xsl:template>, <xsl:variable>, <xsl:when>

\<xsl:copy-of\>

Copies a full tree, including attributes and children, to the destination document. If multiple nodes are matched by the `select` attribute, all of the sub trees are copied. If you have an XML fragment stored in a variable, `<xsl:copy-of>` is the handiest element to send the variables content to the output.

Attributes:

`select` (required)	XPath expression leading to the nodes to be copied.
	Type: `expression`
	Attribute Value Template: no
Implemented:	W3C 1.0 specification (recommendation)
	W3C 1.1 specification (working draft)
	MSXML 2.6 (January 2000 preview)
	MSXML 3.0
	MSXML 4.0
Can contain:	No other elements
Can be contained by:	`<xsl:attribute>`, `<xsl:comment>`, `<xsl:copy>`, `<xsl:document>`, `<xsl:element>`, `<xsl:fallback>`, `<xsl:for-each>`, `<xsl:if>`, `<xsl:message>`, `<xsl:otherwise>`, `<xsl:param>`, `<xsl:processing-instruction>`, `<xsl:template>`, `<xsl:variable>`, `<xsl:when>`

\<xsl:decimal-format\>

Declares a decimal format, which controls the interpretation of a format pattern used by the `format-number()` function. This includes defining the decimal separator and the thousands separator.

Attributes:

`name` (optional)	The name of the defined format.
	Type: `qname`
	Attribute Value Template: no
`decimal-separator` (optional)	The character that will separate the integer part from the fraction part. Default is a dot (.).
	Type: `char`
	Attribute Value Template: no

Table continued on following page

grouping-separator (optional)	The character that will separate the grouped numbers in the integer part. Default is a comma (,).	
	Type:	char
	Attribute Value Template:	no
infinity (optional)	The string that should appear if a number equals infinity. Default is the string 'Infinity'	
	Type:	string
	Attribute Value Template:	no
minus-sign (optional)	The character that will be used to indicate a negative number. Default is minus (-).	
	Type:	char
	Attribute Value Template:	no
NaN (optional)	The string that should appear if a number is Not a Number. Default is the string 'NaN'.	
	Type:	string
	Attribute Value Template:	no
percent (optional)	Character that will be used as the percent sign. Default is %.	
	Type:	char
	Attribute Value Template:	no
per-mille (optional)	Character that will be used as the per-thousand sign. Default is the Unicode character #x2030, which looks like ‰.	
	Type:	char
	Attribute Value Template:	no
zero-digit (optional)	The character used as the digit zero. Default is 0.	
	Type:	char
	Attribute Value Template:	no
digit (optional)	The character used in a pattern to indicate the place where a leading zero is required. Default is 0.	
	Type:	char
	Attribute Value Template:	no
pattern-separator (optional)	The character that is used to separate the negative and positive patterns (if they are different). Default is semicolon (;).	

	Type: char
	Attribute Value Template: no
Implemented:	W3C 1.0 specification (recommendation) W3C 1.1 specification (working draft) MSXML 2.6 (January 2000 preview) MSXML 3.0 MSXML 4.0
Can contain:	No other elements
Can be contained by:	`<xsl:stylesheet>`, `<xsl:transform>`

`<xsl:document>`

Switches the target of the result tree to another document. All output nodes instantiated within the `<xsl:document>` element will appear in the document indicated by the href attribute. All other attributes are identical to the attributes on `<xsl:output>`. Note that this element is not part of the XSLT 1.0 specification; it is an XSLT 1.1 extension.

Attributes:

method (optional)	xml is default.
	html will create empty elements like ` ` and use HTML entities like à .
	text will cause no output escaping to happen at all (no entity references in output).
	Type: xml|html|text|qname-but-not-ncname
	Attribute Value Template: yes
version (optional)	The version number that will appear in the XML declaration of the output document.
	Type: token
	Attribute Value Template: yes
encoding (optional)	The encoding of the output document.
	Type: string
	Attribute Value Template: yes
omit-xml-declaration (optional)	Specifies if the resulting document should contain an XML declaration (`<?xml version="1.0"?>`).
	Type: yes|no

Table continued on following page

	Attribute Value Template:	yes
standalone (optional)	Specifies whether the XSLT processor should output a standalone document declaration.	
	Type:	yes|no
	Attribute Value Template:	yes
doctype-public (optional)	Specifies the public identifier to be used in the DTD.	
	Type:	string
	Attribute Value Template:	yes
doctype-system (optional)	Specifies the system identifier to be used in the DTD.	
	Type:	string
	Attribute Value Template:	yes
cdata-section-elements (optional)	Specifies a list of elements that should have their content escaped by using a CDATA section instead of entities.	
	Type:	qnames
	Attribute Value Template:	yes
indent (optional)	Specifies the addition of extra whitespace for readability.	
	Type:	yes|no
	Attribute Value Template:	yes
media-type (optional)	To specify a specific MIME type while writing out content.	
	Type:	string
	Attribute Value Template:	yes
Implemented:	W3C 1.1 specification (working draft)	
Can contain:	`<xsl:apply-imports>`, `<xsl:apply-templates>`, `<xsl:attribute>`, `<xsl:call-template>`, `<xsl:choose>`, `<xsl:comment>`, `<xsl:copy>`, `<xsl:copy-of>`, `<xsl:document>`, `<xsl:element>`, `<xsl:fallback>`, `<xsl:for-each>`, `<xsl:if>`, `<xsl:message>`, `<xsl:number>`, `<xsl:processing-instruction>`, `<xsl:text>`, `<xsl:value-of>`, `<xsl:variable>`	
Can be contained by:	`<xsl:copy>`, `<xsl:document>`, `<xsl:element>`, `<xsl:fallback>`, `<xsl:for-each>`, `<xsl:if>`, `<xsl:message>`, `<xsl:otherwise>`, `<xsl:param>`, `<xsl:template>`, `<xsl:variable>`, `<xsl:when>`	

<xsl:element>

Generates an element with the specified name in the destination document.

Attributes:

name (required)	Name of the element (this may include a prefix bound to a namespace in the stylesheet).	
	Type:	qname
	Attribute Value Template:	yes
namespace (optional)	To overrule the namespace that follows from the prefix in the name attribute (if any).	
	Type:	uri-reference
	Attribute Value Template:	yes
use-attribute-sets (optional)	To add a predefined set of attributes to the element.	
	Type:	qnames
	Attribute Value Template:	no

Implemented:	W3C 1.0 specification (recommendation) W3C 1.1 specification (working draft) MSXML 2.0 (IE5) MSXML 2.6 (January 2000 preview) MSXML 3.0 MSXML 4.0
Can contain:	`<xsl:apply-imports>`, `<xsl:apply-templates>`, `<xsl:attribute>`, `<xsl:call-template>`, `<xsl:choose>`, `<xsl:comment>`, `<xsl:copy>`, `<xsl:copy-of>`, `<xsl:document>`, `<xsl:element>`, `<xsl:fallback>`, `<xsl:for-each>`, `<xsl:if>`, `<xsl:message>`, `<xsl:number>`, `<xsl:processing-instruction>`, `<xsl:text>`, `<xsl:value-of>`, `<xsl:variable>`
Can be contained by:	`<xsl:copy>`, `<xsl:document>`, `<xsl:element>`, `<xsl:fallback>`, `<xsl:for-each>`, `<xsl:if>`, `<xsl:message>`, `<xsl:otherwise>`, `<xsl:param>`, `<xsl:template>`, `<xsl:variable>`, `<xsl:when>`

<xsl:fallback>

Can be used to specify actions to be executed if the action of its parent element is not supported by the processor.

Implemented:	W3C 1.0 specification (recommendation) W3C 1.1 specification (working draft) MSXML 3.0 MSXML 4.0
Can contain:	`<xsl:apply-imports>`, `<xsl:apply-templates>`, `<xsl:attribute>`, `<xsl:call-template>`, `<xsl:choose>`, `<xsl:comment>`, `<xsl:copy>`, `<xsl:copy-of>`, `<xsl:document>`, `<xsl:element>`, `<xsl:fallback>`, `<xsl:for-each>`, `<xsl:if>`, `<xsl:message>`, `<xsl:number>`, `<xsl:processing-instruction>`, `<xsl:text>`, `<xsl:value-of>`, `<xsl:variable>`
Can be contained by:	`<xsl:attribute>`, `<xsl:comment>`, `<xsl:copy>`, `<xsl:document>`, `<xsl:element>`, `<xsl:fallback>`, `<xsl:for-each>`, `<xsl:if>`, `<xsl:message>`, `<xsl:otherwise>`, `<xsl:param>`, `<xsl:processing-instruction>`, `<xsl:template>`, `<xsl:variable>`, `<xsl:when>`

<xsl:for-each>

For looping through the node selected by the XPath expression in the `select` attribute. The context is shifted to the current node in the loop.

Attributes:

`select` (required)	Expression that selects the nodes to loop through.
	Type: `node-set-expression`
	Attribute Value Template: no
Implemented:	W3C 1.0 specification (recommendation) W3C 1.1 specification (working draft) MSXML 2.0 (IE5) MSXML 2.6 (January 2000 preview) MSXML 3.0 MSXML 4.0
Can contain:	`<xsl:apply-imports>`, `<xsl:apply-templates>`, `<xsl:attribute>`, `<xsl:call-template>`, `<xsl:choose>`, `<xsl:comment>`, `<xsl:copy>`, `<xsl:copy-of>`, `<xsl:document>`, `<xsl:element>`, `<xsl:fallback>`, `<xsl:for-each>`, `<xsl:if>`, `<xsl:message>`, `<xsl:number>`, `<xsl:processing-instruction>`, `<xsl:sort>`, `<xsl:text>`, `<xsl:value-of>`, `<xsl:variable>`

Can be contained by:	`<xsl:attribute>`, `<xsl:comment>`, `<xsl:copy>`, `<xsl:document>`, `<xsl:element>`, `<xsl:fallback>`, `<xsl:for-each>`, `<xsl:if>`, `<xsl:message>`, `<xsl:otherwise>`, `<xsl:param>`, `<xsl:processing-instruction>`, `<xsl:template>`, `<xsl:variable>`, `<xsl:when>`

`<xsl:if>`

Executes the contained elements only if the test expression returns TRUE (or a filled node-set).

Attributes:

`test` (required)	The expression that is tested. If it returns TRUE or a non-empty node-set, the content of the `<xsl:if>` element is executed.
	Type: `boolean-expression`
	Attribute Value Template: no
Implemented:	W3C 1.0 specification (recommendation) W3C 1.1 specification (working draft) MSXML 2.0 (IE5) MSXML 2.6 (January 2000 preview) MSXML 3.0 MSXML 4.0
Can contain:	`<xsl:apply-imports>`, `<xsl:apply-templates>`, `<xsl:attribute>`, `<xsl:call-template>`, `<xsl:choose>`, `<xsl:comment>`, `<xsl:copy>`, `<xsl:copy-of>`, `<xsl:document>`, `<xsl:element>`, `<xsl:fallback>`, `<xsl:for-each>`, `<xsl:if>`, `<xsl:message>`, `<xsl:number>`, `<xsl:processing-instruction>`, `<xsl:text>`, `<xsl:value-of>`, `<xsl:variable>`
Can be contained by:	`<xsl:attribute>`, `<xsl:comment>`, `<xsl:copy>`, `<xsl:document>`, `<xsl:element>`, `<xsl:fallback>`, `<xsl:for-each>`, `<xsl:if>`, `<xsl:message>`, `<xsl:otherwise>`, `<xsl:param>`, `<xsl:processing-instruction>`, `<xsl:template>`, `<xsl:variable>`, `<xsl:when>`

<xsl:import>

Imports the templates from an external stylesheet document into the current document. The priority of these imported templates is very low, so if a template in the importing document is implemented for the same pattern, it will always prevail over the imported template. The imported template can be called from the overriding template using `<xsl:apply-imports>`.

Attributes:

`href` (required)	Reference to the stylesheet to be imported.	
	Type:	`uri-reference`
	Attribute Value Template:	no
Implemented:	W3C 1.0 specification (recommendation) W3C 1.1 specification (working draft) MSXML 3.0 MSXML 4.0	
Can contain:	No other elements	
Can be contained by	`<xsl:stylesheet>`, `<xsl:transform>`	

<xsl:include>

Includes templates from an external document as if they were part of the importing document. This means that templates from the included stylesheet have the same priority as they would have had if they were part of the including stylesheet. An error occurs if a template with the same `match` and `priority` attributes exists in both the including and included stylesheets.

Attributes:

`href` (required)	Reference to the stylesheet to be imported.	
	Type:	`uri-reference`
	Attribute Value Template:	no
Implemented:	W3C 1.0 specification (recommendation) W3C 1.1 specification (working draft) MSXML 2.6 (January 2000 preview) MSXML 3.0 MSXML 4.0	
Can contain:	No other elements	
Can be contained by:	`<xsl:stylesheet>`, `<xsl:transform>`	

\<xsl:key>

Can be used to create index-like structures that can be queried from the key() function. It is basically a way to describe name/value pairs inside the source document (like a Dictionary object in VB, a Hashtable in Java, or an associative array in Perl). However, in XSLT, more than one value can be found for one key and the same value can be accessed by multiple keys.

Attributes:

name (required)   The name that can be used to refer to this key.

	Type:	qname
	Attribute Value Template:	no

match (required)   The pattern defines which nodes in the source document can be accessed using this key. In the name/value pair analogy, this would be the definition of the value.

	Type:	pattern
	Attribute Value Template:	no

use (required)   This expression defines what the key for accessing each value would be. Example: if an element PERSON is matched by the match attribute and the use attribute equals "@name", the key() function can be used to find this specific PERSON element by passing the value of its name attribute.

	Type:	expression
	Attribute Value Template:	no

Implemented: W3C 1.0 specification (recommendation)
W3C 1.1 specification (working draft)
MSXML 3.0
MSXML 4.0

Can contain: No other elements

Can be contained by: \<xsl:stylesheet>, \<xsl:transform>

<xsl:message>

To issue error messages or warnings. The content of the element is the message. What the XSLT processor does with the message depends on the implementation. You could think of displaying it within a message box or logging to the error log.

Attributes:

`terminate` (optional)	If `terminate` is set to `yes`, the execution of the transformation is stopped after issuing the message.

	Type:	yes|no
	Attribute Value Template:	no

Implemented:	W3C 1.0 specification (recommendation) W3C 1.1 specification (working draft) MSXML 3.0 MSXML 4.0
Can contain:	`<xsl:apply-imports>`, `<xsl:apply-templates>`, `<xsl:attribute>`, `<xsl:call-template>`, `<xsl:choose>`, `<xsl:comment>`, `<xsl:copy>`, `<xsl:copy-of>`, `<xsl:document>`, `<xsl:element>`, `<xsl:fallback>`, `<xsl:for-each>`, `<xsl:if>`, `<xsl:message>`, `<xsl:number>`, `<xsl:processing-instruction>`, `<xsl:text>`, `<xsl:value-of>`, `<xsl:variable>`
Can be contained by:	`<xsl:attribute>`, `<xsl:comment>`, `<xsl:copy>`, `<xsl:document>`, `<xsl:element>`, `<xsl:fallback>`, `<xsl:for-each>`, `<xsl:if>`, `<xsl:message>`, `<xsl:otherwise>`, `<xsl:param>`, `<xsl:processing-instruction>`, `<xsl:template>`, `<xsl:variable>`, `<xsl:when>`

<xsl:namespace-alias>

Used to make a certain namespace appear in the destination document without using that namespace in the stylesheet. The main use of this element is in generating new XSLT stylesheets.

Attributes:

`stylesheet-prefix` (required)	The prefix for the namespace that is used in the stylesheet	
	Type:	`prefix|#default`
	Attribute Value Template:	no
`result-prefix` (required)	The prefix for the namespace that must replace the aliased namespace in the destination document.	
	Type:	`prefix|#default`
	Attribute Value Template:	no
Implemented:	W3C 1.0 specification (recommendation) W3C 1.1 specification (working draft) MSXML 3.0 MSXML 4.0	
Can contain:	No other elements	
Can be contained by:	`<xsl:stylesheet>`, `<xsl:transform>`	

<xsl:number>

For outputting the number of a paragraph or chapter in a specified format. It has very flexible features, to allow for different numbering rules.

Attributes:

level (optional)

The value `single` counts the location of the nearest node matched by the `count` attribute (along the ancestor axis) relative to its preceding siblings of the same name. Typical output: chapter number.

The value `multiple` will count the location of all the nodes matched by the `count` attribute (along the ancestor axis) relative to their preceding siblings of the same name. Typical output: paragraph number of form 4.5.3.

The value `any` will count the location of the nearest node matched by the `count` attribute (along the ancestor axis) relative to their preceding nodes (not only siblings) of the same name. Typical output: bookmark number

Type:	`single|multiple|any`
Attribute Value Template:	no

count (optional)

Specifies the type of node that is to be counted.

Type:	`pattern`
Attribute Value Template:	no

from (optional)

Specifies the starting point for counting.

Type:	`pattern`
Attribute Value Template:	no

value (optional)

Used to specify the numeric value directly instead of using `'level'`, `'count'` and `'from'`.

Type:	`number-expression`
Attribute Value Template:	no

format (optional)

How to format the numeric value to a string (1 becomes 1, 2, 3, ...; a becomes a, b, c,).

Type:	`string`
Attribute Value Template:	yes

lang (optional)

Language used for alphabetic numbering

Type:	`token`
Attribute Value Template:	yes

letter-value (optional)	Some languages have traditional orders of letters specifically for numbering. These orders are often different from the alphabetic order.
	Type: `alphabetic|traditional`
	Attribute Value Template: yes
grouping- separator (optional)	Character to be used for group separation.
	Type: `char`
	Attribute Value Template: yes
grouping-size (optional)	Number of digits to be separated. `grouping-separator=";"` and `grouping-size="3"` causes: 1;000;000.
	Type: `number`
	Attribute Value Template: yes
Implemented:	W3C 1.0 specification (recommendation) W3C 1.1 specification (working draft) MSXML 3.0 MSXML 4.0
Can contain:	No other elements
Can be contained by:	`<xsl:attribute>`, `<xsl:comment>`, `<xsl:copy>`, `<xsl:document>`, `<xsl:element>`, `<xsl:fallback>`, `<xsl:for-each>`, `<xsl:if>`, `<xsl:message>`, `<xsl:otherwise>`, `<xsl:param>`, `<xsl:processing-instruction>`, `<xsl:template>`, `<xsl:variable>`, `<xsl:when>`

<xsl:otherwise>

Content is executed if none of the `<xsl:when>` elements in an `<xsl:choose>` is matched.

Implemented:	W3C 1.0 specification (recommendation) W3C 1.1 specification (working draft) MSXML 2.0 (IE5) MSXML 2.6 (January 2000 preview) MSXML 3.0 MSXML 4.0
Can contain:	`<xsl:apply-imports>`, `<xsl:apply-templates>`, `<xsl:attribute>`, `<xsl:call-template>`, `<xsl:choose>`, `<xsl:comment>`, `<xsl:copy>`, `<xsl:copy-of>`, `<xsl:document>`, `<xsl:element>`, `<xsl:fallback>`, `<xsl:for-each>`, `<xsl:if>`, `<xsl:message>`, `<xsl:number>`, `<xsl:processing-instruction>`, `<xsl:text>`, `<xsl:value-of>`, `<xsl:variable>`
Can be contained by:	`<xsl:choose>`

Top-level element for setting properties regarding the output style of the destination document. The `<xsl:output>` element basically describes how the translation from a created XML tree to a character array (string) happens.

Attributes:

method (optional)	xml is default html will create empty elements like ` ` and use HTML entities like `&agrave;`. text will cause no output escaping to happen at all (no entity references in output.)
	Type: `xml|html|text|qname-but-not-ncname`
	Attribute Value Template: no
version (optional)	The version number that will appear in the XML declaration of the output document.
	Type: token
	Attribute Value Template: no
encoding (optional)	The encoding of the output document.
	Type: string
	Attribute Value Template: no

`omit-xml-declaration` (optional)	Specifies if the resulting document should contain an XML declaration (`<?xml version="1.0"?>`)
	Type: `yes`|`no`
	Attribute Value Template: no
`standalone` (optional)	Specifies whether the XSLT processor should output a standalone document declaration.
	Type: `yes`|`no`
	Attribute Value Template: no
`doctype-public` (optional)	Specifies the public identifier to be used in the DTD
	Type: `string`
	Attribute Value Template: no
`doctype-system` (optional)	Specifies the system identifier to be used in the DTD
	Type: `string`
	Attribute Value Template: no
`cdata-section-elements` (optional)	Specifies a list of elements that should have their content escaped by using a CDATA section instead of entities.
	Type: `qnames`
	Attribute Value Template: no
`indent` (optional)	Specifies the addition of extra whitespace for readability
	Type: `yes`|`no`
	Attribute Value Template: no
`media-type` (optional)	To specify a specific MIME type while writing out content.
	Type: `string`
	Attribute Value Template: no
Implemented:	W3C 1.0 specification (recommendation) W3C 1.1 specification (working draft) MSXML 2.6 (January 2000 preview) (No support for methods `html` and `text`) MSXML 3.0 MSXML 4.0
Can contain:	No other elements
Can be contained by:	`<xsl:stylesheet>`, `<xsl:transform>`

<xsl:param>

Defines a parameter in a `<xsl:template>` or `<xsl:stylesheet>`.	
Attributes:	
name (required)	Name of the parameter
	Type: qname
	Attribute Value Template: no
select (optional)	Specifies the default value for the parameter
	Type: expression
	Attribute Value Template: no
Implemented:	W3C 1.0 specification (recommendation)
	W3C 1.1 specification (working draft)
	MSXML 2.6 (January 2000 preview)
	MSXML 3.0
	MSXML 4.0
Can contain:	`<xsl:apply-imports>`, `<xsl:apply-templates>`, `<xsl:attribute>`, `<xsl:call-template>`, `<xsl:choose>`, `<xsl:comment>`, `<xsl:copy>`, `<xsl:copy-of>`, `<xsl:document>`, `<xsl:element>`, `<xsl:fallback>`, `<xsl:for-each>`, `<xsl:if>`, `<xsl:message>`, `<xsl:number>`, `<xsl:processing-instruction>`, `<xsl:text>`, `<xsl:value-of>`, `<xsl:variable>`
Can be contained by:	`<xsl:stylesheet>`, `<xsl:transform>`

<xsl:preserve-space>

Allows you to define which elements in the source document should have their whitespace content preserved. See also `<xsl:strip-space>`.	
Attributes:	
elements (required)	In this attribute you can list the elements (separated by whitespace) for which you want to preserve the whitespace content.
	Type: tokens
	Attribute Value Template: no
Implemented:	W3C 1.0 specification (recommendation)
	W3C 1.1 specification (working draft)
	MSXML 3.0
	MSXML 4.0
Can contain:	No other elements
Can be contained by:	`<xsl:stylesheet>`, `<xsl:transform>`

<xsl:processing-instruction>

Generates a processing instruction in the destination document.

Attributes:

name (required)	The name of the processing instruction (the part between the first question mark and the first whitespace of the processing instruction)

	Type: ncname
	Attribute Value Template: yes

Implemented:	W3C 1.0 specification (recommendation) W3C 1.1 specification (working draft) MSXML 2.0 (IE5) (Caution: the `<xsl:processing-instruction>` element is called `<xsl:pi>` in IE5) MSXML 2.6 (January 2000 preview) MSXML 3.0 MSXML 4.0

Can contain:	`<xsl:apply-imports>`, `<xsl:apply-templates>`, `<xsl:call-template>`, `<xsl:choose>`, `<xsl:copy>`, `<xsl:copy-of>`, `<xsl:fallback>`, `<xsl:for-each>`, `<xsl:if>`, `<xsl:message>`, `<xsl:number>`, `<xsl:text>`, `<xsl:value-of>`, `<xsl:variable>`

Can be contained by:	`<xsl:copy>`, `<xsl:document>`, `<xsl:element>`, `<xsl:fallback>`, `<xsl:for-each>`, `<xsl:if>`, `<xsl:message>`, `<xsl:otherwise>`, `<xsl:param>`, `<xsl:template>`, `<xsl:variable>`, `<xsl:when>`

<xsl:sort>

Allows specifying a sort order for `<xsl:apply-templates>` and `<xsl:for-each>` elements. Multiple `<xsl:sort>` elements can be specified for primary and secondary sorting keys.

Attributes:

select (optional)	Expression that indicates which should be used for the ordering.

	Type: string-expression
	Attribute Value Template: no

lang (optional)	To set the language used while ordering (in different languages the rules for alphabetic ordering can be different).

	Type: token
	Attribute Value Template: yes

Table continued on following page

data-type (optional)	To specify alphabetic or numeric ordering.	
	Type:	text|number|qname-but-not-ncname
	Attribute Value Template:	yes
order (optional)	Specifies ascending or descending ordering.	
	Type:	ascending|descending
	Attribute Value Template:	yes
case-order (optional)	Specifies if uppercase characters should order before or after lower-case characters. Note that case-insensitive sorting is not supported.	
	Type:	upper-first|lower-first
	Attribute Value Template:	yes
Implemented:	W3C 1.0 specification (recommendation) W3C 1.1 specification (working draft) MSXML 2.6 (January 2000 preview) MSXML 3.0 MSXML 4.0	
Can contain:	No other elements	
Can be contained by:	<xsl:apply-templates>, <xsl:for-each>	

<xsl:strip-space>

Allows you to define which elements in the source document should have their whitespace content stripped. See also <xsl:preserve-space>.		
Attributes:		
elements (required)	Specify which elements should preserve their whitespace contents.	
	Type:	tokens
	Attribute Value Template:	no
Implemented:	W3C 1.0 specification (recommendation) W3C 1.1 specification (working draft) MSXML 2.6 (January 2000 preview) MSXML 3.0 MSXML 4.0	
Can contain:	No other elements	
Can be contained by:	<xsl:stylesheet>, <xsl:transform>	

\<xsl:stylesheet\>

The root element for a stylesheet. Synonym to `<xsl:transform>`.

Attributes:

`id` (optional)	A reference for the stylesheet.

Type: `id`

Attribute Value Template: `no`

`extension-element-prefixes` (optional)	Allows you to specify which namespace prefixes are XSLT extension namespaces (like `msxml`).

Type: `tokens`

Attribute Value Template: `no`

`exclude-result-prefixes` (optional)	Namespaces that are only relevant in the stylesheet or in the source document, but not in the result document, can be removed from the output by specifying them here.

Type: `tokens`

Attribute Value Template: `no`

`version` (required)	Version number

Type: `number`

Attribute Value Template: `no`

Implemented:
W3C 1.0 specification (recommendation)
W3C 1.1 specification (working draft)
MSXML 2.0 (IE5)
MSXML 2.6 (January 2000 preview)
MSXML 3.0
MSXML 4.0

Can contain:
`<xsl:attribute-set>`, `<xsl:decimal-format>`,
`<xsl:import>`, `<xsl:include>`, `<xsl:key>`,
`<xsl:namespace-alias>`, `<xsl:output>`, `<xsl:param>`,
`<xsl:preserve-space>`, `<xsl:strip-space>`,
`<xsl:template>`, `<xsl:variable>`

Can be contained by: No other elements

867

<xsl:template>

Defines a transformation rule. Some templates are built-in and don't have to be defined.

Attributes:

match (optional)   Defines the set of nodes on which the template can be applied.

Type:	pattern
Attribute Value Template:	no

name (optional)   Name to identify the template when calling it using `<xsl:call-template>`.

Type:	qname
Attribute Value Template:	no

priority (optional)   If several templates can be applied (through their match attributes) on a node, the priority attribute can be used to make a certain template prevail over others.

Type:	number
Attribute Value Template:	no

mode (optional)   If a mode attribute is present on a template, the template will only be considered for transforming a node when the transformation was started by an `<xsl:apply-templates>` element with a mode attribute with the same value.

Type:	qname
Attribute Value Template:	no

Implemented:
W3C 1.0 specification (recommendation)
W3C 1.1 specification (working draft)
MSXML 2.0 (IE5)
MSXML 2.6 (January 2000 preview) (except for the mode attribute)
MSXML 3.0
MSXML 4.0

Can contain:
`<xsl:apply-imports>`, `<xsl:apply-templates>`, `<xsl:attribute>`, `<xsl:call-template>`, `<xsl:choose>`, `<xsl:comment>`, `<xsl:copy>`, `<xsl:copy-of>`, `<xsl:document>`, `<xsl:element>`, `<xsl:fallback>`, `<xsl:for-each>`, `<xsl:if>`, `<xsl:message>`, `<xsl:number>`, `<xsl:processing-instruction>`, `<xsl:text>`, `<xsl:value-of>`, `<xsl:variable>`

Can be contained by:
`<xsl:stylesheet>`, `<xsl:transform>`

<xsl:text>

Generates a text string from its content. Whitespace is never stripped from an <xsl:text> element.	
Attributes:	
disable-output-escaping (optional)	If set to yes, the output will not be escaped: this means that a string "<" will be written to the output as "<" instead of "&lt;". This means that the result document will not be a well-formed XML document anymore.
	Type: yes|no
	Attribute Value Template: no
Implemented	W3C 1.0 specification (recommendation) W3C 1.1 specification (working draft) MSXML 2.0 (IE5) MSXML 2.6 (January 2000 preview) MSXML 3.0 MSXML 4.0
Can contain:	No other elements
Can be contained by:	<xsl:attribute>, <xsl:comment>, <xsl:copy>, <xsl:document>, <xsl:element>, <xsl:fallback>, <xsl:for-each>, <xsl:if>, <xsl:message>, <xsl:otherwise>, <xsl:param>, <xsl:processing-instruction>, <xsl:template>, <xsl:variable>, <xsl:when>

<xsl:transform>

Identical to <xsl:stylesheet>	
Attributes:	
id (optional)	A reference for the stylesheet.
	Type: id
	Attribute Value Template: no
extension-element-prefixes (optional)	Allows you to specify which namespace prefixes are XSLT extension namespaces (like msxml).
	Type: tokens
	Attribute Value Template: no
exclude-result-prefixes (optional)	Namespaces that are only relevant in the stylesheet or in the source document, but not in the result document, can be removed from the output by specifying them here.

Table continued on following page

	Type:	tokens
	Attribute Value Template:	no
version (required)	Version number	
	Type:	number
	Attribute Value Template:	no
Implemented:	W3C 1.0 specification (recommendation) W3C 1.1 specification (working draft) MSXML 3.0 MSXML 4.0	
Can contain:	`<xsl:attribute-set>`, `<xsl:decimal-format>`, `<xsl:import>`, `<xsl:include>`, `<xsl:key>`, `<xsl:namespace-alias>`, `<xsl:output>`, `<xsl:param>`, `<xsl:preserve-space>`, `<xsl:strip-space>`, `<xsl:template>`, `<xsl:variable>`	
Can be contained by:	No other elements	

`<xsl:value-of>`

Generates a text string with the value of the expression in the `select` attribute.

Attributes:

select (required)	Expression that selects the node-set that will be converted to a string	
	Type:	string-expression
	Attribute Value Template:	no
disable-output-escaping (optional)	You can use this to output < instead of < to the destination document. Note that this will cause your destination to become invalid XML. Normally used to generate HTML or text files.	
	Type:	yes|no
	Attribute Value Template:	no
Implemented:	W3C 1.0 specification (recommendation) W3C 1.1 specification (working draft) MSXML 2.0 (IE5) MSXML 2.6 (January 2000 preview) MSXML 3.0 MSXML 4.0	
Can contain:	No other elements	
Can be contained by:	`<xsl:attribute>`, `<xsl:comment>`, `<xsl:copy>`, `<xsl:document>`, `<xsl:element>`, `<xsl:fallback>`, `<xsl:for-each>`, `<xsl:if>`, `<xsl:message>`, `<xsl:otherwise>`, `<xsl:param>`, `<xsl:processing-instruction>`, `<xsl:template>`, `<xsl:variable>`, `<xsl:when>`	

<xsl:variable>

Defines a variable with a value. Note that in XSLT, the value of a variable cannot change; you can instantiate a variable using `<xsl:variable>`, but it cannot be changed afterwards.

Attributes:

name (required)	Name of the variable	
	Type:	qname
	Attribute Value Template:	no
select (optional)	Value of the variable (if the `select` attribute is omitted, the content of the `<xsl:variable>` element is the value).	
	Type:	expression
	Attribute Value Template:	no
Implemented:	W3C 1.0 specification (recommendation) W3C 1.1 specification (working draft) MSXML 2.6 (January 2000 preview) MSXML 3.0 MSXML 4.0	
Can contain:	`<xsl:apply-imports>`, `<xsl:apply-templates>`, `<xsl:attribute>`, `<xsl:call-template>`, `<xsl:choose>`, `<xsl:comment>`, `<xsl:copy>`, `<xsl:copy-of>`, `<xsl:document>`, `<xsl:element>`, `<xsl:fallback>`, `<xsl:for-each>`, `<xsl:if>`, `<xsl:message>`, `<xsl:number>`, `<xsl:processing-instruction>`, `<xsl:text>`, `<xsl:value-of>`, `<xsl:variable>`	
Can be contained by:	`<xsl:attribute>`, `<xsl:comment>`, `<xsl:copy>`, `<xsl:document>`, `<xsl:element>`, `<xsl:fallback>`, `<xsl:for-each>`, `<xsl:if>`, `<xsl:message>`, `<xsl:otherwise>`, `<xsl:param>`, `<xsl:processing-instruction>`, `<xsl:stylesheet>`, `<xsl:template>`, `<xsl:transform>`, `<xsl:variable>`, `<xsl:when>`	

\<xsl:when\>

Represents one of the options for execution in a `<xsl:choose>` block.	
Attributes:	
`test` (required)	Expression to be tested.
	Type: `boolean-expression`
	Attribute Value Template: no
Implemented:	W3C 1.0 specification (recommendation) W3C 1.1 specification (working draft) MSXML 2.0 (IE5) MSXML 2.6 (January 2000 preview) MSXML 3.0 MSXML 4.0
Can contain:	`<xsl:apply-imports>`, `<xsl:apply-templates>`, `<xsl:attribute>`, `<xsl:call-template>`, `<xsl:choose>`, `<xsl:comment>`, `<xsl:copy>`, `<xsl:copy-of>`, `<xsl:document>`, `<xsl:element>`, `<xsl:fallback>`, `<xsl:for-each>`, `<xsl:if>`, `<xsl:message>`, `<xsl:number>`, `<xsl:processing-instruction>`, `<xsl:text>`, `<xsl:value-of>`, `<xsl:variable>`
Can be contained by:	`<xsl:choose>`

\<xsl:with-param\>

Used to pass a parameter to a template using `<xsl:apply-templates>` or `<xsl:call-template>`. The template called must have a parameter of the same name defined using `<xsl:param>`.	
Attributes:	
`name` (required)	Name of the parameter.
	Type: `qname`
	Attribute Value Template: no
`select` (optional)	XPath expression selecting the passed value.
	Type: `expression`
	Attribute Value Template: no
Implemented:	W3C 1.0 specification (recommendation) W3C 1.1 specification (working draft) MSXML 2.6 (January 2000 preview) MSXML 3.0 MSXML 4.0
Can contain:	No other elements
Can be contained by:	`<xsl:apply-templates>`, `<xsl:call-template>`

Functions

Within expressions in an XSLT stylesheet, you can use all the XPath functions we saw in Appendix F and also a number of special XSLT functions. These functions are described here.

Each function is described by a line of this form:

```
return-type function-name (parameters)
```

For each parameter, we display the type (`object`, `string`, `number`, `node-set`) and where necessary a symbol indicating if the parameter is optional (?) or can occur multiple times (+). The type `object` means that any type can be passed.

If an expression is passed as a parameter, it is first evaluated and (if necessary) converted to the expected type before passing it to the function:

```
node-set current ( )
```

Returns the current context node-set, outside the current expression. For MSXML2 you can use the `context()` function as a workaround. `context(-1)` is synonymous to `current()`

Implemented:

W3C 1.0 specification (recommendation)
W3C 1.1 specification (working draft)
MSXML 2.6 (January 2000 preview)
MSXML 3.0
MSXML 4.0

```
node-set document ( object, node-set? )
```

To get a reference to an external source document.

Parameters:

```
object
```

If of type `String`, this is the URL of the document to be retrieved. If a node-set, all nodes are converted to strings and all these URLs are retrieved in a node-set.

```
node-set
```

Represents the base URL from where relative URLs are resolved.

Implemented:

W3C 1.0 specification (recommendation)
W3C 1.1 specification (working draft)
MSXML 3.0
MSXML 4.0

```
boolean element-available ( string )
```

To query availability of a certain extension element.

Parameters:

```
string
```

Name of the extension element.

Implemented:

W3C 1.0 specification (recommendation)
W3C 1.1 specification (working draft)
MSXML 3.0
MSXML 4.0

```
string format-number ( number, string1, string2? )
```

Formats a numeric value into a formatted and localized string.

Parameters:

```
number
```

The numeric value to be represented.

```
string1
```

The format string that should be used for the formatting.

```
string2
```

Reference to a `<xsl:decimal-format>` element to indicate localization parameters.

Implemented:

W3C 1.0 specification (recommendation)
W3C 1.1 specification (working draft)
MSXML 3.0
MSXML 4.0

```
boolean function-available ( string )
```

To query availability of a certain extension function.

Parameter:

```
string
```

Name of the extension function.

Implemented:

W3C 1.0 specification (recommendation)
W3C 1.1 specification (working draft)
MSXML 3.0
MSXML 4.0

```
node-set generate-id ( node-set? )
```

Generates a unique identifier for the specified node. Each node will cause a different ID, but the same node will always generate the same ID. You cannot be sure that the IDs generated for a document during multiple transformations will remain identical.

Parameter:

node-set

The first node of the passed node-set is used. If no node-set is passed, the current context is used.

Implemented:

W3C 1.0 specification (recommendation)
W3C 1.1 specification (working draft)
MSXML 3.0
MSXML 4.0

```
node-set key ( string, object )
```

To get a reference to a node using the specified `<xsl:key>`.

Parameters:

string

The name of the referenced `<xsl:key>`.

object

If of type `String`, this is the index string for the key. If of type `node-set`, all nodes are converted to strings and all are used to get nodes back from the key.

Implemented:

W3C 1.0 specification (recommendation)
W3C 1.1 specification (working draft)
MSXML 3.0
MSXML 4.0

```
object system-property ( string )
```

To get certain system properties from the processor.

Parameter:

string

The name of the system property. Properties that are always available are `xsl:version`, `xsl:vendor`, and `xsl:vendor-url`.

Implemented:

W3C 1.0 specification (recommendation)
W3C 1.1 specification (working draft)
MSXML 3.0
MSXML 4.0

```
string unparsed-entity-url ( string )
```

Returns the URI of the unparsed entity with the passed name.

Parameter:

```
string
```

Name of the unparsed entity.

Implemented:

W3C 1.0 specification (recommendation)
W3C 1.1 specification (working draft)
MSXML 3.0
MSXML 4.0

Inherited XPath Functions

Check Appendix F for information on the XPath functions. They can all be used in XSLT:

boolean()	ceiling()	concat()	contains()
count()	false()	floor()	id()
lang()	last	local-name()	name()
namespace-uri()	normalize-space()	not	number()
position()	round()	starts-with()	string()
string-length()	substring()	substring-after()	substring-before()
sum()	translate()	true()	

Types

These types are used to specify the types of the attributes for the XSLT elements given in the tables above:

Type	Description
boolean	Can have values TRUE and FALSE.
char	A single character.
expression	A string value, containing an XPath expression.
id	A string value. Must be an XML name. The string value can be used only once as an id in any document.
language-name	A string containing one of the defined language identifiers. American English = EN-US.
name	A string value that conforms to the name conventions of XML. That means: no whitespace should start with either a letter or an underscore (_).
names	Multiple name values separated by whitespace.
namespace-prefix	Any string that is defined as a prefix for a namespace.
ncname	A name value that does not contain a colon.
node	A node in an XML document. Can be of several types, including: element, attribute, comment, processing instruction, text node, and so on.
node-set	A set of nodes in a specific order. Can be of any length.
node-set-expression	A string value, containing an XPath expression that returns nodes.
number	A numeric value. Can be either floating point or integer.
object	Anything. Can be a string, a node, a node-set, anything.
qname	Qualified name: the full name of a node. Made up of two parts: the local name and the namespace identifier.
qnames	A set of qname values, separated by whitespace.
string	A string value.
token	A string value that contains no whitespace.
tokens	Multiple token values separated by whitespace.
uri-reference	Any string that conforms to the URI specification.

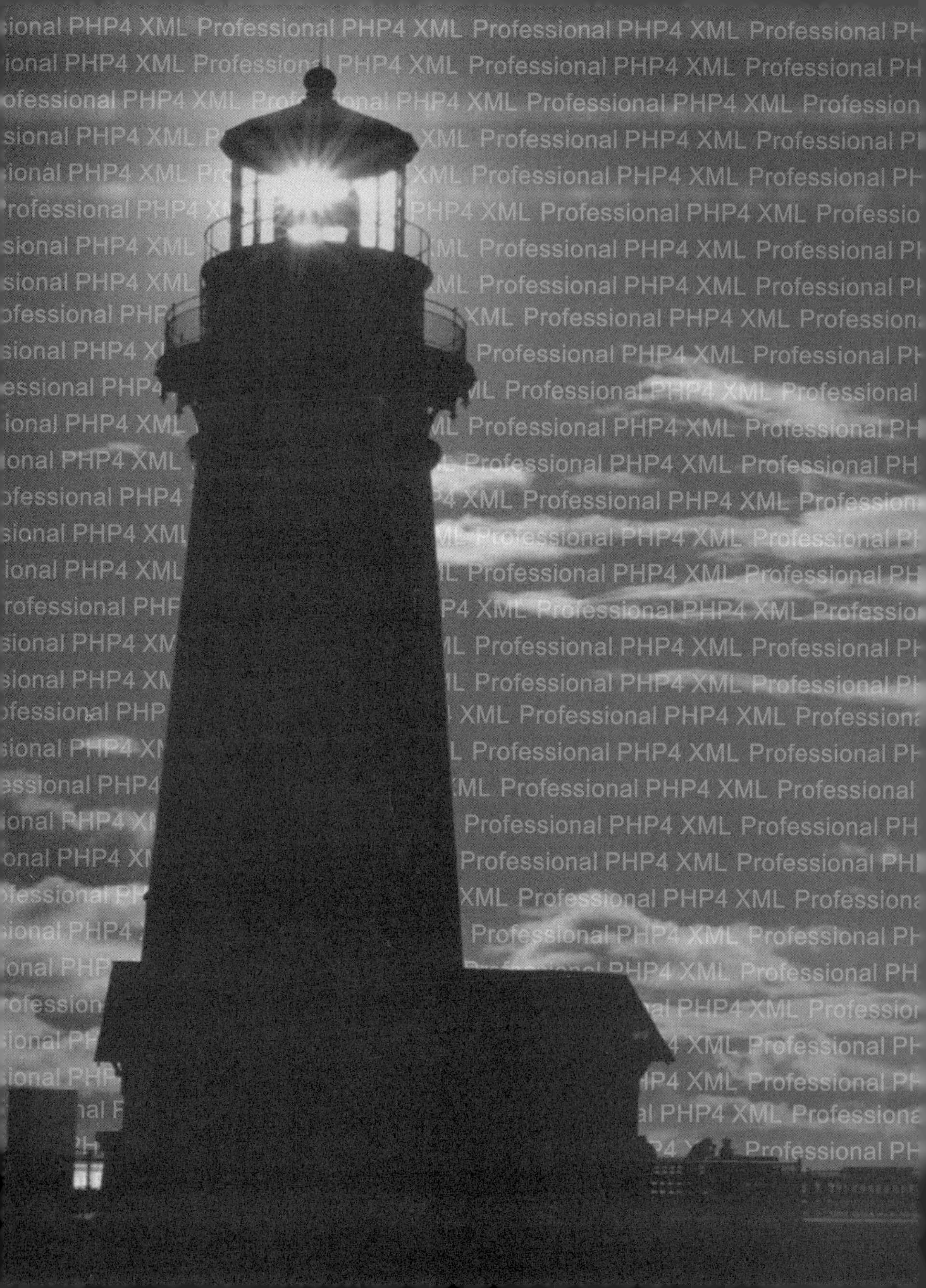
Professional PHP4 XML

XPath Reference

XPath is a W3C Recommendation, describing a syntax for selecting a set of nodes from an XML document. Version 1.0 of XPath reached Recommendation status on 16 November 1999. The requirements document for version 2.0 was a working draft at the time of writing. XPath is an essential part of the XSLT Recommendation.

An XPath location path contains one or more location steps, separated by forward slashes (/). Each location step has the following form:

```
axis-name::node-test [predicate] *
```

In plain English, this is an axis name, then two colons, then a node test, and finally zero or more predicates each contained in square brackets. A predicate can contain literal values (for example, 4, 'hello'), operators (+, -, =, etc.) and other XPath expressions. XPath also defines a set of functions for use in predicates.

The XPath axis defines a part of the document, from the perspective of the context node. This node serves as the 'starting point' for selecting the result set of the XPath expression. The node test makes a selection from the nodes on the given axis. By adding predicates, it is possible to select a subset from these nodes. If the expression in the predicate returns TRUE, the node remains in the selected set, otherwise it is removed.

In this reference we will list the XPath axes, node tests and functions. For each entry, we will list whether it is implemented in version 1.0 of the specification. Also, we will list in which versions of the Microsoft implementation the feature was implemented. Other implementations are not listed.

You can find an online version of the reference at: http://www.vbxml.com/xsl/xpathRef.asp.

We chose to list details on the several MSXML implementations, because Microsoft has chosen to ship several partial implementations of the specification. Although the latest version (MSXML 3.0) is a complete implementation, in many environments the older implementations are still in use. MSXML 2.0 is the version shipped with Internet Explorer 5, causing it to be the most widely installed XSLT implementation (and sadly one of the most incomplete as well). MSXML 2.6 is a version that was released as a preview, but was shipped with certain versions of BizTalk server. Therefore some developers are forced to work with this version.

Other implementations, such as Xalan and Saxon, are not listed here. You can more or less trust their latest versions to implement version 1.0 of the implementation and you will normally not be forced to use a specific version.

Axes

Below, each axis is listed with a description of the nodes it selects. The primary node type of an axis indicates what kind of nodes are selected by the literal node test or the * node test (see under the *literal name* node test for an example). For some axes, XPath defines a shorthand syntax. The form of this syntax and its primary node type are listed for every axis.

ancestor

Description:	Contains the context node's parent node, its parent's parent node, and so on, all the way up to the document root. If the context node is the root node, the ancestor node is empty.
Primary node type:	Element
Shorthand:	None
Implemented:	W3C 1.0 specification (recommendation) MSXML 2.6 (January 2000 preview) MSXML 3.0 MSXML 4.0

ancestor-or-self

Description:	Identical to the ancestor axis, but including the context node itself.
Primary node type:	Element
Shorthand:	None
Implemented:	W3C 1.0 specification (recommendation) MSXML 2.6 (January 2000 preview) MSXML 3.0 MSXML 4.0

attribute

Description:	Contains all attributes on the context node. The axis will be empty unless the context node is an element.
Primary node type:	Attribute
Shorthand:	@
Implemented:	W3C 1.0 specification (recommendation) MSXML 2.6 (January 2000 preview) (erroneously returns namespace declarations as well) MSXML 3.0 MSXML 4.0

child

Description:	Contains all direct children of the context node (that is the children, but not any of the children's children).
Primary node type:	Element
Shorthand:	Default axis if no axis is given
Implemented:	W3C 1.0 specification (recommendation) MSXML 2.0 (IE5) (only shorthand syntax) MSXML 2.6 (January 2000 preview) MSXML 3.0 MSXML 4.0

descendant

Description:	All children of the context node, including all children's children recursively.
Primary node type:	Element
Shorthand:	//
Implemented:	W3C 1.0 specification (recommendation) MSXML 2.0 (IE5) (only shorthand syntax) MSXML 2.6 (January 2000 preview) MSXML 3.0 MSXML 4.0

descendant-or-self

Description:	Identical to the descendant axis, but including the context node itself.
Primary node type:	Element
Shorthand:	None
Implemented:	W3C 1.0 specification (recommendation) MSXML 2.6 (January 2000 preview) MSXML 3.0 MSXML 4.0

following

Description:	Contains all nodes that come after the context node in the document order. This means that the opening tag of the node must come after the closing tag of the context node, and therefore excludes the descendants of the context node.
Primary node type:	Element
Shorthand:	None
Implemented:	W3C 1.0 specification (recommendation) MSXML 3.0 MSXML 4.0

following-sibling

Description:	Contains all siblings (children of the same parent node) of the context node that come after the context node in document order.
Primary node type:	Element
Shorthand:	None
Implemented:	W3C 1.0 specification (recommendation) MSXML 3.0 MSXML 4.0

namespace

Description:	Contains all namespaces available on the context node. This includes the default namespace and the xml namespace (these are automatically declared in any document). The axis will be empty unless the context node is an element.
Primary node type:	Namespace
Shorthand:	None
Implemented:	W3C 1.0 specification (recommendation) MSXML 3.0 MSXML 4.0

parent

Description:	Contains the direct parent node (and only the direct parent node) of the context node, if there is one.
Primary node type:	Element
Shorthand:	..
Implemented:	W3C 1.0 specification (recommendation) MSXML 2.0 (IE5) (only shorthand syntax) MSXML 2.6 (January 2000 preview) MSXML 3.0 MSXML 4.0

preceding

Description:	Contains all nodes that come before the context node in the document order. This includes only elements that are already closed (their closing tag comes before the context node in the document), and therefore excludes all ancestors of the context node.
Primary node type:	Element
Shorthand:	None
Implemented:	W3C 1.0 specification (recommendation) MSXML 3.0 MSXML 4.0

preceding-sibling

Description:	Contains all siblings (children of the same parent node) of the context node that come before the context node in document order.
Primary node type:	Element
Shorthand:	None
Implemented:	W3C 1.0 specification (recommendation) MSXML 3.0 MSXML 4.0

self

Description:	Contains only the context node itself.
Primary node type:	Element
Shorthand:	.
Implemented:	W3C 1.0 specification (recommendation) MSXML 2.0 (IE5) (only shorthand syntax) MSXML 2.6 (January 2000 preview) MSXML 3.0 MSXML 4.0

Node Tests

A node test describes a test performed on each node of an axis to decide whether it should be included in the result set. Appending a predicate can later filter this result set.

*

Description:	Returns TRUE for all nodes of the primary type for the axis.
Implemented:	W3C 1.0 specification (recommendation) MSXML 2.0 (IE5) MSXML 2.6 (January 2000 preview) MSXML 3.0 MSXML 4.0

comment()

Description:	Returns TRUE for all comment nodes.
Implemented:	W3C 1.0 specification (recommendation) MSXML 2.0 (IE5) MSXML 2.6 (January 2000 preview) MSXML 3.0 MSXML 4.0

literal name

Description:	Returns TRUE for all nodes of that name of the primary node type. If the node test is 'PERSON', it returns TRUE for all nodes <PERSON> (if the primary node type is Element).
Implemented:	W3C 1.0 specification (recommendation) MSXML 2.0 (IE5) MSXML 2.6 (January 2000 preview) MSXML 3.0 MSXML 4.0

node()

Description:	Returns TRUE for all nodes, except attributes and namespaces.
Implemented:	W3C 1.0 specification (recommendation) MSXML 2.0 (IE5) MSXML 2.6 (January 2000 preview) MSXML 3.0 MSXML 4.0

processing-instruction(name?)

Description:	Returns TRUE for all processing instruction nodes. If a name parameter is passed (the question mark means that it is optional), it returns TRUE only for processing instruction nodes of that name.
Implemented:	W3C 1.0 specification (recommendation) MSXML 2.0 (IE5) (called pi() in MSXML2) MSXML 2.6 (January 2000 preview) MSXML 3.0 MSXML 4.0

text()

Description:	Returns TRUE for all text nodes.
Implemented:	W3C 1.0 specification (recommendation) MSXML 2.0 (IE5) MSXML 2.6 (January 2000 preview) MSXML 3.0 MSXML 4.0

Functions

To filter a subset from the resultset of nodes that was selected with an axis and node test, we can append a predicate within square brackets. The expression within the brackets can use literal values (numbers, strings, etc.), XPath expressions, and a number of functions described by the XPath specification.

Each function is described below by a line of this form:

```
return-type function-name (parameters)
```

For each parameter, we display the type (`object`, `string`, `number`, `node-set`) and where necessary a symbol indicating if the parameter is optional (?) or can occur multiple times (+). The type `object` means that any type can be passed.

If an expression is passed as a parameter, it is first evaluated and (if necessary) converted to the expected type before passing it to the function.

```
boolean boolean ( object )
```

Converts anything passed to it to a Boolean.

`boolean(attribute::name)` will return TRUE if the context node has a name attribute.

Parameter:

`object`

Numbers result in TRUE if they are not zero or NaN.

Strings result in TRUE if their length is non-zero.

Node-sets return TRUE if they are non-empty.

Implemented:

W3C 1.0 specification (recommendation)
MSXML 2.6 (January 2000 preview)
MSXML 3.0
MSXML 4.0

```
number ceiling ( number )
```

Rounds a passed number to the smallest integer that is not smaller than the passed number.

`ceiling(1.1)` returns 2

Parameter:

`number`

The number that must be rounded.

Implemented:

W3C 1.0 specification (recommendation)
MSXML 3.0
MSXML 4.0

```
string concat ( string1, string2+ )
```

Concatenates all passed strings to one string.

`concat('con', 'c', 'a', 't')` returns `concat`

Parameters:

`string1`

The first string.

`string2`

All following strings.

Implemented:

W3C 1.0 specification (recommendation)
MSXML 2.6 (January 2000 preview)
MSXML 3.0
MSXML 4.0

```
boolean contains ( string1, string2 )
```

Returns TRUE if string1 contains string2.

```
contains('Teun Duynstee', 'uy') returns TRUE.
```

Parameters:

string1

The source string.

string2

The string that must be searched for.

Implemented:

W3C 1.0 specification (recommendation)
MSXML 2.6 (January 2000 preview)
MSXML 3.0
MSXML 4.0

```
number count ( node-set )
```

Returns the number of nodes in the passed node-set.

count(child::*[@name]) returns the number of child elements of the context node that have a name attribute.

Parameter:

node-set

The node-set that is to be counted.

Implemented:

W3C 1.0 specification (recommendation)
MSXML 2.6 (January 2000 preview)
MSXML 3.0
MSXML 4.0

```
boolean false ( )
```

Always returns FALSE. This may seem useless, but XPath does not define a TRUE and FALSE literal value, so the function can be used to construct expressions like:

```
starts-with(@name, 'T') = false()
```

Implemented:

W3C 1.0 specification (recommendation)
MSXML 2.6 (January 2000 preview)
MSXML 3.0
MSXML 4.0

```
number floor ( number )
```

Rounds a passed number to the largest integer that is not larger than the passed number.

`floor(2.9)` returns 2

`floor(-1.1)` returns -2

Parameter:

`number`

The number that must be rounded.

Implemented:

W3C 1.0 specification (recommendation)
MSXML 3.0
MSXML 4.0

```
node-set id ( string )
```

Returns the element identified by the passed identifier. Note that this will only work in validated documents, because for non-validated documents the parser has no way of knowing which attributes represent ID values.

Parameter:

`string`

The ID value.

Implemented:

W3C 1.0 specification (recommendation)
MSXML 2.0 (IE5)
MSXML 2.6 (January 2000 preview)
MSXML 3.0
MSXML 4.0

```
boolean lang ( string )
```

Returns TRUE if the language of the context node is the same as the passed language parameter. The language of the context node can be set using the `xml:lang` attribute on itself or any of its ancestors. This feature of XML isn't used frequently.

`lang('en')` returns TRUE for English language nodes.

Parameter:

`string`

Language identifier.

Implemented:

W3C 1.0 specification (recommendation)
MSXML 3.0
MSXML 4.0

`number last ( )`

Returns the index number of the last node in the current context node-set.

`child::*[position() = last()-1]` selects the penultimate child element of the context node.

Implemented:

W3C 1.0 specification (recommendation)
MSXML 2.0 (IE5) (called end() in MSXML2)
MSXML 2.6 (January 2000 preview) (does not work when used on the descendant axis)
MSXML 3.0
MSXML 4.0

`string local-name ( node-set? )`

Returns the local part of the name of the first node (in document order) in the passed node-set. For example, the local part of an `<xsl:value-of>` element is `value-of`.

Parameter:

`node-set`

If no node-set is specified, the current context node is used.

Implemented:

W3C 1.0 specification (recommendation)
MSXML 2.6 (January 2000 preview)
MSXML 3.0
MSXML 4.0

`string name ( node-set? )`

Returns the name of the passed node. This is the fully qualified name, including namespace prefix.

Parameter:

`node-set`

If no node-set is specified, the current context node is used.

Implemented:

W3C 1.0 specification (recommendation)
MSXML 2.6 (January 2000 preview)
MSXML 3.0
MSXML 4.0

```
string namespace-uri ( node-set? )
```

Returns the full URI that defines the namespace of the passed node.

`namespace-uri(@href)` in an XHTML document might return `'http://www.w3.org/Profiles/XHTML-transitional'`

Parameter:

`node-set`

If no node-set is specified, the current context node is used.

Implemented:

W3C 1.0 specification (recommendation)
MSXML 2.6 (January 2000 preview)
MSXML 3.0
MSXML 4.0

```
string normalize-space ( string? )
```

Returns the whitespace-normalized version of the passed string. This means that all leading and trailing whitespace gets stripped and all sequences of whitespace get combined to one single space.

`normalize-space('   some    text  ')` would return `'some text'`

Parameter:

`string`

If no string is passed, the current node is converted to a string.

Implemented:

W3C 1.0 specification (recommendation)
MSXML 2.6 (January 2000 preview)
MSXML 3.0
MSXML 4.0

```
boolean not ( boolean )
```

Returns the inverse of the passed value.

`not(@name)` returns TRUE if there is no name attribute on the context node.

Parameter:

`boolean`

An expression that evaluates to a Boolean value

Implemented

W3C 1.0 specification (recommendation)
MSXML 2.6 (January 2000 preview)
MSXML 3.0
MSXML 4.0

```
number number ( object? )
```

Converts parameter to a number.

`number(' -3.6 ')` returns the number –3.6

The `number()` function does not use any localized settings, so you must only use this conversion when the format of the numeric data is language-neutral.

Parameter:

`object`

If nothing is passed, the current context node is used.

Implemented:

W3C 1.0 specification (recommendation)
MSXML 2.6 (January 2000 preview)
MSXML 3.0
MSXML 4.0

```
number position ( )
```

Returns the position of the current context node in the current context node-set.

`position()` returns 1 for the first node in the context node-set

Implemented:

W3C 1.0 specification (recommendation)
MSXML 2.6 (January 2000 preview)
MSXML 3.0
MSXML 4.0

```
number round ( number )
```

Rounds a passed number to the nearest integer.

`round(1.5)` returns 2, `round(-1.7)` returns -2

Parameter:

`number`

The number that must be rounded

Implemented:

W3C 1.0 specification (recommendation)
MSXML 3.0
MSXML 4.0

```
boolean starts-with ( string1, string2 )
```

Returns TRUE if string1 starts with string2.

`starts-with(@name, 'T')` returns TRUE if the value of the name attribute starts with a capital T

Parameters:

`string1`

The string that must be checked.

`string2`

The substring that must be searched for.

Implemented:

W3C 1.0 specification (recommendation)
MSXML 2.6 (January 2000 preview) (somehow this fails to work in the test attribute of an
`<xsl:if>` element)
MSXML 3.0
MSXML 4.0

```
string string ( object? )
```

Converts the passed object to a string value.

Parameter:

`object`

If nothing is passed, the result is an empty string.

Implemented:

W3C 1.0 specification (recommendation)
MSXML 2.6 (January 2000 preview)
MSXML 3.0
MSXML 4.0

```
number string-length ( string? )
```

Returns the number of characters in the passed string.

`string-length('Teun Duynstee')` returns 13

Parameter:

`string`

If nothing is passed, the current context is converted to a string.

Implemented:

W3C 1.0 specification (recommendation)
MSXML 2.6 (January 2000 preview)
MSXML 3.0
MSXML 4.0

```
string substring ( string, number1, number2? )
```

Returns the substring from the passed string starting at the number1 character, with the length of number2. If no number2 parameter is passed, the substring runs to the end of the passed string.

substring('Teun Duynstee', 6) returns 'Duynstee'

Parameters:

string

The string that will be used as source for the substring.

number1

Start location of the substring.

number2

Length of the substring.

Implemented:

W3C 1.0 specification (recommendation)
MSXML 2.6 (January 2000 preview)
MSXML 3.0
MSXML 4.0

```
string substring-after ( string1, string2 )
```

Returns the substring following the first occurrence of string2 inside string1. For example, the return value of substring-after('2000/3/22', '/') would be 3/22.

Parameters:

string1

The string that serves as source.

string2

The string that is searched in the source string.

Implemented:

W3C 1.0 specification (recommendation)
MSXML 2.6 (January 2000 preview)
MSXML 3.0
MSXML 4.0

```
string substring-before ( string1, string2 )
```

Returns the string part preceding the first occurrence of the string2 inside the string1. For example, the return value of substring-before('2000/3/22', '/') would be 2000.

Parameters:

string1

The string that serves as source.

string2

The string that is searched in the source string.

Implemented:

W3C 1.0 specification (recommendation)
MSXML 2.6 (January 2000 preview)
MSXML 3.0
MSXML 4.0

```
number sum ( node-set )
```

Sums the values of all nodes in the set when converted to a number.

sum(student/@age) returns the sum of all age attributes on the student elements on the child axis of the context node.

Parameter:

node-set

The node-set containing all values to be summed.

Implemented:

W3C 1.0 specification (recommendation)
MSXML 3.0
MSXML 4.0

```
string translate ( string1, string2, string3 )
```

Translates characters in string1 to other characters. Translation pairs are specified by string2 and string3. For example, translate('A Space Odissei', 'i', 'y') would result in A Space Odyssey, and translate('abcdefg', 'aceg', 'ACE') would result in AbCdEf. The final g gets translated to nothing, because the string3 has no counterpart for that position in the string2.

Parameters:

string1

String to be translated character by character.

string2

String defining which characters must be translated.

string3

String defining what the characters from the string2 should be translated to.

Implemented:

W3C 1.0 specification (recommendation)
MSXML 2.6 (January 2000 preview)
MSXML 3.0
MSXML 4.0

```
boolean true ( )
```

Always returns TRUE.

Implemented:

W3C 1.0 specification (recommendation)
MSXML 2.6 (January 2000 preview)
MSXML 3.0
MSXML 4.0

G

Object-Oriented Programming

This appendix covers the fundamentals of the object-oriented paradigm along with PHP's syntax and capabilities in this aspect. We won't be covering very specific object-oriented concepts like design patterns, delegation, meta patterns, and so on, which many of the frameworks and class libraries were engineered upon. These topics can be learned from other books and are simply too large to cover here.

Object-oriented programming was developed to be a replacement for procedural-based programming. It comes as somewhat of a surprise that PHP has not evolved into an all-out object-oriented language, which tend to be easy to learn if a solid platform (a collection of classes in this case) is available. However, PHP was designed for programmers that want to build more functionality into current static web sites.

PHP was designed to look and behave like C. Because many people already know C's syntax and have written several C programs in school, work, or even as a hobby, it was a natural choice to emulate C syntax to provide some familiarity to newcomers and get people using the language quickly and productively. Although there are some semantic differences between PHP and C, for the most part they are the same. The same goes for PHP's object-oriented features, but in this case they were mainly influenced by the Java programming language. Although PHP does not nearly complete all the list of Java's object-oriented features, keywords like `extends` suggest this adoption.

Objects and Classes

As indicated by the title, object-oriented programs consist of objects. So unlike having functions act on primitives or data structures, objects provide the functionality and behavior for the application. For example, we can have a `Form` object that represents an HTML form on a web page. Inside this form we might have various buttons, text fields, and radio options, which are all modeled as objects as well. To define what these objects are, what they consists of, and what actions they can do, we use the concept of a **class** that defines all these criteria to PHP. To reiterate, a class provides the programmatic definition of the objects that we use in our applications in the same way that a `struct` defines a data structure in C. Let's first talk about classes in more detail.

A class defines a concept or idea that we want to use in the program. For instance, if we want to model the idea of keeping the user's session, we can maintain this information in a `Session` object (or sometimes it can be called `SessionManager`). Classes can model things that are tangible, like forms, sockets, and database connections, and things that are less tangible like proxies, handlers, or listeners. The most important concept is that the class represents a single idea. Usually classes like `MyEntireProgram` and `TheWorldIsInsideOfMe` do not provide great functionality and should be avoided. This usually indicates the class is doing too many things and can probably be split up into several classes. A general rule is that classes should 'do one thing and do it well'.

Now that we know what classes should do, it's time to talk about what they really consist of. In order to be a class, it must consist of data (the object's members and components) and code (the functionality it provides) called **methods**. This means that a class that is missing one of these things is not really a class, but rather a group of functions or a data structure. If we do not pair the code and data that belong together, there is high probability that our class has been incorrectly defined. Now let's take a look at the components of a class.

Members

These are elements which we intend the class to contain. For instance, forms contain buttons, text fields, and combo boxes. These items would be considered members of the `Form` class. As with any class, the members might be intangible things like a `DataValidator` for client-server regular expression validation. The members can also be primitive data types like integers, floats, and strings. For instance, the form's `name` and the `action` can also be members of the `Form` class.

Methods

Methods provide the behavior we expect a particular object to perform. For instance, continuing with our current example, forms provide the ability to validate themselves, populate the fields with data from a data store such as a database, or even process the form to add it to a database or send an e-mail. These methods describe exactly what we intend the forms to do. You wouldn't expect a form to be able to drive a car or do your homework for instance. Although this might sound funny at first, it's true – many programmers simply put methods where they don't belong and this is something you should avoid.

Constructor

A constructor is responsible for initializing the object's ready state. What this means is that if there is any member (objects or primitive types) that need, to be initialized for the methods to work properly, this code usually goes into the class constructor. For instance, we can use the constructor to add all the form elements to the form and specify the regular expression constraints on each form item. One thing to note is that PHP's objects can only have one constructor. This is because PHP does not support a concept called **overloading**. Another thing to note is that it must not return a value.

Here is an example of a `Form` class. It's not a complete example because the intention is to identify and show the various concepts that we've just learned about:

```php
<?php
class Form
{
```

Here we define a class called `Form`. Everything within the curly braces is considered to be a method, member, or a constructor of the class. Notice that the class name is capitalized. This is generally the style that is used throughout PHP classes to distinguish them from other items in the language and has been adopted from Java:

```php
    var $name;
    var $elements;
```

Here we define several member variables that are objects or other primitive type variables that this class contains. The `$name` field stores the name of the form while the `$elements` member actually contains all the objects that get displayed on the form. It is generally considered good practice to add the members at the top of the class rather than anywhere else, just as in a functional program. This provides a good reference for maintenance later on:

```php
    function Form($name = "The Form")
    {
        $this->name = $name;
        $this->elements = array();
        // add the elements to the form
    }
```

Here is the class's constructor. To define the constructor properly, it must have the same name as the class itself. So in this case, the constructor's name is also `Form`. This is actually one reason why the class name has a capital letter, so it makes it very easy to distinguish the constructor from the rest of the methods.

The form's name is assigned the value `The Form` if one is not provided and the `elements` member was assigned an empty array. Later, we will look at adding objects to this array. The `$this` keyword is rather unique to object-oriented programs. Think of `$this` as a variable that points to the object that we are currently writing. Therefore, when we say `$this->name`, we are referring to the `Form` object's name variable that we defined above.

The $this keyword allows PHP to distinguish between any local variables and variables (members) that are contained within the object. So the line $this->name = $name is assigning the value of the argument to the object's name member. Although in other languages the $this keyword is optional and is used to clear up naming conflicts and their associated delays, the PHP interpreter did not adopt this feature for increased speed. This might take a little while to get used to, but with practice and the motivation to avoid interpretation errors the usefulness of this syntax becomes apparent:

```
function validate()
{
    $boolean = true;

    foreach ($this->elements as $element) {
        // check all the elements and set $boolean to false if
        // any errors occur
    }

    return $boolean;
}

function process()
{
    // put the data in the elements into the database
}

function populate()
{
    // populate the elements
}
}
?>
```

These are the object's functions, or rather the methods it provides. Notice that these look exactly as they do in a procedural program except that they are contained within the class { } block. This signifies that they belong to this class only and if another part of the program needs to use these functions, they must go through the object first.

Instances

Now that we defined our Form class, we use the following code to define and create a variable that is of the type Form:

```
$form = new Form("My quick form");
```

Here we use the new operator to create a new Form object. When an object has been created using the new operator, it is said that the object has been **instantiated**. It can also be said that the object is called an **instance** of the Form class. A good analogy between instances and classes is that the blueprints and prototypes for a single car can be called a class while all the cars that are on the road that were built using that particular blueprint can be called instances.

Remember our discussion on constructors? That is what we are calling here, passing the name of the form so that the internal name member can be initialized. With PHP's loosely typed variable concept, we don't have to specify the object's type when we create an object. Constructors always allocate the memory for the object. This is actually done automatically, so once we write the constructor for an object that initializes the members, PHP will do this for us.

Calling Instance Methods

Since the object is created into the $form variable, we can freely use the methods provided by the object. For instance, we can call the validate() method to validate the form using the following code:

```
if ($form->validate()) {
    print ("The form was validated successfully.");
}
```

In this example, we use the -> operator to call the validate() method that belongs to the $form object. Notice that it takes no parameters. That's actually one of the benefits of object-oriented programs. Since each object knows and is associated with its member variables, it does need to have any parameters. This serves several benefits. For one, the programmer using the object doesn't need to know how those elements were coded. The internal data is 'hidden' away from the programmer.

The second benefit is that the implementation could have used other objects to store the elements rather than an array. As far as the calling code knows, the object hasn't changed. This makes each object very abstract and provides a nice candy-like interface. It also improves the maintainability of the system. Lastly, this cleans up the code a lot as well. Since each call to the $form object doesn't need to supply rudimentary data every time a method is invoked, this makes our code much cleaner and simplifies our statements greatly.

How This Works

For those that are interested in the 'how', the interpreter actually adds some information before the code is executed. Within PHP, the engine keeps track of what methods belong to which class, but it doesn't actually tie the members to the object itself. Naturally, like any procedural language, it maintains a data structure that is also linked with the class name. Each time the method is invoked, the object's variable is automatically supplied to it. So in this case, the call is modified to:

```
if ($form->validate($form)) {
    print ("The form was validated successfully.");
}
```

This passes the object back into itself so that the method can access the members of the object that are not declared as local variables. This enables each method to share the same members. So in the class code itself, the $form parameter actually gets transformed into the $this object. Here is the transformation:

```
function validate($this)
{
    $boolean = true;

    foreach ($this->elements as $element) {
        // check all the elements and set $boolean to false if
        // any errors occur
    }

    return $boolean;
}
```

Since the PHP engine automatically puts the $this variable as the first argument to the validate() method, it is more easily seen why $this->elements actually exists and why it is done that way (passing the object back into itself). This also provides an explanation about how the object's members in the $this object do not collide with any local variables or function arguments. Remember that the $this parameter is done automatically – so we don't have to define this variable for our methods. In some languages like Python, we actually have to do this. PHP has made this easy for us so we can think of our object's members as being contained within the class definition rather than being closer to the implementation of the interpreter.

Inheritance

Now that the Form class has been defined, we need to define a class for the buttons, text fields, and other form controls that we would like to add to the form. Since PHP does not supply a type for this, we need to define our own class. These classes that we are about to look into have been taken from the eXtremePHP Form Framework (http://www.extremephp.org/). Since the Form Framework actually uses several classes (around 30), some of the classes have been combined and shortened for this example. Therefore, the example is meant to demonstrate object-oriented code clearly rather than present the most refactored solution.

Now, one way to create text fields and submit buttons would be to create different classes that represent each form control and provide the necessary functionality for each one. Although this can work, it's not the best solution. When we think of HTML form controls, most people think of them as being very similar. Generally, the name of the tag and some of the attributes that are assigned represent the only difference between controls, but each control has a name, a value, might have a regular expression constraint, and can display or convert itself into HTML.

To express these commonalities among all form controls that need to be placed inside the Form object, we first make a FormControl class. Later, when we need a very specific control that puts a text field to the screen or creates a submit button, we can create classes called TextField and SubmitButton, which are called **subclasses**. These classes are said to **inherit** functionality from the FormControl class, meaning they have all the members and methods of that class. FormControl is also said to be the **parent, base,** or **super class** to the TextField and SubmitButton classes.

We can define a new subclass for each type of FormControl by only specifying specific information. Since TextField and other subclasses all **extend** from FormControl, they will posses all the existing functionality from the FormControl – which allows for software reuse. The way this works logically is this: if a TextField is a FormControl, then it should posses all the state and behavior of a FormControl. Notice that the converse is not necessarily true since a FormControl may not contain all the functionality and members of a TextField. This is because a TextField might have additional settings to adjust the field's width, which may not be available to all FormControl objects.

The ability to extend a class by subclassing is the core idea of object-oriented programming. By creating trees of objects, we are able to reuse code, and later we'll see how this makes our programs more generic and easier to work with and maintain.

The Parent Class: FormControl

Here is the code for the FormControl class:

```
<!-- FormControl.class.php -->
<?php
define("NO_VALUE", md5("novalue"));
define("NEWLINE", "\n");
```

Here we provide several constants that are used by the other classes. The NO_VALUE constant is the value that is used to specify that a form control contains no value. Since NULL values are hard to maintain and keep state across HTML, a value that means nothing is sensible to use:

```
class FormControl
{
    var $name;
    var $value;
```

Here we provide two member variables for the name and value of the form. The name provides the unique server-side name that is automatically added to the global variables array and is used when getting the value. The value will be contained within this variable if it is set:

```
function FormControl($name, $value = NO_VALUE)
{
    $this->setName($name);
    $this->setValue($value);
}
```

Our constructor initializes the FormControl with a name and there is an optional parameter to specify the value. Usually when we create a new form and we do not wish to populate it with data, we want to provide just a name. In the case where we want the form control to be initialized to a value before it is displayed to the screen, we can use the second parameter $value. To initialize these values, we use the setName() and setValue() methods. These are usually referred to as **setter** methods and usually contain assignment code. In some cases, we might also want to have rules defined so that the data maintains its integrity:

```
function setName($name)
{
    $this->name = $name;
}

function getName()
{
    return $this->name;
}
```

There is also the concept of a **getter** method that returns the value of a member that is in the object. In the above code, we define a setter and getter for the name member. This allows clients that use the object to be able to manipulate and get the object's name. Instead of saying getter and setter all the time, for a pair, we could say that these two methods are both **data accessor methods**:

```
function setValue($value)
{
    if ($value == NO_VALUE) {
        global ${$this->name};

        if (!isset(${$this->name})) ${$this->name} = '';
            $this->value = ${$this->name};
    } else {
```

```
        $this->value = $value;
    }
}

function getValue()
{
    return $this->value;
}
```

As with the `name` member, there is also a getter and setter for the `value` member. The `setValue()` method is actually more complicated in that it must handle the special case of the `NO_VALUE` constant. If the `NO_VALUE` constant was passed into this function, we check to see if a variable already exists with the `FormControl`'s name. If it does, we can automatically set the value of this form element to that variable. If not, we just make the element contain the empty string. This allows `FormControl` to maintain state as it was when submitted, and it can be very helpful when the form is not validated correctly. This saves the programmer a great deal of time checking the global values and setting them within the `value` attribute of the HTML code. This is now done automatically by the class:

```
function setConstraint(&$validator, $regex, $errorMessage)
{
    $validator->setConstraint($this->getName(), $regex,
                              $this->getValue(), $errorMessage );
}
```

The `setConstraint()` method provides an easy way to add a regular expression check of this form control to an eXtremePHP `DataValidator` object, `$validator`. This component is much like the `Matcher` object in Java or .NET. For the simplicity of this example, we will assume that the `$validator` object has a method called `setConstraint()` as well, and it contains the code to a list of constraints:

```
function validate()
{
    return $validator->validate();
}
```

Once the constraints have been added, they may be also verified using a similar `validate()` method:

```
// template method that calls abstract methods.
function toHtml()
{
    return $this->getHeaderHtml() . $this->getFooterHtml();
}

// abstract
function getHeaderHtml() {}

// abstract
function getFooterHtml() {}
```

The next set of functions provides the base mechanism for displaying the HTML for the `FormControl` component. `toHtml()` is meant to receive the entire HTML document. In some cases, we might only want to view the header or footer of the HTML, so we can use `getHeaderHtml()` or `getFooterHtml()` respectively.

Even though these functions do not provide any functionality, this is actually where the meat of the class is. These methods were left blank intentionally so that they can be redefined in the subclasses of FormControl. For instance, a TextField has its own HTML that it would like to display as compared to a SubmitButton. By **overriding** these methods (as shown in the next class file), we can provide very specific functionality to each subclass of FormControl. We'll take a closer look at overriding methods later on in more detail.

The toHtml() method is actually very powerful in that all subclasses will contain this method. Since every class that inherits FormControl will contain the getHeaderHtml() and getFooterHtml() methods, toHtml() makes sure that every class won't need to bother with creating a duplicate toHtml() method. This **templates** the header and footer methods and the implementer of the subclasses is expected to fill them in.

How do we know when we have to fill them in? Usually in a language that supports full object-orientation like Java, there is a concept called **abstract** methods that forces any subclasses to implement the methods before the class is compiled. Since the compiler tool will not successfully compile a class where the implementer didn't override the methods, it will be impossible to use this in a program. This is extremely helpful since objects are well-defined in this way and we can guarantee that all the methods in the parent class will work in the subclasses.

However, PHP does not contain this feature so it is up to the designer to indicate that these classes are indeed abstract. This is usually done with an empty body { } for the method. A comment just above the method will also help clarify the intentions of the programmer:

```
function display()
{
    echo $this->toHtml();
}

function displayHeader()
{
    echo $this->getHeaderHtml();
}

function displayFooter()
{
    echo $this->getFooterHtml();
}
}
?>
```

The last methods simply make it a bit easier to display the HTML to the screen: they have been separated to make it easy to put the HTML into a string. This can be useful if we'd like insert it into a database or an e-mail message. If we had tied the HTML generation to the display*() methods, some applications may have been very difficult to write.

The Subclasses

The next file shows how to implement a new subclass, TextField, as a subclass of FormControl:

```
<!-- TextField.class.php -->
<?php

require_once('./FormControl.class.php');

class TextField extends FormControl
{
```

Here, we use the extends keyword to tell PHP that the TextField class inherits from the FormControl class. As mentioned before, this means that all the members and methods from the FormControl class are now available to this class as well:

```
function TextField($name, $value = NO_VALUE)
{
    FormControl::FormControl($name, $value);
}
```

Since all FormControl objects were expected to have a name and value, we can use the parent class's constructor to initialize the incoming members rather than rewriting the code again in this class. To do this, we use the class-method call operator to reference the parent function. This is achieved by calling the class name with two colons, followed by the method name we would like to call. Generally, it works like this:

```
ClassName::methodName();
```

So in our example, we use FormControl to replace ClassName and we use the same name for the methodName() because we'd like to call the constructor. By repassing the arguments to the parent method, we can be assured that the name and value members will be set to this object when it is instantiated. This is a huge benefit to programmers because as long as we know the parent class is bug-free, we can be assured that any subclasses will be dealing with error-free code. Thus, this can save great deal of time when debugging applications:

```
function getHeaderHtml()
{
    return '<input type="text" ' .
           'name="' . $this->name . '" ' .
           'value="' . $this->value . '">';
}

function getFooterHtml()
{
    return '</input>' . NEWLINE;
}
}
?>
```

Remember those two abstract methods `getFooterhtml()` and `getHeaderhtml()`? Well, it's our job to implement the code for those for the `TextField` class. In this case, we simply return the `<input>` tag to create a text field in the browser using HTML. Notice the use of `$this->name` and `$this->value`. These fields have been inherited from the `FormControl` superclass, and as such, they are available to use in our code above. As mentioned before, we need not redefine the `toHtml()` method because it has been made to call these overridden methods automatically.

More on Overriding Methods

So how does the parser know which method to call – the one in the superclass or the subclass? Whenever a subclass defines a method that has been previously defined in its parent, it is overriding its behavior. Now, in the previous case, there was no behavior provided by the superclass because the method was blank. In other examples, however, there are times when we may want to override a method that does have an implementation because its current implementation does not suit the more specific object. Consider three classes where `Baby` is a subtype of `Parent` and `Parent` is a subtype of `GrandParent`, and take this code for example:

```
$babyObject = new Baby("");
$babyObject->sayHello();
```

When an instance of the `Baby` subtype is created and the `sayHello()` method is called, the PHP interpreter will first look to see if the method is defined in `$babyObject` class. If it is, it will execute the code within that method. In this case, if the `sayHello()` method overrides the one in a super class, the PHP interpreter skips the superclass entirely.

If no method is defined by `sayHello()` within the `Baby()` interface, PHP will then go to the `Parent` class of `$babyObject` and will attempt to execute the same method using the parent's implementation. If this method is defined in the `Parent` class, PHP will begin executing its code and PHP will commence as normal. If in turn the method wasn't found in the `Parent` class, PHP will search the parent class of each current class until there are no parent classes left. At this time PHP will display an error message saying the following:

```
Fatal error: Call to undefined function: sayHello() in
/websites/babytest.php on line X
```

The Remaining Subclasses: SubmitButton and HiddenField

As we make more `FormControl` objects, we can appreciate how fast it can be to develop various form components. For demonstration purposes, the next two files will be the `SubmitButton` class and the `HiddenField` class which we will use in the following example. Here is the `SubmitButton` class code:

```php
<!-- SubmitButton.class.php -->
<?php

require_once('./FormControl.class.php');

class SubmitButton extends FormControl
{

    function SubmitButton($value)
    {
        FormControl::FormControl('submit', $value);
    }
}
```

```
        function getHeaderHtml()
        {
            return '<input type="submit" ' .
                    'name="' . $this->name . '" ' .
                    'value="' . $this->value . '">';
        }

        function getFooterHtml()
        {
            return '</input>' . NEWLINE;
        }
    }
    ?>
```

Similarly, the code for the `HiddenField` class that models a hidden value for HTML forms, can be written like this:

```
<!-- HiddenField.class.php -->
<?php

require_once('./FormControl.class.php');

class HiddenField extends FormControl
{

    function HiddenField($name, $value = NO_VALUE)
    {
        FormControl::FormControl($name, $value);
    }

    function getHeaderHtml()
    {
        return '<input type="hidden" ' .
                'name="' . $this->name . '" ' .
                'value="' . $this->value . '">';
    }

    function getFooterHtml()
    {
        return '</input>' . NEWLINE;
    }
}
?>
```

Creating the Form Class

Now that we have created various form controls to be placed onto our `Form` class, let's take another look how we might build it:

```
<!-- Form.class.php -->
<?php

require_once('./TextField.class.php');
require_once('./HiddenField.class.php');
require_once('./SubmitButton.class.php');
require_once('./Vector.class.php');
```

To use the classes we developed earlier, we need to include them in the main `Form` class. The `Vector` class is a utility class that was taken right out of the eXtremePHP library. It operates in 90% of the way `Vector` objects behave in Java. For those who haven't used Java, a `Vector` is basically a scalable array. We don't have to worry about indexes and boundaries as the object takes care of all of this information for us. In fact, we won't even realize that it's an array and we'll think of it as a `List` of objects.

A `Vector` provides a very consistent way to iterate over the data contained within the array. Called an `Iterator`, it is analogous to Java `Enumeration` or C++'s `Iterator`. This allows us to traverse all the items within the `Vector`. If we decide to change the `Vector` into another class that supports `Iterator` objects, we won't actually have to change any of the traversal code because it supports the same interface. This is very powerful since program maintenance is reduced. To receive more information on the `Vector` class, please visit http://www.extremephp.org/xpl/docs/Vector.html.

We now define two `Vector` objects that we will use in our `Form`. One `Vector` object, `$formControls`, will store a list of form controls that we developed earlier. Since PHP variables are loosely typed, it is actually possible to have the first position of the `Vector` contain a `TextField` object while the second position contains a `SubmitButton` object, and so on. This is very useful as we can group all these objects together in a generic fashion:

```
class Form
{
    var $formControls;
    var $parameters;
```

The `$parameters Vector` will store the name/value pairs for this `Form`. In this case we also could have used a `Dictionary` object or even a `HashMap`, which resembles an associative array, but again for demonstration purposes this will suffice:

```
function Form($name, $action, $method = "post")
{
    $this->formControls = new Vector();
    $this->parameters   = new Vector();

    $this->setParameter('name', $name);
    $this->setParameter('action', $action);
    $this->setParameter('method', $method);
}
```

Our constructor takes in the name of the form, the PHP page which will process the form when it is submitted, and a `$method` parameter that can either be `POST` or `GET`. This is the same information that would be supplied on an HTML `<form>` tag. Since the constructor is responsible for putting the object into an unwavering state, we must create new instances of the `Vector` objects that we defined above. We can use the `setParameter()` instance method to set up all the properties that were passed into the constructor.

We now define the data accessor methods `getParameter()` and `setParameters()` for the `<form>` tag. In both cases `$name` and `$value` are strings. Vector objects have a `set()` method where they can not only add a new item to the list, but also set it at a defined index. In this case, we use `$name` for the index and place the contents of `$value` at this position. Later we can use the `get()` method on the `$parameters` Vector object to retrieve the value at this position as well:

```
function setParameter($name, $value)
{

    $this->parameters->set($name, $value);

}

function getParameter($name)
{

    return $this->parameters->get($name);

}
```

To make the interface simpler for someone who would like to define several other parameters other than the ones defined in the constructor, there is a setParameters() method that is intended to take in an associative array and then add each name/value pair within the array to the parameter list:

```
function setParameters(&$parameters)
{

    foreach ($parameters as $name => $value) {
        $this->setParameter($name, $value);
    }

}
```

To complete the functionality of parameters, we have a method that easily constructs the HTML code for the parameter list that is meant to be appended to the beginning of an HTML element. Every Vector object has toArray() that converts its contents back into an associative array. This is helpful when we need to retrieve both the indexes (the parameter names) and the values:

```
function constructParameterHtml()
{

    $parameterString = '';

    foreach ($this->parameters->toArray() as $name => $value) {
        $parameterString .= ' ' . $name . '="' .
                            $value . '"';
    }

    return $parameterString;

}
```

After traversing the entire list, we should end up with a string like this "name1=value1", "name2=value2", and so on. Generally, besides the toArray() call, there is nothing very interesting here.

Finally we define an add() method so we can add controls to the form. The argument $control expects any instance of the FormControl class. Because we can take any instance, we don't have to say addTextField() or addSubmitButton() like in a procedural program. We can simply instantiate the class and then pass it into the add() method:

```
function add($control)
{
    if (get_class($control) == 'submitbutton') {
        $submitName = $this->getParameter('name') .
                      ucfirst($control->getName());

        $this->add(new HiddenField( $submitName, $control->getValue()));
    }

    $this->formControls->add( $control );
}
```

So what if we really do want to know the type of an object? Well, PHP has a function called `get_class()` that takes in any object and the function will return a string containing the class name. Since all class and function names are case-insensitive, the function will return the entire string in lowercase letters.

In the eXtremePHP framework, there is a special check to see if a `SubmitButton` instance is being passed to the function, so we can use the `get_class()` function to check the instance type of the object dynamically and add a hidden field with the same name with a capital first letter to the form when this happens. Although for our example, we don't really use the hidden field for anything, the eXtremePHP framework requires a field to be defined to do some fancy tricks and to generally make programming forms much easier and more reusable.

The lesson learned here is that we can check the types of objects in our code and execute extra code for various conditions. For more information on class and object functions within PHP, check out http://www.php.net/manual/en/ref.classobj.php:

```
function getHeaderHtml()
{
    return $this->getTagHeader('form') . NEWLINE;
}

function getFooterHtml()
{
    return $this->getTagFooter('form') . NEWLINE;
}

function getTagHeader($tagName)
{
    return "<$tagName" . $this->constructParameterHtml() . '>';
}

function getTagFooter($tagName)
{
    return "</$tagName>";
}
```

As with the `FormControl`, the `Form` object itself can also get the header and footer HTML. We use some helper methods to generate the HTML more easily. Notice that the `getTagHeader()` method uses the `constructParameterHtml()` method defined earlier. This method places the string containing the generated attributes right after the tag name. In this case, our form options defined in the constructor will be placed after the `<form>` tag as they should be:

```
function getContainedTagsHtml()
{
    $html = '';

    for ($i = $this->createIterator(); !$i->isDone(); $i->next()) {
        $control = $iterator->getCurrent();
        $html .= $control->toHtml();
    }

    return $html;
}
```

Since Form objects can contain other FormControl objects, it is also required that we generate the entire HTML for each control. The result needs to go in between the <form> and </form> tags. The general strategy here is that we create an Iterator on the $formControls member variable (remember, it's a Vector object), and we can traverse all the Form elements as they were added to the Vector. The call to:

```
$html .= $control->toHtml();
```

is actually very interesting. The toHtml() method returns the HTML markup for the TextField or the SubmitButton class. Remember that the Vector object can contain a whole bunch of different FormControl instances. PHP is actually smart enough to call the correct code for each of these controls, regardless of what it is. So when a TextField object is the next object in the iteration, the PHP interpreter will execute the getHeaderHtml() and getFooterHtml() of the TextField class.

This method calling on a group of similar objects is called **polymorphism**. So regardless of what the object is, since PHP knows all FormControl instances have a toHtml() method, it will execute the proper code for each control relieving the programmer from having to decide which method to call. This greatly improves the maintainability of the application since if any new FormControl objects are added, we will not need to modify much of our current code.

How Polymorphism Works

Since the code doesn't specify which code to execute, how does PHP know which method to call? To answer this question, let's look how we might do something like this in a procedural program:

```
if ($control->type == TEXT_FIELD) {
    displayTextField($control);
} elseif() {
    displaySubmitButton($control);
    ...
}
```

As with most procedural programs, we define data structures for complicated types. In this case $control is a record containing the name, value, and so on, of the form control. By testing its type against various constants, we can determine which method to call to draw the correct component. So if it's a text field, it should call displayTextField(). Likewise, if it's a submit button, the code should execute displaySubmitButton() and so on. So where is this code in our object-oriented program?

This is what makes object-oriented programs very different from procedural ones. Recall that all `FormControl` objects contain a `toHtml()` method and that any subclass of `FormControl` will also contain this method. So when we iterate through the `Vector` and call the `toHtml()` method on each `FormControl`, we are guaranteed that each control can deliver this method and return the appropriate HTML for the form control. So how does PHP know which one to call? Let's assume the `Vector` contains the following values:

```
["formControls"]=>
  &object(vector)(2) {
    ["collection"]=>
    array(4) {
      [0]=>
      object(textfield)(3) {
        ["name"]=>
        string(4) "name"
        ["value"]=>
        string(3) "Hey"
      }
      [1]=>
      object(textfield)(3) {
        ["name"]=>
        string(5) "stuff"
        ["value"]=>
        string(3) "You"
      }
      [2]=>
      object(hiddenfield)(3) {
        ["name"]=>
        string(12) "Submit"
        ["value"]=>
        string(6) "submit"
      }
      [3]=>
      object(submitbutton)(3) {
        ["name"]=>
        string(6) "submit"
        ["value"]=>
        string(6) "submit"
      }
    }
    ["size"]=>
    int(4)
```

Upon the first iteration of the `Vector`, the call to `$i->getCurrent();` will return the `TextField` object at index 0. Once a call to `toHtml()` has been made, the PHP interpreter finds that a `toHtml()` method is found in the base class, `FormControl` (as explained in the section about overriding methods). Let's take a look at the code for the `toHtml()` method once more:

```
function toHtml()
{
    return $this->getHeaderHtml() . $this->getFooterHtml();
}
```

915

As PHP executes this code, it comes across $this->getHeaderHtml() first and decides that it has to execute this code. So what is $this really referring to? In this case, $this is still an instance of the TextField class, even though we are currently executing code from the FormControl class. So now that it has to call getHeaderHtml() from the current TextField object, it checks to see if the method exists. As we already know, it does perform this check and the function returns the <input> HTML code for the text field. The same process happens for the getFooterHtml() as well and both results are concatenated together and the result is returned to the caller.

Back To the Form Class

Now that we have all three HTML methods defined, we can create the Form class's toHtml() method as shown below:

```
function toHtml()
{
    return $this->getHeaderHtml() .
            $this->getContainedTagsHtml() .
            $this->getFooterHtml();
}

function display()
{
    echo $this->toHtml();
}
}
```

As with the form controls, the Form needs to be able to display itself. So we defined a display() method for this purpose.

Using the Form

In this application, we are going to create a form with two text fields and a submit button. When the form is submitted, the application will simply type out the contents of the two boxes to the screen. Now that all our classes have been written, we can start to build an application at the problem-domain level. This generally means that we can work with objects that make sense to the problem. This is much like building structures with Lego blocks. Generally, this turns out to be really simple, so let's look at the code:

```
$form = new Form("MyForm", $_SERVER["PHP_SELF"]);
$form->add(new TextField('name'));
$form->add(new TextField('stuff'));
$form->add(new SubmitButton('submit'));
$form->display();
```

Here we create a new instance of the Form object. We give it any random name and use PHP_SELF to tell PHP to use this script to process the form when it has been submitted. At this time, all the internal Vectors are initialized so the object's services are ready to be used. So in this case, we add several form controls using the add() method of the $form object. But create new instances and passing them to add(), we are placing the controls onto the form. Lastly, we can invoke the display() method which displays the generated HTML to the screen. Simple enough:

```
if (isset($_REQUEST['submit'])) {
    echo 'You have typed in "' . $_REQUEST['name'] .
        '" into the first box and ';
    echo '"' . $_REQUEST['stuff'] . '" into the second box';
}
?>
```

Assuming the form has been submitted with the words 'John Doe' and 'Some Stuff', the display of the application would look like this:

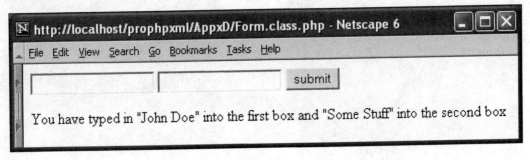

Summary

So in this appendix, we have learned the essential concepts to programming object-oriented code using PHP. Although there are many more concepts we need to learn, this should provide us with a good footing to start with as well as utilize object-oriented capabilities within our applications.

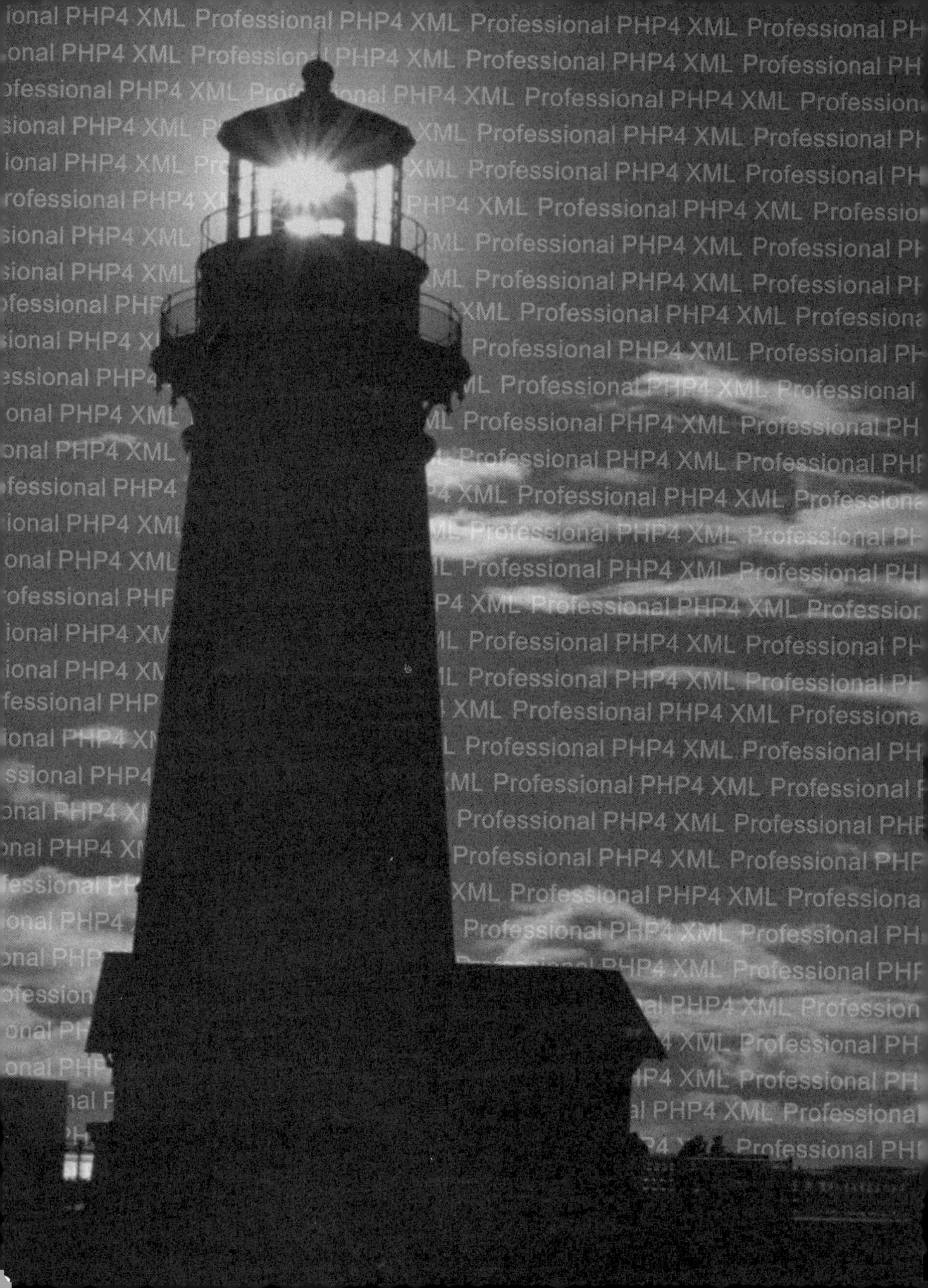
Professional PHP4 XML

Index

A Guide to the Index

The index is arranged hierarchically, in alphabetical order, with symbols preceding the letter A. Most second-level entries and many third-level entries also occur as first-level entries. This is to ensure that users will find the information they require however they choose to search for it.

Symbols

?: (ternary) comparison operator, PHP, 23
=/== (assignment/equality) operators, PHP, 22
  comparing, 22
-> (arrow) operator, PHP
  $this object part, pointing to, 34
& ampersand
  SAX handling, 180
* wildcard, XPath, 258
  *() node test, XPath, 884
    TRUE for all primary nodes, returning, 884
  selecting all children element nodes, 258
// operator, XPath, 258
  elements between slashes, indicating, 258
:: operator
  static method invocation using, 37
@ error handler operator, PHP, 25
@* wildcard, XPath, 258
  @*|node() expression, <xsl:copy> using, 333, 336
  all attributes in given context, selecting, 257, 258
[] (square bracket) syntax, PHP
  arrays, specifying, 16
  empty brackets, pushing values into array, 16
| record separator
  legacy applications, XSLT supporting, 359
<,> and & characters
  NOT allowed in well-formed XML files, 456

A

abstract methods, 907
  abstract parse method, SAX, 404
  Form framework, 906
Access, Microsoft
  storing XML, product solutions, 516
<actor> attribute, SOAP <Header>, 577
  multi-stage message processing example, 577
actuate global attribute, XLink
  link rendering timing, defining, 116

add_child() method, DomNode, 209
  adding child element, 209, 232
  example, 210
add_collection/~_document commands, Xindice, 533
add_root() method, DomDocument, 201
  root element, creating, 201
addChild/~Parent() methods, SvgElement, 616
  child/parent, making passed object, 616
    animated bar chart example, 625, 626, 627
    animated red circle example, 617
addHandlers/~TagHandler() methods, SaxParser, 162
  ArticleParser example, 163
  as hook & template methods pair, 162
adding XML content, 229
  DOM example, 229
    AddApplicationNode(), 231
    AddBugItem(), 232
    architecture, diagram, 231
    HTML table, building, 234
    main program, 233
    output, 230
    WriteNewBugList(), 233
alternatives, RDF containers
  as value/property resource lists, 110
ampersand, see &.
ancestor/~-or-self axes, XPath, 261, 880
  parent (& context) nodes contained, 261-22, 880
<animate> animation element, SVG, 614
  animating single element property, example, 614
    animated bar chart example, 623
    attributes, list of, 615
ANY keyword, CONTENT, 65
Apache web server
  calendar application using, 670
  installation, 747
    UNIX, 760
    Windows, 749
append_child() function, DomNode, 414
  modifying XML using DOM, example, 413
arcrole global attribute, XLink, 115
  URI reference for arc role, defining, 115
arcs, XPath
  inter-graph paths, extended links defining, 116
arguments, XSLT
  xslt_process(), passing to, 343

arithmetic operators, PHP, 22
  list of, 22
arrays, PHP, 16
  [] (square bracket) syntax, specifying arrays, 16
  array() construct, creating array, 16
  multidimensional, declaring, 17
  returning file content as array, file(), 43
  superglobal, 19
  Vectors as scalable arrays, 911
arrays, XML-RPC, 639
  arraysize/~mem(), decoding XML-RPC data, 656
  example, 640
  structs and, example mixing, 641
arrow operator, see -> (arrow).
  $this object part, pointing to, 34
assignment (=) operator, see =/== operators.
assignment, PHP variables, 20
  by value/by reference, 20
  variable variables, 20
ATTLIST declaration, DTD attributes, 71
  MODIFIER, options list & example, 71
Attr interface, DOM Fundamental, 836
  properties, 836
attribute axis, XPath, 264, 881
  context node's attributes, containing, 264, 881
    example, 264
attributeDecl() method, DeclHandler
  attribute-type declaration, reporting, 788
AttributeList deprecated interface, SAX, 780
  methods, AttributeListImpl, 780
Attributes interface, SAX, 776
  get*() methods, list of, 776
attributes() method, DomElement, 222
  all node attributes, returning, 222
attributes, DTD elements, 71
  defining, ATTLIST, 71
    MODIFIER, options list & example, 71
    sample XML document, adding to, 75
  enumerations, 74
  types, 72
    CDATA, 72
    ID/IDREF/IDREFS, 73
    NMTOKEN/~S, 74
    NOTATION, 74
attributes, XML elements, 53
  attribute nodes representing, XPath, 251-52, 257
    attributes in predicates, 265
  create_attribute(), DomDocument, 223
  DomElement attribute methods, 221
  special, 54
    xml:lang, 55
    xml:space, 54
  subelements/attributes, choosing between, 62
  well-formedness rules for, 53
    examples, 54
  <xsl:attribute>/<~:attribute-set>, XSL/XSLT, 845
  XSLT attribute types, 877
  <xupdate:attribute>, XUpdate, 512
Attributes2 interface, SAX Extended, 779
  isSpecified() methods, Attributes2Impl, 779
authentication
  calendar application, 675
  session-based, 675
    steps & advantages, 675
  XML-RPC protocol, 634, 636
    log-/HTTP-based in extended protocol, 636
    NONE in basic protocol, 634
axes, XPath, 259, 879
  list of, 259, 880

B

bags, RDF containers
  as unordered resource lists, 110
base64 binary data, XML-RPC, 639
  base64_encode/~_decode() functions, PHP, 639
batch transformations, 401
  XSLT transforming large XML documents, 401
    transformation server required, 401
Batik Toolkit SVG viewer, Apache XML Project, 590
binary data, see base64.
bindings
  Dispatch Map creating, 657
  writing XML-RPC servers, example, 655
  XBL defining XUL widget bindings, 107
bitwise operators, PHP, 24
  list of, 24
BLOB (Binary Large OBjects), 491
  RDBMS storing XML, 491
<Body> element, SOAP, 568, 570
  invoked method input, containing, 568, 570
    request example, 568
    response example, 570
book overview, 4
  appendices, listing, 6
  chapters, listing, 5
  conventions used, 6
  customer support, 7
    downloading sample code, 7
    e-mail support, 8
    errata, 7
    p2p.wrox.com, subscribing to mailing list, 8
  questions answered, 4
  target audience, 4
boolean variables, PHP/XML-RPC, 13, 638
boolean() function, XPath, 266, 886
  converting anything passed to Boolean, 266, 886
browsers, web
  XSL supporting legacy, 352
buffer, PHP
  erasing, SVG non-fatal error display, 595
byte streams
  getByteStream/set~(), InputSource, 807

C

caching
  querying XML using, 431
  RSS multiple sources & cached content, 446
  XSLT transforming large XML using, 400
calendar client-server application, XML-RPC, 667
  client application, 691
    designing, forms processed, 692
    developing, main.php, 693
      adding/removing events, 695, 696
      getting/setting preferences, 695, 698
      initializing client, 694
      processing login/logout, 697, 698
    developing, section_agenda.php, 703
      abstracting XSLT processor from application, 706
      transforming XML to HTML, 703
    developing, section_preferences.php, 712
      preferences form, 712
    developing, section_schedule.php, 710
      schedule form, 711
    GUI design, layout & sections, 692
    installing client, 713
    layout, code & display, 700
    requirements, 691

calendar client-server application, XML-RPC (continued)
command-line client using Perl, 713
  client, Perl script, 714
  running, 714
  transforming XML agenda to text, 713
finding empty slots for event, 715
  client modifications, section_getslots.php, 719
    client display, 721, 723
    performing search, section_search.php, 722
    search processing, adding to main.php, 721
    transforming XML to HTML, 722
  server modifications, adding GetSlots(), 715
    method inputs, listing, 716
    method source code, 717
    XML string returned, 715
future requirements, 724
  attaching files, attachments table, 725
  describing events, eventDescriptions table, 727
  editing events, 724
  reminders, implementing, 727
  repeating events, 725
  searching for events, 725
    method parameters, listing, 725
  sharing calendar, 726
  task list manager, tasks table, 727
overview, 667
  architecture, diagram, 668
  requirements, 667
server application, 671
  authenticating user, 675
    NOT session-based, 676
  creating database, 673
  errors, listing, 690
  functions, creating, 677
  implementing database tables, 672
  indices, adding, 674
  initializing server, 676
  installing server, 691
  requirements & entities, listing, 671
server functions, 677
  adding/removing events, 679
    AddEvent(), 682
    _findEvent/~OverlappingEvent (), 680-81
    _getEvent(), 679
    RemoveEvent(), 683
  getting agenda, 686
    agenda returned as XML string, advantages, 686
    GetAgenda(), 687
  getting/setting preferences, 684
    _getPreference/GetPreference (), 684-85
    SetPreference(), 685
  other, 689
    GetUnixTimeStamp(), 689
    _lockEvents/_unlock(), 690
  validating users, 677
    _getUserId(), 677
    ValidateUser(), 678
technologies used, 668
  Apache 1.3.24 for web server application, 670
  MySQL for database storage, 670
    RDBMS choices, 670
  overview, diagram, 671
  PHP for server-side programming, 670
  XML-RPC for communication protocol, 669
    pros & cons, 669
cardinality operators, DTD, 66
examples, 67
cards, WML, 102
creating, example, 102
case folding
Expat parsing example, 145
setCaseFolding(), SaxParser, 162
case-order attribute, <xsl:sort>, 327

CDATA sections, XML, 58
CDATA attribute, DTD elements, 72
create_cdata_section(), DomDocument, 200
limitations, 58
startCDATA/end~(), LexicalHandler, 802
CDATASection interface, DOM Extended, 838
ceiling() function, XPath, 267, 887
rounding no. to nearest larger integer, 267, 887
<channel> element, RSS, 112, 440
channel meta data, containing, 112, 440
  /<items>/<textinput> subelements, 440
  subelements, list of, 112
generating content application, RSS, 457
character data, XML, 53
adding to target element, <xsl:element>, 332
NO manipulation methods for, DomElement, 242
  suggested solution, 242
subelements and, mixing, 53
xml_set_character_data_handler(), 141, 738
  characterDataHandler() prototype, 738
character points, XPointer, 118
character references, XML, 56
see also entity references.
character streams
getCharacterStream/set~(), InputSource, 808
CharacterData interface, DOM Fundamental, 836
properties & methods, 836
**characterDataHandler() function prototype, xml_*()
handler, 738**
**characters() methods, ContentHandler/ Document~, 783,
790**
character data, notifying of, 783, 790
characters, XML, 52
list of, 52
child axis, XPath, 259, 881
context node's children, containing, 259, 881
  example, 259
child sequences, XPointer syntax, 117
**child_nodes() methods, DomDocument/~Node,
203, 215**
child nodes, returning, 203, 215
deleting XML content example, 237
<choice> element, RELAX NG, 120
element's choice of subelements, expressing, 120
choose/when/otherwise construct
<xsl:choose>/<~:when>/<~:otherwise>,
  implementing by, 322, 847, 862, 872
<circle> shape element, SVG, 607
circle, example drawing, 607
classes, PHP, 34, 900
as collections of variables & functions, 34, 900
  -> (arrow) operator or $this, 34
  class methods & member variables, 34, 900
  defining, class keyword, 34
built-in functions handling, 38
constructors, 35, 901
extending, extends keyword, 36, 908
  parent operator, parent class methods access, 38
Form class example, 901, 910
  add(), adding controls to form, 912
  application using, code & output, 916
  constructor, 901, 911
  constructParameterHtml(), 912
  extended version, 910
  Form framework, using, 904
  functions, 902
  getParameter/set~/setParameters(), 911
  HTML generation, helper methods, 913

classes, PHP, (continued)
 initial version, 901
 toHtml/display(), 916
 variable definitions, 901
 Vectors, defining, 911
 inheritance, 904
  Form framework, eXtremePHP, 904
 instantiating, new keyword, 34, 35, 902
 public/private variables, PHP NOT supporting, 36
 static method invocation, :: operator, 37
 $this, referencing current object, 901
classes, XML third-party, 363
 phpXML, 381
 XML parser, generic, 363
 XML_Transformer, 376
 XMLFile, 370
cleanup() method, XMLFile
 trimmed down bug list, example, 373
client applications, developing, 537
 Jabber, 550
 SOAP, 563
 TCP/IP, 546
 WDDX, 537
 web services, 554
clone_node() method, DomNode, 214
code property, DOMException
 values, list of, 828
collections
 root collection, organizing XML storage, 503
  additional repository features, listing, 504
  indexing, allowing, 504
commands, XSLT, see <xsl:*> elements.
Comment interface, DOM Fundamental, 837
comment() method, LexicalHandler, 804
comment() node test, XPath, 257, 885
 comment nodes, containing comments, 253
 TRUE for all comment nodes, returning, 257, 885
comments, XML, 57
 create_comment(), DomDocument, 199
 <xsl:comment>, generating comment node, 847
 <xupdate:comment>, XUpdate, 513
comparison operators, PHP, 23
 = (assignment) & == (equality), comparing, 22
 ?: (ternary), 23
 list of, 23
compound variables, PHP, 15
 arrays, 16
 objects, 17
concat() function, XPath, 267, 887
 concatenating all passed strings, 267, 887
conditional structures, PHP, 26
 if/...else/...elseif, 26
 switch...case...default, 27
connect/dis~() methods, DB.php, 467
 database connection/dis~, establishing, 467
  document parts into table, extracting, 475, 478-79
  RSS from database, creating, 470
constants, PHP, 21
 define/defined(), defining constants, 21
constructors, PHP, 35, 901
 as special class functions, 35, 901
  example using, 36
  Form class example, 901
container nodes, XPointer points, 118
containers, RDF resources
 types, bags/sequences/alternatives, 110
  example, 110

contains() function, XPath, 888
 searchable bug list, phpXML example, 385
  programmers reporting database 'string' bugs, 271
 TRUE if string1 contains string2, returning, 888
 XSLT split/recursion example, 357
content event handlers
 getContentHandler/set~(), XMLReader, 812
CONTENT parameter, ELEMENT, 65
 ANY/EMPTY values, 65
ContentHandler interface, SAX, 782
 methods, 782
context, XPath, 255
 evaluating expressions in, example, 255
control structures, PHP, 25
 conditional, 26
  if/...else/...elseif, 26
  switch...case...default, 27
 loops, 27
converting XML documents using XSL, 352
count attribute, <xsl:number>, 330
 bug numbering example, 330
count() function, XPath, 269, 888
 legacy applications, XSLT supporting, 359
 nodes in passed node-set, counting, 269, 888
  bugs no. with different reporting/update date, 272
  total bugs no. in database, 270
create_*() factory methods, DomDocument, 198
 create_attribute(), 223
 create_cdata_section(), 200
 create_comment(), 199
 create_element(), 199
  adding XML content example, 231
  example, 200
 create_entity_reference(), 200
 create_processing_instruction(), 200
 create_text_node(), 199
  adding XML content example, 232
create_root() method, XMLFile
 simplified bug list, example, 374
creating objects from XML files, see objects, creating
 from XML files.
CSS (cascading stylesheets), 603
 inline properties, 604
 SVG, applying styles to elements, 603
  examples, 603
current() function, XSLT, 873
 current context node-set, returning, 873
$curtag member variable, see $roottag/$curtag.
CXD (Coherity XML Database) native XML database,
 Coherity, 517

D

data types, XML-RPC, 637
 arrays, 639
 base64 binary, 639
 Boolean, 638
 date/time, 638
 floats, 637
 integers, 637
 strings, 638
 structs, 640
data types, XPath, 255, 265
databases storing XML, see RDBMS.
data-type attribute, <xsl:sort>, 327
date/time, XML-RPC, 638

DB.php database access class, PEAR, 466
RDBMS storing XML, 466
advantages, 466
methods, 467
connect/dis~(), database connection, 467
fetchRow(), returning database data, 468
query(), querying database, 468
DB2, IBM, 516
DBDOM native XML database, 518
declaration events, DTD
DeclHandler/DTD~ interfaces, 788, 793
declaration, XML Prolog, see XML declaration.
DeclHandler interface, SAX Extended, 788
*Decl() methods, 788
decrement operators, PHP, see increment/ decrement.
default block, PHP, see switch blocks.
default XML namespaces, 86
define/defined() functions, PHP
constants, defining & testing if defined, 21
<defs> container element, SVG, 596
defining elements linked to by other tags, 596
deleting XML content, DOM example, 236
architecture, diagram, 236
FindApplicationNode(), 236
FindBugsNode(), 237
GetTextFromElement(), 238
main program, 238
RemoveBugsItemWithStatus(), 237
derivatives, XML, 89
generic, 92
DOM, 92
SAX, 93
XPath, 95
XSLT, 96
overview, 89
common patterns for XML processing, list of, 90
types, list of, 90
presentation vocabularies, 99
SVG, 103
VoiceXML, 106
WML, 101
XHTML, 99
XUL/XBL, 106
semantic web, 108
RDF, 108
RSS, 110
validating XML, 118
RELAX NG, 118
Schematron, 120
web services, 123
SOAP, 124
XML-RPC, 123
XLink, 114
XPointer, 116
<desc> container element, SVG, 597
SVG file discovery description, containing, 597
animated bar chart example, 622
descendant/~-or-self axis, XPath, 261, 881
context node's children, containing, 261, 881
searchable bug list, phpXML example, 385
trimmed down bug list, phpXML example, 382
description, web services, 560
WSDL, 578
<description> subelement, RSS <channel>, 112
as site/service/info source description, 112
deserialization, WDDX, see serialization/de~.
design, XML documents, 62
subelements/attributes, choosing between, 62
vocabularies, 62

discovery, web services, 560
Dispatch Map, XML-RPC library, 657
introspection, creating binding allowing, 657
DML (Doe's Markup Language)
new XSL tag default settings, deriving, 351
do...while loops, PHP, 28
DOCTYPE declaration, XML Prolog, 75
associating DTD with XML document, 75
SVG syntax including, 591
doctype() method, DomDocument, 203
DTD DOCTYPE, returning, 203
document event handlers
setDocumentHandler() method, Parser, 817
Document interface, DOM Fundamental, 831
properties & methods, 832
document() function, XQuery/XSLT, 508, 873
external source document, referencing, 873
document_element() method, DomDocument, 201
top-level element, returning, 201
DocumentFragment interface, DOM Fundamental, 833
as lightweight Document object, 833
children nodes NOT well-formed XML, 834
DocumentHandler deprecated interface, SAX, 789
HandlerBase implementing functionality, 790
methods, 790
DocumentType interface, DOM Extended, 838
properties, 838
DOM (Document Object Model), 92, 183, 827
as XML parsing & processing interface, 92, 183
functionality diagrams, article example, 184, 195
PHP DOM extension, example, 92
resources, 93
tree, accessing/modifying, 92, 184
adding XML content, 229
advantages, 186
classes/methods, DOM architecture, 193
DomDocument, 198
DomElement, 221
DomNode, 205
inheritance hierarchy, diagram, 194
overview, 193
xml*() factory methods, tree construction, 195
deleting XML content, 236
disadvantages, DOM XML, 187, 239
improper logic distribution, 241
low-level API, 240
NO DomElement character data manipulation, 242
NO internal error checking, 243
creating invalid elements, 243
incomplete DOM Level 1 & 2 standard, 239
OO capability, 244
unsound architecture, 240
DomDocument/~Node, deprecated, 414
Extended Interfaces, 838
CDATASection, 838
DocumentType, 838
Entity/~Reference, 839
Notation, 839
ProcessingInstruction, 838
Fundamental Interfaces, 827
Attr, 836
CharacterData, 836
Comment, 837
Document, 831
DocumentFragment, 833
DOMException, 828
DOMImplementation, 833
Element, 834
NamedNodeMap, 835

DOM (Document Object Model, continued)
    Node, 829
    NodeList, 834
    Text, 837
  installation, Unix, 190
    building program, 191
    downloading libxml, 190
    rebuilding PHP for DOM support, 191
  installation, Windows, 189
    testing, 192
  Levels 1 & 2, 240
    as incomplete standard, disadvantage, 240
  libxml PHP DOM library, GNOME, 189
    PHP version compatibility issues, 193
  modifying XML using, 412
  parsing XML using, 224
  querying XML using, 425
  SAX and, 187, 284
    comparative table, 188
  storing XML implementing, 507
  transforming XML using, 395
  writing XML using, 435
DomDocument class, DOM XML API, 198
  members, list of, 204
  methods, 198
    add_root(), 201
    child_nodes(), 203
    create_*() factory methods, 198
    doctype(), 203
    document_element(), 201
    dump_mem/~_mem_file(), 202
DomElement class, DOM XML API, 221
  methods, 221
    attributes/has_~(), 222, 223
    character data manipulation, lacking, 242
    get_attribute/set_~(), 221
    get_attribute_node/set_~(), 223
    tagname/node_name(), 221
DOMException interface, DOM Fundamental, 828
  code property, value list, 828
DOMImplementation interface, DOM Fundamental, 833
  methods, 833
DomNode class, DOM XML API, 205
  methods, 206
    add_child/new_~(), 209, 211
    clone_node(), 214
    dump_node(), 220
    first_child/last_~/has_~_nodes()/~_nodes(), 215, 216
    insert_before/unlink_node(), 212, 213
      remove_child(), PHP 4.3.0, 214
    node_name/*_value/~_type(), 206
    owner_document(), 218
    parent_node(), 218
    previous_sibling/next_~(), 217
    set_content(), 219
domxml_open_file/~_mem() functions, DOM Extension, 275
  parsing XML document from file/PHP string, 275
    XPath using directly from PHP, example, 275
DSN (Data Source Name), 466
  databases, storing XML, 466
    $dbtype, RDBMS supported, 466
    document parts into table, extracting, 473, 477
    other variables, meanings, 467
    RSS from database, creating, 469
DTD (Document Type Definitions), 65
  associating with XML document, DOCTYPE, 75
    combining both, example, 77
    external DTD, declaring, 76
    internal DTD, declaring, 75

  attributes, 71
    CDATA, 72
    defining, ATTLIST, 71
    defining, sample XML document, 75
    enumerations, 74
    ID/IDREF/IDREFS, 73
    NMTOKEN/~S, 74
    NOTATION, 74
  elements, 65
    cardinality operators, 66
    choices of subelements, 66
    defining, ELEMENT, 65
    defining, sample XML document, 69
    mixed content, 67
    sequences of subelements, 65
    text, #PCDATA, 65
  entities, 74
  shortcomings, 77
    sample XML document, 78
  XML-RPC DTD, writing, 646
DTD event handlers
  getDTDHandler/set~() methods, XMLReader, 812
  setDTDHandler() method, Parser, 818
DTDHandler interface, SAX, 793
  *Decl () methods, 793
  HandlerBase implementing behavior, 793
dump_mem/~_mem_file() methods, DomDocument, 202
  adding XML content example, 233
  deleting XML content example, 239
  dumping content indirectly/directly, 202
dump_node() method, DomNode, 220
  dumping single node into tree, 220
    example, 220

E

Edge table approach, 492
  RDBMS storing XML, element-level mapping, 492
    diagram, example, 493
    Edge tables, 493
    mechanism, describing, 494
ELEMENT declaration, DTD elements, 65
  CONTENT parameter, 65
Element interface, DOM Fundamental, 834
  property & methods, 834
element-available() function, XSLT, 874
  extension element availability, querying, 874
elementDecl() method, DeclHandler
  element-type declaration, reporting, 789
elements, SOAP, 567
  <Body>, 568, 570
  <Envelope>, 567
  <Fault>, subelements, 571
  <Header>, 567
elements, SVG, 596
  container, 596
elements, XML, 50
  create_element(), DomDocument, 199
  element nodes representing, XPath, 252
    selecting elements, writing expressions, 256
  empty, 51
  example, 51
  nesting, 51
  root, 50
  subelements/attributes, choosing between, 62

elements, XML (continued)
 subelements/character data, mixing, 52
 text, #PCDATA, 65
 xml_set_element_handler(), 737
  startElementHandler/end~() prototypes, 738
 xml_set_element_handler(), Expat, 139
 <xsl:comment>, XSLT, 853
 <xupdate:element>, XUpdate, 512
elements, XML DTD, 65
 attributes, 71
 cardinality operators, 66
 choices of subelements, 66
 defining, ELEMENT, 65
  EMPTY/ANY elements, 65
  examples, 68
 defining, sample XML document, 69
  <bugs>/<bug_item>, 70
  limiting subelements to ONE occurence, 70
  root/<application> elements, 70
 mixed content, 67
 sequences of subelements, 65
elements, XML Schema, see <xs:*> elements.
<ellipse> shape element, SVG
 ellipse, example drawing, 608
else/elseif conditional structures, PHP, see if.
<embed> element, HTML, 593
 SVG embedding into HTML, 593
empty elements, XML, 51
 EMPTY keyword, CONTENT, 65
empty() function, PHP
 calendar application, 683
encoding, characters
 encoding/decoding data, XML-RPC to/from PHP, 655
 generating content application, RSS, 456
 getEncoding(), Locator2, 811
 getEncoding/set~(), InputSource, 808
 SOAP encoding, 565
  encodingStyle attribute, values, 565
  features, 566
 use*Encoding(), SaxParser class, 162
encryption
 XML Encryption/Signature, 560
 XML-RPC protocol, 634
end*() methods, see also start*/end*().
endElementHandler() function prototype, xml_*()
handler, 738
entities, DTD, 74
 general, 74
 parameter, 75
 startEntity/end~(), LexicalHandler, 803
Entity interface, DOM Extended, 839
 properties, 839
entity references, XML, 57
 create_entity_reference(), DOMDocument, 200
 external, 739
 predefined entities, list of, 57
 see also character references.
EntityReference interface, DOM Extended, 839
entity resolvers, XML
 getEntityResolver/set~(), XMLReader, 812
 setEntityResolver(), Parser, 818
EntityResolver/~Resolver2 interfaces, SAX/~ Extended, 795-96
 HandlerBase implementing default behavior, 795
 methods, 795-96
enumerations, DTD attributes, 74
<Envelope> element, SOAP, 567
 message, containing, 567
  <Header>/<Body> subelements, 567, 570

Epilog, XML, see XML overview, Epilog.
equality operator (==), see =/== operators.
error codes, XML parsing, 743
 error code constants, list of, 743
 xml_error_string/~_get_error_code(), 743
error/fatalError() methods, ErrorHandler
 recoverable/non-~ errors, notifying of, 800
ErrorHandler interface, SAX, 799
 HandlerBase implementing default behavior, 800
 methods, 800
errors, handling
 @ error handler operator, 25
 calendar application, 690
 getErrorHandler/set~(), XMLReader, 812
 installation, Apache on Windows/UNIX, 752, 762
  configuring Apache for PHP, 755, 767
 installation, PHP4 on Windows/UNIX, 756, 763
  compiling PHP, 765
 NONE internally in DOM XML, 243
 setErrorHandler(), Parser, 818
 SVG displaying fatal/non-~ errors, 594
  buffer, erasing, 595
  error handler, defining/setting, 595
 xml_get_error_code/~_error_string/
  ~_get_currrent_line_number(), Expat, 144
 XML-RPC responses, 645
 <xsl:message>, error messages/warnings, 858
escape characters, string variables, 14
eval() function, Sablotron, 346
 OO XSL example, 346
events, handling, 93
 SAX, event-based XML parsing, 93, 131, 160
  basic SAX events, list of, 93
  example, 94
  article parsing example, 166, 168
 xml_*() functions, Expat, 139, 150
exceptions, XML
 SAXException/SAXParse~ methods, 819
 SAXNotRecognizedException/SAXNotSupported~
  methods, 822
Expat SAX parser, PHP, 94, 135, 731
 functionality, example, 94, 136
  mechanism description, 136
  parsing, circumstances stopping, 141
  source XML document, 136
 installation, UNIX, 287
  Sablotron installation requiring, 288
  testing, 135
 instantiating, xml_parser_create(), 732
 NON well-formed XML content, handling, 178
 overview, 731
 parsing XML document, example, 145
  AppendToGlobal(),148
  CreateParser(), 145
  FreeParser(), 146
  HandleBeginTag(), 147
  HandleCharacterData(), 147
  HandleEndTag(), 148
  OpenFile(), 146
  output display, 149
  Parse(), 146
  SetHandlers(), 145
  SetOptions(), setting case folding to false, 145
 SAX filters transforming XML, example, 404
 whitespace, handling, 173
 xml_*() functions, 137, 150

expressions, XPath, 255
  evaluating correctly, XSLT variable use, 308
  evaluating with namespaces, 276
    query using namespaces, 277
    register_ns(), registering namespaces, 277
  functions, applying to expressions, 269
  precedence rules, XSL predefined templates, 303
  writing, 255
    attributes, selecting, 257
    comments, selecting, 257
    context, evaluating, 255
    elements, selecting, 256
    location paths, writing, 255
    PIs, selecting, 257
    text, selecting, 257
    wildcards, selecting, 258
expressions, XQuery, 507
  basic, 507
  FLWR (FOR, LET, WHERE, RETURN), 508
extended links, XPath, 116
  graph paths, extending links to, 116
    arcs, defining paths, 116
    example, 116
extending PHP classes, 36
  Form framework, 908
  NO constructor/member variable allowed, 37
  parent operator, parent class method access, 38
  syntax, example, 36
external DTD, 76
  private/public, 76
external entity references, XML
  handleExternalEntityRef(), SaxParser, 173
  unparsed, 740
  xml_set_external_entity_ref_handler(), 154, 739
    externalEntityRefHandler() prototype, 740
external markup declaration, XML, 60
  standalone documents lacking, 60
external subsets
  getExternalSubset(), EntityResolver2, 797
externalEntityDecl() method, DeclHandler
  parsed external entity declaration, reporting, 789
externalEntityRefHandler() function prototype, xml_*()
handler, 740
eXtremePHP framework, 157
  Form framework, 904
  installation, 157
    .htaccess, setting up, 157
  SaxParser framework, 159
    ArticleParser/~TagHandler example, 163, 165
  Vector utility class, 911

F

false() function, XPath, 266, 888
  always returning FALSE, 266, 888
<Fault> element, SOAP, 571
  subelements, 571
faults, SOAP responses for, 570
  example, 570
  fault codes, list of, 571
fclose() function, PHP, 41
  closing file handles, 41
  document parts into database, extracting, 473
features, XML
  getFeature/set~(), XMLReader, 812
feof() function, PHP, 550
  end of file, reaching from socket, 550
fetchRow() method, DB.php, 468

database data, returning, 468
  constants as arguments, list of, 468
  document parts into table, extracting, 479
  RSS from database, creating, 470
fgets() function, PHP, 549
  reading line from socket, 549
file handles
  creating/closing, fopen/fclose(), 40
file structures
  special, storing XML using, 501
file system, organizing XML storage, 504
  limitations, 505
file() function, PHP, 43
  returning file content as array, 43
file_exists() function, PHP
  reading multiple sources application, RSS, 449
file_id column, database tables, 465
  databases, storing XML, 465
filemtime() function, PHP, 448
  reading multiple sources application, RSS, 448
files/directories, accessing, 40
  creating file handles, fopen(), 40
    closing, fclose(), 41
    examples, 41
  reading from files, fread(), 42
    placing file content into variable, filesize(), 42
    writing to files, fwrite(), 42
  returning file content as array, file(), 43
    removing line terminators, trim(), 43
filesize() function, PHP, 42
  placing file content into variable, 42
filters, SAX, 403
  modifying XML, 415
    FilterAddProduct, adding products to cart, 415
    FilterRemoveProduct, removing products, 417
    filters chain, building correctly, 416, 418
  modularization use, 403
  objects, creating from XML files, 422
    FilterBuildBooks, creating book objects, 422
    filters chain, building correctly, 423
    NULL filter, using, 423
  querying XML, 429
  transforming XML, 403
    AbstractFilter, SAX event receiver/sender, 405
    AbstractSAXParser, SAX event generator, 403
    ExpatParser, implementing Expat, 404
    FilterName, uppercasing <name> text, 406
    FilterNameBold, bolding <name> text, 407
    FilterOutput, outputting XML for testing, 406
    filters chain, building correctly, 407, 408, 409
    streaming result, example, 408
firewalls, security, 562
  web services use, limitations, 562
first_child/last_~() methods, DomNode, 216
  first/last child nodes, returning, 216
    example, 217
flat files, 464
  legacy applications, XSLT supporting, 358
  storing XML in filesystem, 464
    search/portability disadvantages, 464
    simplicity advantage, 464
floats (floating point variables), PHP/XML-RPC, 14, 637
floor() function, XPath, 267, 889
  rounding no. to nearest smaller integer, 267, 889
FLWR (FOR, LET, WHERE, RETURN) expressions,
XQuery, 508
  examples, 509
    computing document joins, 509
    list bindings, 509

Flyweight optimization pattern, 423
objects, creating from XML files, 423
following/~sibling axes, XPath, 263, 882
following nodes/ siblings, containing, 263, 882
example, 263
fopen() function, PHP, 40
creating file handles, 40
mode argument, values, 40
reading single source application, RSS, 443
for loops, PHP, 28
FOR statement, XQuery, 509
foreach loops, PHP, 29
syntax, versions, 29
<xsl:for-each>, XSLT, 854
Form framework, eXtremePHP, 904
Form class example, using by, 910
FormControl superclass, 904
constructor, 905
display/~Header/~Footer(), 907
setConstraints/validate(), 906
setName/~Value/getName(), data accessors, 905
toHtml/getHeaderHtml/~FooterHtml(), 906
variable definitions, 905
SubmitButton/HiddenField subclasses, 909
TextField subclass, 908
constructor, 908
getHeaderHtml/~FooterHtml(), 908
format attribute, <xsl:number>, 328
accepted values, list of, 328
format-number() function, XSLT, 874
numeric value, formatting, 874
fpassthru() function, PHP, 550
socket response to output stream, sending, 550
fread() function, PHP, 42, 549
reading from files, 42, 549
reading multiple sources application, RSS, 450
fsockopen() function, PHP, 549
communication with host port, opening, 549
TCP/IP client example, 548
function-available() function, XSLT, 874
extension function availability, querying, 874
functions, PHP, 29
built-in handling classes/objects, 38
overloading functions, PHP NOT supporting, 30
returning values, 31
variable types returned, 32
user-defined, 30
variable functions, creating, 32
functions, XPath, 266
applying to expressions, 269
general syntax, overview, 886
list of, 266, 886
boolean, 266
node-set, 269
number, 266
string, 267
fwrite() function, PHP, 42, 549
writing to files, 42, 549

G

<g> container element, SVG, 596
grouping elements with common attributes, 596
animated bar chart example, 623
general entities, DTD, 74
generate-id() function, XSLT, 875
unique ID for specified node, generating, 875

get*/set*() data access methods, 905
Form framework, 905
get_attribute/set~() methods, DomElement, 221
parsing XML example, 226
get_attribute_node/set~() methods, DomElement, 223
get_class() function, PHP, 913
Form class example, 912
get_content() method, phpXML, 381
searchable bug list, example, 385
trimmed down bug list, example, 382
get~/set~/~ByteStream/~CharacterStream() methods, InputSource, 807
get~/set~/~PublicId/~SystemId() methods, InputSource, 808
getColumnNumber/~LineNumber() methods, Locator/SAXParseException, 810, 821
getContentHandler/set~() methods, XMLReader, 812
getDTDHandler/set~() methods, XMLReader, 812
getEncoding() method, Locator2, 811
getEncoding/set~() methods, InputSource, 808
getEntityResolver/set~() methods, XMLReader, 812
getErrorHandler/set~() methods, XMLReader, 812
getException/~Message() methods, SAXException, 819
getExternalSubset() method, EntityResolver2, 797
getFeature/set~() methods, XMLReader, 812
getIndex/~Length() methods, Attributes, 777
getLength/~Name() methods, AttributeListImpl, 780
getLocalName/~QName() methods, Attributes, 777
GetName() method, XmlTagHandler, 164
getParent/set~() methods, XMLFilterImpl, 824
getProperty/set~() methods, XMLReader, 813
getPublicId/~SystemId() methods, Locator/SAXParseException, 810, 822
gettype() function, PHP, 12
getType/~Value() methods, Attributes/ AttributeListImpl, 777, 781
getURI() method, Attributes, 778
getxml() method, xml_sql2xml class, 481
SQL query's XML data results, returning, 481
database to XML, examples storing, 481
nested query example, 483
getXMLVersion() method, Locator2, 811
GUI (graphical user interfaces)
XUL as GUI description language, 106

H

handle*() methods, SaxParser, 172
handleProcessingInstruction(), 172
PI handler, example creating, 172
HandleBeginElement/~EndElement/ ~CharacterData() methods, XmlTagHandler, 164
ArticleTagHandler example, 166
whitespace, handling, 177
handleProcessingInstruction() method, SaxParser, 172
handler functions, XML PHP API, see xml_*().
HandlerBase deprecated class, SAX, 804
interface default behavior, implementing, 804
DocumentHandler, 790
DTDHandler, 793
EntityResolver, 795
ErrorHandler, 800
methods, 804

handlers, events, see events, handling.
has_attributes() method, DomElement, 223
has_child_nodes() method, DomNode, 215
header() function, PHP
  generating content application, RSS, 460
<Header> element, SOAP, 567
  extending messages using, example, 576
    <actor> attribute, allowing multi-stage processing, 577
  namespace qualification required, 568
  SOAP header, describing, 567
    components, 567
    request example, 568
heredoc syntax
  strings, creating, 15
    problematic issues, 15
hook methods, 162
  addHandlers(), SaxParser, 162
  article parsing example, SaxParser, 165, 168
  template methods and, 162
href global attribute, XLink, 115
  resource URI pointed to, containing, 115
.htaccess files, Apache, 157
  eXtremePHP setup using, 157
    advantages, 158
    mechanism description, 158
  overview, 158
HTML (HyperText Markup Language)
  SVG embedding into, 593
  XHTML and, 100
HTTP (HyperText Transfer Protocol), 642
  requests, 642
  responses, 645
  TCP/IP, using, 642

I

id attribute, XML elements
  XPointer syntax using, 117
id() function, XPath, 269, 889
  element identified, returning, 269, 889
ID/IDREF/IDREFS attributes, DTD elements, 73
identity rule
  <xsl:copy> example, 333, 336
if statement, PHP, 26
  if...else/...elseif, 26
  <xsl:if>, 855
ignorableWhitespace() method, ContentHandler/
Document~, 784, 791
image/svg+xml, SVG MIME type, 591
<image> subelement, RSS <channel>, 113, 440
  as image description element, 112, 113, 441
    <title>/<link>/<url> subelements, 112, 113, 441
impxpl() function, eXtremePHP, 163
  including file under document root, 163
include() function, PHP
  impxpl(), eXtremePHP, 163
increment/decrement operators, PHP, 22
indent attribute, <xsl:output>, 295
indexes, XPointer points, 118
indexing, XML documents
  root collection, organizing XML storage, 504
indices, queries
  calendar application using, 674
infinite recursion
  named templates, example invoking, 306
Infonyte DB native XML database, 518

inheritance, classes, 904
  DOM class hierarchy diagram, 194
  Form framework, eXtremePHP, 904
    Form class example, using by, 910
    FormControl superclass, 904
    SubmitButton/HiddenField subclasses, 909
    TextField subclass, 908
  subclasses inheriting from superclasses, 904
    overriding methods, 909
InputSource class, SAX, 806
  get*/set*() methods, 807
    InputSource() constructors, 807
INSERT statement, SQL
  document parts into database, extracting, 475
insert_before() method, DomNode
  inserting node as previous element's child, 212
    example, 212
    post-insertion modifications DON'T affect tree, 213
installing PHP4 & Apache, 747
  choosing, 747
    module/CGI PHP installation, 764, 768
    module/CGI, PHP installed as, 747
    operating system, Windows/UNIX, 747
    PHP installation strategy, 748
    web server, 748
  resources, 770
    Apache, 771
    php.net, 770
    Wrox books & p2p.wrox.com, 770, 771
    zend.com & php4win.de, 771
installing PHP4 & Apache on UNIX, 760
  compiling PHP
    errors, handling, 765
  compiling PHP as CGI, 768
    creating executable PHP scripts, 769
  compiling PHP as module, 764
  installing Apache, 760
    errors, handling, 762
    starting Apache, 760
  installing PHP, 762
    as dynamic shared object instead of module, 763
    errors, handling, 763
  integrating PHP with Apache, 765
    AddType section, 765
    errors, handling, 767
    LoadModule section, 765
    testing, 766
  post-installation, Apache, 761
    Apache running & starting on boot, 761
  post-installation, PHP, 765
installing PHP4 & Apache on Windows, 749
  configuring Apache for PHP, 754
    Action section, 754
    AddType section, 754
    errors, handling, 755
    ScriptAlias section, 754
  installing Apache, 749
    as service/application, choosing, 750
    complete/custom install, choosing, 750
    document root, changing, 751
    errors, handling, 752
  installing PHP, 753
    configuring PHP, 753
    web servers supported, 753
  post-installation, 757
    error reporting, increasing, 757
    PHP extension software, listing & enabling, 758
  testing PHP installation, 756
    errors, handling, 756
  upgrading to ISAPI, 759

instantiating classes into objects, 34, 35, 902
  instance methods, calling, 903
    mechanism explanation, 903
    parameterless call, advantages, 903
instructions, XSL, see <xsl:*> elements.
integers, PHP/XML-RPC, 13, 637
<interface> element, RELAX NG, 119
  XML vocabulary root element, indicating, 119
internal DTD, 75
  shortcomings, 76
internal subset declarations, XML, 60
internalEntityDecl() method, DeclHandler, 789
introspection, XML-RPC library, 658
  describing XML-RPC server services, 658
    system.*() methods, 658
  Dispatch Map creating binding allowing, 657
  integer services library example, 658
    client, 659
    client/server responses, 663
    server, 658
Ipedo native XML database, 518
ISAPI (Internet Server API), Microsoft
  upgrading to, PHP4 Windows installation, 759
isset() function, PHP
  reading multiple sources application, RSS, 452
isSpecified() methods, Attributes2Impl, 779
<item> element, RSS, 441
  content items from channel, displaying, 441
    subelements, 442
  generating content application, RSS, 457
<items> subelement, RSS <channel>, 113, 440
  as channel items list, 112, 113
    subelements, 113
Iterators
  Vectors, traversing, 911

J

Jabber, 550
  as instant messaging protocol, 550
    resources, 554
  connecting to Jabber server, example, 551
    browser creation, 552
    instantiating class, 551
    transform performed on server, 553
JavaScript
  WDDX packet serialization/de~ example, 542

K

key() function, XSLT, 875
  node reference, generating, 875
kindOf property, XML-RPC library, 656
  decoding data, XML-RPC to PHP, 656
Kweelt XQuery implementation, 511
  query testing example, 511
    result, 511

L

lang() function, XPath, 266, 889
  TRUE if language is same as passed, 266, 889
languages
  xml:lang, indicating by, 55

last() function, XPath, 269, 890
  last node's index no., returning, 269, 890
last_child() method, see first_child/last_~().
legacy applications, XSLT supporting, 358
  | record separator, removing after last entry, 359
  DOCTYPE, avoiding addition of, 359
  example, 358
  serializing XML content into flat file, 358
  whitespace, removing, 359
legacy browsers XSLT supporting, 292
  converting XML documents, 352
  limitations, 292
LET construct, XQuery, 508
LexicalHandler interface, SAX Extended, 801
  methods, 801
libxml PHP DOM library, GNOME, 189
  installation, Windows/UNIX, 189, 190
  PHP version compatibility issues, 193
<line> shape element, SVG, 606
  line, example drawing, 606
    animated bar chart example, 622
<link> subelement, RSS <channel>, 112, 441
  as URI pointing to info source, 112
links, XML documents
  XLink, 114
listeners, SAX, 404
literal result element, XSL, 319
  example creating, 319
  limitations, 320
literal-name() node test, XPath, 885
  TRUE for all nodes of that name, 885
local-name() function, XPath, 269, 890
  first node name's local part, returning, 269, 890
location paths, XPath, 255
  writing, 255
Locator interface, SAX, 809
  get*() methods, 810
locator value, XPath type, 115
  extended links containing several, 116
Locator2 interface, SAX Extended, 810
  get*() methods, 810
logical operators, PHP, 23
  list of, 23
loops, PHP, 27
  do...while, 28
  for, 28
  foreach, 29
  while, 27

M

magic_quotes_gpc() function, PHP WDDX
  WDDX packet serialization/de~ example, 543
<marker> shape element, SVG, 611
  shapes linked to by other elements, creating, 611
    animated bar chart example, 622
    marker properties, list of, 612
markup languages
  SGML, 49
  XML, 49
matrix() function, SVG transform, 599
  ellipse rotation example, 602
md5(uniqid(rand())) function, PHP
  calendar application, 683
media-type attribute, <xsl:processing instruction>, 338

member variables, PHP classes, 34, 900
DOM members, list of, 204
example using, 205
messaging, web services, 559
meta data, 48
example, 48
RSS, lightweight meta data description, 108, 439
semantic web, 108
method attribute, <xsl:output>/<~:processing-instruction>, 295, 338
legacy applications, XSLT supporting, 359
<methodCall>/<~Name> elements, XML-RPC, 642
methods, PHP classes, 34, 900
abstract, 906
Form class example, 902
get*/set*() data accessors, 905
instance methods, calling, 903
overriding, 907, 909
static method invocation, :: operator, 37
template, 907
MIME (Multi-purpose Internet Mail Extensions)
image/svg+xml MIME types, SVG, 591
mixed content elements, DTD, 67
modifying XML, 411
abstracting document modifications, 420
DOM, using, 412
addProduct/remove~(), simple example, 412
SAX, using, 415
filters, example using, 415
simple example, 411
XSLT, using, 418
testing stylesheets, 419, 420
XSLT stylesheets, 418, 419
modularization, applications
SAX filters transforming XML, 403
XSL increasing, 290
<module> root element, RELAX NG, 119
RELAX version/namespace, indicating, 119
Mozilla browser
as SVG user agent, 590
multi-tiered applications
XSL, building using, 350
diagram, example, 350
MySQL RDBMS
calendar application using, 670

N

name attribute, <xsl:*>, 305, 306, 338
name() function, XPath, 890
node name, returning, 890
NamedNodeMap interface, DOM Fundamental, 835
property & methods, 835
names, XML elements, 52
namespace axis, XPath, 883
all context node namespaces, containing, 883
namespaces, SOAP, 568
namespaces, XML, 85
declaring, xmlns, 85
evaluating XPath expressions with, 276
register_ns(), registering namespaces, 277
scope declaration & default namespaces, 85
example, 86
using, <prefix:name>, 85
XPath namespace nodes, 253

XSLT using, 294
advantages, 294
<xsl:namespace-alias>, 859
namespace-uri() function, XPath, 269, 891
node's namespace URI, returning, 269, 891
native XML databases, 517
storing XML, product solutions, 517
characteristics, 517
CXD (Coherity XML Database), 517
DBDOM, 518
Infonyte DB, 518
Ipedo XML database, 518
Tamino, 519
Virtuoso Universal Server, 519
X-Hive/DB, 519
Xindice, 520
nesting elements, XML, 51
new_child() method, DomNode, 211
adding XML content example, 232
bug problem, 211
creating child element, 211
example, 211
new_xmldoc() factory method, DOM, see xml*().
next_sibling() method, see previous_~/next_~().
NMTOKEN/~S attributes, DTD elements, 74
Node interface, DOM Fundamental, 829
methods, 831
nodeName/~Type/~Value, comparative list, 830
properties, 829
node tests, XPath, 879, 884
list of, 884
node(), TRUE for all nodes, 258, 885
node_name() method, DomElement, 221
checking node names, 221
node_name()/~_value/~_type() methods, DomNode, 206, 207, 208
node name/value/type, returning, 206, 207, 208
example, 209
return values, list of, 206, 207, 208
parsing XML example, 225
NodeList interface, DOM Fundamental, 834
property & method, 834
nodeName/~Type/~Value properties, Node
comparative values, list of, 830
nodes, XPath, 251
types, list of, 251
attribute, 252
comment, 253
element, 252
namespace, 253
PI, 252
root, 251
text, 252
normalize-space() function, XPath, 268, 891
whitespace-normalized string, returning, 268, 891
open/closed bugs no. in database, example, 271
not() function, XPath, 266, 891
inverse of passed value, returning, 266, 891
NOTATION attribute, DTD elements, 74
notation declarations, DTD, 741
xml_set_notation_decl_handler(), 741
notationDeclHandler() prototype, 741
notation declarations, XML
handleNotationDecl(), SaxParser, 173
xml_set_notation_decl_handler(), Expat, 151
Notation interface, DOM Extended, 839
properties, 839
notationDecl() method, DTDHandler
notation declaration event, notifying of, 794

notationDeclHandler() prototype function, xml_*()
handler, 741
NULL variable, PHP, 18
  SAX filters creating objects from XML files, 423
number() function, XPath, 266, 269, 892
  nodes no. in nodeset, returning, 269
  parameter to number, converting, 266, 892

O

object relational mapping, 495
  RDBMS storing XML, custom solutions, 495
    mapping classes to tables, 495
    mapping DOM objects to tables, 496
      tables, listing, 497
      tables, populating, 499
      tree diagram, 497
<object> element, HTML, 593
  SVG embedding into HTML, 593
objects, PHP, 17, 900
  as class instances, 34, 35, 900
  built-in functions handling, 38
  creating from XML files, 420
    Flyweight pattern, applying, 423
    SAX filter, using, 422
    simple example, 421
  public/private variables, PHP NOT supporting, 36
omit-xml-declaration attribute, <xsl:processing-
instruction>, 338
OOP (object-oriented programming), 32, 899
  classes & objects, 34, 900
    constructors, 901
    Form class example, 901
    members, 900
    methods, 900
    $this, referencing current object, 901
  DOM XML limitations, example, 244
  inheritance, 904
    Form class example, 910
    Form framework, eXtremePHP, 904
    overriding methods, 909
  instantiation, 902
    instance methods, calling, 903
  overview, 899
  PHP support, add-on libraries, 156
    SaxParser framework, eXtremePHP, 157
  polymorphism, 914
  procedural programming and, 33
    comparative diagram, 33
  XSL processing example, 344
    free(), 347
    getXsltProcessLine(), test function, 346
    setSourceXslDocument/~Value() handlers, 345
    testing class, 348
    transform(), 345
    transformDocument/~Value(), 347
    XsltProcessor class, constant definitions, 344
    XsltProcessor() constructor, 344
operators, PHP, 21
  arithmetic, 22
  assignment/increment/decrement, 22
  bitwise, 24
  comparison, 23
  error handler, 25
  logical, 23
  string, 25
Oracle 8/9
  storing XML, product solutions, 517

order attribute, <xsl:sort>, 327
overloadedElements parameter, XML_Transformer
constructor, 378
  XML to HTML table tags transformation, 378
overloading functions
  PHP NOT supporting, 30
overriding methods, 909
  Form framework, 908
  mechanism description, example, 909
owner_document() method, DomNode, 218
  retrieving original document, 218

P

p2p.wrox.com, 8
  subscribing to mailing list, steps, 8
P3P (Platform for Privacy Preferences Project), 561
  as web services security standard, 561
    example, 561
<param>/<params> elements, XML-RPC, 642
parameter entities, DTD, 75
parameters
  <xsl:param>/<~:with-param>, 864, 872
parent axis, XPath, 260, 883
  context node's parent node, contains, 260, 883
    example, 260
parent operator
  parent class methods, accessing, 38
    example, 38
parent_node() method, DomNode, 218
  parent node, returning, 218
parse() method, XML_Parser
  multiple sources application, RSS, 451
  reading single source application, RSS, 443
parse() methods, Parser/XMLReader, 813, 816
  XML document, parsing, 813, 816
parseable entity declarations, XML
  Expat handling, 153
Parser deprecated interface, SAX, 816
  parse/set*() methods, 816
parser functions, XML PHP API, see xml_*().
parsing XML, 129, 284, 731
  DOM, 92
  DOM example, 224
    bug list, 224
    DisplayApplicationTitle(), 226
    DisplayBugItemTable(), 228
    GetTextFromElement(), 226
    output, 229
    ParseApplicationNode(), 225
    ParseBugItemNode(), 227
      variable variables, version using, 228
    ParseBugsNode(), 226
    ParseDocument(), parsing <bug_list>, 225
  Expat XML parser, PHP, 731
  functionality, xml_*() functions, 732
    freeing up resources, xml_parser_free(), 733
    handler functions, 737
    instantiating parser, xml_parser_create(), 732
    parser functions, 733
    parsing data, xml_parse(), 733
    utility functions, 741
  parser types, 130
  SAX, 93, 131
    Expat parsing XML, example, 136, 145
  transforming vs., choosing XSL/DOM/SAX, 284
  XML parser class, generic, 364

<path> shape element, SVG, 610
  vector-based shape, example drawing, 610
    instructions, outlining shape, 610
patterns, Schematron, 121
#PCDATA text elements, DTD, 65
PEAR (PHP Extension & Application Repository), 442
  XML_RSS RSS parser class, 442
Perl (Practical Extraction & Reporting Language)
  calendar application, command-line client, 713
PHP overview, 3, 11
  API, PHP XML, see xml_*() functions.
  basic syntax, 11
    special tags, 11
  calendar application using, 670
  classes & objects, OOP, 32
  constants, 21
  control structures, 25
  files/directories, accessing, 40
  functions, 29
  future developments, listing, 586
  installation, 747
    UNIX, 762
    Windows, 753
  operators, 21
  resources, 770
  variables, 12
    assigning, 20
    types of, 12
  XML and, 3
<?php...?> XML tag, PHP, 11
phpXML class, 381
  methods, 381
  searchable bug list, example, 383
    displaying search results, 387
      output, 387
    expressions for bug titles, creating, 385
    filtering, open/closed bug status-based, 386
      return application name if status OK, 386
    keyword-based search path, creating, 384
    phpXML instantiation & expression evaluation, 385
    search form creation, 383
      form display, 384
  trimmed down bug list, example, 381
    displaying results, 382
      output, 383
    grabbing application names, 382
    storing title nodes data into array, 382
  XPath, using on XML document, 381
PI (processing instructions), XML, 57
  create_processing_instruction(), 200
  handleProcessingInstruction(), SaxParser, 172
  xml_set_processing_instruction_handler(), 739
    processingInstructionHandler() prototype, 739
  xml_set_processing_instruction_handler(), 150
  XPath PI nodes, 252
  <xsl:processing-instruction>, XSLT, 338, 865
  <xupdate:processing_instruction>, XUpdate, 513
points, XPointer, 118
  character points & ranges, defining, 118
  container node & index defining, 118
<polygon>/<polyline> shape elements, SVG, 608
  polygon/polyline, example drawing, 608-09
polymorphism, 914
  as method calling on similar objects' group, 914
    Form class example, 914, 915

position() function, XPath, 892
  current context node position, returning, 892
POST request, HTTP
  XML-RPC request example using, 643, 644
precedence rules, XSL predefined templates, 302
  factors determining, 302
    position of template within stylesheet, 302
    priority assigned to template, 303
    XPath expression specificity, 303
preceding/~sibling axes, XPath, 263-64, 883
  nodes/node siblings preceding context, 263, 883
    example, 263-64
pre-defined variables, PHP, 18
  defined within initial global scope, pre-PHP4.2, 18
    security risks, 19
    superglobal arrays, 19
predicates, XPath, 264, 879
  attributes in predicates, example, 265
    conditions, checking for, 265
  elements matching condition, testing for, 265
    syntax, 265
<prefix:name> syntax, XML namespaces
  using namespaces, 85
presentation vocabularies, XML derivatives, 99
  SVG, 103
  VoiceXML, 106
  WML, 101
  XHTML, 99
  XSL allowing many, 290
  XUL/XBL, 106
previous_sibling/next_~() methods, DomNode, 217
  previous/next node siblings, returning, 217
    example, 217
print() function, Sablotron, 341
  outputting document to file, 341
    example, 341
printElement() method, SvgElement, 616
  animated bar chart/red circle example, 617, 627
procedural programming, 33
  OOP and, 33
    comparative diagram, 33
processing instructions, see PI.
ProcessingInstruction interface, DOM Extended, 838
processingInstruction() method, ContentHandler/
  Document~, 785, 791
  PI, notifying of, 785, 791
processing-instruction() node test, XPath, 885
  TRUE for all PI nodes, 257, 885
processingInstructionHandler() function prototype,
  xml_*() handler, 739
Prolog, XML, see XML overview, Prolog.
properties, CSS inline
  setting within SVG element, <style>, 604
    list of, 605
properties, RDF
  as resource attributes, 109
properties, XML
  getProperty/set~(), XMLReader, 813
public/private variables
  external DTDs, 76
  PHP NOT supporting, 36
publishing
  XSL, using, 354

Q

queries, database
nested, example, 483
non-nested, example, 481
query() method, DB.php, 468
queries, handling, 468
document parts into table, extracting, 475, 478
RSS from database, creating, 470
querying XML, 424
abstracting XML queries, 431
caching, using, 431
choosing alternative, 431
additional alternatives, 430
DOM, using, 425
example, 425
SAX, using, 429
filter example, 429
pros & cons, 430
simple example, 424
XPath, using, 426
example, 426
pros & cons, 428
xpath_eval(), using, 428
XSLT, using, 428
example, 428
pros & cons, 429
Quip XQuery implementation, Software AG, 511

R

ranges, XPointer, 118
RDBMS (Relational Database Management System),
storing XML, 463, 516
advantages, 463
calendar application using MySQL, 670
custom solutions for, 491
document-level mapping (XML as BLOBs), 491
element-level mapping (Edge table), 492
object relational mapping, 495
organizing XML, example, 505
database to XML, storing, 480
example tables, creating, 480
nested query example, 483
output, 485
query, performing, 483
non-nested query example, 481
adjusting <root>/<result>/<row> values, 483
cleaning up XML, 482
output, 482
xml_sql2xml instantiation & performing query, 481
xml_sql2xml class, using, 481
document parts into table, extracting, 472
database table, creating, 472
displaying results, 479
disconnecting from database, 479
output, 479
extracting data, 472
clearing out table, 475
connecting to database, 475
disconnecting from database, 475
freeing memory, 474
INSERT query, performing, 475
opening filehandle & parsing data, 473
parse_bug_list(), examining XML data, 473
variables & DSN, setting up, 473
XMLFile object, instantiating, 473

querying database, 476
connecting to & querying database, 478
HTML header & body, 476
output, 477
variables & DSN, setting up, 477
variables status, checking, 477
product solutions for, 516
Access, 516
DB2, 516
Oracle, 517
SQL Server 2000, 517
RSS from database, creating, 468
connecting to database, 470
database resultset info, returning, 470
database table, creating, 469
output to plaintext, forcing, 469
output, 471
PHP file, 469
query, performing, 470
RSS object, creating, 470
variables & DSN, setting up, 469
storage methods, 464
entire files in database fields, 465
file_id/time_posted columns, advantages, 465
flat files in computer's filesystem, 464
XML to database, storing, 466
database connection, connect(), 467
DB.php, using, 466
document parts into table, extracting, 472
DSN, creating, 466
querying database, query/fetchRow(), 468
RSS from database, creating, 468
see also native XML databases.
RDF (Resource Description Framework), 108
as meta data processing foundation, 108
reasons for RDF, 109
resources, 110
bags/sequences/alternatives as containers, 110
example, 110
resources/properties/sentences, RDF object
model, 109
example, 109
values can be ANY object, 109
<RDF> root element, RSS, 440
read() method, XmlInput
SaxParser handling NON well-formed XML, 179
Read() function example, 180
read_file_handle() method, XMLFile
bug list file, example reading/parsing, 371
document parts into database, extracting, 473
<rect> shape element, SVG, 606
rectangle, example drawing, 606
animated bar chart example, 622
recursion, XSLT example, 355
mechanism description, diagram, 356
running, 357
source & target documents, 355
template rules, creating, 356
XPath functions, using, 357
references, XML, 56
character/entity, 56
register_ns() method, XPathContext, 277
namespaces, registering, 277
evaluating expressions with namespaces, 277
relational databases, see RDBMS.
RELAX NG, 118
as XML validation Schema language, 118
resources, 120
syntax, elements, 119

remove_child() method, DomNode, 214
  unlink_node() and, 214
requests, HTTP, 642
  mechanism, overview, 643
  POST, 643
  SOAP using HTTP request header, 566
  XML-RPC requests, using by, 643
requests, SOAP, 566
  <Body>, containing invoked method input, 568
  client request over HTTP, sending, 571
  client request with WSDL, generating, 578
  <Envelope>, containing message, 567
  header, HTTP request, 566
    SOAPAction HTTP verb, 566
  <Header>, describing SOAP header, 567
requests, XML-RPC, 641
  creating, syntax, 641
    <methodCall>/<~Name>/<param/s>, using, 642
  transmitting to server, 642
    additional headers, 643
    HTTP request mechanism, using, 642
    POST example, 643, 644
  validating, XML-RPC Schema, 646
  writing XML-RPC clients, example, 652
resolveEntity() method, EntityResolver/~Resolver2
  external entities, resolving, 795, 798
resources, PHP, 17
resources, RDF, 109
  containers grouping resources, 110
responses, HTTP
  SOAP using HTTP response header, 569
  XML-RPC responses, using by, 645
responses, SOAP, 569
  <Body>, 570
  header, HTTP request, 569
responses, XML-RPC, 644
  creating, syntax, 644
    defining return artificially, options, 644
  errors, handling, 645
  returning from server, HTTP responses, 645
  validating, XML-RPC Schema, 648
  writing XML-RPC servers, example, 655
retrieve_document command, Xindice, 533
role global attribute, XLink, 115
  link function, defining, 115
root element, XML, 50
root nodes, XPath, 251
  entire XML document, containing, 251
$roottag/$curtag member variables, XMLTag, 371
  root/current tag, referring to, 371
rotate() function, SVG transform, 599
  animated bar chart example, 624
  rectangle example, 601
round() function, XPath, 267, 892
  rounding number to nearest integer, 267, 892
RPC (Remote Procedure Calls), 631
  XML-RPC, 123, 632
RSS (RDF Site Summary), 110, 439
  as syndicating content method, 110, 439
    resources, 114
    sample RSS file, 111
  generating content, class application, 454
    class, 455
    constructor & init(), initializing variables, 455
    driver, generating RSS file, 459
      output, generating/parsing, 460-61

FixEntities(), fixing bad characters, 456
GetRssContent(), 458
  generating <channel> & <item>, 458
  returning result, 459
overview, 455
SetChannel*() subelements, 457
SetEncoding(), 456
StartItem/End~/Add~(), adding <item>s, 457
WriteHeader/~Close(), writing file start/end, 456
overview, elements, 440
  <channel>, 440
  , 441
  <item>, 441
  <RDF> root, 440
  <textinput>, 442
reading multiple sources & cached content, 446
  CacheCurrent(), if cache file is current, 448
    computing time since last cache refreshment, 449
  data source values, checking, 451
  displaying headlines, 452
    data age, displaying, 453
    output, 448, 454
    text inputs, form printing out, 453
  GetRssContent(), writing cache file for data, 449
    checking available cache file, 449
    reading/writing current cache file, 450
    writing data out to cache file, 451
    XML_RSS object, instantiating/parsing, 450
  global variables, declaring, 448
  HTML file, header/body, 447
  overview, 446
  PHP file, 448
  PrintLink(), displaying data, 451
  single <select> form, creating, 447
reading single source, simple application, 443
  arrays/images/textinputs, grabbing, 444
  associative arrays storing search results, 445
  HTML file, header/body, 444
  output from text input, including, 445
  PHP file, 443, 445
  printLink(), displaying data, 444
  sample output, 446
  XML_RSS object, instantiating & parsing, 443
RSS from database, creating, 468
syntax, elements, 112
XML_RSS RSS parser class, PEAR, 113, 442

S

Sablotron XSLT processor, Gingerall, 97, 286
  examples using, 97, 289
    mechanism description & diagram, 289
    output, 99
    sample XML file, 97
    templates, creating, 98
    XSLT/PHP files, 98
  functionality, 341
    OO approach, processing XSL, 344
    print(), outputting document to file, 341
    system-property(), processor compatibility, 349
    xslt_process(), using variables instead of files, 342
  installation, 287
    testing, 288
    UNIX, requires Expat, 287
    Windows, 287
  XSLT 1.0-compliant, 286
    XSLT transforming XML, examples, 400, 419
SAML (Security Assertion Markup Language), 561
  as web services security standard, 561

SAX (Simple API for XML) 2.0, 93, 131, 773
  as event-based XML parsing interface, 93, 131
    basic event types, list of, 93
    example, 94, 132
    history, 131
    resources, 95
    SAX-compliant parser for non-XML data, 94
    stateless SAX, 94
  & ampersand, handling, 180
  additional helper classes, 773
  advantages, 133
    speed, 133
    web applications, ideal for, 134
  class/interface hierarchies, diagrams, 774
  classes, org.xml.sax, 806
    InputSource, 806
    SAXException, 819
    SAXNotRecognizedException, 822
    SAXNotSupportedException, 823
    SAXParseException, 819
  deprecated classes/interfaces, 774
    AttributeList, 780
    DocumentHandler, 789
    HandlerBase, 804
    Parser, 816
  disadvantages, 134
  DOM and, 187
    comparative table, 188
  Expat PHP SAX parser, 94, 135
    example, 94
    parsing XML, example, 136, 145
    xml_*() functions, 137, 150
  filters, modularization use, 403
  interfaces, org.xml.sax, 776
    Attributes, 776
    Attributes2, ~.ext, 779
    DeclHandler, ~.ext, 788
    DTDHandler, 793
    EntityResolver, 795
    EntityResolver2, ~.ext, 796
    ErrorHandler, 799
    LexicalHandler, ~.ext, 801
    Locator, 809
    Locator2, ~.ext, 810
    XMLFilter, 824
    XMLReader, 811
  modifying XML using filters, 415
  new classes/interfaces, 774
  non well-formed XML content, handling, 177
    Expat, 178
    SaxParser framework, eXtremePHP, 179
  objects, creating from XML files, 422
  parser XML class, generic, 364
  querying XML using filters, 429
  SaxParser OO framework, eXtremePHP, 159
    ArticleParser/~TagHandler example, 163, 165
  storing XML implementing, 507
  transforming vs. parsing, XSL/DOM/SAX, 284
  transforming XML using, 402
  whitespace, handling, 173
    Expat, 173
    SaxParser, eXtremePHP, 177
  writing XML using, 436
SAXException* classes, SAX, 819
  SAXException, 819
    methods, 819
  SAXNotRecognizedException, 822
    constructor, 822
    inherited methods, 822

  SAXNotSupportedException, 823
    constructor, 823
    inherited methods, 823
  SAXParseException, 819
    constructors, 820
    get*() methods, 822
SaxParser framework, eXtremePHP, 159
  as OO SAX framework, 159
    classes, listing, 159
    diagram, 159
    parser development, steps, 160
  article application example, 171
  ArticleParser example, extending SaxParser, 163
    addHandlers(),163
    AppendToVariable(), 164
    constructors, 161, 163
    GetVariable(), 164
  ArticleTagHandler example, extending
    XmlTagHandler, 165
    AppendToVariable/GetVariable(), 167
    AuthorTagHandler/Email~ extension classes, 169
    constructor, 165
    DateTagHandler extension class, 169
    functionality, handlers, 165
    HandleBeginElement/~EndElement/
      ~CharacterData(), 166
    IntroTagHandler/Outro~/P~ extension classes, 170
    NameTagHandler extension class, 168
      HandleEndElement/GetName(), 168
      SetOptions(), hook, 168
    SectionTagHandler extension class, 171
    SetHtml/~Store/~Printable(), template, 166, 167
    SetOptions(), hook, 165
    variable declarations, 165
  as white box framework, 161
  NON well-formed XML content, handling, 179
    TexisFileInput example extending XmlInput, 179
  SaxParser class, generic parser, 160
    addHandlers/~TagHandler(), hook/template, 162
    constructor, 161
    functionality, 160
    handle*(), 172
    use*Encoding/setCaseFolding(), 162
  whitespace, handling, 177
  XmlInput, allowing various input sources, 159
  XmlTagHandler, defining handler interface, 164
scalar variables, PHP, 13
  boolean, 13
  floats, 14
  integers, 13
  strings, 14
scalar variables, XML-RPC, 656
  scalartype/~val() methods, 656
    calendar application, 678
scale() function, SVG transform, 599
  animated bar chart example, 623
  ellipses example, 600
Schema, XML, 78
  advantages over DTDs, 78
  constructing, sample XML document, 78
    <application> attributes, adding, 82
    <application> attributes, constraining, 83
    <application> with several <bugs> each, 79
    <bug_item> attributes, adding, 80
    <bug_item> attributes, defining data types for, 81
    <bug_list> with unlimited no. of <application>s, 79
    <bugs> with several <bug_item>s each, 80
  elements, <xs:*>, 79
  XML-RPC Schema, 646

Schematron
  as XML validation Schema language, 120
    examples, 121
    pattern-based language, 121
    resources, 123
    suitable validation targets, 123
    XSLT & XPath, using, 120
      diagram, 120
  PHP XSLT extension, using with, 123
scope, XML namespaces, 85
  default namespaces, 86
<script language="php"></script> tag, PHP, 11
security, web services, 560
  firewalls, using, 562
    limitations, 562
  resources, 562
  standards, listing, 560
select attribute, <xsl:apply-templates>/
  <~:sort, 298, 326
self axis, XPath, 264, 884
  context node itself, containing, 264, 884
    example, 264
semantic web, 108
  as web machines meta data collection, 108
    RDF, 108
    RSS, 110
sentences, RDF
  as resource, property & value combinations, 109
    example, 109
<sequence> element, RELAX NG, 119
  defining when several subelements present, 119
sequences, RDF
  as ordered resource lists, RDF containers, 110
serialization/de~, WDDX, 538
  packet serialization/de~ examples, 539
serialize() function, PHP, 450
  unserialize() and, 450
sessions, server
  authenticating users using, 675
    advantages, 675
    steps, 675
  calendar application NOT using, 676
set*() methods, see also get*/set*().
set_content() method, DomNode, 219
setCaseFolding() method, SaxParser, 162
setDocumentHandler/~DTDHandler() methods,
Parser, 817
setDocumentLocator() method, ContentHandler/
Document~, 785, 792
setEntityResolver/~ErrorHandler() methods,
Parser, 818
setLocale() method, Parser, 818
SetOptions() method, xml_sql2xml class
  <result>/<row> names, changing, 483
    database to XML, example storing, 483, 485
settype() function, PHP, 12
  variable type, setting, 12
SGML (Standard Generalized Markup Language), 49
  example, 49
show global attribute, XLink, 116
  link rendering options, indicating, 116
    values list, 116
SiXDML, 515
  as XML repositories language, 515
    functions, 515
  storing XML implementing, 515
skewX/~Y() functions, SVG transform, 599
  text/rectangles example, 601

skippedEntity() method, ContentHandler, 785
  skipped entity, notifying of, 785
SMTP (Simple Mail Transfer Protocol)
  SOAP over SMTP, example, 564
SOA (Service-Orientated Architecture), web services, 557
  components, 558
    additional, 559
    architecture, diagram, 558
    description, 560
    discovery, 560
    messaging, 559
    security, 560
  web services/consumers/brokers, 557
    model, diagram, 557
    real-life situation, diagram, 558
SOAP (Simple Object Access Protocol), 124, 563
  as data encoding/modular packaging mechanism,
    124, 563
    components, diagram, 565
    document/RPC styles, defining, 563
    example, 125
    mechanism, diagram, 563
    resources, 125, 578, 586
  client request over HTTP, example sending, 571
    request creation, 575
      output, 576
    requirements, 572
    web service defaults, HTML form for, 572
      fields contained, 572
      output, 574
  client request with WSDL, generating, 578
    client class, 579
    extracting info from WSDL, 584
    request creation, 582
    selecting WSDL & input, 581
    sending request using client, 585
    transforming WSDL to SOAP, 580
    ways of, 578
  encoding data structures, 565
  extending messages using <Header>, example, 576
    diagram, 577
    <p:Block/>/<p:data/> headers, attributes, 577
  fault responses, 570
  request-response mechanism, 566
    <Envelope>/<Header>/<Body>, containing, 567, 570
    request, 566
    response, 569
  SMTP, SOAP example over, 564
  version 1.1 to 1.2, changes from, 585
SOAPAction verb, HTTP request header, 566
special file structures, storing XML, 501
  element structure, example, 501
  mechanism, describing, 502
  sample document, storing, 501
special variables, PHP, 17
  NULL, 18
  resources, 17
SQL Server 2000, Microsoft
  storing XML, product solutions, 517
square bracket syntax, see [].
startCDATA/end~() methods, LexicalHandler, 802
startDocument/end~() methods, ContentHandler/
Document~ 786, 792
startDTD/end~() methods, LexicalHandler, 802
startElement/end~() methods, ContentHandler/
Document~, 786, 791, 793
startElementHandler() function prototype, xml_*()
handler, 738
startEntity/end~() methods, LexicalHandler, 803
startPrefixMapping/end~() methods, ContentHandler, 787

starts-with() function, XPath, 267, 893
  TRUE if string1 starts with string2, 267, 893
startup parameter, XML_Transformer constructor, 378
  XML to HTML table tags transformation, 378
state, sessions
  SAX is stateless, 94
  stateless basic XML-RPC, 634
  state-preserving extended XML-RPC, 636
static method invocation, :: operator, 37
storing XML, 489
  APIs, implementing, 490, 506
    DOM, 507
    listing APIs, 490
    proprietary APIs, 516
    SAX, 507
    SiXDML, 515
    XPath, 506
    XQuery, 507
    XSLT, 507
    XUpdate, XMLDB, 512
  custom solutions, 490
  overview, 489
  product solutions, 516
    native XML databases, 517
    RDBMS, 516
  see also RDBMS, storing XML.
storing XML, custom solutions, 490
  APIs, implementing, 503
  organizing XML using, 503
    collections, 503
    file system, 504
    RDBMS, 505
  RDBMS, using, 491
    document-level mapping (XML as BLOBs), 491
    element-level mapping (Edge table), 492
    object relational mapping, 495
  special file structures, using, 501
  text files, using, 491
streaming, SAX filters, 408
  transforming XML, example, 408
    filters chain, building correctly, 409
    FilterStreamer, streaming result, 408
    SimpleStreamer implementation class, 409
string operators, PHP, 25
string/~length () functions, XPath, 267-68, 893
  applications with open bugs, example, 273
strings, PHP, 14
  double quote declarations, 14
    escape characters, list of, 14
  heredoc syntax, 15
  single quote declarations, 15
strings, XML-RPC, 638
  limitations, 638
stripslashes() function, PHP WDDX
  WDDX packet serialization/de~ example, 543
strtoupper() function, PHP
  trimmed down bug list, phpXML example, 386
structs, XML-RPC, 640
  arrays and, example mixing, 641
  example, 640
  structmem/~each(), 657
$structure array, XML parser class, 365
  recreating XML file read in, example, 365
  trimmed down bug list, example, 368
style attribute, SVG elements, 604
  inline CSS properties within element, setting, 604
    animated bar chart example, 622
    list of, 605

<style> element, SVG, 604
  embedded stylesheets in SVG, creating, 604
subelements, see elements.
substring/~after/~before() functions, XPath, 267, 894
  XSLT split/recursion example, 357
sum() function, XPath, 267, 895
  all node values in node-set, summing, 267, 895
    average bug severity, example, 274
superglobal arrays, PHP, 19
  document parts into database, extracting, 477
  example, 20
  list of, 19
SVG (Scalable Vector Graphics), 103, 589
  as XML 2D graphics description, 103, 589
    example, 104
    main features, 104
    resources, 105, 628
  animated bar chart example, 618
    attribute definitions & data collection, 619
      axes attributes & bar heights, calculating, 620
      grabbing file contents & counting strings, 620
      updating & rounding scale up, 620
    output, 619
    SVG generation, embedding PHP directly, 621
      axes, labeling, 624
      bars, drawing, 623
      <desc>/<title>/<marker>, defining, 622
      printing SVG Prolog, 621
      <rect>/<line>, outputting, 622
      <text>, drawing, 623
    SVG generation, using SvgElement, 625
  animation, <animate> creating, 614
  coordinate system, SVG canvas, 597
    initial viewport creation, <svg>, 597
    new user coordinate system, transform, 598
      transformations available, 599
  elements, 596
    container, 596
    shapes/style/text, 604-05, 612
    <svg> root, 597
  embedding into HTML, <embed>/<object>, 593
    nesting both, 594
  errors, displaying, 594
    animated bar chart example, 621, 625
    fatal, 594
    non-fatal, 595
  PHP SVG base class, SvgElement, 616
    animated red circle example, 616
  shapes, elements creating, 605
    <circle>, 607
    <ellipse>, 608
    <line>, 606
    <marker>, 611
    <path>, 610
    <polygon>, 609
    <polyline>, 608
  styles applied to elements, <style>, 603
    external CSS stylesheets, creating/linking, 603
    style attribute, setting inline CSS properties, 604
    <style>, creating embedded CSS, 604
  syntax, components included, 591
    default/xlink namespaces, 592
    DOCTYPE declaration, 591
    document template versions, 592
    image/svg+xml, SVG MIME type, 591
    XML declaration, 591
  text, <text>/<tspan> creating, 612
  user agents, list of, 590
SVG Viewer plug-in, Adobe, 590

<svg> root element, SVG, 597
initial viewport size/units, defining, 597
  display, 598
  unit identifiers, list of, 597
SvgElement base class, PHP SVG, 616
animated bar chart example, 625
  axes label instances, adding to SvgGroup, 627
  bar/text instances, adding to SvgGroup, 626
  printing SVG file, 627
  SvgDocument/~Desc/~Title, instantiating, 625
  SvgMarker/~Defs/~Path, instantiating, 625
  SvgRect/~Group/~Line, instantiating, 626
  SvgText/~Animate, instantiating, 627
animated red circle example, 616
  child-parent relationship, establishing, 617
  printing SVG file, 617
    output, 618
  SvgCircle/~Text objects, instantiating, 617
  SvgDocument/~Group objects, instantiating, 616
methods, 616
switch blocks, PHP, 27
switch...case...break syntax, 27
  default block, always executing, 27
synchronization
asynchronous extended XML-RPC, 635
synchronous basic XML-RPC, 634
syndicated content, using RSS, 110, 439
generating content, class application, 454
reading multiple sources, application, 446
reading single source, application, 443
system.*() methods, XML-RPC introspection, 658
system-property() function, XSLT Sablotron, 349, 875
forward processor compatibility use, 349, 875

T

tagname() method, DomElement, 221
as node_name() alias, 221
Tamino native XML database, Software AG, 519
TCP/IP (Transmission Control Protocol/Internet Protocol), 546, 642
as network communication protocol, 546
  component protocols, 546
  mechanism description, 547
client interrogating server's ports, example, 547
  expanding class, ways of, 549
  instantiating class, PHP script, 548
  scanner class, 547
HTTP, using by, 642
PHP f*() support functions, list of, 549
template methods, 162
addTagHandler(), SaxParser, 162
article parsing example, SaxParser, 166, 167
Form framework, 907
hook methods and, 162
templates, XSLT, 290
named, example invoking, 304
  infinite recursion, avoiding, 306
  output, 305
  template definition, 305
parameterized, examples defining, 306
  passing values, ways of, 307
  variables, referencing, 306
predefined, 302
  precedence rules, 302
  template matching, examples declaring, 303
Sablotron functionality, 289

template rules, example defining own, 294
  <application> translation, rule defining, 297
  HTML content, rule generating, 295
  output, 301
  root node, rule matching, 296
  source & target documents, 296-97, 299
  <title>, rule matching, 298
  transform(), 300
  xslt_create(), 301
  xslt_free(), 301
variables, defining/passing, 308
<xsl:*template>, 303, 844, 846, 868
ternary comparison operator, see ?:.
test attribute, <xsl:if>, 321
text files
storing XML using, 491
<xupdate:text>, XUpdate, 513
Text interface, DOM Fundamental, 837
text nodes, DOM
create_text_node(), DomDocument, 199
representing text elements, 252
text() node test, XPath, 886
TRUE for all text nodes, 257, 886
  applications with open bugs, example, 273
<text> text element, SVG, 612
text, example rendering, 612
animated bar chart example, 623
<textinput> subelement, RSS <channel>, 113, 442
as channel interaction provider, 112, 113, 442
subelements, 113
$this variable, PHP, 901
current object, referencing, 34, 901
  instance methods, calling, 903
time() function, PHP, 448
reading multiple sources application, RSS, 448
time_posted column, database tables, 465
RDBMS storing XML, 465
title global attribute, XLink, 115
human readable link description, containing, 115
<title> container element, SVG, 597
animated bar chart example, 622
<title> subelement, RSS <channel>/<image>, 112, 441
toString() method, SAXException
exception to string, converting, 819
transform attribute, SVG elements, 598
transformations available, 599
  cumulative transformations, 599
  matrix() ellipse rotation example, 602
  rotate() rectangle example, 601
  scale() ellipses example, 600
  skewX/~Y() text/rectangles example, 601
  translate() circles example, 599
user coordinate system, creating new, 598
transformation server
batch transformations, using by, 401
transforming XML, 284, 393
abstracting transformations, 411
DOM, using, 395
  pros & cons, 395
parsing vs., choosing XSL/DOM/SAX, 284
  complex computations, 285
  creating new documents, 285
  document size, 285
  portability, 284
  presentation transformations, 284

transforming XML (continued)
SAX, using, 402
  filters for modularization, example, 403
  limitations, 402
  mechanism description, 402
  pros & cons, 410
  reasons for, 402
  streaming result, example, 408
simple example, 393
ways of, listing, 393
  choosing ways, listing, 410
XSLT, using, 395
  batch transformations, using, 401
  caching mechanism, using, 400
  complex & large documents, options for, 400
  pros & cons, 401
  XSLT implementation/application separation,
    advantages, 399
  simple example, 395
    transformation code/classes, 396
    XSLT stylesheet, 395
translate() function, SVG transform, 599
animated bar chart example, 623, 624, 626
circles example, 599
translate() function, XPath, 269, 896
strings into other characters, translating, 269, 896
trees, DOM, 92
trim() function, PHP
removing line terminators from strings, 43
whitespace, Expat example handling, 175
true() function, XPath, 266, 896
always returning TRUE, 266, 896
<tspan> text element, SVG, 613
text attributes, example changing, 613
type global attribute, XLink, 115
link type, describing, 115
  required/optional attributes, determining, 115
values, list of, 115
types, XSLT element attributes, 877

U

UNIX
installing PHP4 & Apache on, 760
unlink_node() method, DomNode, 213
deleting child node, 213
deleting XML content example, 238
remove_child() and, 214
unparsed external entity declarations, XML
handleUnparsedEntityDecl(), SaxParser, 173
xml_set_unparsed_entity_decl_handler(),152, 740
  unparsedEntityDeclHandler() prototype, 740
unparsedEntityDecl() method, DTDHandler, 794
**unparsedEntityDeclHandler() function prototype, xml_*()
handler, 740**
unparsed-entity-url() function, XSLT, 876
unserialize() function, PHP, 450, 451
reading multiple sources application, RSS, 450
serialize() and, 450
URI (Unifrom Resource Identifiers)
XML-RPC servers, identifying, 633
<url> subelement, RSS <image>, 112, 441
as image URI, 112
use*Encoding() methods, SaxParser
encoding type, setting, 162

user agents, SVG, 590
list of, 590
user interfaces, graphical, see GUI.
user-defined functions, PHP, 30
default variables as arguments, 31
defining, syntax, 30
overloading functions, PHP NOT supporting, 30
passing arguments to, 30
UTF-8 (UCS Transformation Format)
utf8_encode/~_decode() utility functions, 742
utility functions, XML PHP API, see xml_*(), utility.

V

validation, XML documents, 62
derivatives, 118
  RELAX NG, 118
  Schematron, 120
DTDs, 65
Schema, XML, 78
values, RDF
can be ANY object, 109
variables, PHP, 12
assigning, 20
  by value/by reference, 20
  variable variables, 20
compound, 15
  arrays, 16
  objects, 17
member, classes, 34
overview, types, 12
  gettype/set~(), finding/setting type, 12
pre-defined, 18
  superglobal arrays, 19
public/private, PHP NOT supporting, 36
scalar, 13
  boolean, 13
  floats (floating point), 14
  integers, 13
  strings, 14
special, 17
  NULL, 18
  resources, 17
variable functions, creating, 32
variable variables, DOM parsing XML, 228
  <xsl:variable>, XSLT, 871
variables, XSLT, 308
defining/passing, example, 308
  XPath expression, evaluating correctly, 308
Vector utility class, eXtremePHP, 911
Vectors as scalable arrays, 911
  Iterators traversing, 911
viewport, SVG
creating initial, <svg>, 597
**Virtuoso Universal Server native XML database, OpenLink,
519**
vocabularies, XML, 62
standardized/non-~, 62
VoiceXML markup language, 106
example, 106
resources, 106
warning() method, ErrorHandler
warnings, notifying of, 801

W

WDDX (Web Distributed Data eXchange), 537
as application data exchange technology, 538
  serialized XML documents, example, 538
  steps, 538
packet serialization/de~, JavaScript example, 542
packet serialization/de~, XML example, 539
PHP use, circumstances for, 544
PHP wddx_*() support functions, list of, 544
wddx_*() functions, PHP WDDX suppport, 544
wddx_add_vars(), adding variables, 546
  packet serialization/de~, XML example, 540
wddx_deserialize(), deserializing packet, 546
  packet serialization/de~, XML example, 541
wddx_packet_start/~_end(), identifying packet
start/end, 546
  packet serialization/de~, XML example, 540
wddx_serialize_value/~_vars(), creating serialized
packet, 545, 546
web services, 123, 554, 632
as functions accessed from connected machine, 123,
554, 632
  alternative definitions, 554
  organisations specifying architecture, 555
  resources, 556
derivatives, XML, 123
  SOAP, 124
  XML-RPC, 123
future developments, listing, 586
SOA (Service-Orientated Architecture), 557
  description, 560
  discovery, 560
  messaging, 559
  security, 560
W3C role in defining, 555
  standard user scenarios, 556
  Working Groups involved, 555
well-formed XML documents
Expat handling NON well-formed content, 178
  ClearCharacterSet(), removing characters, 179
  FixData(), correcting errors, 178
  Parse() example, inserting FixData() into, 179
SAX handling NON well-formed content, 177
while loops, PHP, 27
white box frameworks, SaxParser, 161
whitespace, 55, 173
Expat XML parsing example handling, 173
  adding whitespace, mechanism, 175
  HandleCharacterData(), modifying, 173, 175
  HandleEndTag(), modifying, 176
  removing whitespace, mechanism, 174
ignorableWhitespace(), ContentHandler/ Document~,
784, 791
normalize-space(), 891
SaxParser ArticleTagHandler example, 177
  HandleCharacterData(), modifying, 177
XML, handling by, 54, 55
  example, 56
  whitespace characters, 55
  xml:space, 54
<xsl:preserve-space>/<~:strip-space>, 864, 866
wildcards, XPath, 258
Windows, Microsoft
installing PHP4 & Apache on, 749

WML (Wireless Markup Language), 101
as WAP content presentation language, 101
  cards, rendering screens as, 102
  example, 102
  resources, 103
PHP generating WML, example, 103
write_file_handle() method, XMLFile
simplified bug list, example, 375
writing XML, 431
DOM, using, 435
  example, 435
  pros & cons, 436
manually, 432
  example, 432
SAX, using, 436
  example, 436
  pros & cons, 437
simple example, 431
WSDL (Web Services Description Language), 578
overview, 578
  details described, 579
SOAP client request, example generating, 578
ways of, 578

X

**XACML (eXtensible Access Control Markup Language),
561**
as web services security standard, 561
Xalan XSLT processor, Apache, 280
XPath using from XSLT, 280
XBL (eXtensible Bindings Language), 106
as XUL widget bindings definition language, 106
see also XUL.
X-Hive/DB native XML database, 519
XHTML (eXtensible HTML), 99
as XML web content presentation language, 99
  advantages, 100
  example, 101
  HTML & XHTML, comparing, 100
  resources, 101
Xindice native XML database, Apache, 520
installing, steps, 523
  XML-RPC plugin, installing, 524
methods list, database access, 520
PHP, example using Xindice from, 522
  counting/listing/retrieving documents, 530
  creating/listing collections, 529
  initialization, 528
  inserting document, 529
  library used, 522
  modifying document, XUpdate, 531
  output, 532
  querying document, result, 531
  removing document/collection, 532
  requirements, 523
  test program, 528
  Xindice class, 524
storing XML using, 520
  APIs supported, 520
  command-line tools, using, 533
  HTTP plugin, retrieving documents, 533
  resources, 533
  XML-RPC plugin, accessing database, 520
Xindice native XML database, Apache, 533

XLink
as inter-document linking language, 114
sample XLink file, 114
syntax, global attributes, 114
extended links, including graph paths, 116
example, 116
xlink namespace
SVG syntax including, 592
XML (eXtensible Markup Language), overview, 1, 47
1.0 specification, overview, 61
API, PHP XML, see xml_*() functions.
body, 50
attributes, 53
CDATA sections, 58
character data, 53
character/entity references, 56
characters, 52
comments, 57
elements, 51
names, 52
PI, 57
root element, 50
whitespace, handling, 54, 55
xml:space/~:lang special attributes, 54
data manipulation, overview, 47
meta data, 48
derivatives, 89
generic, 92
presentation vocabularies, 99
semantic web, 108
validating XML, 118
web services, 123
XLink, 114
XPointer, 116
design, documents, 62
vocabularies, 62
DTD, 65
Epilog, 60
functionality, 1
exchanging info, 2
organizing info, 2
processing info, 3
representing info, 2
future developments, listing, 586
markup languages
SGML, 49
XML, 49
modifying, 411
namespaces, 85
objects, creating from XML files, 420
parsing, see parsing XML.
PHP and, 3
Prolog, 59
DOCTYPE declaration, 75
DTD, 60
valid sections, 59
XML declaration, 59
querying, 424
resources, 4
sample document, 63
bugs elements, 64
DTD declaration, 71, 75, 78
attributes, adding, 75
DTD shortcomings, 78
elements, defining, 69
root/<application> elements, 64
Schema, constructing, 78
source code, 63
Schema, 78

storing, 463, 489
database to XML, storing, 480
storage methods, 464
XML to database, storing, 466
third-party XML classes for PHP, 363
transforming, 393
validation, 62
DTD & Schema, using, 63
well-formed document, parts, 50
<,> and & NOT allowed in XML files, 456
writing, 431
XML Cooktop, 279
XPath console, using XPath from XSLT, 279
example, 279
XML declaration, XML Prolog, 59
internal subset declarations, 60
standalone documents lacking external, 60
SVG syntax including, 591
XML Encryption/Signature, 560
as web services security standards, 560
XML parser class, generic, 364
as PHP SAX API wrapper, overview, 364
downloading, 364
recreating XML file read in, example, 364
$structure array, displaying parsed data, 365
tags/elements/attributes, displaying, 365
displaying results, HTML file, 366
output, 367
ShowStructure(), reconstructing original XML, 365
character data, printing, 366
determining function's next start, 366
tag containing attributes, printing, 365
XMLParseFile(), 364
arguments, 364
functionality, 364
trimmed down bug list, example, 367
$app_data array, storing application data, 369
displaying results, 369
output, 370
global variables, initializing, 367
TraverseXml(), 368
checking if <application> is current tag, 368
examining array case, 368
recursive function part, 368
xml*() factory methods, DOM, 195
new_xmldoc(), creating empty tree, 195
xmldoc(), creating content-filled tree, 196
example, 196
xmldocfile(), creating filename-based tree, 197
deleting XML content example, 238
example, 197
parsing XML example, 228
xmltree(), creating directly accessible tree, 197
example, 198
xml:lang/~:space special attributes, XML, 54-55
language/whitespace, handling, 54-55
preserve/default values, 54
xml_*() functions, PHP XML API, 150, 732, 733
Expat using, 150
handler, 737
as register callback functions, 732
character data, 738
default, 737
elements, 737
external entity references, 739
notation declarations, 741
PIs, 739
unparsed entity declarations, 740
parser, 733
utf8_encode/~_decode(), 742

xml_*() functions, PHP XML API, (continued)
utility, 741
current, 741
error, 743
UTF-8, 742
xml_get_error code/~_error_string/~_get
_current_line_number(),144, 743
xml_get_current_line_number/~_column_number/~_b
yte_index(), 741
xml_parse(), parsing data, 142, 733, 735
4096 bytes block, cutting content off, 143
Expat parsing example, 146
string/file content, examples parsing, 142
xml_parse_into_struct(), 735
xml_parser_create/~_free(), 137, 144, 732-34
Expat parsing example, 145, 146
char encoding parameter, options, 732
xml_parser_get_option/~_set_option(), 138-39, 736
options, additional, 138
SAX parsing example, 145
xml_set_character_data_handler(),141, 738
characterDataHandler() prototype, 738
Expat parsing example, 145
HandleCharacterData(), declaring, 141, 147
parsing, circumstances stopping, 141
xml_set_default_handler(), 156, 737
HandleDefault(), defining, 156
xml_set_element_handler(), 139, 732, 737
Expat parsing example, 145
HandleBeginTag/~EndTag(), declaring, 139, 147
parameters, 140
startElementHandler/end~() prototypes, 738
xml_set_external_entity_ref_handler(), 154, 739
externalEntityRefHandler() prototype, 740
HandleExternalEntity(), declaring, 154
xml_set_notation_decl_handler(), 151, 741
HandleNotationDecl(), declaring, 151
notationDeclHandler() prototype, 741
xml_set_object(), 734
example, 734
xml_set_processing_instruction_handler(), 150, 739
HandlePi(), declaring, 150
processingInstructionHandler() prototype, 739
xml_set_unparsed_entity_decl_handler(), 152, 740
HandleUnparsedEntity(), declaring, 153
unparsedEntityDeclHandler() prototype, 740
XML_Parser base class, PEAR, 442
parse() method, 443
XML_RSS, extending by, 442
XML_RSS parser class, PEAR, 442
downloading & installing, 442
methods, 443
reading multiple sources application, RSS, 450
reading single source application, RSS, 443
XML_Parser, extending, 442
xml_sql2xml class, PEAR, 481
database to XML, storing, 481
nested query example, 483
non-nested query example, 481
methods, 481
constructor, 481, 483
getxml(), returning query results as XML, 481
SetOptions(), changing <result>/<row> names, 483
XML_Transformer class, PEAR, 376
assigning PHP callback functions to XML elements, 377
methods, 377
constructor parameters, 377
XML to HTML table tags transformation, 377
array passing to constructor, defining, 378
displaying results, 379
output, 380

PHP callback functions, writing, 378
reading in XML data, 378
XML_Transformer, instantiating, 379
XMLFile class, 370
document parts into database, extracting, 472
methods, 371
cleanup(), 373
create_root(), 374
read_file_handle(), 371
write_file_handle(), 375
parsing & traversing data in XML file, 370
$roottag/$curtag, 371
best suited for small/medium-sized files, 371
installing class, 370
simplified bug list, example, 374
create_root(), calling, 374
displaying results, 375
output, 376
filling root node with elements, 374
FindBugs(), calling, 374
new XML file, creating, 375
XMLFile & root node, creating new, 374
trimmed down bug list, example, 371
displaying results, 373
output, 373
FindBugs(), 372
if in <APPLICATION>, grab NAME attribute, 372
if in <TITLE>, grab CDATA attribute, 372
read_file_handle(), 371
XMLFilter interface, SAX, 824
getParent/set~() methods, XMLFilterImpl, 824
XmlInput class, SaxParser framework
read() method, 179
SaxParser handling NON well-formed XML, 179
various input sources, allowing, 159
xmlns attribute name, XML namespaces, 294
declaring namespaces, 85
XMLReader interface, SAX, 811
get*/set*() methods, 812
XML-RPC, 123, 632
allowing client-server RPC using XML & HTTP, 123,
632, 633
example, 124
history, 632
protocol overview, 633
resources, 124, 664
basic protocol, 633
authentication & encryption, 634
steps, 633
synchronous & stateless protocol, 634
URIs identifying XML-RPC servers, 633
calendar application using, 667
choosing XML-RPC, reasons for, 669
data types, handling, 637
types list, 637
DTD, writing, 646
extended protocol, 634
asynchronous, 635
diagram, 635
authentication, log-/HTTP-based, 636
state-preserving, 636
PHP XML-RPC library, Usefulinc, 649
decoding data, XML-RPC to PHP, 656
encoding data, PHP to XML-RPC, 655
introspection use, Dispatch Map binding, 657
writing clients, example, 650
writing servers, example, 653
requests, creating/transmitting, 641
POST HTTP request example, 643
responses, creating/transmitting, 644
errors, handling, 645

XML-RPC (continued)
Schema, validating requests/responses, 646
Xindice XML-RPC plugin, 520
installing, 524
XML-RPC PHP library, Usefulinc, 649
as XML-RPC PHP implementation, 649
decoding data, XML-RPC to PHP, 656
arrays, arraysize/~mem(), 656
kindOf property, using, 656
scalars, scalartype/~val(), 656
structs, structmem/~each(), 657
xmlrpc_encode/~_decode() as shortcuts, 657
encoding data, PHP to XML-RPC, 655
xmlrpcval() constructors, using, 655
error codes, list defining, 653
installation, 650
warning, fixing, 650
introspection, using, 658
Dispatch Map, creating binding, 657
example, 658
writing XML-RPC clients, example, 650
client object, creating, 652
client program, 651
errors, handling, 653
multiply(), calling on server, 651
request, creating/sending, 652
steps, 650
writing XML-RPC servers, example, 653
binding, 655
method prototype, 655
output, 654
response, creating/returning, 655
server program, 654
steps, 653
xmlrpc_encode/~_decode() functions, XML-RPC library, 657
xmlrpcval() constructors, XML-RPC library, 655
encoding data, PHP to XML-RPC, 655
XMLTag class, 371
properties used by $roottag/$curtag, 371
XmlTagHandler abstract class, SaxParser framework, 164
ArticleTagHandler example extending, 165
handler object interface, defining, 164
methods, 164
XPath (XML Path Language), 95, 247, 879
as syntax for accessing XML parts, 95, 248
advantages, 248
functionality, overview, 95, 249, 267
limitations, 249
resources, 96, 116
XSLT, XPointer & XQuery, 248
attributes, representing, 251
axes, list of, 259, 880
bugs in database example, questions about, 270
applications with open bugs, string/text(), 273
average bug severity, sum(), 274
bugs no. reporting/update date, count(), 272
bugs reported within given interval, 274
open/closed bugs no., normalize-space(), 271
programmers reporting bugs, contains(), 271
total bugs no., count(), 270
calculations, using for, 309
data types, list of, 255, 265
expressions, writing, 255
functions, list of, 266, 886
node tests, list of, 884
nodes, list of, 251

PHP, using XPath directly from, 96, 275
domxml_open_mem(), parsing document, 275
DomXMLNode objects, processing, 276
evaluating expressions with namespaces, 276
output, 276
XML document, defining, 275
xpath_eval(), evaluating XPath query, 96, 276
XPathContext object, instantiating, 276
phpXML, using XPath on XML document, 381
predicates, 264
querying XML using, 426
Schematron, using by, 120
storing XML implementing, 506
syntax, overview, 250, 879
axes, node tests & predicates, 879
extended syntax, 259
MSXML implementations chosen, 880
tree representation, diagram, 250, 254
XML document representation, example, 253
wildcards, list of, 258
XSLT, using XPath from, 278
basic XSLT stylesheet, 278
Xalan, 280
XML Cooktop's XPath console, using, 279
XSLT split/recursion example, 357
xpath_eval() method, XPathContext, 96, 276
querying XML using XPath, 96, 276, 428
XPointer, 116
as document fragment referencing, 116, 248
child sequence-based syntax, 117
full syntax, 117
ID/child sequence-based syntax, 117
ID-based syntax, 117
resources, 118
points, container node & index defining, 118
character points & ranges, 118
XQuery, 507
as XML query syntax, 248, 507
basic expressions, 507
document(), implementing, 508
FLWR expressions, 508
LET/FOR, using, 508
resources, 512
FLWR expression examples, 509
implementations, listing, 510
Kweelt, 511
Quip, 511
storing XML implementing, 507
<xs:*> elements, XML Schema, 79
<xs:all> container, element list NOT sequence, 81
<xs:complexType>, elements containing sub~, 79
<xs:sequence>, subelement sequence, 79
XSL/XSLT (eXtensible Stylesheet Language/ Transformations), 96, 285, 841
as functional/declarative language, 97, 321, 355
limitations, 321
split/recursion example, 356
string manipulation example, 355
as an XML transformation language, 96, 285
components, 286
diagram, 286
resources, 99
advantages, 290
coding reduction, 291
deployment/productivity, improving, 291
legacy browser support, 292, 352
maintainability/modularity, increasing, 290
many presentation languages, using, 290
portability, increasing, 291

XSL/XSLT (eXtensible Stylesheet Language/ Transformations, continued)
applications, building, 350
attribute types, list of, 877
bugs management example, 309
  Bug Report, main template, 311
    answering questions, 311
    parameters passed, 311
  display-question template, 310
    parameters passed, 310
    result tree, diagram, 310
  output, 313
  questions to answer, 309
calendar application using, 703, 713, 722
commands, <xsl:*>, 331
  comment creation, <xsl:comment>, 333
  copying current node, <xsl:copy>, 333
  element/attribute creation, <xsl:element>/<~: attribute>, 331
  PI generation, <xsl:processing-instruction>, 338
converting XML documents, 352
  multiple transformations, 353
  reasons for, 352
  XML to SQL, example, 352
functions, 873
  general syntax, 873
  list of, 873
  XPath-inherited, list of, 876
functions, Sablotron, 341
  forward processor compatibility, system-property(), 349
  OO approach, processing XSL, 344
  outputting document to file, print(), 341
  using variables instead of files, xslt_process(), 342
instructions, <xsl:*>, 314
  including XSL files, <xsl:include>, 317
  literal result element, 319
  multiple conditional element, <xsl:choose>, 322
  numbering, <xsl:number>, 328
  repetition, <xsl:for-each>, 314
  single conditional element, <xsl:if>, 320
  sorting, <xsl:sort>, 324
legacy applications, supporting, 358
modifying XML using, 418
multi-tiered applications, building, 350
new languages, introducing, 351
  DML, deriving new tag default settings, 351
  suggested new tags, 351
publishing use, 354
PHP using Sablotron processor, 97, 286
  example, 97
  functions, 341
  template rules definition example, 300
querying XML using, 428
Schematron, using by, 120
storing XML implementing, 507
stylesheets, creating, 293
  document structure, diagram, 292
  empty stylesheet, 293
  namespace, defining, 294
  PHP extension, using, 300
  qualifying elements, 294
  template rules example, 294
  XSLT version, specifying, 294
templates, 290
  named, 304
  parameterized, 306
  predefined, precedence rules, 302
  template rules, defining own, 294
transforming vs. parsing, XSL/DOM/SAX, 284
transforming XML using, 395
  complex & large documents, options for, 400
  simple example, 395

variables, defining/passing, 308
XPath using from, example, 248, 278
  basic XSLT stylesheet, 278
  Xalan, using, 280
  XML Cooktop's XPath console, using, 279
<xsl:*> elements, XSLT, 314, 841
overview
  as commands, 331
  as instructions, 314
  qualifying required, 294
  top-level/children, 293
<xsl:apply-imports>, calling from stylesheet, 843
<xsl:apply-templates>, passing context onto another template, 296, 844
  select/mode attributes, 298, 844
  template rules definition example, 296, 298
  <xsl:sort>, using by, 327
<xsl:attribute>, 332, 845
  example, 332
  name/namespace attributes, 845
<xsl:attribute-set>, defining attribute set, 846
  name/use-attribute-sets attributes, 846
<xsl:call-template>, calling by name, 305, 846
  name attribute, 305, 846
  named templates, invoking, 305
<xsl:choose>, implementing choose/when/ otherwise, 322, 847
  <xsl:copy> bug list example, 336
  bug items table, example creating, 323
    output, 324
<xsl:comment>, comment node, 333, 847
  example, 333
<xsl:copy>, context node copy, 333, 848
  identity rule example, 333, 336
  redesigning document structure, bug list, 334
    changes intended, 334
    processing elements, 335
    target document, 336
    target document structure, diagram, 334
  use-attribute-sets attribute, 848
<xsl:copy-of>, full tree copy, 849
  select attribute, 849
<xsl:decimal-format>, 849
  attributes, list of, 849
<xsl:document>, switching target to another document, 851
  attributes, list of, 851
<xsl:element>, 332, 853
  <xsl:copy> bug list example, 335
  character data, example adding, 332
  example, 332
  name/namespace/use-attribute-sets attributes, 853
<xsl:fallback>, specifying fallback actions, 854
<xsl:for-each>, looping through node, 314, 854
  bug items table, example creating, 315
    output, displaying, 316
    source & target document, displaying, 315
  select attribute, 854
  sorting bugs, <xsl:sort> example, 326
  template use, minimizing, 315
  XPath gathering node list, example, 314
<xsl:if>, executing if test expression true, 320, 855
  listing all open bugs, example, 321
    output, 322
  near-programming language behavior, XSL, 320
  test attribute, 321, 855
<xsl:import>, importing templates, 856
  href attribute, 856
<xsl:include>, including templates, 317, 856
  all top-level elements under root, including, 318
  bugs template, example including, 317
  href attribute, 856

<xsl:*> elements, XSLT (continued)

<xsl:key>, describing name/value pairs, 857
 name/match/use attributes, 857
<xsl:message>, issuing error warnings, 858
 terminate attribute, 858
<xsl:namespace-alias>, 859
 stylesheet-prefix/result-~ attributes, 859
<xsl:new-xsl-tag>, forward processor
compatibility, 349
 limitation, 349
<xsl:number>, outputting chapter no., 328, 860
 attributes, list of, 860
 bug items/applications, example numbering, 329
  output, 331
 count attribute, 330
 format attribute, values, 328
 number skipping example, 329
<xsl:otherwise>, implementing choose/when/
 otherwise, 322, 862
 bug items table, example creating, 324
<xsl:output>, output style properties, 295, 862
 attributes, list of, 862
 method/indent attributes, 295
 template rules definition example, 295
<xsl:param>, defining parameter, 306, 864
 name/select attributes, 306, 864
 parameterized templates, 306
<xsl:preserve-space>, preserving whitespace, 864
 elements attribute, 864
<xsl:processing-instruction>, 338, 865
 attributes, 338
 bugs table statical display example, 338
  attributes, declaring, 338
  creating bug items array, 339
  creating HTML table, 339
  output, 340
 name attribute, 865
<xsl:sort>, specifying sort order, 324, 865
 attributes, list of, 326, 865
 sorting bugs, example, 325
  output, 327
  status/severity/title, sorting order, 326
 xsl:apply-templates>, using with, 327
<xsl:strip-space>, stripping whitespace, 866
 elements attribute, 866
<xsl:stylesheet>, stylesheet root element, 293, 867
 attributes, list of, 867
 SAME as <xsl:transform>.
 <xmlns:*>, handling namespaces, 294
<xsl:template>, 293, 868
 attributes, list of, 868
 character & node creation subelements, 293
 name attribute, defining named templates, 305
<xsl:template-match>, matching nodes, 303
 predefined templates examples, 303

<xsl:text>, 869
 disable-output-escape attribute, 869
<xsl:transform>, generating stylesheet, 869
 attributes, list of, 869
 SAME as <xsl:stylesheet>.
<xsl:value-of>, specified value text, 297, 870
 literal result element, example creating, 319
 select/disable-output-escaping attributes, 870
 template rules definition example, 297, 299
 XPath using from XSLT, example, 278, 308
<xsl:variable>, 308, 871
 example, 308
 name/select attributes, 871
<xsl:when>, implementing choose/when/ otherwise,
 322, 872
 bug items table, example creating, 324
 test attribute, 872
<xsl:with-param>, passing parameter, 307, 872
 name/select attributes, 872
 parameterized templates examples, 307
xslt_process() function, Sablotron, 342
 OO XSL example, 346
 using variables instead of files, 342
  arguments, passing to function, 343
  example, 342
   running, 343
  prefixes for reading arguments instead, 343
XUL (XML-based User-interface Language), 106
 as GUI description language, 106
  examples, 107
  graphical element types, creating, 107
  resources, 108
  see also XBL.
XUpdate, XMLDB, 512
 example using, 514
  input, XML file, 514
  modifications, XUpdate file, 514
  output, XML file, 514
 modifications of XML documents, defining, 512
  inserting created nodes, 512
  removing nodes from document, 513
  updating existing nodes, 513
<xupdate:*> elements, XUpdate, 512
 <xupdate:append>, adding child elements, 512
  example, 513
 <xupdate:attribute>/<~:element>, 512
 <xupdate:comment>/<~:text>, 513
 <xupdate:insert-before>/<~:insert-after>, inserting
  child elements, 512
 <xupdate:processing_instruction>, 513
 <xupdate:remove>/<~:rename>, removing/ renaming
  elements, 512
  example, 513
 <xupdate:update>, changing node, 513

Notes

Notes

Notes

Notes

p2p.wrox.com

The programmer's resource centr

A unique free service from Wrox Pre
With the aim of helping programmers to help each

Wrox Press aims to provide timely and practical information to today's programmer.
is a list server offering a host of targeted mailing lists where you can share knowle
with four fellow programmers and find solutions to your problems. Whatever the lev
your programming knowledge, and whatever technology you use P2P can provide yo
the information you need.

ASP Support for beginners and professionals, including a resource page with hundreds of link
and a popular ASP.NET mailing list.

DATABASES For database programmers, offering support on SQL Server, mySQL, and Oracle.

MOBILE Software development for the mobile market is growing rapidly. We provide lists for
the several current standards, including WAP, Windows CE, and Symbian.

JAVA A complete set of Java lists, covering beginners, professionals, and server-side programm
(including JSP, servlets and EJBs)

.NET Microsoft's new OS platform, covering topics such as ASP.NET, C#, and general
.NET discussion.

VISUAL BASIC Covers all aspects of VB programming, from programming Office macros to creating
components for the .NET platform.

WEB DESIGN As web page requirements become more complex, programmer's are taking a more impo
role in creating web sites. For these programmers, we offer lists covering technologies su
Flash, Coldfusion, and JavaScript.

XML Covering all aspects of XML, including XSLT and schemas.

OPEN SOURCE Many Open Source topics covered including PHP, Apache, Perl, Linux, Python and more.

FOREIGN LANGUAGE Several lists dedicated to Spanish and German speaking programmers, categories includ
NET, Java, XML, PHP and XML

How to subscribe:
Simply visit the P2P site, at http://p2p.wrox.com

wroxbase

Got more Wrox books than you can carry around?

Wroxbase is the new online service from Wrox Press. Dedicated to providing online access to books published by Wrox Press, helping you and your team find solutions and guidance for all your programming needs.

The key features of this service will be:

● Different libraries based on technologies that you use everyday (ASP 3.0, XML, SQL 2000, etc.). The initial set of libraries will be focused on Microsoft-related technologies.

● You can subscribe to as few or as many libraries as you require, and access all books within those libraries as and when you need to.

● You can add notes (either just for yourself or for anyone to view) and your own bookmarks that will all be stored within your account online, and so will be accessible from any computer.

● You can download the code of any book in your library directly from Wroxbase

Visit the site at: www.wroxbase.com

Register your book on Wrox.com!

When you download this book's code from
wrox.com, you will have the option to register.

What are the benefits of registering?

- You will receive updates about your book
- You will be informed of new editions, and
  will be able to benefit from special offers
- You became a member of the "Wrox Developer Community", giving
  you exclusive access to free documents from Wrox Press
- You can select from various newsletters you may want to receive

**Registration is easy and only needs to be done once.
After that, when you download code books after logging
in, you will be registered automatically.**

Just go to www.wrox.com

wrox

Programmer to Programmer™

Registration Code: | 7213BNO7LJQ21Y01 |

Wrox writes books for you. Any suggestions, or ideas about how you want
information given in your ideal book will be studied by our team.
Your comments are always valued at Wrox.

Free phone in USA 800-USE-WROX
Fax (312) 893 8001

UK Tel.: (0121) 687 4100   Fax: (0121) 687 4101

Professional PHP4 XML – Registration Card

Name _____

Address _____

_____

_____

City _____ State/Region _____

Country _____ Postcode/Zip _____

E-Mail _____

Occupation _____

How did you hear about this book?

❏ Book review (name) _____

❏ Advertisement (name) _____

❏ Recommendation _____

❏ Catalog _____

❏ Other _____

Where did you buy this book?

❏ Bookstore (name) _____ City _____

❏ Computer store (name) _____

❏ Mail order _____

❏ Other _____

What influenced you in the purchase of this book?

❏ Cover Design ❏ Contents ❏ Other (please specify):

_____

How did you rate the overall content of this book?

❏ Excellent ❏ Good ❏ Average ❏ Poor

What did you find most useful about this book? _____

_____

What did you find least useful about this book? _____

_____

Please add any additional comments. _____

_____

What other subjects will you buy a computer book on soon?

_____

What is the best computer book you have used this year?

_____

Note: This information will only be used to keep you updated
about new Wrox Press titles and will not be used for
any other purpose or passed to any other third party.

7213   Check here if you DO NOT want to receive support for this book ■   7213

wrox

Programmer to Programmer™

Note: If you post the bounce back card below in the UK, please send it to:

Wrox Press Limited, Arden House, 1102 Warwick Road,
Acocks Green, Birmingham B27 6HB. UK.

Computer Book Publishers

Programmer to Programmer™

Registration Code: 72135J12K7K4GO01

Wrox writes books for you. Any suggestions, or ideas about how you want
information given in your ideal book will be studied by our team.
Your comments are always valued at Wrox.

Free phone in USA 800-USE-WROX
Fax (312) 893 8001

UK Tel.: (0121) 687 4100   Fax: (0121) 687 4101

Professional PHP4 XML – Registration Card

Name _____

Address _____

_____

_____

City _____ State/Region _____

Country _____ Postcode/Zip _____

E-Mail _____

Occupation _____

How did you hear about this book?

❏ Book review (name) _____

❏ Advertisement (name) _____

❏ Recommendation _____

❏ Catalog _____

❏ Other _____

Where did you buy this book?

❏ Bookstore (name) _____ City_____

❏ Computer store (name) _____

❏ Mail order_____

❏ Other _____

What influenced you in the purchase of this book?

❏ Cover Design ❏ Contents ❏ Other (please specify):

_____

How did you rate the overall content of this book?

❏ Excellent ❏ Good ❏ Average ❏ Poor

What did you find most useful about this book? _____

_____

What did you find least useful about this book? _____

_____

Please add any additional comments. _____

_____

What other subjects will you buy a computer book on soon?

_____

What is the best computer book you have used this year?

_____

Note: This information will only be used to keep you updated
about new Wrox Press titles and will not be used for
any other purpose or passed to any other third party.

Check here if you DO NOT want to receive support for this book ■

wrox

Programmer to Programmer™

Note: If you post the bounce back card below in the UK, please send it to:

Wrox Press Limited, Arden House, 1102 Warwick Road,
Acocks Green, Birmingham B27 6HB. UK.

Computer Book Publishers